UNDERSTANDING CRIMINAL LAW

SECOND EDITION

Joshua Dressler
Professor of Law
McGeorge School of Law
University of the Pacific

LEGAL TEXT SERIES

MATTHEW BENDER

QUESTIONS ABOUT THIS PUBLICATION?

For questions about the **Editorial Content** appearing in these volumes or reprint permission, please call:

Juliet Turner, J.D., at .... 1-800-252-9257 Ext. 2266
Outside the United States and Canada please call .... (212) 448-2000

For assistance with replacement pages, shipments, billing or other customer service matters, please call:

Customer Services Department at .... (800) 833-9844
Outside the United States and Canada, please call .... (518) 487-3000
Fax number .... (518) 487-3584

For information on other Matthew Bender publications, please call
Your account manager or .... (800) 223-1940
Outside the United States and Canada, please call .... (518) 487-3000

2000 Reprint

Library of Congress Cataloging-in-Publication Data

Dressler, Joshua
    Understanding criminal law / Joshua Dressler. — 2nd ed.
      p. cm. — (Legal Text Series)
    Includes bibliographical references and index.
    ISBN 0-8205-2717-3
      1. Criminal Law—United States 1. Title. II. Series.
KF9219.D74 1995
345.73—dc20   95-9215
[347.305]   CIP

MATTHEW BENDER & CO., INC.
EDITORIAL OFFICES
2 Park Avenue, New York, NY 10016-5675 (212) 448-2000
201 Mission St., San Francisco, CA 94105-1831 (415) 908-3200

Thank You, David B. Dressler

TABLE OF CONTENTS

Page

CHAPTER 3

SOURCES OF THE CRIMINAL LAW

CHAPTER 4

CONSTITUTIONAL LIMITS ON THE CRIMINAL LAW

CHAPTER 5

LEGALITY

CHAPTER 6

PROPORTIONALITY

CHAPTER 7

BURDENS OF PROOF

CHAPTER 10

MENS REA

Page

CHAPTER 18

SELF-DEFENSE

CHAPTER 19

DEFENSE OF OTHERS

Page

CHAPTER 24

INTOXICATION

Page

CHAPTER 25

INSANITY

Page

Page

CHAPTER 28

SOLICITATION

Page

CHAPTER 31

CRIMINAL HOMICIDE

Page

CHAPTER 33

RAPE

Page

PREFACE TO THE SECOND EDITION

As with the First Edition, this Text is primarily designed for use by law students enrolled in a course in Criminal Law. However, as before, I hope and expect that the book will prove helpful to practitioners and scholars alike, who are looking for a survey of criminal law theory and doctrine. The Text considers common law doctrine, statutory reform (with particular emphasis on the Model Penal Code), and constitutional law affecting the substantive criminal law.

I am gratified that the First Edition received a favorable response from its users. Therefore, I have avoided the temptation to tinker. I have clarified certain sections, made slight intra-chapter organizational changes for purposes of clarity, and, of course, have brought the Text up-to-date in light of changes in the law. I have also included citations to new scholarship in the field, in the hope that users will look to some of these sources for additional insight into the various subjects.

In the original Preface, I wrote:

> *Gender Policy of the Text.* For most of Anglo-American legal history men monopolized the critical roles in the system of criminal justice. With only a few exceptions, lawyers, judges, legislators, jurors, and criminals were men. The only place for a woman in the system was as a victim of crime. Such sexual inequality, of course, is changing. . . .
>
> As an author of a book that will be read and used by readers of both sexes I wanted to make sure that the Text recognized the increasing importance of women in the law. Therefore, when discussing hypothetical defendants (D) and victims (V) and when writing in general terms about other parties in the legal system—e.g., lawyers, judges, and legislators—I balance the account between male and female parties. In odd-numbered chapters the parties are female; in the even-numbered chapters males get equal time. I only diverge from this approach when the gender policy would distort history (e.g., I will not talk about property-holders in sixteenth century England as if they were women), be inaccurate as a principle of law, or [confuse] . . . the reader.

The Second Edition follows the same policy.

Acknowledgements. In the first edition, I wrote:

> A book of this length cannot be written without help from many people. A few people, however, deserve special attention. Luckily for me, Robert Abrams was Interim Dean of Wayne State University Law School when I began this book. Robbie believed in the importance of the project. His support—personally and administratively—made it possible for me to complete it on time and, more importantly, in a reasonable frame of mind.
>
> My [Wayne State University] colleague, Leroy Lamborn, should receive the Good Citizen award: although I am not sure that either of us knew what he was getting himself into when it started, Leroy looked at every chapter of this

book as it was finished and provided me with many helpful editorial and substantive suggestions.

Thanks also goes to Nancy Omichinski, [Wayne State] Class of 1987, for her marvelous research work on the book. I also wish to express my appreciation to Wayne State University for providing me with a Career Development Chair, which entitled me to research support and, far more importantly, to leave time to complete the Text.

Finally, and probably most importantly, I want to mention my family. My wife, Dottie, heroically put up with my obsessive desire to work on the manuscript over the past two years; and my son, David, remarkably resisted complaining about the fact that the home computer was never available for his personal use. Their love has always served as the stabilizing influence in my life. I love them dearly.

Many people assisted me in preparing this Second Edition. I received many letters and telephone calls from professors (and some law students) with advice for this edition. I took all of the comments to heart. In this regard, however, the Well-Beyond-the-Call-of-Duty Award must go to Professor Ken Simons (Boston University), who sent me two very long and useful letters commenting on the First Edition. Also, many teachers kindly took the time to complete a questionnaire regarding the First Edition, distributed by the publisher a few years ago. I carefully considered all of the advice therein.

At my new law school home, University of the Pacific (McGeorge School of Law), I thank Dean Gerald Caplan for the support I needed to get the new edition out on schedule. I also received excellent help from my Research Assistants, Syrus Devers and Kristin Engstrom. Also, Sidonie Christian (Class of 1994) provided her usual excellent editorial comments on the manuscript.

My wife, as always, has been there for me. My son no longer frets over the loss of the home computer, as he has gone off to college, graduated, and has his own computer. Although his mother and I miss his physical presence, we experience his spirit with us always, not to speak of his tuition bills.

Joshua Dressler
May 1, 1995

FREQUENTLY CITED SOURCES

The following is a list of sources frequently cited in this Text, and the shorthand form used to cite to them in footnotes.

1. American Law Institute, Model Penal Code and Commentaries (Part I: General Provisions (1985); Part II: Definition of Specific Crimes (1980))—American Law Institute.

    Copyright © 1980 and 1985 by the American Law Institute, as Adopted at the 1962 Annual Meeting of The American Law Institute. Reprinted with the permission of The American Law Institute.

2. William Blackstone, Commentaries on the Laws of England (4 volumes, 1765-1769)—Blackstone.

3. George P. Fletcher, Rethinking Criminal Law (1978)—Fletcher.

4. Matthew Hale, History of the Pleas of the Crown (1736) (2 volumes)—Hale.

5. Jerome Hall, General Principles of the Criminal Law (2d. ed. 1960)—Hall.

6. H.L.A. Hart, Punishment and Responsibility (1968)—Hart.

7. Oliver Wendell Holmes, Jr., The Common Law (1881)—Holmes.

8. Leo Katz, Bad Acts and Guilty Minds: Conundrums of the Criminal Law (1987)—Katz.

9. Herbert L. Packer, The Limits of the Criminal Sanction (1968)—Packer.

10. Rollin M. Perkins & Ronald N. Boyce, Criminal Law (3d ed. 1982)—Perkins & Boyce.

11. Paul H. Robinson, Criminal Law Defenses (1984) (2 volumes)—Robinson.

12. Glanville Williams, Criminal Law: The General Part (2d ed. 1961)—Williams.

CHAPTER 1

CRIMINAL LAW: AN OVERVIEW

§ 1.01   Nature of Criminal Law[1]

The study of the criminal law is the study of crimes and the moral principles of criminal responsibility.

[A]—Crimes

[1]—Comparison to Civil Wrongs

What is a crime? If we are to believe many judicial opinions and treatises, the answer is simple, circular, and useless: a "crime" is anything that lawmakers say is a crime. We need to look deeper for an answer to the question and, thus, to understand how a crime differs from a civil wrong, such as a tort or a breach of contract.

First, unlike torts and contracts, the criminal law involves *public* law. That is, although the direct and immediate victim of a crime may be a private party (e.g., a person who is robbed, assaulted, or kidnapped), and other individuals may be indirectly injured (e.g., a spouse of the direct victim), a crime involves more: a crime is a "social harm,"[2] in that the injury suffered involves "a breach and violation of the public rights and duties, due to the whole community, considered as a community, in its social aggregate capacity."[3] Because of this latter feature, crimes are prosecuted by public attorneys representing the community at large, and not by privately retained counsel.

But, there is more that distinguishes a criminal wrong from its civil counterpart. A person convicted of a crime is punished. The technical definition of "punishment" awaits consideration in the next chapter,[4] but "the essence of punishment . . . lies in the criminal conviction itself."[5] When the factfinder—ordinarily, a jury—determines that a person is guilty of an offense, the resulting conviction is an expression of the community's moral outrage, directed at the criminal actor for her act. The hardship suffered as a result of the criminal conviction may be no greater

---

[1] See generally Henry M. Hart, Jr., *The Aims of the Criminal Law*, 23 Law & Contemp. Probs. 401 (1958); Sanford H. Kadish, *Why Substantive Criminal Law—A Dialogue*, 29 Clev. St. L. Rev. 1 (1980).

[2] For a definition of this term, see 9.10[B], *infra*.

[3] 4 Blackstone at *5.

[4] See § 2.02, *infra*.

[5] George K. Gardner, *Bailey v. Richardson and the Constitution of the United States*, 33 B.U. L. Rev. 176, 193 (1953).

(or even less) than that which results from a civil judgment; it is the societal condemnation and stigma that accompanies the conviction that most of all distinguishes the civil from the criminal process.[6] It follows from this, therefore, that a crime should be defined as "an act or omission and its accompanying state of mind which, if duly shown to have taken place, will incur a formal and solemn pronouncement of the moral condemnation of the community."[7] To the extent that conduct that does *not* justify condemnation is treated as criminal, the line between the civil and criminal process is unwisely blurred.[8]

[2]—Classification of Crimes

The English common law[9] divided crimes into two general categories: felonies and misdemeanors.[10] A felony "comprise[d] every species of crime which occasioned at common law the forfeiture of lands and goods."[11] All common law felonies were punishable by death. The list of felonies was short: felonious homicide (later divided by statute into murder and manslaughter), arson, mayhem, rape, robbery, larceny, burglary, prison escape, and (perhaps) sodomy.[12] All other criminal offenses were misdemeanors.

In modern penal codes, the line between felonies and misdemeanors is drawn differently than in the past. Generally speaking, an offense punishable by imprisonment in a state prison or death is a felony; an offense for which the maximum punishment is a monetary fine, incarceration in a local jail, or both, is a misdemeanor. For sentencing purposes, the Model Penal Code,[13] and the statutory schemes of various jurisdictions,[14] also divide felonies into degrees.[15] Some states, as well, have added an additional classification of crime, e.g., "violations"[16] or

---

[6] Hart, Note 1, *supra*, at 404; see also Katz at 28 ("[P]unishment condemns, the [civil] penalty does not").

[7] Hart, Note 1, *supra.* at 405.

[8] Do not assume, however, that all morally wrongful conduct is criminal. In a society that prizes individual liberty, the criminal law serves a *minimalist* role: it seeks to identify and regulate wrongful conduct of a harmful nature; it does not seek "to purify thoughts and perfect character." *United States v. Hollingsworth*, 27 F.3d 1196, 1203 (7th Cir. 1994) (*en banc*). The latter is the responsibility of religion, family, and other private institutions. For example, telling an untruth may be a sign of a character flaw, but the criminal law punishes only the most harmful lies, e.g., false statements made under oath in judicial proceedings.

[9] The "common law" is judge-made law. See § 3.01[A], *infra*.

[10] Because of its special heinousness, treason was categorized separately, but strictly speaking it was a felony. 4 Blackstone at *95.

[11] *Id.* at *94.

[12] Perkins & Boyce at 14. The authors state that originally sodomy was punished as an ecclesiastical offense, and was made a felony by statute, but it is "old enough to be recognized as common law in this country." *Id.* at 15.

[13] For an explanation of the Model Penal Code, see 3.03, *infra*.

[14] E.g. N.Y. Penal Law § 55.05 (McKinney 1987).

[15] E.g., Model Penal Code § 6.01(1) (dividing felonies into three degrees); § 6.03 and 6.06 (setting out the fines and terms of imprisonment, by degree of felony).

[16] Model Penal Code § 1.04(5).

"infractions." These offenses cover very minor misconduct and cannot result in incarceration. [17]

[B]—Principles of Criminal Responsibility

As one scholar has observed, "[i]t is deeply rooted in our moral sense of fitness that punishment entails blame and that, therefore, punishment may not justly be imposed where the person is not blameworthy." [18]

The study of the criminal law is, therefore, much more than the study of crimes: it is also the investigation of the doctrines that have developed over the centuries for determining when a person may justly be held criminally responsible for harm that she has caused. Put another way, the principles of criminal responsibility, which are at the core of the criminal law, seek to identify the point at which it is fair to go from the factual premise, "*D* caused or assisted in causing X (a social harm) to occur," to the normative judgment, "*D* should be punished for having caused or assisted in causing X to occur."

§ 1.02 Proving Guilt at the Trial

[A]—Right to Trial by Jury

[1]—In General

The Sixth Amendment to the United States Constitution provides that "in all criminal prosecutions, the accused shall enjoy the right to a speedy and public trial, by an impartial jury." The right to trial by jury is "fundamental to the American scheme of justice," and therefore applies in all state criminal proceedings. [19] The constitutional guarantee reflects a "profound judgment about the way in which law should be enforced and justice administered." The right is granted "in order to prevent oppression by the Government . . . . If the defendant prefer[s] the common-sense judgment of a jury to the more tutored but perhaps less sympathetic reaction of the single judge, he [is] to have it." [20]

Despite the Sixth Amendment phrase, "in all criminal prosecutions," the jury-trial right applies only to "non-petty" offenses. According to the Supreme Court, "no offense can be deemed 'petty' for purposes of the right to trial by jury where imprisonment for more than six months is authorized." [21] An offense is also non-petty, even if the maximum authorized period of incarceration is six months or less, if any additional statutory penalties (including fines) "are so severe that they clearly

---

[17] Usually, a violation or infraction involves conduct that does not justify moral condemnation, e.g., breach of a traffic ordinance. To the extent that such an offense is characterized as "criminal," it runs counter to the definition of "crime" set out in subsection [A], *supra*. To avoid this apparent conflict, some scholars state that violations are not "true crimes." Perkins & Boyce at 18.

[18] Kadish, Note 1, *supra*, at 10.

[19] *Duncan v. Louisiana*, 391 U.S. 145, 149 (1968).

[20] *Id.* at 155-56.

[21] *Baldwin v. New York*, 399 U.S. 66, 69 (1970).

reflect a legislative determination that the offense in question is a 'serious' one."[22] As a practical matter, this means that a criminal defendant has a constitutional right to trial by jury in all felony and many misdemeanor prosecutions.

[2]—Scope of the Right

In the federal courts[23] and in most states, a jury in a criminal trial is composed of 12 persons who must reach a unanimous verdict to convict or acquit. Juries as small as six, however, are constitutional.[24] State laws permitting non-unanimous verdicts are also allowed, as long as the vote to convict represents a "substantial majority" of the jurors.[25]

Because the purpose of the jury system is to protect individuals from governmental oppression and to provide the accused with the common-sense judgment of the community, the defendant is entitled to a jury drawn from a pool of persons constituting a fair cross-section of the community.[26] This Sixth Amendment right is violated if large, distinctive groups of persons, such as women, racial minorities, or adherents of a religion, are systematically and unjustifiably excluded from the jury pool.

[B]—Burden of Proof

The Supreme Court has ruled that the due process clauses of the United States Constitution[27] require the prosecutor to persuade the factfinder "beyond a reasonable doubt of every fact necessary to constitute the crime . . . charged."[28] The meaning of this language, and the effect of failing to meet this burden of proof, are matters considered in detail in Chapter 7.

[C]—Jury Nullification[29]

[1]—The Issue

Are there circumstances in which a jury should acquit, even if the prosecutor proves beyond a reasonable doubt that the accused committed the offense charged? For example, should jurors acquit a defendant if they believe that the criminal law

---

[22] *Blanton v. City of North Las Vegas*, 489 U.S. 538, 543 (1989).

[23] Fed. R. Crim. P. 23(a) (size of the jury); 31(a) (unanimity requirement).

[24] *Williams v. Florida*, 399 U.S. 78 (1970) (a jury of six is permissible); *Ballew v. Georgia*, 435 U.S. 223 (1978) (a jury of five is too small).

[25] *Johnson v. Louisiana*, 406 U.S. 356 (1972) (a 9-3 guilty verdict is constitutional).

[26] *Taylor v. Louisiana*, 419 U.S. 522 (1975).

[27] The Fifth and Fourteenth Amendments each contain a due process clause. The Fifth Amendment applies in the federal system, whereas the Fourteenth Amendment pertains to the states.

[28] *In re Winship*, 397 U.S. 358, 364 (1970).

[29] See generally Thomas Andrew Green, Verdict According to Conscience (1985); Alan Scheflin & Jon Van Dyke, *Jury Nullification: The Contours of a Controversy*, 43 Law & Contemp. Probs. 51 (1980); Phillip B. Scott, *Jury Nullification: An Historical Perspective on a Modern Debate*, 91 W. Va. L. Rev. 389 (1989).

she violated is immoral or unwise, or because they feel that she has been "punished enough already."

Juries ordinarily return general verdicts in criminal proceedings. That is, a jury does not explain its verdict; it simply finds the defendant "guilty" or "not guilty."[30] Moreover, the Fifth Amendment of the United States Constitution provides that "[n]o person shall . . . be subject for the same offense to be twice put in jeopardy." Therefore, the government may not prosecute a defendant again after a "not guilty" verdict. Consequently, a jury *can* acquit a defendant without stating its reason and, no matter what its justification may have been, the verdict is non-reviewable. But, *should* juries "nullify" the law?

[2]—The Debate

Advocates of jury nullification point out that the right to trial-by-jury is recognized in order to protect against governmental oppression, and to provide the accused with the common-sense judgment of lay people. Moreover, a finding of guilt is not simply a determination that the accused did the acts charged; it also represents a judgment by the jury—the "conscience of the community"[31] —that the defendant should be subjected to the condemnation and formal punishment that results from a conviction. The jury-nullification power, therefore, serves as the community's safeguard against morally unjust or socially undesirable (albeit legally proper) criminal convictions. An example was the acquittal in 1735, by a colonial jury, of Peter Zenger, the confessed printer of a journal that published articles critical of British authorities, who was prosecuted for seditious libel.[32]

Critics respond that although a jury has the raw power to nullify the law, it should not exercise that power. To the extent that a jury acts on the basis of its conclusion that a law is unjust, the jury-nullification power "[c]ast[s] aside . . . our basic belief that only our elected representatives may determine what is a crime and what is not, and only they may revise that law if it is found to be unfair . . . ."[33] Opponents also argue that if jurors have the right to disregard the law and follow their consciences, they should be told of this "right," yet jurors must swear to obey the law when they serve on the jury. The jury-nullification power, therefore, "would confuse any conscientious citizen serving on a jury."[34] It would also "put untoward strains on the jury system . . . . [The jury-nullification power] is . . . an extreme burden for the jurors' psyche."[35]

[3]—The Law

The issue of jury nullification ordinarily arises in one of two contexts. First, the judge might instruct the jury that, if it finds beyond a reasonable doubt that the

---

[30] One common exception exists: in many states a jury that acquits a defendant on the basis of insanity may return a verdict of "not guilty by reason of insanity." See § 25.02[D], *infra*.

[31] *Witherspoon v. Illinois*, 391 U.S. 510, 519 & n.15 (1968).

[32] See James Alexander, A Brief Narration of the Case and Trial of John Peter Zenger (1963).

[33] *State v. Ragland*, 519 A.2d 1361, 1369 (N.J. 1986).

[34] *Id.* at 1371.

[35] *United States v. Dougherty*, 473 F.2d 1113, 1136 (D.C. Cir. 1972).

defendant committed the crime charged, it "must" find her guilty. The general rule is that such an instruction is not impermissible, although it implicitly denies the jury the right to nullify the law. [36]

Second, the defense may request the judge to instruct the jury that it is entitled to act upon its conscientious feelings to acquit the defendant, or the issue may arise in the context of a defense counsel's call to the jury during closing arguments to exercise its power to nullify the law and acquit. Although a very few courts have allowed jury-nullification arguments to the jury, [37] the overwhelming rule is that such arguments and jury instructions in this regard are impermissible. [38]

---

[36] E.g., *Watts v. United States*, 362 A.2d 706 (D.C. 1976) (*en banc*); *State v. Ragland*, 519 A.2d 1361 (N.J. 1986); contra, *United States v. Hayward*, 420 F.2d 142 (D.C. Cir. 1969).

[37] E.g., *United States v. Datcher*, 830 F.Supp. 411 (M.D. Tenn. 1993) (permitting the defense to put on evidence and argue that the law is unjust; but conceding that there is widespread case law against this position, and stating in dictum that it would not have permitted an instruction on jury nullification if it had been requested).

[38] E.g., *United States v. Dougherty*, 473 F.2d 1113 (D.C.Cir. 1972) (rejecting the appellants' claim that they were entitled to a nullification instruction); *State v. Ragland*, 519 A.2d 1361 (N.J. 1986) (*id.*); *State v. Bjerkaas*, 472 N.W.2d 615 (Wis. Ct. App. 1991) (the trial court properly precluded defense counsel from arguing for jury nullification).

CHAPTER 2

PRINCIPLES OF CRIMINAL PUNISHMENT

§ 2.01 Chapter Overview

The subject of this chapter is punishment, and more specifically the moral theories that are used to justify it. Why should we care about these theories? First, the criminal law is a blunt instrument, used in our name. The criminal justice system, which enforces our criminal laws, inflicts pain on persons convicted of criminal conduct, by taking their lives, liberty, or property (primarily through monetary fines). Any system that intentionally causes such suffering requires a justification. The principles discussed in this chapter provide potential bases for legitimating our criminal justice system.

Second, lawmakers must ascertain not only what conduct is wrongful, but they must determine which persons may properly be held accountable for their wrongful behavior, and when punishment is deemed appropriate, they must decide what and how much punishment fits the offense and the offender. The principles discussed here provide different means for making these determinations.

Third, criminal laws ought to be fair and, to the extent possible, deal coherently with persons charged with crime. The penal theories considered below provide the intellectual foundations for evaluating the fairness and coherence of our criminal laws.

§ 2.02 Definition of "Punishment"[1]

What does it mean to "punish" someone? Clearly, sending a convicted criminal to prison is punishment. Suppose, however, that a wealthy person is required by a court to pay a small fine for violating a criminal statute. Is this punishment? Is a physician "punished" when she is compelled by a criminal court to perform public service in a hospital? What if a convicted criminal must undergo out-patient psychiatric care in lieu of a prison sentence? Is an alleged or convicted wrongdoer "punished" if a mob lynches him? May we say that a lawyer has been punished if she is disbarred for embezzlement of a client's funds?

Virtually all definitions of the term "punishment" are susceptible to the criticism that they are arbitrary. Nonetheless, in the context of the criminal law, D may be

---

[1] See generally Steven Sverdlik, *Punishment*, 7 Law & Phil. 179 (1988). For reflections on, and accounts of, the punitive process, see Michel Foucault, Discipline and Punish (Alan Sheridan, translator 1977); Graeme Newman, The Punishment Response (2d ed. 1985); Robert Blecker, *Haven or Hell? Inside Lorton Central Prison: Experiences of Punishment Justified*, 42 Stan. L. Rev. 1149 (1990).

said to suffer punishment when an agent of the government, pursuant to authority granted to the agent by virtue of *D*'s criminal conviction, intentionally inflicts pain on *D* or otherwise causes *D* to suffer some consequence that is ordinarily considered to be unpleasant.[2]

Pursuant to this definition, payment of a fine by a wealthy individual constitutes punishment, albeit perhaps inadequate punishment, because the fine is a consequence that ordinarily is considered unpleasant. For the same reason, post-conviction court-compelled public service[3] and out-patient psychiatric care constitute punishment. On the other hand, penalties imposed outside the criminal justice system, such as the disbarment of a lawyer by the licensing authority or the actions of a lynch mob, although painful or unpleasant, do not constitute punishment.

§ 2.03   Theories of Punishment[4]

[A]—Forms of Moral Reasoning

Moral reasoning is of two types. One version focuses on actions as means to good ends. According to this "teleological" or "consequentialist" view, actions are morally right if, but only if, they result in desirable consequences. The primary consequentialist theory of punishment is "utilitarianism."

The contrasting form of moral reasoning ("deontology") focuses on actions as ends in themselves. Deontologists seek to determine what actions are morally right, regardless of their ultimate effects on others. The primary nonconsequentialist moral theory of punishment is "retributivism."

---

[2] See Hart at 4-5.

[3] But see *United States v. Bergman*, 416 F. Supp. 496 (S.D.N.Y. 1976), in which *D*, a rabbi and nursing home operator, pleaded guilty to two counts of Medicaid and tax fraud, relating to operation of his nursing homes. *D* proposed to the trial judge that he be required to create and run a program of Jewish vocational and religious high school training or a "Committee on Holocaust Studies." The judge expressed doubt that this would constitute punishment, because the proposed work was "honorific" in nature and "not unlike that done [by *D*] in other projects" prior to his legal difficulties. *Id.* at 500-01.

[4] See generally Hart at 1-27; Packer at 9-70; Sir Walter Moberly, The Ethics of Punishment (1968); Igor Primoratz, Justifying Legal Punishment (1989); Nigel Walker, Why Punish? (1991); Kent Greenawalt, *Punishment*, in 4 Encyclopedia of Crime and Justice 1336 (Sanford H. Kadish ed. 1983); Mark A. Michael, *Utilitarianism and Retributivism: What's the Difference?*, 29 Am. Phil. Q. 173 (1992).

[B]—Utilitarianism [5]

[1]—Basic Principles

According to classical utilitarianism, formulated by Jeremy Bentham,[6] the purpose of all laws is to maximize the net happiness of society. Laws should be used to exclude, as far as possible, all painful or unpleasant events. To a utilitarian, both crime and punishment are unpleasant and, therefore, normally undesirable occurrences. In a perfect world, neither would exist.

As we do not live in a perfect world—some persons are disposed to commit crimes—utilitarians believe that the pain inflicted by punishment is justifiable if, but only if, it is expected to result in a reduction in the pain of crime that would otherwise occur. For example, the imposition of five units of pain (however the "units" are measured) on D is justifiable if it will prevent more than 5 units of pain (in the form of crime) that would have occurred but for D's punishment.

Classical utilitarians reason that the threat or imposition of punishment can reduce crime because, in Bentham's words, [p]ain and pleasure are the great springs of human action," and "[i]n matters of importance every one calculates."[7] Put slightly differently, utilitarians believe that human beings generally act hedonistically and rationally. That is, a person will act according to his immediate desires to the extent that he believes that his conduct will augment his overall happiness. As a calculator, however, a person contemplating criminal activity (to augment his happiness) will balance the expected benefits of the proposed conduct against its risks, taking into account such factors as the likelihood of successful commission of the crime, the risk of detection and conviction, and the severity of the likely punishment. He will avoid criminal activity if the perceived potential pain (punishment) outweighs the expected potential pleasure (criminal rewards).[8]

---

[5] See generally Johannes Andenaes, Punishment and Deterrence (1974); Contemporary Utilitarianism (Michael D. Bayles ed. 1968); Jeremy Bentham, An Introduction to the Principles of Morals and Legislation (J. Bowring ed. 1843); John Stuart Mill, Utilitarianism (1863); Franklin E. Zimring & Gordon J. Hawkins, Deterrence (1973); Louis Michael Seidman, *Soldiers, Martyrs, and Criminals: Utilitarian Theory and the Problem of Crime Control*, 94 Yale L.J. 315 (1984); J.J.C. Smart, *Utilitarianism and Punishment*, 25 Israel L. Rev. 361 (1991); Michael Vitiello, *Reconsidering Rehabilitation*, 65 Tulane L. Rev. 1011 (1991); Andrew von Hirsch, *Selective Incapacitation Reexamined: The National Academy of Sciences' Report on Criminal Careers and "Career Criminals"*, Crim. Just. Ethics, Winter/Spring 1988, at 19; Andrew von Hirsch & Lisa Maher, *Can Penal Rehabilitationism be Revived?*, Crim. Just. Ethics, Winter/Spring 1992, at 25.

[6] Bentham, Note 5, *supra*.

[7] Jeremy Bentham, Principles of Penal Law, in J. Bentham's Works 396, 402 (J. Bowring ed. 1843).

[8] E.g., if D believes that there is a 50 percent chance of being caught, prosecuted, convicted, and subjected to 10 units of punishment, he will commit the crime if his expected gain from the offense is more than 5 units of pleasure (10 units of pain-by-punishment x .50 chance of its infliction = 5 units of expected pain). On the other hand, if D thinks that the risk of detection, conviction, and punishment is 90 percent, he will not commit the crime unless he believes that the likely benefits are much greater (more than 9 units of pleasure).

[2]—Forms of Utilitarianism

Utilitarianism as applied to the criminal law takes different forms. Most commonly, utilitarians stress *general deterrence*. That is, *D* is punished in order to convince the general community to forego criminal conduct in the future. In this model, *D*'s punishment serves as an object lesson to the rest of the community; *D* is used as a means to a desired end, namely, a net reduction in crime. *D*'s punishment teaches us what conduct is impermissible; it instills fear of punishment in would-be violators of the law; and, at least to a limited extent, it habituates us to act lawfully, even in the absence of fear of punishment.

Specific deterrence is an alternative utilitarian goal. Here, *D*'s punishment is meant to deter future misconduct by *D*. Specific deterrence may occur in two ways. First, there is deterrence by incapacitation: *D*'s imprisonment prevents him from committing crimes in the outside society during the period of segregation.[9] Second, upon release, there is deterrence by intimidation: *D*'s punishment reminds him that if he returns to a life of crime, he will experience more pain.

A non-classical variety of utilitarianism is *rehabilitation* (or *reform*). Although the goal is the same—to reduce future crime—advocates of this model prefer to use the correctional system to reform the wrongdoer rather than to secure compliance through the fear or "bad taste" of punishment. The methods of reformation will vary from case to case, but could consist of, for example, psychiatric therapy, lobotomy, or academic or vocational training.[10]

Notice that if an actor believes that there is virtually no chance of detection and punishment, virtually no threat of punishment will deter him. In general, therefore, an increase in the likelihood of punishment will deter more effectively than an increase in the severity of punishment. See Steven Klepper and Daniel Nagin, *The Deterrent Effect of Perceived Certainty and Severity of Punishment Revisited*, 27 Criminology 721 (1989).

[9] This theory does not justify the simplistic notion that society should put all convicts in prison and "throw away the key." To a utilitarian, punishment is unjustifiable on incapacitative grounds unless *D*'s likely future anti-social behavior would cause more pain to society than the pain inflicted on *D* by his lifetime imprisonment.

[10] Adherents of rehabilitation prefer to call the reformative process "treatment" or "healing," rather than "punishment." However, because the process does not require the criminal's consent and is the result of a criminal conviction, reformative procedures constitute "punishment." See § 2.02, *supra*.

[C]—Retributivism [11]

[1]—Basic Principles

Retributivists believe that punishment is justified when it is deserved. It is deserved when the wrongdoer freely chooses to violate society's rules. To an uncompromising retributivist, [12] the wrongdoer should be punished, whether or not it will result in a reduction in crime. As Immanuel Kant made the latter point, "[e]ven if a civil society resolved to dissolve itself . . . the last murderer lying in the prison ought to be executed . . . ." This act of punishment, which can provide no utilitarian benefit, is required because of the "desert of [the murderer's] deeds." [13]

Notice two differences between retributivism and utilitarianism. First, retributivism looks backward and justifies punishment solely on the basis of the voluntary commission of a crime. In contrast, utilitarians look forward. They care about the past only to the extent that it helps them to predict the future. No matter how egregious the wrongdoing, they do not advocate punishment unless they believe it will provide an overall social benefit. Second, whereas the premise of utilitarianism is that people are generally hedonistic and rational calculators, retributivism is based on the view that humans possess free will and, therefore, may justly be blamed when they choose to violate society's mores. [14]

---

[11] See generally Immanuel Kant, The Metaphysical Elements of Justice (J. Ladd translation 1965); Immanuel Kant, The Philosophy of Law (W. Hastie translation 1887); Jeffrie G. Murphy & Jean Hampton, Forgiveness and Mercy (1988); David Dolinko, *Three Mistakes of Retributivism*, 39 UCLA L. Rev. 1623 (1992); David Dolinko, *Some Thoughts About Retributivism*, 101 Ethics 537 (1991); Joshua Dressler, *Hating Criminals: How Can Something That Feels So Good Be Wrong?*, 88 Mich. L. Rev. 1448 (1990); Jean Hampton, *Correcting Harms versus Righting Wrongs: The Goal of Retribution*, 39 UCLA L. Rev. 1659 (1992); Michael S. Moore, *The Moral Worth of Retribution*, in Responsibility, Character and the Emotions 179 (Ferdinand Schoeman, ed. 1987); Herbert Morris, *A Paternalistic Theory of Punishment*, 18 Am. Phil. Q. 263 (1981); Herbert Morris, *Persons and Punishment*, 52 Monist 475 (1968); Jeffrie G. Murphy, *Retributivism, Moral Education, and the Liberal State*, Crim. Just. Ethics, Winter/Spring 1985, at 3; Benjamin B. Sendor, *Restorative Retributivism*, 5 J. Contemp. Leg. Issues 323 (1994); and Roger Wertheimer, *Understanding Retribution*, Crim. Just. Ethics, Summer/Fall 1983, at 19.

[12] Some people support a mixture of retributivism and utilitarianism; others favor a somewhat "softer" version of retributivism than is set out here. See § 2.05, *infra*.

[13] Kant, The Philosophy of Law, Note 11, *supra*, at 197-98. Not all retributivists agree with Kant that the death penalty must be imposed for the offense of murder.

[14] Some philosophers, termed "hard determinists," deny the existence of free will. The thesis of determinism is that every event has a cause. According to hard determinists, humans are little more than marionettes whose strings are pulled by genetic and environmental forces beyond their control. Because free will is a fiction, there is no basis for praising good samaritans or blaming wrongdoers. The hero acts selflessly because he is programmed to act in this manner; the criminal acts selfishly for the same reason. According to this view, a criminal is "more a victim of misfortune than a villain on the cosmic stage." Greenawalt, Note 4, *supra*, at 1338. Hard determinism, therefore, is incompatible with retributivism.

By contrast, "soft determinists" reason that although human actions are caused, they are

[2]—Forms of Retributivism

Although retribution is based on the dual premises that humans possess free will and that punishment is justified when it is deserved, retributivists differ among themselves regarding the best way to defend their "just deserts" philosophy. According to one form of retribution, variously described as *assaultive retribution*,[15] *public vengeance*, or *societal retaliation*, "it is morally right to hate criminals."[16] Because the criminal has harmed society, it is right for society to "hurt him back." This version of retribution is apt to "regard[] criminals rather like noxious insects to be ground under the heel of society."[17]

Some advocates of this view argue that retributive punishment gratifies the passion for revenge that would otherwise be satisfied through private vengeance. However, this justification is a disguised form of utilitarianism, since it defends punishment in order to deter private revenge. On the other hand, Professor Jeffrie Murphy has defended "retributive hatred" this way: when a person is the victim of a crime, he justifiably resents the criminal for violating his rights; such resentment takes the form of righteous anger or hatred, in which the resenter wants to see the wrongdoer suffer; these passions are morally desirable because they demonstrate that the crime victim respects himself, i.e., that he believes that he should be treated with dignity.[18]

A second version of retribution may be called *protective retribution*, or retribution based on the *principle of personhood*.[19] For adherents of this form of retribution, punishment is not inflicted because society wants to hurt wrongdoers, but because punishment is a means of securing a moral balance in the society. As Herbert Morris has explained,[20] society is composed of rules that forbid various form of harmful conduct; compliance with these rules burdens each member of the community that exercises self-restraint. These same rules provide a benefit in the form of "noninterference by others with what each person values, such . . . as continuance of life and bodily security."[21] As long as everyone follows the rules,

---

not always compelled. A person is free, and therefore properly the recipient of praise or blame, if he is able to act according to the determinations of his own will, i.e. if his actions spring from his own rationally-based motives. A person is unfree when he must do something against his own will—the result of external constraints—or when he lacks the capacity to reason. Soft determinism, therefore, is compatible with retributivism.

[15] Margaret Jane Radin, *Cruel Punishment and Respect for Persons: Super Due Process for Death*, 53 S. Cal. L. Rev. 1143, 1168 (1980). Professor Radin also coined the term "protective retribution" discussed in the text, *infra*.

[16] 2 James Fitzjames Stephen, A History of the Criminal Law of England 81 (1883).

[17] Murphy & Hampton, Note 11, *supra*, at 3 (describing the attitude of James Fitzjames Stephen).

[18] *Id.* at 88-110.

[19] Joshua Dressler, *Substantive Criminal Law Through the Looking Glass of Rummel v. Estelle: Proportionality and Justice as Endangered Doctrines*, 34 Sw. L.J. 1063, 1073 (1981).

[20] Morris, *Persons and Punishment*, Note 11, *supra*.

[21] *Id.* at 477.

an equilibrium exists: everyone is similarly benefitted and burdened. If a person fails to exercise self-restraint when he could have—when he renounces a burden which others have assumed—he destroys the balance. He becomes a free rider: he has the benefits of the system of rules, without accepting the same burdens. Thus, a criminal owes a debt to society. It is fair to require payment of the debt, i.e., punishment equal or proportional to the debt owed (i.e. the crime committed).

Advocates of this form of retribution emphasize that by punishing the wrongdoer, society demonstrates its respect for him: by stating that the criminal deserves punishment and is morally blameworthy, society treats him as a responsible moral agent. Indeed, according to this school of thought, the wrongdoer has a *right* to be punished. Punishment permits the offender to pay his debt to society, and to return to it free of moral guilt and stigma.

A third form of retribution might be termed *victim vindication*.[22] As Professor Jean Hampton explains, punishment is a way to "right a wrong." She argues that, by committing an offense, a criminal implicitly sends a message to the victim and society that his (the criminal's) rights and desires are more valuable than those of the victim. Thus, by committing a crime, the offender elevates himself with respect to others. By doing so, the criminal makes a false moral claim as to his relative worth. Retributive punishment corrects this false claim: it reaffirms the victim's worth as a human being in the face of the criminal's challenge. Retributive punishment, therefore, represents a "defeat of the wrongdoer"; he is mastered in much the way that he mastered the victim. Once the criminal receives punishment proportional to the offense, the "score" is made even.

[D]—Denunciation

Most efforts to justify punishment are based on utilitarianism or retributivism. *Denunciation* is probably the most frequently suggested alternative basis of punishment. According to this view, punishment is justified as a means of expressing society's condemnation of a crime.[23] Upon a closer look, however, denunciation turns out to be a hybrid of utilitarianism and retribution.

Why is denunciation desirable? First, it is educative. We inform individuals that the community considers specified conduct improper. Second, public denunciation through the criminal justice system serves an expressive function: it channels community anger away from personal vengeance. The collective expression of condemnation also serves to maintain social cohesion.[24] In all of these ways denunciation is utilitarian in nature.

Denunciation is also retributive, in that it is a form of condemnation: it serves to stigmatize the offender for his offense. By denunciation, society announces that

---

[22] See Hampton, Note 11, *supra*, at 1686 ("retribution is a response to a wrong that is intended to vindicate the value of the victim"), and Murphy and Hampton, Note 11, *supra*, at 111-61; see also Sendor, Note 11, *supra* (defending a somewhat similar version of retribution, which the author describes as "restorative retributivism").

[23] See Royal Commission on Capital Punishment, Minutes of Evidence, Ninth Day, December 1, 1949, Memorandum submitted by the Rt. Hon. Lord Justice Denning (1950).

[24] Emile Durkheim, The Division of Labor in Society 108-09 (G. Simpson translation 1933).

the wrongdoer deserves to be punished and expresses its feelings of hostility toward the offender. These are feelings and beliefs consistent with retributivism.

§ 2.04 The Debate Between the Competing Theories[25]

Debate between utilitarians and retributivists has raged for centuries. It is unlikely to end soon. Nonetheless, it is important to get a sense of the nature of the disagreement. What follows is a brief summary of some of the criticisms of the theories, and common responses to the objections.

[A]—Criticisms of Utilitarianism

[1]—Deterrence

Retributivists criticize general deterrence theory on the ground that it justifies using persons solely as a means to an end. To the utilitarian, the punished individual is an instrument for the improvement of society. This system ignores the dignity and human rights of the wrongdoer. Utilitarians respond that humans possess no immutable rights for utilitarians to ignore.[26] The right each member of society possesses is the right to have the law used to benefit the whole community. Furthermore, since the wrongdoer is a member of society, he benefits from his own punishment. Therefore, he is not used *solely* as a means to an end.

A second criticism of utilitarianism, closely allied to the first charge, is that utilitarianism can justify the punishment of one known to be innocent of wrongdoing.[27] The following hypothetical illustrates this point:[28] A white woman, living in a racially divided community, is brutally raped by an unidentified black male. A mob of white racists respond by surging into an area of town with a predominantly African-American population, intending to lynch and burn the houses of many innocent persons. The town's sheriff lacks the personnel to stop the mob. According to retributivist critics, a utilitarian sheriff could justify immediately arresting and framing an innocent African-American for the crime in order to placate the mob or, even, giving the man over to the mob for a private lynching, in order to sate their vengeance. Retributivism flatly rejects this outcome: an

---

25 See generally Contemporary Utilitarianism, Note 5, *supra*; Murphy & Hampton, Note 11, *supra*; Dolinko, *Three Mistakes of Retributivismeit;, Note 11, supra; Dolinko, Some Thoughts About Retributivismeit;, Note 11, supra; Michael, Note 4, supra; and Moore, Note 11, supra*.

26 Bentham wrote that " *[n]atural rights* is simple nonsense; natural and imprescriptible rights, rhetorical nonsense,—nonsense upon stilts." Bentham, Anarchical Fallacies, in 2 The Works of Jeremy Bentham 501 (J. Bowring ed. 1843).

27 See generally H.J. McCloskey, *A Non-Utilitarian Approach to Punishmenteit;, in Contemporary Utilitarianism, Note 5, supra, at 239; James McCloskey, Convicting the Innocent,* Crim. Just. Ethics, Winter/Spring 1989, at 2; *Jeffrey Reiman & Ernest van den Haag, On the Common Saying that it is Better that Ten Guilty Persons Escape Than That One Innocent Suffer: Pro and Con, Soc. Phil. & Pol'y,* Spring 1990, at 226; *T.L.S. Sprigge, A Utilitarian Reply to Dr. McCloskey, in Contemporary Utilitarianism, Note 5, supra, at 261*.

28 The hypothetical is based on H.J. McCloskey, *A Non-Utilitarian Approach to Punishment,* in Contemporary Utilitarianism, Note 5, *supra*, at 248.

innocent person never deserves punishment because he has no debt to repay society; therefore, punishment of an innocent person is unalterably wrong.

Utilitarians do not usually deny the theoretical possibility that punishment of an innocent person could be justified, but they insist that the factual circumstances supporting such a result would never come into play. In the hypothetical above, for example, the sheriff could have arrested the innocent man, and then released him after the mob dispersed. Furthermore, utilitarians argue, the sheriff ignored the wider consequences of his actions. For example, a sensible utilitarian would consider the possibility that the public would eventually learn that he had framed an innocent person. The public loss of respect for the criminal justice system, anger at the sheriff, and fear of similar treatment would cause more harm than the mob would have committed.

[2]—Rehabilitation

Critics doubt that criminals can be reformed. They ask, in essence: "If family, school, and religion have failed, why should we think that prisons, psychiatric care, or any other form of treatment will succeed?" Opponents of rehabilitation point to studies that suggest that reform efforts have failed. [29] Proponents contend that empirical studies demonstrate "that opponents . . . [have] grossly overstated the case against rehabilitation." [30] Although reformation may not be possible in all circumstances, advocates argue that it will often work if society is prepared to commit the necessary resources to the process.

Retributivists criticize rehabilitation on the ground that, in the name of humanitarianism, the "theory removes from Punishment the concept of Desert . . . . [W]hen we cease to consider what the criminal deserves and consider only what will cure him . . ., we have tacitly removed him from the sphere of justice altogether." [31] Critics state that proponents of rehabilitation treat offenders as if they were sick, childlike, or otherwise unable to act as moral agents. Moreover, a system based on rehabilitation can justify "cures" (e.g. a lobotomy) that violate the criminal's personhood.

Advocates of rehabilitation believe that reformation is preferable to punishment based on fear (classical utilitarian theory) or the "hurt the criminal, he deserves it" attitude of assaultive retribution. They point out that the rehabilitative model preserves the concept of redemption evident in Judeo-Christian values. When such a transformation occurs, "it is difficult to find a continued justification for imposing suffering on that offender." [32]

---

[29] E.g., Robert Martinson, *What Works? Questions and Answers about Prison Reform*, 35 Pub. Interest 22 (1974).

[30] Vitiello, Note 5, *supra*, at 1032. One early critic of rehabilitation (see Note 29, *supra*) has since pointed to successes in the field. Robert Martinson, *New Findings, New Views: A Note of Caution Regarding Sentencing Reform*, 7 Hofstra L. Rev. 243 (1979).

[31] C.S. Lewis, *The Humanitarian Theory of Punishment*, in Contemporary Punishment: Views, Explanations, and Justifications 194 (R. Gerber & P. McAnany eds. 1972).

[32] Vitiello, Note 5, *supra*, at 1051.

[B]—Criticisms of Retributivism

Utilitarians state that punishment—the intentional infliction of pain—is senseless and even cruel if it does no good. Society's goal should be to reduce overall human suffering, not purposely to cause more of it. This criticism focuses on the consequentialist nature of utilitarianism—that actions are right or wrong depending on their consequences—in contrast to the nonconsequentialism of retributivism.[33] Retributivists believe that there are moral imperatives, i.e., acts that are unalterably right or wrong, regardless of their consequences. To a retributivist, once it is determined that a crime has been committed and that the wrongdoer is morally responsible for committing it, a measured response in the form of punishment proportional to the crime is unalterably right.

Second, some utilitarians criticize retributivism because, they say, it glorifies anger and legitimizes hatred.[34] The reality of retribution, therefore, conflicts with its purported respect for the rights of all persons, including criminals. A retributivist response is that this observation, if valid at all, applies only to the assaultive form of retribution.[35]

Third, and closely related to the preceding argument, is the claim that retributivism is irrational, because it is founded on emotions, such as anger, rather than on reason. Retributivists believe, however, that emotion can have a moral content. Just as most people believe that an emotion such as compassion is morally good—it says something good about the character of the person—anger, when directed at a wrongdoer for his wrongdoing, can also be a good emotion. Our anger demonstrates our awareness that the criminal has violated our rights, has acted unjustly and, therefore, deserves punishment. That anger—including the retributive urge to punish—is morally good when it demonstrates that we value ourselves and the rights of other crime victims.

§ 2.05   Mixed Theories of Punishment[36]

Utilitarianism and retributivism conflict with each other. Although adherents of both theories may agree on results in particular cases, a criminal justice system that seeks, exclusively, to prevent future crime will look very different from one that seeks, exclusively, to impose punishment based on a just-deserts philosophy.

The law of crimes that has developed is not philosophically consistent, i.e., some rules of criminal responsibility are primarily retributive in nature, whereas others are utilitarian in character. In part this is because each theory has dominated intellectual thought at separate times, but neither has won the ultimate debate. Consequently, both theories have attracted lawmakers. The result is that the rules

---

[33] See § 2.03[A], *supra.*

[34] Dolinko, *Three Mistakes of Retributivism,* Note 11, *supra,* at 1650.

[35] See § 2.03[C][2], *supra.*

[36] See generally Hart at 8-13; Paul H. Robinson, *Hybrid Principles for the Distribution of Criminal Sanctions,* 82 Nw. U. L. Rev. 19 (1987); Andrew von Hirsch, *Hybrid Principles in Allocating Sanctions: A Response to Professor Robinson,* 82 Nw. U. L. Rev. 64 (1987).

of criminal responsibility and punishment reflect society's attraction to both theories.

Many scholars have sought to justify a mixed theory of criminal punishment. They distinguish between, on the one hand, the general justifying aim of the criminal law and, on the other hand, the rules of criminal responsibility that determine who should be punished and how severe the punishment should be. Many have argued that the general aim of the criminal law—the reason why society has a criminal justice system—is to deter unwanted behavior. Nonetheless, some of these same utilitarians apply retributive concepts of just deserts in determining whether and how much to punish a particular person. For example, suppose that *D*, suffering from a severe mental illness, kills *V*. An advocate of this hybrid penal system might say that, of course, the criminal homicide statutes were enacted to deter unjustified killings, but that *D* should only be punished if he is morally blameworthy, which he might not be in light of his mental illness; and even if he is blameworthy, these mixed theorists would proportion his punishment to his reduced level of blameworthiness. Thus, advocates of this theory might favor less punishment of *D* than would a pure utilitarian, who might treat *D*'s mental illness as additional evidence of dangerousness.

At a minimum, many scholars believe in a hybrid system to this extent: they are unwilling to punish an innocent person, even if it could be justified on utilitarian grounds. [37] Therefore, most commentators, including most utilitarians, favor what is sometimes described as "negative retributivism"—the principle that guilt is a necessary condition of punishment. [38] Except as to innocent persons, however, these hybrid theorists apply utilitarian principles. Thus, like retributivists, they would not punish an innocent person, even if it would do some good; but, like the utilitarians they are, they would not punish a guilty person unless it would do some good. Moreover, in determining how much pain should be inflicted, advocates of this hybrid system would punish a wrongdoer to the extent justifiable under utilitarian, rather than retributive, principles. [39]

---

[37] For discussion of this issue, see § 2.04[A][1], *supra*.

[38] J.L. Mackie, *Morality and the Retributive Emotions*, Crim. Just. Ethics, Winter/Spring 1982, at 3, 4.

[39] For a comparison of utilitarian and retributive conceptions of "proportional punishment," see § 6.04, *infra*.

CHAPTER 3

SOURCES OF THE CRIMINAL LAW

§ 3.01 Origins of the Criminal Law[1]

[A]—Common Law

American criminal law is primarily English in its heritage and judicial in its origin. In large measure, the original thirteen American states and most later states adopted English law as their own.[2]

Originally, English criminal law was "common law" in nature. That is, it was judge-made law: the definitions of crimes and the rules of criminal responsibility were promulgated by courts rather than by the Parliament. When American courts and criminal lawyers use the term "common law," therefore, they are describing the law developed over the centuries by English judges and imported to this country. However, the common law of England was reworked by American courts to meet local needs and mores, so that by the turn of the twentieth century this country's common law diverged in significant respects from its British progenitor.

[B]—Criminal Statutes

During the Enlightenment, there was a movement in eighteenth and nineteenth century Europe and United States to shift the locus of lawmaking from the courts to legislative bodies. In part, the effort to enhance legislative authority was based on the belief that crimes should be defined by an institution more representative than the judiciary of those being governed.[3] The "romance with reason" also inspired reformers of different philosophical stripes (both utilitarians and believers in natural law) to try to codify the criminal law in order to produce "a legislated body of reordered, reformed, and reconceived law" in accordance with their respective principles.[4]

In general, early codification efforts failed. Over time, however, legislatures asserted themselves and enacted penal statutes, initially to supplement, but ultimately

---

[1] See generally Ford W. Hall, *The Common Law: An Account of its Reception in the United States*, 4 Vand. L. Rev. 791 (1951); Sanford H. Kadish, *The Model Penal Code's Historical Antecedents*, 19 Rutgers L.J. 521 (1988); Sanford H. Kadish, *Codifiers of the Criminal Law: Wechsler's Predecessors*, 78 Colum. L. Rev. 1098 (1978).

[2] See Hall, Note 1, *supra*, at 798-805.

[3] See John Calvin Jeffries, Jr., *Legality, Vagueness, and the Construction of Penal Statutes*, 71 Va. L. Rev. 189, 190 (1985).

[4] Kadish, *The Model Penal Code's Historical Antecedents*, Note 1, *supra*, at 521-22.

to replace, the common law. Today, the change-over is virtually complete. The legislature is the pre-eminent lawmaking body in the realm of criminal law.

§ 3.02 Modern Role of the Common Law

Although the legislative branch of government now has primary lawmaking authority, the common law of crimes remains important to modern lawyers.

[A]—"Reception" Statutes

Most states, often by statute, have abolished common law crimes.[5] In these jurisdictions, a person may only be convicted and punished for conduct defined as criminal by statute or other legislative enactment.

A number of states, however, expressly recognize common law offenses. These states have enacted "reception" statutes, which essentially provide that "[a]ny person who . . . commit[s] any . . . offense at the common law, for the punishment of which no provision is expressly made by any statute . . . [is] guilty of a felony [or misdemeanor]."[6] In effect, such a statute "receives" the common law offenses existing at the time of the statute's enactment; the common law crimes become an unwritten part of the state's criminal law, and are defined as they existed at the time of their reception.[7]

As a practical matter, prosecutions of common law offenses in reception-statute jurisdictions are rare. Common law crimes, although not abolished in such states, are superseded by statutes prohibiting similar conduct.[8] A common law prosecution is not possible, therefore, unless there is a gap in the statutory system, and there are now few lacunae; nearly all legislatures have enacted statutes encompassing the common law felonies and most of the misdemeanors.

A lingering issue in states recognizing common law offenses is whether a court may assert its traditional authority to devise new crimes. The authors of early twentieth century treatises assumed that this judicial power remained intact, and a few courts have exercised such authority,[9] but it is now commonly accepted that

---

[5] E.g., Cal. Penal Code 6 (West 1988) ("No act or omission . . . is criminal or punishable, except as prescribed or authorized by this Code . . . ."); Model Penal Code 1.05(1) ("No conduct constitutes an offense unless it is a crime or violation under this Code or another statute of this State").

[6] Mich. Comp. Laws 750.505 (1991).

[7] Where the criminal code is silent on the matter—it has not expressly abolished common law offenses nor does it contain a reception statute—a few courts have held that "so much of the common law as has not been abrogated or repealed by statute [remains] in full force and effect." *Gervin v. State*, 371 S.W.2d 449, 454 (Tenn. 1963).

[8] E.g., *State v. Palendrano*, 293 A.2d 747 (N.J. Super. Ct. 1972) (holding that the common law offense of "being a common scold"—a woman who habitually acts in a quarrelsome manner—was no longer a crime, in part because many of the elements of the offense were encompassed by the state's Disorderly Persons Act).

[9] One scholar discovered two American cases. Jeffries, Note 3, *supra*, at 194 n.13. In *Commonwealth v. Donoghue*, 63 S.W.2d 3 (Ky. 1933), the court upheld an indictment for

"[j]udicial crime creation [in the United States] is a thing of the past."[10] However, some modern courts believe that they are empowered by reception statutes to *abolish* common law offenses that they consider no longer "compatible with . . . local circumstances and situation."[11]

[B]—Statutory Interpretation

Even in states without reception statutes, the common law retains significance. Almost without exception, these jurisdictions have codified the common law felonies and most common law misdemeanors. These offenses are usually defined, at least in part, in common law terms.[12] A familiar maxim of statutory interpretation is that an undefined term in a statute is presumed to have its common law meaning.[13] Therefore, lawyers should be familiar with, and courts must often apply, the common law.

For example, in *Keeler v. Superior Court,*[14] D learned that his ex-wife was pregnant by another man. He intentionally struck her in the abdomen in order to kill the fetus. The fetus was delivered stillborn. D was prosecuted for murder, which was defined by statute, as at common law, as the "unlawful killing of a human being, with malice aforethought."

---

participation in "a nefarious plan for the habitual exaction of gross usury," although no such offense had previously existed. In *Commonwealth v. Mochan*, 110 A.2d 788 (Pa. Super. Ct. 1955), the defendant telephoned the victim, a married woman, and made "filthy, disgusting, and indecent" sexual comments to her. Although this conduct was not prohibited by any statute, the court upheld the conviction for "injuriously affect[ing] public morality." For an example of judicial crime-creation in England, see *Shaw v. Director of Public Prosecutions*, [1962] A.C. 220, in which the House of Lords affirmed a conviction involving the publication of a telephone directory of prostitutes, for conspiracy to corrupt public morals. Viscount Simonds stated that he "entertain[ed] no doubt that there remains in the courts of law a residual power to enforce the supreme and fundamental purpose of the law, to conserve... the moral welfare of the State" against "novel and unprepared for" attacks. *Id.* at 268.

[10] Jeffries, Note 3, *supra*, at 195. However, some courts have maintained that they have authority to expand the definition of *existing* crimes, including statutory offenses. See footnote 15, *infra*.

[11] *Pope v. State*, 396 A.2d 1054, 1078 (Md. 1979) (concluding that the common law offense of "misprision of felony" should be abolished because "its origin, the impractical and indiscriminate width of its scope, its other obvious deficiencies, and its long non-use" rendered it incompatible with the state's "general code of laws and jurisprudence"); see also *State v. Palendrano*, 293 A.2d 747 (N.J. Super. Ct. 1972) (holding that the common law offense of "being a common scold" was no longer an offense, in part because the crime had been ignored by the state legislature and had been mentioned only twice in the reports of judicial proceedings during almost two centuries of statehood).

[12] At times, a state will enact a common law offense but not define it, in which case the common law definition applies. E.g., Mich. Comp. Laws 750.321 (1991) (prohibiting, but not defining, manslaughter).

[13] *Taylor v. United States*, 495 U.S. 575, 592 (1990).

[14] 470 P.2d 617 (Cal. 1970).

D sought to bar his prosecution. He claimed that a fetus born dead was not a "human being" within the meaning of the state's murder statute. Because the statute did not define the critical term, the court looked to the common law of 1850, when the murder statute was enacted and the state legislature abolished common law offenses. The court determined that a fetus born dead was not a "human being" for purposes of homicide law under the common law and, therefore, could not be the basis for a modern-day prosecution, in the absence of legislative action.[15]

The common law may also be used to fill gaps in a penal code. For example, a common law principle is that a person may not be charged with murder if the victim did not die within a year and a day of the assault.[16] Federal law defines murder in common law terms,[17] but is silent regarding the year-and-a-day rule. In the absence of legislative history suggesting that Congress intended to eliminate the rule's requirements, a court may interpret this silence as evidence that the common law rule still applies.[18]

§ 3.03   Model Penal Code[19]

In 1952 the American Law Institute, an organization composed of judges, lawyers, and law professors, began drafting a penal code in the hope that it would induce state legislatures to redraft their criminal laws. Reform was needed. At the time, state laws were usually "disorganized and often accidental in their coverage."[20] Nearly all criminal statutory systems were riddled with archaic statutes, overlapping and inconsistent laws, and gaps.

In 1962, after completion of thirteen tentative drafts and accompanying explanatory commentaries, the American Law Institute approved and published its Proposed Official Draft of the Model Penal Code, a carefully drafted code containing provisions relating to the general principles of criminal responsibility and definitions of specific offenses.

The impact of the Model Code on American criminal law has been "stunning."[21] Although the Code, as such, is not the law in any jurisdiction—it is, after all, a

---

[15] Accord *Meadows v. State*, 722 S.W.2d 584 (Ark. 1987); *People v. Greer*, 402 N.E.2d 203 (Ill. 1980); *State v. Beale*, 376 S.E.2d 1 (N.C. 1989); *State ex rel. Atkinson v. Wilson*, 332 S.E.2d 807 (W. Va. 1985). In jurisdictions in which the judiciary retains residual common law authority, a few courts have expanded the definition of "human being" to include viable fetuses born dead. *Commonwealth v. Cass*, 467 N.E.2d 1324 (Mass. 1984); *Hughes v. State*, 868 P.2d 730 (Okla. Crim. App. 1994); *State v. Horne*, 319 S.E.2d 703 (S.C. 1984). Such changes apply prospectively only, however. See 5.01, *infra*.

[16] See 31.01[C], *infra*.

[17] 18 U.S.C. 1111(a) (1988).

[18] E.g., *United States v. Chase*, 18 F.3d 1166 (4th Cir. 1994).

[19] See generally *Symposium: The 25th Anniversary of the Model Penal Code*, 19 Rutgers L.J. 519-954 (1988).

[20] Herbert Wechsler, *A Thoughtful Code of Substantial Law*, 45 J. Crim. L., Criminology & Police Sci. 524, 526 (1955).

[21] Kadish, *The Model Penal Code's Historical Antecedents*, Note 1, *supra*, at 538.

model penal code—it stimulated adoption of revised penal codes in at least 37 states.[22] As Professor Sanford Kadish has put it, the Model Penal Code "has become a standard part of the furniture of the criminal law."[23] Although some state legislatures have adopted only small portions of the Model Code as their own, other jurisdictions (e.g. New York) have enacted many of its provisions; and courts, on their own, sometimes turn to the Model Code and its supporting commentaries for guidance in interpreting non-Code criminal statutes.

Many criminal law professors treat the Model Code as "the principal text in criminal law teaching,"[24]

[22] Peter W. Low, *The Model Penal Code, the Common Law, and Mistakes of Fact: Recklessness, Negligence, or Strict Liability?*, 19 Rutgers L.J. 539, 539 (1988).

[23] Kadish, *The Model Penal Code's Historical Antecedents*, Note 1, *supra*, at 521.

[24] *Id.*

CHAPTER 4

CONSTITUTIONAL LIMITS ON THE CRIMINAL LAW

§ 4.01 Chapter Overview

Are there limits to a legislature's lawmaking authority? For example, may a state legislature or Congress make it an offense to desecrate an American flag, or prohibit consensual sexual conduct among adults in their home? May it make it a crime to be a drug addict, to suffer from cancer, or to be infected with human immunodeficiency virus (HIV), the causative agent of acquired immune deficiency syndrome (AIDS)? May a state abolish common law defenses, such as self-defense and insanity, and thereby punish persons who kill in self-defense or who act due to an insane delusion?

As explained in Chapter 3, modern legislatures, rather than judges, ordinarily determine what conduct is criminal and the circumstances under which a person may be held accountable for his actions. Their considerable authority, however, is not unlimited: various provisions of the United States Constitution, as interpreted by the judiciary, limit legislative action.[1]

This chapter provides a brief overview of some of the constitutional provisions that limit legislative authority in the realm of criminal law, and which are discussed in this Text.[2] These provisions, however, are not interpreted by judges in a policy vacuum. Therefore, various overarching policy considerations, which may motivate a court to interpret the Constitution either narrowly or broadly, are also considered.

§ 4.02 Relevant Constitutional Provisions

[A]—Bill of Rights

The first ten amendments to the United States Constitution, the so-called "Bill of Rights," restrict the power of the federal government in its relationship to individuals. Various provisions of the Bill of Rights are relevant to the substantive criminal law.

The First Amendment provides, in part, that "Congress shall make no law . . . abridging the freedom of speech." Criminal laws that prohibit speech or chill expression are subject to constitutional attack under this Amendment.[3]

---

[1] A state legislature is also limited by its own state constitution, which may place greater restrictions on it than does the federal Constitution.

[2] See also § 5.01[C], *infra* (bill of attainder and *ex post facto* clauses considered).

[3] See § 9.11, *infra*.

The Fourth Amendment provides in pertinent part that "[t]he right of the people to be secure in their persons, houses, papers, and effects against unreasonable searches and seizures, shall not be violated . . . ." Evidence obtained by the police in violation of this Amendment may be excluded at a defendant's criminal trial.[4] The Amendment also limits the degree of force that a police officer may justifiably use in arresting a suspect or preventing an arrestee from escaping. This limitation can affect the scope of criminal law defenses that would otherwise apply to law enforcement officers.[5]

The Eighth Amendment states that "cruel and unusual punishment [shall not be] inflicted." This Amendment restricts legislative action in two ways: (1) it imposes limitations on what legislators may define as criminal;[6] and (2) it prohibits punishment that is barbarous in its infliction[7] or grossly disproportional to the offense committed.[8]

[B]—Fourteenth Amendment

Whereas the Bill of Rights limits the *federal* government in its relations with individuals, the Fourteenth Amendment to the United States Constitution imposes limits on *state* government. The Amendment reads in full:

No State shall make or enforce any law which shall abridge the privileges or immunities of citizens of the United States; nor shall any State deprive any person of life, liberty, or property, without due process of law; nor deny to any person within its jurisdiction the equal protection of the laws.

The most significant portion of the Fourteenth Amendment as it pertains to the criminal law is the due process clause.[9] Although the meaning of this clause has been the source of great controversy, it is now settled that the due process clause requires states not only to guarantee procedural fairness to criminal defendants, but also to respect substantive principles of justice "so rooted in the traditions and conscience of our people as to be ranked as fundamental."[10] The "fundamental rights" that states must respect are virtually the same as those that the federal government must honor, i.e., most of the Bill of Rights have been incorporated to the states through the Fourteenth Amendment due process clause.

It is also now settled law that the fundamental rights comprised within the constitutional term "liberty" need not be enumerated in the Constitution. In this context, the Supreme Court has held that among the implicit constitutional rights

---

[4] *Mapp v. Ohio*, 367 U.S. 643 (1961); see generally Joshua Dressler, Understanding Criminal Procedure §§ 117-125 (1991).

[5] See § 21.04[B], *infra*.

[6] See § 9.04, *infra*.

[7] *Weems v. United States*, 217 U.S. 349, 368 (1910).

[8] See § 6.05, *infra*.

[9] The Fifth Amendment, which applies to the federal government, includes a due process clause. In most respects, the scope of the two due process clauses are the same. See *West Coast Hotel Co. v. Parrish*, 300 U.S. 379, 391 (1937).

[10] *Snyder v. Massachusetts*, 291 U.S. 97, 105 (1934).

of Americans is a right of privacy.[11] However, the precise contours of this right remain in doubt.[12]

The Fourteenth Amendment also prohibits states from denying their citizens "the equal protection of the laws."[13] A criminal law that on its face,[14] or in the manner in which it is applied, distinguishes between two classes of persons (e.g., men and women, felons and misdemeanants, wealthy and poor people) is subject to constitutional attack.[15]

§ 4.03   Policy Factors in Enforcing the Constitution

[A]—In General

Courts are often called upon to determine whether a criminal statute, or the punishment of an offender under the law, violates one or more of the constitutional principles summarized in Section 4.02. In determining whether a violation has occurred, various competing overarching principles come into play.

In some sense, the Constitution seems to be divided against itself.[16] On the one hand, the document embodies the principles of separation-of-powers and federalism, doctrines which suggest that courts should be slow to intervene in constitutional disputes; on the other hand, the Constitution guarantees certain fundamental rights against government. These competing policies are briefly explained below.

[B]—Separation of Powers

Many judges are reluctant to intrude on the lawmaking domain of the legislature, because members of the latter branch of government are elected, whereas federal judges are appointed and hold office for life. Although judges in many states are elected, legislators are viewed as more immediately subject to the will of the public.

Because criminal laws intimately affect the lives of citizens and are intended to represent the moral values of the community, many judges believe that, whenever possible, they should defer to the wishes of the public as represented by legislative

---

[11] *Griswold v. Connecticut*, 381 U.S. 479 (1965).

[12] See § 9.11, *infra*.

[13] By judicial interpretation this provision applies to the federal government through the Fifth Amendment due process clause. *Bolling v. Sharpe*, 347 U.S. 497, 499 (1954). The Fifth Amendment due process clause is mentioned in footnote 9, *supra*.

[14] E.g., the common law offense of "being a common scold" only applies to women. See § 3.02, note 8, *supra*. As there is no valid justification for the sex-based distinction, the offense violates the equal protection clause. *State v. Palendrano*, 293 A.2d 747, 752 (N.J. Super. Ct. 1972).

[15] This equality right, however, is not absolute. The legislature may lawfully distinguish between groups if there is rational basis for the distinction. Classifications such as race and religion, however, are inherently suspect and subject to much closer judicial scrutiny. See *In re Griffiths*, 413 U.S. 717 (1973).

[16] See Akhil Reed Amar, *Of Sovereignty and Federalism*, 96 Yale L.J. 1425, 1426 (1987).

action. As a consequence, courts presume the constitutionality of criminal statutes, i.e., the party attacking a statute must demonstrate its constitutional invalidity.[17]

[C]—Federalism

State governments have primary authority for defining and enforcing the criminal laws of their respective jurisdictions. The Constitution does not give the federal government the right to compel uniformity in criminal statutes among the states. In fact, legislative experimentation and interstate diversity is welcomed in the federal system.

Left to their own devices, i.e., unless federal courts intrude on the states' sovereignty under the aegis of the Constitution, legislatures are apt to generate codes that differ from each other in key respects. For example, State X might consider prostitution a serious moral offense and prohibit and punish it as a felony, whereas the people of State Y might consider prostitution morally neutral conduct or too trivial a matter to prohibit. On the other hand, State Y, with an agriculturally-based economy, might believe that it needs to punish theft of crops more severely than urban neighbor State X does.

[D]—Protecting Individual Rights

Although the principles discussed above support caution by the judiciary, the Constitution "explicitly compels the States [and federal government] to follow . . . constitutional commands."[18] Among the most important constitutional commands are those found within the Bill of Rights and Fourteenth Amendment. These provisions guarantee that the fundamental rights of individuals will not be trampled upon by the majority.

The legislative branch of government represents the public, as a whole. Some branch of government must protect the constitutional rights of individuals. That branch is the judiciary.[19] Therefore, a court that defers to legislative judgment out of respect for the doctrines of separation-of-powers and federalism may be guilty of abdicating its institutional duty to enforce the Constitution. Judges deeply concerned about potential governmental overreaching, therefore, are apt to de-emphasize these doctrines.

---

[17] *United States v. Watson*, 423 U.S. 411, 416 (1976).

[18] *Rummel v. Estelle*, 445 U.S. 263, 303 (1980) (Powell, J., dissenting).

[19] See *Marbury v. Madison*, 5 U.S. (1 Cranch) 137 (1803).

CHAPTER 5

LEGALITY

§ 5.01 Principle of Legality [1]

[A]—"Legality": Definition

Some conduct is immoral, harmful, or both. Some conduct is criminal and punishable. The fact that conduct is immoral or harmful does not mean, however, that it is criminal and punishable. The American legal system espouses the principle, *nullum crimen sine lege, nulla poena sine lege*, or "no crime without law, no punishment without law." That is, a person may not be punished unless her conduct was defined as criminal before she acted.[2] This is the principle of legality.

Legality is the first principle of American criminal law jurisprudence.[3] It overrides all other criminal law doctrines, and it applies even though its application may result in a dangerous and morally culpable person escaping punishment.[4] As one court stated when it reversed the conviction of a defendant on the basis of the principle of legality:

> That [the defendant] will go largely unpunished . . . is frustrating. There are, however, basic principles upon which this country is founded which compel the result we reach . . . . [Legality] is one of them. The retroactive application of criminal law . . . is so abhorrent that we must occasionally endure some frustration in order to preserve and protect the foundation of our system of law.[5]

There are three interrelated corollaries to the legality principle: (1) criminal statutes should be understandable to reasonable law-abiding people; (2) criminal

---

[1] See generally Packer at 79-102; Francis A. Allen, *The Erosion of Legality in American Criminal Justice: Some Latter-Day Adventures of the Nulla Poena Principle*, 29 Ariz. L. Rev. 385 (1987); Douglas N. Husak & Craig A. Callender, *Wilful Ignorance, Knowledge, and the "Equal Culpability" Thesis: A Study of the Deeper Significance of the Principle of Legality*, 1994 Wis. L. Rev. 29; John Calvin Jeffries, Jr., *Legality, Vagueness, and the Construction of Penal Statutes*, 71 Va. L. Rev. 189 (1985); Paul H. Robinson, *Legality and Discretion in the Distribution of Criminal Sanctions*, 25 Harv. J. on Legis. 393 (1988); A.T.H. Smith, *Judicial Law Making in the Criminal Law*, 100 L.Q. Rev. 46 (1984).

[2] E.g., Model Penal Code § 1.01(2).

[3] Packer at 79-80.

[4] Donald A. Dripps, *The Constitutional Status of the Reasonable Doubt Rule*, 75 Cal. L. Rev. 1665, 1685 (1987) ("[T]he legality principle enjoys nearly complete priority over the public interest in punishing wrongdoers . . . .").

[5] *Hughes v. State*, 868, P.2d 730, 736 (Okla. Crim. App. 1994); *see also* Dripps, Note 4, *supra*, at 1685 ("punishment unauthorized by law is, in civilized communities, simply beyond the pale").

statutes should be crafted so as not to "delegate[] basic policy matters to policemen, judges, and juries for resolution on an *ad hoc* and subjective basis"; [6] and (3) judicial interpretation of ambiguous statutes should "be biased in favor of the accused." [7]

The legality principle is explained in this chapter section. Its corollaries are considered in the following sections of this chapter.

[B]—Rationale

The legality principle serves various purposes. First, it prevents the government from punishing its enemies by enacting vindictive, after-the-fact criminal statutes.

Second, "legislative enactments 'give fair warning of their effect and permit individuals to rely on their meaning until explicitly changed.' " [8] The fair-notice principle "is grounded on the assumption that one should be free to choose between lawful and unlawful conduct." [9] Without fair notice, a citizen lacks adequate opportunity to conform her conduct to the law; in the absence of such an opportunity, the retributive basis for moral condemnation of the actor is lacking. Also, the requirement of fair notice enhances general deterrence principles: a person cannot be deterred from committing a socially unacceptable act unless she has fair notice of the line separating lawful from unlawful conduct.

[C]—Constitutional Law

The legality principle has constitutional foundations.

[1]—Bill of Attainder and *Ex Post Facto* Clauses

Article I, Sections 9 and 10 of the United States Constitution prohibit legislatures from enacting bills of attainder or *ex post facto* (after the fact) legislation. [10] A bill of attainder is special legislation that declares a specific person to be guilty of a crime and subject to punishment without either a trial or conviction. [11] The *ex post facto* clause prohibits:

> 1st. Every law that makes an action done before the passing of the law, and which was innocent when done, criminal; and punishes such action. 2d. Every law that aggravates a crime, or makes it greater than it was, when committed. 3d. Every law that changes the punishment, and inflicts a greater punishment, than the law annexed to the crime, when committed . . . . [12]

---

[6] *Grayned v. City of Rockford*, 408 U.S. 104, 108-09 (1972).

[7] Jeffries, Note 1, *supra*, at 189.

[8] *Miller v. Florida*, 482 U.S. 423, 430 (1987) (quoting *Weaver v. Graham*, 450 U.S. 24, 28-29 (1981)); see also Model Penal Code § 1.02(1)(d) (stating that one purpose of the Code is to "give fair warning of the nature of the conduct declared to constitute an offense").

[9] *Bowers v. State*, 389 A.2d 341, 345 (Md. 1978).

[10] "No Bill of Attainder or ex post facto Law shall be passed." U.S. Const. art. I, § 9, cl. 3. "No State shall . . . pass any Bill of Attainder [or] ex post facto Law." *Id.* § 10, cl. 1.

[11] *Cummings v. Missouri*, 71 U.S. (4 Wall) 277, 325 (1867).

[12] *Calder v. Bull*, 3 U.S. (3 Dall.) 386, 390 (1798) (emphasis omitted).

Under the *ex post facto* clause, if *D* performs lawful act X on January 1, 1994, she cannot be convicted of a criminal offense prohibiting X, enacted by the legislature after her conduct. Similarly, if *D* kills *V* in self-defense on January 1, 1994, *D* may not be convicted of murder if the legislature subsequently abolishes the defense of self-defense. Although murder was an offense on January 1, the legislature may not retroactively criminalize what was an innocent act (a killing in self-defense) at the time of the conduct. It is also impermissible to disadvantage a defendant by applying stricter sentencing guidelines, adopted after the crime was committed. [13]

[2]—Due Process Clause

The *ex post facto* and bill of attainder clauses discussed in subsection [1] apply to state and federal *legislatures*, but not to the judiciary. Nonetheless, the legality principle applies with equal vigor to the judicial branch of government through the Fifth and Fourteenth Amendment due process clauses. As one court has stated, "it is clear the courts cannot go so far as to create an offense by enlarging a statute, by inserting or deleting words, or by giving the terms used false or unusual meanings." [14]

For example, suppose that *D* is prosecuted for murder because she unjustifiably killed a viable fetus, which was born dead. At common law, a fetus born dead was not a "human being" within the definition of murder. [15] Therefore, even if a court (as distinguished from a legislature) may redefine the term "human being" to include fetuses, [16] it would violate the due process clause to apply this expanded definition retroactively in *D*'s prosecution. [17] However, the court could announce the new definition of "human being" in *D*'s case, and apply it prospectively.

§ 5.02 Statutory Clarity

A corollary of the legality principle is that a criminal statute must not be so "vague that men of common intelligence must necessarily guess at its meaning and differ as to its application." [18] A statute must give "sufficient warning that men may conduct themselves so as to avoid that which is forbidden." [19] A person is denied due process of law if she is convicted and punished for violation of a statute that lacks such clarity.

---

[13] *Miller v. Florida*, 482 U.S. 423 (1987).

[14] *Keeler v. Superior Court*, 470 P.2d 617, 625 (Cal. 1970).

[15] See § 31.01[B][1], *infra*.

[16] See § 3.02, *supra* (regarding the respective roles of the two branches of government).

[17] *Commonwealth v. Cass*, 467 N.E.2d 1324 (Mass. 1984); *Hughes v. State*, 868 P.2d 730 (Okla. Crim. App. 1994); *State v. Horne*, 319 S.E.2d 703 (S.C. 1984); see also *Bouie v. City of Columbia*, 378 U.S. 347 (1964) (a trespass statute prohibited nonconsensual *entry* onto private land; the state court unforeseeably and retroactively enlarged the statute to prohibit the separate act of *remaining* on private premises after being asked to leave; held: this retroactive judicial expansion of the statute violated due process).

[18] *Connally v. General Constr. Co.*, 269 U.S. 385, 391 (1926).

[19] *Rose v. Locke*, 423 U.S. 48, 50 (1975) (footnote deleted).

The requirement of reasonable statutory clarity is easy to state but difficult to apply. Supreme Court Justice Felix Frankfurter has conceded that the doctrine

> is itself an indefinite concept. There is no such thing as "indefiniteness" in the abstract. . . . The requirement is fair notice that conduct may entail punishment. But whether notice is or is not "fair" depends on the subject matter to which it relates. [20]

In one particular set of circumstances, courts apply a particularly strict standard: "[s]tatutes governing potential First Amendment and similarly sensitive constitutional rights [are] strictly tested for certainty by interpreting their meaning from the face of the statutes." [21] For example, in *Lewis v. City of New Orleans*, [22] D was prosecuted for breach of the peace. The statute provided that it was an offense "wantonly to curse or revile or to use obscene or opprobrious language toward . . . any member of the city police in the actual performance of his duties." The Supreme Court ruled that the statute could not withstand constitutional attack if it were"susceptible of application to speech, although vulgar or offensive, that is protected by the First . . . Amendment[]." That is, even if a person's conduct *in fact* is not constitutionally protected, her conviction must be overturned if the statute could reasonably be construed to prohibit constitutionally protected speech or other conduct.

Courts are much slower to hold that an ordinary criminal statute—one that does not touch on fundamental constitutional rights—is unconstitutionally vague. Judges do not want to reward ignorance or misunderstandings of law; and they are cognizant of the "practical difficulties in drawing criminal statutes both general enough to take into account a variety of human conduct and sufficiently specific to provide fair warning that certain kinds of conduct are prohibited." [23] The "root of the vagueness doctrine is a rough idea of fairness," [24] and fairness requires only "that there is sufficient warning to one bent on obedience that he comes *near* the proscribed area." [25]

As a consequence, a statute is not invalid "simply because it requires conformity to an imprecise normative standard," [26] such as the requirement that a person not act "negligently," [27] or that she not harm others "by cruel or inhumane treatment." [28] As Justice Holmes observed, "the law is full of instances where a man's fate depends on his estimating rightly, that is, as the jury subsequently estimates it, some matter of degree." [29]

---

[20] *Winters v. New York*, 333 U.S. 507, 524 (1948) (dissenting opinion).

[21] *State v. Flinn*, 208 S.E.2d 538, 543 (W. Va. 1974).

[22] 415 U.S. 130 (1974).

[23] *Colten v. Kentucky*, 407 U.S. 104, 110 (1972).

[24] *Id.*

[25] *Winters v. New York*, 333 U.S. at 539 (Frankfurter, J., dissenting) (emphasis added).

[26] *Eanes v. State*, 569 A.2d 604, 615 (Md. 1990).

[27] See *Nash v. United States*, 229 U.S. 373 (1913).

[28] *Bowers v. State*, 389 A.2d 341 (Md. 1978).

[29] *Nash v. United States*, 229 U.S. at 377.

Furthermore, "[e]ven trained lawyers may find it necessary to consult legal dictionaries, treatises, and judicial opinions before they may say with any certainty what some statutes may compel or forbid."[30] Therefore, the due process clause is not violated unless a law-abiding person would still have to guess as to the meaning of a statute after she or her attorney conducts research into the meaning of the law.[31]

For example, consider a statute that provides that "[w]hoever commits the abominable and detestable crime against nature, either with mankind or beast, shall be guilty of a felony . . . ." On it face, the statute is vague. Ordinary persons would probably have to guess as to the meaning of the critical phrase "crime against nature."[32] Nonetheless, the statute is not unconstitutional if its meaning can be ascertained by reading prior state court opinions construing the law.[33] If these prior opinions indicate that judicial interpretations of a statute in a second state are relevant in ascertaining the first statute's meaning, a person may also be held responsible for learning the applicable law of the other jurisdiction.[34] And, if a statute uses, but does not define, a common law term, a law-abiding person is assumed to have read the treatises of Blackstone, Coke, or other common law sources in order to learn the term's common law meaning.[35]

§ 5.03 Avoiding Undue Discretion in Law Enforcement

A statute that lacks clarity not only provides insufficient notice to law-abiding persons, but is susceptible to enforcement in an arbitrary or discriminatory manner. The Supreme Court has observed that when "the legislature fails to provide . . . minimal guidelines, a criminal statute may permit a standardless sweep [that] allows policemen, prosecutors, and juries to pursue their personal predilections."[36] The

---

[30] *Rose v. Locke*, 423 U.S. at 50.

[31] Can a statute be too *specific*? For example, some statutes provide that it is an offense for a driver to operate a motor vehicle with a specific percentage, e.g., .10%, or more alcohol in her blood. There is usually no way for a drinker to know whether she has reached the physiological point at which she would be in violation of such a statute if she were to drive. Nonetheless, courts have consistently upheld these laws against constitutional attack. They reason that a person of ordinary intelligence should be able to tell when her consumption of alcohol puts her near to violation of the statute, which is sufficient notice to hold her responsible for her later decision to drive. *Fuenning v. Superior Court*, 680 P.2d 121 (Ariz. 1983); *Burg v. Municipal Court*, 673 P.2d 732 (Cal. 1983); *State v. Muehlenberg*, 347 N.W.2d 914 (Wis. Ct. App. 1984).

[32] In its broadest meaning, the crime consists of consensual or nonconsensual oral or anal sexual relations between persons of the same or opposite sex, or sexual relations between a human being and a "brute beast."

[33] *Wainwright v. Stone*, 414 U.S. 21 (1973) (*per curiam*); see also *In re Banks*, 244 S.E.2d 386 (N.C. 1978) (holding that a statute prohibiting "peep[ing] secretly into any room occupied by a female" was not vague, in light of prior judicial interpretative clarifications of the statute).

[34] See *Rose v. Locke*, 423 U.S. at 52-53.

[35] See *Keeler v. Superior Court*, 470 P.2d 617, 620, 633 (Cal. 1970).

[36] *Kolender v. Lawson*, 461 U.S. 352, 358 (1983) (internal quotation marks and emphasis omitted).

due process clause forbids the enforcement of any statute that, due to vagueness in language, "vests virtually complete discretion in the hands of police to determine whether the suspect has satisfied [its requirements]."[37]

So-called vagrancy statutes are prime examples of such impermissible legislation. For example, in *Papachristou v. City of Jacksonville*,[38] a city ordinance prohibited a person from being a "vagrant." Under the ordinance, "[r]ogues and vagabonds," "common drunkards," "persons wandering or strolling around from place to place without any lawful purpose," "habitual loafers," and others, were deemed to be "vagrants."

On its face, of course, this language is vague. What is a "common" drunkard? What makes a person an "habitual loafer"? Worse than its imprecision, however, is that the ordinance gives the police virtually unfettered discretion to determine who is a vagrant. According to *Papachristou*, such laws, "though long common in Russia, are not compatible with our constitutional system." A primary concern is that a prosecution "may be merely the cloak for a conviction which could not be obtained on the real but undisclosed grounds for the arrest,"[39] such as that the "vagrant" was an African-American person "strolling" in a white community,[40] a poorly dressed person found in a wealthy business district, or a person whose lawful conduct, e.g., a male holding hands with another male, offended the sensibilities of the arresting officer.

In contrast, a criminal statute that is drafted more narrowly, for example, to reach persons loitering in a specific location, such as a public toilet, and which requires that the actor intend to commit an illicit act at that location, may withstand constitutional attack.[41]

Model Penal Code § 250.6, drafted prior to *Papachristou*, provides in part that a person commits a violation if she "loiters or prowls in a place, at a time, or in a manner not usual for law-abiding individuals, under circumstances that warrant alarm for the safety of persons or property in the vicinity." Except when it is impracticable, e.g., the suspect flees, the Code requires a police officer, prior to arrest, to "afford the actor an opportunity to dispel any alarm which would otherwise be warranted," and the person may not be convicted if the officer failed to comply with this requirement or if the explanation given by the actor was true and, if believed, would have dispelled the alarm. Courts that have considered statutes patterned on Section 250.6 have reached conflicting conclusions as to its constitutionality under the due process clause.[42]

---

[37] *Id.*

[38] 405 U.S. 156 (1972).

[39] *Id.* at 169.

[40] In *Papachristou*, two black males and two white females driving to a nightclub were arrested for "prowling by auto."

[41] *People v. Superior Court (Caswell)*, 758 P.2d 1046 (Cal. 1988).

[42] Compare *Fields v. City of Omaha*, 810 F.2d 830 (8th Cir. 1987) (invalidating the law) with *State v. Ecker*, 311 So.2d 104 (Fla. 1975) (upholding the law).

§ 5.04   Strict Construction of Statutes (Rule of Lenity)

In response to a "vast and irrational" expansion in the number of capital offenses in eighteenth century England, British courts developed the rule that when a criminal statute is subject to conflicting reasonable interpretations, the statute (including sentencing provisions thereto) should be interpreted strictly against the government. [43] This so-called rule of lenity is not constitutionally compelled, but is thought to support the principle of legality by preventing a court from inadvertently enlarging the scope of a criminal statute through its interpretive powers.

The difficulty with the lenity principle is that even well-drafted criminal statutes are often susceptible to multiple, reasonable interpretations. Strict construction of a statute, therefore, may result in an application contrary to legislative intent. As a result, many American states have abolished the rule of lenity. [44]

The Model Penal Code, as well, does not recognize the lenity principle. It requires instead that criminal statutes be construed according to their "fair import," and that ambiguities be resolved in a manner that furthers "the general purposes [of the Code] and the special purposes of the particular provision involved." [45] That is, although one general purpose of the Code is to provide fair warning regarding the nature of the conduct that is deemed to be criminal, [46] a statute should be interpreted to further, not frustrate, the legislative policies behind the specific law in question.

Jurisdictions that still invoke the lenity principle often treat it, simply, as a tie-breaker. That is, "the touchstone of the rule of lenity is statutory ambiguity." [47] A court will not rely on the rule unless the statute remains susceptible to competing reasonable interpretations after applying *every* interpretive mechanism available to it, including considering "the language and structure, legislative history, and motivating policies" [48] of the statute. [49]

---

[43] Jeffries, Note 1, *supra*, at 198.

[44] *Id.*

[45] Model Penal Code § 1.02(3).

[46] Model Penal Code 1.02(1)(d).

[47] *Moskal v. United States*, 498 U.S. 103, 107 (1990) (internal quotation marks deleted).

[48] *Bifulco v. United States*, 447 U.S. 381, 387 (1980).

[49] *United States v. Bass*, 404 U.S. 336, 347 (1971).

CHAPTER 6

PROPORTIONALITY

§ 6.01 Chapter Overview[1]

"Proportionality" is an important and recurring concept in the criminal law. For example, all justification defenses, e.g., self-defense, defense-of-others, defense-of-property, contain a proportionality requirement: a person is not justified in using force against another unless it is "*proportional* or reasonable in relation to the harm threatened or the interest to be furthered."[2] Thus, a person may not justifiably kill another in order to prevent a minor battery on himself or another, or to prevent a theft of property.

The doctrine of proportionality is also asserted in the context of sentencing, to ensure that an offender receives punishment appropriate to the crime he has committed. Both utilitarians and retributivists recognize proportionality in their theoretical structures.[3] Modern penal codes, as well, acknowledge that one purpose of a criminal code is "to safeguard offenders against excessive, disproportionate or arbitrary punishment."[4] And, according to current Supreme Court case law, the Constitution, through the Eighth Amendment, prohibits grossly disproportional punishment.

This chapter considers two questions relating to proportionality of punishment. First, how much (or what) punishment *is* excessive or disproportionate to a particular crime? Utilitarians and retributivists go about answering this question differently. Punishment that is proportional according to utilitarian principles might be retributively disproportional, or vice-versa. Second, under what circumstances

---

[1] For an understanding of the philosophical underpinnings of the subject, see generally John Kleinig, Punishment and Desert ch. VII (1973); Packer at 139-45; Richard Singer, Just Deserts (1979); C.L. Ten, Crime, Guilt, and Punishment 141-64 (1987); Andrew von Hirsch, Censure and Sanctions (1993); Andrew Ashworth, *Criminal Justice and Deserved Sentences,* 1989 Crim. L. Rev. 340; Lawrence Crocker, *The Upper Limit of Just Punishment,* 41 Emory L.J. 1059 (1992); Andrew von Hirsch, *Proportionality in the Philosophy of Punishment: From "Why Punish?" to "How Much?",* 1 Crim. L.F. 259 (1990); Andrew von Hirsch & Nils Jareborg, *Gauging Criminal Harm: A Living-Standard Analysis,* 11 Oxford J. Legal Stud. 1 (1991); Peter H. Rossi. Emily Waite, Christine E. Bose, & Richard E. Berk, *The Seriousness of Crimes: Normative Structure and Individual Differences,* 39 Am. Soc. Rev. 224 (1974); Jeremy Waldron, *Lex Talionis,* 34 Ariz. L. Rev. 25 (1992); and the sources regarding utilitarianism and retributivism cited in § 2.03, *supra.*

[2] 1 Robinson at 87. See § 18.02, *infra.*

[3] Utilitarianism and retributivism are explained in Chapter 2, *supra.*

[4] Model Penal Code § 1.02(2)(c); see also Cal. Penal Code § 1170(a)(1) (West 1994); N.Y. Penal Law § 1.05(4) (McKinney 1987).

is disproportional punishment, concededly unwise or unfair, also unconstitutional? Few criminal law issues have more sharply divided the United States Supreme Court than this one.

§ 6.02 Utilitarianism and Proportionality

[A]—General Principles

Utilitarian philosophy directs that punishment be neither too little nor too much, but rather that it be proportional, i.e., that punishment be inflicted in the amount required to satisfy utilitarian goals. In his classic account on utilitarianism, Jeremy Bentham announced five rules intended to ensure proportional punishment.[5]

In order to deter crime, the first rule is that punishment must not be less than that required to outweigh the potential profit to the criminal of committing the offense. If too little punishment is imposed, criminal conduct will remain profitable and, therefore, the threat of punishment will be ineffective. It follows, according to the second rule, that "[t]he greater the mischief of the offense, the greater is the expense, which it may be worth while to be at, in the way of punishment."

Utilitarian analysis also directs lawmakers (Rule 3) to grade offenses in a manner that will induce a person "to choose always the least mischievous of two offences," by making sure that "[w]here two offences come into competition, the punishment for the greater offense must be sufficient to induce a man to prefer the less." Punishment should also be set in a manner to induce the criminal "to do no more mischief that what is necessary for his purpose" (Rule 4).

The final rule of proportionality is that "punishment ought in no case to be more than what is necessary to bring it into conformity with the [previous] rules." In other words, because punishment is itself a mischief that should be avoided to the extent possible, punishment is disproportional if more pain is inflicted than is required to satisfy the previous goals.

[B]—Application of the Principles

[1]—General Deterrence

Very dangerous crimes should be punished more severely than less dangerous ones. To the utilitarian concerned with general deterrence, however, the degree of dangerousness of an offense is not measured by calculating the injury caused in a single case by a particular offender, but rather by predicting the overall mischief that is likely to result from commission of the offense in the future by this and other offenders. This means that the appropriate punishment for a crime may differ over time and among jurisdictions. For example, in a rural community in which theft of cattle occurs frequently and is a factor in causing serious economic hardship to its inhabitants, it would be appropriate to punish this conduct more severely than in an urban community where the crime rarely occurs and does not threaten the economic well-being of its people.

---

[5] See generally Jeremy Bentham, An Introduction to the Principles of Morals and Legislation ch. 14 (1789).

In setting the punishment for an offense, however, a utilitarian lawmaker will also consider the extent to which the conduct in question is deterrable. Consider, for example, how a utilitarian might treat the offense of driving an automobile under the influence of alcohol. Little or no injury may occur in a specific case of intoxicated driving. In terms of future mischief, however, the offense is relatively serious, because drunk driving frequently results in loss of life and injury to persons and property. Moreover, some criminologists claim that driving under the influence of alcohol is more-than-ordinarily difficult conduct to deter by threat of punishment.[6] If so, it may be appropriate to impose penalties greater than would be set for equally dangerous, but more easily deterrable, behavior.[7]

[2]—Specific Deterrence

When deterrence of a specific offender is desired, punishment is proportional to the extent that it is necessary to prevent the individual offender from committing future criminal acts more painful to society than the punishment inflicted on the wrongdoer.

Evidence may exist that a specific criminal is less susceptible to deterrence than the ordinary offender. As a result, he may be more likely than the usual criminal to commit future crimes. Consistent with concepts of specific deterrence, the more dangerous offender may properly be punished more severely than the ordinary offender who commits the same crime. For example, the offense of battery may merit "x" units of punishment pursuant to general deterrence principles. D, however, may be more dangerous and less deterrable than the usual batterer, as evidenced by his previous convictions for violent offenses. Enhanced punishment of D, e.g., "x + 5" units of punishment, may be appropriate.

Under the circumstances hypothesized here, D's punishment would be significantly greater than that inflicted for battery under general deterrence principles, and substantially more painful than the harm suffered by the victim of the specific battery. However, utilitarian principles would still demand that the punishment inflicted be no greater than is required to serve its crime-prevention purpose.

---

[6] E.g., Dale E. Berger, John R. Snortum, Ross J. Homel, Ragnar Hauge, & Wendy Loxley, *Deterrence and Prevention of Alcohol-Impaired Driving in Australia, the United States, and Norway,* 7 Justice Q. 453 (1990) (finding general deterrence relatively weak in the United States); Rodney F. Kingsnorth, Lisa Alvis, & Glori Gavia, *Specific Deterrence and the DUI Offender: The Impact of a Decade of Reform,* 10 Justice Q. 265 (1993) (showing no decrease in recidivism associated with an increase in the severity of penalties); Lonn Lanza-Kaduce, *Perceptual Deterrence and Drinking and Driving Among College Students,* 26 Criminology 321 (1988) (finding that perceptions of risk of arrest and severity of punishment were not related to later drinking and driving); H. Laurence Ross, Richard McCleary, & Gary LaFree, *Can Mandatory Jail Laws Deter Drunk Driving? The Arizona Case,* 81 J. Crim. L. & Criminology 156 (1990) (finding that enhanced punishments in Arizona, including mandatory jail sentences, were unsuccessful as a deterrent).

[7] On the other hand, if drunk driving can only be deterred by redirecting law enforcement efforts away from violent crimes, thereby increasing the frequency of the latter offenses, or only by the application of such draconian punitive measures that the community would condemn the law, a utilitarian might favor attacking the problem in a non-penal manner.

[3]—Rehabilitation

Proportionality of punishment has little meaning in a rehabilitative system of treatment. C.S. Lewis has written that it is possible to speak of "just punishment," but not of "just cure," where "just" means "proportional."[8] Although compelled rehabilitation constitutes "punishment" for purposes of the criminal law,[9] Lewis's observation is still pertinent, because the duration of such treatment and the harshness of rehabilitative techniques need not be related to the severity of the offense committed nor to the degree to which the treatment/punishment will deter others from committing the offense. Rehabilitative procedures may theoretically be exercised until they have succeeded.

§ 6.03   Retributivism and Proportionality

[A]—General Principles

Although proportionality is a component of utilitarian sentencing theory, the concept of proportional punishment is more closely allied with retributivism.[10] Retributivists justify punishment on the ground that a crime has been committed. The offender owes a debt to society; punishment is the mode of repayment. The payment due varies with the crime committed, but it must be proportional to the offense committed.

Most modern retributivists reject the concept of *lex talionis*—the infliction upon the wrongdoer of the same injury he has caused the victim—except, perhaps, in the case of murder. To punish a rapist by "raping" him, for example, whatever that would mean in practice, would violate the principle of personhood inherent in one school of retributive theory, which requires that the offender be treated with dignity.[11] Moreover, with the exception of the death penalty for murder, punishment equivalent in kind to the offense committed is impractical. Therefore, retributivists only require that the wrongdoer symbolically repay the debt he owes, by undergoing punishment proportional in severity to the offense committed.

[B]—Application of the Principles

[1]—In General

As discussed more fully in subsequent chapters of this Text, a crime has two basic components: the external part, involving the harm inflicted by the actor; and an internal portion, involving the actor's moral blameworthiness, as represented by the

---

[8] C.S. Lewis, *The Humanitarian Theory of Punishment,* 6 Res Judicatae 224, 225 (1953).

[9] See § 2.02, supra.

[10] Margaret Jane Radin, *Cruel Punishment and Respect for Persons: Super Due Process for Death,* 53 S. Cal. L. Rev. 1143, 1167 n.83 (1980); see also *Harmelin v. Michigan,* 501 U.S. 957, 989 (1991) (opinion of Scalia, J., and Rehnquist, CJ.) ("[I]t becomes difficult even to speak intelligently of 'proportionality,' once deterrence and rehabilitation are given significant weight. Proportionality is inherently a retributive concept . . .").

[11] See § 2.03[C][2], *supra.*

offender's mental state in relation to the harm inflicted. Both components must be considered in calculating the actor's just deserts.

Regarding the harm component, a legislature seeking to impose retributively fair punishment looks backward at the crime committed and determines what harm—physical, psychological, moral, economic, etc.—ordinarily results from the commission of the offense in question. To the extent that a trial judge has sentencing discretion, the judge may consider instead the actual harm inflicted in the case before him.

Regarding the blameworthiness component, retributivists consider a person more deserving of punishment if he intentionally, rather than, for example, negligently, causes the particular harm. Thus, a retributivist would punish an automobile driver who negligently kills a pedestrian less severely than an assassin who purposely takes a human life. The retributivist would take into consideration other factors as well, relating to an offender's moral blameworthiness. For example, if *A* intentionally kills *V1* because *A* is suffering from a severe mental illness that causes him to believe that he has a right to take *V1*'s life, *A* is probably less blameworthy (if he is blameworthy at all) than *B*, a contract killer who equally intentionally, but rationally, kills *V2*.

[2]—Devising a Proportional Retributive System

Developing a retributively fair sentencing system is not easy. In the absence of *lex talionis* punishment, penalties can only roughly approximate the seriousness of the crimes committed. There is no foolproof way to decide what punishment is roughly proportional to most offenses.

One real-world way to scale deserts in a sentencing system based on retribution is to proportion punishment *between* offenses, rather than *to* offenses. For example, consider for a moment a society in which there are only three statutory offenses: criminal homicide; rape; and theft. The first step for the legislator is to rank these crimes in the order of their seriousness. The lawmaker must determine the harmfulness of each offense, taking into consideration the immediate victim, family members, and society as a whole. Empirical studies indicate that people generally consider crimes of violence more serious than non-violent offenses; and, among violent crimes, the unjustifiable taking of human life (criminal homicide) is viewed as the most heinous offense. [12] Therefore, we may assume that the legislature would rank an intentional killing as the most serious offense, rape as less serious, and theft as the least severe.

The next step would be to impose punishment commensurate to the relative gravity of the offenses. One way to do this is to begin with the least serious offense--here, theft--and to set its punishment at the low end of the continuum of acceptable forms and degrees of punishment. For example, theft would receive "x" units of punishment, such as two years' imprisonment. Then, each successively more serious crime would be compared to the last one in terms of increased degree of seriousness, with penalties set in rough proportion to the last crime. If rape is considered approximately five times more serious than the ordinary theft (based on the

---

[12] Rossi, Waite, Bose & Berk, Note 1, *supra.*

comparative harm of the two offenses), then rape would receive "5x" units of punishment (10 years' imprisonment). If an intentional homicide is four times as serious as rape, then the homicide would merit "20x" units of punishment (40 years', or perhaps life, imprisonment). Alternatively, the grading system could start at the top (setting the maximum punishment for murder at death or life imprisonment) and the legislature could work its way down through the lesser offenses.[13]

The preceding analysis considered only the harm component of criminal offenses. As previously indicated, however, the personal blameworthiness of an actor in causing the harm is also relevant. Therefore, a legislature would subdivide criminal homicide and other serious offenses into sub-offenses based on the actor's degree of culpability. For example, an intentional killing would be graded as a more serious offense than a negligent homicide.[14]

§ 6.04 Comparing the Two Theories of Proportionality

For purposes of determining the appropriate punishment for an offense, retribution and utilitarianism differ in two key respects. First, utilitarian punishment is linked to predictions of future harm and the extent to which the undesired conduct is deterrable. In contrast, retributivists seek to proportion punishment to the offense already committed, without consideration of future harm. Second, retributivists believe that punishment for wrongdoing is morally right, perhaps obligatory. Utilitarians contend that punishment is undesirable unless it will result in a net benefit to society. Because of these differences in outlook, utilitarian and retributive versions of proportionality will differ substantially in specific cases.

For example, for many retributivists, especially those impressed by the "eye for an eye" philosophy, the death penalty for the most serious forms of murder is justifiable, but death is disproportional for offenses in which no life is taken. In contrast, utilitarians would favor capital punishment for murder and/or other offenses if it is a proven deterrent, but not otherwise.

The two theories may also lead in very different directions if the offense in question involves dangerous conduct that does not result in significant harm on a specific occasion. For example, as discussed earlier,[15] general deterrence theorists might justify substantial punishment of persons who drive under the influence of intoxicants because such conduct is a major social problem, resulting in great harm on many occasions, and is especially difficult to deter.[16] The retributivist, however, would not consider the difficulty-of-deterrence or likely-future-harm factors in

---

[13] Of course, in a real system, perhaps involving many more than a hundred offenses, the differences in seriousness between crimes will be small. Once the ranking is done, and the upper and lower limits of punishment are set, penalties can be graduated in a relatively simple manner.

[14] What is especially difficult to determine, however, is whether, for example, *intentional* nonconsensual sexual intercourse is more or less serious than the *negligent* taking of a human life.

[15] See § 6.02[B][1], *supra.*

[16] But see footnote 7, *infra.*

calibrating the proper punishment. Instead, the penalty would be based on the harm of drunk driving *per se*, which is apt to be fairly minor,[17] and the actor's culpability in causing the minor harm. Under such circumstances, the penalty is likely to be slight.[18]

Retributivists and specific-deterrence utilitarians may also differ, for example, in their approach to recidivists. As noted before,[19] utilitarians can justify enhanced punishment of repeat offenders. For a retributivist, however, heightened punishment cannot be approved on the basis of the offender's future dangerousness. Also, assuming that the repeat offender has been punished for his prior crimes, i.e., he has paid his debt to society, a retributivist cannot justify punishing the offender more for the present offense merely because of the prior wrongs.[20]

§ 6.05   Constitutional Requirement of Proportionality[21]

[A]—General Principles

The Eighth Amendment to the United States Constitution prohibits the infliction of "cruel and unusual punishment" by agents of the federal government on persons convicted of criminal conduct. Freedom from such punishment is a fundamental

---

[17] If a drunk driver kills another, he may be prosecuted for criminal homicide.

[18] See Douglas N. Husak, *Is Drunk Driving a Serious Offense?*, 23 Phil. & Pub. Aff. 52 (1994) (concluding that the offense is not a serious one, and that drunk drivers should not be imprisoned).

[19] See § 6.02[B][2], *supra*.

[20] This does not mean that retributivists cannot defend enhanced punishment of recidivists. Although some authors have categorically rejected such laws on proportionality grounds, see e.g., Joshua Dressler, *Substantive Criminal Law Through the Looking Class of Rummel v. Estelle: Proportionality and Justice as Endangered Doctrines*, 34 Sw. L.J. 1063 (1981), most retributivists defend at least some forms of recidivist laws. E.g., Michael Davis, *Just Deserts for Recidivists*, 4 Crim. Just. Ethics, Summer/Fall 1985, at 29; Andrew von Hirsch, *Desert and Previous Convictions in Sentencing*, 65 Minn. L. Rev. 591 (1981). However, recidivism laws are generally defended on grounds of specific deterrence.

[21] Thomas E. Baker & Fletcher N. Baldwin, Jr., *Eighth Amendment Challenges to the Length of a Criminal Sentence: Following the Supreme Court "From Precedent to Precedent"*, 27 Ariz. L. Rev. 25 (1985); Dressler, Note 20, supra; Scott W. Howe, *Resolving the Conflict in the Capital Sentencing Cases: A Desert-Oriented Theory of Regulation*, 26 Ga. L. Rev. 323 (1992); David S. Mackey, *Rationality versus Proportionality: Reconsidering the Constitutional Limits on Criminal Sanctions*, 51 Tenn. L. Rev. 623 (1984); Pressly Millen, Note, *Interpretation of the Eighth Amendment—Rummel, Solem, and the Venerable Case of Weems v. United States*, 1984 Duke L.J. 789; Dora Nevares-Muniz, *The Eighth Amendment Revisited: A Model of Weighted Punishments*, 75 J. Crim. L. & Criminology 272 (1984); Kelly A. Patch, Note, *Harmelin v. Michigan: Is Proportionate Sentencing Merely Legislative Grace?*, 1992 Wis. L. Rev. 1697; Charles Walter Schwartz, *Eighth Amendment Proportionality Analysis and the Compelling Case of William Rummel*, 71 J. Crim. L. & Criminology 378 (1980); Peter Mathis Spett, *Confounding the Gradations of Iniquity: An Analysis of Eighth Amendment Jurisprudence Set Forth in Harmelin v. Michigan*, 24 Colum. Hum. Rts. L. Rev. 203 (1993).

right that state governments must also respect.[22] And, in a 1910 ruling, the Supreme Court ruled that an implicit requirement of the Eighth Amendment is that punishment inflicted not be grossly disproportional to the crime committed.[23]

This interpretation of the Eighth Amendment is controversial. Although the Supreme Court has stated that the proportionality doctrine is "deeply rooted" in common law jurisprudence,[24] two members of the Court recently stated that, based on their historical study, "the Eighth Amendment contains no proportionality guarantee."[25] Nonetheless, the Supreme Court is presently wedded to the principle in some form. Accordingly, courts are sometimes called upon to determine whether punishment imposed for violation of a criminal statute was grossly disproportional to the offense.

Proportionality can be calculated by use of either utilitarian or retributive tools of analysis, and results may differ depending upon the approach followed.[26] As seen below, the Supreme Court has sometimes applied retributive theory to invalidate a statute or the sentence in a specific case. On other occasions, however, it has deferred to legislative will, allowing the state to justify punishment on retributive or (more commonly) utilitarian grounds.

[B]—Death Penalty

In 1971, Ehrlich Coker raped a woman and stabbed her to death. Still free eight months later, he kidnapped and twice raped a second woman. Finally caught, Coker was sentenced to three life terms in prison for his offenses. A year and a half later, however, he escaped from prison and robbed and raped a 16-year-old female in front of her husband, threatening her with death. Ultimately caught and convicted for the latest rape and robbery, Coker was sentenced to death by a Georgia jury.

Based on these facts, a compelling utilitarian argument for Coker's execution is possible. He was an exceedingly dangerous man for whom incapacitation had proved to be an insufficient remedy. The community, as represented by the jury that sentenced him to death, had reason to fear that, if he were not executed, Coker would escape prison again and commit additional rapes and, perhaps, murders. On specific deterrence principles, therefore, death was quite arguably proportional punishment for Coker's deed. Nonetheless, in *Coker v. Georgia*,[27] the United States Supreme Court held that death is grossly disproportional punishment for the crime of rape of an adult woman.

Writing for the Court, Justice Byron White utilized two methods of constitutional analysis. First, pursuant to an approach followed in prior death penalty opinions, he considered objective indicia of the nation's attitude regarding the acceptability

---

[22] See *Robinson v. California,* 370 U.S. 660 (1962).

[23] *Weems v. United States,* 217 U.S. 349, 367 (1910).

[24] *Solem v. Helm,* 463 U.S. 277, 284-85 (1983).

[25] *Harmelin v. Michigan,* 501 U.S. 957, 965 (1991) (opinion of Scalia, J. and Rehnquist, CJ.).

[26] See § 6.04, *supra.*

[27] 433 U.S. 584 (1977).

of death as a penalty for rape. At the time, only a few states authorized capital punishment for rape, and Georgia juries rarely sentenced rapists to death. Justice White determined, therefore, that death was a socially unacceptable punishment for rape.[28]

The jury statistics, however, only proved that juries did not want to sentence *all* rapists to death. They did not demonstrate that the penalty was viewed by jurors as excessive in all cases, as the Court ultimately concluded. Also, if concepts of federalism are to be respected,[29] the fact that Georgia was among a small minority of states permitting death as a sentence for rape was not in itself a basis for overturning the legislature's judgment.

Perhaps because of these difficulties with his analysis, Justice White stated that the foregoing evidence did not resolve the issue, "for the Constitution contemplates that in the end our own judgment will be brought to bear on the question of the acceptability of the death penalty under the Eighth Amendment." As a consequence, the Court conducted a second, potentially more subjective, analysis, and again concluded that death was an excessive penalty for Coker's crime.

In effect, Justice White applied a strictly retributive conception of proportionality to the Georgia law. Coker's dangerousness was ignored. As well, the Court did not seriously consider whether death was a suitable penalty according to principles of general deterrence.[30] Instead, as a retributivist would do, Justice White compared the harm caused by rape with the penalty of death. He described rape as "highly reprehensible" and "[s]hort of homicide . . . the 'ultimate violation of self.' " Nonetheless, applying what the dissenters described as the "primitive simplicity" of *lex talionis*, Justice White concluded that rape "does not compare with murder, which . . . involve[s] the unjustified taking of human life . . . . The murderer kills; the rapist, if no more than that, does not." Death, therefore, is a constitutionally inappropriate penalty for rape (or, one would assume from the Court's reasoning, for any other offense), if no life is taken.[31]

[C]—Terms of Imprisonment

The Supreme Court's Eighth Amendment proportionality jurisprudence relating to sentences of imprisonment has not been a model of clarity.

---

[28] Unstated by the Court, but perhaps determinative, was the fact that capital punishment historically has "been reserved overwhelmingly for black defendants, especially those convicted of raping white women." James R. Acker, *Social Science in Supreme Court Death Penalty Cases: Citation Practices and Their Implications,* 8 Just. Q. 421, 431 (1991); see Robert J. Hunter, Paige Heather Ralph, & James Marquart., *The Death Sentencing of Rapists in Pre-Furman Texas (1942-1971): The Racial Dimension,* 20 Am. J. Crim. L. 313 (1993) (historical analysis of executions for rape in Texas demonstrates that decisions to impose death sentences were affected by the race of the offender and the victim).

[29] See § 4.03[C], *supra.*

[30] The issue received one sentence of attention in a footnote. *Coker,* 433 U.S. at 592-93 n.4.

[31] Language in *Coker* suggests that the decision is limited to the rape of adult women, but its reasoning clearly applies to rape of children, as well.

[1]—*Rummel v. Estelle* [32]

In 1973, William Rummel was convicted in Texas of obtaining by false pretenses a check for $120.75, and then cashing it. Although the legislature later reclassified Rummel's offense as a misdemeanor, it was a felony at the time of his trial. The offense carried a two-to-ten year prison term. However, because Rummel previously had been convicted of two other theft offenses (in which he fraudulently amassed property or cash valued at $108.36), he was sentenced as required under the state's habitual offender law to life imprisonment. He was eligible for parole consideration after approximately twelve years in prison.

Rummel argued that his life sentence constituted grossly disproportional punishment because his three offenses were all petty, nonviolent crimes. If the Supreme Court had applied its *Coker* [33] analysis, Rummel's argument probably would have been persuasive. Texas did not, nor could it, seriously claim that pursuant to retributive theory, life imprisonment fit the offense of obtaining $120.75 by false pretenses. Nonetheless, by a vote of 5 to 4, the Supreme Court refused to overturn Rummel's sentence.

Rummel and the dissenting justices asserted that the disproportionality of the life sentence could be established by weighing three objective factors: (1) the gravity of the offense compared to the severity of the penalty; (2) penalties imposed within Texas for similar offenses (*intra*-jurisdictional analysis); and (3) penalties imposed in other jurisdictions for the same offense (*inter*-jurisdictional analysis). Speaking for the majority, however, Justice William Rehnquist rejected the proposition that the excessiveness of Rummel's sentence could be determined by use of this three-prong test.

Regarding the first factor, Rummel reasoned that his offense (indeed all three offenses) were petty, nonviolent crimes, which did not justify the severe sentence he received. The Court rejected his characterization of the offenses as petty. It stated that the state legislature was entitled to draw the line between felony theft and petty larceny as it wished, "subject only to those strictures of the Eighth Amendment that can be informed by objective factors." As for the fact that Rummel's offenses were nonviolent in nature, Justice Rehnquist made the utilitarian observation that the label of violence "does not always affect the strength of society's interest in deterring a particular crime or in punishing a particular criminal."

As for the intra-jurisdictional factor, persons convicted of far more serious offenses in Texas, e.g., first-time rapists, were not subject to the mandatory sentence of life imprisonment. The Court disallowed use of this test, however, because identification of some offenses as more serious than others was "inherently speculative."

Rummel also proved that the Texas habitual offender law was among the three most severe in the country as they related to persons in his situation. Again, the Court was unimpressed. First, it observed that Rummel was eligible for parole consideration after 12 years, which meant that the Court could not know with certainty how long Rummel would actually be imprisoned. Furthermore, even if it

---

[32] 445 U.S. 263 (1980).

[33] *Coker v. Georgia*, 433 U.S. 584 (1977). See § 6.05[B], *supra*.

could be shown that Texas's recidivist law was the harshest in the nation, this would not render Rummel's sentence excessive: "Absent a constitutionally imposed uniformity inimical to traditional notions of federalism, some State will always bear the distinction of treating particular offenders more severely than any other State."

Justice Rehnquist also made the following utilitarian observation about recidivist laws:

> [T]he interest of the State of Texas here is not simply that of making criminal the unlawful acquisition of another person's property; it is in addition the interest . . . in dealing in a harsher manner with those who by repeated criminal acts have shown that they are simply incapable of conforming to the norms of the society . . . . [T]he State of Texas, or any other State, has a valid interest in so dealing with that class of persons.

The clear message of *Rummel*, without consideration of later cases, is that although states are prohibited from inflicting grossly disproportional punishment, the Supreme Court will almost always defer to the state legislature's judgment in non-capital cases. On a more theoretical level, *Rummel* stands for the proposition that legislatures may constitutionally apply utilitarian factors in setting criminal penalties, even if this process results in retributively disproportional sentencing.

[2]—*Solem v. Helm* [34]

Jerry Helm was sentenced to life imprisonment without possibility of parole pursuant to South Dakota's habitual offender law, after he was convicted of fraudulently passing a "no account" check for $100.00. This was Helm's seventh conviction. Although the Court described Helm's prior felonies as nonviolent in nature, his crimes included three burglaries, and driving an automobile while intoxicated.

Helm asserted this his sentence constituted grossly disproportional punishment. Based on *Rummel*, his legal claim seemed weak. Nonetheless, by a vote of 5 to 4, the Court invalidated Helm's sentence. In an opinion written by Justice Lewis Powell, author of the dissent in *Rummel*, the Court reaffirmed the applicability of the constitutional principle of proportionality in non-capital offenses. Although the Justices agreed that reviewing courts should grant substantial deference to legislatures in setting punishments for crimes, Justice Powell warned that "no penalty is *per se* constitutional."

The Court applied the same three-prong test rejected as too subjective in *Rummel*, and concluded that the sentence was excessive on the basis of each prong: Helm received a severe sentence for "relatively minor" conduct; he was treated more harshly than other criminals in South Dakota who committed more serious crimes; and the state's recidivist statute was one of the two toughest in the country. The Court distinguished *Rummel* on the ground that Texas had a relatively liberal parole policy, whereas Helm's life sentence was without possibility of parole.

---

[34] 463 U.S. 277 (1983).

[3]—*Harmelin v. Michigan* [35]

Ronald Harmelin was convicted of possessing 672 grams of cocaine. Although this was his first offense, he received the statutory mandatory term of life imprisonment without possibility of parole. [36] Because there was no death penalty in Michigan, this was the harshest penalty available for any offense in the state, and was reserved for only two other crimes: first-degree murder; and manufacture, distribution, or possession with intent to manufacture or distribute 650 grams or more of narcotics. Moreover, the Michigan drug possession statute was by far the harshest in the nation. Based on the three-prong test of *Solem*, therefore, a strong case of unconstitutionality could be made.

Justice Antonin Scalia announced the judgment of the Court, which was that Harmelin's sentence did *not* violate the Eighth Amendment. However, only Chief Justice Rehnquist joined his opinion. Based on an examination of the background of the Eighth Amendment, Justices Scalia and Rehnquist concluded that the framers of the Constitution did not include within the Eighth Amendment a guarantee against disproportionate sentences. Therefore, they would have flatly overruled *Solem*. [37]

As the *Rummel* Court did, the two Justices rejected as unduly subjective the first two prongs of the test applied in *Solem*. As for the first prong (seriousness of the offense), Justice Scalia said that although violent crimes are serious, "that is only half the equation. The issue is *what else* should be regarded to be *as serious* as these offenses." On this matter, the Justices deferred to the state legislature: "The Members of the Michigan Legislature, and not we, know the situation of the streets of Detroit." [38] Nor would Justices Scalia and Rehnquist compare penalties for offenses within Michigan: "[S]ince deterrent effect depends not only upon the amount of the penalty but upon its certainty, crimes that are less grave but significantly more difficult to deter may warrant substantially higher penalties."

Justice Scalia conceded that the inter-jurisdictional test "can be applied with clarity and ease. The only difficulty is that it has no conceivable relevance to the Eighth Amendment." Just as one state may punish conduct that another state permits, it follows, he said, that one state may "treat with stern disapproval an act that other States punish with the mildest of sanctions."

---

[35] 501 U.S. 957 (1991).

[36] Harmelin was a 45-year-old pool hustler, drug addict, and small-time drug dealer. He was one of more than 125 persons incarcerated for life in Michigan prisons under the statute at issue, which was enacted to imprison drug kingpins. Mark Curriden, *No Mercy: Should Drug Pushers Get Mandatory Life Sentences?*, A.B.A. J., March 1991, at 64.

[37] However, they would not have overruled *Coker v. Georgia*, because the holding in that case was "an aspect of our death penalty jurisprudence, rather than a generalizable aspect of Eighth Amendment law."

[38] In response to the dissent's argument that by this reasoning a legislature could properly make overtime parking a felony punishable by life imprisonment, Justice Scalia responded that it was unlikely "that the horrible example imagined would ever in fact occur, unless, of course, overtime parking should one day become an arguably major threat to the common good, and the need to deter it arguably critical."

Justices Anthony Kennedy, Sandra O'Connor, and David Souter concurred in the judgment against Harmelin, although they refused to overrule *Solem*. In an opinion written by Justice Kennedy, they conceded that the Court's "proportionality decisions have not been clear or consistent in all respects, [but] they can be reconciled . . . ." According to the concurring Justices, the previous cases yielded the following principles: (1) the fixing of prison terms "involves a substantive penological judgment that, as a general matter, is 'properly within the province of legislatures, not courts,'"; (2) "the Eighth Amendment does not mandate adoption of any one penological theory"; (3) substantial divergences in penological theories and in prison sentences are the "inevitable, often beneficial" result of living in a federal system; and (4) proportionality analysis should be informed by objective factors whenever possible.

In light of these principles, Justice Kennedy announced a new way to apply the three-prong test in imprisonment cases: "[I]ntra- and inter-jurisdictional analyses are appropriate only in the rare case in which a threshold comparison of the crime committed and the sentence imposed leads to an inference of gross disproportionality." In other words, hereafter, a federal court will apply the first prong of *Solem*, and if it determines that the offense is a serious one, proportionality analysis will cease and the sentence will be approved. The other prongs of the test will only come into play if the court determines that the offense at issue was petty and the sentence imposed was severe. Ironically, therefore, the courts will now apply the least objective test of the three, and will only resort to the other standards, including the objective inter-jurisdictional test, in rare circumstances. In the present case, the three-Justice plurality determined that the offense for which Harmelin was convicted was a serious one. Therefore, intra-and inter-jurisdictional analysis was unnecessary.

The four dissenters in *Harmelin* not only approved of *Solem*, but would have applied the standards announced in that case without variation. Although Justice White, the author of the primary dissent, agreed that "[d]rugs are . . . a serious societal problem," he did not believe that mere possession of drugs justified a mandatory life sentence. In view of the severity of the penalty in comparison to other laws within the state, and in comparison to similar laws elsewhere, the four dissenters would have held that the Michigan law "fail[ed] constitutional muster."

[4]—Summary

In view of the vote breakdown in *Harmelin*, this much is evident. First, *Solem v. Helm* was not overruled, as there were only two votes for its abandonment. Second, Justice Kennedy's concurrence represents the critical opinion in regard to the application of the *Solem* three-factor test. From now on, therefore, federal courts will provide only minimal proportionality oversight of non-capital sentences.[39]

---

[39] Some state courts have been willing to declare sentences unconstitutional. E.g., *State v. Bartlett*, 830 P.2d 823 (Ariz. 1992) (a 40-year sentence without possibility of early release is grossly out of proportion to the severity of the crimes of two counts of statutory rape); *Naovarath v. State*, 779 P.2d 944 (Nev. 1989) (life imprisonment without possibility of parole, imposed upon a 13-year-old defendant convicted of an especially violent murder, is excessive); *Epps v. State*, 634 A.2d 20 (Md. 1993) (a 20-year prison sentence for an inmate,

The future of proportionality law remains uncertain. Although seven members of the Court reaffirmed the principle that there is a proportionality guarantee in the Eighth Amendment, albeit only a weak one in non-death penalty circumstances, three of the four dissenters in *Harmelin*—the strongest advocates for federal proportionality oversight—have retired from the Court.

---

for projecting a small amount of water upon a correctional officer, constitutes a disproportionate sentence).

Also, a state court may invoke its own state constitution to bar severe penalties. For example, after *Harmelin* was decided, the Michigan Supreme Court ruled that the drug possession statute involved in *Harmelin* was unconstitutional under that state's constitutional prohibition on "cruel or unusual" punishment. *People v. Bullock,* 485 N.W.2d 866 (Mich. 1992).

CHAPTER 7

BURDENS OF PROOF

§ 7.01 Introduction

A criminal trial involves the presentation of evidence pertaining to the crime(s) charged, usually involving a dispute between the State and the defendant regarding some or all of the facts relating to the offense(s). At the conclusion of the trial, the factfinder, usually a jury,[1] must determine whose version of the evidence was more persuasive.

The jury is not wholly free in its deliberative process. Rules exist to ensure that the jury considers only those legal issues about which sufficient factual evidence was presented at trial that it can reach a rational, rather than a speculative, verdict. Moreover, assuming that an issue is properly before it, the jury will be instructed as to "how to decide close cases, and when to regard a case as close."[2]

Among the rules that guide the factfinding process are those establishing two types of burdens of proof: (1) the burden of production;[3] and (2) the burden of persuasion. As to any particular issue raised at a criminal trial, both burdens of proof may fall on a single party, or one party may have the burden of production while the other has the burden of persuasion. Although states have wide discretion in determining on whom the burdens should be allocated, and how substantial the burdens should be, the due process clause of the United States Constitution circumscribes legislative authority.

§ 7.02 Burden of Production

[A]—Nature of the Burden

Prior to trial the prosecution must file a document with the court that indicates the crime or crimes it believes that the defendant has committed. This document provides the accused with notice of the essential elements of the offense(s) charged, and the basic facts that the prosecutor intends to prove at trial to support her allegation that the defendant committed the crime(s).[4] In turn, the defendant is

---

[1] See § 1.02[A], *supra*.

[2] Barbara D. Underwood, *The Thumb on the Scales of Justice: Burdens of Persuasion in Criminal Cases*, 86 Yale L.J. 1299, 1299 (1977).

[3] This is sometimes called the "burden of going forward (with evidence)."

[4] "In all criminal prosecutions, the accused shall enjoy the right . . . to be informed of the nature and cause of the accusation . . . ." U.S. Const. amend. VI. The document that charges the defendant with a crime (called an "indictment" if prepared by a grand jury, or called an "information" if a grand jury is not involved) must "be a plain, concise and definite

sometimes required to provide advance notice to the prosecution of defenses she intends to assert at trial.

At trial, the parties will introduce evidence supporting their pre-trial claims. The rule establishing the burden of production identifies the party on whom is placed the initial obligation to introduce evidence at trial to support the particular legal claim in question.

[B]—To Whom the Burden Is Allocated

Ordinarily, the prosecutor has the burden of production regarding each element of the crime charged.[5] Almost always, the defendant has the burden of producing evidence pertaining to any affirmative defense she wishes to raise. For example, assume that murder is defined by statute as "the killing of a human being by another human being with malice aforethought." For current purposes, this definition may be divided into four elements: (1) a killing; (2) of a human being; (3) by another human being; (4) with malice aforethought. The prosecutor has the burden of producing evidence at trial regarding each of these elements. That is, she must introduce evidence that a life was taken, that the victim was a human being,[6] that the killer was the defendant, and that the killing occurred with the mental state described by the law as "malice aforethought." If the prosecutor fails to introduce sufficient evidence (as discussed below) regarding each of these elements, she has not met her burden of production.

In the preceding example, if the defendant intends to have the jury consider a defense to the murder charge, for example, that she killed in self-defense or that she was insane at the time of the crime, she—not the prosecutor—is usually obligated to introduce evidence at trial supporting the claim.

[C]—Quantum of Evidence Required

The prosecutor must produce enough evidence that a rational trier of fact *can* (but might not in fact) determine that the elements of the crime have been proved beyond a reasonable doubt.[7] Thus, in the hypothetical murder prosecution discussed earlier, the prosecutor has not met her burden of production unless she puts on enough evidence that a rational juror could believe, beyond a reasonable doubt, that the defendant killed another human being with malice aforethought.

As to defenses to crimes, for which the defendant usually has the burden of production, jurisdictions differ as to the amount of evidence required. In some states the defendant meets her burden of production if she simply produces "more than

---

written statement of the essential facts constituting the offense charged." Fed.R.Crim.P. 7(c)(1).

[5] See *Jackson v. Virginia*, 443 U.S. 307, 314-20 (1979); 1 Robinson at § 4.

[6] This would be a serious issue if the victim were a fetus that arguably was born dead. See § 31.01[B][1], *infra*.

[7] See *Jackson v. Virginia*, 443 U.S. at 319. For a definition of the phrase "beyond a reasonable doubt," see § 7.03[C][1], *infra*.

a scintilla of evidence" regarding the affirmative defense;[8] in other states she is required to introduce enough evidence to raise a reasonable doubt as to the defense in question.[9]

[D]—Effect of Failing to Meet the Burden

The trial judge decides whether the parties have met their respective burdens of production. If the judge concludes that the prosecutor failed to satisfy her burden of production regarding any element of the offense, the defendant is entitled to a directed verdict of acquittal at the conclusion of the prosecutor's case-in-chief, or at the end of the trial. This result follows from the fact that, as discussed in the next section, the prosecutor must *persuade* a jury beyond a reasonable doubt that the defendant committed the crime. If the prosecutor failed to introduce enough evidence for a jury to so find, there is no reason for it to deliberate on the matter.

If the defendant fails to meet her burden of production regarding an affirmative defense, the judge will not instruct the jury on the law pertaining to the defense, and the defendant is not entitled to have the issue considered by the jury in its deliberations.

§ 7.03   Burden of Persuasion

[A]—Nature of the Burden

Once a party satisfies her burden of production pertaining to an issue, that matter is properly before the factfinder, i.e., it will decide whose factual claims are more persuasive. But, how is the jury supposed to make this determination? Rules are needed to instruct the jury on how to weigh the conflicting evidence.

The rules establishing the burden of persuasion determine who is obligated to convince the jury of the accuracy of the particular claim in question. Put slightly differently, the party who has the burden of persuasion bears the risk of failing to convince the jury that her factual claim is true.

---

[8] E.g., *McDonald v. United States*, 312 F.2d 847, 849 (D.C. Cir. 1962).

[9] E.g., *People v. Tewksbury*, 544 P.2d 1335, 1343 (Cal. 1962).

[B]—To Whom the Burden Is Allocated[10]

[1]—In General

The Fifth and Fourteenth Amendments to the United States Constitute provide that a person may not be deprived of her life, liberty, or property without due process of law. Pursuant to the due process clause, a person charged with a crime is presumed innocent and, pursuant to what is often called "the *Winship*[11] doctrine," the prosecution is allocated the burden of persuading the factfinder beyond a reasonable doubt of "every fact necessary to constitute the crime charged."

According to *Winship*, the presumption of innocence "lies at the foundation of the administration of our criminal law." Although this presumption increases the risk that a guilty person will go free, "a society that values the good name and freedom of every individual" does "not view the social disutility of convicting an innocent man as equivalent to the disutility of acquitting someone who is guilty."[12]

Unfortunately, the Supreme Court has had difficulty ascertaining the precise scope of the *Winship* doctrine. The prosecutor must prove every fact necessary to constitute the crime charged, but what precisely *are* the "facts" for which the government must carry the burden of persuasion? Three cases illustrate the Court's less-than-straightforward approach to the question.

[2]—*Mullaney v. Wilbur*[13]

D was charged with murder by a Maine prosecutor. Evidence presented at his trial tended to show that *D* intentionally killed the victim, but that he may have done so "in the heat of passion on sudden provocation."

---

[10] See generally Ronald J. Allen, *The Restoration of In re Winship: A Comment on Burdens of Persuasion in Criminal Cases After Patterson v. New York*, 76 Mich. L. Rev. 30 (1977); Donald A. Dripps, *The Constitutional Status of the Reasonable Doubt Rule*, 75 Cal. L. Rev. 1665 (1987); George P. Fletcher, *Two Kinds of Legal Rules: A Comparative Study of Burden-of-Persuasion Practices in Criminal Cases*, 77 Yale L.J. 880 (1968); John Calvin Jeffries, Jr. & Paul B. Stephan III, *Defenses, Presumptions, and Burden of Proof in the Criminal Law*, 88 Yale L.J. 1325 (1979); Note, *Winship on Rough Waters: The Erosion of the Reasonable Doubt Standard*, 106 Harv. L. Rev. 1093 (1993); John Quigley, *The Need to Abolish Defenses to Crime: A Modest Proposal to Solve the Problem of Burden of Persuasion*, 14 Vt. L. Rev. 335 (1990); Irene Merker Rosenberg, *Winship Redux: 1970 to 1990*, 69 Tex. L. Rev. 109 (1990); Louis B. Schwartz, " '*nnocence*"—*A Dialogue with Professor Sundby*, 41 Hastings L.J. 153 (1989); Scott E. Sundby, *The Reasonable Doubt Rule and the Meaning of Innocence*, 40 Hastings L.J. 457 (1989); Barbara D. Underwood, Note 2, *supra*.

[11] *In re Winship*, 397 U.S. 358 (1970).

[12] Voltaire described "the great principle that it is better to run the risk of sparing the guilty than to condemn the innocent." Jean Francois Marie Arouet de Voltaire, *Zadig [Fate]* in Candide and Other Stories 20 (1962). Not everyone agrees. For a thoughtful dialogue on this matter, see Jeffrey Reiman and Ernest van den Haag, *On the Common Saying That It Is Better That Ten Guilty Persons Escape Than That One Innocent Suffer: Pro and Con*, Soc. Phil. & Pol'y, Spring 1990, at 226.

[13] 421 U.S. 684 (1975).

The trial court instructed the jury that Maine recognized two forms of criminal homicide, murder and manslaughter, and that the common elements of both offenses were that the homicide be: (1) "unlawful—*i.e.*, neither justifiable nor excusable"; and (2) that it be committed intentionally. The jury was instructed that the prosecution was required to prove both of these elements (beyond a reasonable doubt), and only if it met this burden was the jury to consider the distinction between murder and manslaughter.

On the distinction between murder and manslaughter, the trial court informed the jury that if the prosecution proved that *D* killed the victim unlawfully and intentionally, then the killing was murder, unless *D* persuaded the jury that the killing was "in the heat of passion on sudden provocation," in which case it constituted the lesser offense of manslaughter. That is, the prosecution had the burden of persuading the jury beyond a reasonable doubt that *D* unlawfully and intentionally killed the victim; if it did, the burden of proof shifted to the defense to prove that *D* was provoked into killing the victim. If *D* failed in this regard, he was guilty of murder; if he succeeded, he was guilty of manslaughter.

D appealed his conviction on the ground that the preceding jury instructions violated the *Winship* doctrine. The State responded, however, that the instructions were constitutional as it interpreted *Winship*: the prosecution only had the constitutional responsibility to prove that *D* was guilty of some form of criminal homicide. Under the instructions given, the State did not require *D* to prove his innocence; he only had the burden of persuasion regarding his level of guilt. In such circumstances, the State argued, "the defendant's critical interests in liberty and reputation are no longer of paramount concern since, irrespective of . . . the heat of passion on sudden provocation, he is likely to lose his liberty and certain to be stigmatized."

The Supreme Court disagreed. In an opinion written by Justice Lewis Powell, the Court summarized the historical roots of homicide law, and concluded that the presence or absence of heat of passion was "the single most important factor in determining the degree of culpability attaching to an unlawful homicide." It observed that "the clear trend has been toward requiring the prosecution to bear the ultimate burden of proving this fact."

The Court criticized the State's argument as unduly formalistic. It pointed out:

> [If the *Winship* doctrine] were limited to those facts that constitute a crime as defined by state law, a State could undermine many of the interests that [the due process clause] . . . sought to protect without effecting any substantive change in its law. It would only be necessary to redefine the elements that constitute different crimes, characterizing them as factors that bear solely on the extent of punishment.

The Court held that the due process clause required the prosecution not only to prove that *D* was guilty of criminal homicide, but also to persuade the jury regarding the facts relating to *D*'s "degree of criminal culpability."

Although the precise contours of the *Mullaney* decision were disputed by scholars, one plausible interpretation of the opinion was that, once a defendant satisfies her burden of *production* regarding an affirmative defense, the prosecution is constitutionally required to disprove the defense.[14]

[3]—*Patterson v. New York*[15]

[a]—The Holding

Patterson dramatically narrowed the import of *Mullaney*. The facts in *Patterson* superficially resembled those in *Mullaney*. *D* was charged with murder. He believed that he was guilty of the lesser offense of manslaughter because he suffered from what New York law described as an "extreme emotional disturbance." This provision, based on the Model Penal Code,[16] was a broader version of the "heat of passion on sudden provocation" doctrine considered in *Mullaney*.

Under New York law, murder required proof of three facts: (1) a human death; (2) that the accused caused it; and (3) that the accused intended the result. The homicide statute explicitly provided that "extreme emotional disturbance" was an affirmative defense to murder that, if proved by the defendant, reduced the criminal homicide to manslaughter. The jury was instructed consistently with these statutory provisions.

D argued that *Mullaney* invalidated the statute because the law permitted the prosecutor to shift to him the burden of proving his lesser level of culpability due to extreme emotional disturbance. Nonetheless, in an opinion written by Justice Byron White, the Supreme Court upheld the statute.

The Court conceded that there was "language in *Mullaney* that has been understood as perhaps construing the Due Process Clause to require the prosecution to prove . . . any fact affecting 'the [defendant's] degree of criminal culpability.' " The Court rejected this reading of *Mullaney* as unduly restrictive of legislative authority to allocate burdens of proof.

The Court reasoned that if the broad reading of *Mullaney* were correct, legislatures might be inclined to repeal defenses or, at least, not to broaden them as New York had done here. Justice White suggested that such a response would serve only to prejudice defendants' interests and undermine legislative reform. The Court stated that it did not intend *Mullaney* to have such a far-reaching effect on legislative conduct.

Following *Patterson*, the prosecution is constitutionally required to prove "every *ingredient* of an offense." As used in this opinion, *Winship*'s "facts" and *Patterson*'s "ingredients" are synonymous with the word "elements." That is, under the due process clause, the prosecution is required to prove every element in the definition of an offense, but the legislature may, if it chooses to do so, allocate to the defendant the burden of persuasion regarding non-elements, i.e., defenses to crimes.

The Court stated that this interpretation of *Winship* was consistent with *Mullaney*. It pointed out that one element of the crime of murder in Maine was that the killing

---

[14] See Allen, Note 10, *supra*, at 33-34.

[15] 432 U.S. 197 (1977).

[16] Model Penal Code § 210.3(1)(b). See § 31.10[C][3], *infra*.

be "unlawful." In turn, "unlawful" meant that the killing be "neither justifiable nor excusable." "Heat of passion," however, is an excuse defense.[17] Therefore, for a Maine homicide to be "unlawful," there had to be an *absence* of heat of passion or any other justification or excuse. This absence of a defense, then, was an ingredient of murder, as defined by Maine law. To require the prosecutor to prove the absence of heat of passion was consistent with the proposition that the government should prove every element of the crime charged.

In New York, however, absence of "extreme emotional disturbance" was not an element of murder; rather, its existence explicitly was an affirmative defense to murder that mitigated the crime to manslaughter. As a non-element of murder, New York could properly place the burden of proving its existence on the defendant.

Justice Powell, author of *Mullaney*, dissented in *Patterson*. He stated that the majority opinion's "explanation of the *Mullaney* holding bears little resemblance to the basic rationale of that decision." Powell condemned the Court's holding as formalistic: he observed that it permitted legislatures to "shift, virtually at will, the burden of persuasion with respect to any factor in a criminal case, so long as it is careful not to mention the nonexistence of that factor in the statutory language that defines the crime."

[b]—Analysis of *Patterson*

Patterson did not expressly overrule *Mullaney*. The Court provided a technically consistent means of distinguishing Maine's criminal homicide statute from New York's version. Nonetheless, whether for good or for ill, *Patterson* ignored or rejected much of the underlying reasoning of *Mullaney*.

Mullaney emphasized the liberty interest of the accused, and her right to avoid undue stigma. In view of the underlying values of the due process clause, as enunciated in *Winship*, a strong case can be developed for the proposition that, since the prosecution is required to prove the elements of an offense, even if the crime is a trivial one that will not result in substantial incarceration or stigma, it should also be required to prove the *degree* of a person's guilt, at least when the factor in question, makes "a substantial difference in punishment of the offender and in the stigma associated with the conviction,"[18] e.g., murder versus manslaughter.

In contrast to *Mullaney*, *Patterson* worried about restricting legislative prerogatives. Should a legislature that chooses to recognize a new defense to a crime, or to expand an old one, be compelled by the due process clause to allocate to the prosecution the duty to disprove the defense? Logically, if the legislature may *abolish* (or refuse to recognize) a defense, does it not have the right to do something *less*, i.e., to recognize the defense, but to require the defendant to bear the risk of failing to convince the jury of the truth of her claim?[19]

---

[17] There is controversy regarding whether heat-of-passion is an excuse or a justification defense. See § 31.07[C], *infra*. For current purposes, however, the dispute is irrelevant: either way, the defense negates the "unlawfulness" requirement.

[18] *Patterson*, 432 U.S. at 226 (Powell, J., dissenting).

[19] But, *may* a legislature abolish a criminal law defense? Are there certain defenses so fun-

Whichever approach is preferable as a matter of policy, the practical effect of *Patterson* is to permit legislatures, at least under the aegis of the due process clause,[20] to avoid most of the restrictions of *Winship* by redrafting their statutes to treat the absence of what previously had been an element of an offense as an affirmative defense.

[4]—Applying *Patterson*: *Martin v. Ohio*[21]

According to *Patterson*, the prosecutor must prove every element of an offense, but the legislature may allocate to the defendant the burden of persuasion regarding defenses. But, as seen in *Mullaney*, sometimes the absence of a defense may be an element of a crime. A difficult issue arises, therefore, when one or more elements of a *defense* effectively negate one or more elements of the *offense*, the latter of which the prosecution must prove beyond a reasonable doubt.

This problem arose in *Martin*, in which *D* was prosecuted for aggravated murder, defined under state law as "purposely, and with prior calculation and design, caus[ing] the death of another." *D* sought to show that he acted in self-defense, the elements of which defense were that he: (1) was not at fault in creating the situation giving rise to the argument; (2) had an honest belief that he was in imminent danger of death or great bodily harm; and (3) did not violate any duty to retreat.

The jury was instructed that to convict *D*, it had to find that, in light of all of the evidence, each of the elements of aggravated murder had been proved by the State beyond a reasonable doubt. However, as the jury was told, *D* had the burden of proving self-defense by a preponderance of the evidence.

D argued that these instructions violated the *Winship* doctrine, as interpreted by *Patterson*. He reasoned that one element of self-defense—the requirement of an "imminent" deadly threat—negated an element of the crime of aggravated murder, "prior calculation and design." In effect, therefore, he argued that the absence of the right to kill in self-defense was an implicit ingredient of the offense charged.

In a 5-4 opinion, the Supreme Court rejected *D*'s argument.[22] In doing so, it emphasized the fact that the trial court did not instruct the jury "that self-defense

---

damental to a concept of justice that it would violate the Constitution not to recognize them? For example, one court stated in dictum that "[i]t is difficult to the point of impossibility to imagine a right in any state to abolish self defense altogether, thereby leaving one a Hobson's choice of almost certain death through violent attack now or statutorily mandated death through trial and conviction of murder later." *Griffin v. Martin*, 785 F.2d 1172, 1187 n.37 (4th Cir.), *aff'd & op. withdrawn*, 795 F.2d 22 (1986) (*en banc*); but see *White v. Arn*, 788 F.2d 338, 347 (6th Cir. 1986) (rejecting the contention that a constitutional right of self-defense is founded in the Eighth, Ninth, or Fourteenth Amendments to the United States Constitution).

[20] Some scholars have argued that other constitutional provisions, such as the Eighth Amendment bar on cruel and unusual punishment, place limits on the legislature's authority to redefine criminal offenses. *E.g.*, Jeffries & Stephan, Note 10, *supra*, at 1365-97. However, in view of the Supreme Court's restrictive reading of the Eighth Amendment, see § 6.05[C], *supra*, this avenue may also be foreclosed.

[21] 480 U.S. 228 (1987).

[22] As in *Patterson*, Justice White wrote the majority opinion, and Justice Powell (the author of *Mullaney*) dissented.

evidence could not be considered in determining whether there was a reasonable doubt about the State's case . . . . Such an instruction would . . . plainly run afoul of *Winship*'s mandate." Although the Court conceded that the instructions to the jury could have been clearer, they conveyed the general point "that all of the evidence, including the evidence going to self-defense, must be considered in deciding whether there was a reasonable doubt about the sufficiency of the State's proof of the elements of the crime."

The Court agreed with *D*'s understanding "that the elements of aggravated murder and self-defense overlap in the sense that evidence to prove the latter will often tend to negate the former." However, a state may allocate to a defendant the burden of persuasion regarding the affirmative defense, as long as the jury may also consider the evidence relating to the defense as a basis for negating an element of a crime.

Notice, however, the confusion that this can create with a jury. A defendant might not prove by a preponderance of the evidence that she killed in lawful self-defense, yet this same evidence might create a reasonable doubt regarding whether she acted with prior calculation and design. If so, she must be acquitted. But, will the jury understand this? As the dissent feared, it might believe instead "that by raising the defense, the accused has assumed the ultimate burden of proving that particular element."

[C]—Quantum of Evidence Required

[1]—Elements of Crimes: Proof Beyond a Reasonable Doubt [23]

According to *In re Winship*, as interpreted by *Patterson*, the due process clause requires the prosecutor to prove every element of a crime "beyond a reasonable doubt."

This burden of proof "defies easy explication."[24] In terms of probability, it is the highest burden in the law. Guilt is not proven on the basis of the traditional civil standard of "preponderance of the evidence" (i.e., 50.1%), or even on the heightened basis of "clear and convincing evidence"; rather, a "very high level of probability [is] required."[25]

"Proof beyond a reasonable doubt" should also be understood to differ in kind, and not simply in degree, from civil standards.[26] We may wish to allocate burdens

---

[23] See generally Barbara J. Shapiro, "Beyond a Reasonable Doubt" and "Probable Cause": Historical Perspectives on the Anglo-American Law of Evidence (1991); Ronald J. Allen, *On the Significance of Batting Averages and Strikeout Totals: A Clarification of the "Naked Statistical Evidence" Debate, the Meaning of "Evidence," and the Requirement of Proof Beyond a Reasonable Doubt*, 65 Tulane L. Rev. 1093 (1991); Barbara J. Shapiro, *"To a Moral Certainty": Theories of Knowledge and Anglo-American Juries 1600-1850*, 38 Hastings L.J. 153 (1986); Richard Uviller, *Acquitting the Guilty: Two Case Studies on Jury Misgivings and the Misunderstood Standard of Proof*, 2 Crim. L. Forum 1 (1990); Henry A. Diamond, Note, *Reasonable Doubt: To Define or Not to Define*, 90 Colum. L. Rev. 1716 (1990); and the sources listed in Note 10, *supra*.

[24] *Victor v. Nebraska*, 114 S.Ct. 1239, 1242 (1994).

[25] *Id*. at 1247.

[26] See Allen, Note 23, *supra*, at 1103-04.

of proof in civil cases in the manner that is most likely to result in factually accurate outcomes. However, the effect of a criminal conviction—probable loss of life or liberty, and certain stigmatization—is so great that, as explained earlier,[27] the due process clause demands that the legal system err on the side of innocence, even at the expense of accuracy.

Chief Justice Shaw of the Massachusetts Supreme Judicial Court crafted the traditional definition of "beyond a reasonable doubt," which has served as the basis for many modern-day jury instructions. In *Commonwealth v. Webster*,[28] he stated, in part:

> [W]hat is reasonable doubt? . . . It is not merely possible doubt; because every thing relating to human affairs, and depending on moral evidence, is open to some possible or imaginary doubt. It is that state of the case, which, after the entire comparison and consideration of all the evidence, leaves the minds of jurors in that condition that they cannot say they feel an abiding conviction, to a moral certainty, of the truth of the charge . . . .

The term "moral certainty," as used by Justice Shaw in the mid-nineteenth century, meant "a state of subjective certitude." In *Victor v. Nebraska*,[29] however, the Supreme Court warned trial courts that this term may have "lost its historical meaning, and that a modern jury [might] understand it to allow conviction on proof that does not meet the beyond a reasonable doubt standard." The critical language in *Webster*, the Court said, is that the jurors must have "an abiding conviction"—a "settled and fixed" conviction—of the defendant's guilt.

[2]—Defenses[30]

Jurisdictions differ in their allocation of the burden of persuasion regarding affirmative defenses. Many states require the prosecution to disprove beyond a reasonable doubt some or all defenses, once the defendant has met her burden of production. In states that allocate to the defendant the burden of persuasion regarding defenses, however, it is typical to require her to prove the validity of the claim by the less strict preponderance-of-the-evidence standard.

[D]—Effect of Failing to Meet Burden

[1]—Elements of Crimes

If the prosecutor fails to prove each element of the crime beyond a reasonable doubt, the defendant must be acquitted of the offense charged. The acquittal may occur in either of two ways. First, after the prosecution completes its presentation of evidence or immediately before the case is due to be submitted to the jury for deliberation, upon motion of the defendant, the court must direct a verdict of acquittal if the evidence, viewed in the manner most favorable to the prosecution,[31]

---

[27] See § 7.03[B][1], *supra.*

[28] 59 Mass. 295, 320 (1850).

[29] 114 S.Ct. at 1247.

[30] See generally 1 Robinson at § 5.

[31] Because the factfinder may rationally decide to believe the prosecutor's rather than the defendant's version of disputed facts, on a motion to direct a verdict in favor of the defendant,

can support no reasonable verdict other than acquittal.[32] Alternatively, upon proper instruction of the burdens of proof, a jury should acquit the defendant if it possesses a reasonable doubt regarding one or more elements of the offense charged.[33]

[2]—Defenses

If a defendant presents sufficient evidence to meet her burden of *production* regarding a defense to the crime charged, the jury must be permitted to evaluate the defense claimed. When the defendant also has the burden of *persuasion*, a jury should reject the claimed defense if she fails to satisfy the stated burden of persuasion. Assuming that the prosecution has proven the elements of the crime beyond a reasonable doubt, and that no other defenses have been proven, the defendant may be convicted.

If the prosecution has the burden of disproving a defense, the jury must find the existence of the defense and acquit the defendant if the prosecution fails to persuade the jury beyond a reasonable doubt of the defense's non-existence.

§ 7.04   Model Penal Code

The prosecution has the burden of production regarding the elements of an offense. The Model Penal Code provides, however, that the prosecutor is not required to disprove an affirmative defense "unless there is evidence supporting such defense."[34] The Code does not specify the strength of the evidence required to satisfy the defendant's burden of production, choosing instead to leave the matter to the courts.[35]

Regarding the burden of persuasion, the general rule is that the prosecution must prove every "element" of an offense beyond a reasonable doubt.[36] The term "element" as used in the Code, however, includes conduct that "negatives an excuse or justification" for the action.[37] That is, the Model Penal Code allocates to the prosecution the duty to disprove defenses, assuming that the defendant has satisfied her burden of production. However, this rule does not apply to defenses that the Code expressly requires the defendant to prove by a preponderance of the evidence.[38]

---

the judge must consider the evidence in the manner most favorable to the opposing side. The same test is applied in any appeal of a conviction. See *Jackson v. Virginia*, 443 U.S. 307, 319 (1979).

[32] *Curley v. United States*, 160 F.2d 229, 232-33 (D.C. Cir. 1947). No matter how overwhelming the evidence of guilt, the prosecution is never entitled to a directed verdict of conviction. *Sullivan v. Louisiana*, 113 S.Ct. 2078, 2080 (1993). The grant of such a motion would deny the accused her constitutional right to trial by jury. See § 1.02[A], *supra*.

[33] Each juror should individually determine whether she has an abiding conviction of the defendant's guilt. If there is no unanimity regarding the matter, a mistrial is declared, and the defendant may be reprosecuted.

[34] Model Penal Code § 1.12(2)(a).

[35] American Law Institute, Comment to § 1.12, at 193.

[36] Model Penal Code § 1.12(1).

[37] Model Penal Code § 1.13(9)(c).

[38] E.g., Model Penal Code § 2.13 (the defense of entrapment).

CHAPTER 8

PRESUMPTIONS

§ 8.01 The Nature of a Presumption [1]

Assume that murder is defined by statute as the "unlawful and intentional killing of a human being by another human being." Under this definition, the prosecutor must prove beyond a reasonable doubt that: (1) a human being was killed; (2) the defendant was the killer; (3) the defendant intended to take a human life; and (4) the killing was unlawful.

Sometimes, a prosecutor will find it difficult to prove an element of an offense. For example, it might be hard to prove the third element--the defendant's subjective intent to kill--in a prosecution based on the hypothetical murder statute. Assume, therefore, that in order to prove that *D* intended to kill *V*, the prosecutor introduces evidence that *D* picked up a loaded gun, pointed it in *V*'s direction, and fired it. Has the prosecutor proved the requisite intent beyond a reasonable doubt? Perhaps, but perhaps not: *D* may have intended only to frighten or wound *V*.

Suppose, however, that a legislature or court establishes the following rule: "Whenever it is proved in a criminal trial that a person fired a loaded gun at another person, the factfinder must [or 'may'] presume that the actor intended to kill the other person."

This rule establishes a presumption. Presumptions operate in the following manner: Upon proof of Fact (or set of Facts) A, a factfinder must (or "may," depending on the language of the instruction) presume Fact B. In the nomenclature of presumptions, Fact A is the *basic* fact, and Fact B is the *presumed* fact. Usually, although not always, the presumed fact in a criminal prosecution is an element of the crime charged. In our hypothetical, the presumption requires (or permits) the

---

[1] See generally Ronald J. Allen, *Structuring Jury Decisionmaking in Criminal Cases: A Unified Constitutional Approach to Evidentiary Devices*, 94 Harv. L. Rev. 321 (1980); Harold A. Ashford & D. Michael Risinger, *Presumptions, Assumptions, and Due Process in Criminal Cases: A Theoretical Overview*, 79 Yale L.J. 165 (1969); Laurie A. Briggs, Note, *Presumptive Mens Rea: An Analysis of the Federal Judiciary's Retreat From Sandstrom v. Montana*, 64 Notre Dame L. Rev. 367 (1989); Michael H. Graham, *Presumptions—More Than You Ever Wanted to Know and Yet Were Too Disinterested to Ask*, 17 Crim. L. Bull. 431 (1981); Shari L. Jacobson, Comment, *Mandatory and Permissive Presumptions in Criminal Cases: The Morass Created by Allen*, 42 U. Miami L. Rev. 1009 (1988); Charles R. Nesson, *Reasonable Doubt and Permissive Inferences: The Value of Complexity*, 92 Harv. L. Rev. 1187 (1979).

jury to presume intent to kill (Fact B) upon proof that D fired a loaded gun at V (Fact A).[2]

If a jury is instructed that it *must* presume Fact B upon proof of basic Fact A, the presumption is a "mandatory presumption." If the jury is told that it *may*, but need not, presume Fact B, the instruction is called a "permissive presumption."[3]

The practical effect of presumptions, especially those of a mandatory nature, is to make it easier for the party with the burden of proof—here, the prosecutor—to persuade the factfinder regarding the issue in question. It is not necessarily improper for the legislature or a court to make the prosecutor's job easier in this manner. At times, however, a presumption runs counter to constitutional protections of the defendant.

This chapter considers the constitutional implications of mandatory and permissive presumptions that affect the burden of persuasion in criminal trials.

§ 8.02 Mandatory Presumptions

[A]—Rebuttable Presumptions

A mandatory rebuttable presumption requires a finding of the presumed fact upon proof of the basic fact, unless that finding is rebutted by the opposing party. Essentially, in a criminal trial, the jury is instructed regarding a presumption that "if the State proves Fact A, then you must find Fact B, unless the defendant disproves Fact B by a preponderance [or other quantum] of the evidence."

The procedural effect of a mandatory rebuttable presumption is to shift to the defendant the burden of persuasion regarding the presumed fact, upon proof by the prosecution of the basic fact. Applying this presumption to the example described in Section 8.01, the jury would be required to find that D intended to kill V [Fact B] if the prosecution proved that D fired a loaded gun at V [Fact A], unless D disproved his intent to kill by a preponderance of the evidence.

Rebuttable mandatory presumptions are unconstitutional when the presumed fact is an element of the crime charged. For example, in *Sandstrom v. Montana*,[4] D was charged with "deliberate homicide," in that D "purposely or knowingly caused the death" of V. At trial, D admitted that he killed V, but he denied that he did so purposely or knowingly. At the conclusion of the trial, the judge instructed the jury that "the law presumes that a person intends the natural and probable consequences of his voluntary acts." As the Supreme Court explained the effect of this presumption, "upon proof by the State of the slaying, and of additional facts not themselves establishing the element of intent, the burden was shifted to the defendant to prove that he lacked the requisite mental state."

---

[2] Of course, the basic fact here is actually a set of facts: (1) that the weapon used was a gun (rather than some other weapon); (2) that it was loaded; (3) that D aimed it at V; and (4) that D fired it. If one or more of these facts is not proved, the presumption does not apply.

[3] As discussed in § 8.03, *infra*, a permissive presumption is more properly described as an "inference."

[4] 442 U.S. 510 (1979).

The Court held that the presumption was unconstitutional. By shifting to *D* the burden of proof regarding his mental state, the presumption "conflict [ed] with the overriding presumption of innocence with which the law endows the accused and which extends to every element of the crime."[5]

Similarly, in a prosecution for theft of a rented car, it is unconstitutional to charge the jury that "intent to commit theft by fraud is presumed if one who has leased or rented the personal property of another pursuant to a written contract fails to return the . . . property . . . within 20 days." By shifting the burden of proof regarding intent, this instruction "subvert[s] the presumption of innocence accorded to accused persons."[6]

A mandatory rebuttable presumption is not saved by the requirement that the prosecution prove the basic fact beyond a reasonable doubt. In the hypothetical case described in Section 8.01, even if *D* undoubtedly fired a loaded gun at *V*, this does not necessarily prove beyond a reasonable doubt that he intended to kill *V*. *D* may have believed that the gun was unloaded, or he may have intended to fire in the direction of, but purposely miss, *V*, in order to frighten him. Yet, pursuant to the presumption, the jury would be required to find the element of the offense, unless *D* disproved his intent to kill. The Constitution does not permit this, because the presumption "invade [s] the truth-finding task assigned solely to juries in criminal cases."[7]

[B]—Irrebuttable ("Conclusive") Presumptions

An irrebuttable or conclusive presumption requires the jury to find the presumed fact upon proof of the basic fact, even if the opposing party introduces rebutting evidence. For example, a jury might be charged that "upon proof that *D* fired a loaded gun at *V*, you must find that *D* intended to kill *V*."

True irrebuttable presumptions are hard to find in the criminal law. However, occasionally a judge will instruct the jury regarding a *rebuttable* presumption in language that could cause a reasonable juror to believe that it is irrebuttable, in which case an appellate court will treat it as such. A mandatory irrebuttable presumption pertaining to an element of an offense is unconstitutional for the same reasons that mandatory rebuttable ones are impermissible.[8]

§ 8.03 Permissive Presumptions

A permissive presumption is one in which the factfinder may, but need not, find the existence of the presumed fact, upon proof of the basic fact.

A permissive presumption is not a true presumption. It is more accurately described as an "inference." An inference is not a formal rule that shifts the burden

---

[5] The State is constitutionally required to prove every element of a crime beyond a reasonable doubt. See § 7.03, *supra*.

[6] *Carella v. California*, 491 U.S. 263, 265 (1989) (*per curiam*).

[7] *Id*.

[8] *Sandstrom v. Montana*, 442 U.S. at 521-24.

of proof from one party to another, as a presumption does. Rather, an inference is a (hopefully) logical bridge between one fact believed to be true and a second fact, the truth of which is at issue. Thus, in the hypothetical posed in Section 8.01, if the jury were informed that it "may"—not "must"—presume Fact B from proof of Fact A, the jury would not be required to find that D intended to kill V on the basis of the evidence that he fired a loaded gun at V, even if D introduced no evidence to disprove his intent to kill. If it wished, however, the jury could cross the inferential bridge and find the intent based on the aiming and firing of the loaded gun.

Because permissive presumptions, or inferences, do not formally affect the prosecution's constitutional obligation to prove every element of an offense beyond a reasonable doubt, they are not unconstitutional *per se*.[9] Nonetheless, an inference is constitutionally impermissible if there is no rational connection between the basic fact and the presumed fact. As the Court stated in *Tot v. United States*,[10] "where the inference [created] is so strained as not to have a reasonable relation to the circumstances of life as we know them," the factfinding process is rendered unreliable, and the defendant is denied due process of law.

To pass scrutiny under the due process clause, a court must determine whether a jury could rationally have drawn the disputed inference on its own. A permissive presumption is unconstitutional if, based on the evidence presented at trial, "there is no rational way the trier [of fact] could make the connection permitted by the inference."[11] For example, in *Tot*, D, a convicted felon, was found in possession of a firearm, in violation of a federal law making it unlawful for a convicted felon to be in possession of any firearm shipped in interstate commerce. Under the law at that time, the jury was permitted to infer that a weapon had been shipped in interstate commerce, if the government proved possession of the firearm by a convicted felon. The Supreme Court held that this presumption/inference violated D's due process rights because there was "no rational connection between the fact proved [that D was in possession of the firearm] and the ultimate fact presumed [that the weapon had been shipped in interstate commerce]."

Likewise, in *Leary v. United States*,[12] the Supreme Court invalidated a presumption that permitted the jury to infer from D's possession of marijuana that he knew it had been illegally imported into the country, which knowledge was an element of the crime charged. The Court stated that, to be valid, it must "more likely than not" be the case (which the Court concluded that it was not) that D knew the marijuana was imported from the simple fact that he was in possession of it.

On the other hand, in *County Court of Ulster County v. Allen*,[13] the Supreme Court upheld an instruction to the jury that permitted it to infer from presence of two firearms in an automobile that all four occupants of the vehicle were in illegal possession of the weapons. In the case, two very heavy, large-caliber handguns were

[9] *County Court of Ulster County v. Allen*, 442 U.S. 140, 157 (1979).

[10] 319 U.S. 463 (1943).

[11] *County Court of Ulster County v. Allen*, 442 U.S. at 157.

[12] 395 U.S. 6 (1969).

[13] 442 U.S. 140 (1979).

positioned crosswise in the open handbag of a 16-year-old female occupant. The bag was either on the front seat or front floor of the car that contained her and three adult males. The Supreme Court held that, as applied to the facts of this case, the inference of constructive possession on the part of the four defendants was rationally based. As the weapons were heavy, large, and in full view, the Court reasoned that it was more likely than not true that the youth was not solely responsible for their being in her purse. More likely that not, the Court said, each of the adult male occupants could exercise control over the weapons, and therefore were in constructive possession of them. In essence, therefore, the jury instruction regarding the inference only made explicit what the jurors might have reasoned for themselves during the deliberative process.[14]

If the evidence at trial had been different, for example, if one of the occupants of the car had been a hitchhiker, the inference of possession by this casual occupant might not have withstood analysis. Or, if the weapons in this case had been small and concealed in the girl's purse, the inference of possession by the adult males might not have satisfied the more-likely-than-not test.

§ 8.04　Model Penal Code

The Model Penal Code does not recognize mandatory presumptions. The drafters of the Code took the position that when a legislature wishes to allocate to the defendant the burden of persuasion regarding a particular issue, it should do so directly by recognizing an affirmative defense, and expressly requiring the defendant to establish the fact by the preponderance of the evidence.[15]

The Code permits *permissive* presumptions regarding elements of criminal offenses. Such presumptions, when established by the legislature, affect a criminal trial in two procedural ways. First, if any evidence of the basic fact is presented at trial, the issue of the existence of the presumed fact—i.e., the element of the crime— must be submitted to the jury unless, in the language of the Code, the trial judge is "satisfied that the evidence as a whole clearly negatives the presumed fact."[16] In essence, the permissive presumption is triggered unless the presumption is so lacking in foundation that the defendant is entitled to a directed verdict on the matter.

Second, assuming that the permissive presumption is not irrational, the Model Code requires the judge to instruct the jury that the element at issue must still be proved by the prosecutor beyond a reasonable doubt, but that the law permits it to regard the basic facts as sufficient evidence of the presumed fact.[17] Thus, with the

---

[14] However, when a judge tells the jury that it may treat proof of the basic fact as sufficient evidence to support the presumed fact, this instruction may have a powerful impact on the jurors. Although they might have inferred the presumed fact on their own, the judge's "permission" to draw the inference may make it much more likely that they will do so. Consequently, some commentators believe that the law should not distinguish between permissive and mandatory presumptions.

[15] American Law Institute, Comment to § 1.12 at 203. See § 7.04, *supra*.

[16] Model Penal Code § 1.12(5)(a).

[17] Model Penal Code § 1.12(5)(b).

ongoing hypothetical considered in this chapter, if the prosecutor introduced evidence that D fired a loaded gun at V, the jury would be instructed (assuming that the inference has a rational foundation) that the prosecutor must prove beyond a reasonable doubt that D intended to kill V, but that the law allows the jury to treat proof of the fact that D fired the loaded gun at V as adequate evidence to meet the prosecutor's burden of persuasion on the matter of D's mental state.

CHAPTER 9

ACTUS REUS

§ 9.01 *Actus Reus*: General Principles [1]

[A]—Definition

Generally speaking, crimes have two components: the "*actus reus*," the physical or external portion of the crime; and the "*mens rea*," the mental or internal feature. The concept of "*actus reus*" is the focus of this chapter.

The term "*actus reus*" was not used by scholars in criminal law treatises prior to the twentieth century,[2] but it has found currency in modern Anglo-American jurisprudence. Unfortunately, it has no single accepted criminal law meaning.

As used in this Text, the term "*actus reus*" includes three ingredients of a crime, which can be encapsulated in a single sentence: the *actus reus* of an offense consists of (1) a voluntary act (or a failure to perform a voluntary act that one has a legal duty to perform); (2) that causes; (3) social harm.[3] For example, if *A* picks up a knife and stabs *B*, killing *B*, the *actus reus* of a criminal homicide has occurred: *A* has performed a *voluntary act* (stabbing *B*) that *caused B*'s death (the *social harm*). As is developed in this chapter, "voluntary act" and "social harm" are legal terms of art that require special attention. The element of causation, which links the defendant's voluntary act (or omission) to the social harm, is discussed in Chapter 14.[4]

---

[1] See generally Michael Moore, Act and Crime (1993); Paul H. Robinson, *Should the Criminal Law Abandon the Actus Reus-Mens Rea Distinction?* in Action and Value in Criminal Law 187 (Stephen Shute, John Gardner, & Jeremy Horder eds. 1993); Exchange, *The Actus Reus Requirement*, Crim. Just. Ethics, Winter/Spring 1991, at 11-26; Symposium, *Act and Crime*, 142 U. Pa. L. Rev. 1443-1839 (1994); Albin Eser, *The Principle of "Harm" in the Concept of Crime: A Comparative Analysis of the Criminally Protected Legal Interests*, 4 Duq. L. Rev. 345 (1965).

[2] Hall at 222.

[3] Eser, Note 1, *supra*, at 386.

[4] Warning: Because "*actus reus*" has no universally accepted meaning, some courts and commentators use the term more narrowly than is suggested in the text, simply to describe the defendant's conduct (in the example given, the voluntary acts of picking up the knife and stabbing *B*) or the result of that conduct (the social harm of *B*'s death), rather than a combination thereof.

[B]—Punishing Thoughts: Why Not?[5]

Suppose that three people separately want the President dead: *A* idly wishes that the President were dead; *B* intends to kill the President; and *C* actually kills the President. A society might plausibly punish all three persons. *A* would be punished for her morally wrongful thoughts; *B* would be punished for her intention, i.e., for developing a morally wrongful plan or expectation to act upon her thoughts; and *C* would be punished for her harmful conduct. In Anglo-American criminal law, however, only *C* is punishable, as "[t]he reach of the criminal law has long been limited by the principle that no one is punishable for his thoughts."[6] Put differently, the legal requirement of conduct resulting in harm—the *actus reus* component of a crime—insures that *A* and *B* are excluded from criminal censure.

Reasons of pragmatism and principle justify the *actus reus* requirement. On a pragmatic level, the requirement of conduct is "[r]ooted in skepticism about the ability . . . to know what passes through the minds of men."[7] We often have difficulty accurately reconstructing our own thoughts, so we can hardly read another person's mind.

Even if there were a way to read a person's mind, punishment for thoughts alone would be objectionable. First, as to *A*, she merely hoped that the President would die; she did not develop a plan to bring her wishes to fruition. Virtually all people, most of whom are entirely law-abiding, occasionally hope that some harm will befall another. A society that would punish for such idle thoughts would be an intolerable place to live.[8]

What about *B*? Many people have momentary antisocial thoughts, but few intend to act upon them. On its face, a rule that allows *B* to escape punishment is counter-utilitarian. For various reasons, however, *B*'s punishment would be unacceptable. First, practically speaking, there is no way to distinguish "between desires of the day-dream variety and fixed intentions that may pose a real threat to society."[9] Second, although conduct may be deterrable, it is doubtful that the thought processes that result in criminal intentions are.

Third, in a society that values individual freedom, use of the criminal law should be limited to situations in which injury is seriously threatened, and not simply "to purify thoughts and perfect character."[10] Respect for individual liberties, therefore, requires that the criminal law be exercised only in response to conduct.[11]

---

[5] See generally Herbert Morris, On Guilt and Innocence 1-29 (1976).

[6] *United States v. Muzii*, 676 F.2d 919, 920 (2d Cir. 1982).

[7] Abraham S. Goldstein, *Conspiracy to Defraud the United States*, 68 Yale L.J. 405, 405 (1959).

[8] 2 James Fitzjames Stephen, A History of the Criminal Law in England 78 (1883) ("If [the law] were not so restricted it would be utterly intolerable; all mankind would be criminals, and most of their lives would be passed in trying and punishing each other . . . .").

[9] *Powell v. Texas*, 392 U.S. 514, 543 (1968) (Black and Harlan, JJ., concurring).

[10] *United States v. Hollingsworth*, 27 F.3d 1196, 1203 (7th Cir. 1994) (*en banc*).

[11] See Packer at 74.

Finally, and perhaps most basically, the *actus reus* requirement is premised on the retributive belief that it is morally wrong to punish people for their unacted-upon intentions. Retributive theory justifies punishment of those who freely choose to harm others; the corollary of this is that society must give people the opportunity to desist from wrongful activity. To a retributivist, therefore, voluntary conduct serves as a moral prerequisite for the infliction of punishment.

§ 9.02 Voluntary Act: General Principles[12]

[A]—General Rule

Subject to a few limited exceptions,[13] a person is not guilty of a crime unless her conduct includes a voluntary act.[14] Few statutes defining criminal offenses expressly provide for this requirement. Nonetheless, the voluntary act requirement has common law support, modern courts usually treat it as an implicit element of criminal statutes,[15] and an increasing number of states now include a general statutory provision, cast in terms similar to the Model Penal Code, that sets out this rule.[16]

For analytical purposes the voluntary act rule should be separated into its two components, the "act" and its "voluntary" nature.

[B]—The "Act"

For purposes of the *actus reus* requirement, an "act" is simply a bodily movement, more specifically, a muscular contraction.[17] A person "acts" when she pulls the trigger of a gun, raises her arm, turns the ignition key in an automobile, or simply puts one leg in the front of the other to walk. Understood this way, an act involves *physical*, although not necessarily *visible*, behavior. For example, the muscular contractions involved in talking—the movements of the vocal chords and tongue—constitute "acts" for present purposes. However, the term "act" *excludes* the internal

---

[12] See generally Katz at 103-135; Larry Alexander, *Reconsidering the Relationship Among Voluntary Acts, Strict Liability, and Negligence in Criminal Law*, Soc. Phil. & Pol'y, Spring 1990, at 84; Michael Corrado, *Automatism and the Theory of Action*, 39 Emory L.J. 1191 (1990); Sanford J. Fox, *Physical Disorder, Consciousness, and Criminal Liability*, 63 Colum. L. Rev. 645 (1963); Douglas Husak & Brian P. McLaughlin, *Time-Frames, Voluntary Acts, and Strict Liability*, 12 Law & Phil. 95 (1993); Michael S. Moore, *Responsibility and the Unconscious*, 53 S. Cal. L. Rev. 1563 (1980); Kevin W. Saunders, *Voluntary Acts and the Criminal Law: Justifying Culpability Based on the Existence of Volition*, 49 U. Pitt. L. Rev. 443 (1988); and the sources in Note 1, *supra*.

[13] See § 9.07, *infra*.

[14] *State v. Massey*, 747 P.2d 802, 805 (Kan. 1987).

[15] E.g., *Martin v. State*, 17 So.2d 427 (Ala. Ct. App. 1944) (*D* was charged with violation of an offense that provided that "[a]ny person who, while intoxicated or drunk, appears in any public place . . . and manifests a drunken condition [shall be convicted of an offense]"; the court interpreted the word "appears" to presuppose a voluntary appearance in public, which was not proven at *D*'s trial).

[16] Model Penal Code § 2.01. See § 9.05, *infra*.

[17] Holmes at 54.

mental processes of thinking about, or of developing an intention to do, a physical act (e.g., "mental acts").

Two aspects of the term "act" should be noted here. First, the term does *not* apply to the *results* of a person's bodily movements. For example, suppose that *D*, intending to kill *V*, places dynamite around *V*'s house, where *V* is asleep, and then activates a detonator that causes an explosion, killing *V*. In a criminal homicide prosecution, the pertinent acts by *D* are the positioning of the dynamite around *V*'s house and her activation of the detonator. The term "act," however, does *not* include the result of *D*'s conduct, i.e., *V*'s death. The latter constitutes the "social harm" element of the *actus reus*.[18]

Second, some courts and scholars contend that, to be an "act," the muscular contraction must be voluntarily performed. As one court put it, "[a]n [involuntary] 'act' . . . is in reality no act at all. It is merely a physical event . . . ."[19] Most modern lawyers, however, use the term "act" as it is defined in this subsection, as a bodily movement that can be voluntarily or involuntarily performed, as these terms are discussed immediately below.

[C]—"Voluntary"

Unfortunately, the word "voluntary" is used by criminal lawyers in two different senses. The two usages of the term are often confused.

[1]—Broad Meaning: In the Context of Defenses

The word "voluntary" is often used in discussing criminal law defenses to express the general conclusion that the defendant possessed sufficient free will to be blamed for her conduct.[20] Thus, it is sometimes said that a person who acted under duress or as the result of a mental disorder acted "involuntarily." This simply means that, due to the excusing condition, the actor does not deserve to be punished for her actions.

[2]—Narrow Meaning: In the Context of the *Actus Reus*

The term "voluntary" has a much narrower meaning when used to determine whether the *actus reus* of an offense has occurred. Nineteenth century scholar John Austin defined a "voluntary act" in this sense as a "movement of the body which follows our volition."[21] Similarly, Holmes described it as a "willed" contraction of a muscle.[22]

What did Austin mean by "volition," or Holmes by a "willed" act? Austin posited a view of human behavior, in which a person consciously decides to move a part of the body, and then that part of the body "invariably and immediately [follows]

---

[18] See § 9.10, *infra*.

[19] *State v. Utter*, 479 P.2d 946, 950 (Wash. Ct. App. 1971).

[20] Fletcher at 803.

[21] 1 John Austin, Lectures on Jurisprudence 426 (3d. ed. 1869); see also Katz at 125 (it is "a movement, a contraction of one's muscles, *preceded by a volition*").

[22] Holmes at 54.

our wishes or desires for those same movements."[23] Applying this definition, nearly all human acts are voluntary,[24] and thus it may be more useful to give examples of *involuntary* acts. Examples of these include reflexive actions, spasms, epileptic seizures,[25] and bodily movements while the actor is unconscious[26] or asleep.[27]

Austin's explanation of volition is too simplistic. Today, we realize that bodily movements occur as the result of complicated physiological and psychological mechanisms, many of which are not fully understood even now. However, no human act occurs simply as the result of wishing it to take place. Instead, a person receives stimuli from outside and from within herself, which themselves act as further stimuli, some of which produce electrical impulses from the brain that result in bodily movements.[28]

So, what does it *really* mean to say that a person may not be punished unless her conduct includes a voluntary—"willed"—act? The concept of volition is tied to the notion that criminal law responsibility should only attach to those who are accountable for their actions in a very personal way. As Professor Sanford Kadish has explained, the criminal law distinguishes

> between genuine human actions, which are susceptible of praise and blame, and mere events brought about by physical causes which happen to involve a human body . . . . When a person claims the involuntary-act defense he is conceding that his own body made the motion but denies responsibility for it.[29]

Professor Kadish's point can be seen if one considers the difference in meaning of the following two sentences: (1) "I raised my arm;" and (2) "My arm came up."[30] Both statements suggest that a bodily movement has occurred. Yet, the difference in language expresses our intuitive understanding of the difference between a voluntary act (as described in the first sentence) and an involuntary one (the second sentence). In both cases, the arm movement was the result of impulses from the actor's brain. But, in the first sentence, the implication is that the act was the result of something more than mere physiological brain activity. That extra "something"

---

[23] Austin, Note 21, *supra*, at 426 (emphasis omitted).

[24] Notice that if X points a gun at D and threatens to kill her unless she shoots V, D's coerced act of pulling the trigger of a gun to shoot V is "voluntary" in the Austinian sense, although it is arguably "involuntary" in the broader sense described in subsection [1], *supra*.

[25] E.g., *People v. Williams*, 99 Cal.Rptr. 103 (Ct. App. 1972).

[26] E.g., *People v. Newton*, 87 Cal.Rptr. 394 (Ct. App. 1970); *State v. Massey*, 747 P.2d 802 (Kan. 1987); *State v. Utter*, 479 P.2d 946 (Wash. Ct. App. 1971); *Fulcher v. State*, 633 P.2d 142 (Wyo. 1981). The "defense" of unconsciousness is sometimes described as "automatism."

[27] *Fain v. Commonwealth*, 78 Ky. 183 (1879).

[28] D. O'Connor, *The Voluntary Act*, 15 Med. Sci. Law 31, 32 (1975).

[29] Sanford H. Kadish, *Excusing Crime*, 75 Cal. L. Rev. 257, 259 (1987).

[30] Ludwig Wittgenstein, Philosophical Investigations 161 (G. Anscombe trans. 3d ed. 1958) ("[W]hat is left over if I subtract the fact that my arm goes up from the fact that I raise my arm?").

was the more sophisticated thought process that goes into the "decision" to raise one's arm. Put slightly differently, a voluntary act involves the use of the human *mind*; an involuntary act involves the use of the human *brain*, without the aid of the mind. [31] With a voluntary act, a human being—a person—and not simply an organ of a human being, causes the bodily action.

Thus, when D's arm strikes V as the result of an epileptic seizure, we sense that D's *body*, but not D the person, has caused the impact. The movement of D's arm is similar to a tree branch bending in the wind and striking V. When D "wills" her arm to move, however, we feel that D, and not primarily her body, is responsible for V's injury. Her "acting self" is implicated. A personal, human agency is involved in causing the bodily contact. [32] Another way of making this point is to say that involuntary acts are "inappropriate" actions, i.e., they are bodily movements not "required for any action . . . which the agent believed himself to be doing." They are "wild" acts, "not 'governed by the will' in the sense that they are not subordinated to the agent's conscious plans of action." [33]

One should be careful not to assume that an act is involuntary simply because the actor is unaware of what she is doing as she is doing it. For example, people act habitually: a chain-smoker may light up a cigarette "without thinking"; a driver coming home from work may change lanes on the freeway at precisely the same place each day, without even noticing that she is doing this. Although, at our best, we are aware of both our external and internal (mental) surroundings, sometimes we "don't notice that [we] notice . . . . [We are] aware of everything except [ourselves]." [34] In this sense, consciousness is a matter of degree, and the law treats habitual acts as falling on the voluntary side of the continuum. This conclusion follows from the fact that an habitual act is an appropriate way to fulfill an actor's plan of action, even if it is true that she may not be aware that she has a plan of action.

---

[31] See *Bratty v Attorney-General*, [1963] A.C. 386, 409 (House of Lords) (an involuntary act is one "which is done by the muscles without any control by the mind").Sometimes, there can be bodily movement without even the "order" from the brain. For example, if D's car strikes X, and X's body is propelled through the air into V, we say that D acted by driving her vehicle into X. X, however, has not acted at all, voluntarily or involuntarily. Neither X's brain, nor her mind, had anything to do with causing her body to move as it did. Her body struck V the way a stone thrown by D might strike V. It makes no more sense to say that X "acted" in striking V than to say that the stone "acted" by flying through the air.

[32] Moore, Note 12, *supra*, at 1576.

[33] Hart at 105.

[34] Katz at 120.

[3]—"Voluntariness": At the Edges

[a]—Hypnotism[35]

Suppose that X hypnotizes D to immediately shoot and kill V, or suppose that X uses post-hypnotic suggestion to get D to kill V. When D shoots V, is she acting "voluntarily," in the narrow sense of the term?

Depending on our ultimate understanding of how hypnotism works upon the human mind, D's acts might be classified as involuntary. The idea to kill V was planted in D's mind by X. If D lacked the ability to disregard X's "suggestions"—a matter of considerable dispute[36] —it would be plausible to view D as little more than a marionette whose strings were pulled by X. The hypnotized subject might be equated to a sleepwalker, whose acts are involuntary.

On the other hand, a strong case can be developed for the proposition that acts under hypnosis or as the result of hypnotic suggestion are voluntary. D willed her finger to pull the trigger of the gun. Although this willed act was in response to X's suggestion, it is difficult to draw a principled line between such acts and those of a person not under hypnosis whose self-esteem is so low that she submits "blindly" to the suggestions of a more dominant personality.

[b]—Multiple Personality Disorder[37]

As suggested in subsection [2], a voluntary act involves the use of the mind, and not simply of the brain. But, is it possible for more than one mind to inhabit a single brain?[38] William James reported[39] that in 1811 a melancholy Pennsylvania woman fell into a profound sleep from which she could not be awakened, and woke up 18 hours later as a "different person," with an exuberant personality and no memory of her past. Five weeks later, after another deep sleep, her old personality returned. This woman may have suffered from what is described as "multiple personality disorder" (MPD), a recognized mental disease.[40]

A person suffering from MPD may be insane, but the condition may also implicate the voluntary act requirement. For example, in State v. Grimsley,[41] D

---

[35] See generally Jack Solomon, Note, *Hypnotism, Suggestibility and the Law*, 31 Neb. L. Rev. 575 (1952); William P. Swain, Note, *Hypnotism and the Law*, 14 Vand. L. Rev. 1509 (1961); see also Richard Delgado, *Ascription of Criminal States of Mind: Toward a Defense Theory for the Coercively Persuaded ("Brainwashed") Defendant*, 63 Minn. L. Rev. 1 (1978); Joshua Dressler, *Professor Delgado's "Brainwashing" Defense: Courting a Determinist Legal System*, 63 Minn. L. Rev. 335 (1979).

[36] The scientific evidence in this regard is summarized in Ernest R. Hilgard, *Hypnosis*, 26 Ann. Rev. Psych. 19 (1975).

[37] See generally Elyn R. Saks, *Multiple Personality Disorder and Criminal Responsibility*, 25 U.C. Davis L. Rev. 383 (1992).

[38] See Katz at 104.

[39] William James, The Principles of Psychology 359-63 (1981).

[40] American Psychiatric Association, Diagnostic and Statistical Manual of Mental Disorders 257 (4th ed. 1994) (now describing the condition as "dissociative identity disorder").

[41] 444 N.E.2d 1071 (Ohio Ct. App. 1982).

(Robin), who suffered from MPD, drove an automobile under the influence of alcohol while she was dissociated from her primary personality. *D* introduced psychiatric evidence that she had a secondary personality, Jennifer, who had a drinking problem, and which was in control when she was in the automobile. As a consequence, she argued that she—*D* (Robin)—was unconscious while Jennifer was acting. The court rejected *D*'s reasoning. It stated:

> There was only one person driving the car and only one person accused of drunken driving. It is immaterial whether she was in one state of consciousness or another, so long as in the personality then controlling her behavior, she was conscious and her actions were a product of her own volition.

But, who is the "her" in the phrase "product of her own volition"? Robin and Jennifer had separate identities; Jennifer did not think of herself as Robin, or vice-versa. With separate memories, separate feelings, and separate characters, can we genuinely treat *D* as a single volitional agent, as *Grimsley* did? Although few courts have confronted this question, the court's approach in *Grimsley* is typical. As another court that has confronted the MPD issue has put the matter, "we will not begin to parcel criminal accountability out among the various inhabitants of the mind."[42]

[D]—Rationale for the Voluntary Act Requirement

Granted that a person should not be convicted for her thoughts alone,[43] why should an involuntary actor who causes harm escape punishment? One frequent explanation is that the law cannot deter involuntary movement.[44]

This utilitarian explanation is insufficient. Although the threat of punishment cannot deter a person while she is acting involuntarily, e.g., during a seizure, it can motivate her to adjust her behavior, e.g., to take medication or not use a dangerous instrumentality, so as to reduce the risk to others from her involuntary conduct. Moreover, even if the *threat* of the criminal sanction cannot deter, its *use* is one rational way to segregate (or in some other manner render less dangerous) involuntary actors. To a utilitarian lawmaker, whose overall goal is to protect society from dangerous people, the criminal justice system is "simply another method of social control."[45] That is, the line between civil commitment and criminal punishment is blurry, at best, in a purely utilitarian system of laws,[46] so there is no reason categorically to exclude liability for involuntary actions.

---

[42] *Kirkland v. State*, 304 S.E.2d 561, 564 (Ga. Ct. App. 1983).

[43] See § 9.01[B], *supra.*

[44] American Law Institute, Comment to § 2.01, at 214-15.

[45] Richard Singer, *The Resurgence of Mens Rea: II—Honest But Unreasonable Mistake of Fact in Self Defense*, 28 B.C. L. Rev. 459, 512 n.285 (1987).

[46] Packer at 77-78; see also George P. Fletcher, *The Right Deed for the Wrong Reason: A Reply to Mr. Robinson*, 23 UCLA L. Rev. 293, 302 (1975) ("The instrumentalist theory rejects the importance of criminal law as a separate discipline and locates the criminal sanction within a matrix of devices designed to further the all-encompassing goal of social protection.").

The voluntary act requirement is far more closely linked to the retributivist's respect for human autonomy. Retributive theory is premised on the view that "the critical distinction between criminal law and other systems of confinement . . . is that the criminal sanction carries with it something more—the stigmatization of moral blameworthiness."[47] Criminal punishment, with its attendant pain, stigma and formal condemnation of the offender, should only be imposed on those who deserve it, i.e., on those who act as the result of free choice. In the absence of a voluntary act, there is no basis for social censure.

[E]—Burden of Proof

Courts frequently describe "involuntariness" as a "defense."[48] To the extent that the word "involuntariness" is used in the broad sense of the term,[49] this characterization is appropriate. However, omissions aside,[50] a "voluntary act" (in the narrow sense of the term) is a prerequisite to criminal responsibility, i.e, it is an element of every criminal offense.[51]

This distinction—that a voluntary act is an element of a criminal offense and not simply a defense to it—is of procedural significance. Under the due process clause, the prosecution must prove beyond a reasonable doubt every element of an offense, but it is not constitutionally required to carry the burden of persuasion regarding defenses.[52] Despite the appellation "defense," therefore, the prosecution should be required to prove beyond a reasonable doubt that a defendant's conduct included a voluntary act.[53]

In view of this distinction, one who is unconscious at the time of the alleged act, but whose unconsciousness was not the result of a mental disease or defect, need not plead insanity and, if acquitted on the basis of unconsciousness, is not subject to commitment to a mental hospital.[54]

[F]—The Issue of "Time-Framing"[55]

As explained in this chapter section, a person is not ordinarily guilty of an offense in the absence of a voluntary act. The prosecution does not need to show, however,

---

[47] Singer, Note 45, *supra*, at 512 n.285.

[48] E.g., *People v Newton*, 87 Cal. Rptr. 394, 404-05 (Ct. App. 1970); *People v Grant*, 377 N.E.2d 4, 7 (Ill. 1978); *Fulcher v. State*, 633 P.2d 142, 145 (Wyo. 1981).

[49] See § 9.02[C][1], *supra*.

[50] See § 9.07, *infra*.

[51] 2 Robinson at 263.

[52] See § 7.03[B], *supra*.

[53] E.g., *Baird v. State*, 604 N.E.2d 1170, 1176 (Ind. 1992).

[54] *Fulcher v. State*, 633 P.2d at 145 (quoting *State v. Caddell*, 215 S.E.2d. 348, 360 (N.C. 1975)).

[55] See generally Alexander, Note 12, *supra*; Husak & McLaughlin, Note 12, *supra*; Leo Katz, *Proximate Cause in Michael Moore's Act and Crime*, 142 U. Pa. L. Rev. 1513 (1994); Mark Kelman, *Interpretive Construction in the Substantive Criminal Law*, 33 Stan. L. Rev. 591 (1981).

that *every* act, or even that the defendant's *last* act, was voluntary in order to establish criminal liability.[56] It is sufficient that the defendant's conduct *included* a voluntary act.

But, what does it mean to say that the defendant's "conduct" must "include" a voluntary act? If one identifies the defendant's conduct broadly enough, it will always include a voluntary act. After all, even if *D*, a killer, was unconscious at the time of the homicide, she was surely conscious and acting voluntarily some time prior to the moment of death, if only when she woke up in the morning, dressed, and drove to the scene of the crime.

Professor Mark Kelman has suggested that courts can choose between narrow and broad time-frames in identifying the conduct that must include a voluntary act.[57] He contends that the time-framing choice is "arational"; the decision to frame the actor's conduct broadly—or narrowly—is based (if only subconsciously) on the desired outcome. If a court wants to convict a defendant who acted involuntarily at some point during the commission of an offense, it will construct a time-frame broad enough to include some remote, but voluntary, act; if it wants the defendant to escape responsibility, it will construct a narrower time-frame, which excludes the prior voluntary movements. If Kelman is right in this regard, of course, the voluntary act requirement is "vacuous."[58]

Manipulation of the voluntary act requirement can be avoided if a court applies the fully stated rule of criminal responsibility: *a person is not guilty of an offense unless her conduct, which must include a voluntary act, and which must be accompanied*[59] *by a culpable state of mind (the mens rea of the offense),*[60] *is the actual and proximate cause*[61] *of the social harm, as proscribed by the offense.* That is, a court may not properly choose *any* conduct it wishes; it must focus on the *relevant* conduct, i.e., the conduct (performed with the requisite *mens rea*) that actually and proximately caused the social harm of the offense. Once it identifies this conduct, the court can determine whether it includes a voluntary act.

To see how a court should construct the proper time-frame, consider, first, a simple example. *D* decides to kill *V*. She builds a bomb and mails it to *V* in a package. The bomb reaches its destination three days later. Coincidentally, at precisely the moment *V* opens the package and is killed in the ensuing explosion, *D* is unconscious 3000 miles away. *D* is prosecuted for murder, which for current purposes is defined as the "intentional killing of another human being."

At the murder trial, it will do no good for *D* to point out that she was unconscious at the time of *V*'s death. *D*'s relevant conduct—the acts that were the actual and

---

[56] *State v. Burrell*, 609 A.2d 751, 753 (N.H. 1992).

[57] Kelman, Note 55, *supra*, at 593-94, 603-05.

[58] Alexander, Note 12, *supra*, at 91 (largely sympathetic to Kelman's analysis); Moore, Note 1, *supra*, at 35 (critical of Kelman's analysis).

[59] See Chapter 15 (Concurrence of Elements), *infra*.

[60] See Chapter 10 (*Mens Rea*), *infra*.

[61] See Chapter 14 (Causation), *infra*.

proximate cause of *V*'s death, and which were accompanied by the requisite intent to kill—occurred three days earlier, when *D* acted voluntarily.

Now, consider a more difficult case. In *People v. Decina*,[62] *D* was an epileptic who killed four children when the car he was driving went out of control during a seizure. The prosecutor alleged that *D* knew that he was highly susceptible to seizures and failed to take proper precautions. As a result, *D* was prosecuted for "criminal negligence in the operation of a vehicle, resulting in death."

Notice that if a court constructed an extremely narrow time-frame—specifically, the conduct at the instant the car struck the victims—*D*'s conduct did not include a voluntary act. A broader time-frame, however, would include the voluntary actions of entering the car, turning the ignition key, and driving.

The appellate court properly affirmed *D*'s conviction. The *actus reus* of the offense was "the operation of a vehicle resulting in death." It was perfectly appropriate, therefore, for the prosecution to include in its focus the voluntary acts immediately preceding the seizure, which constituted the arguably negligent operation of the car.

In contrast is *Martin v. State*:[63] *D*, while intoxicated, was taken from his home by the police and placed by them on a public highway, where he used loud and profane language. *D* was charged with an offense that provided in relevant part that "[a]ny person who, while intoxicated . . ., appears in any public place . . . and manifests a drunken condition by boisterous or indecent conduct" is guilty of a misdemeanor.

A broad time-frame might suggest that *D* was guilty because he became drunk voluntarily, before the police arrived at his home. However, the court applied a narrower time-frame, one that discounted these prior voluntary acts; it held that *D*'s conviction had to be overturned because the statute required a voluntary appearance on the highway, which did not occur here.

A careful inspection of the statute shows that the *Martin* court was correct in its analysis. To be guilty of this offense, *D* had to: (1) appear in public: and (2) act there in a boisterous or indecent manner; (3) while intoxicated. The conduct stated in (1) and (2) had to include a voluntary act. By the express wording of the statute, this conduct had to occur "while" *D* was intoxicated; it did not matter how *D* became intoxicated, only that *while* he was in that condition he voluntarily appeared in public and acted boisterously. Thus, the court was right to focus on how *D* ended up on the highway, rather than on how he previously became intoxicated.

§ 9.03　Voluntary Act: Supposed (But Not Real) Exceptions to the Requirement

[A]—Poorly Drafted Statutes

Some statutes appear to dispense with the requirement of a voluntary act. For example, a Vermont statute prohibited persons not married to one another "to be

---

[62] 138 N.E.2d 799 (N.Y. 1956).

[63] 17 So.2d 427 (Ala. Ct. App. 1944).

found in bed together."[64] Read literally, this statute would unfairly and implausibly allow the conviction of a person who, while unconscious, was placed in a bed with someone to whom she was not married. Although a court could conceivably apply such a statute literally,[65] it is likely that it would interpret the law to require a voluntary act.

[B]—Status Offenses

In the past, many legislatures enacted so-called status offenses. For example, vagrancy laws made it an offense to "be a vagrant." Likewise, a California statute prohibited one "to be addicted to the use of narcotics." These offenses required proof of a status (vagrancy or addiction), rather than conduct.

The Supreme Court has not looked kindly upon status offenses. It invalidated a typical vagrancy law on the ground that it was unduly vague and could result in arbitrary police enforcement;[66] and it held that a California addiction statute violated the Eighth Amendment bar on cruel and unusual punishment.[67] Very likely any statute that punishes a person for a mere propensity to act will run afoul of constitutional principles.[68]

[C]—Crimes of Possession

Virtually all states prohibit possession of contraband (e.g., cocaine) or criminal instrumentalities (e.g., "burglars' tools"[69]). On their face, these penal provisions do not require the defendant to act, only that she passively possess the prohibited objects.

Crimes of possession are "inchoate," or incomplete, offenses. That is, their real purpose is to provide the police with a basis for arresting those whom they suspect will later commit a socially injurious act (e.g., sell narcotics, or use the tools to commit a burglary).

Possession crimes do not necessarily dispense with the voluntary act requirement. In order to convict, the prosecution must ordinarily prove that the defendant knowingly procured or received the property possessed (thus, a voluntary act must be proven), or that she failed to dispossess herself of the object after she became

---

[64] See *State v. Woods*, 179 A. 1 (Vt. 1935) (applying Vt. Pub.L. § 8602 (1933), repealed in 1979) (emphasis added).

[65] E.g., *Reg. v. Larsonneur*, (1933) 24 Cr. App. R. 74 (upholding the conviction of *D*, a French citizen, for being an alien "found" in the United Kingdom without permission, based on the following facts: she entered England with permission; when English authorities learned she was committing acts of prostitution there, she left for Ireland; Irish officials arrested her and handed her back to English police, upon which she was charged with the offense).

[66] *Papachristou v. City of Jacksonville*, 405 U.S. 156 (1972). See § 5.03, *supra.*

[67] *Robinson v. California*, 370 U.S. 660 (1962).

[68] See § 9.04, *infra.*

[69] E.g., Cal. Penal Code § 466 (West 1988) ("Every person having upon him or her in his or her possession a picklock, crow, keybit, . . . or other instrument or tool with intent feloniously to break or enter into any building . . . is guilty of misdemeanor.").

aware of its presence.[70] In the latter case, "possession" is equivalent to an omission, in which the defendant has a statutory duty to dispossess herself of the property.[71] She is not guilty if the contraband was "planted" on her, and she did not have sufficient time to terminate her possession after she learned of its presence.

§ 9.04 Voluntary Act: Constitutional Law[72]

Twice in the 1960s, the Supreme Court considered the question of whether the Eighth Amendment bar on cruel and unusual punishment prohibits states from enacting laws that authorize punishment in the absence of voluntary conduct.

[A]—*Robinson v. California*[73]

The California legislature enacted a law making it an offense, punishable by incarceration of from 90 days to one year, for a person to "be addicted to the use of narcotics." No act by the defendant—just his present addiction—was required for conviction. The Supreme Court ruled that the statute violated the Eighth and Fourteenth Amendments to the United States Constitution.

The Court focused on the fact that the statute made the illness of drug addiction (a status that it pointed out could be contracted innocently or involuntarily) a criminal offense. The Justices analogized drug addiction to other illnesses—mental illness, leprosy, venereal disease, and the common cold: if a state were to punish persons for suffering from these ailments, it would "doubtless be universally thought to be an infliction of cruel and unusual punishment." The Court believed that the same discernment should be shown the status of drug addiction.

The Court did not state that the statute subjected Robinson to grossly disproportional punishment. That is, the constitutional infirmity in this case was not that a drug addict might receive a 90-day or longer jail sentence, but rather that he could be punished at all. "Even one day in prison," the Justices intoned, would have rendered Robinson's fate impermissible. Essentially, the Court held that California lacked constitutional authority to treat Robinson as a criminal solely because of his addiction.

The Justices indicated that a legislature may constitutionally attack the social problems arising from drug addiction through health education, civil commitment, and other non-penal programs; they may also use criminal sanctions against the unauthorized manufacture, sale, purchase, or possession of narcotics. What states may not constitutionally do, however, is punish for the addiction itself.

The Court's approach to the Eighth Amendment is intriguing. Following *Robinson*, a state may use the criminal sanction to prohibit harmful acts by drug addicts,

---

[70] See, e.g., *People v. Ackerman*, 274 N.E.2d 125, 126 (Ill. App. Ct. 1971); *State v. Flaherty*, 400 A.2d 363, 366 (Me. 1979).

[71] See § 9.07, *infra*.

[72] See generally Lionel H. Frankel, *Narcotic Addiction, Criminal Responsibility, and Civil Commitment*, 1966 Utah L. Rev. 581; Kent Greenawalt, *"Uncontrollable" Actions and the Eighth Amendment: Implications of Powell v. Texas*, 69 Colum. L. Rev. 927 (1969).

[73] 370 U.S. 660 (1962).

but the Eighth Amendment bars it from using its criminal laws to punish drug addiction *per se*. In so ruling, the Court (perhaps unwittingly) invoked retributive, rather than utilitarian, values of punishment. That is, retributivism is based on the principle that punishment should not be inflicted unless a person voluntarily chooses to commit a socially harmful act; the condemnatory feature of criminal punishment should not be used against one whose only "crime" is her illness. In contrast, a utilitarian would not categorically rule out the use of the criminal justice system to deal with drug addiction. To utilitarians, there is no special significance to the civil/criminal commitment distinction; the law should be permitted to use every weapon available to it to reduce net social pain.

Essentially, the message of *Robinson* was a retributive one: although drug addicts constitute a danger to society and, therefore, it may be *rational* to incarcerate some of them, it is *indecent* to punish them simply because they are sick.

[B]—*Powell v. Texas*[74]

Leroy Powell was charged with violation of a Texas statute that prohibited "get[ting] drunk or be[ing] found in a state of intoxication in any public place." Powell attempted to prove at trial that he suffered from the disease of chronic alcoholism and that, therefore, he was unable to avoid appearing in public in a drunken condition. His punishment, he argued not unreasonably, violated the underlying principles enunciated in *Robinson*. After all, Powell was a sick person. To the extent that he represented a social problem, Texas should be required to deal with him in a non-criminal manner.

Speaking for only four Justices, Justice Thurgood Marshall upheld Powell's conviction and $20 fine. He distinguished *Robinson* on the ground that Powell "was convicted, not for being a chronic alcoholic, but for being in public while drunk on a particular occasion." As such, Texas was punishing conduct, not an illness.[75] The plurality explained the import of *Robinson* as follows:

> The entire thrust of *Robinson*'s interpretation of the Cruel and Unusual Punishment Clause is that criminal penalties may be inflicted only if the accused has committed some act, has engaged in some behavior, which society has an interest in preventing, or perhaps in historical common law terms, has committed some *actus reus*.

Although this statement of *Robinson* may be correct in terms of its holding, *Powell*'s underlying reasoning runs counter to *Robinson*'s retributivist thrust. In *Powell*, Justice Marshall said that the Court was "unable to assert that the use of the criminal process as a means of dealing with the public aspects of problem

---

[74] 392 U.S. 514 (1968).

[75] Justice Marshall hesitated to attach the label "disease" to alcoholism. He observed that alcoholism was a "disease" simply because the medical profession considered it one. Interestingly, however, in *Robinson* the Justices quoted the statement in the appellee's brief that "[o]f course it is generally conceded that a narcotic addict . . . is in a state of mental and physical illness. *So is an alcoholic*." *Robinson v. California*, 370 U.S. at 667 n.8 (emphasis added).

drinking can never be defined as rational." He said it would be "tragic to return large numbers of helpless, sometimes dangerous and frequently unsanitary inebriates to the streets of our cities without even the opportunity to sober up adequately which a brief jail term provides."

Thus, the plurality blurred the line drawn in *Robinson* between the civil and criminal processes. If Justice Marshall's test of rationality had been applied in *Robinson* to drug addicts, the Court might have determined that the use of the criminal sanction was one rational way to deal with the addiction problem. To the *Robinson* Court, however, rational punishment can be unconstitutionally cruel: under *Robinson*, it would have been wrong to punish an addict for her disease, even if housing her in a prison until she could "get clean" was one sensible approach to her rehabilitation.

Why did the Court back off from the possible implications of *Robinson*? The answer lies in Justice Marshall's observation that a broad reading of *Robinson* would have made the Supreme Court, "under the aegis of the Cruel and Unusual Punishment Clause, the ultimate arbiter of the [states'] standards of criminal responsibility."[76] That is, if the Eighth Amendment prevents a state from punishing an alcoholic for the act of becoming drunk in public, a state could also be barred from punishing a drug addict for possessing drugs,[77] or even for committing a robbery in order to secure the money necessary to feed her habit. It would be just a small step to the proposition that the Eighth Amendment requires states to draft specific criminal law defenses (e.g., insanity and duress) that would exculpate persons whose conduct was "involuntary," in some sense of that term. The Court was unwilling to intrude.

[C]—Current Law: *Powell* in Light of *Robinson*

The Court was splintered in *Powell*: there was a four-Justice plurality, a concurrence in the result by a fifth Justice, and a four-Justice dissent. Nonetheless, this much is clear: (1) *Powell* did not overrule *Robinson*; and (2) these two cases stand for the proposition that a state may not dispense with the criminal law requirement of an *actus reus*. That is, the government may not punish a person for her thoughts alone, or for her mere propensity to commit crimes. The special rule of omissions aside,[78] some conduct by the defendant, *at least of an involuntary nature*, is required.

Powell might stand for more than this, however. The four-vote dissent would have held that a person may not constitutionally be punished for exhibiting "a characteristic part of the pattern of [a] disease . . . which . . . [is] not the consequence of [her] volition." Following this reading, an addict could be punished

---

[76] In concurrence, too, Justices Black and Harlan observed that a broad reading of *Robinson* "would have [had] a revolutionary impact on the criminal law."

[77] See *United States v. Moore*, 486 F.2d 1139 (D.C. Cir. 1973) (rejecting the petitioner's claim that he could not be convicted of possession of heroin because of his overpowering addiction to drugs).

[78] See § 9.06, *infra*.

if she robbed a bank to support her habit, but she could not be punished for possession or use of narcotics, a "characteristic part of the pattern" of drug addiction.

Because this broader reading of the Constitution "cancels out" the four-Justice plurality opinion, the views of the remaining Justice, Byron White, are especially critical. He observed:

> If it cannot be a crime to have an irresistible compulsion to use narcotics, Robinson v. California, . . . I do not see how it can constitutionally be a crime to yield to such a compulsion. Punishing an addict for using drugs convicts for addiction under a different name. Distinguishing between the two crimes is like forbidding criminal conviction for being sick with flu or epilepsy but permitting punishment for running a fever or having a convulsion.

In this case, however, Powell was not prosecuted for using or possessing alcohol, but for the "voluntary" act (in the willed-muscular-contraction sense of the term) of going from a private place into a public area in an intoxicated condition.[79] Therefore, Justice White did not dissent, but instead concurred in the result. Justice White's reasoning suggests, however, that unless *Robinson* were overruled,[80] he was prepared to recognize a constitutional defense to involuntary conduct that is an inevitable part of the disease syndrome from which the person suffers. In light of the dissent, therefore, there were five votes—a majority—for this proposition.

None of the Justices involved in *Powell* still sit on the bench. In light of the more conservative nature of the present-day Supreme Court, it would be foolhardy to assume that today's high court would constitutionalize the voluntary act requirement if the proper case came along. Therefore, the only safe proposition is the one set out at the start of this subsection.

§ 9.05   Voluntary Act: Model Penal Code[81]

[A]—General Principles

The Model Penal Code provides that no person may be convicted of a crime in the absence of conduct that "includes a voluntary act or the omission to perform an act of which he is physically capable."[82] The Code allocates to the prosecution the responsibility to persuade the factfinder beyond a reasonable doubt of the existence of a voluntary act.[83]

---

[79] Justice White suggested that some homeless alcoholics might be entitled to a defense under the Texas statute: "I would think that a showing [by them] could be made that resisting drunkenness is impossible and that avoiding public places when intoxicated is also impossible."

[80] Justice White dissented in *Robinson*.

[81] See generally James W. Child, *Donald Davidson and Section 2.01 of the Model Penal Code*, Crim. Just. Ethics, Winter/Spring 1992, at 31.

[82] Model Penal Code § 2.01(1).

[83] Model Penal Code § 1.12(1).

The Code defines the term "act" as a "bodily movement whether voluntary or involuntary."[84] It does not define the term "voluntary," except "partially and indirectly,"[85] by listing bodily movements that are involuntary: reflexes; convulsions; conduct during unconsciousness, sleep, or due to hypnosis;[86] and, generally, any conduct that "is not a product of the effort or determination of the actor, either conscious or habitual."[87] The Model Code also provides that, for purposes of the voluntary act rule, "possession" is an "act" if the possessor either knowingly obtained the object possessed or knew she was in control of it "for a sufficient period to have been able to terminate . . . possession."[88]

[B]—Exception to the Rule

Section 2.01 of the Model Penal Code applies to liability for "crimes," i.e., felonies, misdemeanors, and petty misdemeanors.[89] However, Section 2.05(1) of the Code provides that the requirements set out in Section 2.01 do not apply to offenses that constitute "violations," unless a court determines that application of Section 2.01 is "consistent with effective enforcement of the law defining the offense." A "violation" is an offense for which the maximum penalty is a fine or civil penalty.[90]

Thus, under Section 2.05, a driver who suffers an unforeseeable blackout and, as a consequence, fails to halt at a stop sign, may be convicted of a motor vehicle violation in the absence of proof of a voluntary act. The Commentary to Section 2.05 concedes that the fairness of this outcome is "debatable";[91] but with extremely minor offenses, the drafters of the Code determined that litigation of involuntary act claims should not be permitted to undermine effective law enforcement.

[84] Model Penal Code § 1.13(2).

[85] American Law Institute, Comment to § 2.01, at 219.

[86] The drafters of the Code justified this controversial inclusion on the ground that conduct during hypnosis or resulting from hypnotic suggestion is "characterized by the subject's dependence on the hypnotist, [so] it does not seem politic to treat conduct [in such circumstances] as voluntary, despite the state of consciousness involved." *Id.* at 221 (footnote deleted). The Commentary acknowledged, however, that the general view is that a hypnotized subject will not follow suggestions contrary to her moral views. For more on hypnosis, see § 9.02[C][3][a], *supra*.

[87] Model Penal Code § 2.01(2)(d).

[88] Model Penal Code § 2.01(4).

[89] Model Penal Code § 1.04(1) (classifying crimes).

[90] Model Penal Code § 1.04(5).

[91] American Law Institute, Comment to § 2.05, at 292.

§ 9.06   Omissions: General Principles[92]

[A]—General Rule

Consider the following two incidents. First, in *People v. Beardsley*,[93] a married man failed to come to the aid of the woman with whom he was having an affair after she took a lethal dose of poison in his presence. She died. Second, in an infamous after-midnight 1964 assault in Queens, New York, a young woman by the name of Kitty Genovese cried out for help for approximately thirty minutes as she was repeatedly attacked and, ultimately, killed outside her apartment building. It was later learned that 38 of her neighbors heard her cries and saw the attack in progress from their apartment windows, but did nothing.[94]

In both situations, a human being died. In both situations, one or more persons knew that a life was in jeopardy. In both situations, the harm that occurred might have been prevented or mitigated at no risk to those aware of the victim's plight. Nonetheless, adulterer Beardsley was not held criminally responsible for his omission; and none of Genovese's neighbors were prosecuted in relation to her death.

The lesson to be learned from these two incidents is that not every moral obligation to act creates a concomitant legal duty. Subject to a few limited exceptions, a person has no criminal law duty to rescue or render aid to another person in peril, even if the person imperiled may lose her life in the absence of assistance.[95] In essence, the criminal law distinguishes between an act that affirmatively causes harm, on the one hand, and the failure of a bystander to take measures to prevent harm, on the other hand. As Professor Woozley has described the principle: "the law should see to it that we do not do harm, but not see to it that, in the absence of a specific statutory duty, we do things to prevent harm."[96] As a matter of criminal law doctrine, we are not our brothers' and sisters' keepers.

[B]—Criticisms of the General Rule

Many critics of the omission rule consider it morally repugnant. As one scholar stated in relation to *Beardsley*, "[i]n a civilized society, a man who finds himself

---

[92] See generally Hall at 190-211; Katz at 135-53; Andrew Ashworth, *The Scope of Criminal Liability for Omissions*, 105 L.Q. Rev. 424 (1989); George P. Fletcher, *On the Moral Irrelevance of Bodily Movements*, 142 U. Pa. L. Rev. 1443 (1994); Lionel H. Frankel, *Criminal Omissions: A Legal Microcosm*, 11 Wayne L. Rev. 367 (1965); Graham Hughes, *Criminal Omissions*, 67 Yale L.J. 590 (1958); F.M. Kamm, *Action, Omission, and the Stringency of Duties*, 142 U. Pa. L. Rev. 1493 (1994); Arthur Leavens, *A Causation Approach to Criminal Omissions*, 76 Cal. L. Rev. 547 (1988); Alison McIntyre, *Guilty Bystanders? On the Legitimacy of Duty to Rescue Statutes*, 23 Phil. & Pub. Aff. 157 (1994); A.D. Woozley, *A Duty to Rescue: Some Thoughts on Criminal Liability*, 69 Va. L. Rev. 1273 (1983).

[93] 113 N.W. 1128 (Mich. 1907).

[94] See generally Abraham M. Rosenthal, Thirty Eight Witnesses (1964).

[95] *People v. Oliver*, 258 Cal.Rptr. 138, 142 (Ct. App. 1989).

[96] Woozley, Note 92, *supra*, at 1273.

with a helplessly ill person who has no other source of aid should be under a duty
to summon help, whether the person is his wife, his mistress, a prostitute or a Chief
Justice."[97] The implication is that there is no inherent moral difference between an
act and an omission: there is no moral difference between walking into the Pacific
Ocean and drowning oneself, and sitting on the beach until one is submerged by
the incoming tide;[98] there is no meaningful difference between slamming shut
one's open door to bar entry of a child trying to escape a wild animal, and failing
to open a closed door for the same child.[99]

The effect of the omission rule is to exonerate people who are guilty of moral
indifference, such as Kitty Genovese's neighbors in Queens. The rule may even
absolve one who is guilty of a more culpable state of mind. For example, consider
S, an Olympic-level swimmer, who stands by and watches an infant (not her own)
drown in a wading pool. S is not criminally responsible for the death, although she
could have saved the child at no risk to herself. It does not matter why S failed to
act: perhaps she was on her way to a party and did not consider the child's life worth
the delay; or, even worse, she might be a person who experiences sadistic pleasure
watching others suffer.

From a utilitarian perspective, the callousness of the omission rule may breed
contempt for society's system of criminal justice. In contrast, a rule that requires
people to assist others in peril might promote social cohesion; and some wrongdoers
might desist from planned criminal activity if they knew that others were likely to
intervene.

[C]—Defense of the General Rule

[1]—Practical Arguments

In a criminal case, the State must prove beyond a reasonable doubt that the
defendant had a culpable mental state (*mens rea*) at the time of the crime, and it
must also show that the defendant caused the social harm for which she is being
prosecuted. It is far more difficult to ascertain these two elements—*mens rea* and
causation—in an omission case than in one in which the defendant acted. For
example, if Beardsley had poisoned his mistress, a jury could easily have inferred
that he intended to kill her. But, omissions are more ambiguous: the omitter may
have wanted the harm to occur to the victim; but the omitter may simply have frozen
from shock in the situation. Similarly, in the Genovese tragedy, it is possible that
some of the apartment residents assumed that someone else had called the police.[100]

---

[97] Hughes, Note 92, *supra*, at 624.

[98] *Cruzan v. Director, Missouri Dept. of Health*, 497 U.S. 261, 296 (1990) (Scalia, J., concurring).

[99] Katz at 140.

[100] See Bibb Latan & John Darley, *Group Inhibition of Bystandr Intervention in Emergencies*, 10 J. Personality & Soc. Psych. 215, 215 (1968) ("We have found that the mere
perception that other people are also witnessing the event will markedly decrease the
likelihood that an individual will intervene in an emergency."); Katz at 150 ("For Kitty
Genovese, then, there was no safety in numbers.").

Regarding the element of causation, if a man poisons another, it should be comparatively easy to determine that he caused her death. It is far more difficult, however, to say that Beardsley's failure to secure medical care for his paramour caused her death; she might have died from the poison despite his best efforts. Similarly, even if one of Genovese's neighbors had called the police, how can we know whether help would have come in time?

Beyond this, serious line-drawing problems would arise in omission prosecutions. For example, in the Genovese case, should all 38 people who heard her cries be held responsible, or only those that heard her in the early moments and, therefore, had the maximum time to help? Also, to what extent should liability depend on the extent of the omitter's knowledge, e.g., should liability be limited to those who fully comprehended the extreme seriousness of the situation?

[2]—Moral Arguments

Defenders of the act/omission distinction reject the argument that there is no moral difference between a voluntary act and an omission. Intuitively, they say, the difference is obvious if one considers the implication of treating acts and omissions alike: the outcome in the Kitty Genovese case would be that some or all of her neighbors could be prosecuted, along with the mugger, for her death. But, surely there is a moral difference between stabbing a victim to death, and failing to call the police or otherwise coming to the victim's aid.

Or, consider the drowning child and S, the Olympic swimmer. Suppose that we learned that X pushed the child into the pool. Even assuming that S obtained sadistic pleasure from watching the child die, would we say that there is no moral difference between X's act and S's omission? X *caused* the child to die; S merely *permitted* it. X changed the state of affairs by putting the child in jeopardy; S merely failed to put things right. X killed the child; S withheld a benefit. Advocates of the no-liability-for-omissions rule contend that the positive duty not to make the world worse is, morally speaking, more stringent than the duty to make it better.[101]

The latter point leads to a second justification for the omission rule, which is that the omission doctrine is consistent with the principle of autonomy. In a society that values individual freedom and limited governmental power, the criminal justice system should be used discriminately. Even if a person is morally obligated to come to the aid of others, not every violation of a moral duty should result in criminal punishment.[102] It is the role of religion and other moral institutions to perfect human character; the purpose of the criminal law is limited to deterring or punishing persons for causing harm.[103] If it were otherwise, the criminal justice system would intrude too deeply into peoples' lives.

[3]—Utilitarian Arguments

A rule that treats acts and omissions alike could be counter-productive. First, "good samaritans" sometimes do more harm that good when they come to aid of

---

[101] See Kamm, Note 92, *supra*, at 1493; Moore, Note 1, *supra*, at 25.

[102] *Reg. v. Instan*, [1893] 1 Q.B. 450, 453 ("It would not be correct to say they every moral obligation involves a legal duty; but every legal duty is founded on a moral obligation.").

[103] See § 1.01[A][1][a], *supra*.

others. Second, if the law required good samaritanism, people might become less, rather than more, involved in their neighbors' problems, in order to avoid the risk of criminal liability. Finally, a legal system in which omissions generally are punishable would be an expensive one, requiring more police to search out omitters, and courts to handle the additional prosecutions.

§ 9.07 Omissions: Exceptions to the No-Liability Rule

[A]—Overview

In the limited circumstances described below, liability for an offense may be predicated on an omission, rather than on a voluntary act. The exceptions to the no-liability-for-omissions rule are divisible into two main categories. The first category is considered in subsection [B]: by special statutory prohibition, failure to perform an act may itself be punishable.

The remaining exceptions involve common law duties to act that can result in "commission by omission"[104] liability. That is, a defendant's omission of a common law duty to act, *assuming that she was physically able to perform the act*, will serve as a substitute for a voluntary act; and, if the remaining elements of an offense are proven, the defendant may be convicted of that crime. For example, it is possible for a person to "commit" a murder by omission: if the defendant had a duty to act, but she omitted to do so, she may be convicted of murder if her omission caused the death of another person,[105] and if she possessed the requisite *mens rea* for the crime.

[B]—Statutory Duty

A duty to act may be statutorily imposed. Examples of such statutes are those that require: a person to pay taxes on earned income;[106] a driver of a motor vehicle involved in an accident to stop her car at the scene;[107] and parents to provide food and shelter to their minor children.[108] Absent a valid defense, failure to satisfy a statutory duty constitutes an offense.

[C]—Status Relationship

Even in the absence of a statute, a person may have a common law duty to act because she stands in a special status relationship to another. Such a relationship is usually founded on the dependence of one party on the other, or on their

---

[104] Fletcher, Note 92, *supra*, at 1447.

[105] The typical murder statute defines the social harm of murder as the "killing" of a human being by another human being. Can a person "kill" another by omission, as distinguished from "letting die"? An action verb such as "killing" seems inapt in the case of an omission, but liability generally is permitted, assuming that the other elements of the offense are proven.

[106] 26 U.S.C. § 7203 (Supp.1994).

[107] E.g., Cal. Vehicle Code § 20001 (West 1988 & Supp. 1994).

[108] E.g., Tex. Fam. Code Ann. § 1204 (West 1986 & Supp. 1994).

interdependence. Such status relationships include: parents to their minor children;[109] married couples to one another;[110] and masters to their servants.[111] For example, a mother who allows her children to remain with their father, whom she knows is abusing them, is herself guilty of child abuse by her omission;[112] and, a parent's failure to seek medical attention for her seriously ill child, which omission results in the child's death, will support a conviction for criminal homicide, assuming that the parent acted with the requisite *mens rea.*[113]

[D]—Contractual Obligation

A duty to act may be created by implied or express contract. For example, a person who breaches an agreement to house, feed, and provide medical care to an infirm stranger,[114] or to care for one's mentally and physically disabled parent,[115] may be held criminally responsible for an ensuing death. Similarly, a baby-sitter owes an implied contractual duty to protect her ward, and a doctor has a duty to provide ordinary medical care for her patient.

[E]—Omissions Following an Act

In some circumstances an act, followed by an omission, will result in criminal responsibility for the omission, even when there is no liability for the act.

[1]—Creation of a Risk

A person who wrongfully, or perhaps even innocently, harms another or another's property, or who places a person or her property in risk of harm, has a common law duty to aid the injured or endangered party. If she breaches her duty in this regard, she may be held criminally responsible for the harm arising from the omission. For example, if *D* negligently injures *V*, *D* has a common law duty to render aid to *V*. If *D* fails to do so, and *V* dies as the result of the omission, *D* may be held criminally responsible for *V*'s death, even if she is not guilty of any offense regarding the initial injuries.[116]

Although there is less case law in this regard, a duty to act may arise from non-culpable risk-creation. For example, various courts have held that one who accidentally starts a house fire, and who, therefore, is free of liability for the initial blaze, may be convicted of arson if she fails to act to extinguish the fire or prevent

---

[109] *Jones v. United States*, 308 F.2d 307 (D.C. Cir. 1962).

[110] *State v. Smith*, 65 Me. 257 (1876).

[111] *Rex v. Smith*, 2 Car. & P. 449, 172 Eng. Rep. 203 (1826).

[112] *State v. Williquette*, 385 N.W.2d 145 (Wis. 1986).

[113] *Commonwealth v. Twitchell*, 617 N.E.2d 609 (Mass. 1993).

[114] *Commonwealth v. Pestinikas*, 617 A.2d 1339 (Pa. Super. Ct. 1992).

[115] *Davis v. Commonwealth*, 335 S.E.2d 375 (Va. 1985).

[116] See also *Jones v. State*, 43 N.E.2d 1017 (Ind. 1942) (*D* raped *V*; emotionally distraught, *V* jumped or fell into a creek; *D* did not attempt to rescue *V*, although he was aware of her peril; *D* was convicted of murder for *V*'s death resulting from his omission).

damage to property therein.[117] On the other hand, according to another court,[118] one who shoots an aggressor in self-defense, seriously wounding the latter, does not have a duty to obtain medical aid for the injured person.

[2]—Voluntary Assistance

One who voluntarily commences assistance to another in jeopardy has a duty to continue to provide aid, at least if a subsequent omission would put the victim in a worse position than if the actor had not initiated help. This rule applies even if the omitter had no initial responsibility to rescue the victim.

Thus, a well-meaning individual who takes a sick person into her home, but then fails to provide critical care, may be held responsible for a death arising from this failure. By letting the victim rely on her for care, and by secluding the victim so that others are unaware of her deteriorating condition, the defendant has made matters worse than if she had never become involved.[119]

§ 9.08   Omissions: Model Penal Code

The Model Penal Code does not differ significantly from the common law regarding omissions. A person is not guilty of any offense unless his conduct "includes a voluntary act or the omission to perform an act of which he is physically capable."[120]

Liability based on an omission is permitted in two circumstances: (1) if the law defining the offense provides for it;[121] or (2) if the duty to act is "otherwise imposed by law."[122] The latter category incorporates duties arising under civil law, such as torts or contract law.[123]

---

[117] *Regina v. Miller*, [1983] 1 All ER 978 (House of Lords); see *Commonwealth v. Cali*, 141 N.E. 510 (Mass. 1923).

[118] *King v. Commonwealth*, 148 S.W.2d 1044 (Ky. 1941).

[119] E.g., *People v. Oliver*, 258 Cal. Rptr. 138 (Ct. App. 1989) (*D* permitted *V*, who was extremely intoxicated, to come to her home, and then allowed *V* to use her bathroom, where *V* injected himself with narcotics; when *V* collapsed, *D* did not summon aid; held: *D* was guilty of manslaughter because "she took [*V*] from a public place where others might have taken care to prevent him from injuring himself, to a private place—her home—where she alone could provide such care"); *Regina v. Instan*, 17 Cox Crim. Cas. 602 (1893) (*D*, who lived alone with *V*, her elderly and sick aunt, in *V*'s house, failed to obtain needed food and medical care for *V*, who died as a result; held: *D* was properly convicted of manslaughter).

[120] Model Penal Code § 2.01(1).

[121] E.g., Model Penal Code § 220.1(3) (failure to control or report a dangerous fire).

[122] Model Penal Code § 2.01(3)(b).

[123] American Law Institute, Comment to § 2.01, at 222-23.

§ 9.09　Medical "Omissions": A Special Problem [124]

[A]—The Problem

Consider this all-too-common problem. Patient, *P*, is in an irreversible coma, kept alive by use of a respirator. *P*'s doctor, *D*, concludes that future medical treatment would be useless, so she turns off the respirator, aware that the effect will be to cause *P*'s imminent death, which occurs.

The traditional common law analysis of this scenario is this: *D* committed a voluntary act by turning off the respirator; this conduct resulted in the death of *P*, the social harm of murder; *D* caused *P*'s death knowingly or intentionally, the *mens rea* of murder; therefore, the elements of common law murder have been proven. As there is no defense of euthanasia, *D* is guilty of murder.

Arguably, this analysis is too simplistic. It fails to consider the moral subtleties of the situation. It equates the physician's act of pulling a plug on medical machinery attached to a comatose patient with the ordinary murderer's voluntary act of stabbing or shooting a conscious victim. Whatever society's ultimate evaluation of *D*'s behavior may be, something more seems to be going on in the medical case than in the usual criminal homicide.

On the other hand, perhaps this simple analysis is correct. Suppose that *P* had not been on a respirator, but similarly was in a hopeless, chronic vegetative state. Suppose, further, that *D* had purposely injected *P* with a deadly dose of morphine in order to end her patient's (and *P*'s family's) misery. Should this "merciful" act be treated any differently than the ordinary act of a murderer, who kills for reasons of hatred or greed? If they should be treated alike, is there any reason why a physician who turns off a patient's respirator should be seen in a better light than one who injects a drug in her patient's veins?

In the absence of a euthanasia defense, some courts have analyzed the issues raised in this context in terms of the act/omission dichotomy.

[B]—Act or Omission?

The traditional approach begins with the characterization of *D*'s behavior as a voluntary act. Is it self-evident, however, that *D* is performing an act, rather than omitting conduct, when she turns off a respirator on a comatose patient? Literally, of course, *D*'s conduct *does* include the voluntary act of pulling the plug or turning off the switch on the respirator. But, does this scenario differ significantly from one in which *D* fails to turn on the respirator in the first place (a clear-cut omission)? Indeed, from a purely semantic point of view, the act/omission distinction seems

---

[124] See generally George P. Fletcher, *Prolonging Life*, 42 Wash. L. Rev. 999 (1967); John C. Hall, *Acts and Omissions*, 39 Phil. Q. 399 (1989); Sanford H. Kadish, *Letting Patients Die: Legal and Moral Reflections*, 80 Cal. L. Rev. 857 (1992); Arthur Leavens, Note 92, *supra*; H.M. Malm, *Killing, Letting Die, and Simple Conflicts*, 18 Phil. & Pub. Aff. 238 (1989); Jeff McMahan, *Killing, Letting Die, and Withdrawing Aid*, 103 Ethics 250 (1993); Gregory C. Sarno, Annotation, *Homicide: Physician's Withdrawal of Life Supports From Comatose Patients*, 47 ALR4th 18 (1986).

to fail us. One can as sensibly describe what occurred by saying "*D* failed to provide medical treatment to *P*" as by saying, "*D* voluntarily turned off the machine."

Probably what troubles us about *D*'s behavior (if anything does) is that a doctor, trained to heal others, has chosen to deny future treatment to her patient. The voluntary act of turning off the machine is merely the means for omitting medical care. Arguably, therefore, we ought to analyze *D*'s behavior as an omission.

[C]—Analysis as an Omission

Even if the act of turning off a respirator or discontinuing other medical treatment is properly analyzed as an omission, this does not necessarily save the doctor from a criminal prosecution. A physician has a contractual duty to provide medical treatment to her patients; therefore, she may be held criminally responsible for an omission of this duty.

But, what is the scope of a doctor's duty to her patient? Modern technology has required courts to consider this question, and it is often stated that a physician owes a duty to provide "ordinary," but not "extraordinary," care.[125] If the process of keeping a comatose person artificially alive is considered "extraordinary," a doctor does not violate her duty of care when she discontinues the treatment.

Considering the issue in terms of "ordinary" versus "extraordinary" care only raises more questions. What is "extraordinary" care? Human heart transplants once seemed extraordinary; today they are commonplace. Would the physician who fails to perform a needed transplant operation be violating a duty of ordinary care to her patient? More importantly, *who* should decide what constitutes "ordinary" and "extraordinary" care? Is this a matter solely for medical evaluation, based on the custom of the profession?

[D]—The *Barber* Approach[126]

In *Barber*, the defendants were physicians charged with murder and conspiracy to commit murder, of Clarence Herbert, their patient. Herbert had been in a deep coma from which he was unlikely to recover. After they received permission from the patient's family, the doctors caused life-sustaining equipment to be turned off and, when Herbert continued to survive, they removed intravenous tubes that provided needed hydration and nourishment to their patient. Herbert eventually died from the loss of fluids and nourishment.

The court stated that the physicians' conduct amounted to a withdrawal or omission of further treatment, rather than an affirmative act. It reasoned that although the life-support devices were "self-propelled," each drop of fluid introduced into the patient's body by intravenous feeding was "comparable to a manually administered injection or item of medication." Therefore, it concluded, the disconnection of the mechanical device was tantamount to withholding medical treatment.

---

[125] See *Superintendent of Belchertown State School v Saikewicz*, 370 N.E.2d 417, 424 (Mass. 1977); *In re Quinlan*, 355 A.2d 647, 667-68 (N.J. 1976).

[126] *Barber v. Superior Court*, 195 Cal. Rptr. 484 (Ct. App. 1983).

The court framed the resulting omission issue in terms of what "duties [are] owed by a physician to a patient who has been reliably diagnosed as in a comatose state from which any meaningful recovery of cognitive brain function is exceedingly unlikely." In resolving this issue, the court expressed the view that the ordinary/extraordinary care distinction begged the real question. Instead, the court substituted the test of "whether the proposed treatment [was] proportionate . . . in terms of the benefits to be gained versus the burdens caused." The court reasoned that medical treatment that is even minimally painful or intrusive is apt to constitute disproportionate treatment when the patient has no meaningful chance of medical improvement.

Who determines whether the proposed medical treatment is disproportionate? The court's answer was that "the patient's interests and desires are the key ingredients of the decision making process." When the patient is unable to indicate her wishes, the court ruled that the immediate family is the proper "surrogate" for the patient. In the absence of legislation to the contrary, the court held that medical personnel, along with the family, were permitted to decide whether to withdraw treatment without prior judicial authorization.

[E]—Reflections and Questions Regarding *Barber*

The act/omission distinction is based, at least in part, on the premise that the law should prevent people from actively causing harm, but that it should not compel them to benefit others.[127] Based on this reasoning, did the doctors here withhold a benefit from their patient, or did they actually cause his death?

Before the respirator was turned off, Herbert was alive. Even after the physicians shut off the machinery, he was not in imminent danger of death. Only after the doctors stopped providing nourishment and fluids to Herbert did he die. Therefore, as Professor Arthur Leavens has observed, "it is difficult to avoid concluding that the doctors caused [Herbert's] death."[128] From this perspective, the situation was no different than if Herbert's wife had starved her comatose husband to death at home. Whether family members or health professionals should be allowed to cut off food and fluids to a chronically comatose person is a matter of considerable moral complexity. Arguably, however, the matter ought to be resolved directly—through debate regarding whether euthanasia should be recognized as a defense—rather than indirectly through the act/omission, duty/no-duty analysis. But, as Leavens said, "[g]iven that euthanasia is not legally justified . . ., such intentional conduct seems unavoidably to constitute criminal homicide."[129]

Second, even if the doctors' behavior was properly analyzed as an omission, should the court have treated the cessation of fluids and nourishment as a withdrawal of *medical* treatment? After all, they did not stop a course of treatment intended to combat a disease-process; as a practical matter, they starved their patient to death. Whether or not this was the right decision, was it a *medical* one? It was,

---

[127] See § 9.06[C][2], *supra*.

[128] Leavens, Note 92, *supra*, at 586.

[129] *Id.* at 586-87.

in the sense that they made a medical determination that their patient's prognosis was bleak and irreversible; but perhaps the law should treat discontinuance of basic sustenance differently than it does termination of, for example, dialysis treatment, radiation therapy, or medication.[130]

Third, at a minimum, should physicians and families be required to receive prior judicial authorization before termination of treatment? On the one hand, judicial authorization is costly, time consuming, and, as a consequence, wasteful of finite resources. On the other hand, without oversight, a premature decision might be made, perhaps motivated by a family's greed or understandable emotional turmoil.[131]

§ 9.10 Social Harm: General Principles

[A]—Overview

Holmes has written that the "aim of the law is not to punish sins, but is to prevent certain external results."[132] Joel Feinberg has stated that "[a]cts of *harming* . . . are the direct objects of the criminal law.[133] These statements remind us that, to be guilty of an offense, a person must do more than think bad thoughts; she must be guilty of wrongdoing. The voluntary act is the "doing"; the harm caused by the voluntary act is the "wrong."[134] The harm is the body of the crime. Because crimes are public wrongs,[135] however, we may describe the harm caused in a criminal case as "social harm."

Some scholars state that "social harm" is an essential element of every crime.[136] This is true, but only if the term "social harm" is broadly defined. Some conduct that is criminal may cause no injury in the usual sense of the term. What is the "social harm," for example, in driving while intoxicated, if nobody is hurt and no property is damaged? Or, if D, intending to kill V, pulls the trigger of what turns

---

[130] For discussion of the medical-ethical issues in this regard, see Willard Green, *Setting Boundaries for Artificial Feeding*, The Hastings Center Report, Dec. 1984, at 8; and Gilbert Meilaender, *On Removing Food and Water: Against the Stream*, The Hastings Center Report, Dec. 1984, at 11.

[131] As a constitutional matter, a competent patient has a "liberty" interest encompassed by the due process clause of the United State Constitution, to refuse medical treatment. This interest must be weighed against the state's legitimate interest in preserving life. However, in the case of an incompetent patient, as in *Barber*, the Supreme Court has held that a state has the right to refuse to accept the substituted judgment of a close family member, and it may refuse to permit the cessation of medical care in the absence of clear and convincing evidence of the person's pre-incompetency expressed desire for withdrawal of medical care in such circumstances. *Cruzan v. Director, Missouri Dept. of Health*, 497 U.S. 261 (1990).

[132] *Commonwealth v. Kennedy*, 48 N.E. 770, 770 (Mass. 1897).

[133] Joel Feinberg, Harm to Others 31 (1984).

[134] Obviously, in the unusual case in which a person may be punished for an omission, the term "wrongdoing" does not literally describe the situation.

[135] See § 1.01[A][1], *supra*.

[136] E.g., Eser, Note 1, *supra*, at 346.

out to be an unloaded gun, *D* may be charged with attempted murder, but where is the harm in *D*'s conduct? If all crimes require "social harm," must such conduct go unpunished?

To a utilitarian, there is no reason why harm should be a prerequisite to criminal liability, as long as the actor's conduct threatens to cause injury. Dangerous conduct should be deterred, so that *no* harm occurs; dangerous people should be detained *before* they cause harm. In contrast, many retributivists believe that punishment of an actor is unjustified in the absence of social injury. Only then has the actor taken something from society. Only then is it right for society to take something from the actor, by means of punishment.

In most circumstances the views of both schools of thought converge. Murder causes harm and needs to be deterred, so both retributivists and utilitarians can justify punishing murderers. Moreover, even in the case of an intoxicated driver who threatens future harm, the non-utilitarian may be able to justify punishment. A drunk driver weaving on the highway, for example, endangers others by her conduct, which endangerment frequently causes apprehension in other drivers. Disturbing the public repose[137] is a form of intangible, albeit real, injury that may justify penal sanction.

Frequently, however, it is hard to conclude that dangerous conduct has hurt anyone, even intangibly. If nobody is on the highway to see an intoxicated driver weaving, for example, there is no public alarm. If *V* is asleep and alone when *D* pulls the trigger of an unloaded gun, nobody is put in fear by *D*'s conduct. In these situations, of course, the intoxicated driver and attempted murderer *are* subject to criminal punishment. This need not mean that social harm is not an essential element of these crimes, but it does mean that "social harm" must be carefully defined.

[B]—Definition of "Social Harm"

Society values and has an interest in protecting people and things. The "things" that society values and has an interest in protecting may be tangible (e.g., an automobile) or intangible (e.g., emotional security, reputation, personal autonomy). Society is wronged when an actor invades *any* socially recognized interest and diminishes its value.[138] Specifically, "social harm" may be defined as the "negation, endangering, or destruction of an individual, group or state interest which was deemed socially valuable."[139]

This definition is broad enough ("endangering . . . an individual, group, or state interest") to meet the concerns of those who wish to deter future wrongdoing; it also serves as a reminder that punishment is inappropriate in the absence of proof that the actor has wronged society, at least by jeopardizing a socially valued interest.

---

[137] See *Clark v. State*, 8 S.W. 145, 147 (Tenn. 1888).

[138] See Hall at 217.

[139] Eser, Note 1, *supra*, at 413.

[C]—Finding the "Social Harm" Element in a Criminal Statute

Every crime contains an *actus reus* and, as discussed in the next chapter, nearly all crimes require proof of a culpable state of mind (*mens rea*). The definition of an offense will set out the *actus reus* component of the crime. More specifically, the definition of the offense will identify the proscribed social harm.

For example, the common law definition of murder is "**the killing of a human being by another human being** *with malice aforethought*." The italicized words constitute the *mens rea* of the offense, i.e., the culpable state of mind required to be guilty of the crime. The words in bold express the *actus reus*. More specifically, these words tell us what society does not want to occur (the social harm): the taking of a human life by another human being. The voluntary act/omission component of the *actus reus* is implicit in this definition: the "killing" of a human being must be the result of conduct that includes a voluntary act or an omission (when there is a duty to act).

Of course, in actuality the social harm of murder is not simply the loss of one human life. This is the definitional social harm. The underlying social harm—the full reason why society prohibits murder—is broader and deeper: when a human life is taken by another person, there are deep psychological injuries to loved ones and friends; there may be financial losses suffered by family members and by those with whom the victim worked; there is harm to strangers who, upon learning of the homicide, become fearful for their safety, and consequently restrict their public activities; and, of course, there is the tear to the fabric of society as a whole that results when one of its members unjustifiably takes the life of another.

[D]—Dividing "Social Harm" Into Sub-Elements

The social harm of an offense, as defined by statute or at common law, may consist of wrongful conduct, wrongful results, or both. Moreover, the offense will contain so-called "attendant circumstance" (or, simply "circumstance") elements. Frequently, it is necessary for a lawyer or court to distinguish between "conduct," "result," and "attendant circumstance" elements of the *actus reus* of the crime.

[1]—"Conduct" Elements (or "Conduct" Crimes)

Some crimes are defined in terms of harmful conduct; harmful results are not required. An example of a "conduct" crime would be the offense of "intentionally **driving under the influence of alcohol**." The words in bold state the *actus reus* of the offense. More specifically, they state the social harm of the crime: the wrongful conduct of driving a car in an intoxicated condition, which conduct implicitly must include a voluntary act. This is a "conduct" crime because no harmful result is required; the offense is complete whether or not anyone or any property is tangibly injured because of the intoxicated driving. It is enough that socially valuable interests have been jeopardized by the actor's conduct.

[2]—"Result" Elements (or "Result" Crimes)

An offense may be defined in terms of a prohibited result. For example, common law murder is a "result" crime, in that the social harm is the death of another human being. [140] Although the death must be the result of conduct, the *nature* of the actor's conduct definitionally is irrelevant. That is, it does not matter *how* the result occurs, just that it does.

On the other hand, some offenses contain both "conduct" and "result" elements. For example, assume that a statute defines first-degree murder as the "killing of another human being, by means of a destructive device or explosive, poison, or torture." [141] The *actus reus* of this statute includes a result (another person's death) brought about by a certain type of conduct (use of explosives, poison, or torture).

[3]—Attendant Circumstances

In order for any offense to occur, certain circumstances—usually called "attendant circumstances"—must be present when the actor performs the prohibited conduct and/or causes the prohibited result that constitutes the social harm of the offense.

Some attendant circumstances are not elements of a crime. For example, if *D* intends to kill *V*, the gun that *D* uses must be loaded and in good working condition. Although these circumstances must be present for *V*'s death to occur, they are not part of the definition of the crime.

An attendant circumstance, however, may be an element of an offense. That is, included in the definition of a particular offense may be one or more facts or conditions that must be present during the prohibited conduct, or must be part of the prohibited result, in order for the actor to be guilty of the crime. For example, the social harm of common law burglary is the "breaking and entering of the dwelling house of another at nighttime." This means that for a burglary to occur, the breaking and entering by the actor must be of a "dwelling house" (not, for example, of a commercial structure); the dwelling must belong to someone other than the actor; and the events must occur at night. These elements of the offense—"dwelling house," "of another," and "at night"—are attendant circumstances of burglary. In the absence of these facts or conditions, the social harm of burglary has not occurred (although the social harm of another offense, e.g., trespass, may have occurred).

§ 9.11 Social Harm: Constitutional Limits

Various constitutional provisions limit the extent to which a legislature may proscribe harmful conduct. For example, the First Amendment bars a state from making it an offense to deface an American flag in a manner that the actor knows "will seriously offend one or more persons," [142] or to place on property a Nazi swastika, burning cross, or other symbol that the actor should know "arouses anger, alarm or resentment in others on the basis of race, color, creed, religion, or gender." [143] By these and other rulings, the Supreme Court is *not* suggesting that

---

[140] Although the word "killing"—a conduct term—is used in the common law definition, it is clear that the law is really concerned with the resulting death.

[141] See, e.g., Cal. Penal Code §§ 187(a) (West 1988), and 189 (West 1988 & Supp. 1994).

[142] *Texas v. Johnson*, 491 U.S. 397 (1989).

[143] *R.A.V. v. City of St. Paul*, 112 S.Ct. 2538 (1992).

social harm does not occur in the circumstances under consideration, but rather is saying that constitutional rights—here, freedom of speech—outweigh the society's interest in preventing the harm.

In the 1960s and 1970s, as well, the Supreme Court wrote in rather sweeping terms about the right of Americans "to be free, except in very limited circumstances, from unwanted governmental intrusions into one's privacy."[144] Based on an expansive view of the right of privacy, the high court invalidated laws that prohibited women from obtaining abortions before fetal viability,[145] physicians from dispensing contraceptive information to married and unmarried persons,[146] and adults from possessing obscene literature in their homes.[147]

Language and holdings in recent Supreme Court opinions suggest that the privacy doctrine is not likely to expand much past these areas. Indeed, in *Bowers v. Hardwick*,[148] the Supreme Court ruled, 5-4, that the Constitution does not prohibit a state from punishing adults for committing consensual homosexual acts in their home.[149]

The significance of *Bowers* goes well beyond the homosexual activities it refused to protect. Justice White warned that "[t]he Court is most vulnerable and comes nearest to illegitimacy when it deals with judge-made constitutional law having little or no cognizable roots in the language or design of the Constitution." Therefore, the majority announced, they were not "inclined to take a more expansive view of [their] . . . authority to discover new fundamental rights."

Bowers gives legislatures exceedingly wide latitude to punish "victimless" conduct. *Bowers* states that a "presumed belief of a majority of the electorate" that particular conduct is "immoral and unacceptable" provides sufficient justification for a state to prohibit it, as long as the conduct is not otherwise constitutionally protected.

---

[144] *Stanley v. Georgia*, 394 U.S. 557, 564 (1969).

[145] *Roe v. Wade*, 410 U.S. 113 (1973); *Planned Parenthood of Southeastern Pennsylvania v. Casey*, 112 S.Ct. 2791, 2804 (1992) (reaffirming, as the "essential holding" of *Roe*, the "right of [a] woman to choose to have an abortion before viability and to obtain it without undue [governmental] interference.").

[146] *Griswold v. Connecticut*, 381 U.S. 479 (1965); *Eisenstadt v. Baird*, 405 U.S. 438 (1972).

[147] *Stanley v. Georgia*, 394 U.S. 557 (1969).

[148] 478 U.S. 186 (1986); see generally Anne B. Goldstein, *History, Homosexuality, and Political Values: Searching for the Hidden Determinants of Bowers v. Hardwick*, 97 Yale L.J. 1078 (1988); Jed Rubenfeld, *The Right to Privacy*, 102 Harv. L. Rev. 737 (1989); Kendall Thomas, *Beyond the Privacy Principle*, 92 Colum. L. Rev. 1431 (1992); Norman Vieira, *Hardwick and the Right of Privacy*, 55 U. Chi. L. Rev. 1181 (1988).

[149] Lewis Powell, one of the five Justices in the majority, told law students at New York University after his retirement that "I probably made a mistake in that one," referring to *Bowers*. Barry Friedman, *How a Supreme Court Vote Set Back Gay Rights*, San Francisco Chronicle, January 14, 1991, at A17. Only three of the Justices who heard the *Bowers* appeal remain on the high court. Two of them (Justices Rehnquist and O'Connor) voted to uphold the law; the third (Justice Stevens) dissented.

CHAPTER 10

MENS REA

§ 10.01 General Principle [1]

Actus non facit reum nisi mens sit rea, or "an act does not make [a person] guilty, unless the mind be guilty," expresses the modern principle that a crime contains not only an *actus reus*, but also a *mens rea*. That is, except in rare circumstances,[2] a person is not guilty of an offense unless he performs a voluntary act (or omits an act that is his legal duty to perform) that causes social harm (the *actus reus*), with a *mens rea* (literally, a "guilty mind").

In ancient English law, criminal responsibility was based solely on proof of the commission of an *actus reus*; the actor's state of mind while causing the prohibited harm was irrelevant. By as early as the thirteenth century, however, English courts had begun to require proof that the person charged with a criminal offense had a culpable state of mind.[3]

By the twentieth century, the concept of *mens rea* had become so deeply entrenched in American law that the Supreme Court could state that "[t]he contention that an injury can amount to a crime only when inflicted by [*mens rea*] is no provincial or transient notion. It is . . . universal and persistent in mature systems of law . . . ."[4] Today, the existence of *mens rea* as a prerequisite to criminal responsibility "is the rule of, rather than the exception to, the principles of Anglo-American criminal jurisprudence."[5] It is "the criminal law's mantra."[6]

---

[1] See generally Hall at 70-104; Hart at 105-45; Katz at 165-209; Rebecca Dresser, *Culpability and Other Minds*, 2 S. Cal. Interdisciplinary L.J. 41 (1993); Gerhard O.W. Mueller, *On Common Law Mens Rea*, 42 Minn. L. Rev. 1043 (1958); Jeffrey S. Parker, *The Economics of Mens Rea*, 79 Virg. L. Rev. 741 (1993); Rollin M. Perkins, *A Rationale of Mens Rea*, 52 Harv. L. Rev. 905 (1939); Frank J. Remington and Orrin L. Helstad, *The Mental Element in Crime — A Legislative Problem*, 1952 Wis. L. Rev. 644; Paul H. Robinson, *A Brief History of Distinctions in Criminal Culpability*, 31 Hastings L.J. 815 (1980); Francis Bowes Sayre, *Mens Rea*, 45 Harv. L. Rev. 974 (1932); Richard A. Wasserstrom, *H.L.A. Hart and the Doctrines of Mens Rea and Criminal Responsibility*, 35 U. Chi. L. Rev. 92 (1967).

[2] See Chapter 11 (Strict Liability), *infra*.

[3] Robinson, Note 1, *supra*, at 821-46; Sayre, Note 1, *supra*, at 975-994.

[4] *Morissette v. United States*, 342 U.S. 246, 250 (1952).

[5] *Dennis v. United States*, 341 U.S. 494, 500 (1951).

[6] *United States v. Cordoba-Hincapie*, 825 F.Supp. 485, 490 (E.D.N.Y. 1993).

§ 10.02   Definition of *"Mens Rea"*

[A]—Ambiguity of the Term

Professor George Fletcher has observed that "there is no term fraught with greater ambiguity than that venerable Latin phrase that haunts the Anglo-American criminal law: *mens rea*."[7] Holmes, too, has noted "that most of the difficulty as to the *mens rea* was due to having no precise understanding what the *mens rea* is."[8]

"Mens rea" has been described as "chameleon-like, [because it] takes on different colors in different surroundings."[9] Professor Sanford Kadish has ruefully observed that "the term '*mens rea*' is rivalled [by few legal terms] for the varieties of senses in which it has been used and for the quantity of obfuscation it has created."[10]

Generally speaking, *"mens rea"* has two meanings. Particularly during the early development of the doctrine, the term had a broad—indeed, "exceedingly vague"[11]—meaning, described below in subsection [B]. Over time, however, "the law [has] embarked upon a long journey of refinement and development"[12] of the doctrine, resulting in a narrower, more precise meaning, considered in subsection [C]. Although the latter meaning has gained prominence, both usages of the term *"mens rea"* persist today.

[B]—Broad Meaning: The "Culpability" Meaning of *"Mens Rea"*

Broadly speaking, *"mens rea"* is defined as "a general immorality of motive,"[13] "vicious will,"[14] or an "evil-meaning mind."[15] Although each of these phrases has a slightly different connotation, *"mens rea"* as used here suggests a general notion of moral blameworthiness, i.e., that the defendant committed the *actus reus* of an offense with a morally blameworthy state of mind.[16] For current purposes, this may be termed the "culpability" meaning of *"mens rea."*

According to this definition of *"mens rea,"* guilt for an offense is not dependent on proof that an actor caused the proscribed harm with any specific mental state, i.e., it is not necessary to show that he committed the offense "intentionally," "knowingly," or with any other particular frame of mind. Indeed, common law definitions

---

[7] Fletcher at 398.

[8] Holmes-Laski Letters 4 (Mark DeWolfe Howe ed. 1953) (letter of Oliver Wendell Holmes to Harold J. Laski, dated July 14, 1916).

[9] Francis Bowes Sayre, *The Present Signification of Mens Rea in the Criminal Law*, in Harvard Legal Essays, 399, 402 (1934) (italics omitted).

[10] Sanford H. Kadish, *The Decline of Innocence*, 26 Cambridge L.J. 273, 273 (1968).

[11] Sayre, Note 1, *supra*, at 994.

[12] *United States v. Cordoba-Hincapie*, 825 F.Supp. at 491.

[13] Sayre, Note 9, *supra*, at 411-12.

[14] 4 Blackstone at *21.

[15] *Morissette v United States*, 342 U.S. at 251.

[16] See *Commonwealth v. Buckley*, 238 N.E.2d 335, 337 (Mass. 1968) ("blameworthy condition of the mind").

of most offenses failed to specify any *mens rea*.[17] It was sufficient that the defendant committed the proscribed acts in a manner that demonstrated his bad character, malevolence, or immorality.

For example, in *Regina v. Cunningham*,[18] *D* entered the cellar of a building, where he tore the gas meter from the gas pipes and stole the coins deposited in the meter. As a consequence, gas escaped from the pipes, seeped through the cellar wall, and nearly asphyxiated *V*. Although *D* had not intended to endanger anyone's life by his actions, he was charged with an offense that provided, in part, that "[w]hosoever shall . . . maliciously . . . cause to be administered to or taken by any other person any poison . . .or noxious thing, so as thereby to endanger the life of such person, . . . shall be guilty of a felony . . . ."

The evidence presented at trial demonstrated that *D* committed the *actus reus* of the offense: as a result of his voluntary conduct, *D* "caused to be administered" to *V* a "noxious thing" that endangered *V*'s life. The primary issue was whether *D* had the requisite *mens rea*. The trial judge instructed the jury that the statutory term "maliciously" meant only that the prosecution was required to show that the defendant acted "wickedly." Thus, the court invited the jury to convict *D* if it found that he caused the social harm with a morally culpable state of mind. Since *D* caused the harm, albeit unintentionally, while attempting to steal money from the meter, the jury found the requisite wickedness.[19]

[C]—Narrow Meaning: The "Elemental" Meaning of *"Mens Rea"*

"*Mens rea*" may also be defined, simply, as "the particular mental state provided for in the definition of an offense." This is the "elemental" meaning of "*mens rea*."

For example, assume that murder is defined by statute as "the intentional killing of a human being by another human being." The *actus reus* of the offense is "the killing of a human being by another human being." The "*mens rea*"—the particular mental state provided for in the definition of the offense—is "intentional." Applying the elemental meaning of "*mens rea*," *D* is not guilty of murder unless he intentionally killed another human being. If he killed *un*intentionally, albeit with a morally blameworthy state of mind, e.g., if he *recklessly* took another's life, he would *not* be guilty of the crime, because he lacked the particular mental state required in the definition of the offense.

---

[17] Some offenses did specify a particular mental state in their definition. These offenses came to be known as "specific intent" crimes. See § 10.06, *infra*.

[18] 41 Crim. App. 155, 2 Q.B. 396, 2 All. E.R. 412 (1957) (Court of Criminal Appeal).

[19] However, the Court of Criminal Appeal in *Cunningham* allowed *D*'s appeal on the ground that the trial judge's *mens rea* instruction was erroneous. See § 10.04[E], *infra*.

§ 10.03   Rationale of the *Mens Rea* Requirement [20]

[A]—Utilitarian Arguments

Some persons justify the *mens rea* requirement on grounds of deterrence. A person cannot be deterred from criminal activity, it is argued, unless he "appreciate[s] that punishment lies in store" if he persists in his actions. [21] Therefore, punishment of one who lacks a culpable state of mind will be ineffective and, as a consequence, wasteful. It may also be reasoned that one who causes harm accidentally, rather than intentionally or with an "evil-meaning mind," is harmless and not in need of reformation.

These claims are only partly persuasive. Even if a person acting without a *mens rea* cannot be deterred, his punishment may serve as a useful warning to others to be more careful in their activities, thereby reducing the number of accidentally inflicted injuries. [22] Furthermore, although one who acts with a *mens rea* is apt to be dangerous and in need of reformation, the accidental harmdoer may also need incapacitation or some other corrective influence. Some people may be accident-prone; the criminal sanction may be a rational way to protect society from them. At a minimum, their punishment may influence them to change their lifestyle and to avoid activities that may result in injury to others.

The *mens rea* requirement may be counter-productive for another reason. The prosecution is constitutionally required to prove beyond a reasonable doubt every element of a criminal offense, including the defendant's *mens rea*. [23] This is often a difficult burden to satisfy; consequently, some persons who *do* act with a *mens rea* are able to avoid conviction. In turn, this means that some dangerous people escape punishment, and the law sends the counter-utilitarian message to potential wrongdoers that they might also be able to escape the criminal sanction.

[B]—Retributive Arguments

The Supreme Court once observed that "[a] relation between some mental element and punishment for a harmful act is almost as instinctive as the child's familiar exculpatory [statement], 'But I didn't mean to'. . . ." [24] Oliver Wendell Holmes has made the same point with animals rather than children when he suggested that "even a dog distinguishes between being stumbled over and being kicked." [25]

---

[20] See generally the sources in Note 1, *supra*; for a scholarly judicial discussion of *mens rea*, see *United States v. Cordoba-Hincapie*, 825 F.Supp. 485 (E.D.N.Y. 1993) (opinion of Senior District Judge Jack B. Weinstein).

[21] Williams at 30.

[22] Richard A. Wasserstrom, *Strict Liability in the Criminal Law*, 12 Stan. L. Rev. 731, 736-37 (1960).

[23] See § 7.03, *supra*.

[24] *Morissette v. United States*, 342 U.S. at 250-51.

[25] Holmes at 3.

Whether Holmes's observation is right or wrong, the preceding observations assist in making the point that the principle of *mens rea* has its roots far deeper in retributive than in utilitarian soil. Although a society certainly wants to deter harmful conduct, the *mens rea* requirement "flows from our society's commitment to individual choice"; [26] the principle is founded on the belief that it is morally unjust to punish those who accidentally, rather than by choice, cause social injury.

Crimes are public wrongs; a finding of guilt implies that the convicted party wronged the community as a whole. By convicting a criminal defendant, society denounces the actor; it condemns and stigmatizes him as a wrongdoer. [27] Respect for human dignity suggests, if it does not dictate, that stigma should not attach and liberty should not be denied to one who has acted without a culpable state of mind.

§ 10.04   Common *Mens Rea* Terms [28]

[A]—"Intentionally"

[1]—Definition

Many criminal offenses are defined in terms of "intent," that is, the prosecution must prove that the defendant intentionally committed the social harm that constitutes the *actus reus* of the offense. At common law, a person "intentionally" causes the social harm [29] of an offense if: (1) it is his desire (i.e., his conscious object) to cause the social harm; or (2) he acts with knowledge that the social harm is virtually certain to occur as a result of his conduct. [30]

For example, suppose that bomb expert *D* wants to kill *V*, his wife, in order to obtain the proceeds from her life insurance policy. *D* constructs a bomb and places it on an airplane on which *V* is a passenger. He sets the bomb to explode while the plane is in air. Although *D* does not want anyone on the plane other than *V* to die— indeed, he fervently prays that the others will survive—he knows that the bomb will destroy the airplane. The bomb goes off as planned, killing *V* and the other 100 persons on board.

According to the preceding definition, how many people did *D* "intentionally" kill? Clearly, *D* "intentionally" killed *V*. This follows from the simple fact that *D* wanted *V* to die; it was his conscious object to take her life. Under the first prong of the definition of "intent," it does not matter how likely it is that the result will occur; it is sufficient that the outcome is desired.

D's mental state as to the other victims must be analyzed differently. He did not desire their deaths; in fact, he prayed that they would live. Nonetheless, assuming

---

[26] *United States v. Cordoba-Hincapie*, 825 F.Supp. at 495.

[27] See § 1.01[A][1], *supra*.

[28] See generally Kenneth W. Simons, *Rethinking Mental States*, 72 B.U. L. Rev. 463 (1992).

[29] As explained in § 9.10, *supra*, the prohibited "social harm" may be an unwanted result (e.g., the death of a human being) or wrongful conduct (e.g., receiving stolen property). The "intent" definition encompasses both types of offenses; however, because most "intent" issues arise in the context of "result" crimes, the examples here focus on such offenses.

[30] *Mill v. State*, 585 P.2d 546, 549 (Alaska 1978); Williams at §§ 16, 18.

that D was a person of ordinary intelligence, it is reasonable to conclude that he "intended" their deaths as well. According to the second meaning of "intent" set out above, he knew that the social harm of their deaths was virtually certain to occur when his bomb exploded. This second version of "intent" does not require proof that the actor *wanted* the harm to occur; it is enough that he *knew* that their deaths were virtually certain to occur as a result of his actions. This second prong may be termed the "known certainties" prong, for it is not satisfied if the outcome was merely highly probable; the actor must realize that, short of a divine or secular "miracle," the undesired event will occur "for sure."[31]

Both versions of "intent" involve subjective fault. An actor's fault is "subjective" if he possesses a wrongful state of mind—in this case, the conscious desire to cause the social harm, or the conscious awareness that the harm will almost certainly result from his conduct. If the defendant lacks either of these states of mind, he has not "intentionally" caused the harm.

The significance of the subjective nature of "intent" is seen by a minor change in the bombing hypothetical. Suppose that D belonged to a religious sect that espoused the view that members of the faith always have their wishes fulfilled by God. Therefore, as a member of the sect, D genuinely believed that his fervent prayers would save the remaining persons on board the airplane.

Based on these revised facts, D (as before) "intentionally" killed his wife, because he desired her death. However, assuming that a jury believes his testimony about his religious faith, D did not "intentionally" kill the other passengers; he was not subjectively aware that their deaths were a near certainty. "Intent" requires such awareness; it is insufficient that he should have been aware, as a reasonable person, that they would be killed.

[2]—"Motive" Distinguished[32]

Some legal scholars state that motive is irrelevant in the substantive criminal law.[33] This statement is only correct if they mean that the "intention" to cause social harm is no less "intentional" simply because the actor's motive may not have been evil. For example, a doctor who kills his terminally ill patient to "put him out of his misery" arguably has a good motive, but he has still killed the victim "intentionally."[34]

---

[31] Glanville Williams, *Oblique Intention*, 46 Cambridge L.J. 417, 418 (1987).

[32] See generally Walter Wheeler Cook, *Act, Intention and Motive in the Criminal Law*, 26 Yale L.J. 645 (1917); Martin R. Gardner, *The Mens Rea Enigma: Observations on the Role of Motive in the Criminal Law Past and Present*, 1993 Utah L. Rev. 635; Kent Greenawalt, *Reflections on Justifications for Defining Crimes by the Category of the Victim*, 1992/1993 Ann. Surv. Am. L. 617; Douglas N. Husak, *Motive and Criminal Liability*, Crim. Just. Ethics, Winter/Spring 1989, at 3; Paul H. Robinson, *Hate Crimes: Crimes of Motive, Character, or Group Terror?*, 1992/1993 Ann. Surv. Am. L. 605.

[33] E.g., Hall at 88 ("[H]ardly any part of penal law is more definitely settled than that motive is irrelevant").

[34] Even here, however, the doctor's motive is relevant to the criminal law, in the sense that proof of his motive reinforces the prosecution's claim that the doctor acted with the requisite intent.

A defendant's motive is often relevant in the criminal law. First, some offenses (called "specific intent" crimes[35]) *by definition* require proof of a specified motive. For example, common law larceny is the trespassory taking and carrying away of the personal property of another *with the intent to steal, i.e., with the intent to permanently deprive the other of the property.* Although the law uses the term "intent"—many scholars call it an "ulterior intention"—the italicized language denotes the actor's motive for committing the *actus reus* of the offense. In the absence of this motive, e.g., if the defendant intentionally took and carried away property, but intended to return it the next day, a larceny has not occurred.

Second, motive is relevant to claims of defense. That is, if the defendant's motive for his intentional actions is legally justifiable, e.g., he intentionally killed the victim in self-defense, he will be acquitted. But, as this example demonstrates, the existence of a justifiable motive does not render the defendant's conduct or the consequences of it any less intentional.

Third, motive is relevant at the sentencing phase of a criminal proceeding. For example, if it wishes to do so, a state may impose enhanced punishment for an offense if the actor selected his victim on account of a factor such as race, religion, disability, or sexual orientation.[36] Likewise, in jurisdictions permitting sentencing discretion, a defendant's good motive for wrongful conduct may be considered in mitigation.

[3]—"Transferred Intent"

[a]—General Doctrine

Assume that *D1* wrongfully fires a gun at *X*, intending to kill him, but the bullet instead strikes and kills *V*, a bystander. Although *D1* did not intend to kill *V*, he may successfully be prosecuted for intent-to-kill murder. Similarly, if *D2* attempts to kick *X*, but instead strikes *V*, he may be convicted of battery (for current purposes, defined as "intentional touching or striking of another").[37]

Many courts reach this outcome by applying the legal fiction of "transferred intent." This doctrine, which originated in the sixteenth century,[38] provides that "if one intends injury to the person [or property] of another under circumstances in which such a mental element constitutes *mens rea*, and in the effort to accomplish this end he inflicts harm upon a person [or property] other than the one intended, he is guilty . . . as if his aim had been more accurate."[39]

The stated purpose of the rule is "to ensure that prosecution and punishment accord with culpability."[40] That is, one who accidentally harms an innocent

---

[35] See § 10.06, *infra.*

[36] E.g., Wis.Stat. § 939.645(1)(b) (1989-1990) (upheld against constitutional attack in *Wisconsin v. Mitchell*, 113 S.Ct. 2194 (1993).

[37] See *Mordica v. State*, 618 So.2d 301 (Fla. Dist. Ct. App. 1993).

[38] *Regina v. Saunders*, 2 Plowd. 473, 75 Eng.Rep. 706 (1576) (if *A* shoots an arrow at *B* with intent to kill him, and a person to whom *A* bore no evil intent is killed by it, it is the same offense as if he had killed *B*).

[39] *Gladden v. State*, 330 A.2d 176, 188 (Md. 1974).

[40] *People v. Czahara*, 250 Cal.Rptr. 836, 839 (Ct. App. 1988).

bystander, while failing to inflict precisely the same injury upon the intended victim, acts with the culpability of an intentional wrongdoer, and should be punished as such.

[b]—When the Doctrine Does Not Apply

The transferred intent doctrine does not apply in all circumstances seemingly involving unintended victims. First, the doctrine does not apply—it is unnecessary—in cases of misidentification, rather than mis-aim. That is, if A intentionally shoots B, mistakenly believing that B is C, there is no need to "transfer" the intent to another:[41] A successfully shot the body of the person at which he aimed.

Second, many courts do not apply the doctrine if A intends to cause harm to B, *and causes that harm*, but also unintentionally causes the same type of harm to C, a bystander.[42] For example, if A, with the intent to kill B, fires one bullet at B, who is standing in front of C, and the bullet enters and exits B's body, striking and killing C, A may be convicted of only one count of intent-to-kill homicide. A's intention to harm B cannot be transferred to C because the "intent" has been "used up" against B. This is a sensible result because application of the transferred intent doctrine in such circumstances would result in disproportional punishment of A; it would make two intentional crimes out of one, in the sense that the actor intended to cause harm to only one victim, but is convicted for two.[43] Notwithstanding the wisdom in such reasoning, some courts *do* permit use of the transferred intent doctrine in such circumstances, on the ground that "intent is not regarded as a limited commodity that, once satisfied, is totally expended."[44]

Third, the transferred intent doctrine does not apply if the crime, by definition, precludes it. For example, in *Ford v. State*,[45] D threw rocks at X, the driver of an automobile on the highway, with the intention of maiming X. The rocks struck the car, and seriously hurt V, a passenger in the car. D's conduct constituted an assault—an attempted battery—of X. In relation to V, D was convicted of the offense of "assault[ing] or beat [ing] any person with intent to maim, disfigure, or disable *such person*." The conviction was overturned because D's intent to "main, disfigure, or disable" X was nontransferable to V. By the express wording of the statute, an actor must have the intent to main, disfigure, or disable a specific person, namely, the person assaulted or beaten (in this case, X, not V).

---

[41] E.g., *Martinez v. State*, 844 S.W.2d 279 (Tex. Ct. App. 1992).

[42] E.g., *People v. Czahara*, 250 Cal.Rptr. 836 (Ct. App. 1988); *Ford v. State*, 625 A.2d 984 (Md. 1993).

[43] Such cases must be distinguished from those in which A intentionally creates a "kill zone" by firing a barrage of bullets in the direction of a crowd of persons that contains B, A's primary victim. When B and others are killed, it may be possible to show that A "concurrently intended to kill everyone in [B]'s immediate vicinity to ensure [B]'s death." *Ford v. State*, 625 A.2d at 1001. If A intended to kill multiple victims, there is no need to transfer any intent. There is enough intent to go around.

[44] *State v. Hinton*, 630 A.2d 593, 596 n.8 (Conn. 1993); see *Mordica v. State*, 618 So.2d 301 (Fla. Dist. Ct. App. 1993) (D intentionally kicked X, but also hit V; in dictum, the court stated that the transferred intent doctrine could be applied).

[45] 603 A.2d 883 (Md. Ct. Spec. App. 1992), *aff'd*, 625 A.2d 984 (Md. 1993).

Fourth, the transferred intent doctrine serves to transfer the intent to a different victim, but it does not transfer the intent to cause one type of social harm to another. For example, if *A* intends to kill a dog, but the bullet strikes and kills a human, it would be impermissible to transfer the intent from the dog to the human. Similarly, if *D* throws a rock at *X*, intending to injure him, but the rock instead breaks a window in a building behind *X*, the intent to batter *X*—one type of social harm— may not be used to prove that he intended to cause property damage—a different social harm.[46]

[c]—Do We Even Need the Doctrine?

The transferred intent doctrine is unnecessary and, in light of the subtle exceptions to it, potentially misleading. Consider the typical case: *A* intends to kill *B*, but instead kills *C*, and is prosecuted for intent-to-kill murder. In this case, there is no need to transfer *A*'s intention to kill *B* to *C*; *A* has the requisite intent *without* the doctrine. The social harm of murder is the "killing of a human being by another human being." The requisite intent, therefore, is the intent to kill *a*, not a specific, human being. In the present case, *A* intended to kill *a* human being (*B*), and he did in fact kill a human being (*C*). Thus, the *actus reus* and *mens rea* of murder are proved without invoking the legal fiction of transferred intent.[47]

[B]—"Knowingly" or "With Knowledge"[48]

As explained in subsection [A] [1], a person who knowingly causes social harm is commonly said to have "intended" the harm. Sometimes, however, knowledge of a material fact—an "attendant circumstance"[49] —is a required element of an offense. For example, it is a federal crime for a person knowingly to import into the United States any controlled substance.[50] Under this statute, a person who drives an automobile containing marijuana into the country is not guilty unless he "knows" of the presence of the contraband—the attendant circumstance—when he enters the United States.

A person has "knowledge" of a material fact if he is aware of the fact or he correctly believes that it exists. Thus, in the marijuana importation hypothetical, *D*

---

[46] *Regina v. Pembliton*, 12 Cox C.C. 607 (1874) (Court of Criminal Appeal); see also *Mordica v. State*, 618 So.2d 301 (Fla. Dist. Ct. App. 1993) (*D*, a prison inmate attempted to kick *X*; *D*'s foot hit *V*, a prison guard; held: the transferred intent doctrine does not apply in a prosecution for "battery upon a law enforcement officer"; *D* intended to commit a battery, but not of a police officer, a different and more serious social harm).

[47] Furthermore, if the offense, as defined, *did* require proof of the intent to kill a specific person, the transferred intent doctrine would *not* apply anyway, as explained in subsection [b], *supra*.

[48] See generally Robin Charlow, *Wilful Ignorance and Criminal Culpability*, 70 Tex. L. Rev. 1351 (1992); Douglas N. Husak & Craig A. Callender, *Wilful Ignorance, Knowledge, and the "Equal Culpability" Thesis: A Study of the Deeper Significance of the Principle of Legality*, 1994 Wis. L. Rev. 29; Ira P. Robbins, *The Ostrich Instruction: Deliberate Ignorance as a Criminal Mens Rea*, 81 J. Crim. L. & Criminology 191 (1990).

[49] See § 9.10[D][3], *supra*.

[50] 21 U.S.C. § 952(a) (1988).

"knows" of the presence of the marijuana if he concealed it in the vehicle himself or personally observed its presence ("actual knowledge"); he also "knows" of the marijuana's existence if he smells it and, as a consequence, believes that it is present ("correct belief" form of "knowledge").

Many jurisdictions also permit a finding of knowledge in a third circumstance: if the person is aware of a high probability of the existence of the fact in question, and he deliberately fails to investigate in order to avoid confirmation of the fact.[51] This form of "knowledge" is described as "wilful blindness" or "deliberate ignorance." An instruction to the jury in this regard is sometimes called the "ostrich instruction." One federal judge has explained the ostrich analogy this way:

> [Supposedly, real ostriches] do not just fail to follow through on their suspicions of bad things. They are not merely *careless* birds. They bury their heads in the sand so that they will not see or hear bad things. They *deliberately* avoid acquiring unpleasant knowledge. The ostrich instruction is designed for cases in which there is evidence that the defendant, knowing or strongly suspecting that he is involved in shady dealings, takes steps to be sure that he does not acquire full or exact knowledge . . . .[52]

Thus, in the importation hypothetical, *D* would be guilty of "wilful blindness" or "deliberate ignorance" if, for example, he agreed to drive *X*'s car into the country, although he was highly suspicious that drugs had been concealed in it, and he purposely avoided looking in the trunk or elsewhere because he was afraid that it would confirm his suspicions.[53]

The latter form of "knowledge" is controversial. First, notwithstanding the ostrich analogy, the actor need not "take steps" of an active nature, equivalent to putting his head in the sand, to be found guilty of wilful blindness; as a practical matter, his culpability can be based on his *failure* to take obvious and simple steps to confirm or dispel his suspicions. The risk in giving an ostrich instruction is that a jury might convict a defendant for merely being a careless bird, i.e., upon a finding of negligence, which is a less culpable *mens rea* than knowledge.[54] At most, one who suspects the existence of a circumstance is reckless in acting on the basis of a known suspicion.[55]

Advocates of the doctrine contend that in the real world, absolute knowledge is hard to come by, if ever.[56] Therefore, a strict interpretation of the term

---

[51] E.g., *United States v. Lara-Velasquez*, 919 F.2d 946 (5th Cir. 1990); *United States v. Jewell*, 532 F.2d 697 (9th Cir. 1976); *State v. LaFreniere*, 481 N.W.2d 412 (Neb. 1992); Williams at § 57; contra, *State v. Bogle*, 376 S.E.2d 745 (N.C. 1989) (refusing to recognize the "willful blindness" doctrine).

[52] *United States v. Giovannetti*, 919 F.2d 1223, 1228 (7th Cir. 1990).

[53] See *United States v. Jewell*, 532 F.2d 697 (9th Cir. 1976).

[54] See *United States v. Ramsey*, 785 F.2d 184, 190 (7th Cir. 1986); Robbins, Note 48, *supra*, at 227-31.

[55] Robbins, Note 48, *supra*, at 220-27. "Recklessness" is defined at § 10.04[D][3], *infra*.

[56] See Perkins & Boyce at 865.

"knowledge" would reward persons who seek to avoid criminal responsibility by purposeful ignorance. Such a person is as culpable as one who is actually aware of a fact or correctly believes that it exists. However, even if "wilful blindness" is morally equivalent to "knowledge," that is not the same as saying that "wilful blindness" *is* "knowledge." As long as an offense is defined in terms of "knowledge," the principle of legality suggests that an equivalent—but different—state of mind (such as "purposeful avoidance of knowledge") is insufficient for conviction.[57]

[C]—"Wilfully"[58]

"Wilful" is a "word of many meanings."[59] It is often a synonym for "intentional."[60] Sometimes, however, the term means "an act done with a bad purpose"[61] or with "an evil motive."[62] "Wilful" may also connote an "intentional violation of a known legal duty,"[63] or "a purpose to disobey the law."[64]

Usually intentional wrongdoers act with a bad purpose or evil motive, and with knowledge that they are violating the law, so it does not matter what meaning of "wilful" is applied. Occasionally, however, the difference is significant. For example, in one federal case, *D* asserted what he believed to be his constitutional privilege not to incriminate himself, by refusing to answer questions propounded to him by a government agency. As it turned out, the constitutional provision did not apply in his circumstances, so he was charged with "wilfully" refusing to answer the questions.[65]

If "wilful" means "intentional," *D* was guilty because he intentionally refused to answer the questions. *D*'s conviction was overturned, however, because his refusal, although intentional, was based on an erroneous belief that he had a lawful right to refuse to answer. Therefore, he lacked an evil motive for the violation, and did not act with the purpose of disobeying the law. It should be noted that if the latter meaning of "wilful" is applied, the presence of this term in the definition of an offense can result in an exception to the usual rule that a mistake of law is not a basis for exculpation of an actor.[66]

---

[57] See Husak & Callender, Note 48, *supra*.

[58] See generally Michael E. Tigar, *"Willfulness" and "Ignorance" in Federal Criminal Law*, 37 Cleve. St. L. Rev. 525 (1989).

[59] *Ratzlaf v. United States*, 114 S.Ct. 655, 659 (1994) (quoting *Spies v. United States*, 317 U.S. 492, 497 (1943)).

[60] E.g., *Commonwealth v. Welansky*, 55 N.E.2d 902, 910 (Mass. 1944).

[61] See *Townsend v. United States*, 95 F.2d 352, 358 (D.C. Cir. 1938).

[62] *United States v. Murdock*, 290 U.S. 389, 395 (1933), *overruled on other grounds* in *Murphy v. Waterfront Commission*, 373 U.S. 52 (1964).

[63] *Cheek v. United States*, 498 U.S. 192, 200 (1991).

[64] *Ratzlaf v. United States*, 114 S.Ct. at 659.

[65] *United States v. Murdock*, 284 U.S. 141 (1931), *overruled* in *Murphy v. Waterfront Commission*, 378 U.S. 52 (1964).

[66] See § 13.02[D][2], *infra*.

[D]—"Negligence" and "Recklessness"

[1]—Overview

Risk-taking is an ever-present aspect of life. Virtually every human act may cause harm to the actor or others. Nonetheless, society rewards some risk-taking, even as it requires some risk-takers to compensate those who are injured by their conduct, and punishes still others for their risk-taking.

Basically risk-taking falls into four categories: (1) socially desirable or morally neutral risk-taking; (2) risk-taking that justifies civil liability ("civil negligence"); (3) criminally negligent risk-taking ("criminal negligence"); and (4) reckless conduct ("recklessness"). The lines between these categories are not bright. And, unfortunately, courts have often used terms such as "negligence" and "recklessness" interchangeably, so it is sometimes very difficult to distinguish between these types of risk-taking.

[2]—"Negligence"[67]

[a]—In General

A person's conduct is "negligent" if it constitutes a deviation from the standard of care that a reasonable person would have observed in the actor's situation. Conduct constitutes such a deviation if the actor takes an unjustifiable risk of causing harm to another. Thus, "negligence" constitutes *objective* fault, i.e., an actor is not blamed for a wrongful state of mind, but instead is punished for his failure to live up to the standards of the fictional "reasonable person."[68]

Three factors come into play when determining whether a reasonable person would have acted as the defendant did: (1) the gravity of harm that foreseeably would result from the defendant's conduct; (2) the probability of such harm occurring; and (3) the burden to the defendant of desisting from the risky conduct. Judge Learned Hand described the relationship of these factors in algebraic terms: "if the probability [of harm] be called P; the [gravity of] injury, L; and the burden, B; liability depends upon whether B is less than L multiplied by P: i.e., whether BPL."[69] Although this formula cannot be applied with scientific precision, its expression emphasizes the point that, as the gravity and/or probability of harm increases, the more substantial the actor's justification for taking the risk must be.

For example, suppose that *D* darts between lanes in his car at a very fast rate of speed on a busy public road, in order to get to a friend's birthday party. As a result, *D* is an accident and kills *V*. If *D* were sued or prosecuted for negligence in *V*'s

---

[67] See generally Hall at 105-145; Larry Alexander, *Reconsidering the Relationship Among Voluntary Acts, Strict Liability, and Negligence in Criminal Law*, Social Phil. & Pol'y, Spring 1990, at 84; James B. Brady, *Punishment for Negligence: A Reply to Professor Hall*, 22 Buff. L. Rev. 107 (1972); George P. Fletcher, *The Theory of Criminal Negligence: A Comparative Analysis*, 119 U. Pa. L. Rev. 401 (1971); Jerome Hall, *Negligent Behavior Should be Excused from Penal Liability*, 63 Colum. L. Rev. 632 (1963); Note, *Negligence and the General Problem of Criminal Responsibility*, 81 Yale L.J. 949 (1972).

[68] The nature of the "reasonable person" is considered in § 10.04[D][3][d], *infra*.

[69] *United States v. Carroll Towing Co.*, 159 F.2d 169, 173 (2d Cir. 1947).

death, a jury might find that D's conduct was negligent: the gravity of harm was substantial (loss of life); the probability of such harm occurring was not insubstantial; the burden to defendant of driving in a safer manner was small (he could have obeyed traffic laws and reached his party late). On the other hand, if D drives in precisely the same manner in order to get his gravely ill child to the hospital, a jury might determine that D took a justifiable risk, in light of the child's condition.

[b]—Distinguishing Civil from Criminal Negligence

A person who breaches his duty of care to another has acted negligently, as defined in subsection [a]. However, not every breach constitutes a crime. As Jerome Hall has observed, " '[b]lame' is a very wide notion and, like praise, it permeates almost all of daily life. Important differences exist between raising an eyebrow and putting a man in jail . . . ."[70] More specifically, the blame expressed in a civil finding of negligence is not the same as the blame communicated by a jury when it returns a verdict of guilty of criminal negligence in a criminal prosecution.

Although rare exceptions exist, "civil negligence ordinarily is [considered] an inappropriate predicate by which to define . . . criminal conduct."[71] That is, to establish criminal responsibility for negligence, the prosecution must ordinarily show more than the mere deviation from the standard of care that would constitute civil negligence.[72]

"Criminal negligence" is conduct that represents a *gross* deviation from the standard of reasonable care, i.e., a person is criminally negligent if he takes a *substantial* and unjustifiable risk of causing the social harm that constitutes the offense charged. Applying the Learned Hand formula, criminal negligence exists when "PL" *far* outweighs "B"; the level of negligence should be so great "that it would be shocking to allow the actor's lack of awareness to excuse his actions in the circumstances."[73]

Frequently courts describe criminal negligence as "gross negligence," "culpable negligence," or "recklessness." However, as explained in subsection [3], *infra*, the term "recklessness" should not be equated with criminal negligence.

[c]—Should Negligence Be Punished?

Punishment for negligence is controversial. After all, "*mens rea*" means "guilty mind," but the negligent actor is blamed and punished for his *lack* of the state of mind of a reasonable person.

Some opponents of punishment for negligence contend that, by definition, a negligent actor fails to perceive the risks of his conduct and, therefore, cannot be deterred. Since utilitarians believe that punishment should be avoided if it will not

---

[70] Hall, *Negligent Behavior Should be Excluded from Penal Liability*, Note 67, *supra*, at 641.

[71] *Santillanes v. State*, 849 P.2d 358, 365 (N.M. 1993).

[72] *State v. Jones*, 126 A.2d 273, 275 (Me. 1956).

[73] *Commonwealth v. Heck*, 491 A.2d 212, 225 (Pa. Super. Ct. 1985).

result in a net reduction in societal pain,[74] negligent harmdoers should not be punished.

The utilitarian defense of punishment for negligence primarily focuses on general deterrence. Holmes has bluntly observed that "public policy sacrifices the individual to the general good."[75] In this context, punishment of an individual negligent actor, even if he was undeterrable on this occasion, is justified on the ground that it promotes safer conduct by others. It may also have an incidental specific deterrence benefit: the negligent actor who is punished may act more carefully in the future.

A more significant criticism of punishment based on negligence is founded in retributive principles of just punishment. The basis for just punishment, it is argued, is voluntary wrongdoing.[76] People who intentionally cause harm choose to act wrongly and may properly be punished. Similarly, one who is aware that his proposed conduct is unjustifiably risky, but proceeds anyway, exercises a choice for which he may fairly be held responsible. The negligent actor's risk-taking, however, is inadvertent: he does not appreciate that his conduct is dangerous; he may not even be capable of appreciating it, since an offender might be held to a standard of care that he is physically or mentally incapable of satisfying. Negligent persons should bear civil responsibility for the injuries they cause; but retributive opponents of punishment for negligence assert that negligent actors should not be stigmatized and have their liberty restrained due to their inadvertence.

Retributive defenders of punishment for negligence point out that the label "criminal negligence" implies that the "act has been done so heedlessly, so indifferently, and so grossly contrary to common experience that it becomes intolerable to reasoning minds that the actor did not perceive the risk of harm created by his conduct."[77] Such a person manifests an ethical insensitivity to the rights of others. If "*mens rea*" implies that the actor is morally blameworthy, or that his conduct demonstrates a character flaw, then the ethically insensitive wrongdoer may possess sufficient "*mens rea*" to deserve punishment.[78] Additionally, the negligent actor's explanation for the injury he caused is frequently something like: "But, I just didn't think." Defenders of punishment for negligence argue that if a person can be blamed because he failed to act, there is no reason why he should not be blamed because he failed to think.[79]

---

[74] See § 2.03[B][1], *supra*.

[75] Holmes at 48.

[76] Hall, *Negligent Behavior Should be Excluded from Penal Liability*, Note 67, *supra*, at 635.

[77] *Commonwealth v. Heck*, 491 A.2d at 225.

[78] Fletcher, Note 67, *supra*, at 416-18. This argument presupposes that the actor was capable of perceiving the risks in his conduct.

[79] Hart at 151-52.

[d]—Who *Really* Is the "Reasonable Person"?: Initial Observations[80]

Jurists have struggled for centuries to identify the "reasonable person," or what used to be called the "reasonable prudent *man*." He was once described as "an ideal, . . . the embodiment of all those qualities which we demand of the good citizen."[81] In the context of civil negligence, the leading torts treatise states that "[h]e is not to be identified with any ordinary individual, who might occasionally do unreasonable things; he is a prudent and careful person, *who is always up to standard.*"[82] According to this description, of course, everyone occasionally acts negligently, at least at the civil level of this standard, although they may be fortunate enough not to injure others in the process.

Although the standard is objective—the defendant's conduct is compared to this external ideal—courts frequently are called upon to "subjectivize" the "reasonable person," by infusing him with the mental and/or physical characteristics of the defendant, and by incorporating in him the defendant's personal life experiences. For example, if the defendant is of low education, should his conduct be judged by the standard of a reasonable person with a similar level of education? Or, if the defendant is a woman, African-American, blind, a former mugging victim, or a person suffering from "battered woman syndrome," should these characteristics be considered in determining whether the defendant acted reasonably?

The general issue raised by these questions, namely, whether the law should retain a purely objective standard, is considered in various places in thes Text.[83] Generally speaking, however, the current position of the law—but one that is under considerable attack—is that the defendant's unusual physical characteristics (e.g., blindness), if relevant to the case, may be incorporated into the "reasonable man" standard, but that the defendant's unusual mental characteristics are not. Holmes expressed the traditional view that the law does not take "account of the infinite varieties of temperament, intellect and education which make the internal character of a given act so different," and that it "does not attempt to see men as God sees them."[84]

[3]—"Recklessness"

In the past, "recklessness" was a synonym for "criminal negligence." Today, however, a line is drawn between these two concepts, with "recklessness" falling on the more culpable side of the line.

---

[80] See generally Ronald K.L. Collins, *Language, History and the Legal Process: A Profile of the "Reasonable Man"*, 8 Rut.-Cam. L.J. 311 (1977); Osborne M. Reynolds, Jr., *The Reasonable Man of Negligence Law: A Health Report on the "Odious Creature"*, 23 Okla. L. Rev. 410 (1970); Robert Unikel, Note, *"Reasonable" Doubts: A Critique of the Reasonable Woman Standard in American Jurisprudence*, 87 Nw. U. L. Rev. 326 (1992).

[81] A.P. Herbert, Misleading Cases in the Common Law 12 (1930).

[82] Dan B. Dobbs, Robert E. Keeton, & David G. Owens, Prosser and Keeton on Torts 175 (5th ed. 1984).

[83] See §§ 18.06[A], 31.07[B][2][b][ii], *infra*.

[84] Holmes at 108.

As an independent concept, two definitions of "recklessness" have developed. According to the tort law definition, which also has some support in the criminal law, a person acts "recklessly" if he takes a *very* substantial and unjustifiable risk. According to this approach, "civil negligence," "criminal negligence," and "recklessness" lie on a continuum: each involves unjustifiable risk-taking; they differ only in respect to the degree of the actor's deviation from the standard of due care.

Today, however, most jurisdictions reject this definition of "recklessness." Instead, a finding of recklessness requires proof that the actor disregarded a substantial and unjustifiable risk *of which he was aware.* [85] According to this prevailing view, the line between "criminal negligence" and "recklessness" is *not* drawn on the basis of the extent of the actor's deviation from the standard of reasonable care—the deviation is gross in both cases—but rather is founded on the actor's state of mind. Criminal negligence involves inadvertent risk-taking (we are saying that the defendant, as a reasonable person, *should have been aware* of the substantial and unjustifiable risk he was taking); in contrast, recklessness implicates *subjective* fault, in that the actor was aware of the substantial and unjustifiable risk he was taking, and yet he consciously disregarded it and proceeded with his dangerous conduct.

[E]—"Malice"

"Malice" is a critical common law and statutory *mens rea* term. Although the term has a more complicated meaning in the context of murder,[86] in most circumstances a person acts with "malice" if he *intentionally* or *recklessly* causes the social harm prohibited by the offense.[87] Although language to the contrary can be found in some common law treatises,[88] the term "malice" is rarely employed in its popular, nonlegal sense, as meaning "ill-will," "spite," or "wickedness."

For example, in *Regina v. Cunningham,*[89] *D*, a thief, wrenched a gas meter from gas pipes in the cellar of a building in which *V* resided, in order to steal coins inside the meter. Gases escaped into *V*'s living quarters, unintentionally harming *V*. *D* was prosecuted for "maliciously" causing the injury to *V*. The trial judge defined "malice" in terms of wickedness; in that sense, *D* did act maliciously.

But, according to the proper definition of "malice" described above, the issue is more complicated. *D* did not intentionally cause the social harm to *V*, but did he recklessly cause it? By tearing the meter from the gas pipes, *D* arguably disregarded a substantial and unjustifiable risk to *V*'s safety; if *D* was aware of this risk and

---

[85] *Farmer v. Brennan,* 114 S.Ct. 1970, 1978-79 (1994); Williams at § 23.

[86] See § 31.02[B][2], *infra.*

[87] *Regina v. Cunningham,* 41 Crim. App. 155, 2 Q.B. 396, 2 All. E.R. 412 (1957) (Court of Criminal Appeal).

[88] 4 Blackstone at *198-99 (in the context of common law murder, defining "malice aforethought" as "any evil design in general; the dictate of a wicked, depraved, and malignant heart").

[89] *Regina v. Cunningham,* 41 Crim. App. 155, 2 Q.B. 396, 2 All. E.R. 412 (1957) (Court of Criminal Appeal). The case is more fully discussed in § 10.02[B], *supra.*

consciously disregarded it, he recklessly caused the social harm and, therefore, acted with "malice." If he did not have such foresight—if he should have been aware of the risk, but was not—then he acted in a criminally negligent manner, which is an insufficient *mens rea* to prove "malice."

§ 10.05   Statutory Interpretation: What Elements Does a *Mens Rea* Term Modify? [90]

In *People v. Ryan*,[91] *D* asked *X*, a friend, to order and receive a shipment of hallucinogenic mushrooms on his behalf, which *X* did. Tipped off to the transaction, the police intervened, took *X* into custody, and subsequently arrested *D* for attempted criminal possession of a controlled substance. A subsequent chemical test indicated that the shipment contained approximately two pounds of mushrooms, which contained 796 milligrams of psilocybin, a hallucinogen. *D* was charged with "knowingly possess[ing] . . . 625 milligrams [or more] of a hallucinogen." At his trial, *D* did not deny that he attempted to possess the hallucinogenic mushrooms, but he claimed that he did not know that the mushrooms contained 625 milligrams or more of the hallucinogen.

Was *D* guilty of the offense charged? *D* committed the *actus reus* of the offense, but did he have the requisite *mens rea*? When "*mens rea*" was simply a synonym for "moral blameworthiness," this issue rarely arose, because no *mens rea* term was expressed in the definition of most offenses.[92] The only question to be answered, therefore, was whether the defendant, in committing the *actus reus* of the crime, manifested a morally blameworthy state of mind.

Today, the definitions of many, if not most, felonies expressly include a specific mental-state element, in this case "knowingly." In *Ryan*, *D* admitted that he knew that the mushrooms contained hallucinogens, so it may fairly be said that he "knowingly possessed" the hallucinogens. The critical question, however, is whether the *mens rea* term "knowingly" also modifies the statutory attendant circumstance of the weight of the controlled substance.

Unfortunately, there is no foolproof answer to this question. The general rule is that if a statute is ambiguous, the court should determine the legislature's intent, which may in turn require consideration of legislative debates and common law history (if the statute was derived from the common law). In seeking to determine the legislature's intent, the court will look at the policies underlying the law, in order to determine what interpretation of the statute would best promote that policy.

In seeking to divine legislative intent, a court will often consider the structure of the statute, taking into consideration rules of grammar. For example, if there is only one statutory *mens rea* term, and it is set out at the beginning of the statute, a court may interpret this to mean (as it did in *Ryan*) that the word modifies every *actus*

---

[90] See generally Michael Vitiello, *Does Culpability Matter?: Statutory Construction Under 42 U.S.C. § 6928*, 6 Tul. Envtl. L.J. 187 (1993).

[91] 626 N.E.2d 51 (N.Y. 1993).

[92] See § 10.02[B], *supra*.

reus element that follows it.[93] A different result would probably apply, however, if the *mens rea* term *follows* various *actus reus* elements, but *precedes* others, in which case the court is likely to conclude that the *mens rea* element applies in a "forward" direction, but not "backward." For example, assume that a statute is drafted in this form: "A person is guilty of a felony if he [Does X] with the intent of [Causing Y and Z]." Here, the term "intent" probably modifies Y and Z, but not X.[94]

If the lawmakers' intent still cannot be ascertained with any degree of confidence, courts often look to "background assumption[s] of our criminal law,"[95] one of which is that, in the absence of clear legislative intent to the contrary, some level of culpability should be required as to each material element of an offense,[96] although not necessarily the same level of *mens rea* as to each ingredient. Thus, in the preceding hypothetical statute, although a court would not likely conclude that the element of intent applies to X, it might still require some guilty state of mind, such as negligence, as to that element.

§ 10.06   "Specific Intent" and "General Intent"

The terms "specific intent" and "general intent" are the bane of criminal law students and lawyers. This is because the terms are critical to understanding various common law rules of criminal responsibility,[97] yet the concepts are so "notoriously difficult . . . to define and apply . . . [that] a number of text writers recommend that they be abandoned altogether."[98]

---

[93] Be careful, however, of statutes containing parenthetical phrases or clauses. Consider, for example, a statute that prohibits "intentional seizure of another person with intent to cause him, *without authorization of law*, to be confined." See *People v. Weiss*, 12 N.E.2d 514 (N.Y. 1938). Although "intentional" is set out at the beginning of the statute, and again preceding the italicized language, it is plausible that these *mens rea* terms do not modify the italicized words, which are separated by the commas. Thus, if *D* intentionally seized and confined *V*, but did so believing that he had authorization of law, he should be acquitted if "intent" modifies "without authorization of law"; he may be convicted if a determination were made that "intent" skips past the italicized words, because of the commas.

[94] E.g., *United States v. Yermian*, 468 U.S. 63 (1984) (a federal offense provided that "whoever, in any matter within the jurisdiction of any department or agency of the United States knowingly . . . makes any false . . . statements . . . shall be fined . . . ."; *D* admitted that he knowingly made false statements in a questionnaire sent by his employer to the Department of Defense, but he denied that he knew that the false statements pertained to any "matter within the jurisdiction of any department or agency of the United States"; held: "knowingly" did not modify the introductory phrase).

[95] *Liparota v. United States*, 471 U.S. 419, 426 (1985).

[96] *United States v. X-Citement Video, Inc.*, 115 S.Ct. 464, 469 (1994) ("the presumption in favor of a scienter requirement should apply to each of the statutory elements which criminalize otherwise innocent conduct").

[97] E.g., see §§ 12.05-.06 (mistake of fact); 13.02[D] (mistake of law); 24.03 [B] (voluntary intoxication); and 26.02[B][3] (diminished capacity), *infra*.

[98] *People v Hood*, 462 P.2d 370, 377 (Cal. 1969).

Historically, "general intent" referred to any offense for which the only *mens rea* required was a blameworthy state of mind; "specific intent" was meant to emphasize that the definition of the offense expressly required proof of a particular mental state.[99] In other words, an offense that only required proof of "*mens rea*" in the "culpability" sense of the term was a "general intent" crime; offenses that required "*mens rea*" in the "elemental" sense were "specific intent" in nature.[100] This dichotomy was understandable: the definitions of most common law and early statutory offenses were silent in regard to *mens rea*; those offenses that expressly required a particular state of mind—e.g., murder ("malice aforethought"), larceny ("intent to steal"), and burglary ("intent to commit a felony [inside a dwelling]"— stood out, and were thus denominated as "specific intent."

Today, however, most criminal statutes expressly include a *mens rea* term, or a particular state of mind is judicially implied, so the distinction between "general" and "specific" intent is much more difficult to draw. Making matters worse, there is no universally accepted meaning to the terms. Generally speaking, however, a "specific intent" offense is one in which the definition of the crime: (1) includes an intent to do some future act, or achieve some further consequence (i.e., a special motive for the conduct), *beyond the conduct or result that constitutes the actus reus of the offense*;[101] or (2) provides that the actor must be aware of a statutory attendant circumstance. An offense that does not contain either of these features is termed "general intent."

For example, consider common law burglary, defined as "breaking and entering of the dwelling of another in the nighttime with intent to commit a felony."[102] The *actus reus* of this offense is complete when the offender breaks and enters another person's dwelling at night; he need not commit a felony inside to be convicted of burglary. The requisite *mens rea*, therefore, pertains to a planned future act (commission of a felony) that is not part of the *actus reus*. Consequently, common law burglary is a specific-intent offense.

Similarly, larceny is the trespassory taking and carrying away of the personal property of another *with the intent to permanently deprive the other person of his property* ("intent to steal"). That is, a person is not guilty of the offense if he, merely, intentionally takes and carries away another person's property. Instead, he must intend to achieve a further consequence, namely, to deprive the owner of the property permanently (and not, simply, temporarily). Therefore, larceny is a specific-intent offense.

Another example of a specific-intent crime would be "receiving stolen property with knowledge that it is stolen." According to this definition, the actor who receives the stolen property (the *actus reus* of the offense) must have knowledge of the attendant circumstance that the property was "stolen" in nature.

---

[99] *Commonwealth v. Sibinich*, 598 N.E.2d 673, 675 n.2, 676 n.3 (Mass. App. Ct. 1992).

[100] For discussion of the "culpability" and "elemental" meanings of "*mens rea*," see § 10.02, *supra*.

[101] *People v. Hood*, 462 P.2d at 378; *Dorador v. State*, 573 P.2d 839, 843 (Wyo. 1978).

[102] See 4 Blackstone at *224.

In contrast to these offenses, consider battery, often defined statutorily as "intentional application of unlawful force upon another." This is a general-intent crime, for the simple reason that the definition does not contain any specific intent. The only mental state required in its definition is the intent to "apply force upon another," the *actus reus* of the crime.

§ 10.07   Model Penal Code[103]

No aspect of the Model Penal Code has had greater influence on the direction of American criminal law than § 2.02 of the Code, which sets out the "General Requirements of Culpability." As one commentator has observed, "[t]he Code's provisions concerning culpable mental states introduced both reason and structure to a previously amorphous area of Anglo-American law."[104]

[A]—Section 2.02: In General

Section 2.02 takes an exclusively "elemental"[105] approach to the concept of *mens rea*. Subsection (1) provides that, except in the case of offenses characterized as "violations,"[106] a person may not be convicted of an offense unless "he acted purposely, knowingly, recklessly or negligently, as the law may require, with respect to each material element of the offense." In other words, the Code requires the prosecution to prove that the defendant committed the *actus reus* of the offense—*indeed, each ingredient of the offense*—with a culpable state of mind, as defined in the specific statute.

This provision is noteworthy in various regards. First, under the Code, a person may not be convicted solely on the ground that he acted with a morally blameworthy state of mind, i.e., the Code eschews the "culpability" meaning of *"mens rea."* Second, the common law distinction between "general intent" and "specific intent"[107] is discarded.

Third, the Model Penal Code would remove the clutter of common law and statutory *mens rea* terms, and replace them with just four carefully defined terms: "purposely"; "knowingly"; "recklessly"; and "negligently."[108]

Fourth, the phrase "material element of the offense," as used in § 2.02 and throughout the Code, includes "elements" relating to the existence of a justification

---

[103] See generally Ronald L. Gainer, *The Culpability Provisions of the Model Penal Code,* 19 Rutgers L.J. 575 (1988); Paul H. Robinson & Jane A. Grall, *Element Analysis in Defining Criminal Liability: The Model Penal Code and Beyond,* 35 Stan. L. Rev. 681 (1983).

[104] Gainer, Note 103, *supra,* at 575.

[105] See § 10.02[C], *supra.*

[106] A "violation" is an offense (but not a "crime"), for which no sentence other than a fine or civil penalty is authorized. Model Penal Code § 1.04(5). Section 2.05, rather than § 2.02, pertains to violations.

[107] See § 10.06, *supra.*

[108] Because "wilful" was one of the most common pre-Code statutory terms, see § 10.04 [C], *supra,* the drafters of the Code saw fit to deal expressly with the term: a person who acts "knowingly" satisfies the requirement of wilfulness. Model Penal Code § 2.02(8).

or excuse for the actor's conduct,[109] i.e., defenses to crimes. As a consequence, since § 2.02 states that one of the four culpability terms applies to *every* material element of the crime, this Section is also relevant in determining whether a person is entitled to be acquitted on the grounds of an affirmative defense.

[B]—Culpability Terms

[1]—"Purposely"

The term "purposely" has two definitions, depending upon whether the material element of the offense pertains to a result or conduct, on the one hand, or to an attendant circumstance, on the other. In the context of a result or conduct, a person acts "purposely" if it his "conscious object to engage in conduct of that nature or to cause such a result."[110] So defined, "purposely" is a mental state comparable to the first of the two alternative common law definitions of the word "intentional."[111] For example, in the airplane bombing hypothetical discussed in § 10.04 [A], the killing of *V*, *D*'s wife, was "purposeful" because it was *D*'s conscious object to take *V*'s life, but the deaths of the remaining passengers were not purposeful.

A person acts "purposely" with respect to attendant circumstances if he "is aware of the existence of such circumstances or he believes or hopes that they exist."[112] For example, if *D* enters an occupied structure in order to commit a felony inside, he has acted "purposely" regarding the attendant circumstance that the structure was occupied, if he was aware it was occupied or hoped that it would be.

[2]—"Knowingly"

The Code provides two definitions of the term "knowingly," one that applies to results, and the second that pertains to conduct and attendant circumstances.

A result is "knowingly" caused if the actor "is aware that it is practically certain that his conduct will cause such a result."[113] Thus, in the airplane bombing hypothetical, *D* knowingly killed *V*'s fellow passengers, assuming *D* was aware that

---

[109] Model Penal Code § 1.13(10)(ii).

[110] Model Penal Code § 2.02(2)(a)(i). The Code effectively applies the common law "transferred intent" doctrine. See § 10.04[A] [3], *supra*. Section 2.03(2)(a) provides that when purposely causing a particular result is an element of an offense, that element is established if "the actual result differs from that designed or contemplated . . ., only in respect that a different person or different property" is harmed. For example, if *D*'s purpose is to kill *X*, but he accidentally kills *V*, the requisite element of "purpose" is established. Or, if *D*, intending to set *X*'s house on fire, causes *V*'s home to burn down instead, *D* may be convicted of an offense prohibiting the purposeful destruction of another's property.

The Code also provides that a defendant is not relieved of liability for an offense if *less* harm occurs than it was his conscious object to cause. For example, if *D*'s conscious object is to kill two persons, but he only succeeds in killing one, the element of "purpose" is established. Model Penal Code § 2.03(2)(a).

[111] See § 10.04[A], *supra*.

[112] Model Penal Code § 2.02(2)(a)(ii).

[113] Model Penal Code § 2.02(2)(b)(ii).

his bomb would almost certainly kill those on board.[114] If *D* lacked normal mental faculties, or for any other reason had a distorted sense of reality, so that he was not subjectively aware that their deaths were practically certain to result, then a finding of "knowledge" would not be appropriate.

With "attendant circumstances" and "conduct" elements, one acts "knowingly" if he is "aware that his conduct is of that nature or that such [attendant] circumstances exist."[115] For example, if *D* fired a loaded gun in *V*'s direction, and was prosecuted for "knowingly endangering the life of another," *D* would be guilty if he was aware that his conduct endangered the life of another person. If he was not aware (perhaps because he did not see anyone in the vicinity), then *D* did not act "knowingly," no matter how obvious *V*'s presence was.

The same approach is used with attendant circumstances. If *D* purchased stolen property and was prosecuted for "knowingly receiving stolen property," *D* would be guilty of the offense if, when he received the property, he was aware that it had been stolen. In order to deal with the problem of "wilful blindness"[116] the Code includes a special provision that states that knowledge is established, if "a person is aware of a high probability of . . . [the attendant circumstance's] existence, unless he actually believes that it does not exist."[117]

[3]—"Recklessly" and "Negligently"

[a]—In General

Under the Code, a person acts "recklessly" if he "consciously disregards a substantial and unjustified risk that the material element exists or will result from his conduct." A risk is "substantial and unjustifiable" if "considering the nature and purpose of the actor's conduct and the circumstances known to him, its disregard involves a gross deviation from the standard of conduct that a law-abiding person would observe in the actor's situation."[118]

A person's conduct is "negligent" if the actor "should be aware of a substantial and unjustifiable risk that the material element exists or will result from his conduct."[119] The definition of "substantial and unjustifiable" is the same as that provided for in the definition of "recklessness," except that the term "reasonable person" is substituted for "law-abiding person."

"Negligence" and "recklessness," therefore, require the same degree of risk-taking: "substantial and unjustifiable." The difference between them lies in the fact that the reckless actor "consciously disregards" the risk, whereas the negligent actor's risk-taking is inadvertent. This tracks the modern common law approach to these

---

[114] Observe, therefore, that the common law term "intent" is separated into two Model Code terms, "purposely" and "knowingly." This separation permits the legislature, if it chooses to do so, to make finer culpability distinctions than the common law permits.

[115] Model Penal Code § 2.02(2)(b)(i).

[116] See § 10.04[B], *supra.*

[117] Model Penal Code § 2.02(7).

[118] Model Penal Code § 2.02(2)(c).

[119] Model Penal Code § 2.02(d).

doctrines; indeed, it is fair to say that the Model Penal Code influenced modern courts, and not vice-versa, in this regard.

[b]—Nature of the "Reasonable Person"

The conduct of the "reasonable person" (and "law-abiding person" in the context of "recklessness") is evaluated from the perspective of a person "in the actor's situation." This phrase is ambiguous, but the Commentary opines that physical characteristics, such as an actor's blindness, or the fact that he has just suffered a heart attack, "would certainly be facts to be considered in judgment involving criminal liability,"[120] but hereditary factors, and matters of intelligence and temperament, may not properly be considered.

[C]—Principles of Statutory Interpretation

The Model Code provides solutions to some of the difficult problems of statutory interpretation that have confounded courts dealing with pre-Code statutes.[121] First, according to § 2.02(4), if a statute defining an offense "prescribes the kind of culpability that is sufficient for the commission of the offense, without distinguishing among the material elements thereof," a court will interpret such *mens rea* provision as applying to *every* material element of the offense, "unless a contrary purpose plainly appears." In other words, a single *mens rea* term—whatever it is—modifies each *actus reus* element of the offense, absent a plainly contrary purpose of the legislature.

For example, § 212.3 (False Imprisonment) provides, in part, that it is an offense to "knowingly restrain another unlawfully." Applying § 2.02(4), this means that the prosecution must prove that the defendant knowingly restrained the victim, *and* that he knew that the restraint was unlawful.[122]

In contrast, if the single *mens rea* term is placed in the middle of the statute, i.e., some material elements of the offense precede the culpability term and some come after, this would suggest a contrary purpose. For example, § 221.1 (Burglary) provides in part that it is an offense to "enter an occupied structure with purpose to commit a crime therein." The placement of "purpose" after the phrase "enter an occupied structure" plainly demonstrates the drafters' intention not to require "purpose" as to the preceding phrase (or else it would have placed the word "purposely" at the start).[123]

Does this mean that *no mens rea* is required as to the "entry of the occupied structure"? No. When the definition of a criminal offense is silent regarding the matter of culpability as to *any* material element of the offense, such as here, subsection (3) of § 2.02 provides an interpretive solution: the material element "is established if a person acts purposely, knowingly, or recklessly."

---

[120] American Law Institute, Comment to § 2.02, at 242.

[121] See § 10.05, *supra.*

[122] American Law Institute, Comment to § 2.02, at 245-46.

[123] See American Law Institute, Comment to § 2.02, at 246.

Here, the phrase "entry of an occupied structure" actually consists of two material elements: (1) the conduct element of "entry"; and (2) the attendant circumstance that the entry be of an "occupied structure." Therefore, according to § 2.02(3), a person may not be convicted of burglary under the Code, unless he purposely, knowingly, or recklessly entered an occupied structure (with the purpose to commit a crime inside). For example, if *D*, with the purpose to commit a crime therein, entered an occupied structure, *believing it was unoccupied*, he could *not* be convicted of burglary if he was negligent in his belief that the structure was unoccupied. He could be convicted, however, if he was reckless in this regard.

CHAPTER 11

STRICT LIABILITY

§ 11.01 Chapter Overview[1]

The subject of strict liability, or conviction in the absence of *mens rea*, arises in two contexts: in relation to strict-liability *doctrines* and to strict-liability *crimes*. A strict-liability doctrine is a rule of criminal responsibility that authorizes the conviction of a morally innocent person for violation of an offense that, by definition, requires proof of a *mens rea*. An example of such a doctrine is the rule that a person who misunderstands a criminal law, even one that contains an element of *mens rea*, may be punished for violating it, even if that person's mistake was reasonable. Strict-liability doctrines such as this one are discussed, as relevant, elsewhere in the Text.[2]

The focus of this chapter is on strict-liability offenses, or crimes that, by definition, do not contain a *mens rea* requirement regarding one or more elements of the *actus reus*. This chapter considers the nature, wisdom, and constitutionality of such offenses.[3]

---

[1] See generally Hall at 325-59; Sanford H. Kadish, *The Decline of Innocence*, 26 Cambridge L.J. 273 (1968); Laurie L. Levenson, *Good Faith Defenses: Reshaping Strict Liability Crimes*, 78 Cornell L. Rev. 401 (1993); Gerhard O.W. Mueller, *Mens Rea and the Law Without It*, 58 W. Va. L. Rev. 34 (1955); Steven S. Nemerson, Note, *Criminal Liability Without Fault: A Philosophical Perspective*, 75 Colum. L. Rev. 1517 (1975); Herbert L. Packer, *Mens Rea and the Supreme Court*, 1962 Sup. Ct. Rev. 107; Francis Bowes Sayre, *Public Welfare Offenses*, 33 Colum. L. Rev. 55 (1933); Richard G. Singer, *The Resurgence of Mens Rea: III—The Rise and Fall of Strict Criminal Liability*, 30 B.C. L. Rev. 337 (1989); Richard A. Wasserstrom, *Strict Liability in the Criminal Law*, 12 Stan. L. Rev. 731 (1960).

[2] See, e.g., §§ 13.01, 19.01, *infra*.

[3] Do not confuse "strict liability" with "vicarious liability." With a strict-liability offense, the prosecution must prove that *D* committed the *actus reus*, but does not have to prove any *mens rea* in regard to the *actus reus*. In contrast, liability is "vicarious" if *D* may be punished for the acts of another, i.e., if the *actus reus*, committed by *X*, is imputed to *D*. For example, a statute may provide that the owner of a bar or restaurant is liable for her employee's act of selling liquor to a minor. E.g., *Commonwealth v. Koczwara*, 155 A.2d 825 (Pa. 1959). Such liability is an exception to the general rule that criminal responsibility must be personal, rather than vicarious.

Often, vicarious and strict liability are joined: *D*, who lacks any personal *mens rea*, is held vicariously liable for *X*'s acts. Some courts have declared such statutes unconstitutional, when their violation results in imprisonment. E.g., *Davis v. Peachtree City*, 304 S.E.2d 701 (Ga. 1983); *State v. Guminga*, 395 N.W.2d 344 (Minn. 1986); *Commonwealth v. Koczwara*, *supra*.

§ 11.02　General Principles

[A]—Presumption Against Strict Liability

As discussed more generally in Chapter 10, "[t]he contention that an injury can amount to a crime only when inflicted by [*mens rea*] is no provincial or transient notion. It is . . . universal and persistent in mature systems of law . . . ."[4] As a consequence, the Supreme Court warned in *United States v. United States Gypsum Co.*,[5] offenses that do not contain a *mens rea* element have a "generally disfavored status," and "at least with regard to crimes having their origin in the common law, an interpretative presumption [exists] that *mens rea* is required" in federal statutes. Generally speaking, state courts apply the same presumption against strict liability.[6]

Courts consider various factors in determining whether a statute that appears on its face to be one of strict liability should be treated as such. Judge (later Justice) Harry Blackmun set out in *Holdridge v. United States*[7] various factors that may overcome the presumption against strict liability: (1) that the statutory crime is not derived from the common law; (2) that there is an evident legislative policy that would be undermined by a *mens rea* requirement; (3) that the standard imposed by the statute is "reasonable and adherence thereto properly expected of a person"; (4) that the penalty is small; and (5) that the "conviction does not gravely besmirch."

[B]—Public-Welfare Offenses

Until the middle of the nineteenth century, Anglo-American criminal offenses generally proscribed conduct *malum in se* (conduct inherently wrongful), such as murder, arson, rape, and larceny. Conviction for such offenses, which required proof of *mens rea*, was gravely stigmatizing, and the penalties for their violation were usually very severe.

After the advent of the Industrial Revolution, legislative bodies found it necessary to deal with conduct that, although not morally wrongful, could gravely affect public health, safety, or welfare. As a consequence, Congress and state legislatures enacted laws, most of which contained no express *mens rea* requirement, that came to be characterized as "public-welfare offenses." Such crimes involve *malum prohibitum* conduct (conduct that is wrong because it is prohibited). Examples of such offenses are those that prohibit the sale of intoxicating liquors to minors, and impure food and drugs to the public, as well as traffic and motor-vehicle regulations.[8]

---

[4] *Morissette v. United States*, 342 U.S. 246, 250 (1952).

[5] 438 U.S. 422 (1978).

[6] E.g., *People v. Hager*, 124 Misc.2d 123, 128, 476 N.Y.S.2d 442, 446 (1984) ("What is certain is that the principle of statutory construction is one that requires, emphasizes and insists that intent be engrafted upon *every* element of the offense unless the intent to limit is patently clear.").

[7] 282 F.2d 302, 310 (8th Cir. 1960).

[8] Some scholars exclude public-welfare offenses from the class of wrongs called "crimes," treating them instead as "civil offenses." Perkins & Boyce at 880-86. Inasmuch as these "civil" offenses are prosecuted in criminal courts and can result in criminal punishment, this terminology is not convincing.

Courts usually hold that criminal liability may be permitted without regard to fault in the case of public-welfare offenses. The factors set out in subsection [A] often support such an outcome: (1) public-welfare offenses are not derived from the common law; (2) a single violation of such an offense, e.g., production of an impure drug, can simultaneously injure a great number of people, which may explain the legislature's desire to disregard questions of personal moral guilt, in favor of a "sense of the importance of collective interests"[9] (3) the standard imposed by the law, e.g., "do not sell alcohol to minors," or "be in possession of an unexpired license when driving a motor vehicle," is reasonable; (4) the penalty for violation is relatively minor, sometimes involving only a fine; and (5) conviction rarely damages the reputation of the violator.

[C]—Non-Public-Welfare Offenses

A few traditional, i.e., non-public-welfare, offenses permit conviction in the absence of proof that the defendant possessed a *mens rea* regarding a material element of the offense. For example, in many states, the offense of statutory rape, i.e., consensual intercourse with an underage female, is characterized as "strict liability" because the statute does not require, and most courts have not implied, any *mens rea* element regarding the defendant's knowledge of the girl's age. That is, a male may be convicted of statutory rape, even if he reasonably believed that the female was old enough to consent to intercourse.

Traditional strict-liability offenses differ from their public-welfare counterparts in at least two regards. First, whereas public-welfare crimes usually carry only minor penalties, traditional strict-liability offenses often result in severe punishment. Second, traditional strict-liability crimes sometime involve conduct *malum in se*. Violators of such laws, therefore, are apt to be stigmatized, although proof of moral fault was not required. Therefore, strict-liability non-public-welfare offenses are aberrant.

§ 11.03 Policy Debate Regarding Strict-Liability Offenses[10]

[A]—Justification for Strict Liability

Most modern criminal law scholars do not look kindly upon the abandonment of the *mens rea* requirement. Such support for strict liability as exists is largely limited to its use in the enforcement of public-welfare offenses, and is premised on utilitarian grounds.

As developed elsewhere,[11] the requirement of *mens rea* is consistent with the retributive principle that one who does not choose to cause social harm, and who is not otherwise morally to blame for its commission, does not deserve to be punished. In most circumstances, society places the interest of the blameless harmdoer

---

[9] Sayre, Note 1, *supra*, at 67.

[10] See generally Nemerson, Note 1, *supra*; Singer, Note 1, *supra*; and Wasserstrom, Note 1, *supra*.

[11] See § 10.03[B], *supra*.

above its concern for deterring social harm, by requiring proof of the actor's *mens rea.*

Society balances the competing interests differently with public-welfare offenses. Punishing innocent actors is still retributively unfair, but the penalties attached to such offenses usually are slight. Society is willing to permit this "mitigated unfairness"[12] to the individual, in order more effectively to deter socially dangerous conduct.

Among the utilitarian arguments for strict liability are: (1) the absence of a *mens rea* requirement may have the desirable effect of keeping a relatively large class of people, namely those who doubt their capacity to act safely, from participating in dangerous activities, such as manufacturing drugs or other dangerous instrumentalities; (2) those who do choose to engage in the risky activity will act with greater caution in light of the strict-liability nature of the law; and (3) an inquiry into the actor's *mens rea* "would exhaust courts, which have to deal with thousands of 'minor' infractions every day."[13]

[B]—Alternatives to Strict Liability

Even if public-welfare offenses should be treated differently than traditional crimes, mechanisms other that the abandonment of the *mens rea* requirement are available to legislatures seeking to protect the public. First, a legislature might require proof of recklessness, but set much higher penalties, including stiff prison sentences, for violation of public-welfare offenses. This approach with a non-corporate defendant[14] might be a more effective means of deterring dangerous conduct.

Second, a legislature might retain the minor penalties that apply to public-welfare offenses, but require proof of an extremely low level of *mens rea*, such as civil negligence.

Third, a legislature might continue to define public-welfare offenses in strict-liability terms, but permit a "lack of *mens rea*" affirmative defense.[15] For example, if a person sold liquor to a minor, she would be convicted unless she persuaded the factfinder by a preponderance of the evidence that she took all reasonable care to determine the customer's age.

[C]—Lady Wootton's Proposal[16]

British criminologist Lady Barbara Wootton has advanced a dramatic proposal: she would dispense with the requirement of *mens rea* for *all* criminal offenses. All that would be required for conviction is proof that the person charged with the crime

---

[12] The unfairness is not really mitigated. If a person has a moral right not to be punished in the absence of moral blameworthiness, as retributivist principles would suggest, that right is no less violated simply because the punishment imposed is slight.

[13] Singer, Note 1, *supra*, at 389.

[14] Corporations, of course, cannot be imprisoned.

[15] E.g., *Regina v. City of Sault Ste. Marie*, 85 D.L.R.3d 161 (1978) (Canada).

[16] Barbara Wootton, Crime and Criminal Law 32-57 (1963).

caused the requisite social harm. For example, *D1* would be guilty of theft if she nonconsensually took *V1*'s property. It would not matter to the issue of guilt whether *D1* knew the property belonged to *V1*, or instead picked it up thinking it was her own. Likewise, *D2* would be guilty of criminal homicide if she caused *V2*'s death, regardless of whether she maliciously shot *V2* or, instead, accidentally struck *V2* with her car on the highway as the result of an unforeseeable icy patch on the road.

Wootton's contention is not that *mens rea* is irrelevant, but rather that it arises in the criminal law in the wrong place. She would permit consideration of an actor's *mens rea* (or lack of it) *after* a finding of guilt, in order to determine what punishment or treatment, if any, is appropriate.

Wootton supports her proposal on utilitarian grounds. As she understands the concept of *mens rea*, its purpose is solely retributive in nature, in that it precludes conviction of "non-wicked" harmdoers. According to Wootton, however, the modern purpose of the criminal justice system is to prevent harm, not to punish persons for acting wickedly. The *mens rea* requirement, therefore, gets in the way of satisfying this goal.[17]

H.L.A. Hart has provided the best known rejoinder to Wootton's proposal.[18] He contends that there is a utilitarian justification for retaining the *mens rea* requirement: in Lady Wootton's system, "the occasions for official interferences with our lives and for compulsion will be vastly increased."[19] For example, every time a person strikes another person, even accidentally, this would constitute a criminal assault, requiring police intervention. This would be wasteful of finite police resources, would increase police power over individuals' lives, and make daily life vastly less tolerable.

§ 11.04 Constitutionality of Strict-Liability Offenses

The late professor Herbert Packer once summarized the constitutional law regarding strict-liability offenses this way: "*Mens rea* is an important requirement, but it is not a constitutional requirement, except sometimes."[20] Packer only partially had his tongue in his cheek.

[A]—Due Process of Law

In *United States v Balint*,[21] *D* and others were indicted for sale of narcotics without a required order form supplied by the Commissioner of Internal Revenue. The maximum penalty for the strict-liability public-welfare offense was five years' imprisonment. In a single sentence that cited dictum from an earlier opinion,[22] the

---

[17] See § 10.03[A], *supra*.

[18] See Hart, at 195-209; H.L.A. Hart, Book Review, 74 Yale L.J. 1325 (1965) (reviewing Wootton's book); see also Kadish, Note 1, *supra*, at 285-90.

[19] Hart at 206.

[20] Packer, Note 1, *supra*, at 107.

[21] 258 U.S. 250 (1922).

[22] *Shevlin-Carpenter Co. v. Minnesota*, 218 U.S. 57 (1910). Professor Packer has described *Shevlin-Carpenter* as "constitutional adjudication at its worst." Packer, Note 1, *supra*, at 111.

Supreme Court held that strict-liability offenses do not violate the Fifth Amendment due process clause. The Justices provides no principled explanation for this assertion, nor did they mention the offense's potential substantial prison sentence.

In contrast, in *Morissette v. United States*,[23] the Supreme Court spoke of the common law *mens rea* requirement in glowing terms, stating that it "is no provincial or transient notion. It is . . . universal and persistent in mature systems of law . . . ." Nonetheless, the Court observed that, "wisely or not," legislatures usually do not require proof of *mens rea* with public-welfare offenses, and that courts "not . . . without expressions of misgiving" have approved such statutes. With offenses that have evolved from the common law, however, the Court stated that "mere omission . . . of any mention of intent will not be construed as eliminating that element from the [crime]." For example, at trial, Morissette was convicted of conversion of government property that he had believed had been abandoned. The statute did not expressly require proof of an intent to steal property. However, because the statute evolved from the common law offense of larceny, which contains such a requirement, the Supreme Court construed the conversion statute as requiring this specific intent.

Morissette's finding of a *mens rea* requirement was not constitutionally-based. It left *Balint*'s constitutional holding intact in the context of public-welfare offenses. Moreover, the Court did not state that a legislature could not abandon the *mens rea* requirement with traditional criminal offenses; it held only that a requirement of *mens rea* would be presumed in the absence of a contrary legislative purpose.[24]

[B]—Cruel and Unusual Punishment

Grossly disproportional punishment violates the Eighth Amendment bar on cruel and unusual punishment. The Supreme Court has never ruled on the applicability of this provision to strict-liability legislation.

Arguably, under retributive theories of proportionality,[25] a person who causes social harm in a morally faultless manner, i.e., without any *mens rea*, should not be punished, although she may properly be subject to a civil judgment. At a minimum, following this reasoning, any significant punishment, such as incarceration, would be grossly disproportional to the offense.

This argument is very unlikely to succeed. As described more fully elsewhere,[26] the Supreme Court will almost always defer to a legislature's determination of the proper sentence for a non-capital offense, and the state may reach its conclusion on utilitarian grounds, if it wishes.

The Court considered the *mens rea* issue in *Shevlin-Carpenter* although the corporate petitioner was appealing from a civil, not criminal, judgment, and although the strict-liability issue had not been raised by the defense in lower court proceedings, as is ordinarily required.

[23] 342 U.S. 246 (1952).

[24] See § 11.02 [A], *supra*, for discussion of the factors that may suggest such a contrary legislative purpose.

[25] See § 6.03, *supra*.

[26] See § 6.05[C], *supra*.

§ 11.05   Model Penal Code

The Code "makes a frontal attack on . . . strict liability in the penal law."[27] Section 2.02, subsection (1), expresses the general rule that no criminal conviction may be obtained unless the prosecution proves some form of culpability regarding each material element of an offense. The only exception is found in § 2.05, which provides that the voluntary act and *mens rea* requirements do not apply to offenses graded as "violations," rather than "crimes." "Violations" are offenses that cannot result in imprisonment or probation but may result in fines.[28]

---

[27] American Law Institute, Comment to § 2.05, at 282 (footnote omitted).

[28] Model Penal Code § 1.04(5).

CHAPTER 12

MISTAKES OF FACT

§ 12.01 Chapter Overview[1]

D1, a hunter, shoots and kills *V1*, believing he is killing a wild animal. *D2* has nonconsensual sexual intercourse with *V2*, mistakenly believing that *V2* has consented. *D3* takes property belonging to *V3*, incorrectly thinking that he has permission to take it. *D4* drives above the speed limit because his speedometer is inaccurate.

In each of these cases the actor has caused proscribed social harm. One might also infer from the defendants' conduct that they intended to cause the harms inflicted. In fact, however, each actor was either unaware of, or mistaken about, a fact relevant to an element of the definition of the offense for which he might be prosecuted. *D1*, for example, did not know that he was shooting a human being, yet the death of a human being is an element of murder; *D2* erroneously believed that *V2* was willing to have sexual intercourse with him, which, if true, would negate the "lack of consent" element of rape; *D3* believed that he had the right to *V3*'s property, which, if true, would mean that he did not intend to steal the property; and *D4* did not know that he was speeding, which is the *actus reus* of the traffic offense.

The issue considered in this chapter is how a mistake or ignorance[2] of a fact relating to an element of an offense[3] affects an actor's criminal responsibility for

---

[1] See generally Fletcher at §§ 9.1-9.3.3; Hall at 360-76; Williams at §§ 52-73; Edwin R. Keedy, *Ignorance and Mistake in the Criminal Law*, 22 Harv. L. Rev. 75 (1908); Peter W. Low, *The Model Penal Code, The Common Law, and Mistakes of Fact: Recklessness, Negligence, or Strict Liability?*, 19 Rutgers L.J. 539 (1988); Rollin M. Perkins, *Ignorance and Mistake in Criminal Law*, 88 U. Pa. L. Rev. 35 (1939); Benjamin B. Sendor, *Mistakes of Fact: A Study in the Structure of Criminal Conduct*, 25 Wake Forest L. Rev. 707 (1990); Kenneth W. Simons, *Mistake and Impossibility, Law and Fact, and Culpability: A Speculative Essay*, 81 J. Crim. L. & Criminology 447 (1990); Richard Singer, *The Resurgence of Mens Rea: II—Honest But Unreasonable Mistake of Fact in Self Defense*, 28 B.C. L. Rev. 459 (1987); A.T.H. Smith, *Rethinking the Defence of Mistake*, 2 Oxford J. of Legal Studies 429 (1982).

[2] "Ignorance" and "mistake" are not synonyms. "Ignorance" implies a total want of knowledge—a blank mind—regarding the matter under consideration, whereas "mistake" suggests a wrong belief about the matter. See Williams at 151-52. Because this distinction is not drawn in mistake-of-fact cases, no effort will be made in this chapter to distinguish between the terms.

[3] It should be reiterated that the focus of this chapter is on factual mistakes pertaining to *elements* in the definition of crimes. Frequently, however, a defendant will allege that he was

the social harm he causes. As will become evident, the common law's resolution of this issue is complicated and, at times, questionable. The Model Penal Code's solution is straightforward and less controversial.

§ 12.02   Basis for Exculpation Due to Mistake

One aspect of the doctrine of "mistake of fact" is clear: a person's misperception of reality, even when not caused by insanity, intoxication, or some other unusual mental condition, may sometimes exculpate him for the harm that he has caused.

Why does a mistake of fact exculpate? Aristotle believed that a person is not morally responsible for his actions unless he acts voluntarily, and that "[b]y the voluntary I mean . . . any of the things in a man's own power which he does with knowledge, i.e. not in ignorance . . . ."[4]

Use of the word "voluntary" in this context is potentially confusing because the word has multiple meanings in the criminal law;[5] nonetheless, it points us in the proper direction. An actor who is mistaken about some fact "does not have the same kind of opportunity to avoid doing evil that he would have if he knew what he was doing."[6] Consequently, the mistaken actor's freedom of choice—and ultimately the moral basis for punishing him—is undermined.

Perhaps a better way to understand why a mistake of fact may exculpate an actor is to observe that what makes a person's mistaken action "involuntary" has more to do with his cognition (i.e., what he is aware of) than with his volition (i.e., his capacity to control his conduct). From this realization, "the trail leads plainly to *mens rea*."[7]

Unfortunately, if the trail leads to "*mens rea*," then the common law leads us down two paths. This is so because courts use the term "*mens rea*" in two ways: in a general sense to describe the actor's "vicious will," or his moral culpability for causing the social harm; and, in the narrower sense, to describe the mental state that is an express element of the offense. A mistake of fact may negate the actor's "*mens rea*" in either sense of the term.

In some cases, proof that a person was factually mistaken demonstrates that, despite appearances, he acted in a morally blameless manner, that his will was not

---

mistaken as to the existence of facts that would provide a *defense* to his conduct (e.g., D kills in "self-defense" because he mistakenly believes that V is a deadly aggressor). This subject is considered elsewhere in the Text. See § 17.04, *infra*.

A person may also be mistaken about some factor unrelated to the harmfulness or blameworthiness of his conduct. For example, D may be unaware of the fact that the person he has intentionally killed was standing on the Ohio side of the Michigan-Ohio border, and, therefore, he does not know that his murder falls within Ohio's jurisdiction. Such mistakes are never exculpatory.

[4] Aristotle, *Nicomachean Ethics* 1135a (W.D. Ross trans.) in 2 *The Complete Works of Aristotle* 1791 (Jonathan Barnes ed. 1984).

[5] See § 9.02[C], *supra*.

[6] Michael S. Moore, *Causation and the Excuses*, 73 Cal. L. Rev. 1091, 1149 (1985).

[7] Hall at 360.

"vicious," and that, therefore, he is not morally deserving of punishment for causing the social harm. In this sense a mistake negates "*mens rea*" in the "culpability" sense of the term.

A mistake of fact may also negate "*mens rea*" in the "elemental" sense. That is, because of a mistake, a defendant may not possess the particular mental state element required in the definition of the crime. When this occurs, the defendant ought to be acquitted because the prosecutor has failed to prove an express element of the offense. Understood this way, the rule that a mistake of fact is exculpatory is not a special rule; rather, "the law could be stated equally well without reference to mistake."[8] Either the defendant had the *mens rea* required in the definition of the crime, or he did not.

So understood, a mistake-of-fact claim is not a true defense. It is only a "defense" in that the defendant may have the initial burden to produce evidence that he was mistaken. The prosecution, however, must persuade the factfinder beyond a reasonable doubt that the defendant possessed the requisite *mens rea* of the offense (i.e., that *D* was *not* mistaken, or that his mistake did not negate the *mens rea*).[9]

§ 12.03   Common Law Rules: General Approach

Common law rules regarding mistakes of fact, although complicated, are understandable if the reader reconsiders the historical context in which the rules developed.[10] Originally, common law definitions of most crimes omitted any mention of a mental-state requirement; a person was guilty if he committed the *actus reus* under circumstances that manifested his moral culpability. A few crimes, however, included a particular mental-state element in their definitions. The latter offenses came to be known as "specific intent" crimes.

From these two types of crimes (and two types of "*mens rea*") came a dual approach to mistakes of fact. With specific-intent crimes,[11] common law jurists developed the rule that a mistake of fact is exculpatory if it negates the particular element of *mens rea*—the "specific intent"—in the definition of the offense. That is, the common law adopted an *elemental* approach to mistakes. However, with general-intent offenses, i.e., crimes that did not include an express mental-state element, the jurists sought to determine if the actor's mistake negated his moral culpability for the crime. This is the *culpability* approach to mistakes.

This dual system, as sensible as it might have been centuries ago, is difficult to justify today in light of the fact that, strict-liability offenses aside, virtually every felony or serious misdemeanor in a modern penal code specifies a particular *mens rea* element in its definition. Logically, therefore, the elemental approach should be

---

[8] Williams at 173; see also Fletcher at 687-90; American Law Institute, Comment to § 2.04 at 269-71.

[9] The difference between a "true defense" and a defense of the sort described here is clarified at § 16.02, *infra*.

[10] See § 10.02, *supra*.

[11] The concepts of "specific intent" and "general intent" are defined at § 10.06, *supra*, and should be reviewed here.

followed with all crimes today. Although the trend is in this direction, largely as the result of the promulgation of the Model Penal Code,[12] the common law's two approaches to mistakes, depending on whether the offense charged is characterized as general-intent or specific-intent, has endured.

As a consequence, the first step in analyzing a mistake-of-fact claim in a jurisdiction that follows common law doctrine is to identify the nature of the crime for which the defendant is being prosecuted: is it a strict-liability, specific-intent, or general-intent crime? The separate rules for each type of offense are described in the following chapter sections.

§ 12.04 Common Law Rules: Strict-Liability Offenses

The mistake-of-fact rule for strict-liability crimes is straightforward: under no circumstances does a person's mistake of fact negate his criminal responsibility for violating a strict-liability offense.

This rule is sensible. By definition, a strict-liability offense is one that does not require proof of any *mens rea*. Inasmuch as the basis for exculpation on the ground of mistake is that it negates the actor's "*mens rea*" in some sense of that term, the absence of any *mens rea* to negate necessarily precludes the use of this defense. For example, if *D* drives above the lawful speed limit because his speedometer is inaccurate, he will be convicted of a strict-liability driving offense, even if the speedometer's faulty calibration was unknown and unforeseeable to him.

Similarly, statutory rape ordinarily is considered to be a strict-liability offense, at least regarding the attendant circumstance of the girl's age. Thus, *D*'s erroneous belief, no matter how reasonable, that the female with whom he is having intercourse is old enough to consent, will not exculpate him.[13] Any perceived unfairness in this outcome is a function of the strict-liability nature of the offense, and not of the mistake rule pertaining to such offenses.

§ 12.05 Common Law Rules: Specific-Intent Offenses

[A]—Mistakes Relating to the "Specific Intent"

Typically, a defendant's mistake-of-fact claim in a prosecution of a specific-intent offense relates directly to the specific-intent portion of that offense. Consider two cases in this regard. First, *D1* takes *V1*'s property, incorrectly believing that the property has been abandoned and, therefore, does not belong to anyone.[14] *D1* is charged with larceny, a specific-intent offense defined at common law as the "trespassory taking and carrying away of the personal property of another with intent to permanently deprive the other of the property."

---

[12] See § 12.07, *infra*.

[13] E.g., *State v. Stiffler*, 788 P.2d 220 (Idaho 1990); *Garnett v. State*, 632 A.2d 797 (Md. 1993). A few courts permit a reasonable-mistake-of-fact defense in statutory rape cases. *State v. Guest*, 583 P.2d 836 (Alaska 1978); *People v. Hernandez*, 393 P.2d 673 (Cal. 1964); *Perez v. State*, 803 P.2d 249 (N.M. 1990). In such circumstances, statutory rape must be considered a general-intent offense. See § 12.05, *infra*.

[14] E.g., *People v. Navarro*, 160 Cal.Rptr. 692 (Ct. App. 1979).

In the second case, *D2* attempts to have sexual intercourse with *V2*, whom he believes is a consenting prostitute; because of a language barrier, he is unaware that *V2* has not consented to the intercourse.[15] *D2* is arrested before the intercourse occurs, so he is charged with the specific-intent crime of "assault with the intent to commit rape."

In each case, the defendant's mistake relates to the specific-intent portion of the applicable offense: *D1*'s mistaken belief that the property does not belong to anyone is relevant in determining whether he had the "intent to permanently deprive [*V1*] of the property," the specific intent of larceny; *D2*'s mistaken belief that *V2* consented to intercourse is pertinent to the question of whether he intended to rape *V2*, the specific intent in the prosecuted offense.[16]

The rule of law here is simple: A defendant is not guilty of an offense if his mistake of fact negates the specific-intent portion of the crime, i.e., if he lacks the intent required in the definition of the offense. Thus, if *D1* genuinely believed that the property he took had been abandoned, then *D1* did not intend to permanently deprive *V1* of the property; if *D2* truly believed that *V2* was consenting to intercourse, then *D2* did not intend to rape *V2*.[17] It does not matter that the defendants' mistakes in these cases may have been unreasonable under the circumstances. Acquittal follows inextricably from the fact that a person may not be convicted of an offense unless every element thereof, including the mental-state element, is proved, which did not occur here.

On the other hand, suppose that *D3* obtains heroin from *X*, believing that the substance is cocaine. *D3* is prosecuted for "knowingly receiving a controlled substance," a specific-intent offense.[18] In this case, *D3* may properly be convicted, notwithstanding his mistake, because his error, whether reasonable or unreasonable, does not negate the requisite specific intent. *D3* knew that he was receiving a controlled substance; he was only mistaken regarding its nature.

[B]—Mistakes Relating to the "General Intent"

In rare cases, a defendant will assert a mistake-of-fact claim that pertains to the general-intent portion of a specific-intent offense. For example, suppose that *D* touches a 13-year-old girl for his sexual gratification. He is charged with the offense of "touching the body of a child under the age of 14, with the intent of gratifying a sexual desire of that person or of the child." *D* claims that he mistakenly believed that the girl was 14 years old.

---

[15] *United States v. Short*, 4 C.M.A. 437, 16 C.M.R. 11 (1954).

[16] The assumption here is that "intent to rape" only exists if the actor knows or believes that the woman is not consenting.

[17] *United States v. Langley*, 33 M.J. 278 (1991); but see *United States v. Short*, 4 C.M.A. 437 (1954) (criticized by *Langley*; in *Short*, Judge Quinn, in his lead opinion [each of the three military judges wrote separate opinions, so there was no majority opinion] incorrectly applied the mistake-of-fact rule pertaining to *general*-intent offenses, and concluded that *D2*'s mistake as to the victim's consent had to be genuine and reasonable).

[18] This is a specific-intent offense because it requires proof that the actor was aware of an attendant circumstance of the offense, i.e., that he has received a "controlled substance."

In this case, *D*'s mistake does not relate to the specific-intent portion of the offense ("intent of gratifying a sexual desire"). Rather, his mistake involves the *actus reus* portion of the crime ("touching the body of a child under the age of 14"), which presumably must occur with a culpable state of mind if he is to be convicted. Because the specific intent of the crime is not implicated by *D*'s mistake claim, a court is likely to apply the rules relevant to general-intent offenses, as described immediately below.

§ 12.06   Common Law Rules: General-Intent Offenses

[A]—Ordinary Approach: Was the Mistake Reasonable?

The ordinary rule is that a person is not guilty of a general-intent crime if his mistake of fact was reasonable, but he is guilty if his mistake was unreasonable.[19] For example, suppose that *D* has nonconsensual sexual intercourse with *V*, whom he incorrectly believes is consenting. *D* is charged with rape, defined for current purposes as "sexual intercourse by a male with a female not his wife, without her consent." Inasmuch as rape is a general-intent offense, courts utilize the culpability approach to analyze *D*'s mistake of fact: if his mistake regarding *V*'s "consent" was reasonable, then he is not guilty of the offense; the *actus reus* of the offense has occurred, but *D*'s state of mind in regard to the prohibited conduct was nonculpable, i.e., his belief that she was consenting was one that a reasonable person might have harbored. If *D*'s belief as to *V*'s "consent" was unreasonable, however, then he acted with a culpable state of mind that justifies his conviction of the offense.[20]

This rule is not without its critics. The practical effect of denying the defense to those who act on the basis of an unreasonable mistake of fact is to permit punishment on the basis of negligence. Punishment for negligence is controversial in its own right,[21] but in the mistake context its potential unfairness is aggravated in two ways. First, when a crime is defined in terms of "negligence," a person is not ordinarily liable unless his negligence is "gross." With mistakes of fact, however, "unreasonableness" is not always defined in a manner that requires this heightened degree of fault. Therefore, the unreasonably mistaken actor, although perhaps responsible for conduct that would constitute no more than civil negligence, may be punished as a criminal wrongdoer.

Second, the mistake-of-fact rule permits conviction and punishment of a negligent wrongdoer as if he were guilty of intentional wrongdoing. For example, a male who genuinely, but unreasonably, believes that a female is consenting to intercourse

---

[19] *People v. Williams*, 841 P.2d 961 (Cal. 1992); *United States v. Adams*, 33 M.J. 300 (C.M.A. 1991); see Ind. Code Ann. § 35-41-3-7 (West 1986) ("It is a defense that the person who engaged in the prohibited conduct was reasonably mistaken about a matter of fact, if the mistake negates the culpability required for commission of the offense.").

[20] Notice the anomaly in the common law approach: if *D*'s mistake was unreasonable, he is convicted of rape; if he is arrested before the intercourse occurs, and he is charged with the specific-intent offense of assault with intent to commit rape, his unreasonable mistake of fact will exculpate him. See § 12.05, *supra*.

[21] See § 10.04[D][2][c], *supra*.

will be convicted of the same degree of offense, and will be subject to the same punishment, as one who has full knowledge that he is acting against the will of the victim. Although the former wrongdoer may be sufficiently culpable to merit criminal punishment, his culpability (and, probably, his dangerousness) is not of the same degree as the intentional wrongdoer.

[B]—Moral-Wrong Doctrine [22]

[1]—Background

As noted in the preceding subsection, the usual approach to a mistake-of-fact claim in the prosecution of a general-intent offense is to evaluate the mistaken actor's moral culpability on the basis of his blameworthiness for making the mistake. Moral culpability, however, can be measured in other ways. One can make a *reasonable* mistake and yet manifest a bad character or otherwise demonstrate worthiness of punishment. The "moral-wrong doctrine," as described below, was developed in this context.

It should be kept in mind that the moral-wrong doctrine represents a departure from the ordinary common law rule. It is most often applied in prosecution of sex offenses and crimes against family interests.

[2]—Rule

According to the moral-wrong doctrine, "there should be no exculpation for mistake where, if the facts had been as the actor believed them to be, his conduct would still be . . . immoral."[23] Essentially, the intent to commit an immoral act furnishes the requisite culpability for the related, but unintended, outcome.[24]

Consider the moral-wrong doctrine in light of the classic case of *Regina v. Prince*.[25] In *Prince*, D was prosecuted for "unlawfully tak[ing] or caus [ing] to be taken, any unmarried girl, being under the age of sixteen years, out of the possession . . . of her father." The girl in question, V, was only 13 years old, but the jury found that D honestly and reasonably believed that she was 18 years of age.

All but one of the seventeen judges ruled that D was guilty of the offense. Judge Blackburn, speaking for a majority of ten, interpreted the offense as one of strict liability as to the statutory element of the girl's age. The remaining judges, however, agreed with Baron Bramwell that *mens rea* had to be proven. The difficulty with this view was that if the court applied the usual mistake rule pertaining to general-intent offenses, D would have to be acquitted.

Bramwell voted to affirm D's conviction, however, on the basis of the moral-wrong doctrine. Pursuant to this rule, the first matter to be determined is whether the actor's mistake of fact was reasonable or unreasonable. If it was the latter, the usual mistake rule applies, and he may be convicted.

---

[22] See generally Williams at § 69.

[23] *Bell v. State*, 668 P.2d 829, 833 (Alaska. Ct. App. 1983).

[24] *Garnett v. State*, 632 A.2d 797, 813 (Md. 1993) (Bell, J., dissenting).

[25] L.R. 2 Cr. Cas. Res. 154 (1875).

Here, *D*'s mistake was reasonable, so Bramwell took the second step, which is to look at the factual panorama from the actor's perspective. Suppose that Bramwell had asked *D*, "What is it that you thought you were doing?" If *D* had answered candidly, he would have responded, "I thought that I was taking an *18*-year-old girl out of the possession of her father, without his permission."

The third step is for the court to evaluate the morality of the actor's conduct, *based on the facts as the actor believed them to be*. To Bramwell, *D*'s conduct as he supposed it to be— "the taking of a female of such tender years [as age 18] that she is properly called a *girl*" from the care and possession of her father—was morally wrong. Indeed, this conclusion was self-evident to Bramwell: "no argument is necessary to prove [the immorality of *D*'s conduct]; it is enough to state the case."

In light of Bramwell's belief that *D*'s conduct was self-evidently wrong, he imputed to *D* knowledge that he was acting immorally. Pursuant to the moral-wrong doctrine, a person who knowingly performs a morally wrong act assumes the risk thereby that the factual circumstances are not as they reasonably appear to be and that, therefore, his conduct is not only immoral but is also illegal. In *Prince*, *D* knowingly assumed the risk that *V*, whom he immorally took away from her father, was also underage. Thus, according to the moral-wrong doctrine, *D* was properly convicted of the offense. [26]

The moral-wrong doctrine is not triggered unless the defendant's conduct would be immoral had the situation been as he supposed. Suppose, for example, that *D* had known *V*'s true age, but instead had erroneously and reasonably believed that she was homeless and, therefore, not in anyone's lawful possession. In these circumstances, *D*'s answer to the question, "What did you think you were doing?" would have been, "I thought I was taking a homeless girl of fourteen off the streets and into my possession." Presumably, this conduct is not immoral. Consequently, *D* would not have to assume the risk that he was mistaken about the attendant circumstances. As his mistake of fact was reasonable, he would have been acquitted (assuming the offense was not strict-liability in nature).

[3]—Criticisms of the Rule

The moral-wrong doctrine is controversial. First, it permits conviction of a person who did not know, and had no reason to know, that his conduct would violate the law. In *Prince*, *D* may have known that his behavior was immoral; immorality and illegality, however, are not identical concepts. Even if all criminal offenses implicated immoral conduct (which, in light of the existence of public-welfare offenses, is not the case [27]), not all immoral conduct is illegal. The moral-wrong

---

[26] Accord, *White v. State*, 185 N.E. 64, 65 (Ohio Ct. App. 1933) (*D* abandoned his wife; when he left her she was pregnant, although he had no reason to know this; held: *D* was guilty of the offense of "abandoning one's pregnant wife"; according to the court, "[h]e must make sure of his ground when he commits the simple wrong of leaving her at all"; *Bell v. State*, 668 P.2d 829 (Alaska Ct. App. 1983) (*D* was charged with inducing a person under the age of sixteen to engage in prostitution; the court held that *D*'s claim of mistake as to the age of the prostitute was irrelevant, in part on the basis of the moral-wrong doctrine).

[27] See § 11.02[B], *supra*.

doctrine conflates the two concepts in a manner that runs afoul of the principle of legality. [28] That is, if Parliament had wanted to prohibit the "immoral" act of taking an 18-year-old female away from her parents (which is what D reasonably thought he was doing and for which, in essence, he was convicted) it could have done so, but it did not. A person should only be punished for conduct that the legislature, the lawmaking branch of government, has prohibited.

Second, the doctrine is founded on the premise that it is fair to punish a person for unintentionally committing the *actus reus* of an offense, if he knew that his conduct was immoral. Even if this is an accurate premise, there remains the question of whether the actor knew that his conduct was immoral. The moral-wrong doctrine, as it is applied, simply assumes that people know when their conduct violates social mores. Perhaps in the English society in which the doctrine developed, this was a fair assumption. In today's culturally heterogeneous American society, however, this will sometimes be an inaccurate conclusion.

[C]—Legal-Wrong Doctrine

[1]—Rule

Some courts apply a less extreme alternative to the moral-wrong doctrine, usually termed the "legal-wrong doctrine." This rule simply substitutes the word "illegal" for "immoral" in the description of the former doctrine, but is otherwise applied in the same manner. That is, D is guilty of criminal offense X, despite a reasonable mistake of fact, if he would be guilty of a different, *albeit lesser*, crime Y, if the situation were as he supposed. [29]

For example, assume that a jurisdiction prohibits the promotion of prostitution in the following manner: the intentional procurement of a person under 16 years of age to engage in prostitution constitutes a felony (crime X); the intentional procurement of a prostitute who is 16 years of age or older constitutes a separate, less serious, offense (crime Y). Suppose that D procures a 15-year-old female, *whom he reasonably believes is 16 years of age*, to perform acts of prostitution. Put somewhat differently, D has committed the *actus reus* of crime X, with the *mens rea* of crime Y.

Looking at the facts from D's perspective, he committed crime Y. Under the legal-wrong doctrine, however, he would be convicted of the more serious offense X. D intentionally did acts that he knew constituted a crime; [30] therefore, he assumed the risk that, unbeknownst to him or a reasonable person, the attendant circumstances were such that his conduct constituted an even greater offense than he imagined.

---

[28] See § 5.01, *supra.*

[29] Judge Brett applied this doctrine in *Regina v. Prince*, L.R. 2 Cr. Cas. Res. 154 (1875), discussed in subsection [B] [2], *supra*. D's conduct, as he supposed it to be, did not constitute any other offense, so Brett voted to overturn the conviction.

[30] The common law conclusively presumes that people know and understand the relevant criminal laws. See generally Chapter 13, *infra.*

[2]—Criticism of the Doctrine

The legal-wrong doctrine authorizes punishment based on the harm that an actor caused—i.e., the *actus reus* of the greater offense—while it ignores the fact that the actor's *mens rea* was at the level of the lesser crime. If society were concerned only with consequences, i.e., the offense is one of strict liability, this result would follow. With offenses that require proof of *mens rea*, however, punishment should be graduated on the basis of the social harm caused *and* the blameworthiness of the person who caused it.

For example, in *Bell v. State*,[31] the offense of promoting prostitution by procuring a person under the age of 16 was a felony, subject to substantial punishment; the offense of promoting prostitution by procuring someone older constituted a mere misdemeanor. Under the legal-wrong doctrine, the defendant would be punished as a felon, although his culpability was that of a misdemeanant. Under some circumstances, this may result in punishment grossly disproportional to the offender's blameworthiness.[32]

[D]—*Regina v. Morgan*[33]: Common Law in Transition or an Aberration[34]

*D*s, three men, were convicted of forcibly raping *V*, *X*'s wife. According to *D*s, *X* invited them to have intercourse with *V*, falsely telling them that if she struggled they should not worry, because she "was 'kinky' and this was the only way in which she could be turned on." At trial, the jury was instructed that *D*s should only be acquitted if their mistake regarding *V*'s consent was reasonable. On appeal, however, *D*s argued that this instruction was faulty, and that the jury should have been informed that even an unreasonable mistake of fact would exculpate them.

Under ordinary principles, the tendered instruction and resulting convictions would have been proper. Nonetheless, a majority of the Law Lords held that a man who acts on the basis of an honest but unreasonably mistaken belief in the woman's consent is not guilty of rape, because the mistake prevents the man from having the *mens rea* required to be proved for that offense.

Lord Cross explained the issue raised in the case this way:

[T]he . . . question to be answered in this case, as I see it, is whether according to the ordinary use of the English language a man can be said to have committed rape if he believed that the woman was consenting to the intercourse and would not have attempted to have it but for his belief, whatever his grounds for so

---

[31] 668 P.2d 829 (Alaska Ct. App. 1983).

[32] See *People v. Olsen*, 685 P.2d 52, 59 (Cal. 1984) (Grodin, J., concurring and dissenting) (discussing the proportionality issue in constitutional terms).

[33] [1976] A.C. 182.

[34] See generally David Cowley, *The Retreat from Morgan*, [1982] Crim. L. Rev. 198; R.A. Duff, *Recklessness and Rape*, 3 Liverpool L. Rev. 49 (1981); James Faulkner, *Mens Rea in Rape: Morgan and the Inadequacy of Subjectivism, or Why No Should Not Mean Yes in the Eyes of the Law*, 18 Melbourne U. L. Rev. 60 (1991).

believing. I do not think that he can. Rape, to my mind, imports at least indifference as to the woman's consent.

Lord Cross may have been wrong. The average person using the English language in the "ordinary" way would probably say that *V was* raped, even if *D*s believed that she had consented. What Lord Cross may have meant, however, was expressed more clearly by Lord Hailsham:

[E]ither the prosecution proves that the accused had the requisite intent, or it does not. In the former case it succeeds, and in the latter it fails. Since honest belief clearly negatives intent, the reasonableness or otherwise of that belief can only be evidence for or against the view that the belief and therefore the intent was actually held . . . .

Essentially, Lord Hailsham's remarks demonstrate that he was analyzing the defendants' mistake claim elementally,[35] a process ordinarily restricted to specific-intent offenses. That is, according to Hailsham, once it is established that the definition of a crime requires proof of "intention," then this *mens rea* term modifies each of the *actus reus* elements, including the attendant circumstance that the intercourse was nonconsensual.[36] Therefore, if *D*s negligently believed that *V* was consenting, they did not possess the requisite *mens rea* of the offense, i.e., the intention to act without *V*'s consent.

Morgan has proved to be a highly controversial decision, one from which the House of Lords has largely retreated in non-rape contexts.[37] The controversy is hardly surprising in light of the fact that the rule announced in *Morgan* would have authorized the acquittal of men who had forcible intercourse with a nonconsenting woman, and who manifested extreme indifference to her wishes.[38]

As a matter of *mens rea* analysis, however, *Morgan* is a sensible decision. As a matter of modern penal reform, the definitions of most offenses now expressly provide for some culpable mental-state element. The dichotomy between "general intent" and "specific intent," therefore, makes no sense in this context: either a person possesses the mental element required in the definition of the offense (in this case, the *mens rea* of intent) or he does not. The elemental approach used by

---

[35] See §§ 10.02[C], 12.02, and 12.05 *supra*.

[36] Notice: if the word "intentional" modifies the attendant circumstance of "without her consent" in the definition of rape, as Lord Hailsham assumes by his remark, he has effectively converted the offense of rape into a specific-intent crime. It would be as if rape were defined as follows: "intentional nonconsensual sexual intercourse by a male, with a female, not his wife, *with the knowledge or belief* that she is not consenting." If rape is a specific-intent offense, of course, the Lords' elemental approach to the mistake issue is correct. Historically, however, rape has been treated as a general-intent crime.

[37] See Cowley, Note 34, *supra. Morgan* is not followed in United States jurisdictions. See § 33.05, *infra*.

[38] The defendants' appeal in *Morgan* was dismissed—their convictions were not overturned—because the Lords believed that the trial judge's erroneous instruction did not prejudice *D*s' rights. In essence, they concluded that *D*s knew full well that *V* was not consenting, and that a jury would have reached the same outcome, even on the basis of a proper instruction.

common law jurists in the prosecution of specific-intent offenses, therefore, should be applied to all offenses, including rape.[39]

§ 12.07   Model Penal Code[40]

[A]—General Rule

The Model Code uses a straightforward elemental approach to matters of *mens rea*, including mistakes of fact. Section 2.02, subsection (1), states the general rule that one is not guilty of an offense unless he acted "purposely, knowingly, recklessly, or negligently, as the law may require, with respect to each material element of the offense." Specifically as to mistakes of fact, § 2.04(1) provides that a mistake is a defense if it negates the mental state required to establish *any* element of the offense. It is irrelevant whether the offense would be identified as general-intent or specific-intent at common law.

For example, consider how the facts in *Morgan*,[41] discussed in § 12.06 [D] of this Text, would be analyzed under the Code. Model Penal Code § 213.1 provides that rape occurs when "a male has sexual intercourse with a female not his wife if he compels her to submit by force . . . ." Because this definition is silent regarding the applicable *mens rea*, the Code provides that each material element is established if the defendant acted purposely, knowingly or recklessly with respect thereto.[42]

Therefore, *D*s in *Morgan* could be convicted of rape if they recklessly compelled the victim to have sexual intercourse by force, but they could not be convicted on the basis of negligence. For example, if *D*s realized that *X*'s statement to them about his wife's "kinkiness" might be false, and yet they consciously disregarded the substantial and unjustifiable risk that *V* was not consenting, i.e., they were reckless, their mistaken belief that she was consenting would not be a defense. In contrast, they would be acquitted if *D*s were not aware of this risk, but should have been, i.e., they negligently compelled her to have sexual intercourse by force.[43]

[B]—Exception to the Rule

The Model Penal Code provides one exception to the general rule described above. In a variation on the common law legal-wrong doctrine,[44] the Code provides

---

[39] This does not mean that a person who acts on the basis of an unreasonable mistake of fact must be acquitted. The legislature may redefine a statute to permit conviction based on a lesser *mens rea*, as Parliament did in reaction to *Morgan*. See § 1(1) of the Sexual Offenses (Amendment) Act of 1976 (permitting conviction on the basis of knowledge or recklessness as to the victim's lack of consent).

[40] See generally George P. Fletcher, *Mistake in the Model Penal Code: A False False Problem*, 19 Rutgers L.J. 649 (1988); Low, Note 1, *supra*.

[41] *Regina v. Morgan*, [1976] A.C. 182.

[42] Model Penal Code § 2.02(3)-(4). See § 10.07[C], *supra*.

[43] The Model Code definition of rape does not include the element of "non-consent," but the Commentary states that the statutory element of "[c]ompulsion plainly implies non-consent." American Law Institute, Comment to § 213.1, at 306.

[44] See § 12.06[C], *supra*.

that the defense of mistake-of-fact is not available if the actor would be guilty of another offense, had the circumstances been as he supposed. [45] However, unlike the common law legal-wrong doctrine, which maintains that the defendant is guilty of the higher offense in such circumstances, the Code only permits punishment at the level of the lesser offense. [46]

For example, under Model Penal Code § 221.1, a burglary involves the reckless entry of a building or occupied structure with the purpose of committing a crime inside. The offense is graded as a felony of the third degree, except that it is a felony of the second degree if the building entered is a dwelling of another and the entry occurs at night. Suppose that D enters the dwelling of another at night with the purpose of committing a felony inside, but he reasonably believes that the building he is entering is a store. That is, he has committed the *actus reus* of the more serious degree of burglary (felony of the second degree), whereas he has the *mens rea* of the lesser degree of burglary (felony of the third degree). According to the common law legal-wrong doctrine, D is guilty of the higher degree of burglary; under the Model Code, however, in harmony with his lesser *mens rea*, D will be punished as if he committed a felony of the third degree. [47]

---

[45] Model Penal Code § 2.04(2).

[46] American Law Institute, Comment to § 2.04, at 273.

[47] *Id.* at 272.

CHAPTER 13

MISTAKES OF LAW

§ 13.01 General Principles[1]

[A]—General Rule

Subject to very few exceptions, the common law rule is straightforward: *ignorantia legis neminem excusat*, or ignorance of the law excuses no one.[2] Expressed in slightly different terms, an actor's ignorance or mistake[3] of law does not negate the *mens rea* of an offense, as a comparable mistake of fact may do, because neither knowledge nor recklessness or negligence as to whether conduct constitutes an offense, or as to the meaning of an offense, is ordinarily an element of that offense. This "dogmatic common-law maxim"[4] is deeply imbedded in Anglo-American jurisprudence.[5]

[B]—Rationale of the Rule

[1]—Certainty of the Law

According to some common law scholars, the law is "definite and knowable."[6] Therefore, it may be argued that there is no such thing as a *reasonable* mistake of law: anyone who misunderstands the "definite and knowable" law has simply not tried hard enough to learn it.

---

[1] See generally Hall at 382-414; Douglas Husak & Andrew von Hirsch, *Culpability and Mistake of Law* in Action and Value in Criminal Law 157 (1993); Larry Alexander, *Inculpatory and Exculpatory Mistakes and the Fact/Law Distinction: An Essay in Memory of Myke Bayles*, 12 Law & Phil. 267 (1980); A.J. Ashworth, *Excusable Mistake of Law*, [1974] Crim. L. Rev. 652; Ronald A. Cass, *Ignorance of the Law: A Maxim Reexamined*, 17 Wm. & Mary L. Rev. 671 (1976); Bruce R. Grace, Note, *Ignorance of the Law as an Excuse*, 86 Colum. L. Rev. 1392 (1986); Livingston Hall & Selig J. Seligman, *Mistake of Law and Mens Rea*, 8 U. Chi. L. Rev. 641 (1941); Kenneth W. Simons, *Mistake and Impossibility, Law and Fact, and Culpability: A Speculative Essay*, 81 J. Crim. L. & Criminology 447 (1990).

[2] *United States v. International Minerals & Chemical Corp.*, 402 U.S. 558, 563 (1971); *People v. Marrero*, 507 N.E.2d 1068, 1069 (N.Y. 1987).

[3] "Ignorance" and "mistake" involve different states of mind. See § 12.01, note 2, *supra*. However, the terms will be used interchangeably in this chapter, except when distinguishing between them will enhance clarity.

[4] *People v. Marrero*, 507 N.E.2d at 1069.

[5] *Lambert v. California*, 355 U.S. 225, 228 (1957).

[6] 1 J. Austin, Lectures on Jurisprudence 497 (4th ed. 1879); see 4 Blackstone at *27 ("[E]very person of discretion . . . is bound and presumed to know [the law].").

147

At common law, this claim might have had the ring of plausibility. The courts recognized few criminal offenses, and those that existed involved conduct *malum in se*. Few people could seriously allege surprise in learning that stealing another person's property, intentionally burning another person's house, or unjustifiably taking another person's life was illegal.

However, even at common law, the principle that laws were definite and knowable was often a fiction. Criminal laws were not enacted by legislatures and published, as they are today. Instead, judges shaped the law on a case-by-case basis, which meant that the criminal law changed incrementally every time a new decision was handed down. Moreover, the definitions of some common law offenses were not models of clarity.[7]

Whatever its plausibility centuries ago, the "definite and knowable" claim cannot withstand modern analysis. There has been a "profusion of legislation making otherwise lawful conduct criminal (*malum prohibitum*)."[8] Therefore, even persons with a clear moral compass are frequently unable to determine accurately whether particular conduct is prohibited. Furthermore, many modern criminal statutes are exceedingly intricate. In today's complex society, therefore, a person can reasonably be mistaken about the law.

[2]—Avoiding Subjectivity in the Law

Jerome Hall has provided a more sophisticated explanation for the common law rule.[9] In stark contrast to the assertion that criminal laws are definite and knowable, Hall claimed that laws are "unavoidably vague" and that persons can "disagree indefinitely regarding the[ir] meaning." At some point, Hall reasoned, debate regarding the meaning of a law must end. Certain competent officials and institutions, particularly courts, must determine its meaning. Their official declarations provide an objective definition of penal provisions.

If mistake-of-law could excuse, Hall argued, the result would be that the law would lose its objective meaning; it would mean whatever a person subjectively (and perhaps incorrectly) thought that it meant. Yet, a "legal order implies the rejection of such contradiction." The legal system favors "objectivity to subjectivity and judicial process to individual opinion."[10]

Hall's thesis, however, misconceives the nature of a mistake-of-law claim. A legally mistaken actor does not claim, nor would her acquittal imply, that the law means whatever she thinks it does. An acquittal would not contradict the conclusion that she violated the law, i.e., that she did something legally wrong. Rather, an acquittal would simply mean that it is unfair to punish a person for violating the

---

[7] For example, sodomy was considered so shocking an offense that Blackstone not only did not define it with clarity, but he also refused to name it, calling it simply "the infamous *crime against nature*." 4 Blackstone at *215. Also, some offenses, e.g., common law larceny, contained exceedingly intricate rules that required judges (and inferentially citizens) to make "hair-splitting distinctions." Perkins & Boyce at 291.

[8] *People v. Marrero*, 507 N.E.2d at 1075 (Hancock, J., dissenting).

[9] Hall at 382-87.

[10] *Id.* at 383.

law, if an ordinary law-abiding person would have misunderstood the law in question. To punish in such circumstances "is contrary to 'the [retributive] notion that punishment should be conditioned on a showing of subjective moral blameworthiness.'"[11]

[3]—Fraud

A pragmatic justification for the rule is that recognition of a mistake-of-law defense would provide "opportunities for wrong-minded individuals to contrive [claims of mistake] solely to get an exculpatory notion before the jury."[12] Courts would become hopelessly enmeshed in insoluble questions regarding the extent of the defendants' knowledge of the law. Some false claims would doubtlessly succeed because the truth of the allegations "could scarcely be determined by any evidence accessible to others."[13]

As Holmes observed, however, "it may be doubted whether a man's knowledge of the law is any harder to investigate than many questions which are gone into,"[14] including the defendant's *mens rea*, and whether the actor suffers from an excusing condition, such as insanity. Moreover, the risk of fraud can be mitigated by allocating to the defendant the burden of persuasion regarding most mistake-of-law claims.[15]

[4]—Sacrificing the Individual for the Public Good

Ultimately the most plausible explanation for the general rule—"frankly pragmatic and utilitarian"[16]—comes from Holmes:

> The true explanation of the rule is the same as that which accounts for the law's indifference to a man's particular temperament, faculties, and so forth. Public policy sacrifices the individual to the general good . . . . It is no doubt true that there are many cases in which the criminal could not have known that he was breaking the law, but to admit the excuse at all would be to encourage ignorance . . . and justice to the individual is rightly outweighed by the larger interests on the other side of the scales.[17]

That is, if a reasonable mistake of law were a defense, this rule would foster lawlessness by encouraging ignorance of the law, rather than respect for and adherence to law. The best way to discourage ignorance is to enforce a strict rule that mistakes of law will not be countenanced.

Holmes's explanation provides the strongest rationale for the general rule, but it also suggests why it is controversial. A reasonable, law-abiding person can be

---

[11] *People v. Marrero*, 507 N.E.2d at 1074 (quoting White, *Reliance on Apparent Authority as a Defense to Criminal Prosecution*, 77 Colum. L. Rev. 775, 784 (1977)).

[12] *Id.* at 1073.

[13] 1 Austin, Note 6, *supra*, at 498.

[14] Holmes at 48.

[15] As a constitutional matter, the prosecutor must carry the burden of persuasion regarding one type of mistake-of-law claim. See § 13.02[A] & [D], *infra*.

[16] *People v. Marrero*, 507 N.E.2d at 1074.

[17] Holmes at 48.

mistaken about the meaning of a criminal law, or occasionally even be unaware of its existence. To the extent that a defense is denied to a defendant in such circumstances, this constitutes strict liability, subject tᴠ the moral objections that apply to such legislation. [18]

§ 13.02 Exceptions to the General Rule

[A]—Overview

Although the no-defense rule stated in § 13.01 [A] is strict, three mistake-of-law exceptions are recognized. They are described in this chapter section.

The first two exceptions (reasonable reliance and fair notice) are true defenses. That is, under the circumstances set out below, the defendant may be excused for violating an offense, although all of the essential elements of the crime, including *mens rea*, have been satisfied.

The third exception is different: here, the defendant claims that because of a mistake of law, she did not have the requisite *mens rea* to be convicted of the offense charged. To the extent that this type of claim is exculpatory, it is like a mistake of *fact* in that the defendant is acquitted for the simple reason that the prosecution has failed in its constitutional burden of proof regarding an essential element of the offense.

[B]—Reasonable-Reliance Doctrine

[1]—Personal Interpretation of the Law

A person is *not* excused for committing a crime if she relies on her own erroneous reading of the law, even if a reasonable person—even a reasonable law-trained person—would have misunderstood the law.

For example, in *People v. Marrero*, [19] *D*, a federal corrections officer, was arrested for possession of a loaded .38 caliber automatic pistol, in violation of a statute that prohibited the carrying of a handgun without a permit. *D* sought dismissal of his indictment on the ground that peace officers were expressly exempted from liability under the statute. The statutory definition of "peace officers" included "correction officers of any state correctional facility or *of any penal correctional institution*." As a federal corrections officer, *D* believed that he was exempt.

D's reading of the statute surely was a reasonable one. Indeed, the trial judge agreed with *D*'s interpretation. Nonetheless, an appellate court concluded, by a 3-2 vote, that he was not a "peace officer" within the meaning of the statute. Although this means that three of the six judges who considered the question interpreted the statute as *D* did, *D* was not entitled to claim mistake-of-law at his subsequent trial, because his mistake was founded solely on his personal understanding of the law.

---

[18] See §§ 10.03 and 11.03, *supra*.

[19] 507 N.E.2d 1068 (N.Y. 1987).

[2]—Official Interpretation of the Law

A person *is* excused for committing a criminal offense if, at the time of the offense, she reasonably relied on an official statement of the law, later determined to be erroneous, obtained from a person or public body with responsibility for the interpretation, administration, or enforcement of the law defining the offense.[20]

This exemption applies for various reasons. First, the threat of punishment can have no deterrent effect on an individual whose conduct has been authorized by an appropriate person or legal body. Second, a person who acts on the basis of an official, but erroneous, interpretation of the law has acted as we would want her to do, i.e., in obedience of the law as it was then understood, and, therefore, she lacks moral culpability for her actions. Third, the prosecuting authorities should come to court with "clean hands." It is fundamentally unfair for an official to authorize conduct, and then prosecute a person who relies on that authorization, if it later turns out that the original interpretation of the law was incorrect.

The reasonable-reliance doctrine is quite narrowly applied. For a statement of the law to be "official," it must be contained in: (1) a statute later declared to be invalid;[21] (2) a judicial decision, later determined to be erroneous, of the highest court in the jurisdiction;[22] or (3) an official, but erroneous, interpretation of the law, secured from a public officer in charge of its interpretation, administration, or enforcement, such as the Attorney General of the state[23] or, in the case of federal law, of the United States.[24] Although there is very little case law on the matter, there is precedent for the proposition that a person may *not* reasonably rely on an interpretation of the law provided by a local prosecuting attorney.[25]

---

[20] *Commonwealth v. Twitchell*, 617 N.E.2d 609, 619 (Mass. 1993).

[21] See *Brent v. State*, 43 Ala. 297 (1869); *State v. Godwin*, 31 S.E. 221 (N.C. 1898).

[22] *State v. O'Neil*, 126 N.W. 454 (Iowa 1910). The law is divided on whether a person may rely on a lower court ruling. E.g., *State v. Chicago, M. & St. P. Ry.*, 153 N.W. 320 (Minn. 1915) (recognizing the excuse); *State v. Striggles*, 210 N.W. 137 (Iowa 1926) (rejecting the defense); see also *Ostrosky v. State*, 913 F.2d 590 (9th Cir. 1990) (holding that the due process clause does not require a defendant to be allowed to rely on a lower court decision, if that decision has been stayed while the state appeals).

[23] See *Commonwealth v. Twitchell*, 617 N.E.2d 609 (Mass. 1993).

[24] But see *United States v. Barker*, 546 F.2d 940 (D.C.Cir. 1976), which involved the prosecution of two "footsoldiers" in the Watergate activities that resulted in President Richard Nixon's resignation. *X*, who was on the Nixon Administration payroll, instructed the defendants to break into *V*'s office in order to acquire files for the Central Intelligence Agency. *X* assured them that their conduct was justified under principles of national security. However, *X* lacked authority to provide an official interpretation of the law. Despite this fact, the court stated that "in certain situations there is an overriding societal interest in having individuals rely on the authoritative pronouncements of officials whose decisions we wish to see respected." The court concluded that public policy favored providing a defense to persons who act at the behest of a government official, as long as such reliance is otherwise reasonable. *Barker* is discussed in Stephen M. Kristovich, Comment, *United States v. Barker: Misapplication of the Reliance on an Official Interpretation of the Law Defense*, 66 Cal. L. Rev. 809 (1978).

[25] *Hopkins v. State*, 69 A.2d 456 (Md. 1949).

Even if a person obtains an interpretation of the law from the proper source, that interpretation must come in an "official" way. For example, a person may rely on an official "opinion letter" from the state Attorney General, formally interpreting the statute in question. However, an informal interpretation of the law will not do. For example, a fisherman may not reasonably rely on a quick interpretation of a fishing regulation, provided by a Fish and Wildlife Patrol Officer at the scene. [26]

[3]—Advice of Private Counsel

Reliance on erroneous advice provided by a private attorney is not a defense to a crime. [27] This blanket rejection of the defense is hard to justify. Society is far better off if a person acts on the basis of a lawyer's advice, than if she acts on her own untutored reading of the applicable law. A rule that encourages a citizen to seek a lawyer's assistance would likely promote, rather than discourage, knowledge of the law. [28]

Occasionally it is suggested, however, that if reliance on private legal advice could excuse a person's unlawful conduct, she might purposely turn to an unethical or incompetent lawyer in order to obtain advice that authorizes the improper conduct. [29] However, this argument exaggerates the dangers in recognizing the excuse. Unqualified lawyers exist, but ordinarily courts presume that attorneys are competent, unless evidence to the contrary is presented. [30] Nor is the risk of fraud substantial: an attorney is subject to professional discipline or criminal prosecution for fraudulent conduct. [31]

Probably the most serious problem with permitting the defense in these circumstances would be one of line-drawing. Should the advice of any lawyer qualify, or only advice from a specialist in the field? Must a person turn to an experienced lawyer, or may she turn to a new member of the bar? Ultimately, however, any reliance that would result in exculpation would have to be reasonable. A jury could determine whether the defendant made reasonable efforts to obtain accurate legal advice.

[C]—Fair Notice: The *Lambert* Principle[32]

At common law, "every one is *conclusively* presumed to know the law." [33]

---

[26] *Haggren v. State*, 829 P.2d 842 (Alaska Ct. App. 1992).

[27] *State v. Huff*, 36 A. 1000 (Me. 1897).

[28] See *Long v. State*, 65 A.2d 489 (Del. 1949) (not following the ordinary rule, and holding that evidence of *D*'s efforts to ascertain the law from an attorney was admissible to establish a mistake-of-law claim).

[29] See *State v. Downs*, 21 S.E. 689, 689 (N.C. 1895).

[30] See *Strickland v. Washington*, 466 U.S. 668, 687-91 (1984).

[31] A lawyer who purposely gives incorrect advice so that her client can assert a mistake-of-law defense could be prosecuted for obstruction of justice, or for conspiracy with her client to violate the statute in question.

[32] See generally A.F. Brooke II, Note, *When Ignorance of the Law Became an Excuse: Lambert & Its Progeny*, 19 Am. J. Crim. L. 279 (1992).

[33] *State v. Woods*, 179 A. 1, 2 (Vt. 1935) (emphasis added).

Nonetheless, the Supreme Court held in *Lambert v. California*[34] that, under limited circumstances, a person who is unaware of a duly enacted and published criminal statute may successfully assert a constitutional defense in a prosecution of that offense.

In *Lambert*, *D* was a Los Angeles resident and convicted felon. A local ordinance required felons residing in the city for more than five days to register their presence with the police. Violation of the ordinance was punishable by a maximum sentence of six months in jail, five hundred dollars, or both. *D* never registered, and was prosecuted under the ordinance. She was convicted after the trial court barred evidence of her claim that she was unaware of the law.

The Supreme Court ruled that her conviction violated the due process clause of the Constitution. The high court acknowledged that the common law rule that ignorance of the law is no excuse is "deep in our law." Nonetheless, it warned that the due process clause places limits on this doctrine. Specifically, "actual knowledge of the duty to register or proof of the probability of such knowledge" was a constitutional prerequisite to conviction for violation of the registration statute.

Literal application of this language would seem to invite fraudulent claims, and diminish the incentive of persons to ascertain the laws governing their activities.[35] Therefore, it is important to determine what features of the Los Angeles ordinance troubled the Supreme Court. Perhaps the Court's most significant observation was that *D*'s situation was atypical, because "we deal here with conduct that is wholly passive—mere failure to register. It is unlike the commission of acts, or the failure to act under circumstances that should alert the doer to the consequences of his deed."

This statement suggests that three aspects of the ordinance concerned the Justices: (1) it punished an omission (failure to register); (2) the duty to act was imposed on the basis of a status (presence in Los Angeles), rather than on the basis of an activity; and (3) the offense was *malum prohibitum*. As a result of these factors, there was nothing to alert *D* or a reasonable person to the need to inquire into the law.[36]

Lambert might require all three factors to be present in order to entitle a law violator to a constitutional defense. For example, suppose that a statute requires pharmacists to keep written records of all prescription sales of specified dangerous drugs. *D*, a pharmacist, is unaware of the law, and consequently fails to keep the requisite records. The *Lambert* doctrine would almost certainly not apply: although two of the three factors—(1) and (3)—are present, the act of selling dangerous prescription drugs should alert a pharmacist to the possibility of legislation relating to their sale.

What if a legislature enacts an uncommonly silly statute, in which one of the three factors is lacking? For example, suppose that a city enacts and duly publishes an

---

[34] 355 U.S. 225 (1957).

[35] American Law Institute, Comment to § 204, at 276-77.

[36] See also *United States v. Mancuso*, 420 F.2d 556 (2nd Cir. 1970) (holding that *Lambert* applied to a statute requiring a citizen to register with customs officials, on leaving and entering the United States, as a narcotics law violator, user, or addict).

ordinance making it a violation to water the lawn on any February 29th. *D* moves into the city, and waters the lawn on the first February 29th that arises, and is prosecuted for violation of the offense. The statute prohibits conduct—watering the lawn—rather than an omission; on the other hand, this conduct is not illegal unless it is February 29 (a status), and the conduct is *malum prohibitum*, not *malum in se*. In such circumstances, should *D* be permitted to testify that she was unaware of the law?

There was nothing about the fact that it was February 29 that would or should have alerted *D* to the consequences of her deed of watering the law. However, if *D* is provided a defense in these circumstances, this would seriously undermine the common law rule that ignorance of the law is no excuse, and would jeopardize the enforcement of many *malum prohibitum* offenses. Therefore, although the Supreme Court has never clarified *Lambert*'s meaning, and nine new Justices now sit on the Court, it is doubtful that the current high court would invalidate this or any similar statute.

[D]—Ignorance or Mistake That Negates *Mens Rea*

[1]—General Approach

As noted in § 13.01 [A], neither knowledge nor recklessness or negligence as to whether conduct constitutes an offense, or as to the meaning of an offense, is ordinarily an element of that offense. Therefore, a mistake of law, whether reasonable or unreasonable, will not usually negate any *mens rea* element found in the definition of the crime.

Under very rare circumstances, knowledge that the prohibited conduct constitutes an offense is itself an express element of the crime.[37] Somewhat more often, however, a defendant's lack of knowledge of, or misunderstanding regarding the meaning or application of, *another* law—usually, it will be a nonpenal law—will negate the *mens rea* element in the definition of the criminal offense.

For example, consider these three cases. *D1* takes her automobile to *X*, a mechanic, for repair. Upon receiving what she believes to be an excessive bill, she refuses to pay, whereupon *X* refuses to deliver the car. That night *D1* returns to *X*'s lot, finds her car, and drives it away. She is prosecuted for larceny.[38] *D1* is unaware of the fact that a lien law provides that a mechanic may retain possession of a repaired automobile until the bill is paid.

D2 is charged with rape after he has nonconsensual sexual intercourse with *V*. At the time of his actions, *D2* believed that *V* legally was his wife, thus taking his

---

[37] For example, the Michigan Campaign Finance Act makes it illegal for any person to make or accept a campaign cash contribution in excess of $20.00. The statute further provides that "[a] person who knowingly violates this section is guilty of a misdemeanor." Mich. Comp. Laws § 169.241 (1989). It is a defense under this statute, therefore, that the defendant, a campaign contributor, did not know it was against the law for him to make a cash contribution in excess of $20.00. *People v. Weiss*, 479 N.W.2d 30 (Mich. Ct. App. 1991).

[38] See *State v Cude*, 383 P.2d 399 (Utah 1963)

conduct outside the proscription of common law rape, which prohibits nonconsensual intercourse with a female "not his wife." In fact, the marriage ceremony in which he and *V* participated was legally invalid.

D3 is prosecuted for bigamy; she responds that she believed that she had obtained a legally valid divorce before remarrying.

What do these cases have in common? Each defendant presumably was aware of, and understood the meaning of, the criminal statute (larceny, rape, or bigamy) that was the basis of her of his prosecution. At the same time, however, each defendant was unaware of, or misunderstood the import of, another law (mechanics' lien law, marriage law, or divorce law), under circumstances in which this mistake of law arguably is relevant to the defendant's criminal liability. For short-hand purposes, a mistake-of-law claim of this sort will be termed a "different-law mistake," because the claimed mistake relates to a law other than the criminal offense for which the defendant has been charged.

When a defendant seeks to avoid conviction for a criminal offense by asserting a different-law mistake, on the ground that the different-law mistake negates her *mens rea*, the first matter for determination is whether the offense charged is one of specific-intent (as in *D1*'s case), general-intent (*D2*), or strict-liability (*D3*).

[2]—Specific-Intent Offenses

A different-law mistake, whether reasonable or unreasonable, is a defense in the prosecution of a specific-intent offense, if the mistake negates the specific intent in the prosecuted offense. [39] This doctrine parallels the rule relating to mistakes-of-*fact* in the prosecution of specific-intent crimes. [40]

For example, in *D1*'s larceny prosecution described in the preceding subsection, the prosecutor must prove that *D1* had the specific intent "to steal the property of another." For purposes of larceny law, the automobile belonged to the mechanic, [41] so *D1* committed the *actus reus* of larceny when she drove away in "*X*'s" car. However, because *D1* was unaware of the lien law, she erroneously believed that she had a right to possession of the vehicle, without paying the bill. Therefore, this different-law mistake negated *D1*'s "intent to steal the property of another." As she understood the legal situation, she was simply taking lawful possession of what rightfully was hers. *D1*, therefore, is not guilty of the offense, even if her mistake of law was unreasonable.

Cheek v. United States [42] provides another example of this rule. In *Cheek*, *D*, an anti-tax activist, failed to file federal income tax returns for six years, although he received wages each year as an airline pilot. As a result, *D* was charged with six

---

[39] *Id.*; *State v. Varszegi*, 635 A.2d 816 (Conn. Ct. App. 1993).

[40] See § 12.05[A], *supra*.

[41] Ownership of property is not determinative in larceny law. The offense is intended to protect the person in lawful possession of personal property. See Chapter 32, *infra*. In this case, the mechanic was in lawful possession of the car.

[42] 498 U.S. 192 (1991); see generally Michael E. Tigar, *"Willfulness" and "Ignorance" in Federal Criminal Law*, 37 Clev. St. L. Rev. 525 (1989).

counts of "willfully" failing to file federal income tax returns. For purposes of this statute, "wilfully" means "a voluntary and intentional violation of a known legal duty."[43]

D testified in his own defense at trial. He admitted that he had not filed personal income tax returns during the years in question, but he explained that during this period he attended seminars sponsored by an anti-tax organization that provided advice on tax matters. D introduced evidence that an attorney from that group indicated, among other things, that investment profits ("capital gains"), but not wages, constituted "income," under the Internal Revenue Code. Therefore, D testified, he believed that he was not required to report his wages to the Internal Revenue Service. As a consequence, D requested the judge to instruct the jury that D was not guilty of the offense if he believed, even unreasonably, that he was not legally required to report his wages.

The trial court did not instruct the jury as D requested, but the Supreme Court held that it should have done so: if the jury believed D's testimony, his mistake regarding the meaning of the term "income" under the Revenue Code (a "different law") disproved that he "intentionally violated a *known* legal duty."

[3]—General-Intent Offenses

Although there is very little case law on point, a different-law mistake, whether reasonable or unreasonable, apparently[44] is not a defense to a general-intent crime.[45] Thus, in the rape hypothetical described in subsection [1], D2 may be convicted of V's rape because the D2-V marriage was legally invalid. Even if D2's mistake regarding the legality of the marriage was reasonable—and, thus, D2 did not intend to have intercourse with a "female not his wife"—the common law does not exculpate D2.

This result does not conform with the comparable mistake-of-fact rule.[46] If D2 had made an equivalent mistake of *fact*, e.g., if D2 had believed, as a reasonable person, that he was having forcible intercourse with his wife, but it turned out that the victim was her twin sister, he would be acquitted of rape.[47] Presumably, the

---

[43] See § 10.04[C], *supra*.

[44] Perkins & Boyce state the following as to general-intent offenses: if "by reason of mistake of some nonpenal law the defendant lacked the [general] mens rea needed for guilt, the obvious conclusion is that he is not guilty; *but this has often been overlooked by the courts*." Perkins & Boyce at 1036 (emphasis added). Based on the "correct" view, these scholars state that "[i]n sum, . . . if the offense charged requires . . . only the general mens rea, this element can be negated by a mistake that is reasonable but not by one that is unreasonable." *Id.*

[45] E.g., *People v. Snyder*, 652 P.2d 42 (Cal. 1982) (D was prosecuted for the general-intent offense of "possession of a concealable firearm by a convicted felon"; D was denied the opportunity to prove at trial that she believed that her prior conviction for marijuana possession was a misdemeanor; held: the trial court's ruling was correct; D's different-law mistake, i.e., the status of marijuana possession as a felony, was irrelevant to her guilt for the firearm-possession charge).

[46] See § 12.06[A], *supra*.

[47] This statement assumes that a jury believes D2's mistake claim, and that the jurisdiction does not apply the controversial moral-wrong or legal-wrong doctrine. See § 12.06[B]-[C],

difference in result is a function of the very strong policy arguments against encouraging ignorance of the law. However, the outcome is inconsistent with the general principle that one who believes that her conduct is lawful, based on a reasonable mistake of law, has acted without culpability as to her mistake and, therefore, should be acquitted.

[4]—Strict-Liability Offenses

A different-law mistake, whether reasonable or unreasonable, is not a defense to a strict-liability offense. Thus, in the bigamy case noted in subsection [1], *D3* will be convicted of bigamy even though she believed, perhaps reasonably, that she had obtained a proper divorce before she remarried.[48]

As with the comparable rule regarding a mistake of fact,[49] this result is logical. By definition, a strict-liability offense contains no element of *mens rea* in its definition. There is no *mens rea* or culpability, therefore, that can be negated. Consequently, *D3*'s mistake-of-law claim is not relevant to her guilt.

§ 13.03 Model Penal Code

[A]—General Rule

Like the common law, the Model Penal Code does not generally recognize a mistake-of-law defense. Unless the definition of a crime so provides, "[n]either knowledge nor recklessness or negligence as to whether conduct constitutes a crime or as to the existence, meaning or application of the law determining the elements of an offense is an element of such offense."[50]

[B]—Exceptions to the General Rule

[1]—Reasonable-Reliance Doctrine

In nearly all respects, the Model Penal Code codifies the common law reasonable-reliance doctrine. A person's belief that her conduct is lawful constitutes a defense if: (1) she relies on an official, but erroneous, statement of the law; (2) the statement of the law is found in a statute, judicial decision, administrative order or grant of permission, or an official interpretation by a public official or body responsible for the interpretation, administration, or enforcement of the law; and (3) the reliance is otherwise reasonable.[51] A person is excused in these circumstances because,

---

supra. Assuming that he were acquitted, *D2* would be guilty of another offense, e.g., aggravated battery. And, of course, it should be kept in mind that this hypothetical assumes that the jurisdiction applies the common law marital-immunity rule in rape prosecutions. Many states have abolished the rule, so that a husband may be convicted of the rape of his wife. See § 33.06, *infra.*

[48] See *State v. Woods*, 179 A. 1 (Vt. 1935) (despite *D*'s reasonable belief in the lawfulness of a prior divorce, she may be convicted of violation of a statute prohibiting a person to be "found in bed" with another person's spouse).

[49] See § 12.04, *supra.*

[50] Model Penal Code § 2.02(9).

[51] Model Penal Code § 2.04(3)(b).

according to the Commentary, she has acted in law-abiding fashion, the danger of fraud is slight, and her claim is not unduly difficult to prove or disprove.[52]

Because of the danger of collusion, the Model Code, like the common law, does not recognize an excuse for reliance on the advice of a private attorney. The Commentary concedes, however, that cases can "be imagined in which a client is unfairly taxed with his lawyer's bad advice."[53]

[2]—Fair Notice

The Model Code provides that a defendant is not guilty of an offense if she does not believe that her conduct is illegal, and the statute defining the offense: (1) is not known to her; and (2) was "not published or otherwise reasonably made available" to her before she violated the law.[54]

The modern Commentary to the Code concedes that *Lambert v. California*[55] may require exculpation "in some extraordinary situations not reached by the section."[56] The Code defense applies only if the statute was neither published nor otherwise made reasonably available to the actor before she committed the crime. *Lambert* would apply to a situation in which the statute or ordinance *was* published, but the prohibited conduct itself would not alert an actor to the need to investigate whether there is a relevant statute on the books.

[3]—Ignorance or Mistake that Negates *Mens Rea*

The Model Penal Code requires proof of some culpable state of mind regarding every material element of an offense.[57] Furthermore, § 2.04(1) provides that a mistake of law is a defense if it negates a material element of the offense, or if the law expressly provides for a mistake-of-law defense.[58]

As noted in subsection [A], unless the definition of an offense so provides, neither knowledge (nor any other specified state of mind) as to whether conduct constitutes an offense, or as to the meaning of the law, is an element of the offense. Therefore, generally speaking, § 2.04(1) relates to "different-law" mistakes.[59] A claim that a different-law mistake negates the *mens rea* of the offense is handled in the same manner as a claim of a mistake of *fact* under the Code.[60]

---

[52] American Law Institute, Comment to § 2.04, at 275.

[53] *Id.* at 280.

[54] Model Penal Code § 2.04(3)(a).

[55] 355 U.S. 225 (1957). See § 13.02[C], *supra.*

[56] American Law Institute, Comment to § 2.04, at 276.

[57] Mode Penal Code § 2.02(1).

[58] For an example of the latter type of mistake-of-law defense, see the statute discussed in note 37, *supra.*

[59] For the meaning of "different-law mistakes," see § 13.02[D][1], *supra.*

[60] See § 12.07, *supra.*

CHAPTER 14

CAUSATION

§ 14.01 General Principles[1]

[A]—"Causation": An Element of Criminal Responsibility

D points a gun at *V*, intending to kill *V*. A few seconds before *D* pulls the trigger, *X*, independently[2] of *D*, shoots and instantly kills *V*. The bullet in *D*'s gun strikes the already dead *V*. Is *D* guilty of murder?

The answer is "no." A crime (here, murder) is composed of an *actus reus* and, usually, a *mens rea*. As described elsewhere,[3] the "*actus reus*" of an offense consists of a voluntary act (or an omission, when there is a duty to act) that results in the social harm prohibited by the offense. The "*mens rea*" is the culpable state of mind.

In the hypothetical, *D*'s conduct included a voluntary act—pulling the trigger of the gun. The social harm of murder—the killing of a human being by another human being—occurred. Moreover, *D* intended to kill *V*, a sufficient *mens rea* for murder. It would appear, then, that everything is in place for *D*'s conviction of murder. Common sense, however, tells us that *D* is guilty of attempted murder, rather than murder.

Common sense is confirmed by another prerequisite to criminal responsibility: causation. Analytically, "causation" is an ingredient of a crime's *actus reus*.[4] A careful look at the definition of "*actus reus*," provided above, indicates that it

---

[1] See generally Hall at 247-95; H.L.A. Hart & Tony Honore, Causation in the Law (2d ed. 1985); Katz at 210-51; Sanford H. Kadish, *The Criminal Law and the Luck of the Draw,* 84 J. Crim. L. & Criminology 679 (1994); Kimberly D. Kessler, Comment *The Role of Luck in the Criminal Law,* 142 U. Pa. L. Rev. 2183 (1994); Alan Norrie, *A Critique of Criminal Causation* 54 Modern L. Rev. 685 (1991); Paul F. Rothstein, *Causation in Torts, Crimes, and Moral Philosophy: A Reply to Professor Thomson,* 76 Geo. L.J. 151 (1987); Paul K. Ryu, *Causation in Criminal Law,* 106 U. Pa. L. Rev. 773 (1958); Stephen J. Schulhofer, *Harm and Punishment: A Critique of Emphasis on the Results of Conduct in the Criminal Law,* 122 U. Pa. L. Rev. 1497 (1974); Jane Stapleton, *Law, Causation, and Common Sense,* 8 Oxford J. Legal Studies 111 (1988); Judith Jarvis Thomson, *The Decline of Cause,* 76 Geo. L.J. 137 (1987).

[2] Throughout this chapter the word "independently" is used to describe a person who is not acting in concert with (i.e., is not an accomplice or co-conspirator of) another actor.

[3] See § 9.01[A], *supra.*

[4] Albin Eser, *The Principle of "Harm" in the Concept of Crime: A Comparative Analysis of the Criminally Protected Legal Interests,* 4 Duq. L. Rev. 345, 386 (1965).

contains three rather than two elements. In addition to the voluntary act (or omission) and the social harm, there must be a link between the two: the defendant's voluntary act (or omission) must "result in"—i.e., cause—the social harm.

As all offenses contain an *actus reus*, causation is an implicit element of all crimes.[5] As a practical matter, however, "causation" only turns up as an issue in the prosecution of "result" crimes, i.e., when the social harm of an offense is an unwanted result (e.g., the death of another human being).[6] Indeed, causation problems seldom arise outside the context of homicide prosecutions.[7]

Returning to the initial hypothetical, *D* will not be guilty of murder for the simple reason that *X*—not *D*—caused *V*'s death. *D* is not legally responsible for a result that he did not cause. He may be held responsible, however, for the harm he *did* cause, for example the social harm that results from the commission of an attempted murder.

[B]—"Causation": Its Role in Criminal Law Theory[8]

Causation analysis is so common a part of everyday thought processes that it is easy to ignore or downplay its importance in the criminal law. In fact, however, "causation" is a concept deeply imbedded "in human thought and expressed even among the most [ancient] people in their effort to understand 'the way of things.'"[9]

The role of causality in the criminal law is the same as it is in the evaluation of any everyday event: to determine why something occurred. More specifically, principles of causation assist us in deciding who or what among the various people and forces existing in the world should be held responsible for resulting harm.

---

[5] See Michael Moore, Act and Crime 219-20 (1993).

[6] Where is the causation requirement with a "conduct" crime? For example, if *D* is charged with attempted murder of *V* in the hypothetical shooting episode, isn't *D* guilty of an attempt precisely because he did *not* cause the social harm of the offense? Not quite.

As discussed in § 9.10 of the Text, "social harm" is defined broadly to include the endangerment of any socially valuable interest. As discussed more fully in Chapter 27, the social harm of attempted murder may be described as "a substantial step" toward a killing, or conduct that is in "dangerous proximity" to killing, etc. In such circumstances, the endangerment of a socially valuable interest (a human life) occurs.

Theoretically, *D* is not guilty of attempted murder simply because he performs the voluntary act of pulling the trigger of the gun (with the requisite *mens rea*). He must also bring about a state of affairs in which he has endangered a socially valuable interest, which he does by taking a substantial step toward the killing, or by coming dangerously close to causing the death. In practical terms, however, this requirement is satisfied without any event occurring after *D*'s voluntary act: *D*'s act of pulling the trigger of the gun *causes* a state of proximity to the destruction of a socially valuable interest (a human life), thereby endangering that social interest, and, thus, causing the social harm of attempted murder. *Id.* at 218.

[7] *People v. Superior Court (Aishman)*, 22 Cal.Rptr.2d 311, 319 (Ct. App.), *appeal granted*, 862 P.2d 663 (Cal. 1993) (quoting 1 Witkin, Cal. Crimes (1963) § 78, p. 79).

[8] See Joshua Dressler, *Reassessing the Theoretical Underpinnings of Accomplice Liability: New Solutions to an Old Problem*, 37 Hastings L.J. 91, 103-08 (1985).

[9] Hall at 248.

The value of "causation" in determining criminal responsibility is virtually irrefutable. Imagine a law that provided that any person in physical proximity to an accident could be punished for the resulting harm, even if he had nothing to do with causing the injury. Such a draconian rule would have immense negative social consequences. People would rationally fear that the lightning bolt of the law might strike them at any time; therefore, they would be deterred from socially desirable, and not simply unduly dangerous, activities.

This utilitarian argument, however, does not adequately explain the moral importance of the causation requirement in the criminal law. It does not explain why, in the hypothetical at the beginning of this chapter, *D* should not be held responsible for *V*'s death, simply because *X* intervened a split second earlier and killed *V*. After all, *D* is not an innocent party selected at random for punishment. Presumably, he is as dangerous as *X*; certainly he is no less dangerous than he would have been but for the fortuity of *X*'s involvement in the events. Yet, *D* will be convicted of attempted murder, a lesser offense than murder.

The role of causation in the criminal law finds its primary moral justification in retributive concepts of just deserts. Unlike tort law, in which morally innocent people are frequently held vicariously responsible for the wrongful acts of others, the criminal law is wedded to the concept of personal responsibility for crimes. This notion is rooted in the "inarticulate, subconscious sense of justice of the man on the street."[10]

The principle of causation is the instrument society employs to ensure that criminal responsibility is personal. It is the basis that links the actor to the social harm. Moreover, "causation" serves as the mechanism for determining how much the wrongdoer owes society and ought to repay it, i.e., causation principles help to quantify his just deserts. Under retributive principles, a wrongdoer's punishment should not exceed the harm that he has caused. This principle explains, for example, why an attempted murder is punished less severely than a murder at common law.

[C]—"Causation": Criminal Law versus Tort Law

Causation is a litigated issue in both tort and criminal law. However, causal problems are fewer and often less factually complex in criminal cases. Consequently, much that we think we know about causation in the criminal law springs from tort law and from scholarly literature focused on that area.

Nonetheless, tort theories of causation should not be equated with criminal law conceptions of causation. This is because of the different purposes of the two systems of law. Tort law generally seeks to identify the most suitable party on whom to place financial responsibility for negligently or innocently caused harm, whereas the criminal law seeks to determine whether and to what extent an intentional wrongdoer ought to be condemned by the community and punished.

Because of the higher stakes in the criminal law, and its especially strong commitment to personal, rather than vicarious, responsibility, some courts expressly

---

[10] Francis Bowes Sayre, *Criminal Responsibility For the Acts of Another*, 43 Harv. L. Rev. 689, 717 (1930).

provide that a tort conception of causation is insufficient to impose criminal responsibility.[11] Instead, a stricter test, requiring a closer connection between the defendant's conduct and the resulting harm, is applied. This dichotomy is observable in the criminal law's treatment of the second prong of the causation inquiry, i.e., "proximate causation."[12]

§ 14.02   Actual Cause

[A]—"But-For" ("*Sine Qua Non*") Test

Causation analysis is divisible into two parts. "Actual cause," or what is sometimes called "factual cause" or "cause-in-fact," constitutes the first prong. There can be no criminal liability for resulting social harm "unless it can be shown that the defendant's conduct was a cause-in-fact of the prohibited result."[13] In order to make this determination, courts traditionally apply the "but-for" or "*sine qua non*" test. This test may be stated as follows: "*But for D's voluntary act(s),*[14] *would the social harm have occurred when it did?*" If the answer is in the negative, i.e., if the social harm would *not* have occurred when it did but for *D*'s voluntary conduct, *D* is an actual cause of the result.

The but-for test serves a limited, but critical, purpose. It functions in a negative manner to exclude certain forces, including human ones, from responsibility for ensuing harm. That is, subject to one possible and very limited exception,[15] *D* cannot be held criminally responsible for social harm unless the prosecution proves beyond a reasonable doubt that he is a but-for cause of the harm.[16]

The fact that *D*'s conduct is determined to be an actual cause of a result does not mean, however, that he will be held criminally responsible for the harm. To be guilty, *D* must have acted with the requisite *mens rea*, and he must also be the *proximate* cause of the social harm. The latter causal issue represents the second part of the causation analysis, discussed in § 14.03.

---

[11] E.g., *Commonwealth v. Rementer*, 598 A.2d 1300, 1304 (Pa. Super. Ct. 1991); see *Commonwealth v. Root*, 170 A.2d 310, 311 (Pa. 1961) ("the accused is not guilty unless his conduct was a cause of death sufficiently direct as to meet the requirements of the *criminal*, and not the *tort*, law").

[12] See § 14.03, *infra*.

[13] *Velazquez v. State*, 561 So.2d 347, 350 (Fla. Ct. App. 1990).

[14] In the prosecution of a culpable omission, of course, this test would be rephrased to begin "but for *D*'s *omission*."

[15] See subsection [C][2][b], *infra*.

[16] See *Welch v. State*, 45 Ala. App. 657, 235 So.2d 906 (1970) (in a murder prosecution, a doctor testified that a blot clot, which originated in *V*'s left leg and then lodged in *V*'s lung, was "probably associated" with a gunshot wound to the *right* leg inflicted by *D*; held: in the absence of testimony as to how blood clots form and circulate, and in the absence of an autopsy, this evidence was insufficient to support a murder conviction).

[B]—"Causes" versus "Conditions"

D pulls the trigger of a gun, and a bullet is propelled from the gun into *V*'s chest, causing *V*'s death. Common sense tells us that *D* was the cause of the death: but for *D*'s voluntary act of pulling the trigger of the gun, *V* would not died when he did.

In fact, however, there are additional "actual causes" of *V*'s death. For example, *V* would not have died but for the fact that his heart muscle was too weak to withstand the intrusion of the bullet. Other causes of the death are found in certain principles of physics that explain how and why the pulling of the trigger results in a bullet moving at a fast rate of speed. Indeed, if *V*'s mother had not given birth to *V*, he could not have been killed by *D*.

Usually a court will either ignore these latter "causes" or identify them more realistically as necessary "conditions" for the harm to occur. Although conditions may technically meet the *sine qua non* test of causation, their exclusion from the latter category is consistent with a common sense view of the issue.

In determining causation, people focus on what is interesting in an event. They focus on the abnormal, the matters that seem out of the ordinary.[17] "Conditions" are normal events or circumstances that, although necessary for the result to occur, do not positively contribute to it. *D*'s firing of the gun is the act that is interesting and out of the ordinary. It is *D*'s conduct, therefore, and not the laws of physics, the structure of *V*'s heart, or *V*'s prior birth, that affirmatively contributed to the death.

[C]—Special "Actual Cause" Problems

[1]—Confusing "Causation" With "*Mens Rea*"

"Actual causation" and "*mens rea*" are independent concepts, both of which must be proven in a criminal prosecution.[18] Frequently, however, these doctrines are confused.

[a]—Causation Without *Mens Rea*

D has a minor argument with her husband, *V. V*, upset about the argument, leaves the house, and walks across the street. As he does, he is struck and killed by an automobile driven by *X*. Is *D* an actual cause of *V*'s death? Unless *V* had planned to cross that street at that moment anyway, the answer is "yes": but for *D* having the argument with *V*, *V* would not have crossed the street at that moment and, therefore, would not have been struck by *X*.

This does not mean, however, that *D* may be convicted of a crime pertaining to *V*'s death. First, *D* was not the sole cause of the harm. *X*'s conduct was another cause. So, too, was *V*'s decision to leave the house and cross the street. "Actual cause," it will be remembered, serves only to *eliminate* candidates for responsibility; it does not resolve the matter of ultimate causal responsibility, which awaits

---

[17] Hall at 249-50; Hart & Honore, Note 1, *supra*, at 32-37.

[18] See *State v. Boles*, 613 A.2d 770, 773-74 (Conn. 1992)

proximate-causation analysis. Second, but more immediately to the point, the facts do not suggest that *D* possessed a culpable state of mind—any *mens rea*—regarding *V*'s death. Thus, we have a case of but-for causation without a *mens rea*.

[b]—*Mens Rea* Without Causation

Just as a person may be the actual cause of resulting harm without having a *mens rea*, he may also possess a culpable state of mind without being the actual cause of the harm.

For example, suppose that *D1*, with the intent to kill *V*, shoots *V*, barely nicking him. At the same moment, *D2* independently and accidentally, shoots *V* in the heart. *V* dies instantly. *D1* intended to kill *V*. *D2* did not intend to kill *V*. Nonetheless, *D2*'s conduct is the sole cause of *V*'s death: but for *D2* accidentally firing the gun, *V* would not have died when he did. *D1*'s conduct was ineffectual. As a result, *D1* should not be convicted of *V*'s death.[19] *D2* is the only possible candidate for criminal prosecution, although he may be acquitted because he lacked the requisite *mens rea*.

[2]—Multiple Actual Causes

[a]—Accelerating a Result

D1 intentionally shoots *V* in the stomach. Assume that medical testimony would prove that *V* would have died from the wound in one hour. However, simultaneously and independently of *D1*, *D2* intentionally shoots *V* in the stomach. Medical evidence would show that *V* would have died from the latter wound in one hour. As a result of the two wounds, *V* dies in five minutes.

Who is the cause of *V*'s death? At first glance it may appear that application of the but-for test will result in the conclusion that *neither D1* nor *D2* was an actual cause of the death. In fact, however, *both* actors may properly be described as actual causes of *V*'s death. Both may successfully be prosecuted for murder.

A careful application of the but-for test supports this conclusion. It must be remembered that this test asks whether, but for the voluntary act of the defendant, the harm would have occurred *when it did*. The italicized words are essential to the correct application of the test. After all, ultimately everyone dies. No act can do more than accelerate the process.

With this point in mind it is evident that *D1* accelerated *V*'s death. Ask the *sine qua non* question: "but for *D1*'s voluntary act [firing the gun], would *V* have died *when he did* [in five minutes]?" The answer is that he would *not* have died when he did; he would have died in one hour as the result of the wound simultaneously inflicted by *D2*. Because *D1*'s actions accelerated the death process, *D1* is an actual cause of the death. One need only substitute *D2* for *D1* in this analysis to reach the same causal conclusion regarding *D2*.

Or, consider the facts in *Oxendine v. State*.[20] *V* was the tragic victim of two separate acts of child abuse: first, he sustained internal injuries from a beating

---

[19] Of course, he may be convicted of attempted murder.

[20] 528 A.2d 870 (Del. 1987).

inflicted by *X*; one day later, *D*, *V*'s father, inflicted additional injuries. *V* died later that day. *X* and *D* were prosecuted for *V*'s death. The state introduced evidence regarding the cause of death: one physician testified that he could not determine whether one or both injuries caused *V*'s death; a second doctor stated that the earlier injury inflicted by *X* was the underlying cause of the death; he could not state whether *D*'s actions accelerated the process.

Based on this evidence, the court held that *D* was entitled to a directed verdict of acquittal. However, if the state had introduced evidence that the beating inflicted by *D* had hastened *V*'s death by even the slightest degree, *D* could properly have been found to be an actual cause of the death.

[b]—Concurrent Sufficient Causes

D1 shoots *V* in the heart; simultaneously and independently, *D2*'s shoots *V* in the head. *V* dies instantly. Medical evidence indicates that either attack alone would have killed *V* instantly.

In the real world such events rarely occur. More often, *D1* and *D2* will be acting in concert, so that their joint conduct may be analyzed as if they were one party. Or, one wound will accelerate the result caused by the other. Another possibility in a dual attack is that neither wound will be mortal, but acting together they result in the death. As the facts are described here, however, *D1* and *D2* are "concurrent sufficient causes" of *V*'s death. That is, either act alone was sufficient to cause the result that occurred *when it did*.

Our intuitions probably suggest that both actors should be convicted of murder. Yet, the but-for test seems to fail us here: but for *D1*'s act of shooting *V* in the heart, *V* would have died when he did (instantly) as the result of *D2*'s gunshot to V's head. Applying the same test to *D2*'s conduct, *D2* also is relieved of responsibility. If this analysis is correct, and if no other principle is applicable, *D1* and *D2* may be convicted of attempted murder, but of no more.[21]

Two ways to avoid this result have been suggested. First, some criminal law courts import from tort law its solution in comparable circumstances, which is to rephrase the causation test to ask whether the defendant was a "substantial factor" in causing the prohibited harm.[22]

The difficulty with the "substantial factor" test is not only that the critical term is never defined,[23] but that it is difficult to comprehend how a person's conduct

---

[21] What is wrong with this? Reconsider the hypothetical at the beginning of this chapter. In that situation, *D* is given the benefit of the fortuity of *X*'s independent action; he is convicted of the lesser offense of attempted murder. Why should we not give the actors here the benefit of the fortuity, and convict them both of attempted murder? The reason why we balk at this outcome is that in the first case there is someone—*X*—who can be convicted of murder; here, however, use of the but-for test results in *nobody* being convicted of murder.

[22] *Anderson v. Minneapolis, St. P. & S. Ste. M. Ry. Co.*, 179 N.W. 45, 46 (Minn. 1920), *overruled on other grounds, Borshein v. Grant N.R. Co.*, 183 N.W. 519 (Minn. 1921); see also Jeremiah Smith, *Legal Cause in Actions of Tort*, 25 Harv. L. Rev. 223, 229-30 (1912).

[23] According to various torts scholars the phrase "is sufficiently intelligible . . . that it is neither possible nor desirable to reduce it to any lower terms." W. Page Keeton, Dan B. Dobbs, Robert E. Keeton, & David G. Owen, *Prosser and Keeton on Torts* 267 (5th ed. 1984).

can ever be a "substantial factor" in causing a result if the harm was going to occur when it did without his contribution. The only way in which it may fairly be said that a concurrent sufficient cause is a substantial factor in the outcome is to point out that the force *would have been* the cause of the harm if circumstances had been different (i.e., if the other force had not materialized). However, this is not the way we ordinarily talk about causation. If it were, the would-be killer in the example that began this chapter would have been guilty of murder, rather than attempted murder.

A second method of resolving the causal quandary is to retain the but-for test in these circumstances, but to elaborate on it. Two extra words are added, so that the test becomes: "but for *D*'s voluntary act would the social harm have occurred when *and as* it did."[24] In essence, this technique refines the description of the result for which the defendants are prosecuted. Thus, in the present example, the result would not be described as "the death of *V*," but rather as "the death of *V* by two simultaneous mortal wounds." Applying the but-for test in this manner, both *D1* and *D2* satisfy the causation standard, because the result—death from two mortal wounds— could not have occurred without the presence of both actors.

[3]—Obstructed Cause

D1 shoots *V* in the stomach. Simultaneously and independently, *D2* shoots *V* three times in the head, killing him instantly.

Although it may appear that *D1* is causally linked to *V*'s death, this may not be the case. A coroner might testify that the wound inflicted by *D1* did not contribute to *V*'s death, i.e., that the three bullets in the head would have killed *V* instantly, even in the absence of the abdominal wound. Under such circumstances, *D1* is no more the cause of *V*'s death than if, just a split-second before *D1* fired the gun, *V* had been struck by a bolt of lightning that killed him instantly. In the latter case we would not say that *D1* killed *V*; rather, we would say that he attempted to kill *V*, but that his efforts were obstructed by a separate force (the lightning), which actually caused the result. The same analysis applies to *D1* and *D2*: *D1* attempted to take *V*'s life; he was thwarted in this goal because *D2* was a more effective killer.

§ 14.03 Proximate Cause

[A]—Overview

"Mankind might still be in Eden, but for Adam's biting an apple."[25] The present point of this remark is to remind us that the sole purpose of the but-for test of causation is to identify candidates for responsibility for an event. From this pool, which may include many actors stemming over an extended period of time,[26] the

---

[24] See Perkins & Boyce at 773; Hart & Honore, Note 1, *supra* at 124-25.

[25] *Welch v. State*, 235 So.2d 906, 907 (Ala. App. 1970).

[26] E.g.,, in *State v. Govan*, 744 P.2d 712 (Ariz. Ct. App. 1987), *D* shot *V*, paralyzing *V* from the neck down. *D* was charged with assault, but the charges were dropped when *V* married *D*. Due to her quadriplegia, *V* suffered from various ailments and needed constant care thereafter. Five years after the shooting, *V* contracted pneumonia and died. *D* was

"proximate" or "legal" cause of the social harm must be selected. [27]

The concept of "proximate causation" is obscure. [28] In the process of determining proximate causation, courts and lawyers frequently bandy about conclusory terms like "superseding intervening cause," "direct cause," and "remote cause." An observer might assume from this language that a formula exists to produce uniform and reliable results in proximate-causation analysis. In fact, however, a court or jury does not *discover* the proximate cause of harm. It *selects* it. The decision to attach causal responsibility for social harm to one, rather than to another, event is made in a common sense manner, [29] or by application of moral intuitions, a community sense of justice, and/or public policy considerations. [30]

[B]—Direct Cause

In many cases, no serious litigable issue of proximate causation arises. For example, suppose that *D* shoots *V*, and *V* dies instantly. Or, suppose that *D* shoots *V*, and *V* is taken to the hospital where he dies after proper medical care. In both cases, courts are apt to say that *D* was the "direct" cause of the result. That is, no event of causal significance intervened between *D*'s conduct and the social harm for which he is being prosecuted. In the first case, the death occurred instantly; in the second hypothetical, nothing done by the medical personnel aggravated *V*'s injuries or accelerated *V*'s death.

The closest thing to a bright-line rule in the realm of proximate cause is this: *an act that is a direct cause of social harm is also a proximate cause of it.* This rule makes sense. By definition, a "direct cause" is a force already determined to be an "actual cause" of the undesired result. Inasmuch as no other causal factors have intervened, there is no more proximate party to whom to shift legal responsibility for the result.

[C]—Intervening Causes

[1]—Overview

An "intervening cause" is an independent force that operates in producing harm to another *after* the defendant's voluntary act has been committed or his omission

---

charged with her murder, based on the initial shooting, and convicted of manslaughter. The appellate court upheld the conviction, ruling that the evidence created a jury question as to whether *D*'s conduct five years earlier was the proximate cause of her death.

[27] Usually there will be only one proximate cause of a result, but this is not always so. For example, in the case of concurrent sufficient causes, see § 14.02[C][2][b], *supra*, each cause is proximate.

[28] American Law Institute, Comment to § 2.03, at 255.

[29] See Roscoe Pound, *The Theory of Judicial Decision*, 36 Harv. L. Rev. 940, 952 (1923) ("[W]e must rely on the common sense of the common man as to common things . . . .").

[30] In the latter regard, some scholars have pointed out that the process of seeking the "proximate" cause of a result will inevitably exclude the "deeper causes" of crime, such as poor social environment, discrimination, and other social inequities. Norrie, Note 1, *supra*, at 691.

has occurred.[31] That is, if one were to draw a line, put the words "*D*'s voluntary act/omission" at the beginning of the line, and mark down "social harm" at its end, the intervening causes would be those but-for causal forces that arose during the time period represented by the line.

Although not exhaustive of the circumstances in which intervening causes arise, many cases fit this general pattern: *D* gravely harms *V*. Thereafter, another force intervenes. This intervening cause aggravates *V*'s injuries or accelerates the inevitable (i.e., *V*'s death). The intervention usually comes in the form of wrongdoing by *X*, a third party, or as the result of a dangerous or suicidal act by *V*, the victim. Sometimes the intervening cause is a natural force ("an act of God").

The legal issue for consideration in such cases is the following: Under what circumstances does the intervening conduct of a third party, the victim, or a natural force make "it no longer seem[] fair to say that the [social harm] was 'caused' by the defendant's conduct"?[32] Framing the issue more precisely: Under what circumstances should *D*, who acts with the requisite *mens rea*, and who commits a voluntary act that *is* a cause-in-fact of the social harm, be relieved of criminal responsibility because of the existence of an intervening cause? When an intervening cause does relieve the defendant of criminal responsibility, the law generally describes that intervening event as the "superseding cause" of the social harm.

One early twentieth century scholar observed that all efforts to set down universal tests that explain the law of causation are "demonstrably erroneous."[33] In particular, there are no hard-and-fast rules for determining when an intervening cause supersedes the defendant's conduct. However, there are various factors that assist the factfinder in the evaluative process.

[2]—Factor 1: *De Minimis* Contribution to the Social Harm

Sometimes, a defendant's causal responsibility for ensuing harm is insubstantial in comparison to that of an intervening cause. For example, suppose that *D* wrongfully wounds *V*. Although the wound is not life-threatening, it does require medical attention, so *V* drives himself to the doctor. On the way, his car is struck by lightning. *V* dies instantly. Is *D* guilty of criminal homicide? Or, suppose that after *D* slightly wounds *V*, *X* shoots *V* in the stomach, causing his death an hour later.

From a causal perspective, *D* was an actual cause of the ensuing death-by-lightning: but for *D*'s wrongful actions, *V* would not have been in the car, and thus would not have been at the spot where the lightning struck. In the second scenario, it is possible that the wound *D* inflicted took a few seconds or a minute off *V*'s life (although it might be hard to obtain expert testimony to this effect). Nonetheless, the law is likely to treat *D*'s causal connection in either scenario as *de minimis*, and relieve him of criminal liability for *V*'s death.[34]

This outcome conforms to our common-sense analysis of causal events. If a small pebble is followed immediately by a giant meteor striking Jupiter, our attention

---

[31] *State v. Marti*, 290 N.W.2d 570, 586 (Iowa 1980).

[32] *State v. Malone*, 819 P.2d 34, 37 (Alaska Ct. App. 1991).

[33] Smith, Note 22, *supra*, at 317.

[34] Of course, *D* could be prosecuted for battery in either hypothetical.

focuses on the meteor; although the pebble may have contributed slightly to the ensuing damage, we treat the giant force as the "real" cause of the harm. The same principle applies in the criminal law: some wrongdoers have too minor a causal role to justify criminal punishment. The law will treat the substantial, intervening cause as the proximate cause of the social harm.[35]

[3]—Factor 2: Foreseeability of the Intervening Cause

[a]—In General

According to some courts, the "linchpin"[36] of proximate causation is whether the intervening party's acts were reasonably foreseeable. This may be a slight overstatement, but it is certainly true that foreseeability is a matter of great significance in proximate-causation analysis.

Cases can be found in which it is said, simply, that the defendant cannot escape liability if the intervening act was reasonably foreseeable,[37] whereas an unforeseeable intervening cause is superseding in nature. Proper analysis, however, is usually a little more sophisticated than this. The law tends to distinguish between "responsive" (or "dependent") and "coincidental" (or "independent") intervening causes.[38]

[b]—Responsive (Dependent) Intervening Causes

A responsive intervening cause is an act that occurs in reaction or response to the defendant's prior wrongful conduct. For example, suppose that *D1* operates his boat at an unsafe speed, causing it to capsize. *V1*, his drunken passenger, drowns while foolishly attempting to swim to shore.[39] *V1*'s actions constitute a responsive intervening cause in his own death, i.e., his life-saving efforts were in response to *D1*'s initial improper conduct. Or, suppose that *D2* seriously wounds *V2*. *V2* is taken to a hospital where he receives poor medical treatment by physician *X* and dies.[40] In *D2*'s prosecution for the death, *X*'s negligent conduct constitutes a responsive intervening cause: *X*'s medical actions were in response to *D2*'s act of wounding *V2*.

Generally speaking, a responsive intervening cause does not relieve the initial wrongdoer of criminal responsibility, unless the response was highly abnormal or

---

[35] The *de minimis* rule should not be confused with the "substantial factor" test described at § 14.02[C][2][b], *supra*. The latter test is used when two forces, each of which is sufficient to cause the result, simultaneously occur. It is a pragmatic substitute for the but-for test. The *de minimis* proximate-causation principle only applies after a determination that the defendant was a but-for cause of the result.

[36] *State v. Dunn*, 850 P.2d 1201, 1215 (Utah 1993).

[37] *Id.* at 1216.

[38] In their treatise, Professors LaFave and Austin use the "responsive/coincidental" terms, Wayne R. LaFave & Austin W. Scott, Jr., Criminal Law 289-90 (2d ed. 1986), whereas Professors Perkins and Boyce describe intervening causes as "dependent/independent." Perkins & Boyce at 791, 809.

[39] *People v. Armitage*, 239 Cal.Rptr. 515 (Ct. App. 1987).

[40] *Fairman v. State*, 513 So.2d 910 (Miss. 1987).

bizarre.[41] This outcome is justifiable: since the intervening cause was a response to the defendant's initial wrongdoing and, therefore, the defendant is responsible for the presence of the intervening force, the defendant should not escape liability unless the intervening force was so out-of-the-ordinary that it is no longer fair to hold him criminally responsible for the outcome.

Applying this analysis, case law provides that the accused bears criminal responsibility for the death of a person who seeks to extricate himself or another from the dangerous situation created by the defendant, even if the victim was contributorily negligent in his efforts.[42] Similarly, many cases provide that one who wrongfully injures another is responsible for the ensuing death, notwithstanding subsequent negligent medical treatment that contributes to the victim's death or accelerates it.[43] On the other hand, grossly negligent or reckless medical care is sufficiently abnormal to supersede the initial wrongdoer's causal responsibility.[44]

[c]—Coincidental (Independent) Intervening Causes

A coincidental intervening cause is a force that does not occur in response to the initial wrongdoer's conduct. The only relationship between the defendant's conduct and the intervening cause is that the defendant placed the victim in a situation where the intervening cause could independently act upon him. For example, suppose that *D1* robs *V1*, a passenger in *D1*'s car, and then abandons *V1* on a rural road. Sometime later, driver *X1* strikes and kills *V1*, who is standing in the middle of the road.[45] *X1*'s conduct is a coincidental intervening cause: nothing *D1* did caused *X1* to drive down that road on that particular occasion; *D1* simply put *V1* on the road where *X1*'s independent conduct could act upon *V1*.

Or, suppose that *D2* wounds *V2*. *V2* is taken to a hospital for medical treatment, where he is killed by *X2*, a "knife-wielding maniac" who is running through the hospital killing everyone in sight.[46] Again, *X2* is a coincidental intervening cause: he was going to be running through that hospital killing victims whether or not *V2* was there. This is a case in which *V2* was in the wrong place at the wrong time, as the result of *D2*'s original wrongdoing.

---

[41] *Kibbe v. Henderson*, 534 F.2d 493, 498 n.6 (2nd Cir. 1976); *State v. Malone*, 819 P.2d at 37; *State v. Hall*, 633 P.2d 398, 403 (Ariz. 1981).

[42] *People v. Armitage*, 239 Cal.Rptr. 515 (Ct. App. 1987) (see the facts described in the text accompanying footnote 39); *State v. Leopold*, 147 A. 118 (Conn. 1929) (one who knowingly set fire to a building is responsible for the death or injury of one who enters the building to save his property); *People v. Kern*, 554 N.E.2d 1235 (N.Y. 1990) (*Ds* chased *V* with a baseball bat, with the intention of beating or killing him; *V* attempted to escape by running onto a highway, where he was struck and killed by a third party; *Ds* are responsible for *V*'s death); *State v. Johnson*, 615 A.2d 132 (Vt. 1992) (*D* attempted to kill *V*; *V*, fearing for his life, walked into a river to escape, and drowned; *D* is guilty of murder).

[43] E.g., *Fairman v. State*, 513 So.2d 910 (Miss. 1987); *State v. Baker*, 742 P.2d 633 (Or. Ct. App. 1987); see *People v. Kane*, 107 N.E. 655 (N.Y. 1915).

[44] *Regina v. Jordan*, 40 Crim. App. Rep. 152 (1956).

[45] *Kibbe v. Henderson*, 534 F.2d 493 (2nd Cir. 1976).

[46] This is a slight embellishment on hypothetical 6(c) in Sanford H. Kadish & Stephen J. Schulhofer, Criminal Law and Its Processes 588 (5th ed. 1989).

The common law rule of thumb is that a coincidental intervening cause relieves the original wrongdoer of criminal responsibility, unless the intervention was foreseeable. In the present examples, therefore, it would be necessary to determine whether *D1* and *D2*, as reasonable people, should have foreseen, respectively, that *V1* would be struck by another car, and that *V2* would be the victim of a criminal intermediary. In the first case, it may have been foreseeable that another car would drive down that road and strike *V1*. In the second hypothetical, *X2*'s criminal activities were probably bizarre enough to relieve *D2* of liability for the ensuing death, unless (perhaps) it turned out that all of the events occurred in a high-security institution for the criminally insane.

[4]—Factor 3: The Defendant's *Mens Rea* (Intended-Consequences Doctrine)

"The legal eye reaches further in the examination of intentional crimes than in those in which this element is wanting."[47] As two scholars on causation have explained, a voluntary act intended to "bring about what in fact happens, and in the manner in which it happens, has a special place in causal inquiries."[48] That special place is this: *we usually trace the cause of social harm backwards through other causes until we reach an intentional wrongdoer.* Or, as is sometimes said, although a bit too strongly: "Intended consequences can never be too remote."[49]

For example, in a classic case,[50] *D*, with the intent to kill *V*, her child, furnished poison to *X*, a home nurse, falsely informing *X* that the substance was medicine to be administered to *V*. *X* did not believe that *V* needed the "medicine," so she did not administer it. Instead, she placed the substance on a mantel where some time later *C*, a young child, discovered it and gave it to *V*, killing *V*. *D* was prosecuted for murder.

D intended *V*'s death. Her voluntary act of providing the poison to *X* was a but-for cause of the death. On the other hand, at least two other causes intervened: *X*'s negligent act of placing the "medicine" where it could be reached by *C*; and *C*'s innocent act of administering it to *V*. Despite these intervening acts, at least one of which was a coincidental intervening cause,[51] *D* was declared to be the proximate cause of *V*'s death.

This outcome is hardly surprising. *D* wanted her child poisoned, which is exactly what she got.[52] As a matter of moral intuitions, the intervening actions—*X*'s

---

[47] *State v. Cummings*, 265 S.E.2d 923, 927 (N.C. Ct. App. 1980) (emphasis deleted) (Clark, J., dissenting) (*quoting* Perkins, Criminal Law 693 (2d ed. 1969)).

[48] Hart & Honore, Note 1, *supra*, at 42.

[49] *Id.* at 170 (emphasis omitted); see Henry T. Terry, *Proximate Consequences in the Law of Torts*, 28 Harv L. Rev. 10, 17 (1914).

[50] *Regina v. Michael*, 169 Eng. Rep. 48 (1840).

[51] *X*'s negligent act of putting the poison on the mantel was coincidentally acted upon by *C*.

[52] The intended-consequences doctrine is most often applied when the result *and the means of its commission* were intended by the defendant.

possible negligence and *C*'s innocent conduct—should not override *D*'s intentional wrongdoing. It is as if the jurors were to say: "You got *exactly* what you wanted. What right do you have to complain if we hold you responsible for the intended consequence?"

[5]—Factor 4: Dangerous Forces That Come to Rest (Apparent-Safety Doctrine)

One scholar has observed that when a "defendant's active force has come to rest in a position of apparent safety, the court will follow it no longer."[53] For example, consider a somewhat simplified version of the facts in *State v. Preslar*:[54] *D* threatened the life of *V*, his spouse. As a consequence, *V* was forced to leave the house on a freezing night in order to protect herself. *V* walked to within 200 yards of her father's home, where she would have been welcome, but she chose to spend the night in the extreme cold, rather than bother her father by entering the house. *V* froze to death during the night. Clearly, *D* was an actual cause of *V*'s death: but for *D*'s threatening conduct, *V* would not have gone out into the cold. But, *V*'s decision to sleep outside was also a but-for cause of her own death. Is *D* the proximate cause of *V*'s death? The court in *Preslar* answered this question in the negative.

The result may be explained in terms of the apparent-safety doctrine:[55] *D* did not follow *V* from their home; when *V* reached the vicinity of her father's house, and she knew that she could enter in complete safety, *D* no longer constituted an immediate threat to *V*'s safety. Therefore, her decision to sleep outside constituted a superseding intervening cause.[56]

[6]—Factor 5: Voluntary Human Interventions

A defendant is far more apt to be relieved of criminal responsibility in the case of a "free, deliberate, and informed,"[57] i.e., voluntary, intervention of a human agent than in the case of an intervention of a natural force or the actions of a person whose conduct is less than fully free. This rule is consistent with the retributive principle that accords special significance to the free-will actions of human beings.

---

[53] Joseph H. Beale, *The Proximate Consequences of an Act*, 33 Harv. L. Rev. 633, 651 (1920).

[54] 48 N.C. 421 (1856).

[55] Notice that the facts in *Preslar* could be analyzed in terms of the foreseeability factor: *V*'s decision to leave the house and seek shelter was a responsive intervening cause; was her decision to sleep out at night, however, highly abnormal? If so, *D* may be relieved of liability on this independent ground. On the other hand, should the intended-consequences doctrine apply to these facts? *D* intended to kill *V*, and she *did* die. This would argue in favor of his liability. However, the means of *V*'s death—death by freezing—was unintended, so this would argue against liability. See note 52, *supra*.

[56] Cf., *Commonwealth v. Rementer*, 598 A.2d 1300 (Pa. Super. Ct. 1991) (*D* assaulted *V*, his girlfriend, in a bar; *D* continued to pursue *V* when she left; *V* fell to the ground and was run over by a car as she approached *X*, a motorist, for aid; held: *D*'s conduct remained an operative force that justified holding him criminally responsible for her death).

[57] Hart & Honore, Note 1, *supra*, at 326.

For example, the result in the *Preslar* case,[58] described in subsection [5], can be explained in terms of the voluntary-human-intervention factor. *V* chose to sleep in the cold rather than to enter her father's home. Her decision was free, deliberate, and with full knowledge of the fact that it was exceedingly cold outside. Under these circumstances, the responsibility for her death is shifted from *D* to *V*.

The same analysis applies if, for example, *D* and *V* operate their vehicles in a reckless manner as part of a drag race, at the end of which race *V*, acting under his own volition, turns his car around and speeds through a guardrail, killing himself or another. Regardless of *D*'s initial responsibility for the race, *V*'s decision to "ad lib" by continuing the race after it was over relieves *D* of responsibility for the ensuing harm.[59]

Of course, the critical issue in applying the present factor is whether the human intervention was "free, deliberate, and informed." Frequently, it is not. For example, if *V* escapes *D*, a home-intruder, by jumping out of a second-story window of his house, his actions would not be considered free. Therefore *D* would be liable for *V*'s injuries or death from the jump.[60] Likewise, if *D* kidnaps and rapes *V*, after which despondent *V* commits suicide, *V* could be held responsible for her death.[61]

[7]—Factor 6: Omissions

"Doing nothing . . . is just that—nothing—so far as the law is concerned . . . ."[62] Therefore, an omission will rarely, if ever, serve as a superseding intervening cause.[63] For example, if *D* drives his automobile in a negligent manner, causing the death of *V* (a passenger in *D*'s car or a driver of another vehicle), *V*'s

---

[58] *State v. Preslar*, 48 N.C. 421 (1856).

[59] *Velazquez v. State*, 561 So.2d 347 (Fla. Ct. App. 1990).

[60] *Rex v. Beech*, 23 Cox Crim.Case. 181 (1912).

[61] See *Stephenson v. State*, 179 N.E. 633 (Ind. 1932). Considerably more doubtful under this analysis was the result in *Regina v. Blaue*, [1975] 1 W.L.R. 1411. In the case, *D* seriously wounded *V*. *V*, informed that she needed a blood transfusion or else she would die, refused it on religious grounds. The court, stating that *D* had to take his victim—including *V*'s religious views—as he found her, concluded that he was the proximate cause of *V*'s death. This result may be wrong. Quite arguably, *V*'s decision to refuse medical treatment should be accorded the respect of being treated as a free, deliberate, and informed decision. It is often said, as in *Blaue*, that a wrongdoer takes his victim as he finds him. E.g., *People v. Webb*, 415 N.W.2d 9, 10 (Mich. Ct. App. 1987). However, this doctrine is typically applied in cases in which the victim has a pre-existing and hidden medical condition, such as hemophilia or a weak heart. In such circumstances, it cannot be said that the victim chooses for his blood not to coagulate, or that he chooses to have a heart attack. In contrast, the victim in *Blaue* chose to "suffer" from a pre-existing religious "condition," and to act upon it.

[62] Perkins & Boyce at 820.

[63] This assertion assumes that the defendant's dangerous conduct has not already come to rest. For example, in *State v. Preslar*, 48 N.C. 421 (1856), discussed in subsections [5] and [6], *V* failed to enter her father's home. However, by this time, *V* had reached apparent safety; *D*'s conduct was no longer operative. Therefore, the omission principle would not come into play.

failure to wear a seat belt, although causally related to his own death,[64] will not absolve *D* from liability for the death.[65]

This principle applies, even if the intervening actor has a duty to act. Therefore, a parent's failure to intervene to stop another person from beating his (the parent's child), will not absolve the attacker for the ensuing homicide, although the parent may also be responsible for the death on the basis of omission principles.

§ 14.04 Model Penal Code[66]

[A]—Actual Cause

The Model Penal Code applies the but-for (*sine qua non*) rule. To be guilty of an offense, a person's conduct must cause the prohibited result. "Cause" is defined under the Code as "an antecedent but for which the result in question would not have occurred."[67] The common law principles that clarify the meaning of this test also apply in Code jurisdictions.[68]

[B]—Proximate Cause (Actually, Culpability)

Unlike the common law, the Code treats but-for causation as the exclusive meaning of "causation" in the criminal law. The Code treats matters that the common law would consider in terms of "proximate causation" as issues relating instead to the actor's culpability.

Specifically, subsections (2)(b) and (3)(b)[69] of Section 2.03 deal with situations in which the actual result of the defendant's conduct (considering both the precise harm caused and the manner in which it occurred) diverges from that which was

---

[64] There is substantial philosophical debate regarding whether an omission can "cause" a resulting event. See Moore, Note 5, *supra*, at 267-78 (also citing literature on the topic). How can "nothing" be the cause of something? As evidenced by the fact that some omissions are punishable, however, the criminal law accepts the premise that they can be causally relevant. See Model Penal Code § 1.13(5) (defining "conduct" as an "act *or omission* and its accompanying state of mind"); and § 2.03(1)(a) (providing the circumstances under which "conduct" is the "cause" of a result).

[65] *Bowman v. State*, 564 N.E.2d 309 (Ind. Ct. App. 1990); *People v. Clark*, 431 N.W.2d 88 (Mich. Ct. App. 1988).

[66] See generally David J. Karp, Note, *Causation in the Model Penal Code*, 78 Colum. L. Rev. 1249 (1978).

[67] Model Penal Code § 2.03(1)(a).

[68] In the case of concurrent sufficient causes, see § 14.02[C][2][b], *supra*, e.g., when *D1* and *D2* independently inflict immediately-lethal wounds on *V*, the Commentary to the Code states that "the result in question" should be described as "death from two mortal wounds." Thus, the jury would determine whether "but for [*D1*'s]/[*D2*'s] act, the result [death from two mortal wounds] would have occurred." This way, each party is a but-for cause of the result. American Law Institute, Comment to § 2.03, at 259.

[69] Subsection (2)(b) applies to crimes in which purposely or knowingly causing a result is the requisite element; subsection (3)(b) is invoked with crimes of recklessness or negligence.

designed, contemplated, or (in the case of a crime of recklessness or negligence) risked. In such circumstances, the issue in a Model Code jurisdiction is not whether, in light of the divergences, the defendant was a "proximate cause" of the resulting harm, but rather whether it may still be said that he caused the prohibited result with the level of culpability—purpose, knowledge, recklessness, or negligence—required by the definition of the offense.

According to the Code, the defendant has *not* acted with the requisite culpability (which, in this context, is the same as saying that the common law proximity standard is *not* satisfied), unless the actual result, including the way in which it occurred, was not "too remote or accidental in its occurrence to have a [just] bearing on the actor's liability or on the gravity of his offense."[70] Thus, under the Code, the "varying and sometimes inconsistent"[71] proximate-causation doctrines developed by the common law are replaced with a single standard, which invites the jury to reach a result based on common sense and fairness.

In the rare circumstance of an offense containing no culpability element,[72] the Code provides that causation "is not established unless the actual result is a probable consequence of the actor's conduct."[73] This would mean that in a jurisdiction that recognizes the common law felony-murder rule,[74] but which applies Model Penal Code causation principles, a defendant may not be convicted of felony-murder if the death was not a probable consequence of his felonious conduct. For example, if *D* attempted to rob a bank, and the bank teller was accidentally electrocuted attempting to press the burglar alarm switch, *D* would not be liable for the death because the actual result—death by electrocution—was not a probable consequence of robbing a bank.[75]

---

[70] The word "just" was placed in brackets by the American Law Institute as a possible addition to the formulation. Disagreement existed among its members regarding the desirability of submitting undefined questions of justice to a jury. American Law Institute, Comment to § 2.03, at 261 n.16.

[71] *Id.* at 256.

[72] Under the Code, some element of *mens rea* is required regarding every material element of an offense, except in the case of "violations." Model Penal Code §§ 2.02(1), 2.05. See §§ 10.07[A] and 11.05, *supra*.

[73] Model Penal Code § 2.03(4).

[74] Basically, this rule permits a person to be convicted of murder for an accidental killing that occurs during the commission of a felony. See § 31.06, *infra*.

[75] American Law Institute, Comment to § 2.03, at 264.

CHAPTER 15

CONCURRENCE OF ELEMENTS

§ 15.01 General Principle[1]

A crime contains an *actus reus* and, usually, a *mens rea*. More specifically, a person may not be convicted of an offense unless the prosecutor proves beyond a reasonable doubt that the defendant, with the requisite mental state, performed a voluntary act that actually and proximately caused the proscribed social harm. Implicit in this statement is an additional prerequisite to criminal liability: the *concurrence* of the *actus reus* and the *mens rea*.[2]

The principle of concurrence contains two components. First, there must be temporal concurrence. That is, the defendant must possess the requisite *mens rea* at the same moment that her voluntary conduct (or omission) causes the social harm (the *actus reus*). Second, there must be motivational concurrence. That is, even if the *mens rea* and *actus reus* temporally concur, the relationship between the two must be more than coincidental. As explained below, the defendant's conduct that caused the social harm must have been set into motion or impelled by the thought process that constituted the *mens rea* of the offense.

§ 15.02 Temporal Concurrence

Lack of temporal concurrence occurs when the *mens rea* of an offense exists before or after, but not during, the commission of the *actus reus*.

[A]—*Mens Rea* Preceding *Actus Reus*

Occasionally, a defendant's *mens rea* will precede the *actus reus* of the offense, but be absent when she acts. For example, suppose that *D* intends to kill *V*, plans the killing, but never has the opportunity to implement the plan. Later, she changes her mind, abandons the scheme, and befriends *V*. Thereafter, *D* and *V* go hunting, during which time *D* innocently (non-negligently) kills *V*. Obviously, *D* is not guilty of criminal homicide. When she had the *mens rea*, there was no *actus reus*. When she subsequently killed *V*, she had no culpable state of mind.

The concurrence principle is satisfied, however, if the *voluntary act* that causes the social harm concurs with the *mens rea*, although the social harm itself occurs

---

[1] See Hall at 185-90.

[2] The concurrence principle is codified in a few state penal codes. E.g., Cal. Pen. Code § 20 (West 1988), which provides that "[i]n every crime . . . there must exist a *union, or joint operation* of act and intent, or criminal negligence." The Model Penal Code also requires concurrence, albeit inferentially, by defining "conduct" as "an action or omission and *its accompanying* state of mind." Model Penal Code § 1.13(5) (emphasis added).

later. For example, suppose that *D*, intending to kill *V*, mortally wounds *V*. *V* dies in the hospital three months later, by which time *D* has expressed genuine remorse, and no longer wants *V* to die. Here, *D* is guilty of murder. The critical issue is whether the lethal act—the firing of the gun—concurred with the *mens rea*, and not whether the *mens rea* was present at the time of the death.

[B]—*Actus Reus* Preceding *Mens Rea*

Temporal concurrence is absent if the *actus reus* precedes the *mens rea*. For example, suppose that *D1* wrongfully breaks into and enters *V1*'s home at night in order to get out of the rain. After she enters, *D1* decides to steal *V1*'s property. *D1* is prosecuted for burglary, defined as "breaking and entering the dwelling house of another at night, with intent to commit a felony therein." On these facts, *D1* is not guilty of burglary because the specific intent of the offense ("intent to commit a felony therein") arose after the occurrence of the voluntary acts that caused the social harm ("breaking and entering the dwelling house of another at night").[3] Likewise, *D2* is not guilty of murder if she innocently takes *V2*'s life, even if she decides later that she is glad that she killed *V2*.

§ 15.03   Motivational Concurrence

The impelling force or motivation behind the act that causes the social harm must be the *mens rea* of the offense, and not some other thought process, such as the mental state of preparing to commit the offense.

For example, suppose that *D* intends to shoot and kill her spouse, *V*, when he arrives home. Incorrectly believing the gun is still unloaded, *D* tests the trigger by pulling it. As she does, *V* unexpectedly enters the house and is struck and killed by the bullet. Based on these facts, the requisite motivational concurrence is missing. Although *D* had the intent to kill *V* when she voluntarily performed the act that caused the death (i.e., temporal concurrence existed), the *mens rea*—the intent to kill—was not the actuating force behind the *actus reus*. The lethal act of pulling the trigger was intended as a preparatory act; it was "not done in order to give effect to [the] desire to kill."[4]

§ 15.04   Special Problem: Temporally Divisible Acts and/or Omissions

In most cases application of the concurrence principle is straightforward. Difficulties arise, however, when a person commits temporally divisible acts only one of which causes the social harm, or when the defendant's *mens rea* concurs with an omission that follows an innocent act.

For example, in *State v. Rose*,[5] *D*, an automobile driver, was prosecuted for negligent homicide, in the death of *V*, a pedestrian. The evidence showed that *D* apparently non-negligently struck *V*, whose body wedged underneath *D*'s car. *D*

---

[3] See *State v. Moore*, 12 N.H. 42 (1841).

[4] 1 W. Russell, Crime 54 (12th ed. 1964).

[5] 311 A.2d 281 (R.I. 1973).

continued to drive some distance, dragging V's body along. Medical experts could not determine whether V died at impact or as the result of being dragged.

Based on this evidence, the court properly reversed D's conviction. Although all of the elements of manslaughter were present—D committed a voluntary act; she caused the death of V; and as to her post-impact conduct, D acted with the requisite *mens rea*—the prosecutor did not prove beyond a reasonable doubt that the elements of manslaughter concurred. Essentially, D committed two divisible voluntary acts or series of acts: first, she collided with V; second, she dragged V's body after impact. Regarding the first voluntary act, D lacked a *mens rea*. Regarding the second voluntary act (or, if you will, D's omission of failing to stop), D was criminally negligent. There was insufficient medical testimony, however, to prove beyond a reasonable doubt that *this* negligent conduct/omission caused the social harm.[6]

Sometimes courts ignore the concurrence requirement. In one case $D1$, intending to kill $V1$, poisoned $V1$. Although the poison left $V1$ unconscious, it did not kill her. Thereafter, believing that $V1$ was dead, $D1$ decapitated $V1$, causing her death.[7] In another case, $D2$ struck $V2$ over the head; thinking that $V2$ was dead, $D2$ threw $V2$ over a cliff, in order to make it appear that $V2$ had died as a result of an accident. $V2$ died from exposure after the fall.[8]

In both of these cases, a defendant, with the intent to kill the victim, performed a voluntary act (poisoning $V1$; striking $V2$) that did *not* cause death, and then committed a second voluntary act (decapitating $V1$; throwing $V2$ over a cliff) that *did* cause death but without the requisite *mens rea*. Nonetheless, the convictions in both cases were affirmed. The probable, but unstated, rationale in such circumstances is that "[o]rdinary ideas of justice and common sense require that such [cases] . . . be treated as murder,"[9] rather than attempted murder.

---

[6] See also *Fagan v. Commissioner of Metropolitan Police*, [1969] 1 Q.B. 439 (*D*, perhaps accidentally, drove his car onto V's toes; D purposely failed to move his vehicle off V's toes; held: in a prosecution for assault, D may not be convicted if D's initial voluntary act was accidental; he cannot be convicted on the basis of his culpable omission, because the social harm of the offense had already occurred).

[7] *Jackson v. Commonwealth*, 38 S.W. 422 (Ky. 1896).

[8] *Thabo Meli v. Regina*, [1954] 1 W.L.R. 228, 1 All E.R. 373.

[9] Williams at 174 (footnote deleted).

CHAPTER 16

DEFENSES: AN OVERVIEW

§ 16.01 Chapter Overview[1]

In criminal trials in the United States, the prosecution has the burden of producing evidence, and of persuading the factfinder beyond a reasonable doubt, of the concurrence of four elements of criminal responsibility: (1) a voluntary act (or an omission when there is a duty to act) by the defendant; (2) the social harm prohibited by the offense; (3) the defendant's *mens rea* (strict-liability crimes aside); and (4) an actual and proximate causal connection between elements (1) and (2).

Even if the prosecution proves the concurrence of these four elements, the defendant may seek to raise one or more defenses, which, if proven, will result in his acquittal of the offense charged.[2] Unfortunately, the term "defense" is used in various ways in the criminal law. For reasons that are explained below, it is important to distinguish between so-called "failure-of-proof" defenses and true defenses. This chapter examines the difference between these types of defenses, and it categorizes the true defenses.

§ 16.02 Failure-of-Proof "Defenses"[3]

A failure-of-proof "defense" is one in which the defendant introduces evidence at his trial that demonstrates that the prosecution has failed to prove an essential element of the offense charged.

For example, suppose that *D1*, charged with an intentional homicide, seeks to prove that he mistakenly believed that the object at which he fired his gun was a tree stump rather than a human being. Or, suppose that *D2* claims that he was unconscious when he killed *V*. Or, *D3* introduces evidence that he was not at the scene of the crime and, therefore, was misidentified as the wrongdoer. Each of these defendants is raising what courts often describe as a "defense." *D1* claims a mistake-of-fact "defense"; *D2* asserts an unconsciousness (or what is sometimes termed "automatism") "defense"; *D3* alleges an alibi "defense."

---

[1] See generally 1 Robinson at 62-200; Douglas N. Husak, *The Serial View of Criminal Law Defenses*, 3 Crim. L. Forum 369 (1992); Paul H. Robinson, *Criminal Law Defenses: A Systematic Analysis*, 82 Colum. L. Rev. 199 (1982).

[2] Some so-called "partial" defenses result in the defendant's conviction of a lesser offense. For example, the "heat of passion" (or "provocation") defense to murder, if successfully proven, results in conviction of the defendant for voluntary manslaughter. See § 31.07, *infra*. Partial defenses are complete, however, in the sense that the defendant is acquitted of the crime originally charged, e.g., murder.

[3] 1 Robinson at 72.

These are not true defenses. Rather, the purpose of the defendant's evidence is to raise a reasonable doubt regarding an element of the prosecutor's case-in-chief. The mistake-of-fact "defense" negates the *mens rea* of the crime; *D2*'s unconsciousness, if believed, demonstrates that the prosecutor has failed to prove beyond a reasonable doubt that *D2*'s conduct included a voluntary act; and the alibi "defense" goes to the question of whether *D3* performed the *actus reus* of the offense.

The distinction between a true defense and a failure-of-proof "defense" is a matter of considerable significance. As a matter of constitutional law, the legislature may allocate to the defendant the burden of production and the burden of persuasion regarding true defenses.[4] In contrast, the *prosecution* must shoulder the burden of *disproving* beyond a reasonable doubt a defendant's failure-of-proof claim. This rule follows from the fact that the prosecution has the constitutional duty to prove every element of a criminal offense.

§ 16.03   True Defenses

[A]—In General

A true defense is one that, if proved, results in the acquittal of a defendant, although the prosecutor has proved beyond a reasonable doubt every element in the definition of the crime.

The burden of producing evidence regarding a true defense is allocated to the defendant; and, because a true defense does not negate an element of the crime, the legislature may place on the defendant the burden of persuasion regarding the defense. When the defendant does shoulder the burden, he is usually required to convince the factfinder of his claim by a preponderance of the evidence.

The criminal law recognizes four categories of true defenses, which are described briefly below. The two most important categories, justifications and excuses, are more fully examined in the next chapter.

[B]—Justification Defenses

A "justification" defense is one that defines conduct "otherwise criminal, which under the circumstances is socially acceptable and which deserves neither criminal liability nor even censure."[5] Justified conduct is conduct that is "a good thing, or the right or sensible thing, or a permissible thing to do."[6] That is, a justified act is an act that is right or, at least, not wrong.

For example, killing a human being ordinarily is wrongful conduct. When D kills V in self-defense, however, society says that D's conduct is "justified." Although D has committed the *actus reus* of criminal homicide, the special circumstance of the situation—D killed V because V was about to use deadly force upon him for

---

[4] See §§ 7.02[B], 7.03[B], *supra*.

[5] Peter D.W. Heberling, Note, *Justification: The Impact of the Model Penal Code on Statutory Reform*, 75 Colum. L. Rev. 914, 916 (1975).

[6] J.L. Austin, *A Plea for Excuses* in Freedom and Responsibility 6 (Herbert Morris ed. 1961).

no lawful reason—renders the homicide socially acceptable. By providing *D* with the justification defense of self-defense, society announces that *D*'s act of killing *V* was the right or, at least, a permissible, thing to do. Or, put slightly differently, the result of *D*'s conduct—*V*'s death—was not a socially undesirable outcome under the circumstances.

[C]—Excuse Defenses

An excuse defense, e.g., insanity, differs from a justification defense in a fundamental way. Whereas a justification claim generally focuses upon an *act* (i.e., *D*'s conduct), and seeks to show that the act was not wrongful, an excuse centers upon the *actor* (i.e., *D*), and tries to show that the actor is not morally culpable for his wrongful conduct. Thus, an excuse defense "is in the nature of a claim that although the actor has harmed society, [he] should not be blamed or punished for causing that harm."[7] A defendant who asserts an excuse defense claims, "in essence, 'I admit, or you have proved beyond a reasonable doubt, that I did something that I should not have done, but I [still] should not be held criminally accountable for my actions.'"[8]

An insane actor, for example, does not deny that the prosecutor has proved the essential elements of the crime nor that, all things considered, his conduct was wrongful, intolerable, and censurable (i.e., unjustified). He seeks to avoid criminal liability, however, by demonstrating that, as a result of his mental disease or defect, he lacks the moral blameworthiness ordinarily attached to wrongdoers.

[D]—Specialized Defenses ("Offense Modifications")

Justification and excuse defenses apply to all crimes. Some defenses, however, pertain to just one or a few crimes. For example, "legal impossibility" is a common law defense to the crime of attempt. In some jurisdictions "abandonment" is a defense to the crimes of attempt and conspiracy. And, "Wharton's Rule" is a defense peculiar to the crime of conspiracy.[9]

Crime-specific defenses have one common feature: they authorize acquittal of a defendant whose conduct satisfies the elements of the offense, when the underlying purpose for prohibiting the conduct is negated by the defense. Professor Paul Robinson terms such defenses "offense modifications."[10]

For example, the Model Penal Code crime of criminal attempt[11] serves the utilitarian purpose of providing society with a basis for arresting and punishing a person who has demonstrated his culpability and dangerousness by taking a substantial step toward committing a criminal offense. If *D* purposely takes a

---

[7] Joshua Dressler, *Justifications and Excuses: A Brief Review of the Concepts and the Literature*, 33 Wayne L. Rev. 1155, 1162-63 (1987).

[8] *Id.* at 1163.

[9] See §§ 27.07[D] (legal impossibility), 27.08 (abandonment of an attempt), 29.09[B] (abandonment of a conspiracy), and 29.09[C] (Wharton's Rule), *infra*.

[10] 1 Robinson at 77.

[11] Model Penal Code § 5.01.

substantial step toward committing a murder (i.e., he commits the *actus reus* and *mens rea* of an attempted murder), but then voluntarily abandons his criminal enterprise (i.e., if he proves the defense of "abandonment"), the underlying reason for punishing *D* is negated. His decision to abandon his criminal goal negates his culpability and dangerousness and, therefore, renders his punishment unnecessary.

[E]—Extrinsic Defenses ("Nonexculpatory Defenses")

Justification, excuse, and offense-modification defenses are similar in this regard: these defenses relate to the culpability or dangerousness of the defendant or the wrongfulness of his conduct. Some defenses, however, bar a defendant's conviction, *or even his prosecution*, for reasons unrelated to these factors. These claims, which Professor Robinson terms "nonexculpatory" defenses,[12] raise public-policy factors extrinsic to substantive criminal law doctrine. Examples of such defenses are the statute of limitations, diplomatic immunity, and incompetency to stand trial.

Each nonexculpatory defense serves an important public policy interest unrelated to the social harm committed by the actor or to his blameworthiness for causing it. Legislative recognition of such a defense implies that the social interest served by it outweighs the utilitarian and/or retributive reasons for punishing the offender.

---

[12] 1 Robinson at 102.

CHAPTER 17

JUSTIFICATIONS AND EXCUSES

§ 17.01 Chapter Overview [1]

Two classes of criminal law defenses are the subject of this chapter: justifications and excuses. [2] In very early English legal history the distinction between justifications and excuses was a matter of profound practical significance. In the case of felonies, a justified actor was acquitted of the offense; an excused actor, however, was subject to the same punishment as a convicted offender (the death penalty and forfeiture of his property), although he could escape the death sentence with a pardon from the Crown.

This dichotomy blurred over time, as excused actors were pardoned by the Crown on an increasingly *pro forma* basis; and they were allowed to regain their property by means of a writ of restitution. [3] Nonetheless, the excused wrongdoer was not on the same footing as the justified actor, since the former party was subject to incarceration while he petitioned for a pardon and for restitution of his property. The justified actor was free of all legal impediments.

Today, justified and excused actors are treated the same by the criminal courts: each is acquitted of the offense and neither is punished for her conduct. [4] As a result, many courts, legislatures, and commentators have become inattentive to the inherent differences between the two classes of defenses, even to the point of using the terms "justification" and "excuse" interchangeably. [5]

---

[1] See generally Fletcher at 759-875; Joshua Dressler, *Justifications and Excuses: A Brief Review of the Concepts and the Literature*, 33 Wayne L. Rev. 1155 (1987) (and the sources cited therein); Albin Eser, *Justification and Excuse*, 24 Am. J. Comp. L. 621 (1976); Kent Greenawalt, *Distinguishing Justifications From Excuses*, 49 Law & Contemp. Probs., Summer 1986, at 89; Jerome Hall, *Comment on Justification and Excuse*, 24 Am. J. Comp. L. 638 (1976); Donald L. Horowitz, *Justification and Excuse in the Program of the Criminal Law*, 49 Law & Contemp. Probs., Summer 1986, at 109; Finbarr McAuley, *The Theory of Justification and Excuse: Some Italian Lessons*, 35 Am. J. Comp. L. 359 (1987).

[2] See § 16.03[B]-[C], *supra*.

[3] 4 Blackstone at *188. Forfeiture was statutorily abolished in 1838. 9 Geo. 4, c. 13, § 10 (1838).

[4] However, a person excused on the ground of insanity is subject to civil commitment. See § 25.05, *infra*.

[5] E.g., *State v. Cozzens*, 490 N.W.2d 184, 189 (Neb. 1992) ("Therefore, the *justification* . . . defense operates to legally *excuse* conduct that would otherwise subject a person to criminal sanctions.") (emphasis added); for citations to other judicial, legislative, and scholarly misuses of the terms, see Joshua Dressler, *New Thoughts About the Concept of Justification in the Criminal Law: A Critique of Fletcher's Thinking and Rethinking*, 32

This inattention has not gone without objection by an increasing number of scholars.[6] These writers have clarified the nature of the concepts of "justification" and "excuse," demonstrating how the two defenses differ, and explaining why they believe lawyers should care about the distinctions. Because of renewed interest in the subject, including among courts who are increasingly sensitive to the distinctions, this chapter provides a close inspection of these contrasting concepts.

§ 17.02 Underlying Theories of "Justification"[7]

[A]—Initial Comments

As explained in the last chapter,[8] justified conduct is conduct that under ordinary circumstances is criminal, but which under the special circumstances encompassed by the justification defense is not wrongful and is even, perhaps, affirmatively desirable.[9] A justified act is one that "the law does not condemn, or even welcomes."[10]

The question for consideration in this section is: What makes ordinarily bad conduct justifiable? Why is it, for example, that D is justified in killing V to protect herself from V's unlawful lethal assault or from V's intrusion into her home, but she is not justified in killing V to protect her dog or her television set from theft? Are the justification defenses of self-defense, defense-of-habitation, and defense-of-property, for example, no more than a conglomeration of rules unrelated to one

UCLA L. Rev. 61, 65-66 (1984); Paul H. Robinson, *A Theory of Justification: Societal Harm as a Prerequisite for Criminal Liability*, 23 UCLA L. Rev. 266, 276 (1975).

[6] "Crying in the wilderness . . . are a few possibly prophetic voices, among which the loudest and most eloquent is George Fletcher's." Kent Greenawalt, *The Perplexing Borders of Justification and Excuse*, 84 Colum. L. Rev. 1897, 1897-98 (1984) (footnote omitted).

[7] See generally Dressler, Note 1, *supra*; Dressler, Note 5, *supra*; George P. Fletcher, *The Right and the Reasonable*, 98 Harv. L. Rev. 949 (1985); George P. Fletcher, *The Right Deed for the Wrong Reason: A Reply to Mr. Robinson*, 23 UCLA L. Rev. 293 (1975); Greenawalt, Note 1, *supra*; Greenawalt, Note 6, *supra*; Peter D.W. Heberling, Note, *Justification: The Impact of the Model Penal Code on Statutory Reform*, 75 Colum. L. Rev. 914 (1975); Robinson, Note 5, *supra*.

[8] See § 16.03[B], *supra*.

[9] Notice that "justification," as defined in the text, may imply a positive judgment about conduct (it is "right," "good," or "desirable"), or it may constitute a weaker value judgment (that the conduct is "not wrong"). Some scholars believe, however, that the concept of "justification" necessarily implies the stronger meaning.

The significance of this debate is more than semantic. For example, suppose that a legislature's view is that killing a human being in self-defense is "not wrong," but that it is unwilling to say that it is affirmatively "right" or "good." If "justification" implies only the latter concept, then lethal self-defense cannot be recognized as a justification defense. For an explanation of the larger significance of this debate, compare George P. Fletcher, *Should Intolerable Prison Conditions Generate a Justification or an Excuse for Escape?*, 26 UCLA L. Rev. 1355 (1979) (contending that justification involves "right conduct") with Dressler, Note 5, *supra* and Greenawalt, Note 6, *supra* (contending that a justification defense may involve "nonwrongful conduct").

[10] Hart at 13 (footnote deleted).

another, or is there a single moral principle that provides theoretical unity among the justification defenses?

It would be ideal if there were a unifying principle of justification, but there is none. In fact, the ingredients of a single justification defense may reflect the influence of various moral theories. What follows is a brief summary of some of the more common justification principles.

[B]—"Public Benefit" Theory

At early common law, justification defenses had a strong public-benefit cast to them. Generally speaking, conduct was not justified unless it was performed in the public's interest, and in most cases was limited to the actions of public officers.

For example, Blackstone identified three sets of circumstances in which homicides were justifiable:[11] (1) when a public officer was commanded to take a life (e.g., when the warden executed a convicted felon); (2) when a public officer, although not commanded to do so, took a life in order to advance the public welfare (e.g., when an officer killed a felon resisting arrest); and (3) when a private party took a life in order to prevent the commission of a forcible, atrocious felony.[12]

A homicide in these circumstances is considered justifiable because society benefits from the actor's conduct. But, there is more to this justification principle: the benefit to society is not incidental to some selfish goal of the actor;[13] it is the underlying motivation for the actor's conduct. Although strands of the public-benefit concept remain today, it is no longer the dominant theory of justification.

[C]—"Moral Forfeiture" Theory

The public-benefit justification principle discussed in the preceding subsection attaches to conduct that benefits society. Some theories of justification, however, are more limited in their focus: a person's conduct is justified as long as it does not result in a socially undesirable outcome.

The moral-forfeiture principle of justification fits this category. It is based on the view that people possess certain moral rights or interests that society recognizes through its criminal laws, e.g., the right to life, but which may be forfeited by the holder of the right.

The *forfeiture* of a right must be distinguished from its *waiver*. Some moral interests are not waivable. For example, a person may not legally consent to her own death. The right to life is inviolable in this sense. Nonetheless, even this nonwaivable right can be *forfeited*—nonconsensually lost—as the result of an actor's voluntary decision to violate the rights of another. In such circumstances, society may determine unilaterally that it will no longer recognize the wrongdoer's interest in her life.

---

[11] 4 Blackstone at *177-88.

[12] A person who killed another to prevent a rape, robbery, burglary, or other forcible felony acted justifiably, presumably because she was benefiting others; however, if a person killed in self-defense, this conduct constituted excusable, rather than justifiable, homicide.

[13] See Note 12, *supra*.

The moral-forfeiture doctrine is frequently called upon to explain why an aggressor or fleeing felon may justifiably be killed: as a result of V's freely-chosen decision to wrongfully threaten D's life or to commit a dangerous felony, V forfeits her right to life; consequently, when D kills V in self-defense or in order to prevent V's escape, no socially recognized harm has occurred. From the law's perspective, V's life is worth no more than that of an insect or inanimate body.[14]

The forfeiture principle, although widespread in the common law, is morally troubling to some people because it involves the nonconsensual loss of a valued right. When the forfeiture principle is applied to the interest in human life, it runs counter to the "good and simple moral principle that human life is sacred."[15] To equate human life with that of an insect or an inanimate object is troubling to those who believe in the sanctity of human life.

[D]—"Moral Rights" Theory

Conduct may be justified on the ground that the actor has a right to protect a particular moral interest. This theory of justification differs significantly from the moral-forfeiture principle described in the preceding subsection. The forfeiture doctrine focuses on the wrongdoing of the "victim," whereas the moral-rights theory focuses on the interests of the defendant. Whereas forfeiture works in a negative way to deny that there is a socially protected interest lost when the wrongdoing victim is injured or killed, the moral-rights theory work in a positive sense to provide the actor with an affirmative right to protect her threatened moral interest.

For example, when D kills or seriously injures V, a lethal aggressor, her conduct may be justified because she was enforcing a natural right of autonomy that V's conduct threatened. D is a right-holder protecting her interest against V, the outlaw who would violate her right. This principle of justification does not treat V's death as socially irrelevant, as the forfeiture doctrine does; rather, it views D's conduct as affirmatively proper.

This concept is not without its critics. Because the theory focuses on the person whose rights are being threatened rather than on the interest of the wrongdoer, some commentators claim that the principle "filters out shades and nuances and trans-forms all situations into black and white relief."[16] That is, once it is determined that V has intruded on a right belonging to D, the theory suggests that D may do whatever is necessary to enforce her right, no matter how minor the intrusion may be. After all, she is in the right, and V is in the wrong, and Right should never give way to Wrong.[17] Unless limits are placed on it, therefore, this justification theory may permit a disproportional response to the harm threatened.

---

[14] Hugo Bedau, *The Right to Life*, 1968 Monist 550, 570 ("[The wrongdoer] no longer merits our consideration, any more than an insect or a stone does.").

[15] Working Party, Board for Social Responsibility, Church of England, On Dying Well—An Anglican Contribution to the Debate on Euthanasia 24 (1975), quoted in Sanford H. Kadish, *Respect for Life and Regard for Rights in the Criminal Law*, 64 Cal. L. Rev. 871, 878 (1976).

[16] George P. Fletcher, *Proportionality and the Psychotic Aggressor: A Vignette in Comparative Criminal Theory*, 8 Israel L. Rev. 367, 381 (1973).

[17] Edmond Coke, Third Institute *55 (1644) (no "man shall [ever] give way to a thief, etc., neither shall he forfeit anything").

[E]—"Superior Interest" (or "Lesser Harm") Theory

Another theory of justification authorizes conduct when the interests of the defendant outweigh those of the person she harms. Pursuant to this principle, the interests of the parties, and, more broadly, the values that they seek to enforce, are balanced. In each case there is a superior, or at least a non-inferior, interest. As long as such an interest is pursued the conduct is justified.

For example, if *D* trespasses by entering *V*'s house in order to avoid a tornado, her conduct is justified. Protection of human life is more important than property protection. Similarly, the use of nonlethal force upon a lethal aggressor is justifiable because preservation of life is more important than prevention of injury to another. As these examples suggest, the superior-interest theory of justification is consistent with the utilitarian goal of promoting individual conduct that reduces overall harm. It is also consistent with the non-utilitarian concept of weighing moral rights and identifying the superior one.

§ 17.03 Underlying Theories of "Excuse"[18]

[A]—Initial Comments

As explained earlier,[19] an excuse defense "is in the nature of a claim that although the actor has harmed society, she should not be blamed or punished for causing that harm."[20] The question that must be answered here is: Is there a single principle that determines when the law will abstain from blaming a person who has caused social harm?

As with justifications, no single theory explains every excuse defense. Moreover, some of the theories partially overlap. Unlike the concept of justification, however,

---

[18] See generally Fletcher at § 10.3; Hart at 28-53, 158-85; Packer at 103-35; Peter Arenella, *Convicting the Morally Blameless: Reassessing the Relationship Between Legal and Moral Accountability*, 39 UCLA L. Rev. 1511 (1992); Peter Arenella, *Character, Choice and Moral Agency: The Relevance of Character to Our Moral Culpability*, 7 Soc. Phil. & Pol., Spring 1990, at 59; Michael Corrado, *Notes on the Structure of a Theory of Excuses*, 82 J. Crim. L. & Criminology 465 (1991); Anne N. Coughlin, *Excusing Women*, 82 Cal. L. Rev. 1 (1994); Deborah W. Denno, Comment, *Human Biology and Criminal Responsibility: Free Will or Free Ride?*, 137 U. Pa. L. Rev. 615 (1988); Joshua Dressler, *Reflections on Excusing Wrongdoers: Moral Theory, New Excuses and the Model Penal Code*, 19 Rutgers L.J. 671 (1988); Dressler, Note 1, *supra*; George P. Fletcher, *The Individualization of Excusing Conditions*, 47 S. Cal. L. Rev. 1269 (1974); Jeremy Horder, *Criminal Culpability: The Possibility of a General Theory*, 12 Law & Phil. 193 (1993); Sanford H. Kadish, *Excusing Crime*, 75 Cal. L. Rev. 257 (1987); Michael S. Moore, *Choice, Character, and Excuse*, 7 Soc. Phil. & Pol., Spring 1990, at 29; Michael S. Moore, *Causation and the Excuses*, 73 Cal. L. Rev. 1091 (1985); Stephen J. Morse, *Culpability and Control*, 142 U. Pa. L. Rev. 1587 (1994); Samuel H. Pillsbury, *The Meaning of Deserved Punishment: An Essay on Choice, Character, and Responsibility*, 67 Ind. L.J. 719 (1992); George Vuoso, *Background, Responsibility, and Excuse*, 96 Yale L.J. 1661 (1987); Glanville Williams, *The Theory of Excuses*, 1982 Crim. L. Rev. 732.

[19] See § 16.03[C], *supra*.

[20] Dressler, Note 1, *supra*, at 1162-63.

which can (but need not) be explained on utilitarian grounds, excuses in the criminal law are more plausibly defended in non-utilitarian terms. As Professor Sanford Kadish has observed, "[s]omething is missing" in the utilitarian account of excuses:

> What is missing is an account of the concern for the innocent person who is the object of a criminal prosecution . . . . [¶] To blame a person is to express a moral criticism, and if the person's action does not deserve criticism, blaming him is a kind of falsehood and is, to the extent the person is injured by being blamed, unjust to him. It is this feature of our everyday moral practices that lies behind the law's excuses.[21]

After brief comment on the utilitarian theory of excuses, various nonconsequentialist moral theories are surveyed.

[B]—Deterrence Theory

According to Jeremy Bentham, the leading classical utilitarian, excuses are recognized in the criminal law because they identify the circumstances in which conduct is undeterrable, e.g., when a person is insane or coerced to commit an offense. In such situations, punishment of the actor is wrong because it is inefficacious.[22]

This argument has been denounced as a "spectacular *non sequitur*."[23] The threat of punishment may not deter a person who is suffering from a mental illness or is acting under duress, but its actual infliction may deter misconduct by "normal" persons, who might otherwise believe that they could fraudulently convince a jury of their undeterrability. Abolition of all excuses, therefore, might be socially useful: the pain inflicted on the undeterrable actor might be outweighed by the prevention of harm caused by the law's imposition of a stricter form of liability.[24]

Professor H.L.A. Hart has offered a more sophisticated utilitarian account of excuses. He has argued that excuses "function as a mechanism for . . . maximizing within the framework of coercive criminal law the efficacy of the individual's informed and considered choice in determining the future and also his power to predict that future."[25] That is, the rule that criminal liability is limited to voluntary wrongdoing allows each person to derive satisfaction from being able to plan her life with reasonable confidence that she can avoid the sanctions of the law, as long as she chooses to obey society's dictates.

[C]—Causation Theory

Perhaps the broadest non-utilitarian theory of excuse states that a person should not be blamed for her conduct if it was caused by factors outside her control.[26] For

---

[21] Kadish, Note 18, *supra*, at 264.

[22] Jeremy Bentham, An Introduction to the Principles of Morals and Legislation 160-62 (J. Burns and H.L.A. Hart eds. 1970).

[23] Hart at 19.

[24] *Id.* at 19-20; Fletcher at 813-17; Packer at 108-11.

[25] Hart at 46.

[26] For a full exposition of this theory, which the author ultimately rejects, see Moore, Note 18, *supra*, at 1101-12.

example, *D* is morally blameless and, therefore, should be excused, if her criminal conduct was the result of a mental illness or a coercive threat, but not if her criminal conduct was caused by self-induced intoxication or by any other factor for which she is responsible.

Although this principle is plausible on its face and represents the views of some scholars and courts, it does not accurately explain the whole of current excuse law. For example, as is developed elsewhere,[27] only a single, largely discredited, definition of insanity applies the causation principle; most people who commit criminal offenses due to mental disease are held criminally responsible. Likewise, if a person commits a crime because she is threatened with economic ruin not of her own making, her conduct is not legally excused.[28]

It is also not evident that the causation principle conforms with our moral intuitions. A person who commits a crime due to self-induced intoxication, for example, may be able to show that her strong propensity to become intoxicated was caused by genetic or environmental factors over which she had no control. Thus, acceptance of the causal principle of excuses could threaten to lead society down "the cul-de-sac of . . . determinism,"[29] in which nobody can be blamed or punished for her wrongful acts.

[D]—Character Theory

Various theorists treat a person's moral character as central to the concept of deserved punishment. According to one character theory, punishment should be proportional to a wrongdoer's moral desert, and that desert should be measured by the actor's character.[30] Normally, we infer bad character from an actor's wrongful conduct; these character theorists argue that excuses should be recognized in the law in those circumstances in which bad character cannot be inferred from the offender's wrongful conduct.

For example, if *D* robs a bank, we would ordinarily infer that she is a greedy person who lacks concern for the rights of others, i.e., that she possesses a bad character. However, we would not infer bad character if we learned that she robbed the bank because terrorists threatened to kill her child if she did not cooperate. In such circumstances, we assume that even a person of good moral character would probably violate the law. Therefore, we excuse her actions.

This theory may conform with our moral intuitions. We assume that people who commit crimes are "bad people." When a "good person" commits a "bad act" we sometimes say that her act was "out of character." We look for some explanation independent of her character that explains and excuses her conduct.

Nonetheless, critics raise various objections to the character theory of excuses. First, if excuse law were genuinely based on the concept of character, a court would

---

[27] See § 25.04[C][4], *infra.*

[28] See § 23.01[B], *infra.*

[29] Fletcher at 801.

[30] *Id.* at 800.

need to look at a person's entire life, and not solely at the circumstances surrounding the particular criminal act, in order to judge her moral desert. Yet the law does not do this, nor is it likely that most people would want courts involved in God-like investigation of a person's character.

Second, the theory does not explain why we *do* punish people of *good* character who commit out-of-character offenses, e.g., if *D*, unemployed, in a moment of frustration, batters *V*. Although *D* is a good person, she has acted in a blameworthy manner and is (and most people would probably say, should be) held accountable for her actions.

Third, causal theorists[31] argue that the character theory assumes that people are responsible for their character, but this may not be the case. They argue that one's character is shaped by powerful genetic and environmental factors beyond the individual's control. Defenders of the character theory argue, however, that a person may be held responsible for her character traits, even if she did not initially choose them, because she is responsible for retaining them.[32]

[E]—"Free Choice" (or Personhood) Theory

Advocates of the free-choice theory claim that a person may properly be blamed for her conduct "if, but only if, [s]he had the capacity and fair opportunity to function in a uniquely human way, *i.e.,* freely to choose whether to violate the moral/legal norms of society."[33] According to this account, "free choice" exists if, at the time of the wrongful conduct, the actor has the substantial capacity and fair opportunity to: (1) understand the facts relating to her conduct; (2) appreciate that her conduct violates society's mores; and (3) conform her conduct to the dictates of the law. A person lacking in any of these regards does not deserve to be punished, because she lacks the basic attributes of personhood that qualify her as a moral agent.

Another way to express the personhood principle is to state that a person is excused if she lacks the substantial capacity or opportunity to use practical reasoning skills. "Practical reasoning" requires the ability to: (1) formulate action-goals; (2) "form a belief about how certain actions will or will not advance the objects of our desires";[34] and (3) act in furtherance of one's desires and beliefs. Thus, we excuse people whose ability to reason practically is grossly disturbed or underdeveloped (e.g. insane people and infants); we also partially or fully excuse those whose opportunity to reason practically is seriously undermined on an individual occasion (e.g., due to passion or coercion).

---

[31] See § 17.03[C], *supra*.

[32] Pillsbury, Note 18, *supra*, at 730-31 (describing, but not defending, this proposition).

[33] Dressler, Note 18, *supra*, at 701 (footnote omitted); see Hart at 181 ("Thus a primary vindication of the principle of responsibility could rest on the simple idea that unless a man has the capacity and a fair opportunity . . . to adjust his behaviour to the law its penalties ought not to be applied to him.").

[34] Moore, *Causation and the Excuses*, Note 18, *supra*, at 1148.

Critics of the free-choice/personhood theory believe that it is too narrow. Causal theorists argue, for example, that because "free choice" is defined in terms of the actor's capacity and opportunity, *at the moment of the criminal act*, to obey the law, morally significant events arising earlier are excluded from the picture. For example, although a person may have had "free choice" regarding whether to rob a particular liquor store on a particular occasion, she may not have had a fair opportunity to avoid the conditions that hardened her character and made committing the crime seem inevitable.

Professor Peter Arenella, a character theorist,[35] is also critical. He contends that the free-choice theory provides too "thin" an account of what it means to be a moral agent. He argues that one cannot be a moral decisionmaker, and thus qualify as a morally accountable actor, unless the person has the capacity to empathize. One who lacks the ability to care about other human beings, Arenella contends, lacks such an important human characteristic that she is undeserving of blame and punishment, even if she "freely" causes harm, as "free choice" is defined above.

§ 17.04 Justification Defenses and Mistake-of-Fact Claims[36]

[A]—The Issue

Consider the following hypothetical: *D* intentionally kills *V*. At trial, *D* claims that she killed *V* because she believed that *V* was about to kill her. In fact, *V* did *not* constitute an imminent unlawful deadly threat to *D*, i.e., *D* did not need to kill *V*. This very common scenario involves the convergence of two "defense" concepts: a traditional justification defense (here, self-defense); and a mistake-of-fact claim (*D*'s erroneous belief that *V* posed an imminent unlawful deadly threat).

Two questions arise when a defendant asserts a justification defense, and yet also claims a mistake of fact: (1) Is a defendant entitled to be acquitted if she is mistaken as to the existence of facts that would justify her conduct; and (2) If she is entitled to be acquitted, should the law describe her conduct as justified or excused? For current purposes, these questions will be answered in relation to self-defense (considered fully in Chapter 18), but the principles here have application to the other justification defenses, as well.

---

[35] See Arenella, *Convicting the Morally Blameless,* and Arenella, *Character, Choice, and Moral Agency, Note 18, supra.*

[36] See generally Fletcher at 762-68; 2 Robinson at § 184; Russell L. Christopher, *Mistake of Fact in the Objective Theory of Justification: Do Two Rights Make Two Wrongs Make Two Rights . . . ?*, 85 J. Crim. L. & Criminology 295 (1994); Dressler, Note 5, *supra*; Greenawalt, Note 6, *supra*; Terry L. Price, *Faultless Mistake of Fact*, Crim. Just. Ethics, Summer/Fall 1993, at 14; Benjamin B. Sendor, *Mistake of Fact: A Study in the Structure of Criminal Conduct*, 25 Wake Forest L. Rev. 707 (1990); Richard Singer, *The Resurgence of Mens Rea: II—Honest But Unreasonable Mistake of Fact in Self-Defense*, 28 B.C. L. Rev. 459 (1987).

[B]—The General Rule

The law is clear-cut in situations of the sort described here. A defendant *is* entitled to be acquitted on the basis of self-defense if her mistake of fact regarding the threat was reasonable. However, she will be convicted of some form of criminal homicide if her mistake was unreasonable.[37] More specifically, the rule is that a defendant is justified—and not merely excused—in using deadly force if, at the time of the homicide, she had reasonable grounds for believing, and did believe, that she was in imminent danger of death or grievous bodily injury, and that deadly force was necessary to repel the threat, *although it turned out later that these appearances were false.*

[C]—Criticisms of the General Rule

There is little disagreement with the principle that a defendant who acts on the basis of reasonable appearances should be acquitted,[38] but there is considerable debate about the propriety of treating such a mistaken actor's conduct as justifiable, rather than excusable. For example, in the self-defense hypothetical at the beginning of this section, how can it be that *D* is *justified* in taking *V*'s life, if *V* was an innocent person or, at worst, intended only a minor battery upon *D*?

Critics of the general rule—the rule that a person is justified in acting on the basis of reasonable, albeit inaccurate, appearances—argue that it confuses the difference between justifications, which go to the propriety of the defendant's *act*, and excuses, which relate to the blameworthiness of the *actor*. The critics maintain that a reasonable-but-mistaken *actor* is morally blameless and, therefore, should be excused; but it is wrong to suggest that the *act* of killing an innocent person or one who does not pose a threat to the life of the actor is justifiable.

These critics are making more than a semantic argument. As discussed more fully in the next section of this chapter, the justification/excuse distinction can have practical implications. In the current situation, critics contend, it is wrong to allow *D* (in the hypothetical) a justification defense in the killing of innocent-*V*, because this would seemingly leave *V* without her own right of self-defense, which is unjust. Alternatively, the law would have to recognize incompatible justifications: *D* is justified in killing *V*, based on incorrect-but-reasonable appearances; *V* is justified in killing *D*, based on the reality that *D* is (justifiably) trying to take *V*'s life. To critics, this is an anomalous outcome: one (specifically *V*), but not both, are justified in killing the other. Moreover, critics argue, unless the law properly characterizes *D*'s and *V*'s conduct, a third person who arrives on the scene will not know whether she may come to the aid of *D*, *V*, both, or neither.[39]

---

[37] Under traditional common law principles, she is guilty of murder; in some jurisdictions today, however, she would be convicted of manslaughter. See §§ 18.02, 18.04, *infra*. Under the Model Penal Code, she is guilty of manslaughter or negligent homicide, depending on whether she was reckless or negligent as to her mistake of fact. See § 18.07[B], *infra*.

[38] But see § 19.01, *infra*.

[39] See § 17.04[E], *infra*.

[D]—Defense of the General Rule

Defenders of the general rule point out that "[t]he criminal law does not demand ideal behavior from people."[40] All that the law can fairly expect of a person is that she make a conscientious effort to determine the true state of affairs before acting. If she does this, the defenders claim, her conduct is justifiable, although the result of her conduct (in the hypothetical, V's death) may prove to be tragic.

The defenders of the rule may be right. Consider that a police officer is legally entitled to arrest a person if she has probable cause to believe that the suspect has committed a felony. An officer acting on probable cause is justified in making the arrest, even if the suspect turns out to be innocent. Critics of the general rule would say that an officer in such circumstances has acted *un*justifiably, no matter how carefully she has investigated the situation. Yet, few would agree that a police officer is acting outside the law, i.e., unjustifiably, simply because her knowledge of the circumstances proves to be imperfect.

Moreover, defenders of the general rule argue, there is no inherent anomaly in recognizing incompatible justifications. For example, in the arrest situation, suppose that the innocent person uses nondeadly force to resist the arrest. If the citizen is later charged with battery upon the police officer, there is no reason why the law must be so inflexible as to deny a justification defense to the citizen, although the officer was also justified in making the arrest.[41]

The reader should appraise these competing arguments, and their practical effects, while considering the specifics of the justification defenses, as set out in Chapters 18-22.

§ 17.05　Justification v. Excuse: Why Does it Matter?[42]

[A]—In General

Why should the legal profession care about the conceptual differences between justification and excuse defenses, if they both result in acquittal of a defendant?

Not everyone believes that the distinctions are sufficiently important to merit close attention. The drafters of the Model Penal Code, for example, were skeptical that they could draw sensible lines between justifications and excuses; and, even if they could, they concluded that the increased complexity of the statutory system would have outweighed the benefits from drawing distinctions.[43]

Advocates of drawing distinctions offer a number of justifications for their position, some of which are summarized below.[44]

---

[40] Greenawalt, Note 6, *supra*, at 1905.

[41] The point here is not that the law *should* permit a justification defense to the citizen in the battery prosecution, but rather that it is not inherently unreasonable to permit one.

[42] See Fletcher at 664-70, 759-69; Dressler, Note 1, *supra*; Dressler, Note 5, *supra*; George P. Fletcher, *Rights and Excuses*, Crim. Just. Ethics, Summer-Fall 1984, at 17; Fletcher, Note 9, *supra*; Greenawalt, Note 6, *supra*; Robinson, Note 5, *supra*.

[43] American Law Institute, Comment to art. 3, at 2-4.

[44] Also, review the justification-versus-excuse arguments considered in § 17.04, *supra*, which also raise potential practical implications.

[B]—Moral Guidance

The criminal law represents a moral compass that people should use to decide which of various potential paths they should take in particular circumstances. For example, when a battered woman kills her abusive partner while he is asleep, is she acting justifiably, excusably, or neither?[45] People should take justifiable, rather than wrongful-but-excusable, paths. If the law does not label the paths clearly, then the system has failed to provide adequate guidance.

[C]—Retroactivity[46]

Suppose that conduct A constitutes a defense when D acts, but that the defense is repealed before D's trial. Is D entitled to assert conduct A as a defense at her trial? The answer arguably depends on whether A was a justification or an excuse.

D should be entitled to raise any justification defense recognized at the time of her conduct. A justification defense defines conduct that society wishes to encourage or, at least, tolerate. People should be allowed to rely on these representations. To deny D the opportunity at trial to justify her conduct on the basis of the subsequently-repealed defense would be unfair and counter-utilitarian.

The same cannot be said for excuses. Excuse defenses are not directives to would-be actors regarding the permissibility of particular conduct; excuses identify the circumstances under which a person ought to be relieved of criminal responsibility for her conduct because she is undeterrable or is not morally to blame for her conduct. Any person who investigates excuse law and relies on it before she acts, however, is not the type of person to whom the excuses are meant to apply. Therefore, to the extent that retroactivity principles are based on conceptions of justifiable reliance, it is fair to deny her the opportunity to raise a repealed excuse.

[D]—Accomplice Liability[47]

Suppose that D wishes to perform conduct A. D needs assistance to do so, so she turns to X for aid. If X assists, what is *her* criminal responsibility? If conduct A is justified, D has acted properly. X, therefore, should be acquitted as an accomplice in the commission of the justified act. Thus, if X provides D with a gun used to kill V in justifiable self-defense, X is guilty of no crime.[48]

Suppose, however, that D kills V due to an insane delusion. X, who is sane, provides D with the gun used in the crime. Although D may be acquitted on the basis of insanity, no logical reason precludes the conviction of X of the murder in which she sanely assisted. After all, a wrongful act has occurred, i.e., the death of

---

[45] See § 18.06[B][4], *infra*.

[46] See generally Chapter 5, *supra*.

[47] See § 30.06[B][2], *infra*.

[48] Should X be acquitted, however, if she had a malicious motive for helping, e.g., X wanted V dead because V was a business rival? Compare Robinson, Note 5, *supra* (saying yes) with Fletcher, Note 7, *supra* (saying no, in comparable circumstances).

V. The fact that *D* is relieved of responsibility due to mental illness should not bar conviction of a sane person who assists in the wrongful act.

[E]—Third Party Conduct

Generally speaking, justifications are universalized, whereas excuses are individualized.[49] That is, if *D* is justified in performing act A to protect her own rights, a third person, *X*, is also justified in doing A to protect *D*. An excuse, however, may only be invoked by the person who suffers from the excusing condition.

In some cases this generalization works easily and straightforwardly. For example, if *D* is justified in killing *V*, an aggressor, in self-defense, it would ordinarily follow that *X*, an onlooker, is justified in killing *V* in order to save *D*. On the other hand, if *D* is only excused in killing *V*, e.g., *D* is insane, no right attaches to *X* to kill *V*. Assuming that *X* is sane (and is not the victim of any other excusing condition), she is subject to prosecution.

Some cases are far more difficult to resolve. Consider the case of a person who kills a morally innocent aggressor in self-defense:[50] *V*, a very young child—a child too young to understand the consequences of her actions—points a loaded gun at *D* under circumstances in which *D* accurately believes that her life is in imminent jeopardy, and that the only way to protect herself is to take *V*'s life.[51] If *D* kills *V*, *D* will be acquitted, but it is unclear whether her defense should be treated as one of justification or excuse. She is *justified* in killing the youth under the moral-right theory of justification,[52] since her right of autonomy is being threatened; she is *not justified*, however, in killing the youth under the moral-forfeiture doctrine,[53] since the child is too young to know what she is doing and, therefore, has not forfeited her right to life.

The legal rights of *X*, a stranger who comes upon the situation when *V* is about to kill *D*, may depend on the label attached to *D*'s defense. If *D* is justified in killing *V*, it would follow from the universalization premise[54] that *X* is also justified in killing *V* to save *D*. If *D* is merely excused in killing *V*, however, *X* could be convicted if she killed the youth, unless she could allege some excuse personal to her.

---

[49] See Fletcher at 810-13. Some commentators believe that this proposition, although generally accurate, is not true in all circumstances or would lead to undesirable conclusions if it were followed without exception. See Dressler, Note 5, *supra*, at 95-98; Greenawalt, Note 6, *supra*, at 1915-16.

[50] See generally Fletcher, Note 16, *supra*; Mordechai Kremnitzer, *Proportionality and the Psychotic Aggressor: Another View*, 18 Israel L. Rev. 178 (1983); Jeff McMaham, *Self-Defense and the Problem of the Innocent Attacker*, 104 Ethics 252 (1994); Michael Otsuka, *Killing the Innocent in Self-Defense*, 23 Phil. & Pub. Aff. 74 (1994).

[51] Sanford H. Kadish & Stephen J. Schulhofer, Criminal Law and Its Processes 876 (5th ed. 1989).

[52] See § 17.02[D], *supra*.

[53] See § 17.02[C], *supra*.

[54] But see Note 49, *supra*.

CHAPTER 18

SELF-DEFENSE

§ 18.01 Chapter Overview[1]

Every state in the United States recognizes self-defense, including the use of deadly force in self-protection, as a justification defense. Although the right to protect oneself from an aggressor has never been held to be a fundamental constitutional right,[2] one court has observed:

> It is difficult to the point of impossibility to imagine a right in any state to abolish self-defense altogether, thereby leaving one a Hobson's choice of almost certain death through violent attack now or statutorily mandated death [or life imprisonment] through trial and conviction of murder later.[3]

Most issues regarding the application of defensive force arise in the context of homicide and attempted murder prosecutions. Therefore, most of this chapter focuses on the question of when *deadly* force may be used in self-defense.

§ 18.02 General Principles

At common law, a person who is not an aggressor is justified in using force upon another if he reasonably believes that such force is necessary to protect himself from imminent use of unlawful force by the other person.[4] However, *deadly* force is *un*justified in self-protection unless the actor reasonably believes that its use is necessary to prevent imminent and unlawful use of *deadly* force by the aggressor.[5] And, in some jurisdictions, a person may not use deadly force against an aggressor if he knows that he has a completely safe avenue of retreat.

These principles are subject to substantial clarification, as discussed in the next chapter section. However, it should be noted at the outset that the defense of self-defense, as is the case with other justification defenses,[6] contains: (1) a "necessity"

---

[1] See generally Joseph H. Beale, *Homicide in Self-Defense*, 3 Colum. L. Rev. 526 (1903). Citations to specific self-defense topics are set out below, at the beginning of appropriate sections and/or subsections.

[2] The issue rarely arises. However, at least two federal courts have held that the right of self-defense is not a constitutional right. *White v. Arn*, 788 F.2d 338 (6th Cir. 1986); *Rowe v. DeBruyn*, 17 F.3d 1047 (7th Cir. 1994).

[3] *Griffin v. Martin*, 785 F.2d 1172, 1186 n.37 (4th Cir.), *aff'd and op. withdrawn*, 795 F.2d 22 (1986) (*en banc*).

[4] *People v. Rodriguez*, 631 N.E.2d 427, 430 (Ill. App. Ct. 1994).

[5] *United States v. Peterson*, 483 F.2d 1222, 1230-31 (D.C. Cir. 1973); *People v. Murillo*, 587 N.E.2d 1199, 1204 (Ill. App. Ct. 1992).

[6] See 1 Robinson at 86-88.

component; (2) a "proportionality" requirement; and (3) a reasonable-belief rule that overlays the defense.

The *necessity* rule provides that force should not be used against another person unless, and only to the extent that, it is necessary. Therefore, a person may not use deadly force to combat an imminent deadly assault if some nondeadly response will apparently suffice. For example, if *V*, an elderly or infirm aggressor, attempts to stab *D*, *D* may not kill him if he knows or should know that he could avoid death by disarming *V*,[7] or by using *non*deadly force.[8]

The *proportionality* rule provides that a person is not justified in using force that is excessive in relation to the harm threatened. Therefore, a person is not permitted to use deadly force to repel a nondeadly attack, even if deadly force is necessary to prevent the battery. For example, if *V* threatens to strike *D* on a public road, and the only way that *D* can avoid the battery is to push *V* into the way of a fast-moving car, *D* must abstain, and seek compensation for the battery after the fact.

Finally, the privilege of self-defense is based on reasonable appearances, rather than on objective reality. That is, as discussed elsewhere,[9] a person is justified in using force to protect himself if he has reasonable grounds for believing, and actually believes, that such force is necessary to repel an imminent unlawful attack, although appearances prove to be false.[10] The defense is unavailable to one whose belief in this regard was genuine, but *unreasonable*. Therefore, in a murder prosecution involving the use of deadly force, the traditional rule is that an unreasonably mistaken actor is guilty of murder, notwithstanding his belief that he was acting in legitimate self-defense. However, some states permit an unreasonably mistaken actor to assert an "imperfect" or "incomplete" claim of self-defense, which mitigates the offense to manslaughter.[11]

§ 18.03 Deadly Force: Clarification of the General Principles

As stated in § 18.02, a person who is not an aggressor is justified in using deadly force upon another if he reasonably believes that such force is necessary to protect himself from imminent use of unlawful deadly force by the other person. This rule is explained immediately below.

---

[7] E.g., *State v. Garrison*, 525 A.2d 498 (Conn. 1987) (*V*, who was intoxicated, moved menacingly toward *D* with a gun in his waistband; *D* was able to disarm *V*; *V* then pulled out a knife; *D* shot *V* to death; *D*'s conviction was upheld, in part on the ground that *D* knew, or should have known, that he could have disarmed *V* again).

[8] E.g., *State v. Dill*, 461 So.2d 1130 (La. Ct. App. 1984) (*D* was in his car preparing to leave a public parking lot; *V* requested help in starting his car; *D* said he would not help unless *V* paid him; after a verbal exchange, *V* lunged at *D* with a knife through *D*'s car window; *D* shot *V* in the head; held: conviction upheld on the ground that *D* could have rolled up his window and driven away or shot *D* in a less vital area than the head).

[9] See § 17.04[B], *supra*.

[10] See *State v. Simon*, 646 P.2d 1119, 1120-21 (Kan. 1982); *People v. Goetz*, 497 N.E.2d 41, 46-48 (N.Y. 1986); *Fresno Rifle and Pistol Club, Inc. v. Van de Kamp*, 746 F.Supp. 1415, 1421 (E.D.Cal. 1990).

[11] See § 18.04, *infra*.

[A]—"Deadly Force": Definition

"Deadly force" is force likely to cause death or grievous bodily injury.[12] That is, force is characterized as deadly if death or grievous injury is the likely outcome, regardless of the actor's intentions or the actual result. For example, if D stabs V in self-defense, this constitutes deadly force, even if D intended only to wound V slightly,[13] and regardless of whether V dies, is grievously injured, or neither.

On the other hand, a minor battery does not ordinarily constitute deadly force, even if death unexpectedly results.[14] A battery constitutes deadly force, however, if the person being struck is an infirm individual who is likely to die or be grievously harmed by the battery.[15]

[B]—The "Non-Aggressor" Limitation

[1]—Definition of "Aggressor"

An aggressor "has no right to a claim of self-defense."[16] An "aggressor" is a person whose "affirmative unlawful act [is] reasonably calculated to produce an affray foreboding injurious or fatal consequences."[17] For example, if D unlawfully brandishes a knife and threatens to kill V, D is not justified in defending himself if V responds to D's threats by attacking him.

Courts frequently state that a person is not privileged to use force to resist an attack unless he is "free from fault in the difficulty,"[18] but this is an over-statement.[19] In some circumstances, a person *is* justified in using deadly force, although he is not free from fault in creating the situation that results in another person's death. For example, if D calls V, an acquaintance, "a jerk," to which V take such umbrage that he pulls out a gun and menaces D with it, D is justified in killing V (assuming that the other requirements of the defense are met), although D was

---

[12] *State v. Clay*, 256 S.E.2d 176, 182 (N.C. 1979), *overruled on other grounds, State v. Davis*, 290 S.E.2d 574 (N.C. 1982) and *State v. McAvoy*, 417 S.E.2d 489 (N.C. 1992). This definition applies whether one is considering the force used by the aggressor or the innocent person being threatened.

[13] Of course, if D did not intend to kill V, he would not have the requisite *mens rea* to be convicted of intent-to-kill murder.

[14] E.g., V throws a fist at D; D protects himself by lightly pushing V away. V unexpectedly dies. D may successfully claim self-defense because the force he used was not like to cause death or serious bodily injury. Presumably, too, D would not be guilty of murder or manslaughter for lack of *mens rea*.

[15] Depending upon D's awareness of V's infirmity, however, D may lack the *mens rea* for murder.

[16] *Bellcourt v. State*, 390 N.W.2d 269, 272 (Minn. 1986); see *Loesche v. State*, 620 P.2d 646, 651 (Alaska 1980) ("The law of self-defense is designed to afford protection to one who is beset by an aggressor and confronted by a necessity not of his own making.").

[17] *United States v. Peterson*, 483 F.2d 1222, 1233 (D.C. Cir. 1973).

[18] *Id.* at 1231; Perkins & Boyce at 1115.

[19] *State v. Corchado*, 453 A.2d 427, 433 (Conn. 1982) (stating that "[i]t is not difficult to visualize self-defense situations where . . . there is some fault on both sides").

not entirely free from fault in the conflict. *D* was not the aggressor because his mild insult was not an "affirmatively unlawful act reasonably calculated to produce an affray foreboding injurious or fatal consequences."

Two features of the concept of "aggression" merit brief attention here. First, a person is an aggressor even if he merely starts a *non*deadly conflict. Second, a person is *not* an aggressor if his conduct, no matter how provocative, is lawful. For example, if *D*, a police officer, comes upon a fight and threatens to use force against the combatants if they do not desist, his conduct cannot reasonably be interpreted as an aggression. [20]

[2]—Removing the Status of "Aggressor"

The initial aggressor in a conflict may purge himself of that status and regain the right of self-defense. The issue always is: Who was the aggressor *at the time the defensive—in this context, deadly—force was used*? In this regard, it is important to distinguish between "deadly" (or "felonious") and "nondeadly" aggressors.

[a]—Deadly Aggressor

A "deadly" (or "felonious") aggressor is a person whose acts are reasonably calculated to produce fatal consequences. The only way such a person may regain the right of self-defense is by withdrawing from the affray and successfully communicating this fact, either expressly or impliedly, to his intended victim. [21]

This rule is strictly applied. For example, suppose that *D* initiates a deadly attack on *V* in the street, whereupon *V* responds with sufficient force that *D* is fearful for his own life. If *D* runs behind a parked car, and *V* pursues him, *D* is still not entitled to act in self-defense, unless by actions or words he communicates to *V* that he no longer is a threat to *V*, i.e., that *D*'s retreat is not simply a temporary strategic act of avoiding *V*'s resistance. In the absence of notice to *V* of the termination of the conflict, *D* is guilty of murder if he kills *V* in "self-defense."

[b]—Nondeadly Aggressor

Suppose that *D* attempts to slap *V*. *V* improperly responds to the threat by pulling out a knife and attempting to kill *D*. In this conflict, *D* was the initial aggressor, because he started an "affray foreboding *injurious* consequences." On the other hand, *V*'s response was disproportional to *D*'s attack, as he wrongfully converted a minor altercation into a deadly assault. Thus, *V* is also an aggressor, indeed, a worse one than *D*. May *D*, therefore, now kill *V* in self-defense?

Case law is split in this regard. Many courts provide that when the victim of a nondeadly assault responds with deadly force, the original aggressor immediately regains his right of self-defense. [22] Thus, in the hypothetical, although *D* was the

---

[20] An alternative way to reach the same result is to state that the force threatened by the officer does not constitute *unlawful* force. See § 18.03[D][2], *infra*.

[21] *People v. Gleghorn*, 238 Cal.Rptr. 82, 85 (App. Ct. 1987); *State v. Diggs*, 592 A.2d 949, 951 (Conn. 1991); *Bellcourt v. State*, 390 N.W.2d at 272.

[22] E.g., *People v. Gleghorn*, 238 Cal.Rptr. at 85; *Watkins v. State*, 555 A.2d 1087, 1088 (Md. Ct. Spec. App. 1989).

initial aggressor (and is subject to prosecution for assault), he may defend himself, including by use of deadly force if required.

Some courts, however, do not provide D, the initial nondeadly aggressor, with an automatic right of self-defense. [23] In these jurisdictions, D is not entitled to use deadly force against V unless he avails himself of an obviously safe retreat, if one exists. [24] If no safe place exists, or if D does retreat and V pursues him, D may resort to deadly force. If D does not retreat when he obviously could do so, he does not lose his status as an aggressor, and is not justified in killing V. However, in such circumstances, aggressor D will usually be convicted of manslaughter, rather than murder. [25]

The rationale for reducing the offense to manslaughter in such circumstances is not always explained. Frequently, D's manslaughter verdict can be explained on non-self-defense grounds: V's deadly response to D's nondeadly assault constitutes "adequate provocation," which brings D's conduct within the "sudden heat of passion" doctrine of homicide law. [26]

Sometimes, however, a court will state that a nondeadly aggressor has an "imperfect" or "incomplete" right of self-defense, which results in the manslaughter conviction. [27] This is an unfortunate way to describe the defense: it is a contradiction in terms to say that a person has a "right" to use deadly force in self-defense, and yet convict and punish him for enforcing this "right." It would be preferable to say that D has an *excuse* for the killing, but one that is imperfect or incomplete due to his culpability in the conflict.

[C]—Necessity Requirement: The Issue of Retreat [28]

[1]—Contrasting Approaches

The general rule is that self-defense "is measured against necessity," [29] i.e., that deadly force may not be used to repel aggression if such force is unnecessary. [30] One potential exception to this principle is the "no-retreat" rule applied in most states.

---

[23] See American Law Institute, Comment to § 3.04, at 50-51.

[24] Perkins & Boyce at 1128-29.

[25] *State v. Hill.* 20 N.C. 629, 633-34 (1839); Perkins & Boyce at 1128-29; 1 Oscar Leroy Warren & Basil Michael Bilas, Warren on Homicide 693 (1938).

[26] See § 31.07[B][2], *infra.*

[27] See § 18.04, *infra.*

[28] See generally Richard Maxwell Brown, No Duty to Retreat (1992); Joseph H. Beale, *Retreat from a Murderous Assault*, 16 Harv. L. Rev. 567 (1903); Garrett Epps, Further Developments, *Any Which Way But Loose: Interpretive Strategies and Attitudes Toward Violence in the Evolution of the Anglo-American "Retreat Rule"*, 55 Law & Contemp. Probs., Winter 1992, at 303.

[29] *State v. Abbott*, 174 A.2d 881, 884 (N.J. 1961).

[30] See § 18.02, *supra.*

Although American courts are sharply split on the issue of retreat, a majority of jurisdictions have adopted the rule that a non-aggressor[31] is permitted to use deadly force to repel an unlawful deadly attack, even if he is aware of a place to which he can retreat in complete safety.[32]

The no-retreat rule is justified on various grounds. First, the law "should not denounce conduct as criminal when it accords with the behavior of reasonable men."[33] Specifically, it is said that the "manly" reaction to an unlawful attack is to stand one's ground, rather than to retreat. Second, "Right" should never give way to "Wrong,"[34] yet this is what the retreat doctrine demands of "Right." Third, the retreat rule would have a counter-utilitarian effect: it would embolden aggressors; and innocent people, if required to retreat, might be killed while fleeing.

Notwithstanding these claims, a minority of states provide that an innocent person threatened by deadly force must retreat rather than use deadly force,[35] if he is aware that he can do so in complete safety.[36] Proponents of this position declare that the retreat requirement properly places protection of human life above the "manly" right of standing up to aggression.[37] They also assert that the retreat rule does not increase the risk of harm to innocent persons, because retreat is not demanded when it would imperil the would-be defender.[38]

In fact, in retreat jurisdictions, the duty to retreat is not triggered unless there is a place of *complete* safety to which the non-aggressor can turn.[39] Furthermore, the issue is not simply whether a place of such safety exists, but rather whether the person under siege is aware of its existence.[40] The practical effect of these two conditions is that people under attack rarely are compelled to retreat, especially when the aggressor is armed with a gun: there is almost never a place of complete

---

[31] *Aggressors* who wish to defend themselves are required to retreat, even in no-retreat jurisdictions. See § 18.03[B][2], *supra*.

[32] See *State v. Anderson*, 631 A.2d 1149, 1154 (Conn. 1993) (stating, but rejecting, the majority rule); *Idrogo v. People*, 818 P.2d 752, 756 (Colo. 1991) (applying the no-retreat rule).

[33] *State v. Abbott*, 174 A.2d at 884.

[34] See § 17.02[D], *supra*.

[35] Even in retreat jurisdictions, an innocent person is not required to retreat if he can repel the deadly assault with *non*deadly force. *State v. Sherman*, 18 A. 1040, 1041 (R.I. 1889).

[36] E.g., *State v. Abbott*, 174 A.2d at 84; *State v. Charles*, 647 P.2d 897, 901 (Or. 1982).

[37] *State v. Anderson*, 631 A.2d at 1155; Beale, Note 28, *supra*, at 581 (in which the author states that "a really honorable man . . . would perhaps always regret the apparent cowardice of a retreat, but he would regret ten times more . . . the thought that he had the blood of a fellow-being on his hands.").

[38] *State v. Gardner*, 104 N.W. 971, 975 (Minn. 1905) ("Self-defense has not, by statute nor by judicial opinion, been distorted, by an unreasonable requirement of the duty to retreat, into self-destruction.").

[39] *State v. Anderson*, 631 A.2d at 1155 (holding that a judge's "retreat" instruction to the jury was erroneous because it failed to include the word "complete"; "the term 'complete safety' connotes a standard that is more absolute than mere 'safety' ").

[40] *Commonwealth v. Palmer*, 359 A.2d 375, 378 (Pa. 1976).

safety to which a person can turn when confronted by a gun; and even when a place of safety exists, the person is apt to be unaware of it because of the attendant excitement of the situation.[41]

[2]—The "Castle" Exception to the Retreat Requirement

So-called "retreat jurisdictions" have developed exceptions to the rule. A universally recognized one[42] is that a non-aggressor need not retreat if he is attacked in his dwelling place[43] or within its curtilage, even though he could do so in complete safety.[44] This exception is based on the common law view of a man's home as his castle, i.e., a natural sanctuary from external aggression.[45] A few states have expanded the "castle" rule beyond its historic rationale to permit a non-aggressor to stand his ground in his business office or in another person's home in which he is a guest.[46]

May a person in his home stand his ground if the assailant is a co-dweller? This is a matter of considerable significance, in view of the fact that "[i]n the great majority of homicides the killer and the victim are relatives or close acquaintances."[47] A majority of retreat jurisdictions (which, it will be remembered, constitute a *minority* of the states overall) have adopted the rule that the assailant's status as a co-dweller is irrelevant, i.e., the innocent person need not retreat from the home, even if the aggressor also lives there.[48]

---

[41] *State v. Abbott*, 174 A.2d at 884-86.

[42] Another exception to the retreat requirement, but one rarely litigated, is that a police officer is permitted (indeed, he may have a duty) to stand his ground when confronted by deadly resistance to the officer's use of lawful force in the enforcement of the law. *Boykin v. People*, 45 P. 419, 422 (Colo. 1896).

[43] Occasionally, courts have to determine what constitutes a dwelling place for purposes of this exception. E.g., *State v. Marsh*, 593 N.E.2d 35, 38 (Ohio Ct. App. 1990) (D's tent at a campground constituted a home, for purposes of the no-duty-to-retreat exception).

[44] *Gainer v. State*, 391 A.2d 856, 860 (Md. Ct. Spec. App. 1978). The "curtilage" is "the land immediately surrounding and associated with the home . . . to which extends the intimate activity associated with the 'sanctity of a man's home and the privacies of life.' " *Oliver v. United States*, 466 U.S. 170, 180 (1984) (quoting *Boyd v. United States*, 116 U.S. 616, 630 (1886)). For example, a person is not required to retreat from his front porch, although he could do so in complete safety. *State v. Bonano*, 284 A.2d 345, 347-48 (N.J. 1971).

[45] *Gainer v. State*, 391 A.2d at 860; see *Jones v. State*, 76 Ala. 8, 16 (1884) ("Why, it may be inquired, should one retreat from his own house, when assailed by . . . a stranger who is . . . upon the premises? Whither shall he flee, and how far, and when may he be permitted to return?").

[46] E.g., *Kelley v. State*, 145 So. 816, 819 (Ala. 1933) (another person's home); *State v. Baratta*, 49 N.W.2d 866, 871 (Iowa 1951) (place of business).

[47] *State v. Shaw*, 441 A.2d 561, 566 (Conn. 1981).

[48] *Id.* at 565-66 (stating the majority rule, but rejecting it on the ground that it "cannot conclude that the [state] legislature intended to sanction the reenactment of the climactic scene from 'High Noon' in the familial kitchens of this state").

[D]—Nature of the Threat: "Imminent, Unlawful Deadly Force"

[1]—"Imminent"

At common law, deadly force may only be used in temporally narrow circumstances, i.e., when deadly force by the aggressor is imminent. In the context of self-defense, force is "imminent" if it will occur "immediately,"[49] "upon the instant" or "at once."[50] Force is not imminent if an aggressor threatens to harm another person at a later time. Until the threat is imminent, use of force is premature.

Strict application of the imminency rule may result in unfairness. For example, suppose that *D* is regularly beaten by *V*, her husband. On a particular day, *V* informs *D* that he is going to kill her; as *V* leaves the house in order to go to his car to obtain a weapon, *D* kills *V*. Strictly speaking, *D*'s use of force was premature; yet, if *D* had waited for the threat to become imminent, she probably would have been unable to protect herself.

[2]—"Unlawful Force"

A person may not defend himself against the imposition of *lawful*, i.e., justified, force. For example, force applied by a police officer in the performance of his duties is justified; excessive force, however, is unjustified and, therefore, unlawful. Consequently, a citizen may not use deadly force to resist an officer's proper use of force against him; however, in the absence of special legislation restricting his rights, a person may defend himself against excessive police force.[51]

Conduct that would constitute a crime or a tort is "unlawful," even if the actor could escape conviction or liability by assertion of an *excuse* defense. For example, if *V*, an insane person or an infant, uses unjustifiable force upon another, this constitutes "unlawful force," notwithstanding *V*'s potential excuse claim.

---

[49] *State v. Norman*, 378 S.E.2d 8, 13 (N.C. 1989). According to Professor Holly Maguigan, the terms "imminent" and "immediate" are not precisely interchangeable in the self-defense, particularly battered-woman, context. Holly Maguigan, *Battered Women and Self-Defense: Myths and Misconceptions in Current Reform Proposals*, 140 U. Pa. L. Rev. 379, 414-16 (1991). Her research suggests that courts that use the term "imminent" are somewhat more likely than courts that use the word "immediate" to permit jury instructions regarding the relevancy of the decedent's prior violence, and to permit broader use of battered woman syndrome testimony. See generally § 18.06 [B], *infra*. However, many courts and scholars, even in the battered-woman context, use the terms "imminent" and "immediately" interchangeably. E.g., *State v. Norman, supra*; *State v. Kelly*, 478 A.2d 364, 385 n.23 (N.J. 1984); Richard A. Rosen, *On Self-Defense, Imminence, and Women Who Kill Their Batterers*, 71 N.C. L. Rev. 371, 373 (1993); Robert F. Schopp, Barbara J. Sturgis, & Megan Sullivan, *Battered Woman Syndrome, Expert Testimony, and the Distinction Between Justification and Excuse*, 1994 U. Ill. L. Rev. 45, 64-65.

[50] Black's Law Dictionary 750 (6th ed. 1990) (definition of "imminent danger" in the context of self-defense).

[51] See § 18.06[D], *infra*.

§ 18.04   Deadly Force: "Imperfect" Self-Defense Claims

In general, the defense of self-defense is a full defense, resulting in exoneration of the person acting in self-protection. Moreover, the traditional common law rule is that if any of the elements of the defense are missing, the defense is wholly unavailable to a defendant. [52] Some states, however, recognize a so-called "imperfect" or "incomplete" defense of self-defense to murder, which results in conviction for the lesser offense of manslaughter.

There are two versions of imperfect self-defense. First, some courts provide that a *non-deadly* aggressor who is the victim of a *deadly* response must retreat to any known place of complete safety before using deadly force. If he fails to do so, his right of self-defense is considered imperfect. [53]

Second, some states provide that a person who kills another because he *unreasonably* believes that factual circumstances justify the killing, is guilty of manslaughter, rather than murder. [54] That is, *D* is guilty of manslaughter if he kills *V* in either of the following circumstances: (1) *D* unreasonably believes that *V* is about to use deadly force although, in fact, *V* intends no harm or nondeadly harm; [55] or (2) *V* intends to use deadly force, but *D* fails to realize, as a reasonable person, that nondeadly protective force will suffice. [56] In such cases, *D*'s culpability does not reach the level required for murder. As Justice Tobriner of the California Supreme Court explained:

> [T]he state has no legitimate interest in obtaining a conviction of murder when, by virtue of defendant's unreasonable belief, the jury entertains a reasonable doubt whether defendant harbored malice [the common law *mens rea* of murder]. Likewise, a defendant has no legitimate interest in complete exculpation when acting outside the range of reasonable behavior. The vice is the element of malice; in its absence the level of guilt must decline. [57]

---

[52] *Ross v. State*, 211 N.W.2d 827, 833 (Wis. 1973) (quoting Moreland, The Law of Homicide 91 (1952)).

[53] E.g., *People v. Amos*, 414 N.W.2d 147, 150 (Mich. Ct. App. 1987); *State v. McAvoy*, 417 S.E.2d 489, 497 (N.C. 1992). See § 18.03[B][2][b], *supra*.

[54] E.g., *In re Christian S*, 872 P.2d 574, 575 (Cal. 1994); *State v. Faulkner*, 483 A.2d 759, 769 (Md. 1984); *Commonwealth v. Carter*, 466 A.2d 1328, 1332 (Pa. 1983); *State v. Kelley*, 319 N.W.2d 869, 873 (Wis. 1982).

[55] E.g., *People v. Flannel*, 603 P.2d 1, 4 (Cal. 1979); but see *Peterson v. State*, 643 A.2d 520, 522 (Md. Ct. Spec. App. 1994) (*D* shot *V* while *V* sat in a chair watching television; held: "the imperfect self-defense instruction should not be given unless the evidence generates the issue of whether, under the circumstances, the defendant was entitled to take *some* action against the victim").

[56] E.g., *Ross v. State*, 211 N.W.2d at 830.

[57] *People v. Flannel*, 603 P.2d at 7 (citations omitted).

§ 18.05   Deadly Force in Self-Protection: Rationale for the Defense [58]

[A]—Self-Defense as an Excuse

Although some dispute about the matter exists, use of deadly force in self-defense apparently constituted an excuse, rather than a justification, in early English legal history. It is not difficult to appreciate why the use of deadly force in such circumstances is, at least, excusable.

Each of the three non-utilitarian moral theories of excuse outlined elsewhere [59] can explain self-defense as an excuse. First, under the causation theory of excuses, an innocent person is not responsible for the condition that causes him to commit the crime: but for the aggressor's actions, the defendant would not have taken a life. Therefore, the innocent person is not to blame for the killing. Second, a character theorist would point out that it is the aggressor, and not the innocent person acting in self-defense, whose actions manifest a bad moral character.

Third, the choice theory would support an excuse for self-defense, as the innocent actor finds himself figuratively, if not literally, with his back to the wall, without a fair opportunity to choose *not* to kill. As Blackstone suggested, the common law "respects the passions of the human mind." [60] Killing in self-defense, therefore, may be "excusable from the great universal principle of self-preservation, which prompts every man to save his own life preferably to that of another." [61] The act of killing another person to save one's own life is nearly instinctual; it represents the "the primary law of nature." [62]

[B]—Self-Defense as a Justification

[1]—Utilitarian Explanations

Killing in self-defense may be socially desirable. One utilitarian argument is that if someone must die in a deadly conflict it is better that the aggressor, an anti-social

---

[58] See generally George P. Fletcher, A Crime of Self-Defense: Bernhard Goetz and the Law on Trial (1988); Suzanne Uniacke, Permissible Killing: The Self-Defense Justification of Homicide (1994); A.J. Ashworth, *Self-Defence and the Right to Life*, 34 Camb. L.J. 282 (1975); George P. Fletcher, *Punishment and Self-Defense*, 8 Law & Phil. 201 (1989); George P Fletcher, *Proportionality and the Psychotic Aggressor: A Vignette in Comparative Criminal Theory*, 8 Israel L. Rev. 367 (1973); Sanford H. Kadish, *Respect for Life and Regard for Rights in the Criminal Law*, 64 Cal. L. Rev. 871 (1976); David McCord & Sandra K. Lyons, *Moral Reasoning and the Criminal Law: The Example of Self-Defense*, 30 Am. Crim. L. Rev. 97 (1992); Nancy M. Omichinski, Comment, *Applying the Theories of Justifiable Homicide to Conflicts in the Doctrine of Self-Defense*, 33 Wayne L. Rev. 1447 (1987); Cheyney C. Ryan, *Self-Defense, Pacifism, and the Possibility of Killing*, 93 Ethics 508 (1983); Judith Jarvis Thompson, *Self-Defense*, 20 Phil. & Pub. Aff. 283 (1991); David Wasserman, *Justifying Self-Defense*, 16 Phil. & Pub. Aff. 356 (1987).

[59] See § 17.03, *supra*.

[60] 3 Blackstone at *3.

[61] 4 Blackstone at *186.

[62] 3 Blackstone at *4.

individual as manifested by his conduct, is the victim.[63] If it were otherwise, a dangerous person would remain alive and a threat to others, unless and until he is taken into custody.

This argument might somewhat overstate the case. Many self-defense homicidal conflicts occur between mutually intoxicated actors, or start with fisticuffs and escalate into deadly affairs. In many cases in which self-defense becomes an issue, therefore, it is hard to argue convincingly that the aggressor is the "bad" or dangerous person, and the defender is the "good" or more socially desirable individual. Matters are often not so clear-cut.

Another utilitarian claim is that rules of self-defense will function over time to preserve life, because the permission to kill provided to innocent people will operate as a sanction against unlawful aggression.[64] That is, at least in a fair number of cases, the aggressor will be deterred by the fear that his intended victim will resist the attack.

The difficulty with this argument is that it is uncertain that *any* rule of self-defense can successfully affect the actions of parties involved in deadly confrontations. Self-preservation is the "primary law of nature." A person subjected to a deadly attack will likely defend himself, whether or not the law permits it: if an innocent person under attack weighs the circumstances before acting, which is doubtful, the threat of immediate death at the aggressor's hands is surely more relevant to his decision whether to act than the law's identification of the proposed conduct as justifiable, excusable, or punishable. Therefore, what will deter an aggressor from attacking another person is his expectation that the person being assailed will follow the law of nature, irrespective of the law of society.

[2]—Non-Utilitarian Explanations

Various moral theories justify the use of deadly force in self-defense. First, it is frequently said that a defensive killing is justifiable because the aggressor, by his culpable act of threatening an innocent person's life, forfeits his right to life.[65] As a result, the aggressor's death constitutes no cognizable social harm.[66]

Second, "[t]he idea of physical security as one of the 'natural rights' of mankind has a long history."[67] Consequently, when an aggressor "breaches an implicit

---

[63] See Kadish, Note 58, *supra*, at 882.

[64] Herbert Wechsler & Jerome Michael, *A Rationale of the Law of Homicide: I*, 37 Colum. L. Rev. 701, 737 (1937).

[65] E.g., Ashworth, Note 58, *supra*, at 283; Joel Feinberg, *Voluntary Euthanasia and the Inalienable Right to Life*, 7 Phil. & Pub. Aff. 93, 111 (1978); Kadish, Note 58, *supra*, at 883. The moral-forfeiture theory is discussed at § 17.02[C], *supra*.

[66] Not all self-defense rules are consistent with this theory. First, the law permits D to kill V if he reasonably believes that V is about to kill him. Yet, if V is not a genuine threat, he could hardly have forfeited his right to life. Second, the requirement of necessity (and, more specifically, retreat) violates the forfeiture principle. If V has forfeited his right to life, why should D have to abstain from unnecessary deadly force? Following the forfeiture principle, there is no recognized harm in killing someone who has no right to life.

[67] Ashworth, Note 58, *supra*, at 282.

contract among autonomous agents . . . to respect the living space of all others,"[68] he creates a "state of war" between himself and the person wrongfully threatened,[69] which justifies the innocent person vindicating his autonomy by taking the aggressor's life.[70]

A third rationale of self-defense is that the right of an innocent person to life is morally superior to an aggressor's right to life. Therefore, by balancing moral interests, the safety of the innocent person represents the greater moral good; the aggressor's death is the lesser social evil.[71] Ultimately, however, this argument returns to the principle of forfeiture: ordinarily, human beings are equally deserving of protection, so this theory only makes sense if the aggressor's interest in life is, at least partially, forfeited by his culpable conduct.

Fourth, self-defense may be justified as a form of private punishment of a wrongdoer, in which the individual being threatened "acts in the place of the state in inflicting on wrongdoers their just deserts."[72] Self-defense as punishment "avoid[s] the injustice of suffering unsanctioned crime."[73]

---

[68] Fletcher, *Proportionality and the Psychotic Aggressor*, Note 58, *supra*, at 380.

[69] John Locke, Second Treatise of Civil Government: An Essay Concerning the True Original, Extent, and End of Civil Government 23 (DeKoster ed. 1978).

[70] Like the moral-forfeiture principle, the autonomy theory, see generally § 17.02[D], *supra*, is inconsistent with some features of current law. The autonomy theory, at least in its pure form, does not require a proportional response by the defender: an innocent person, if necessary, may kill a *non*deadly aggressor who breaches the implicit contract of physical security. Yet, the law prohibits such a disproportional response.

[71] Of course, a *utilitarian* balancing of social interests is also possible, as is discussed in subsection [1], *supra*.

[72] Fletcher, A Crime of Self-Defense, Note 58, *supra*, at 27-28.

[73] Fletcher, *Punishment and Self-Defense*, Note 58, *supra*, at 215. As with the other theories, this explanation does not perfectly conform with all of the self-defense rules. It is not always the case that a person acting in self-defense is, simply, providing the private punishment that would otherwise be imposed by the courts. For example, death is a constitutionally disproportionate punishment for rape. *Coker v. Georgia*, 433 U.S. 584 (1977). See § 6.05 [B], *supra*. In contrast, the proportionality doctrine of self-defense is not so finely tuned: a woman is permitted to kill a forcible rapist in self-defense, assuming that such force is necessary to avoid the serious bodily injury arising from the rape. *People v. Heflin*, 456 N.W.2d 10, 23 (Mich. 1990). This outcome follows from the fact that, as explained at § 18.03 [A], *supra*, "deadly force" is force likely to cause death *or grievous bodily injury*. Therefore, the rapist is using "deadly force," which in turn justifies the rape victim's use of similar force.

§ 18.06 Self-Defense: Special Issues

[A]—The Reasonable-Belief Standard: More Reflections[74] About the "Reasonable Person" [75]

[1]—The Issue

The law of self-defense represents a compromise. The right of self-defense is not based on objective reality, but neither is it based solely on the actor's subjective impressions: a person may defend himself if, and to the extent that, a reasonable person would believe it is appropriate under the circumstances. The crux of the issue, therefore, is: Who is the "reasonable person" with whom the defendant is compared?

Consider in this regard two controversial self-defense cases. In *People v. Goetz*,[76] Goetz shot and wounded four African-American youths on a New York City subway after one or two of them approached him and requested five dollars. Goetz, a three-time prior mugging victim, claimed that he shot the youths because he believed that their request for money was a precursor to an armed robbery. At his trial,[77] Goetz claimed that he acted as a reasonable person would have acted in the same situation, i.e., that a reasonable person would have believed, as he did, that deadly force was necessary to repel impending use of deadly force by the youths. Among the questions that one may pose about the "reasonable person" in this case are: (1) Like Goetz, is he a prior mugging victim?; (2) Is he an experienced New York subway user?; and (3) To what extent would he consider the race, age, sex, body language, and/or wearing apparel of the victims in determining whether deadly force was necessary?

In *State v. Wanrow*,[78] Wanrow, a 5'4" woman with a broken leg and crutches, killed Wesler, a large and visibly intoxicated man, in her home. Although Wesler did not menace Wanrow at the moment of the shooting,[79] Wanrow suspected

---

[74] See § 10.04[D][2][d], *supra*, for "initial observations" on the topic.

[75] See generally Jody D. Armour, *Race Ipsa Loquitur: Of Reasonable Racists, Intelligent Bayesians, and Involuntary Negrophobes*, 46 Stan. L. Rev. 781 (1994); Mark Kelman, *Reasonable Evidence of Reasonableness*, 17 Critical Inquiry 798 (1991); Shirley Sagawa, *A Hard Case for Feminists: People v. Goetz*, 10 Harv. Women's L.J. 253 (1987); Kenneth W. Simons, *Self-Defense, Mens Rea, and Bernhard Goetz*, 89 Colum. L. Rev. 1179 (1989); Richard Singer, *The Resurgence of Mens Rea: II—Honest But Unreasonable Mistake of Fact in Self Defense*, 28 B.C. L. Rev. 459 (1987); Michael Andrew Tesner, *Racial Paranoia as a Defense to Crimes of Violence: An Emerging Theory of Self-Defense or Insanity?*, 11 B.C. Third World L.J. 307 (1991).

[76] 497 N.E.2d 41 (N.Y. 1986).

[77] Goetz originally claimed that his indictment was invalid because the prosecutor instructed the grand jurors to measure the accused's actions against an objective standard. According to Goetz, state law applied a subjective standard: the question was whether he subjectively believed that he acted in a reasonable manner. The New York Court of Appeals rejected this argument.

[78] 559 P.2d 548 (Wash. 1977).

[79] Wanrow turned her back for a moment on Wesler, and when she turned around, he was standing directly behind her, at which point she became "gravely startled" and shot him.

Wesler of a prior attempted sexual molestation of her son. Furthermore, a neighbor girl had identified Wesler as the man who had molested her, and Wanrow had previously been told that Wesler was a former inmate of a mental institution. At trial, the judge instructed the jury on self-defense, but used the male pronoun "he" in describing the circumstances under which deadly force could properly be used. Among the questions that one may pose about the "reasonable person" in this case are: (1) Is the "reasonable person" male or female?; (2) Is (s)he diminutive and on crutches?; and (3) What knowledge or beliefs would (s)he possess regarding Wesler's background?

These two cases pose difficult problems for the law. For example, the traditional description of the "reasonable person" is in male—"reasonable *man*"—terms. [80] Yet, such an approach to self-defense is unfair when the defender is a small woman and the aggressor is a large man, as in *Wanrow*. The effect of a "reasonable man" instruction is that a woman will be held to the standard of conduct of a person whose size, weight, strength, and experience in combat, exceeds that of the defendant. A strong male, for example, might be able to repel an attack with nondeadly force under circumstances in which a woman might be unable to protect herself except by use of a deadly weapon. [81] Therefore, at first (and, perhaps, later) glance, it seems fairer to test a woman's conduct by the standards of a "reasonable woman." On the other hand, some women are taller, stronger, and better able to defend themselves than some men. Is it fair to hold a diminutive and weak man who lacks self-defense skills to the standard of a "reasonable man"?

Some commentators and courts favor virtual subjectivization of the "reasonable person." According to one court, the "accused's actions are to be viewed from the standpoint of a person whose mental and physical characteristics are like the accused's and who sees what the accused sees and knows what the accused knows." [82] Under this test, as the court acknowledged, a timid, diminutive male would be judged by the standard of a reasonable timid, diminutive male; and a "strong, courageous and capable female" would be judged by the latter standard. [83]

But, where does such a subjective standard leave the law? The risk is that the normative message of the criminal law will be lost if the reasonableness of an actor's conduct is measured by the standard of one who may be unreasonable by nature. At some point, the defendant's real claim is not (or should not be) that he is acting *justifiably*, but rather that he should be *excused* because of his unusual mental characteristics.

---

[80] It would be nice to think that although the common law used a gender-specific term, it had a gender-neutral concept in mind, but this would be an unrealistic expectation, in light of the subservient position of women in early Anglo-American society.

[81] *State v. Wanrow*, 559 P.2d at 558 (footnote deleted) ("In our society women suffer from a conspicuous lack of access to training in and the means of developing those skills necessary to effectively repel a male assailant without resorting to the use of deadly weapons.").

[82] *State v. Leidholm*, 334 N.W.2d 811, 818 (N.D. 1983).

[83] See also *State v. Wheelock*, 609 A.2d 972, 976 (Vt. 1992) ("Our law does not hold a nervous coward and fearless bully to an identical reasonable person standard.").

For example, in *State v. Simon*,[84] the defendant, an elderly man, fired a weapon at Steffan Wong, a young Asian-American male, although Wong was not acting aggressively. According to some testimony at trial, Simon was a "psychological invalid" who feared persons of Asian ancestry, and who believed that by virtue of Wong's racial heritage the young man was an expert in martial arts. If a judge were to instruct the jury to incorporate Simon's beliefs and mental characteristics into the "reasonable person," would it not be inviting the jury to measure him by the standard of a "reasonable psychological invalid who fears Asian-Americans and believes that they are all experts in the martial arts"? Is this not equivalent to a standard of the "reasonable unreasonable person," "reasonable racist," or "reasonable mentally ill person"?

[2]—The Law

The law is undergoing significant but uneven change in this area. In general, the law provides that, in determining whether the defendant's self-protective acts were reasonable, the factfinder should hold the accused to the standard of the "reasonable person in the actor's situation." This language is found in the Model Penal Code definitions of the terms "recklessness" and "negligence."[85] As the Commentary to the Code concedes, the word "situation" in the phrase is ambiguous—inevitably and designedly so.[86]

Most courts have rejected the wholesale subjectivization of the "reasonable person" standard. Nonetheless, in determining what a reasonable person in the actor's situation or circumstances would do, the defendant is entitled to consider

> more than the physical movements of the potential assailant . . . . [The] terms ["situation" and "circumstances"] include any relevant knowledge the defendant has about that person. They also necessarily bring in the physical attributes of all persons involved, including the defendant. Furthermore, the defendant's circumstances encompass any prior experiences he had which could provide a reasonable basis for the belief that another person's intentions were to [harm] . . . him or that the use of deadly force was necessary under the circumstances.[87]

Thus, arguably, Goetz's prior mugging experiences were relevant in determining the reasonableness of his belief that he was about to be attacked,[88] and Wanrow was properly measured by a standard of a woman of her height, weight, strength, and physical handicap. And, applying this standard, a battered woman who uses

---

[84] 646 P.2d 1119 (Kan. 1982).

[85] See § 10.07[B][3], *supra*.

[86] American Law Institute, Comment to § 2.02, at 242; ("[t]here is an inevitable ambiguity in 'situation' "); *id.*, Comment to § 210.3, at 62 ("[t]he word 'situation' is designedly ambiguous").

[87] *People v. Goetz*, 497 N.E.2d at 52.

[88] On the one hand, Goetz's experiences may have made him more sensitive than the average person to the behavior of robbers. On the other hand, a neighbor of Goetz's compared his reaction to his first mugging experience to that of a rape victim, who thereafter feels highly vulnerable and fragile. Kelman, Note 75, *supra*, at 804 n.7. Does this mean that the reasonable person is a "hypersensitive multiple-mugging victim"? *Id.* at 804.

deadly force against her abusive partner should be held to a standard of a reasonable woman who has experienced the same abuse as has the battered woman.[89]

But, this standard still leaves many issues open. For example, would a reasonable person in Wanrow's situation consider Wesler a child molester and former resident of a mental hospital, although Wanrow had no first-hand knowledge of these "facts"? The answer should be that a reasonable person would only consider allegations that are based on reliable information. If this is so, to what extent is it appropriate for the reasonable person in Goetz's shoes to take into consideration the race, age, sex, clothing, and body language of the youths in the subway, in order to measure *their* dangerousness? This remains a difficult and sensitive issue,[90] one that the "designedly ambiguous" standard of the "reasonable person in the actor's situation" leaves to the jurors to resolve for themselves.

---

[89] See § 18.06[B], *infra.*

[90] On this subject, see especially the articles by Armour and Kelman, cited in Note 75, *supra.* These articles identify the arguments that a person in Goetz's situation might attempt to develop at trial, or which might be raised by jurors on their own during their deliberations. First, Goetz could claim that he is a "reasonable racist." That is, he is a "product of a particularly racist subculture that led him to overestimate the risk of violence by young black males." Kelman, Note 75, *supra*, at 804. But, as an express argument, this must fail. Even if he is empirically correct—that his subculture is racist—it would defeat the normative message of the criminal law, *and would conflict with the fact that self-defense is a justification defense*, to treat the "reasonable person" as a racist.

Alternatively, Goetz might claim "that his racial fears rest on a valid factual basis, rather than on a racial basis." Armour, Note 75, *supra*, at 809. That is, it may be that persons fitting the victims' description—black young males acting in concert—represent a disproportionate threat to New York subway passengers. When reasonable people have to make split-second decisions, Goetz might claim, they take race, gender, age, wearing apparel, and body language into account. Professor Armour contends, however, that a defendant should not be allowed overtly to raise race as a factor, because it enhances the risk of racial bias in the jury box.

[B]—"Battered Woman Syndrome"[91]

[1]—Issue Overview

Men are more prone to violence than women are.[92] The number of women sentenced for violent offenses has risen slightly in recent years,[93] but it is still true that "[w]omen rarely kill" and, to the extent that they do, "female homicide is so different from male homicide that women and men may be said to live in two different cultures, each with its own 'subculture of violence.' "[94]

In recent years, however, an increasing number of women have been prosecuted for killing their abusive partners.[95] In many of these cases, the women have sought

---

[91] See generally Charles Ewing, Battered Women Who Kill: Psychological Self-Defense as Legal Justification (1987); Cynthia Gillespie, Justifiable Homicide: Battered Women, Self-Defense, and the Law (1989); Lenore E. Walker, The Battered Woman Syndrome (1984); B. Sharon Byrd, *Till Death Do Us Part: A Comparative Law Approach to Justifying Lethal Self-Defense By Battered Women*, 1991 Duke J. Comp. & Int'l L. 169; Anne M. Coughlin, *Excusing Women*, 82 Cal. L. Rev. 1 (1994); Donald L. Creach, Note, *Partially Determined Imperfect Self-Defense: The Battered Wife Kills and Tells Why*, 34 Stan. L. Rev. 615 (1982); Developments—Domestic Violence, 106 Harv. L. Rev. 1498, 1574-97 (1993); David L. Faigman, Note, *The Battered Woman Syndrome and Self-Defense: A Legal and Empirical Dissent*, 72 Va. L. Rev. 619 (1986); Kit Kinports, *Defending Battered Women's Self-Defense Claims*, 67 Ore. L. Rev. 393 (1988); Deborah Kochan, *Beyond the Battered Woman Syndrome: An Argument for the Development of New Standards and the Incorporation of a Feminine Approach to Ethics*, 1 Hastings Women's L.J. 89 (1989); Maguigan, Note 49, *supra*; McCord & Lyons, Note 58, *supra*; Marilyn Hall Mitchell, Note, *Does Wife Abuse Justify Homicide?*, 24 Wayne L. Rev. 1705 (1978); Cathryn Jo Rosen, *The Excuse of Self-Defense: Correcting a Historical Accident on Behalf of Battered Women Who Kill*, 36 Am. U. L. Rev. 11 (1986); Rosen, Note 49, *supra*; Schopp, Sturgis, & Sullivan, Note 49, *supra*; Stephen J. Schulhofer, *The Gender Question in Criminal Law*, Soc. Phil. & Policy, Spring 1990, at 105.

[92] See James Q. Wilson & Richard J. Herrnstein, Crime & Human Nature 117 (1985); Federal Bureau of Investigation, U.S. Dep't of Justice, Sourcebook of Criminal Justice Statistics—1991 442 (1991) (reporting that males represent 89.6% of arrestees for murder and nonnegligent manslaughter in 1991).

[93] U.S. Dep't of Justice, Bureau of Justice Statistics Special Report, Women in Prison 3 (March 1994) (from 1986 to 1991, the number of women sentenced for violent offenses rose from 8,045 to 12,400).

[94] Laurie J. Taylor, Comment, *Provoked Reason in Men and Women: Heat-of-Passion Manslaughter and Imperfect Self-Defense*, 33 UCLA L. Rev. 1679, 1680, 1681 (1986) (footnotes omitted); see also Wilson & Herrnstein, Note 92, supra, at 114 (quoting D.A. Ward, M. Jackson, & R.E. Ward, *Crimes of Violence by Women* in Crimes of Violence (D.J. Mulvihill & M.M. Tumin eds. 1969) ("The male and female style of offending was so different even within crime categories that [criminologists] concluded 'that female criminality is a separate and distinct order of criminal behavior.' ").

[95] Although attention has centered on male-on-female abuse, some men have reportedly been victims of abuse by their female partners. Also, gay men and lesbians are reportedly "as likely [as heterosexual couples], proportionally, to encounter violence in their intimate relationships. Furthermore, typical gay and lesbian violence and its patterns and effects appear to be virtually identical to heterosexual intimate violence." Denise Bricker, Note,

exculpation by asserting the defense of self-defense, and they have attempted to introduce evidence of "battered woman syndrome."

Battered-women cases, and the legal issues that arise in the prosecutions, may be divided into three categories. First, there are "confrontational" homicides, i.e., cases in which the battered woman kills her partner during a battering incident.[96] Many, probably most,[97] prosecutions, fall into this category. The primary issue in these cases is whether the defendant is entitled to introduce history-of-abuse evidence and offer expert battered woman syndrome testimony.

Second, in a relatively few circumstances, the battered woman kills her abuser while he is asleep[98] or during a significant lull in the violence (a "nonconfrontational" homicide).[99] Two inter-related legal issues commonly arise in these cases. One issue is whether the defendant may introduce battered woman syndrome evidence in order to show that she subjectively and reasonably believed that her actions were necessary to combat an imminent deadly assault. Such evidence is critical to her case, in view of the abuser's passivity at the time of the homicide. A second issue is whether the defendant is entitled to a jury instruction on self-defense in the absence of proof of some aggressive act by the decedent at the time of the killing.

Finally, in a very few cases, the battered woman has hired someone to kill her husband, and then pled self-defense at trial.[100] In these cases, the defendant seeks to introduce evidence of battered woman syndrome in order to show that her response—soliciting a homicide—was reasonable under the circumstances.

Although the primary issue in battered-woman cases are those already mentioned—the admissibility of syndrome evidence, and whether a jury instruction on self-defense is permitted in non-confrontational cases—another issue lurks behind the scenes, particularly in the minds of the jurors: in view of his horrific conduct, is the decedent's death justifiable, even if a traditional self-defense claim is not viable?

[2]—Jury Instructions on Self-Defense

A defendant is entitled to an instruction on a defense if he presents some credible evidence in support of the claim.[101] A trial court must give an instruction on a

---

Fatal Defense: An Analysis of Battered Woman's Syndrome Expert Testimony for Gay Men and Lesbians Who Kill Abusive Partners, 58 Brooklyn L. Rev. 1379, 1383-84 (1993).

[96] E.g., *State v. Hundley*, 693 P.2d 475 (Kan. 1985) (during a long battering incident, the decedent hit, choked, raped, and threatened to kill *D*; *D* picked up a gun and demanded that the decedent leave; decedent laughed and said, "You are dead, bitch, now," and reached for a beer bottle; *D* closed her eyes and fired the gun, killing the decedent).

[97] In one study of appellate decisions, 75% of the prosecutions involved confrontational homicides. Maguigan, Note 49, *supra*, at 394-97.

[98] E.g., *State v. Norman*, 378 S.E.2d 8 (N.C. 1989).

[99] E.g., *State v. Allery*, 682 P.2d 312 (Wash. 1984) (abuser shot while he was lying on a couch).

[100] E.g., *People v. Yaklich*, 833 P.2d 758 (Colo. Ct. App. 1991); *State v. Leaphart*, 673 S.W.2d 870 (Tenn. Ct. Crim. App. 1983).

[101] See § 7.02[C], *supra*.

defense, therefore, if it determines that a jury could reasonably be persuaded to accept the defense on the basis of the evidence introduced, i.e., that there is evidence to support each element of the defense claim.

In confrontational battered-woman cases, an instruction on self-defense is almost always given, as it should be. In these cases, by the very nature of the confrontation, there are sufficient grounds to support a jury instruction, [102] although the jury may decide, of course, that one or more of the elements of the defense were not adequately proven.

Court are divided on whether self-defense may be claimed if there is no evidence of threatening conduct by the abuser at the time of the homicide, i.e., in nonconfrontational circumstances. [103] And, courts have unanimously refused to permit instructions in third-party hired-killer cases. [104]

[3]—Evidentiary Issues

[a]—Prior Abuse by the Decedent

Courts do not ordinarily want to put the victim of a homicide on trial, because it focuses the jury's attention on the decedent's character, rather than on the events occurring at the time of the homicide. On the other hand, courts increasingly believe that in homicide prosecutions of battered women, "the law can no longer ignore the fact that in reality what occurred involved two victims."[105]

In general, a battered woman may introduce evidence of the decedent's prior repeated abusive treatment of her, in support of her claim of self-defense. [106] This is consistent with the proposition that a reasonable person in the defendant's shoes would take into consideration the decedent's prior violence in determining whether he is a threat on the present occasion. [107]

[b]—Expert Testimony Regarding Battered Woman Syndrome

According to Dr. Lenore Walker, [108] battering relationships go through cycles commencing with comparatively minor incidents of abuse, escalating to the "acute battering incident," followed by a period of time when the abuser expresses

---

[102] For example, consider the facts in *State v. Hundley*, 693 P.2d 475 (Kan. 1985), set out in Note 97, *supra*. A prior victim of domestic violence, in *D*'s shoes, could reasonably have believed that her life was in imminent jeopardy, based on the aggressor's words ("You are dead, bitch, *now*") and actions (reaching for a beer bottle, which could serve as a weapon).

[103] Compare *State v. Stewart*, 763 P.2d 572 (Kan. 1988) and *State v. Norman*, 378 S.E.2d 8 (N.C. 1989) (not permitting the defense) with *State v. Gallegos*, 719 P.2d 1268 (N.M. Ct. App. 1986), *State v. Leidholm*, 334 N.W.2d 811 (N.D. 1982), and *State v. Allery*, 682 P.2d 312 (Wash. 1984) (permitting self-defense instructions).

[104] See *People v. Yaklich*, 833 P.2d at 762 (discussing the hired-assassin cases to date).

[105] *People v. Evans*, 631 N.E.2d 281, 288 (Ill. App. Ct. 1994).

[106] Maguigan, Note 49, *supra*, at 423-24 (describing acceptance of such evidence as "routine").

[107] See § 18.06[A][2], *supra*.

[108] See Walker, Note 91, *supra*, at 75-85; Lenore Walker, Battered Woman 32-51 (1979).

contrition and love for the partner, after which the abuse resumes. Dr. Walker also reports that battered women have low self-esteem and suffer from "learned helplessness" as the result of their inability to prevent the abuse. As a consequence of the latter condition, a battered woman is apt to remain in her relationship rather than seek to escape.

In the typical homicide prosecution of a battered woman, defense counsel seeks to introduce expert testimony regarding battered woman syndrome, including testimony that the defendant suffers from the condition and acted pursuant to it. The purpose of such evidence is to enhance the defendant's credibility, explain to jurors why the defendant *subjectively* believed that the decedent was about to kill her (when he may have been asleep or otherwise passive); and to demonstrate that this belief was *objectively* reasonable to a person suffering from the syndrome. Evidence of learned helplessness is especially useful in explaining to jurors why the defendant did not leave the abusive relationship. In the absence of an explanation, especially in nonconfrontational homicides, jurors are apt to disbelieve the defendant's claim that self-defense was the motive for her conduct, blame the woman for her plight, or conclude that deadly force was unnecessary given the option of escape.

The legal difficulty in introducing such evidence is that in most states expert testimony is inadmissible in a criminal trial unless three conditions are satisfied: (1) the subject matter is beyond the understanding of the average lay-person; (2) the witness has sufficient skill, knowledge, or experience in the field that his testimony will aid the jury in its search for the truth; and (3) the state of the pertinent art or scientific knowledge permits a reasonable opinion to be asserted by an expert.[109]

The third prong is a major stumbling block when novel scientific evidence is involved. The traditional rule is that scientific evidence is inadmissible unless the principle upon which it is based is "sufficiently established to have gained general acceptance in the particular field in which it belongs."[110]

Initially, many courts doubted that battered woman syndrome was a generally accepted scientific phenomenon.[111] Today, however, it is said that "battered woman's syndrome has . . . gained general acceptance in the scientific community. Equally compelling is the clear trend across the United States towards admissibility of expert testimony on battered woman's syndrome"[112] in appropriate self-defense cases.[113]

---

[109] *Dyas v. United States*, 376 A.2d 827, 832 (D.C. App. 1977).

[110] *Frye v. United States*, 293 F. 1013, 1014 (D.C. Cir. 1923). Although *Frye* is a federal court opinion, most states have adopted this or a similar standard. However, the United States Supreme Court recently announced a new, more liberal, test to be applied in federal courts: evidence may be admitted if the expert's testimony rests on a reliable scientific foundation, even if the theory or technique in question lacks general acceptance. *Daubert v. Merrell Dow Pharmaceuticals, Inc.*, 113 S.Ct. 2786, 2799 (1993).

[111] E.g., *Ibn-Tamas v. United States*, 455 A.2d 893, 894 (D.C. App. 1983).

[112] *Rogers v. State*, 616 So.2d 1098, 1099 (Fla. Ct. App. 1993) (footnotes deleted).

[113] Some states have passed legislation permitting battered woman syndrome testimony. E.g., Md.Cts. & Jud.Proc.Code Ann. § 10-916 (1993 supp.). Although battered woman syndrome evidence is admissible in most courts, Dr. Walker's research has been criticized

Although battered woman syndrome evidence is admissible in most battered-woman self-defense cases, states vary as to the purposes for which it may be introduced. [114] A few courts permit evidence of the syndrome, but do not permit the expert to testify as to whether the defendant suffers from the syndrome or what its affect may have been on the defendant at the time of the homicide. [115] Other courts allow the expert to state an opinion as to whether the defendant *subjectively* believed that deadly force was necessary under the circumstances, but will not allow the evidence to be used to show that her conduct was *objectively* reasonable under the circumstances. [116] Still other courts apparently permit syndrome evidence to assist the jury in determining whether the defendant's perceptions were reasonable, i.e., to test the defendant's conduct by the standard of a reasonable battered woman suffering from battered woman syndrome. [117]

The latter proposition—that battered woman syndrome testimony is admissible to show that the defendant reasonably believed that the decedent was about to kill her—is debatable, at least in nonconfrontational cases. Seemingly, the expert's testimony shows that the defendant suffers from a condition that renders her different from the ordinary woman—that is why the expert testimony is needed. [118] Much of the evidence relates to her mental condition, including the psychological paralysis from which she suffers. This evidence more clearly supports a claim that she should be *excused* for her conduct due to her mental condition, or that she is entitled to an imperfect defense of self-defense (in jurisdictions that recognize such a claim), rather than that her act of killing her sleeping (or otherwise passive) partner was *justifiable* under the circumstance.

The distinction as to whether or not a battered woman's self-defense claim based on syndrome testimony should constitute a justification or an excuse is not without moral and practical significance, as discussed immediately below.

[4]—Should There Be a "Battered Woman Defense"?

Although a court may permit a battered woman in nonconfrontational circumstances to introduce evidence that she suffers from battered woman syndrome, this testimony may be of only limited value to her if the jury is required to apply a reasonableness standard of a woman who is *not* a victim of learned helplessness and/or of the other conditions associated with the syndrome. In the absence of jury

---

on various grounds, including the absence of control groups, her use of self-reporting survey data, and "the apparent lack of clear support in the data for [some of] the conclusions drawn." Schopp, Sturgis, & Sullivan, Note 49, *supra*, at 54-55.

[114] See Maguigan, Note 49, *supra*, at 429-31.

[115] E.g., *People v. Wilson*, 487 N.W.2d 822, 825 (Mich. Ct. App. 1992); *State v. Hennum*, 441 N.W.2d 793, 799 (Minn. 1989).

[116] E.g., *People v. Aris*, 264 Cal.Rptr. 167, 176 (Ct. App. 1989).

[117] See, e.g., *State v. Kelly*, 685 P.2d 564, 570 (Wash. 1984).

[118] This is not the view of some scholars, who object to the proposition that "reasonable battered woman" is an oxymoron. E.g., Kinports, Note 91, *supra*, at 417. Essentially, they believe that the syndrome "is more appropriately understood as a normal response to an abnormally stressful situation." Schopp, Sturgis, & Sullivan, Note 49, *supra*, at 95 (reporting, but rejecting, this view).

nullification,[119] a woman who kills her partner during a lull in the violence or while he is asleep, cannot seriously claim self-defense in a jurisdiction rigidly enforcing the imminency requirement.

Implicit in some arguments for permitting battered woman syndrome evidence is a much broader claim: that the killing of an abuser is justifiable on its own merits, i.e., independent of any imminent self-defense claim that might be made. A utilitarian might defend the homicide on the ground that the abuser constitutes an ongoing danger to the woman and, very possibly, to other persons. Therefore, his immediate death results in a net social benefit. However, ultimately, a more socially acceptable utilitarian solution is for society to offer abused women places of sanctuary from the abusers, as well as to devise more efficient mechanisms for bringing abusers to justice.

A non-utilitarian justification for killing the abuser, even when he is not an imminent threat, may be found in the principle of moral forfeiture:[120] as a result of the abuser's ongoing culpable conduct, he has forfeited his right to life. This may have been what Justice Harry C. Martin of the North Carolina Supreme Court had in mind when he said about one abuser, who was killed by his wife while he was asleep:

> By his barbaric conduct over the course of twenty years, [he] reduced the quality of the defendant's life to such an abysmal state that, given the opportunity to do so, the jury might well have found that she was justified in acting in self-defense for the preservation of her tragic life.[121]

Even if the moral-forfeiture doctrine is an otherwise acceptable principle, its application here is troubling. First, in the traditional self-defense context, an aggressor only temporarily forfeits his right to life. If he withdraws from the conflict, or once the aggression is thwarted, his right to protect himself is restored. In the case of the abuser, however, the implication is that the constancy of his immoral conduct renders his right to life nearly permanently forfeited. He becomes fair game for killing day or night, awake or asleep, in ambush or otherwise.[122] Second, the logic of the forfeiture position is that the abuser is fair game for killing *by anyone*, even if the battered woman hires an assassin. After all, if the abuser has no right to life, why should it matter *who* kills him? It is unlikely that many people would take the forfeiture doctrine that far.

An alternative rationale for a special battered woman defense is that an abused woman may need to kill her tormenter when the opportunity arises, in order to protect her natural right of autonomy. Indeed, it may be argued, the abuser not only represents an ongoing threat to her physical security, but that she needs to kill him

---

[119] See § 1.02[C], *supra*.

[120] See § 17.02[C], *supra*.

[121] *State v. Norman*, 378 S.E.2d at 21 (dissenting opinion).

[122] See *Jahnke v. State*, 682 P.2d at 997 (in a case in which a battered child ambushed his father, the court warned that "although many people, and the public media, seem to be prepared to espouse the notion that a victim of abuse is entitled to kill the abuser[,] that special justification defense is antethetical [sic] to the mores of modern civilized society.").

to prevent her psychological disintegration.[123] However, should the right to protect one's personal security include the right to conduct "defensive preemptive strikes"?[124] It is tempting to answer the question in the affirmative, but if it is, it will prove difficult to determine how early the assailant may act, and who else, besides abused women, should be granted the right to kill in non-imminent circumstances.

A different approach to the issue, but one which is sharply criticized by many advocates of abused women, is to provide a full or partial *excuse* to the battered woman who kills her abusive partner, either on traditional grounds of insanity, duress, diminished capacity, or provocation, or by carefully crafting a new excuse defense.

The question of whether a battered woman should be justified or only excused for her actions raises intriguing moral questions, but also a practical one. Suppose that the abused party is about to shoot or set on fire[125] her sleeping husband, when he unexpectedly awakens. What are *his* rights of self-defense at that moment? If she is justified in killing him, the traditional rule would be that he is not justified in killing her, because he would be combatting an imminent, *lawful* exercise of deadly force. If she is *excused* (partially or wholly) in killing him, however, he would be *justified* in taking her life in self-defense, assuming that all of the elements of the defense are satisfied.

[C]—Risk to Innocent Bystanders

Assume that *D* is justified in killing *V* in self-defense. *D* fires a gun at *V* but misses him, instead killing or wounding *X*, an innocent bystander. May *D* use his self-defense right against *V* as a basis of exculpation for the harm he inflicted on *X*?

Courts have infrequently confronted this issue and few non-Model Code jurisdictions have statutes dealing with the problem.[126] In general, however, courts apply a transferred-justification doctrine, similar to the transferred-intent rule:[127] a defendant's right of self-defense "transfers" (just as his intent to kill does) from the intended to the actual victim.[128]

---

[123] The leading advocate of the concept of psychological self-defense is Charles Ewing. See Ewing, Note 91, *supra*. For a critique of his position, see Stephen J. Morse, *The Misbegotten Marriage of Soft Psychology and Bad Law*, 14 Law & Hum. Behav. 595 (1990).

[124] See Peter Arenella, *When Victims Strike Back*, Los Angeles Times, Aug. 4, 1994, at B7 (justifying such strikes by children against their abusive parents "when nonviolent alternatives are not readily available").

[125] This was the method-of-killing by Francine Hughes in a famous battered-woman case recounted in an NBC-TV movie, The Burning Bed, and in a 1980 book of the same name, written by Faith McNulty.

[126] The Model Penal Code resolution of this issue is discussed at § 18.07[C], *infra*.

[127] See § 10.04[A][3], *supra*.

[128] *People v. Mathews*, 154 Cal.Rptr. 628, 631-32 (Ct. App. 1979); *Smith v. State*, 419 S.E.2d 74, 75 (Ga. Ct. App. 1992); *People v. Adams*, 291 N.E.2d 54, 55-56 (Ill. App. Ct. 1972).

This rule is not absolute. If the defendant, acting justifiably in self-defense against an aggressor, fires a weapon "wildly or carelessly,"[129] thereby jeopardizing the safety of known bystanders, some courts may hold the defendant guilty of manslaughter of a bystander, or of reckless endangerment if no bystander is killed.[130]

This result is correct from a utilitarian perspective, at least when an innocent person's act of self-defense jeopardizes multiple innocent bystanders:[131] if the actor's self-protective behavior creates an unjustifiable risk of death to others, it may be socially desirable for him to choose some less dangerous (but also less protective) means of defending himself. This outcome is also consistent with at least one non-utilitarian rationale of self-defense, the moral-forfeiture doctrine:[132] the death of an innocent bystander is unjustified, because he is not guilty of any culpable act that would merit loss of his life.

[D]—Resisting an Unlawful Arrest[133]

Suppose that V, a police officer, attempts to arrest D. The arrest is unlawful. Therefore, D uses moderate or deadly force to resist the arrest, and is subsequently prosecuted for the harm caused by his resistance, e.g., battery or murder. D defends his actions on the ground that he had a right to resist the unlawful arrest. Is such a defense recognized?

An English common law right to resist an unlawful arrest was established early on in this country. But the scope of the rule, and its current vitality, depends in part on the basis for the conclusion that the arrest was unlawful.

An arrest may be illegal for various reasons. First, an arrest is unlawful if the officer uses excessive force in effectuating it. Under common law doctrine, an officer may use only as much force as necessary to make an arrest, and may never use deadly force to arrest a misdemeanant.[134] Therefore, if a police officer uses excessive force in making an arrest, he is to that extent the aggressor, and the citizen is justified in protecting himself. The rule here is simple: general self-defense doctrines apply. That is, the victim of excessive police force is entitled to use reasonable force to protect himself, including deadly force if his life reasonably appears to be in jeopardy.[135]

---

[129] *People v. Adams*, 291 N.E.2d at 56.

[130] See *id.* (dictum); *People v. Jackson*, 212 N.W.2d 918 (Mich. 1973).

[131] For example, in *People v. Goetz*, 497 N.E.2d 41 (N.Y. 1986), D, a New York subway passenger, fired shots in rapid succession at four youths whom he suspected were going to rob him. As a consequence, bystanders were forced to take cover. Among the charges brought against D was a count of reckless endangerment of the bystanders. (D was acquitted of the charge.)

[132] See § 18.05[B][2], *supra*.

[133] See generally Paul G. Chevigny, *The Right to Resist an Unlawful Arrest*, 78 Yale L.J. 1128 (1969); Jeffrey F. Ghent, Annotation, *Modern Status of Rules as to Right to Forcefully Resist Illegal Arrest*, 44 A.L.R.3d 1078 (1993).

[134] See § 21.03[B][1], *infra*. The Constitution set limits on police use of deadly force in some felony circumstances. See § 21.04, *infra*.

[135] *People v. White*, 161 Cal.Rptr. 541, 545 (Ct. App. 1980); *Commonwealth v. French*, 611 A.2d 175, 178 (Pa. 1992)..

Many unlawful arrests, however, do not implicate traditional self-defense concerns. For example, an arrest is unlawful (even if reasonable force is used) if the arresting officer lacks probable cause to believe that the suspect is guilty of the crime for which he is being taken into custody.[136] And, even if an officer has probable cause, he must respect other constitutional and statutory arrest procedures. For example, an officer must usually have a warrant to make an arrest in a suspect's home.[137] Also, an arrest is unlawful if the warrant was improperly issued (e.g., the judge who issued the warrant failed to sign it) or executed (e.g., the arresting officer failed to knock and demand admittance before entering the home[138]). Thus, as may be seen from this summary, some unlawful arrests are evident on their face, e.g., the officer enters a home without permission, whereas others may not be evident to the arrestee until after he is taken into custody, e.g., the warrant was not signed.

The generally-stated common law rule is that a person may use as much force as is reasonably necessary, *short of deadly force*, to resist an illegal arrest.[139] If the arrestee uses deadly force, he is guilty of manslaughter, rather than murder.[140] However, there is some question as to whether these rules apply to all unlawful arrests, or only to those that occur under provocative circumstances, i.e., in which the person being arrested is aware of the illegality of the police action.[141] For example, there is some very early authority for the view that a person may not use force to resist an arrest the illegality of which is technical, e.g., an otherwise valid warrant was signed in pencil,[142] and not evident to him. Even today, there is a split of authority in homicide cases: some courts treat an unlawful arrest as a trespass to the person, which automatically reduces the homicide to manslaughter, even if the arrestee is unaware of the illegality; other courts refuse to permit reduction of the offense unless the actor is aroused to passion by the unlawfulness of the arrest,[143] in which case the heat-of-passion manslaughter doctrine comes into play.

Today, the right to resist an excessive-force arrest remains untrammeled. However, a few states by statute[144] or case law[145] have abolished or limited the defense in non-excessive-force circumstances. The argument for retrenchment is that the original reasons for the defense no longer apply. At common law, a person who was unlawfully arrested had little hope for early release. He could petition for

---

[136] See *Dunaway v. New York*, 442 U.S. 200, 207-08 (1969) (an arrest without probable cause violates the Fourth Amendment bar on unreasonable searches and seizures).

[137] See *Payton v. New York*, 445 U.S. 573, 576 (1980).

[138] E.g., Cal. Pen. Code § 844 (West 1994).

[139] See *People v. Curtis*, 450 P.2d 33, 35 (Cal. 1969).

[140] *Davis v. State*, 102 A.2d 816, 820-21 (Md. Ct. App. 1954).

[141] Chevigny, Note 133, *supra*, at 1129-32 (interpreting early Anglo-American law as requiring provocation).

[142] *United States v. Thompson*, 28 F. Cas. 89, 90 (No. 16,484) (C.C.D.C. 1823).

[143] *Davis v. State*, 102 A.2d at 820-21 (summarizing the contrasting rules).

[144] E.g., Cal. Pen. Code § 834a (West 1985) (abolishing the defense).

[145] *State v. Wright*, 162 S.E.2d 56, 62 (N.C. Ct. App.), *aff'd*, 163 S.E.2d 897 (N.C. 1968) (no defense if the officer is acting under authority of a warrant, although it is defective or irregular in some respect).

a writ of habeas corpus,[146] but this was an expensive and slow process. Post-trial civil suits for damages could not remedy the harm already inflicted. Moreover, jail conditions were harsh: death from disease and maltreatment in jails were not uncommon. When these evils were balanced against the social harm of a battery upon an officer, resistance could be viewed as justifiable.

Today, the balancing process is apt to result in a different conclusion. Jail conditions, although harsh, are not as severe as before. Bail is easier to obtain than it was centuries ago. The lawfulness of an arrest can now be determined comparatively rapidly,[147] so that the extent of wrongful incarceration is reduced. Finally, it is much more difficult today than it was in the past to successfully resist an unlawful arrest without using deadly force. In light of these changes, it may be preferable for the arrestee to forego resistance and seek post-custodial remedies.

These arguments for abandonment of the common law rule make sense if the defense is perceived as a justification, based on a balancing of utilities. But, the defense can also be justified on the ground that a person should be permitted to use force to protect his autonomy. This right is no less applicable today than it was centuries ago.

Moreover, perhaps the common law defense should be understood as an excuse, rather than a justification. That is, the "right" to resist unlawful arrests may be a misnomer; perhaps the underlying basis for the rule is that when one is patently mistreated by government officials, he is apt to become enraged, and that response (expressed in the form of nondeadly resistance to the arrest) is morally blameless under the circumstances.

§ 18.07   Model Penal Code

This section does not describe each aspect of the Model Penal Code's extensive treatment of the doctrine of "self-protection." Instead, the defense is described with a broad brush; more careful analysis is reserved for those portions that represent a significant departure from the common law.

[A]—General Rules

[1]—Force, in General

[a]—Permissible Use

Subject to various limitations, a person is justified in using force upon another person if he believes that such force is immediately necessary to protect himself

---

[146] A writ of habeas corpus is a civil court order to a jail or prison official to bring the petitioner before the court to determine if the petitioner is being unlawfully confined.

[147] E.g., a person arrested without a warrant who is not released on bail is constitutionally entitled to a probable-cause hearing within 48 hours of arrest. *County of Riverside v. McLaughlin*, 500 U.S. 44, 56 (1991).

against the exercise of unlawful force[148] by the other on the present occasion.[149]

This rule diverges from the common law in two noteworthy ways. First, it is drafted in terms of the actor's subjective belief in the need to use force; his belief need not be reasonable. However, nearly all of the Code justification defenses, including the defense of self-protection, are modified by § 3.09, which re-incorporates a reasonableness component, although not in the fashion of the common law. This feature of the Code is discussed in subsection [B] below.

Second, the Code substitutes the phrase "immediately necessary . . . on the present occasion," for the common law imminency requirement. This shift in language is intended to authorize self-protective force sooner than is allowed at common law. For example, reconsider the domestic violence hypothetical discussed earlier,[150] in which D, a battered woman, killed V, her abusive husband, as he left the house to go to his car to obtain a gun to kill her. Under traditional common law principles, D's self-defense claim would fail, because V did not yet represent an imminent threat. In contrast, under the Code, D would be justified in using deadly force against V, if she believed that she could not afford to wait until V returned with a weapon.[151]

[b]—Impermissible Use: Resisting an Unlawful Arrest

In a departure from common law principles, a person may not use force to resist an arrest that he knows is being made by a police officer, even if the arrest is unlawful (e.g., without probable cause).[152] However, this rule, which was opposed by a substantial minority of the members of the American Law Institute,[153] does *not* prohibit use of force by an arrestee who believes that the officer intends to use excessive force in effectuating the arrest.[154]

[2]—Deadly Force, in General

[a]—"Deadly Force": Definition

Section 3.11, subsection (2), of the Code provides that "deadly force" is force

---

[148] The Model Penal Code definition of "unlawful force" (§ 3.11(1)) is cumbersome. The definition, however, does not appreciably differ from the meaning accorded to the phrase at common law. See § 18.03[D][2], *supra.* One difference, however, is that "force" under the Code includes "confinement." That is, if the other provisions of the defense are met, a person may use force to resist an unlawful effort to imprison him, even if he is aware that the imprisoner will not need to touch him in order to confine him. For example, D may use force to prevent V from unlawfully locking him in a cellar.

[149] Model Penal Code § 3.04(1).

[150] See § 18.03[D][1], *supra.*

[151] See American Law Institute, Comment to § 3.04, at 39-40.

[152] Model Penal Code § 3.04(2)(a)(i).

[153] For a summary of the minority's position, see American Law Institute, Comment to § 3.04, at 43.

[154] *Id.*

used for the "purpose of causing or that [the actor] knows to create a substantial risk of causing death or serious bodily injury." The section expressly provides that the act of purposely firing a gun in the direction of a person or of a vehicle that the actor believes is occupied constitutes "deadly force." However, a mere threat (without the purpose) to cause death or serious injury to another is not "deadly force," even if the actor produces a weapon to back up his threat.

This definition is broader than the common law version in one respect. At common law, force that is not likely to cause death or serious bodily injury does not constitute "deadly force," even if the actor's purpose is to kill.[155] Under the Code, however, one who acts with the purpose of causing death or serious injury, although such an outcome is highly unlikely, falls within the Code's "deadly force" prohibitions.

[b]—Permissible Use

Deadly force is unjustifiable unless the actor believes that such force is immediately necessary to protect himself on the present occasion against: (1) death; (2) serious bodily injury; (3) forcible rape; or (4) kidnapping.[156]

The first three categories in which deadly force may be used are not problematical. The provision regarding kidnapping, however, is of questionable legitimacy. As the Commentary concedes,[157] the appropriateness of its inclusion in the Code will depend on how kidnapping is defined by state law. A kidnapping need not involve a threat of death or great bodily injury to the kidnap victim, for example, when a parent abducts a child from the custody of another parent. In such a circumstances, deadly force would be a disproportional (yet, under the Code, permissible) response.

[c]—Impermissible Use

Even if deadly force is otherwise permitted, as described immediately above, the Code prohibits its use in two key circumstances.

[i]—Deadly Force by Aggressors

The Code prohibits the use of deadly force by a person who, "with the purpose of causing death or serious bodily injury, provoked the use of force against himself in the same encounter."[158] This concept of aggression is narrower than the common law version because it does not include within its scope the "nondeadly aggressor," i.e., the actor who provokes a *non*deadly conflict. Therefore, in a Model Code jurisdiction, if *D* unlawfully starts a nonlethal conflict, he does not lose his privilege of self-defense if *V* escalates it into a lethal assault.

It should be observed that an actor only loses his privilege to use deadly force in self-protection if he is the aggressor "in the same encounter." This language is

---

[155] See § 18.03[A], *supra.*

[156] Model Penal Code § 3.04(2)(b).

[157] American Law Institute, Comment to § 3.04, at 48.

[158] Model Penal Code § 3.04(2)(b)(i).

consistent with the common law treatment of deadly aggressors.[159] That is, if *D* unlawfully commences a deadly assault upon *V*, he may regain the right of self-protection if he breaks off the struggle, and *V* continues to threaten him. In these circumstances, *V*'s threat is viewed as a "distinct engagement."[160]

[ii]—Retreat

The Model Code applies a version of the minority common law rule relating to retreat: a person may not use deadly force against an aggressor if he "knows that he can avoid the necessity of using such force with complete safety by retreating."[161]

As a result of policy disagreements among members of the American Law Institute and subsequent compromising,[162] the retreat rule is subject to various exceptions and counter-exceptions.[163] The most significant exception is that, as in common law retreat jurisdictions, retreat is not necessary if the actor would have to retreat from (or in) his home or place of work.

This exception, however, is subject to its own exception, which is that retreat from the home or office *is* required: (1) if the actor was the initial aggressor, and wishes to regain his right of self-protection; or (2) even if he was not the aggressor, if he is attacked by a co-worker in their place of work. However, largely in order to protect women in domestic disputes, the Code does not require retreat by a non-aggressor in the home, even if the assailant is a co-dweller.

[iii]—Applying the MPC Rules

The Code's deadly-force rules add up to this. First, if *D* did not start the unlawful conflict, he may use deadly force against *V* if he believes that such force is necessary on the present occasion to combat an unlawful deadly assault by *V*, if any of the following circumstances exist: (1) *D* has retreated, and *V* continues to pursue him; (2) *D* knows of no safe place to retreat; or (3) even if *D* could have retreated and did not, if *D* is in his home or place of work, and *V* is not in his place of work.

Second, if *D* *did* start the unlawful conflict but did so without the purpose of provoking a deadly conflict—e.g., he lightly struck *V*, but *V* escalated matters by menacing *D* with a knife—*D* may still use deadly force in all of the circumstances noted above. In such circumstances, however, *D* may be prosecuted for the initial unlawful assault or battery that commenced the conflict.[164]

Third, *D* may *not* kill *V* in self-defense if he started the conflict with the intent to cause death or great bodily harm, unless he withdraws from the conflict. If he does so, *D*'s privilege to kill is restored, although he may be charged with a crime pertaining to the initial acts that commenced the conflict.

---

[159] See § 18.03[B][2][a], *supra*.

[160] American Law Institute, Comment to § 3.04, at 52.

[161] Model Penal Code § 3.04(2)(b)(ii).

[162] See generally American Law Institute, Comment to § 3.04, at 52-57.

[163] See Model Penal Code § 3.04(2)(b)(ii).

[164] American Law Institute, Comment to § 3.04, at 50.

[B]—Mistake-of-Fact Claims and Model Code Justification Defenses[165]

As previously explored, the common law rule is that a person is justified in acting on the basis of reasonable appearances.[166] For example, if D kills V because he reasonably believes that V, unlawfully, is about to kill him, D may successfully claim self-defense, even if turns out later that V did not pose a genuine threat. A justification defense is not available, however, to one who acts on the basis of an unreasonable belief, although some states recognize an "imperfect" defense in such circumstances.[167]

The Model Penal Code follows the minority rule that recognizes an imperfect defense, but it takes a two-step process to get to this point. Initially each justification defense dealing with the use of defensive force is defined solely in terms of the defendant's subjective belief in the necessity of using the force, or in terms of his subjective belief regarding other circumstances that are material to the particular justification claimed.[168]

Each of these defenses, however, is subject to the provisions of § 3.09(2), which provides that when the defendant is reckless or negligent in regard to the facts relating to the justifiability of his conduct, the justification defense is unavailable to him in a prosecution for an offense for which recklessness or negligence suffices to establish culpability. For example, if D intentionally kills V because he *unreasonably* (let us assume, negligently) believes that V is about to kill him, the defense of self-protection is available to D if he is charged with purposely, knowingly, or recklessly killing V, but the defense is not available to him if he is prosecuted for negligent homicide, in light of his negligent mistake of fact. Similarly, if D *consciously* disregards a substantial and unjustifiable risk that V is not an aggressor, D's recklessness as to the relevant facts would render him guilty of an offense based on that state of mind.

The practical effect of the conjunction of § 3.09 and the various justification defenses is that the Code recognizes imperfect defenses. This outcome is sensible. In the hypothetical above, the common law rule allows conviction of D for a more serious offense that his culpability would suggest is appropriate: he may be convicted of a crime of intent, although he is really a negligent or reckless wrongdoer (in light of his negligent or reckless mistake). The Code (and minority common law) approach permits conviction of an offense in accord with his culpability as to the mistake.[169]

---

[165] The concepts described in this section apply to the defenses of execution of public duty (§ 3.03), self-protection (§ 3.04), protection of other persons (§ 3.05), protection of property (§ 3.06), law enforcement (§ 3.07), and use of force by persons with special responsibility for care, discipline, or safety of others (§ 3.08).

[166] See §§ 17.04 (justification defenses generally) and 18.02 (self-defense), *supra*.

[167] See § 18.04, *supra*.

[168] American Law Institute, Comment to § 3.09, at 150.

[169] *Id.* at 151-52.

[C]—Justification Defenses and Risks to Innocent Bystanders

If a person justifiably uses force against an aggressor, but uses such force in a manner that is reckless or negligent in regard to the safety of an innocent bystander, the justification defense, which is available to the person in regard to the aggressor, is unavailable to him in a prosecution for such recklessness or negligence as to the bystander.[170] For example, if D shoots at A, an aggressor, in a crowded subway, thereby recklessly causing X's death or recklessly endangering the lives of X and others, D may successfully assert self-protection as a defense in any prosecution for his actions against A, but he is not entitled to use this defense in a prosecution for manslaughter of X, or for the offense of reckless endangerment of the bystanders.

However, convictions in this regard are difficult to obtain. In order to show that a defendant acted recklessly or negligently as to bystanders, the prosecution must show that he took an *unjustifiable* risk as to their safety, because "unjustifiability" is an element in the definition of both "recklessness" and "negligence."[171] When the justification for risky conduct is to save one's own life, however, this factor is apt to weigh very heavily on the defender's behalf, unless the method of self-protection jeopardizes many innocent people. For example, if a terrorist is shooting at D from a window of a schoolroom occupied by 100 children, and D protects himself by throwing a live hand grenade into the room, D justifiably may claim self-defense (assuming that he could not safely retreat) in the death of the terrorist, but this method of self-protection, which jeopardizes the lives of the 100 children, might not protect him in a prosecution for their deaths.[172]

---

[170] Model Penal Code § 3.09(3).

[171] See § 10.07[B][3], *supra*.

[172] See American Law Institute, Comment to § 3.09, at 154-55.

CHAPTER 19

DEFENSE OF OTHERS

§ 19.01 General Rule

Generally speaking, a person is justified in using force to protect a third party from the unlawful use of force by an aggressor.[1] The intervenor's right to use force in such circumstances parallels the third party's right of self-defense; that is, she may use force when, and to the extent that, the third party would apparently be justified in using force to protect herself.[2]

Some potential limits to this rule exist. First, the defense was originally limited to the protection of persons related to the intervenor by consanguinity, marriage, or employment relation.[3] This limitation is enforced only infrequently today.[4]

Second, a majority of jurisdictions once held that an intervenor could only use force to defend a third party if the party being defended would *in fact* have been justified in using the same degree of force in self-defense.[5] That is, *D*, the intervenor, is placed in the shoes of *X*, the party being defended, and acts at her peril: if *X* had no right of self-defense, even though a reasonable person would have believed that *X* did, *D* is not justified in using force to protect *X*. This rule represents an exception to the common law rule that an actor is justified in using force based on reasonable appearances.

Jurisdictions that follow the act-at-peril rule are impressed by the not uncommon circumstance in which the defense is raised: *D* comes upon an apparently unlawful attack by *V* on *X*; *D* defends *X*; later *D* learns that *V* was an undercover police officer properly using force against an unlawfully resistant *X*. Permitting *D* to act on reasonable appearances, it is said, creates "a dangerous precedent . . . that plain-clothes police officers attempting lawful arrests over wrongful resistance are subject to violent interference by strangers ignorant of the facts."[6]

Some states retain the act-at-peril rule. However, largely due to the influence of the Model Penal Code, the more prevalent modern view is that an intervenor may

---

[1] *Commonwealth v. Martin*, 341 N.E.2d 885, 889-90 (Mass. 1976).

[2] See *Hughes v. State*, 719 S.W.2d 560, 564 (Tex. Crim. App. 1986).

[3] *Commonwealth v. Martin*, 341 N.E.2d at 891-92.

[4] E.g., *State v. Marsh*, 593 N.E.2d 35, 37 (Ohio Ct. App. 1990) (recognizing the privilege to defend a member of one's family).

[5] See *People v. Young*, 183 N.E.2d 319, 319-20 (N.Y. 1962) (stating and applying the then-majority rule).

[6] *People v. Young*, 210 N.Y.S.2d 358, 367 (N.Y. App. Div. 1961) (Valente, J., dissenting), *rev'd*, 183 N.E.2d 319 (N.Y. 1962).

use deadly or nondeadly force to the extent that such force *reasonably appears* to the intervenor to be justified in defense of the third party.[7]

Advocates of the reasonable-appearance rule justify it on utilitarian and retributive grounds. From a utilitarian perspective, a consequence of the act-at-peril doctrine was that onlookers hesitated to intervene in disputes. As one court explained, "[e]ven if their hearts had been stout enough to enter the fray in defense of a stranger being violently assaulted, the fear of legal consequences chilled their basic instincts."[8] The reasonable-appearance rule seeks "to afford protection to a defender who acts while injury may still be prevented."[9] The act-at-peril rule also violates concepts of just deserts, because it results in liability and punishment without fault. [10] The reasonable-appearance rule ensures that people who act reasonably, albeit mistakenly, are not punished for their good motives.

§ 19.02　Model Penal Code

Under the Model Code, subject to retreat provisions discussed in the next paragraph, an intervenor is justified in using force upon another person in order to protect a third party if three conditions are met: (1) the intervenor uses no more force to protect the third party than the intervenor would be entitled to use in *self*-protection, based on the circumstances as she believes them to be; (2) under the circumstances as the intervenor believes them to be, the third party would be justified in using such force in self-defense; and (3) the intervenor believes that her intervention is necessary for the protection of the third party.[11]

The Code's self-protection retreat rules[12] have limited applicability in the context of the defense of another person. First, if the intervenor would be required to retreat to a place of known safety if she were protecting *herself* in such circumstances, she is *not* required to retreat before using force in protection of the third party, except in the unlikely circumstance that she knows that such retreat will assure the latter's complete safety.[13] Second, she is required to attempt to secure the defended party's retreat in those circumstances in which the latter would be required to retreat under the rules of self-protection, assuming that the intervenor knows that the third party can obtain complete safety by retreating.[14]

The Model Code does not apply the act-at-peril rule that represented the majority position at the time of the Code's adoption. As with other justification defenses,[15]

---

[7] E.g., *Alexander v. State*, 447 A.2d 880, 885-87 (Md. Ct. Spec. App. 1982); Danny R. Veilleux, Annotation, *Construction and Application of Statutes Justifying the Use of Force to Prevent the Use of Force Against Another*, 71 A.L.R.4th 940, 947 (1989).

[8] *Alexander v. State*, 447 A.2d at 881.

[9] *Id.* at 887.

[10] American Law Institute, Comment to § 3.05, at 65-66.

[11] Model Penal Code § 3.05(1).

[12] See § 18.07[A][2][c][ii], *supra*.

[13] Model Penal Code § 3.05(2)(a).

[14] Model Penal Code § 3.05(2)(b).

[15] See § 18.07[B], *supra*.

the applicability of the defense-of-others provision is based on the intervenor's subjective beliefs. Thus, if *D* is prosecuted for purposely killing *V*, a police officer who was lawfully pointing a gun at *X*, *D* is entitled to raise a defense-of-others claim if she believed that *V* was an unlawful attacker.[16] However, if *D*'s belief in this regard was negligent or reckless, the justification would be unavailable to her in a prosecution for negligent or reckless homicide.

---

[16] Notice the interesting possibility: *D* is justified in using deadly force upon *V*, based on her belief that she was acting in *X*'s defense; simultaneously, *V* is justified in killing *D* in self-protection if *V* believes that *D* is *X*'s accomplice. In such circumstances, the officer would be acting on the belief that she is repelling unlawful force by *D*. Model Penal Code § 3.04(1).

CHAPTER 20

DEFENSE OF PROPERTY AND HABITATION

§ 20.01 Chapter Overview

This chapter focuses on two related defenses. The first is the defense of property, which is implicated when a person uses force to prevent another person from dispossessing him of real or personal property, or in order to regain possession of the property immediately after dispossession. The second is the defense of habitation, which is involved when the dweller of a home uses force to prevent unlawful entry into the actor's "castle" by an intruder. This defense is distinguishable from the property defense in that its purpose is to safeguard the dweller's bodily security and privacy in his home; dispossession of the home or its contents need not be implicated.

Some courts and statutes treat the habitation defense as part of a broader property defense. It is easy to see why: when *V* enters *D*'s home wrongfully and forcibly in order to dispossess him or to take property from within it, *D* simultaneously has the right to protect his property from dispossession (defense of property) and to protect his right to inhabit his home in privacy and safety (defense of habitation). Realistically, there is usually no way to separate the two interests. Nonetheless, it is preferable to distinguish the claims because the common law treats them differently in one significant respect: deadly force is *never* permitted to protect property, as such; deadly force is justified in certain circumstances, however, in order to defend habitation.

These two defenses often overlap other justification claims, as well. For example, one who uses force in his residence might simultaneously claim one or more of the following defenses: defense of property; defense of habitation; crime prevention (which itself subsumes multiple defenses); self-defense; and defense of others. Frequently, some of these defenses overlap nearly completely, so that it is irrelevant which defense is claimed; sometimes, however, subtle differences exist so that it may be important to distinguish between the claims.

§ 20.02 Defense of Property [1]

[A]—General Rule

Despite the high value placed on property rights in Anglo-American society, the law prefers the resolution of property disputes by nonforcible means, including the

---

[1] See generally David Lanham, *Defence of Property in the Criminal Law*, 1966 Crim. L. Rev. 368 & 426.

use of judicial orders. Forcible self-help is discouraged. Nonetheless, in narrow circumstances, a person may use force to protect his property.

As more fully examined in subsection [B], a person in possession of real or personal property is justified in using nondeadly force against a would-be dispossessor if he reasonably believes that such force is necessary to prevent imminent and unlawful dispossession of the property.[2] Under no circumstances may a person use deadly force to prevent dispossession. And, subject to one exception considered in subsection [B][6] below, once a person is dispossessed of his property, his right to use force to defend his interest in it is extinguished.

[B]—Clarification of the Rule

[1]—Possession versus Title to Property

The privilege of defense-of-property entitles a person to use necessary force to retain rightful possession of, as distinguished from title to, personal or real property.[3] For example, assuming the other aspects of the defense are satisfied, D, a mechanic doing repairs on X's car, may use nondeadly force against V, a thief, in order to prevent V from taking the vehicle. Similarly, T, a tenant in an apartment, may use nondeadly force, if necessary, to prevent L, the owner of the property, from wrongfully evicting him from the premises.

[2]—Necessity for the Use of Force

A person may use no more force than reasonably appears to be necessary to defend his possessory interest in the property. The necessity component has two elements. First, a person should not use force until he has sought to avoid a physical conflict by requesting desistance by the would-be dispossessor.[4] A request is unnecessary if it would be futile or would jeopardize the defender's or another person's safety, such as when the wrongdoer attempts to take property by force rather than by stealth.

Second, even if force reasonably appears to be necessary, a defender of property must not use force beyond that which the urgency of the occasion reasonably requires. For example, D may "gently lay hands" on V to force him off D's land or to keep V away from D's personal property,[5] but he may not severely kick V when lesser force would suffice to protect the property.[6]

[3]—Deadly Force

Deadly force is never permitted in defense of property, even if it is the only means available to prevent the loss.[7] However, the right to use nondeadly force to protect

---

[2] *People v. Goedecke*, 730 P.2d 900, 901 (Colo. Ct. App. 1986); *Laney v. State*, 361 S.E.2d 841, 843 (Ga. Ct. App. 1987).

[3] See *State v. Rullis*, 191 A.2d 197, 202 (N.J. Super. Ct. 1963).

[4] *State v. Elliot*, 11 N.H. 540, 544-45 (1841).

[5] 1 Hale at *485.

[6] *Wild's Case*. 2 Lewin 214, 168 Eng. Rep. 1132 (1837).

[7] *Russell v. State*, 122 So. 683, 685 (Ala. 1929); *People v. Ceballos*, 526 P.2d 241, 249 (Cal. 1974).

property is sometimes transformed into an independent right to use deadly force in self-protection or defense of a third party. For example, suppose that *V* threatens to steal *D*'s property; *D* resists by use of nondeadly force; but in an effort to overcome *D*'s lawful resistance, *V* pulls a knife and attempts to stab *D*. In these circumstances, *D* may use deadly force against *V*. This right, however, is based on *D*'s privilege to protect himself from an imminent, unlawful deadly attack, and not on the basis of his interest in the property.

[4]—Threat to Use Deadly Force

Although a person may not *use* deadly force to protect his property, may he *threaten* it as a way to prevent dispossession? For example, suppose that *V* unlawfully cuts timber on *D*'s land. *D* points a gun at *V* and, although he has no intention of using the weapon, threatens to kill *V* unless he leaves the land. If *D* is charged with assault,[8] and asserts the claim of defense-of-property, should he be denied the defense because he threatened a forbidden act?

States are divided on this question.[9] An argument in favor of recognizing the defense is that a threat of deadly force will often deter a wrongdoer, without harming him. Thus, a *threat* of *deadly* force may be preferable to *implementation* of *non-deadly* force, which the common law permits. On the other hand, a threat of deadly force is itself a dangerous act, because it may provoke a deadly response, so it may be desirable to deter threats that the issuer has no right to implement.

[5]—Claim of Right

Occasionally, a person may assert a "claim of right" to possession of property and, therefore, seek to dispossess another person of the disputed property. For example, *V*, a landlord, may have a right to retake real property from *D*, a tenant; or *V* may seek to recapture an automobile from *D*, who has failed to make timely car payments.

V's claim of right to possession of the property is relevant to *D*'s claim of defense-of-property in one circumstance: if *D* knows, believes, or as a reasonable person should believe, that *V* has a legitimate claim of right to possession of the property in question, it follows that *D* cannot reasonably believe that *V* represents a threat to dispossess him *unlawfully*. From *D*'s (or the reasonable person's) perspective, *V*'s threatened act of dispossession is *lawful*. Therefore, in these circumstances, *D* is not privileged to use force against *V*.

---

[8] Common law assault is defined as an attempted battery. See § 27.02[E] [1], *infra*. *D* did not intend to batter *V*, so *D* is not guilty of common law assault, regardless of the defense-of-property claim. However, most states have redefined the offense of assault to include the tort definition of assault (i.e., intent to place another person in reasonable apprehension of an imminent battery). E.g. Ariz. Rev. Stat. Ann. § 13-1203(A)(2) (West 1989). Under such a statute, *D* would be guilty of assault, subject to any applicable defense.

[9] Compare *State v. Yancey*, 74 N.C. 244 (1876) (permitting the defense) with *State v. Murphy*, 500 P.2d 1276 (Wash. Ct. App. 1972) (rejecting it).

[6]—Recapture of Property

In order to discourage self-help and consequent breaches of the peace, a person may not ordinarily use force to recapture property of which he has been unlawfully dispossessed.[10]

One exception to this rule exists. A person who acts promptly after dispossession may use nondeadly force, as reasonably necessary, to regain or recapture his property. Thus, a person wrongfully evicted from his land may immediately re-enter the property and attempt to retake it; likewise, one who is unlawfully dispossessed of his personal property may follow the dispossessor in hot pursuit and use nondeadly force, if necessary, to recapture it.[11]

§ 20.03   Defense of Habitation[12]

[A]—General Comments

If jurists have treated the use of force in defense of property with considerable caution, they have always treated the related interest of safe and private habitation of one's home with reverence.

The reason for the difference in attitude—as with the rule permitting people to kill in self-defense rather than to retreat in their home—is that the home represents the person's "castle." As with a castle, the home is a dweller's fortress, "as well for his defence against injury and violence, as for his repose."[13] The house serves as a sanctuary from external attack, "for where shall a man be safe if it be not in his house?"[14]

The home is also a source of privacy where the most intimate activities in life are conducted, and from which people seek to exclude the prying eyes and ears of strangers and of the government. The Supreme Court has observed:

The [Constitution] protects the individual's privacy in a variety of settings. In none is the zone of privacy more clearly defined than when bounded by the unambiguous physical dimensions of an individual's home—a zone that finds its roots in clear and specific constitutional terms: "The right of the people to be secure in their . . . houses . . . shall not be violated."[15]

Although this quotation concerns a person's right to be free from unreasonable intrusions by the government, this constitutional right is itself based on the pre-constitutional common law reverence for the home as a place of security.

---

[10] The fourteenth century English Statute of Forcible Entry made it a crime for one entitled to possession of land to regain it by use of force. 5 Rich. 2, ch. 8 (1381). This statute "has been substantially reenacted by nearly all the states." American Law Institute, Comment to § 3.06, at 86.

[11] *Woodward v. State*, 855 P.2d 423, 428 n.14 (Alas. Ct. App. 1993).

[12] See generally William Wilbanks, The Make My Day Law (1990); J. David Jacobs, *Privileges for the Use of Deadly Force Against a Residence-Intruder: A Comparison of the Jewish Law and the United States Common Law*, 63 Temple L. Rev. 31 (1990).

[13] *Semayne's Case*, 5 Co.Rep. 91a, 91b, 77 Eng. Rep. 194, 195 (1620).

[14] Edmond Coke, Third Institute *162 (1644).

[15] *Payton v. New York*, 445 U.S. 573, 589 (1980).

When a wrongdoer seeks to enter a person's dwelling, therefore, more than property is invaded. In common law terms, the fortress has been attacked; a person's primary source of safe and private habitation has been jeopardized.

[B]—Rules Regarding Use of Deadly Force

A person may use deadly force to defend his home. The scope of this privilege, however, has changed over time; and, no single common law or statutory rule applies today. Instead, the right extends along a continuum. Three approaches will be noted.

[1]—Early Common Law Rule

The broadest right to use deadly force is found in the original common law principle that a home-dweller may use deadly force upon another person if he reasonably believes that such force is necessary to prevent an imminent and unlawful[16] entry of his dwelling.[17]

A careful look at the elements of this defense demonstrates its wide scope. The right to use deadly force is triggered by the immediacy of the unlawful entry; the unlawful purpose of the intruder, and the degree to which he constitutes a threat to the physical safety of the occupants, is immaterial. For example, D may kill V, an apparent intruder, whether V is an armed burglar intending to kill him or to steal his property, an unarmed intruder seeking to dispossess him of his property, or even an unarmed and intoxicated neighbor mistakenly entering what he thinks is his own home.[18] Indeed, pursuant to this rule, the right to kill exists even if D knows that V is his intoxicated neighbor, as long as he reasonably believes that deadly force is the only way to prevent the entry.[19]

---

[16] Courts frequently state that the entry must be forcible. E.g., *People v. Stombaugh*, 284 N.E.2d 640, 643 (Ill. 1992) (the defense applies if the intruder enters in a "violent, riotous or tumultuous manner"). However, many courts require simply that there be an unlawful entry. E.g., *State v. Lumpkin*, 850 S.W.2d 388, 391 (Mo. Ct. App. 1993). And, at least one court has stated that the right to use deadly force does not depend on the dweller closing his door. See *State v. Bell*, 160 N.W. 727 (S.D. 1916). It would seem that, open doors aside, any unlawful entry of a closed door would be considered forcible for purposes of the defense.

[17] See *State v. Reid*, 210 N.E.2d 142, 147 (Ohio Ct. App. 1965).

[18] Notice the practical irony: pursuant to the property defense, D may not use deadly force to prevent V from stealing his car in the driveway, nor may he kill a trespasser on his land (but outside the dwelling). D may not even use deadly force if he is outside his own dwelling and seeks to prevent V from wrongfully boarding up the doors to his house. Once D is inside the dwelling and V is on the outside, however, and regardless of V's purpose for the apparently wrongful entry, D has the right to use deadly force. Technically—but only technically—this is because D is protecting his habitation and not his possessory interest in property *per se*.

[19] Of course, D may know that a simple warning or nondeadly force will prevent his neighbor's intrusion. However, if D unsuccessfully calls out to V, and if D has no other way to prevent V's entry, deadly force is justifiable.

[2]—"Middle" Approach

A less broad approach to the defense of habitation provides that a person may use deadly force if he reasonably believes that: (1) the other person intends an unlawful and imminent entry of the dwelling; (2) the intruder intends to injure him or another occupant, or to commit a felony therein; and (3) deadly force is necessary to repel the intrusion. [20]

This rule is narrower than the original common law defense. Under this formulation, for example, *D* may not justifiably shoot *V* if he knows or should know that the intruder is *D*'s intoxicated neighbor mistakenly attempting to enter his own house. Under such circumstances, *V* (presumably) does not represent a threat to an occupant's physical well-being, and *V*'s entry would not constitute a burglary [21] or any other felony.

[3]—"Narrow" Approach

A narrow version of the defense provides that a person is justified in using deadly force upon another if he reasonably believes that: (1) the other person intends an unlawful and imminent entry of the dwelling; (2) the intruder intends to commit a forcible felony therein or to kill or seriously injure an occupant; [22] and (3) such force is necessary to prevent the intrusion. [23] A "forcible" felony is one "committed by forcible means, violence, and surprise, such as murder, robbery, burglary, rape, or arson." [24]

This version of the defense differs from the immediately preceding one in two significant ways. First, deadly force is impermissible if the occupant knows or should know that the intruder intends to commit a minor battery. Second, the resident may not use deadly force if he knows or should know that the intruder's purpose is to commit a nonforcible felony, such as larceny. [25]

[C]—Observations About the Rules

[1]—May the Occupant Use Force After the Intruder Has Entered?

The privilege of defense-of-habitation is triggered when an intruder attempts to enter the dwelling unlawfully. Suppose, however, that *D* awakens at night and finds

---

[20] *Falco v. State*, 407 So.2d 203, 208 (Fla. 1981); *People v. Eatman*, 91 N.E.2d 387, 390 (Ill. 1950).

[21] Burglary requires a specific intent to commit a felony inside the dwelling; *V* does not intend to commit a crime inside.

[22] The rule often is stated in these terms. In fact, however, any effort by the intruder to kill an occupant is itself a forcible felony, e.g., attempted murder, so that the addition of this last phrase is superfluous.

[23] *State v. Garrison*, 525 A.2d 498, 501 (Conn. 1987); *Crawford v. State*, 190 A.2d 538, 542 (Md. Ct. App. 1963).

[24] *Crawford v. State*, 190 A.2d at 542 (quoting 1 F. Wharton, Wharton's Criminal Law and Procedure § 206, at 453-55 (Anderson ed. 1957)).

[25] On the other hand, if the intruder seeks to enter at night in order to commit a larceny, he is guilty of common law burglary, a forcible felony. See 20.03[C][2], *infra*.

V already in the house, or he returns home and finds *V* on the premises? Is the defense still applicable?

Case law is split in this regard. Some courts consider the defense inapplicable once the intrusion has occurred. [26] In these states, if *D* uses deadly force, he must assert some other defense, such as self-defense (once the threat of unlawful attack is imminent, as it may be by the time the dweller becomes aware of the entry) or crime prevention.

Other jurisdictions permit application of the defense. [27] Nonetheless, the changed circumstances may affect the right. Once *V* is in the dwelling, *D* is apt to know more about the intruder's intentions than he would have known prior to entry. In some circumstances, e.g., if *D* observes that the intruder is his well-meaning but intoxicated neighbor, the occupant's right to use deadly force will no longer be available.

[2]—Are the Differences in the Habitation Rules Significant?

The differences among the rules regarding use of deadly force in defense of habitation are more theoretical than real. First, as with all other justification defenses, the right to defend the dwelling is based on reasonable appearances rather than on objective reality. This is an especially significant point in the application of the habitation defense because the right to use force is triggered *before* the intruder's entry of the dwelling and, therefore, often before the occupant is able to determine the intruder's intentions. In these days of ready access to weapons, an occupant can reasonably believe that nearly *any* intruder represents a serious threat to the dwellers' safety. In most cases, therefore, a home-dweller who uses deadly force will be able to satisfy the elements of even the narrowest version of the habitation defense.

Second, even under the narrow version of the defense, a home-dweller will often be permitted to kill an intruder whom he knows intends to commit a *non*violent felony, such as larceny. This result follows from the inclusion of burglary in the category of forcible felonies. At common law, a person who intends to enter another person's home in order to commit larceny, a felony, is a burglar if he breaks in at night. Indeed, many modern burglary statutes dispense with the nighttime requirement, thus expanding the right to use deadly force still further. [28]

---

[26] *State v. Brookshire*, 353 S.W.2d 681, 691-92 (Mo. 1962).

[27] *People v. Stombaugh*, 284 N.E.2d at 643 (applying a statute that permits the defense if "entry is made or attempted"); see *People v. Godfrey*, 600 N.E.2d 225, 226 (N.Y. 1992) (the defense is "intended to protect those individuals who suddenly find themselves the victim of an intrusion upon their premises by one bent on a criminal end").

[28] But see *People v. Ceballos*, 526 P.2d 241, 245 (Cal. 1974), in which the court concluded that deadly force is impermissible in order to prevent an intruder from committing a burglary, unless the burglar intends to commit some other forcible or dangerous act within the dwelling.

[3]—Relationship of the Defense to Other Defenses

[a]—Self-Defense and Defense-of-Others

The defense of habitation is broader than the right to kill in self-defense or to protect a third person. First, under the original common law and "middle" approaches to habitation, a home-dweller may properly use deadly force against an intruder, even if the dweller does not reasonably believe that his life or that of an occupant is jeopardized. The habitation defense, therefore, permits use of force disproportional to the physical harm threatened.

Second, the common law defense of self-defense is not triggered until physical harm is imminent. The right to defend the home begins when entry of the dwelling is imminent, which may be well before the dweller's physical well-being is in imminent jeopardy. [29]

[b]—Law Enforcement Defenses

The privilege to use deadly force to defend one's house will often overlap one of the law enforcement defenses discussed in the next chapter. To the extent that an occupant reasonably believes that the intruder intends to commit a felony inside the home, the resident's right to use deadly force to defend his habitation will coincide with his right to kill in order to prevent the commission of a felony (i.e., the defense of "crime prevention"). [30]

§ 20.04 Spring Guns

[A]—The Issue [31]

"Spring guns" or "trap guns" are mechanical devices that are set off when a person opens a door or other entryway into or within a building. They usually have the capacity to kill or seriously injure the intruder. Such devices are frequently placed in unoccupied homes (e.g., while the residents are on vacation) or other structures (e.g., garages, barns, chicken-coops on farms). Sometimes they are placed in occupied homes, in order to wound or kill an intruder while the occupant is asleep.

The problem with these devices springs from their advantage: they act mechanically—"without mercy or discretion." [32] A trap gun will as quickly kill an innocent child as an armed robber; it will kill an intoxicated neighbor mistakenly entering the premises, as well as a police officer or firefighter lawfully entering. Moreover, the device cannot determine whether deadly or nondeadly force is needed, or even

---

[29] See *State v. Jenkins*, 443 S.E.2d 244, 251 n.11 (W. Va. 1994).

[30] Sometimes, however, deadly force in crime prevention is limited to prevention of forcible felonies, whereas the habitation defense may authorize deadly force against intruders intending to commit nonforcible crimes. In these circumstances, a defendant should be careful to raise the proper defense.

[31] The issue discussed in this section applies to the privileges of defense-of-property, defense-of-habitation, self-defense, defense-of-others, and crime prevention.

[32] *People v. Ceballos*, 526 P.2d at 244.

whether a warning to desist would be sufficient. The lives of innocent people, therefore, may needlessly be lost by use of such devices.

Advocates of spring guns argue that as long as the law permits use of deadly force to protect a dweller of a home, the means used to inflict it—personally or by his "agent," the spring gun—should not matter. Indeed, from the occupant's perspective, a mechanical device may provide special protection: it will stop the intruder immediately upon entry, before a confrontation can occur; in the case of an elderly or infirm resident, or one who is not well-trained in firearm use, the spring gun may be an especially effective mechanism for limiting unlawful entries.

The risks and benefits of spring guns are amply demonstrated by the facts reported in *People v. Ceballos*.[33] Ceballos placed a spring gun in his garage, a structure in which he kept valuable property and sometimes slept at night, after an unknown intruder attempted unsuccessfully to enter. One afternoon thereafter, while Ceballos was absent, two unarmed teenagers, after looking in a window to make sure that nobody was present, entered the garage in order to steal property. As they did so, the spring gun fired, striking one youth in the face.

Ceballos was charged with assault with a deadly weapon. He raised several claims in support of his right to use the spring gun, including defense-of-property, defense-of-habitation, prevention of a felony, and apprehension of a felon. The applicability of these defenses are considered below.

[B]—Common Law Rule

At common law, a mechanical device may be used "where the intrusion is, in fact, such that the person, were he present, would be justified in taking the life or inflicting the bodily harm with his own hands."[34]

The words "in fact" in this rule are significant. One who deliberately places a spring gun on his property acts at his peril: his right to use force by this means is based on reality, rather than on reasonable appearances. Thus, if *D* is present and reasonably believes that *V*, a police officer, is a felonious intruder, he may kill *V* in defense of his habitation. If *D*'s spring gun kills the same officer under the same circumstances, however, *D* is not entitled to the defense.

How does the common law rule apply to the events in *Ceballos*, described in subsection [A]? The answer depends on whether Ceballos would have been justified in using deadly force "by his own hands," when the youths entered the garage. The answer to *that* question depends, in turn, on the nature of the defense being claimed. For example, Ceballos would not have been justified in using deadly force to defend his property in the garage, so a spring gun, as well, was impermissible for that purpose.

Ceballos's privilege to use deadly force in defense of habitation was more problematical. Assuming that the garage were determined to be part of his dwelling (on the ground that he sometimes slept in it, or because it was physically connected

---

[33] 526 P.2d 241 (Cal. 1974).

[34] *Id.* at 244.

to the house), he could have justifiably used deadly force by his own hands under the original, "middle," and perhaps "narrow," versions of the habitation defense.[35] In light of this, Ceballos had a common law right to use a deadly mechanical device in his absence.[36]

The common law rule regarding spring guns is slowly changing. An increasing number of states now support the proposition that a resident may not justifiably use a mechanical device designed to kill or serious injure an intruder, even if he would be permitted to use deadly force in person.[37]

§ 20.05 Model Penal Code

[A]—Permissible Use of Nondeadly Force

[1]—Force to Protect Property

Subject to the limitations described in subsection [B], the Code provides that a person may use nondeadly force upon another person to prevent or terminate an entry or other trespass upon land, or the carrying away of personal property, if he believes that three conditions exist: (1) the other person's interference with the property is unlawful; (2) the intrusion affects property in the actor's possession,[38] or in the possession of someone else for whom he acts; and (3) nondeadly force is immediately necessary.[39] In general, this provision conforms with the common law.

[2]—Force to Recapture Property

Subject to the limitations described in subsection [B], the Code provides that a person may use nondeadly force to re-enter land or to recapture personal property if: (1) he believes that he or the person for whom he is acting was unlawfully dispossessed of the property; and either (2a) the force is used immediately after dispossession; or (2b) even if it is not immediate, he believes that the other person has no claim of right to possession of the property. In the (2b) situation, however, re-entry of land (as distinguished from recapture of personal property) is not

---

[35] Under the narrow habitation defense, a home-dweller must reasonably believe that the intruder intends to commit a forcible felony upon entry. See § 20.03[B] [3], *supra*. The youths intended to commit larceny, a non-forcible crime; and, as it was daytime when they entered, they were not guilty of common law burglary, a forcible felony. Under the law in Ceballos's jurisdiction, however, entry of a garage in the daytime constituted statutory burglary; as a result, deadly force by Ceballos would have been allowed, even under the narrow version of the habitation defense. However, the state supreme court held that deadly force may not be used unless a burglar's entry creates a reasonable apprehension of serious harm to human life.

[36] The justifiability of the use of spring guns in crime prevention depends on the class of crimes for which deadly force may be used in such circumstances. See § 21.03[B][1], *infra*.

[37] E.g., *People v. Ceballos*, 526 P.2d 241 (Cal. 1974); *Falco v. State*, 407 So.2d 203 (Fla. 1981); *State v. Britt*, 510 So.2d 670 (La. Ct. App. 1987).

[38] Although the American Law Institute believes that the concept of possession should be "left largely to the courts," American Law Institute, Comment to § 3.06, at 77, the Code clarifies the meaning of "possession" in subsection (2).

[39] Model Penal Code § 3.06(1)(a).

permitted unless the actor also believes that it would constitute an "exceptional hardship" to delay re-entry until he can obtain a court order.[40]

This recapture provision expands on the common law. It extends the right to use nondeadly force to circumstances in which hot pursuit of the dispossessor is no longer involved, namely, when the actor believes that he was dispossessed at an earlier time by a person who had no claim of right to the property. In this situation, the American Law Institute believes that the law "should not deny a privilege that a well conducted person would expect to have."[41] However, force may *not* be used to regain property if the dispossessed party believes that the dispossessor acted on the basis of a claim of right, even if the dispossessed party believes that the other's claim ultimately will be rejected by the courts. In the latter circumstance, the Institute agrees with the common law that absent immediacy, the best approach is for the parties to resolve their conflicting claims in court.

[B]—Impermissible Use of Nondeadly Force

Nondeadly force that is otherwise permitted in defense of property is unjustified in three circumstances. First, force is not "immediately necessary" unless the defender first requests desistance by the interfering party. A request is not required, however, if the defender believes that a request would be useless, dangerous to himself or to another, or would result in substantial harm to the property before the request can effectively be made.[42]

Second, a person may not use force to prevent a trespass to personal or real property if he knows that to do so would expose the trespasser to a substantial risk of serious bodily injury.[43] For example, it would be impermissible to evict a trespasser from a moving vehicle.[44]

Third, the Code addresses the situation in which both the dispossessor of land or personal property (*A*) and the person seeking to regain it (*B*) believe that they have a right to the property in dispute.[45] For example, suppose that *A*, believing that he has a right to a television set in *B*'s possession, dispossesses *B* of it. *B* is unaware that *A* has a right to the set, however, so he immediately seeks to recapture his property. Pursuant to the Code's recapture provisions described above, *B* is justified in using nondeadly force to retake the property.[46] However, since *A*'s original dispossession was based on a claim of right to the property, the Code would appear to authorize *A* to use nondeadly force against *B* to protect his newly-obtained

---

[40] Model Penal Code § 3.06(1)(b). "Exceptional hardship" would exist, for example, if the land contained a crop that would be lost if it were not immediately harvested, or if the land were the site of a small business that would suffer substantial economic damage if the owner could not enter to carry on his duties. American Law Institute, Comment to § 3.06, at 87.

[41] American Law Institute, Comment to § 3.06, at 85.

[42] Model Penal Code § 3.06(3)(a).

[43] Model Penal Code § 3.06(3)(b).

[44] American Law Institute, Comment to § 3.06, at 91.

[45] Model Penal Code § 3.06(3)(c).

[46] This case would fall within the (2), hot pursuit, category.

possessory interest in the television set. Thus, without a special rule to deal with the situation, the Code seems to allow both parties, justifiably, to fight over the property.

In such circumstances, the Code prefers that the original dispossessor (in the hypothetical, *A*) forego the use of force and permit the recaption to occur. Specifically, the Code provides that *A*, a prior dispossessor, may *not* use force to resist re-entry or recaption of property by *B*, even if he believes that *B* is acting unlawfully, if *B*'s re-entry or recaption is otherwise justifiable. [47]

[C]—Use of Deadly Force [48]

[1]—In General

Deadly force in defense of property is prohibited except in two circumstances.

[a]—Dispossession of a Dwelling

A person may use deadly force upon an intruder if he believes that: (1) the intruder is seeking to dispossess him of the dwelling; (2) the intruder has no claim of right to possession of the dwelling; and (3) such force is immediately necessary to prevent the dispossession. [49] The actor may use deadly force although he does not believe that his or another person's physical well-being is jeopardized.

This provision is both broader and narrower than the common law. It is broader in that the right to use deadly force is not predicated on the actor's right to safe and private habitation, but rather is founded on his right to possession of the dwelling. The Commentary to this Code section concedes that "[t]o kill a man is, on a dispassionate view, an evil both more serious and more irrevocable than the loss of possession of a dwelling for a period during which a court order is being obtained." [50] Nonetheless, describing an illegal ouster from one's home as a "provocation that is not to be depreciated," the Institute determined that the right to use deadly force should be permitted in this class of cases.

On the other hand, this provision does not authorize deadly force merely to prevent an unlawful entry into the home, as the common law originally permitted. The actor must believe two things: that the intruder's purpose for entry is to dispossess him of the dwelling, and that the intruder is acting without a claim of right.

[b]—Prevention of Serious Property Crimes

A person may use deadly force upon another, inside a dwelling *or anywhere else*, if he believes that: (1) the other person is attempting to commit arson, burglary, robbery, or felonious theft or property destruction; (2) such force is immediately

---

[47] For further explanation of this provision, see American Law Institute, Comment to § 3.06, at 89-90.

[48] See generally Comment, *The Use of Deadly Force in the Protection of Property Under the Model Penal Code*, 59 Colum. L. Rev. 1212 (1959).

[49] Model Penal Code § 3.06(3)(d)(i).

[50] American Law Institute, Comment to § 3.06, at 93.

necessary to prevent the commission of the offense; and either (3a) the other person previously used or threatened to use deadly force against him or another person in his presence, or (3b) use of nondeadly force to prevent commission of the offense would expose him or another innocent person to substantial danger of serious bodily injury. [51]

This provision is highly controversial. It justifies use of deadly force in protection of property, under circumstances that go well beyond any concern relating to habitation. Moreover, the right to kill is not based upon the actor's perceived need to protect his or another person's life. For example, if *V*, a burglar or a robber on the street, uses or threatens to use deadly force against *D* or *X*, but is disarmed by *D* and seeks to flee with the fruits of his crime, *D* may kill *V* if he believes that this is the only way to prevent *V* from successfully consummating the crime. As the Institute puts it, "deadly force may be used in order to prevent [*V*] from capitalizing upon his offense."[52]

The Model Code's position is surprising. Another section of the Code[53] provides that a private person (i.e., one who is neither a law enforcement officer nor a person assisting him) may *not* use deadly force in order to effectuate a felony arrest. Yet, when the actor's justification for using deadly force is protection of personal property—presumably, a less socially valuable interest than law enforcement—the Code authorizes its use. The Commentary recognizes that this result is inconsistent with the judgment underlying the arrest provisions.[54]

[2]—Spring Guns

The Model Code prohibits the use of a mechanical device to protect property if it is intended to cause, or is known by the user to create a substantial risk of causing, death or serious bodily injury.[55] Thus, in those circumstances in which deadly force is permitted in defense of property, the actor must personally commit the lethal acts rather than use a spring gun.

---

[51] Model Penal Code § 3.06(3)(d)(ii).

[52] American Law Institute, Comment to § 3.06, at 96.

[53] Model Penal Code § 3.07(2)(b). See § 21.05[C][2], *infra.*

[54] American Law Institute, Comment to § 3.06, at 96-97.

[55] Model Penal Code § 3.06(5)(a).

CHAPTER 21

LAW ENFORCEMENT

§ 21.01 Chapter Overview[1]

Society wants its criminal laws enforced. Ideally, crimes should be prevented, people involved in criminal activity arrested, and suspects who flee restrained. In order to meet these goals, police officers must perform acts that ordinarily would be criminal: they must apply force upon suspected criminals, deprive them of their life or liberty, or both.[2] When such acts occur in the reasonable enforcement of the criminal laws, they are justified.

The label attached to the defense that authorizes such conduct is problematic. Sometimes, courts speak generically of the defense of "law enforcement." This term, however, encompasses three sub-defenses. Courts and commentators use different labels to describe these sub-defenses, but they will be described here as: (1) public authority; (2) crime prevention; and (3) effectuation of an arrest. The third defense may itself be sub-divided into two temporal components: (3a) the arrest; and (3b) prevention of the escape of the arrestee.

This chapter examines the law enforcement defenses and the extent to which they justify restrictions on the liberty of, and use of force upon, people suspected of criminal activity. As will become evident, common law rules relating to law enforcement often differentiate between police officers (or government officials in general) and private individuals; in general, the law enforcement defenses provide somewhat broader authority to police officers than to private persons.

---

[1] See generally Floyd R. Finch, Jr., Comment, *Deadly Force to Arrest: Triggering Constitutional Review*, 11 Harv. C.R.-C.L. L. Rev. 361 (1976); Kevin P. Jenkins, *Police Use of Deadly Force Against Minorities: Ways to Stop the Killing*, 9 Harv. BlackLetter J. 1 (1992); Edward J. Littlejohn, *Deadly Force and its Effects on Police-Community Relations*, 27 Howard L.J. 1131 (1984); Roy Moreland, *The Use of Force in Effecting or Resisting Arrest*, 33 Neb. L. Rev. 408 (1953); Rollin M. Perkins, *The Law of Arrest*, 25 Iowa L. Rev. 201 (1940); Lawrence W. Sherman, *Execution Without Trial: Police Homicide and the Constitution*, 33 Vand. L. Rev. 71 (1980); Jerry R. Sparger & David J. Giacopassi, *Memphis Revisited: A Reexamination of Police Shootings After the Garner Decision*, 9 Just. Q. 211 (1992); Abraham N. Tennebaum, *The Influence of the Garner Decision on Police Use of Deadly Force*, 85 J. Crim. L. & Criminology 241 (1994); Gregory Howard Williams, *Controlling the Use of Non-Deadly Force: Policy and Practice*, 10 Harv. BlackLetter J. 79 (1993).

[2] Of course, other harm can occur in the law enforcement context. For example, the police may trespass on land in order to execute an arrest or search warrant, or drive above the posted speed limit on a highway in the apprehension of a fugitive. These comparatively unproblematic issues are not considered in this chapter.

§ 21.02   Restraint on Liberty in Law Enforcement: "Public Authority" Defense

[A]—How the Issue Arises

D arrests *X*. Ordinarily, "*D*" is a police officer taking into custody a person whom she believes committed a crime. Sometimes, *D* arrests *X* pursuant to an arrest warrant;[3] often, however, she acts without a warrant. Infrequently, *D* is a private (i.e., non-government) person, assisting an officer in making the arrest, or independently conducting a so-called "citizen's arrest."

In rare circumstances, *D*, the arresting party, may be prosecuted for false imprisonment ("unlawful confinement") of *X*, or for a related offense.[4] In such a prosecution, *D* may raise a claim described at common law as the defense of "public authority" or "public duty." Today, the justifiability of *D*'s conduct, in restricting *V*'s liberty by making an arrest, is regulated by statute; most statutes, however, codify the common law rules regarding arrests.

[B]—By Police Officers

[1]—Common Law

A police officer is authorized to make an arrest, whether for a felony or for a misdemeanor, if it is made pursuant to an arrest warrant based upon "reasonable" or "probable" cause.[5]

At common law, an officer was also justified in making a felony arrest *without* a warrant, as long as the arrest was based on probable cause;[6] warrantless misdemeanor arrests, however, were valid only if the offense occurred in the officer's presence.[7]

---

[3] An arrest warrant is an order of a judicial officer commanding law enforcement officials to arrest a particular person for a specified crime. Arrests, whether with or without warrants, must be based on probable cause to believe that the arrestee committed the specified offense. U.S. Const. amend. IV. For the definition of "probable cause" see note 5, *infra*.

[4] E.g., 18 U.S.C. § 242 (1982) ("Whoever, under color of any law . . . willfully subjects any inhabitant of any State . . . to the deprivation of any rights [such as freedom from unreasonable arrest] . . . secured or protected by the Constitution . . . by reason of his race shall be fined . . . or imprisoned . . . .").

[5] "Reasonable cause," a common law term, is equivalent to the constitutional phrase "probable cause." *Draper v. United States*, 358 U.S. 307, 310 n.3 (1959). "Probable cause" exists when the facts and circumstances within an officer's knowledge and of which she has reasonably trustworthy information are sufficient in themselves to cause a person of reasonable caution to believe that an offense has been committed and that the person to be arrested committed it. *Carroll v. United States*, 267 U.S. 132, 162 (1925).

[6] See *United States v. Watson*, 423 U.S. 411, 418 (1985); *Baltimore & O.R.R. v. Cain*, 31 A. 801, 803 (Md. 1895).

[7] "Presence" has been broadly construed to mean that commission of the offense is "apparent to the officer's senses." *People v. Brown*, 45 Cal.2d 640, 642 (1955). This may include hearing the offense committed over a telephone. *People v. Cahill*, 328 P.2d 995 (Cal. Ct. App. 1958).

[2]—Constitutional Limits on the Common Law

The Fourth Amendment to the United States Constitution prohibits unreasonable searches and seizures. Generally speaking, this provision protects people in their legitimate expectations of privacy.[8]

Nowhere is the zone of privacy more clearly defined and more rigorously protected than in a person's home. Consequently, in the absence of an emergency or consent, warrantless felony arrests in the home are unconstitutional.[9] Moreover, virtually no emergency will justify a warrantless *misdemeanor* arrest in the home.[10]

[C]—By Private Persons

Private persons have common law authority to make arrests. The common law provides that a private citizen may arrest another person for a felony, or for a misdemeanor involving a breach of the peace,[11] if: (1) the crime actually occurred; and (2) she reasonably believes that the suspect committed the offense.[12] With misdemeanors, the offense must also occur in the arresting person's presence.[13]

Under this rule, the arresting party acts at her criminal peril regarding the first element of the defense, but is permitted a reasonable mistake of fact regarding the second element. For example, suppose that *D* observes *V* flee from a bank as the bank alarm goes off. *D* believes that *V* robbed the bank and, therefore, arrests *V*. If it later turns out that *V* did not rob the bank, and *D* is prosecuted for false imprisonment of *V*, *D* may not successfully assert a public authority defense unless the bank was robbed. If it was robbed, however, *D* may successfully claim the defense, although *V* was not the robber (e.g., she was a customer fleeing the scene), as long as *D*'s belief in *V*'s guilt was a reasonable one.

The Fourth Amendment applies solely to governmental activity.[14] Therefore, private parties who make arrests are not subject to the constitutional rules that apply to police officers.

---

[8] *Katz v. United States*, 389 U.S. 347 (1967).

[9] *Payton v. New York*, 445 U.S. 573, 589-90 (1980).

[10] *Welsh v. Wisconsin*, 466 U.S. 740, 753 (1984) ("[I]t is difficult to conceive of a warrantless home arrest that would not be unreasonable under the Fourth Amendment when the underlying offense is extremely minor.").

[11] "Breach of the peace" is conduct that causes or tends to cause a disturbance of the peace and tranquility of other persons. *Cantwell v. Connecticut*, 310 U.S. 296, 308 (1940). Sometimes, "breach of the peace" is a specific offense; in other cases, it is a general term that encompasses crimes such as "disorderly conduct" and "disturbing the peace."

[12] *United States v. Brown*, 551 F.2d 639, 645 (5th Cir. 1977), *rev'd en banc on other grounds*, 569 F.2d 236 (1978) (rule regarding felonies); *Baltimore & O.R.R. v. Cain*, 31 A. at 803 (rule regarding misdemeanors).

[13] *Baltimore & O.R.R. v. Cain*, 31 A. at 803.

[14] *Burdeau v. McDowell*, 256 U.S. 465 (1921).

§ 21.03   Force Used in Law Enforcement: Common and Statutory Law

[A]—Nondeadly Force

A police officer or private citizen will often use force in law enforcement, either to prevent the commission or consummation of a crime, or to make an arrest after the offense has been committed. Criminal prosecutions for the use of nondeadly force in such circumstances are rare.

The common law rule regarding the use of nondeadly force may be summarized simply: a police officer or private person is justified in using nondeadly force upon another if she reasonably believes that: (1) such other person is committing or has committed a felony, or a misdemeanor amounting to a breach of the peace; and (2) the force used is necessary to prevent the commission of the offense, or to effectuate an arrest, i.e., to make the arrest or to prevent the arrestee's escape. [15]

[B]—Deadly Force

[1]—Crime Prevention

Deadly force may never be used in the prevention of a misdemeanor offense. [16] Deadly force is permitted, however, in the prevention of a felony. A split of authority exists regarding the scope of the right to use deadly force in felony crime prevention.

[a]—Broad Defense: Minority Rule

The broad view is that a police officer or private person is justified in using deadly force upon another if she reasonably believes that: (1) such other person is committing any felony; and (2) deadly force is necessary to prevent the commission of the crime. [17]

This rule is remarkably broad in that it authorizes the use of necessary force to prevent nonviolent felonies. Thus, *D* may kill *V*, a felonious thief, if it is the only means to prevent her from taking the personal property of *D* or a third person, even though no life is jeopardized by *V*'s criminal activities.

The right to use deadly force in crime prevention is broader than the scope of the common law justification of defense-of-property, which bars the use of deadly force to protect a person's possessory interest in property. [18] This difference results in an undesirable anomaly: if a defendant kills a would-be thief, she may avoid

---

[15] Restatement (Second) of Torts §§ 141-143 (1965). There is some authority for the view that when a private party (and perhaps a police officer not in uniform) intends to make an arrest, she must first inform the arrestee of her intentions. American Law Institute, Comment to § 3.07, at 110 (citing authority).

[16] *Durham v. State*, 159 N.E. 145, 147 (Ind. 1927). Also, deadly force may not be used to arrest or prevent the escape of a misdemeanant. See *Tennessee v. Garner*, 471 U.S. 1, 12 (1985).

[17] *State v. Rutherford*, 8 N.C. 457 (1821).

[18] See § 20.02[A], *supra*.

conviction if she claims the defense of crime prevention, but may be convicted of murder if she raises a defense-of-property claim.

[b]—Narrow Defense: Majority Rule

Most states do not enforce as broad a defense of crime prevention as that mentioned in the preceding subsection. Usually, the right to use deadly force is limited to the prevention of "forcible" or "atrocious" felonies.[19] Thus, under this rule, a store owner may shoot a would-be robber, if necessary, to prevent the commission of the offense, but she may not justifiably kill one who takes property and attempts to leave without paying for it, as the latter offense is a misdemeanor or, at most, the nonviolent felony of larceny.[20]

[2]—Effectuation of an Arrest

[a]—By Police Officers

[i]—Early Common Law Rule

Until the fourteenth century, a law enforcement officer had the right (perhaps even the duty) to use deadly force against any person who the officer reasonably believed had committed any felony. The officer was justified in killing the felon *even if deadly force was unnecessary to effectuate the felon's detention.*

This extreme approach was based on the premise that felons were outlaws at war with society.[21] Society was justified, therefore, in treating them as dangerous combatants whose lives could be taken for the community's benefit. This view was strengthened by the fact that all felonies were subject to the penalty of death and forfeiture of property. Thus, it was said, by committing a capital offense, a felon forfeited his right to life;[22] his killing was merely "a premature execution of the inevitable judgment."[23]

[ii]—Modification of the Rule

The stark approach of pre-fourteenth century England is no longer followed. Necessity, not part of the original common law rule, is now included as an element of the defense. Thus, deadly force is permitted only as a last resort.[24] Nonetheless, under the modified rule, which became the majority rule,[25] a person may use deadly

---

[19] 4 Blackstone at *180; 1 Hale at *488; *Laney v. State,* 361 S.E.2d 841, 843 (Ga. Ct. App. 1987) (applying a statute).

[20] *Laney v. State,* 361 S.E.2d 841 (Ga. Ct. App. 1987) (upholding *D*'s conviction for manslaughter in the death of *V*, who attempted to leave *D*'s convenience store with a beer without paying for it; but stating that deadly force would have been permitted if *D* had reasonably believed that *V* was planning to rob the store).

[21] See *Schumann v. McGinn,* 240 N.W.2d 525, 532-33 (Minn. 1976).

[22] *Petrie v. Cartwright,* 70 S.W. 297, 299 (Ky. 1902).

[23] Note, *Legalized Murder of a Fleeing Felon,* 15 Va. L. Rev. 582, 583 (1925).

[24] *Schumann v. McGinn,* 240 N.W.2d at 532-33; 4 Blackstone at *289; 2 Hale at *85.

[25] See *Tennessee v. Garner,* 471 U.S. at 15-16 (summarizing the law up to 1985). The state of the law today is uncertain in various jurisdictions, so that no single rule is clearly followed by a majority of states.

force upon another if she reasonably believes: (1) the suspect committed a forcible *or nonforcible* felony; and (2) such force is necessary to make the arrest or to prevent the suspect from escaping. It should be observed that this rule is broader than the majority common law rule pertaining to the use of deadly force in crime prevention, which only authorizes the use of deadly force to repel *forcible* felonies.

Beginning in the late nineteenth century, some jurisdictions, by statute or common law, narrowed the scope of the defense still further. In these states, deadly force is only permitted when necessary to effectuate an arrest for a forcible or atrocious felony.[26]

The rules described here are subject to constitutional limitations, discussed in § 21.04.

[b]—By Private Persons

A private person may use deadly force, if reasonably necessary, to arrest or apprehend a felon, but the defense is narrower than the comparable right held by police officers. The special limitations are the result of lawmakers' concerns about "uncontrolled vigilantism and anarchistic actions . . . [as well as] the danger of death or injury of innocent persons at the hands of untrained volunteers using firearms."[27]

Although the rules vary among the states, some of the special requirements that often must be satisfied before a private person may justifiably use deadly force in connection with a felony arrest include: (1) the offense must be a forcible felony;[28] (2) the arresting party must give the suspect notice of her intention to make the arrest;[29] and (3) the arresting party must be correct in her belief that the person against whom the force is used actually committed the offense in question, i.e., a reasonable mistake of fact in this regard neither justifies nor excuses the use of deadly force.[30]

§ 21.04   Force Used in Law Enforcement: Constitutional Limits

[A]—Background: The Controversy

Many commentators have criticized the breadth of the common law law-enforcement defense, set out in § 21.03[B][2][a][ii], *supra*, which authorizes the use of deadly force, when reasonably necessary, to arrest or prevent the escape of persons suspected of nonforcible, as well as forcible, felonies.[31]

---

[26] E.g., *Storey v. State*, 71 Ala. 329, 339 (1882).

[27] *Commonwealth v. Klein*, 363 N.E.2d 1313, 1317-18 (Mass. 1977).

[28] E.g., *id.* at 1319.

[29] E.g., *Commonwealth v. Chermansky*, 242 A.2d 237, 240 (Pa. 1968).

[30] E.g., *id.* at 240.

[31] The common law rule has had little scholarly support. Perhaps its bluntest supporter stated that narrowing the defense would be equivalent to saying to the non-resistant criminal, " 'You are foolish. No matter what you have done you are foolish to submit to arrest. The officer dare not take the risk of shooting at you. If you can outrun him, outrun him . . . .

Critics maintain that police officers too often kill or seriously injure innocent people, including suspects who are innocent of any crime and bystanders caught in the gunfire.[32] Additionally, police use of lethal force may have an undesirable effect on police-community relations.[33] Sometimes, police shootings appear to be racially motivated, or the result of "trigger-happy" law enforcement officers.[34] Even when these appearances are inaccurate, police use of deadly force can increase tension between law enforcement agencies and the communities they serve. In the short run, this may result in disorder; in the long run, it may result in disrespect for the police.

Critics of the common law defense have also claimed that the underlying justifications for the rule no longer apply. The law no longer considers a felon an outlaw whose life may be taken at any time, regardless of necessity. Nor does the forfeiture theory withstand modern scrutiny: only the crime of murder carries the penalty of death today, and even here it is not mandatory; it cannot be said, therefore, that any felon's "execution" on the street merely speeds up an inevitable process.[35]

Perhaps as a consequence of changes in circumstances, police departments in many large American cities began in the late 1970s to develop policies restricting their officers' use of firearms to circumstances in which the arrestee presented a threat of death or serious bodily injury.[36] These changes in departmental policy have received the imprimatur of the Supreme Court, as discussed immediately below.

[B]—*Tennessee v. Garner*: The Common Law Restricted[37]

[1]—Holding

According to the Supreme Court, a police officer violates the Fourth Amendment prohibition on unreasonable searches and seizures if she uses deadly force to effectuate an arrest unless: (1) she "has probable cause to believe that the suspect

---

If you are faster than he is you are free, and God bless you.' I feel entirely unwilling to give that benediction to the modern criminal." Quoted in American Law Institute, Comment to § 3.07, at 120 n.31.

[32] For one exhaustive survey of empirical research on police use of deadly force against civilians, see William A. Geller, *Deadly Force: What We Know*, 10 J. Pol. Sci. & Adm. 151 (1982).

[33] *The President's Commission on Law Enforcement and Administration of Justice Task Force Report: The Police* 189-90 (1967); see Littlejohn, Note 1, *supra*.

[34] See Eric Lichtblau, *LAPD Officers Faulted in 3 of 4 Shooting Cases*, Los Angeles Times, August 14, 1994, at A1 (according to a review of nearly 700 shooting reports in 1989, police officers succumbed to "the John Wayne Syndrome" and, in 75% of the cases, fired their weapons inappropriately).

[35] Of course, the forfeiture theory never withstood analysis when the suspected felon was innocent of the crime. See *Petrie v. Cartwright*, 70 S.W. 297, 299 (Ky. 1902).

[36] *Tennessee v. Garner*, 471 U.S. 1, 18-19 (1985).

[37] 471 U.S. 1 (1985).

poses a significant threat of death or serious physical injury to the officer or others"; [38] and (2) such force is necessary to make the arrest or prevent escape. In regard to the necessity element, a warning, if feasible, must be given to the suspect before deadly force is employed.

[2]—Facts Underlying *Garner*

In *Garner*, two officers were dispatched at night to answer a "prowler inside call." At the scene, a witness told the officers that she had heard glass breaking and that "they" were, or "someone" was, breaking into the house next door.

One officer investigated while his partner went to the police car to call the dispatcher. The investigating officer saw someone run into the backyard of the apparently-burglarized home. He chased the suspect, Cleamtree Garner, a fifteen-year-old eighth-grader, to a six-foot high chain-link fence where Garner crouched at the base. The officer shone a flashlight on Garner's hands and face, saw no sign of a weapon, and determined that he was "reasonably sure" that the youth was unarmed.

Garner began to climb the fence. The officer concluded that if the youth made it over the fence he would elude capture. The officer called out "police, halt"; when Garner did not stop, the officer shot him. The bullet struck the boy in the back of the head, killing him.

Garner's suspected conduct constituted burglary. As such, the officer's use of deadly force was justified under Tennessee law, which authorized the use of deadly force to arrest a suspect for any felony. Nonetheless, Garner's family brought a federal action against the police seeking damages for violation of the youth's constitutional rights.

[3]—Reasoning of the Supreme Court

An arrest of a suspect constitutes a "seizure" of that person. Consequently, the Fourth Amendment ban on unreasonable seizures is implicated when a police officer makes an arrest. In order to determine whether Garner's seizure by deadly force was reasonable, the Supreme Court balanced the suspect's interests against those of society. According to the Court, the intrusion on a suspect's rights is "unmatched" when an arresting officer uses deadly force: Garner's fundamental interest in life was jeopardized by the officer's use of deadly force; such force also frustrated his and society's interest in obtaining a judicial determination of his guilt and punishment.

The Court concluded that society's interest in the arrest of nonviolent felons is outweighed by the competing interests: "it is not better that all felony suspects die than that they escape." The Court reasoned that "[w]here the suspect poses no immediate threat to the officer and no threat to others, the harm resulting from failing to apprehend [the nonviolent felon] does not justify the use of deadly force"; as Justice White, author of *Garner*, put it, "[a] police officer may not seize an unarmed, nondangerous suspect by shooting him dead."

---

[38] 471 U.S. at 3.

[4]—Observations Regarding *Garner*

Because the Fourth Amendment only applies to governmental conduct, common law and statutory provisions relating to the use of deadly force by private persons are not effected by *Garner*. [39] It is also unclear whether the rule of *Garner* has application in prosecutions of police officers who shoot nonviolent felons; it is arguable that the rule simply provides a civil remedy, as in *Garner*, for use of excessive police force. [40]

Assuming that states must modify their criminal laws to conform with the holding of *Garner*, it is evident that deadly force may no longer be used by police officers against persons suspected of nonforcible felonies. Less evident, but also true, is that deadly force is sometimes barred by *Garner*, even when it is necessary to effectuate the arrest of a person suspected of committing a *forcible* felony. Burglary—the crime that Garner was suspected of committing—is a forcible felony; nonetheless, the Court held that the officers were not entitled to kill Garner, because Garner was apparently unarmed.

The underlying basis of the holding in *Garner* is that police use of deadly force is constitutionally unreasonable unless, based on the circumstances as they would appear to a reasonable police officer in the situation, the suspect poses a threat of death or serious bodily harm to the officer or others, if she is not immediately apprehended. This means that the dangerousness of the felon must be determined on the facts of the individual case, and not on the basis of an abstract characterization of the felony as a "forcible" or "atrocious" crime. [41]

§ 21.05   Model Penal Code

[A]—Authority to Arrest

The Model Penal Code defense of "execution of public duty" provides that conduct is justified when it is required or permitted by: (1) a law defining the duties of a government officer; (2) a law pertaining to the execution of legal process; (3) an order of a court; or (4) any other law imposing a public duty on the actor. [42]

This defense is also available in two circumstances in which an actor *lacks* legal authority to act, but believes that she does. Essentially, these two situations constitute special mistake-of-law rules. First, a law enforcement officer acts justifiably if she believes, albeit incorrectly, that her conduct is authorized "by the judgment or direction of a competent court or tribunal or in the lawful execution of legal process." [43] For example, if *D* makes an arrest based on a warrant (i.e., legal

---

[39] *People v. Couch*, 461 N.W.2d 683 (Mich. 1990).

[40] *State v. Clothier*, 753 P.2d 1267 (Kan. 1988) (holding that *Garner* does not apply in criminal prosecutions).

[41] In dictum the Court provided two examples of circumstances in which necessary deadly force would be justified: (1) if the officer has probable cause to believe that the suspect committed a crime involving the infliction or threatened infliction of serious physical harm; or (2) if the felon threatens the officer with a weapon.

[42] Model Penal Code § 3.03(1).

[43] Model Penal Code § 3.03(3)(a).

process) that later proves to be defective (e.g., it was issued on less than probable cause), she is not subject to criminal prosecution for restricting the arrestee's liberty in an unlawful manner.

Second, the defense is available to an actor who believes that she is authorized to assist a public officer in the performance of her duties, although it turns out that the officer was acting beyond her authority.[44] For example, if an officer requests assistance from a bystander in making an arrest, the private citizen is not subject to prosecution if the officer lacked authority to arrest the suspect, e.g., lacked probable cause for the arrest or did not have a required warrant.

[B]—Crime Prevention

[1]—Use of Force, In General

A police officer or private person is justified in using force upon another if she believes that: (1) such other person is about to commit suicide, inflict serious bodily injury upon herself, or commit a crime involving or threatening bodily injury, damage to or loss of property, or a breach of the peace; and (2) the force is immediately necessary to prevent the commission of the aforementioned act.[45] Deadly force is impermissible except as discussed in subsection [2].

The Code does not impose special limitations on the use of nondeadly force in crime prevention. Instead, it states that any limitation on the use of force imposed by another justification provision applies to the use of force in crime prevention.[46]

[2]—Use of Deadly Force

A police officer or private person may not use deadly force to prevent the commission of a crime unless she believes that: (1) a substantial risk exists that the suspect will cause death or serious bodily injury to another person unless she prevents the suspect from committing the offense; and (2) use of deadly force presents no substantial risk of injury to bystanders.[47]

This provision should be compared to the Code's deadly-force provisions in analogous circumstances. First, it largely parallels the effectuation-of-arrest defense discussed below, except that the crime prevention defense applies to all persons, public or private, whereas only public officers and those aiding them may use deadly force in the arrest process. The Institute's justification for this difference is that "[i]n modern conditions, the arrest of suspected criminals is peculiarly the concern of the police. The prevention of crime, on the other hand, is properly the concern of everybody."[48]

Second, the crime prevention defense is somewhat narrower than the rules regarding defense of property.[49] The present defense, but not the defense of

---

[44] Model Penal Code § 3.03(3)(b).

[45] Model Penal Code § 3.07(5)(a).

[46] Model Penal Code § 3.07(5)(a)(i).

[47] Model Penal Code § 3.07(5)(a)(ii)(A).

[48] American Law Institute, Comment to § 3.07, at 132.

[49] Id., Comment to § 3.06, at 95 n.48.

property, prohibits the use of deadly force if it would jeopardize the safety of bystanders. Moreover, deadly force may be used in defense of property in some circumstances in which the safety of the actor is not threatened,[50] but deadly force is not permitted in crime prevention unless the actor believes that there is a related threat of death or serious bodily injury connected to the commission of the crime.

[C]—Effectuation of an Arrest

[1]—Use of Force, In General

A police officer or private person is justified in using force upon another to make or assist in making an arrest, or to prevent the suspect's escape, if the actor: (1) believes that force is immediately necessary to effectuate a lawful arrest or to prevent the suspect's escape;[51] and (2a) makes known to such other person the purpose of the arrest or (2b) believes that such other person understands the purpose of the arrest or that notice cannot reasonably be provided.[52] Deadly force is impermissible except as discussed immediately below.

[2]—Use of Deadly Force

Deadly force may never be used by a private person, acting on her own, to make an arrest or to prevent a suspect's escape. However, deadly force may be employed by a police officer, or a private person assisting someone she believes is a law enforcement officer, to make an arrest or to prevent the suspect's escape if: (1) the arrest is for a felony; (2) the requirements for the use of force set out in subsection [1] are satisfied; (3) the actor believes that the use of deadly force creates no substantial risk of harm to innocent bystanders; and either (4a) the actor believes that the crime included the use or threatened use of deadly force; or (4b) the actor believes that a substantial risk exists that the suspect will kill or seriously harm another if her arrest is delayed or if she escapes.[53]

This Code provision is considerably narrower than the common law. First, the common law permits private citizens acting alone to use deadly force in making arrests. Second, deadly force may not be used unless the actor affirmatively believes that its use will not seriously jeopardize the safety of bystanders. For example, suppose that D, a police officer, purposely shoots and kills V, a dangerous fleeing felon, on a crowded street. At common law, D's conduct as to V would be justified; under the Code, D would be denied the law enforcement defense, and could be convicted of purposely killing V, unless she believed that her actions did not jeopardize the bystanders' safety.[54]

---

[50] See § 20.05[C][1][b], *supra*.

[51] The defense is not available, however, if the arrest was unlawful and if the person's belief in its lawfulness was the result of a mistake of law regarding provisions of the criminal law or the law governing the scope of her power to arrest. Model Penal Code § 3.09(1). See generally American Law Institute, Comment to § 3.07, at 107.

[52] Model Penal Code §§ 3.07(1), 3.07(2)(a), 3.07(3).

[53] Model Penal Code § 3.07(2)(b).

[54] This provision represents a departure from the rule set out in Model Penal Code § 3.09(3), as discussed at § 18.07 [C], *supra*. Under § 3.09, a person whose conduct in relation to V

Third, unlike the common law, the Code does not permit use of deadly force in making arrests for nonforcible felonies. The Code provision appears to conform to the dictates of *Tennessee v. Garner.*[55] The Code, as required by *Garner*, does not justify use of deadly force in effectuating arrests unless the arrestee appears to pose such a high level of risk to the safety of another that her immediate capture overrides her constitutionally recognized interest in her life.[56]

---

is justified, but whose conduct recklessly or negligently threatens the safety of *X*, a bystander, is entitled to the defense in a prosecution for use of force against *V*, but may be convicted of an offense based on recklessness or negligence regarding *X*. Under § 3.07, however, *D*'s recklessness regarding the safety of a bystander results in the loss of the defense in relation to *V*. The drafters of the Code believed that this was an appropriate way of emphasizing the priority that police officers must accord to the safety of bystanders. American Law Institute, Comment to § 3.07, at 118.

[55] 471 U.S. 1 (1985). See § 21.04, *supra.*

[56] American Law Institute, Comment to § 3.07, at 120.

CHAPTER 22

NECESSITY

§ 22.01 Basic Nature of the Defense[1]

This chapter considers the defense of necessity, also called the "lesser evil" or "choice of evils" defense. Unfortunately, "[t]he origins and present status of the defense . . . are shrouded in uncertainty and confusion."[2] Indeed, at the foundational level, there is uncertainty whether the defense should be classified as a justification defense, an excuse, or has characteristics of both. Also, this defense is often confused with, or is treated as part of, a broader defense encompassing the defense of duress. The excuse characteristics of "necessity" (to the extent that they exist) and the relationship of necessity to the defense of duress, are considered in the next chapter.[3] This chapter considers only necessity as a justification defense.

The defense of necessity can arise in a myriad of circumstances, but it is most often invoked successfully when an actor encounters the following dilemma: as a result of some force or condition, he must choose between violating a relatively minor offense, on the one hand, or suffering (or allowing others to suffer) substantial harm to person or property, on the other hand. For example, the necessity defense applies if a seaman violates an embargo by putting into a foreign port due to dangerous and unforeseeable weather conditions,[4] a person drives on a suspended license in order to take a loved one to the hospital in a dire emergency,[5] or a motorist exceeds the speed limit in order to pass another car and move to the right lane, so that an emergency vehicle can pass.[6]

---

[1] See generally Fletcher at § 10.2; Kent Greenawalt, Conflicts of Law and Morality 286-310 (1987); Hall at 415-36; Katz at 8-81; Williams at §§ 229-239; Edward B. Arnolds & Norman F. Garland, *The Defense of Necessity in Criminal Law: The Right to Choose the Lesser Evil*, 65 J. Crim. L. & Criminology 289 (1974); Alan Brudner, *A Theory of Necessity*, 7 Oxford J. Legal Studies 339 (1987); P.R. Glazebrook, *The Necessity Plea in English Criminal Law*, 30 Cambridge L.J. 87 (1972); Mirian Gur-Arye, *Should the Criminal Law Distinguish Between Necessity as a Justification and Necessity as an Excuse?*, 102 L.Q. Rev. 71 (1986); Heidi M. Hurd, *Justifiably Punishing the Justified*, 90 Mich. L. Rev. 2203 (1992); Edward M. Morgan, *The Defence of Necessity: Justification or Excuse?*, 42 U. Toronto Fac. L. Rev. 165 (1984); Rollin M. Perkins, *Impelled Perpetration Restated*, 33 Hastings L.J. 403 (1981); Lawrence P. Tiffany & Carl A. Anderson, *Legislating the Necessity Defense in Criminal Law*, 52 Denver L.J. 839 (1975); Michelle R. Conde, Comment, *Necessity Defined: A New Role in the Criminal Defense System*, 29 UCLA L. Rev. 409 (1981).

[2] Greenawalt, Note 1, *supra*, at 288.

[3] See §§ 23.03, 23.05-.06, *infra*.

[4] *The William Gray*, 29 Fed. Cas. 1300 (No. 17,694) (1810).

[5] *State v. Baker*, 579 A.2d 479 (Vt. 1990).

[6] *State v. Messler*, 562 A.2d 1138 (Conn. Ct. App. 1989).

Not all litigated necessity cases fit the preceding paradigm. For example, courts have been required to determine whether it is justifiable for a person to possess marijuana when it is used to reduce the effects of glaucoma,[7] to distribute clean hypodermic needles to drug addicts in an effort to combat the spread of acquired immune deficiency syndrome (AIDS),[8] to escape confinement because of intolerable prison conditions,[9] to steal food out of economic necessity,[10] to kidnap a person in order to remove her from the influence of a "religious cult,"[11] or to kill an innocent person in order to save several innocent lives.[12] Occasionally, too, the defense is raised when a person commits civil disobedience in order to signal his opposition to a law or governmental policy.[13]

Generally speaking, "necessity" is a residual justification defense. That is, it is a defense of last resort: it legitimizes technically illegal conduct that common sense, principles of justice, and/or utilitarian concerns convince us is justifiable, but which does not fall within any other recognized justification defense. Thus, the necessity defense serves as "a supplement to legislative judgment."[14] It may be used by a jury in extreme cases to uphold conduct that lawmakers would have allowed, if given the opportunity.

Despite many uncertainties regarding the defense, there is little doubt that the principle of necessity—the principle that, if circumstances compel a choice among various evils, an actor should not be punished if he chooses the least harmful option—is one so "essential to the rationality and justice of the criminal law, [that it] is appropriately addressed in a penal code."[15]

§ 22.02   General Rules

Necessity may not have been a common law defense in England,[16] but it is a part of the common law tradition of the United States.[17] Despite this, the defense has no single accepted definition. Indeed, at any given time in history it was exceedingly difficult to determine the standing and scope of the defense in any particular jurisdiction.[18]

---

[7] *Jenks v. State*, 582 So.2d 676 (Fla. Ct. App. 1991) (permitting a medical necessity defense); *State v. Hanson*, 468 N.W.2d 77 (Minn. Ct. App. 1991) (disallowing the defense).

[8] *Commonwealth v. Leno*, 616 N.E.2d 453 (Mass. 1993) (disallowing the defense).

[9] See § 23.05, *infra*.

[10] *State v. Moe*, 24 P.2d 638, 640 (Wash. 1933) (stating that "economic necessity has never been accepted as a defense to criminal charge").

[11] *People v. Brandyberry*, 812 P.2d 674 (Colo. Ct. App. 1991) (disallowing the defense).

[12] See § 22.04, *infra*.

[13] See § 22.03, *infra*.

[14] Greenawalt, Note 1, *supra*, at 289.

[15] American Law Institute, Comment to § 3.02, at 9.

[16] Glanville Williams states "somewhat confidently" that it was a defense in England. Williams at § 231. Others disagree. See English Law Commission, No. 83, Criminal Law Report on Defences of General Application 20 (1977).

[17] American Law Institute, Comment to § 3.02, at 10.

[18] *Id.* at 10-11.

Much of this has changed. Largely as the result of the inclusion of a choice-of-evils provision in the Model Penal Code, [19] approximately one-half of the states now statutorily recognize the defense. Some of the statutes define "necessity" in general terms; others are more specific in their descriptions. In states without a statutory defense, the vague contours of the common law apply.

The parameters of the common law defense may be deduced from its purpose as described in the preceding chapter section. Subject to three potential limitations mentioned below, a person is justified in violating a criminal law if the following six conditions are met. First, the actor must be "faced with a clear and imminent danger." [20] For example, in *United States v. Paolello*, [21] *D*, a convicted felon, was threatened with bodily harm by *X*, who put his hand in the air with a gun and fired it. To save himself, *D* grabbed the gun from *X* and ran down the street with it. *D* was prosecuted for violation of a statute that made it an offense for a convicted felon to possess a firearm. Based on these facts, however, *D* was entitled to an instruction on the necessity defense, as the danger to *D* was clear and imminent. In contrast, in *Commonwealth v. Leno*, [22] *D* participated in a needle exchange program run by AIDS activists, in which he and others furnished clean needles to drug addicts in order to reduce the spread of the deadly disease. *D* was charged with possession and distribution of hypodermic needles without a prescription. The Supreme Judicial Court of Massachusetts held that *D* was not entitled to a jury instruction on necessity because the harm—spread of AIDS—was not imminent in any given case in which the needles were exchanged.

Second, the defendant must expect, as a reasonable person, that his action will be effective in abating the danger that he seeks to avoid, i.e., there must be a direct causal relationship between his action and the harm to be averted. [23] For example, an inmate who flees confinement because of a raging prison fire, has chosen a path that will directly save his life.

Third, the defendant may not successfully claim necessity if there is an effective legal alternative for averting the harm. [24] For example, in *Nelson v. State*, [25] *D* drove his four-wheel-drive truck onto a side road off the highway, where it became stuck in a marsh. After spending an hour trying to free the vehicle, *D* and *X* went to a nearby Highway Department Yard where they took equipment, including a dump truck, without permission, and unsuccessfully used it to try to pull *D*'s vehicle out of the mud. *D* was prosecuted for reckless destruction of the Highway Department's property and of driving the truck without consent. The court held that the facts did

---

[19] See § 22.05, *infra*.

[20] *Commonwealth v. Schuchardt*, 557 N.E.2d 1380, 1381 (Mass. 1990) (quoting *Commonwealth v. Burgmann*, 433 N.E.2d 457 (Mass. Ct. App. 1982).

[21] 951 F.2d 537 (3rd Cir. 1991).

[22] 616 N.E.2d 453 (Mass. 1993).

[23] *Id.* at 455; *United States v. Schoon*, 971 F.2d 193, 195 (9th Cir. 1991).

[24] *Commonwealth v. Leno*, 616 N.E.2d at 455; *People v. Gray*, 571 N.Y.S.2d 851, 853 (N.Y. City Crim. Ct. 1991).

[25] 597 P.2d 977 (Alaska 1979).

not support the defense of necessity, in part on the ground that *D* had lawful alternatives in his situation, since various people came by on several occasions and offered their services in the form of physical aid, rides, or offers to call for tow trucks or the police.

Fourth, the defense does not apply unless the harm that the defendant will cause by violating the law is less serious than the harm that he seeks to avoid.[26] Two features of this lesser-harm rule must be understood. First, in balancing the harms, the defendant's actions "should be weighed against the harm reasonably foreseeable at the time, rather than the harm that actually occurs."[27] For example, if *D*'s car loses its brakes and *D* must choose between striking one of two parked automobiles, one of which is occupied by one person (who will be injured by the collision) and another that is apparently unoccupied, *D* should choose the latter option. He does not lose the defense, however, if it later turns out that there were two persons asleep in the car he struck, who were injured by his actions. Second, given the facts as they reasonably appear, the issue is not whether the *defendant* believes that he made the right choice, but rather is "whether the defendant's value judgment was [in fact] correct,"[28] as determined by the judge or the jury. In making the value determination, the judge or jury may apply utilitarian values,[29] or make the judgment on the basis "of what is [morally] right and proper conduct under the circumstances."[30]

A fifth condition of the necessity defense is that lawmakers must not have "anticipated the choice of evils and determined the balance to be struck between the competing values" in a manner in conflict with the defendant's choice.[31] For example, a defendant may not defend his illegal use of marijuana for medical purposes if the legislature previously "weighed the competing value of medical use of marijuana against the values served by prohibition of its use or possession,"[32] and rejected the former claim.

The final feature of the necessity defense is that the defendant must come to the situation with clean, sometimes immaculate,[33] hands. That is, he must not have wrongfully "placed himself in a situation in which he would be forced to engage in criminal conduct."[34] For example, suppose that *D* recklessly starts a fire. He realizes that the fire is likely to quickly spread and burn down a number of residences, so he purposely burns *V*'s farm land in order to create a "fire line" that will prevent a major conflagration. Although *D*'s act satisfies all of the other

---

[26] *State v. Warshow*, 410 A.2d 1000, 1001-02 (Vt. 1979).

[27] *Nelson v. State*, 597 P.2d at 979-80.

[28] *Id.* at 980 n.6.

[29] *United States v. Schoon*, 971 F.2d at 196 ("Necessity is, essentially, a utilitarian defense.").

[30] *Id.* at 200 (Fernandez, J. concurring).

[31] *State v. Tate*, 505 A.2d 941, 946 (N.J. 1986); *Commonwealth v. Leno*, 616 N.E.2d at 455.

[32] *State v. Tate*, 505 A.2d at 946.

[33] Katz at 42.

[34] *United States v. Paolello*, 951 F.2d at 541.

elements of the defense, he will be denied the defense of necessity because he was responsible for creating the emergency.[35]

Even if these elements of the necessity defense are proven, three potential limitations on the application of the necessity defense may come into play. First, some states limit the defense to emergencies created by natural forces.[36] Thus, in these jurisdictions, *D* may trespass on property in order to avoid a tornado, but not to escape an armed robber. Likewise, *D*, a prison inmate, may be able to claim necessity if he flees the prison as the result of a fire, but not if another inmate threatens to assault him. Assuming that the defendant has chosen the lesser of two evils, and the other elements of the defense are satisfied, this natural-versus-human distinction is arbitrary and should not be drawn.

Second, the necessity defense may not apply in homicide cases.[37] Third, some states limit the defense to protection of persons and property; a person may not act, for example, to protect his reputation or economic interests.[38]

§ 22.03 Civil Disobedience[39]

"Civil disobedience" may be defined as "a nonviolent act, publicly performed and deliberately unlawful, that has as its purpose to protest a law, government policy, or action of a private body whose conduct has serious public consequences."[40]

Civil disobedience may be direct or indirect. Direct civil disobedience involves protesting a particular law by breaking it.[41] An example occurred in the early 1960s when civil rights demonstrators sat-in at all-white lunch counters in the South to

---

[35] From a utilitarian perspective, this rule is unwise. The law should provide *D* with an incentive, i.e., the necessity defense, to save the houses from the fire. *D* would remain liable in tort for his original reckless conduct, and he would be subject to criminal prosecution for any offense committed when he recklessly started the fire. From a retributivist perspective, as well, the rule is unsound, for it may result in an actor being punished in excess of his culpability. In the current example, *D* will be convicted of *purposely* setting fire to *V*'s land, although his true culpability is that of recklessness for setting the original fire. See Paul H. Robinson, *Causing the Conditions of One's Own Defense: A Study in the Limits of Theory in Criminal Law Doctrine*, 71 Va. L. Rev. 1, 3-4, 8-10 (1985).

[36] E.g., Wis. Stat. Ann. § 939.47 (1993) ("pressure of natural physical forces").

[37] See § 22.04, *infra*.

[38] E.g., *State v. Moe*, 24 P.2d 638 (Wash. 1933) (no economic-necessity defense).

[39] See generally Carl Cohen, Civil Disobedience (1971); Abe Fortas, Concerning Dissent and Civil Disobedience (1968); Greenawalt, Note 1, *supra*; Howard Zinn, Disobedience and Democracy (1968); Steven M. Bauer & Peter J. Eckerstrom, Note, *The State Made Me Do It: The Applicability of the Necessity Defense to Civil Disobedience*, 39 Stan. L. Rev. 1173 (1987); James L. Cavallaro, Jr., *The Demise of the Political Necessity Defense: Indirect Civil Disobedience and United States v. Schoon*, 81 Cal. L. Rev. 351 (1993); Matthew Lippman, *The Necessity Defense and Political Protest*, 26 Crim. L. Bull. 317 (1990); Laura J. Schulkind, Note, *Applying the Necessity Defence to Civil Disobedience Cases*, 64 N.Y.U. L. Rev. 79 (1989).

[40] See Cohen, Note 39, *supra*, at 1-40.

[41] Schulkind, Note 39, *supra*, at 79 n.5.

protest, and ultimately to prove the unconstitutionality, of segregationist laws. The necessity defense rarely arises in these circumstances, as the protesters seek to have the protested law declared unconstitutional or otherwise invalidated.

In contrast, indirect civil disobedience involves the violation of a law that is not the object of the protest. In this category, for example, are protesters who violate a trespass statute, although they have no objection to trespass laws, in order to express their opposition to the performance of abortions in a nearby clinic,[42] or who sit in a Congressman's office in order to protest governmental actions in a foreign country.[43]

Do the facts alleged in a typical indirect civil disobedience case state a credible claim of necessity, so as to justify a jury instruction on the defense? The issue usually arises prior to trial as part of a prosecutor's motion *"in limine"* ("on or at the threshold") to bar evidence on the necessity claim, or during trial when the prosecutor objects to the introduction of such evidence. If the prosecutor's motion or objection is granted, which it nearly always is,[44] the defendant is left without any realistic basis to avoid conviction. Therefore, on appeal from the conviction, the defendant will argue that he was improperly denied the opportunity to raise the necessity claim with the jury.

Appellate courts consistently reject the claim that a defendant is entitled to assert a necessity defense in cases of indirect civil disobedience.[45] Indeed, one federal Circuit Court has ruled that the defense is unavailable as a matter of law in all such cases.[46] Typically, the requisites of a traditional necessity claim are lacking in indirect civil disobedience cases: the harm to be avoided is not imminent; the protest does not directly abate the danger; protesters have legal options, such as the ballot

---

[42] E.g., *City of Wichita v. Tilson*, 855 P.2d 911 (Kan. 1993) (the defense is inapplicable); *Jones v. City of Tulsa*, 857 P.2d 814 (Okla. Crim. App. 1993) (same). The line between civil disobedience—a public protest—and a traditional necessity claim can be very thin. If anti-abortion demonstrators attempt to stop particular abortions in a clinic, rather than simply to express their opposition to the procedures, their actions fall outside the mantle of "civil disobedience"; instead, their claim is one of ordinary necessity.

[43] *People v. Craig*, 585 N.E.2d 783 (N.Y. 1991) (protesting governmental policy in Nicaragua; held: the defense is inapplicable); *State v. Cram*, 600 A.2d 733 (Vt. 1991) (protest of shipment of guns to El Salvador; held: same); see *United States v. Schoon*, 939 F.2d 826 (9th Cir. 1991) (Ds were convicted of obstructing activities of the Internal Revenue Service, and of failing to comply with an order of a police officer, as part of a protest against United States involvement in El Salvador; held: the defense is unavailable as a matter of law in *all* indirect civil disobedience cases).

[44] Occasionally, a trial judge permits the defendant to raise the claim. E.g., Terry Wilson, *26 Found Not Guilty of Trespassing At Base*, Chicago Tribune, May 18, 1988, at 3 (26 protesters were acquitted of trespassing to dramatize their opposition to United States policy in Central America). If the defendant is acquitted, the government has no recourse, as the Fifth Amendment double jeopardy clause prohibits retrial following an acquittal. *United States v. Ball*, 163 U.S. 662 (1896).

[45] E.g., *State v. Warshow*, 410 A.2d 1000 (Vt. 1979); *United States v. Kroncke*, 459 F.2d 697 (8th Cir. 1972); see, also, the citations in Notes 42-43, *supra*.

[46] *United States v. Schoon*, 971 F.2d at 196.

box, to change the disputed policy; and the legislature (or, in the case of issues such as abortion, the judiciary) has calculated the comparative harms differently than the protesters.

As a matter of technical application of the necessity defense, the claim should be unavailable to protesters. However, advocates of a "political necessity" defense contend that such a defense should be recognized because it "empowers the individual primarily by presenting a forum in which stifled minority or unheeded majority viewpoints receive a public hearing."[47] Also, the defense empowers the jury, by giving them an opportunity to nullify the law[48] and "weigh in" on a controversial subject.

Opponents of such a defense believe that it would undesirably erode the principle of traditional civil disobedience, which is that people who are compelled by conscience to violate the law, but who also believe in the democratic system, should accept their punishment (as Gandhi and Martin Luther Kind did) as part of their protest.[49] As one philosopher put it, "[w]e must pay a certain price to convince others that our actions have . . . a sufficient moral basis in the political convictions of the community."[50]

§ 22.04 "Necessity" as a Defense to Homicide[51]

[A]—The Issue

Assume for a moment that A, B, and C, are riding in a horse-drawn carriage that is being pursued by a pack of very hungry wolves. If it becomes clear to the passengers that the horse cannot outrun the wolves and that all of them will likely be devoured by the animals, may A push B out of the carriage, so that the wolves devour him, thereby saving the lives of the two remaining occupants of the carriage?[52]

Or, suppose that D, a surgeon, wants to save the lives of five critically ill patients, one of whom needs a new heart, two of whom need a healthy lung each, and two of whom require a kidney transplant to survive. Each of his patients is likely to die within 24 hours without the needed operation. Along comes E, who possesses two good lungs, too good kidneys, and a very healthy heart. Amazingly, E's has the proper blood type and tissue-match to serve as an organ donor for D's patients. May

---

[47] Bauer & Eckerstrom, Note 39, *supra*, at 1184.

[48] The jury nullification principle is discussed at § 1.02[C], *supra*.

[49] Bauer & Eckerstrom, Note 39, *supra*, at 1194.

[50] John Rawls, A Theory of Justice 367 (1971).

[51] See generally A.W. Brian Simpson, Cannibalism and the Common Law (1984); Lon L. Fuller, *The Case of the Speluncean Explorers*, 62 Harv. L. Rev. 616 (1949); John Makdisi, *Justification in the Killing of an Innocent Person*, 38 Cleve. St. L. Rev. 85 (1990); Judith Jarvis Thomson, *The Trolley Problem*, 94 Yale L.J. 1395 (1985); Andrew von Hirsch, *Lifeboat Law*, Crim. Just. Ethics, Summer/Fall 1985, at 88.

[52] Perkins, Note 1, *supra*, at 406.

D harvest *E*'s organs, on the ground that he has saved five people at the expense of just one?[53]

Finally, suppose that *T*, a terrorist, threatens to kill 100 children in a nearby school by use of a remotely-controlled bomb unless *F* immediately kills *G*, who is standing next to *F*. Assuming that *F* has every reason to believe that *T*'s threat is real, is *F* justified in killing *G*?[54]

Each of these hypotheticals raises the same issue: Assuming that all of the requirements for a necessity defense are satisfied, may a person justifiably kill an innocent person in order to save a greater number of innocent lives? Fortunately, this issue rarely arises. Perhaps the most celebrated case involved a lifeboat containing four hungry men.

[B]—*Regina v. Dudley and Stephens*[55]

Three adult seamen and a 17-year-old youth were forced to survive on an open boat after their sailing vessel sank. After 20 days on the boat, the last nine days of which were without food, and the last seven of which were without water, the seamen were exceedingly weak. The boy was seriously ill, as well, from drinking seawater. As a consequence, two of the men, *D* and *S*, killed *V*, the youth, in order to eat his flesh to survive.[56] Four days later, the three survivors were discovered and saved. *D* and *S* were prosecuted for *V*'s murder. They raised the defense of necessity, arguing that they reasonably believed that, had they not killed *V*, all of the occupants of the boat would have perished.

Their claim was rejected. Lord Coleridge, describing the defense argument as "new and strange," canvassed the common law authority and concluded that no decided case or scholar, with one possible exception,[57] supported the claim that "in order to save your own life you may lawfully take the life of another, when that other is neither attempting nor threatening [to take] yours, nor is guilty of any illegal act whatever toward you or any one else."

Lord Coleridge stated that, although "preserv[ing] one's life is generally speaking a duty, . . . it may be the plainest and highest duty to sacrifice it." Thus, he said, it is the duty of a captain to sacrifice his life for the crew, and of the crew to do

---

[53] Thomson, Note 51, *supra*, at 1396.

[54] Notice that in this hypothetical the necessity defense does not apply if the jurisdiction limits the defense to *natural*, i.e., non-human, threats. See § 22.02, *supra*.

[55] 14 Q.B.D. 273 (1884).

[56] The third man did not approve of, or participate in, the homicide, but he joined in eating the flesh.

[57] Lord Coleridge discounted the views of Lord Bacon, who asserted that one is justified by necessity to thrust another person off a plank in the ocean to save one's own life. Coleridge stated that if Bacon intended "to lay down a broad proposition that man may save his life by killing . . . an innocent and unoffending neighbour, it certainly is not law at the present day." In any case, Bacon's example can hardly constitute a lesser-evil justification: it involves *equal* evils of one innocent life for another. Lord Bacon's hypothetical would have more plausibly stated an *excuse* claim.

so' for the passengers, and of soldiers to give up their lives for women and children. Although Coleridge conceded that the principle he was espousing was harsh, he remarked that "[w]e are often compelled to set up standards that we cannot reach ourselves, and to lay down rules which we could not ourselves satisfy." As a consequence, D and S were convicted of murder and sentenced to death, although the sentence was commuted by the Crown to a six months' imprisonment.

Based on *Dudley and Stephens*, and an American case that also rejected the necessity defense in somewhat similar circumstances,[58] some commentators have concluded that the common law does not recognize the defense of necessity in homicide prosecutions, and some statutes expressly so provide.[59]

[C]—What Does *Dudley and Stephens* Really Say?

Some commentators believe that *Dudley and Stephens* did not (or, at least, did not have to) categorically reject the defense of necessity in homicide cases.[60] The argument may be made that D and S, although exceedingly weak, acted precipitously; in necessity terms, the harm they were seeking to avoid was not yet imminent. It may be noted that Lord Coleridge focused on the special finding of the jury that it was only "probable" that the three men would have died had they not killed the youth. As Coleridge weighed the evils, D and S "with certainty" deprived V of his life, merely "upon the chance" of preserving their own lives. Arguably, therefore, had the seamen's plight been more extreme, the case might have received more favorable treatment.[61]

The weaknesses in the defendants' case are highlighted by comparing it to the following hypothetical:[62] D and V are mountaineers tied together by a rope. V loses his footing, falls off the cliff, and is about to drop to his certain death, pulling D down with him. D holds on as long as he can. When D feels himself about to be pulled over the cliff, may he justifiably cut the rope and permit V to fall?

---

[58] *United States v. Holmes*, 26 F.Cas. 360 (C.C.E.D. Pa. 1842) (No. 15,383) was a case "replete with incidents of deep romance, and of pathetic interest." *Id.* at 363. Holmes and other crew-members of an American ship threw 14 male passengers of a lifeboat overboard after it began to leak. The trial judge told the jurors that "in applying the law, we must look, not only to the jeopardy in which the parties are, but also to the relations to which they stand." *Id.* at 366. He explained that the sailors were bound to sacrifice their lives to save the passengers. He also expressed the view that when the life of one person must be taken "to appease the hunger of others, the selection is by lot." *Id.* at 367. The defendants were convicted of manslaughter, sentenced to a term of six months, although the maximum potential penalty was three years' imprisonment. President Tyler refused to grant a pardon, despite public pleas on their behalf.

[59] E.g., Wis. Stat. Ann. § 939.47 (1993) (but reducing the offense to second-degree murder).

[60] E.g., Glazebrook, Note 1, *supra*, at 113-14.

[61] The difficulty with this argument is that D and S had no reason to believe that they would be found, nor is it clear that they would have survived the four days had they chosen to forego the homicide.

[62] See American Law Institute, Comment to § 3.02, at 15.

Dudley and Stephens should not compel a negative answer. First, unlike the facts in that case, climber-*D*'s plight is clear. The threat is imminent; he must act now or never. Second, *V*'s status is different from that of the "unoffending" youth in the lifeboat. *V* may fairly be characterized as an aggressor, albeit an innocent one. That is, by slipping, *V* threatened *D*'s life.

Third, in *Dudley and Stephens*, the means of selection of the potential victim may have bothered the court. The youth was likely, but not doomed, to die. He died because *D* and *S* chose to kill him. Selection by lot might have been fairer.[63] Climber-*V*'s death, however, was a certainty. *D* did not choose for him to die; circumstances did.

Finally, and closely related to the previous point, *D* and *S* *caused* the boy to die. They chose him for death, and they shortened his life by more than a *de minimis* amount. In light of the certainty of mountaineer-*V*'s death, however, it would be preferable to say that *D*'s act of cutting the line on the rope merely *permitted* nature to take its course.

Therefore, it is at least plausible that a court might justify a homicide of an innocent person in necessitous circumstances.

[D]—Reconsidering the Moral Issue

To repeat, the issue is: Assuming that all of the requirements for a necessity defense are satisfied (which perhaps they were not in *Dudley and Stephens*), may a person justifiably kill an innocent person in order to save a greater number of innocent lives?

From a utilitarian perspective, an affirmative answer is proper. The calculus in a case such as *Dudley and Stephens* is simple: one person's life should be taken so that three may survive. Indeed, the calculus may be put more starkly: the choice was between doing nothing, in which case all four occupants of the lifeboat were likely to die, and acting, in which case only one life would be lost.[64] To utilitarians, the end (reduction in aggregate harm) justifies the means (an intentional homicide).[65]

---

[63] See Note 58, *supra*. On the other hand, the youth was more likely to die than the men, so his selection was not irrational.

[64] This may unduly simplify the calculus. As pointed out in *Dudley and Stephens*, if *D* and *S* were justified in taking *V*'s life to save three lives, would they also have been justified in taking the third man's life to save their own, assuming that they were not rescued in time? If so, two lives were taken to save two lives, although the calculus looked quite different at each step along the way.

[65] How would a utilitarian resolve the three hypotheticals in subsection [A]? Probably *A* did not act justifiably, as the method of selection—*A*'s might and quick wits—is not socially desirable and should not be encouraged.

Arguably, a utilitarian would approve *D*'s decision to harvest *E*'s organs, assuming that less extreme options were unavailable. This also assumes, of course, that a utilitarian would value lives equally, which is not self-evident. Suppose that *E* was a brilliant young scientist with unbounded potential to do good for society, and *D*'s patients were five old men who reached their current state of bad health as a result of dissolute living?

A negative answer to the question posed here is far more easily made from a nonutilitarian perspective. The argument is that *D* and *S* used *V* solely as a means to an end—their survival—in violation of a moral imperative not to take innocent human life. *V* was "unoffending;" he did not forfeit his right to life by any misconduct. Therefore, the correct principle is that an innocent person's life may *never* justifiably be taken, even to save a larger number of lives.

This does not mean that a retributivist would punish *D* and *S*. They might deserve to be *excused*, on the ground that, as a result of the extraordinary natural circumstances in which they found themselves, they were compelled to take a life.[66] Therefore, they should not be blamed for giving in to the coercive circumstances.[67]

§ 22.05 Model Penal Code

The Model Code recognizes a "choice of evils" defense. A person's conduct is justified if: (1) he believes that his conduct is necessary to avoid harm to himself or another; (2) the harm to be avoided by his conduct is greater than that sought to be avoided by the law prohibiting his conduct; and (3) no legislative intent to exclude the conduct in such circumstances plainly exists.[68] The determination of what constitutes a lesser harm is not left to the actor's evaluation, but rather to the judge and jury at trial. The Code does not resolve whether the balancing-of-harms should be determined by the judge, as a matter of law, or should be submitted to the jury for its evaluation.[69]

This defense is broader than the common law in various respects. First, the Code rejects the common law imminency requirement. Second, a person does not automatically lose the defense because he was at fault in creating the necessitous situation. Instead, the Code provides that the defense is unavailable if the actor is prosecuted for a crime of recklessness or negligence, and he acted with that level of culpability in bringing about the emergency or in evaluating the necessity of his conduct.[70] For example, in the hypothetical in which *D* recklessly started a fire that threatened to burn down a number of homes,[71] *D* would be justified in purposely burning *V*'s property, although he could be prosecuted for criminal mischief,[72] due to his original reckless act.

On the other hand, a utilitarian analyzing the organ-harvesting case on a broader front might conclude that a rule justifying *D*'s conduct would shock the community, deter normal organ donations, and destroy important doctor-patients relationships.

Most likely of all, a utilitarian would defend the homicide in the terrorist case.

[66] However, if an excuse were recognized in these circumstances, *V* would be justified in defending himself from *D*'s and *S*'s homicidal assault, because their *excused* conduct would constitute an *unlawful* attack on *V*.

[67] For further discussion of an excuse-based necessity defense, see § 23.06, *infra*.

[68] Model Penal Code § 3.02(1).

[69] American Law Institute, Comment to § 3.02, at 12.

[70] Model Penal Code § 3.02(2).

[71] See the text accompanying Note 35, *supra*.

[72] Model Penal Code § 220.3(1) ("damag[ing] tangible property of another . . . *recklessly* . . . in the employment of fire . . .") (emphasis added).

Third, unlike some common law and statutory definitions of the defense, the Code provision is one of general applicability. All forms of necessity qualify: the defense is not limited to emergencies created by natural forces, is not limited to physical harm to persons or property, and may be employed in homicide prosecutions. The Commentary states that it would be "particularly unfortunate" to deny the defense in appropriate homicide cases; it contends that the sanctity of human life is promoted by a law that permits an actor to kill to save a larger number of lives.[73]

---

[73] American Law Institute, Comment to § 3.02, at 14-15.

CHAPTER 23

DURESS

§ 23.01   General Principles[1]

[A]—Overview

"Duress" or "coercion" is a common law defense to criminal conduct. As has been written about the defense:

> Our society has a love-hate relationship with the . . . defense. Although "of venerable antiquity," the defense was frequently condemned as illegitimate, narrowly defined at common law, comparatively rarely invoked in criminal prosecutions, and not often successfully pleaded. [¶] Nonetheless, our society also seems to love the plea or, at least, to be intrigued by it. Despite criticisms, our society has retained the defense, expanded it over the years, and paid close attention to the calls of those who would apply the defense in novel ways.[2]

[B]—Elements of the Defense

The contours of the duress defense differ by jurisdiction. However, generally speaking, a person will be acquitted of any offense *except murder*[3] if the criminal act was committed under the following circumstances: (1) another person threatened to kill or grievously injure the actor or a third party, particularly a near relative, unless she committed the offense; (2) the actor reasonably believed that the threat was genuine; (3) the threat was "present, imminent, and impending" at the time of the criminal act;[4] (4) there was no reasonable escape from the threat except through

---

[1] See generally Fletcher at §§ 10.4.2-10.4.3; Hall at 436-48; Katz at 62-81; Williams at §§ 242-50; Craig L. Carr, *Duress and Criminal Responsibility*, 10 Law & Phil. 161 (1991); Joshua Dressler, *Exegesis of the Law of Duress: Justifying the Excuse and Searching for Its Proper Limits*, 62 S. Cal. L. Rev. 1331 (1989); Herbert Fingarette, *Victimization: A Legalist Analysis of Coercion, Deception, Undue Influence, and Excusable Prison Escape*, 42 Wash. & Lee L. Rev. 65 (1985); Walter Harrison Hitchler, *Duress as a Defense in Criminal Cases*, 4 Va. L. Rev. 519 (1917); Lawrence Newman & Lawrence Weitzer, *Duress, Free Will and the Criminal Law*, 30 S. Cal. L. Rev. 313 (1957); Robert Nozick, *Coercion*, in Philosophy, Science, and Method: Essays in Honor of Ernest Nagel 440 (1969); Martin Waslik, *Duress and Criminal Responsibility*, 1977 Crim. L. Rev. 453.

[2] Dressler, Note 1, *supra*, at 1331-32 (footnotes omitted).

[3] Regarding murder, see § 23.04, *infra*.

[4] *State v. Crawford*, 861 P.2d 791, 797 (Kan. 1993); *State v. Toscano*, 378 A.2d 755, 760 (N.J. 1977).

compliance with the demands of the coercer; and (5) the actor was not at fault in exposing herself to the threat.[5]

As this description of the defense suggests, a person will not be exculpated unless she acts as a result of a very specific type of threat. First, the threat must emanate from a human being. For example, if *D* breaks into *V*'s home because a rabid dog is threatening her in the street, or a severe lightning storm is underway, she might be able to claim the defense of *necessity* if she is charged with criminal trespass,[6] but the defense of duress is inapplicable.

Second, the coercer must threaten to cause death or serious bodily harm. Force that is likely to cause death or serious bodily harm is commonly termed "deadly force" in the criminal law;[7] therefore, it is accurate to state that a person may not claim common law duress unless a threat of deadly force is issued. A lesser threat, such as a threat to cause property damage, economic hardship, or to damage another person's reputation, is insufficient.[8]

Third, the deadly force threatened must be imminent, or as some courts put it, "present, imminent, and impending." The word "present" suggests that the threat must be operating on the actor's will at the time of the criminal act.[9] The remaining requirement is that the threatened harm will occur immediately, unless the actor complies. Courts rarely explain this requirement any further, except to state that a threat of future harm is insufficient, or that the harm must be likely to occur so quickly that there is no realistic way for the actor to escape the situation (which brings into play the fourth element of the defense, as listed above).[10] For example, in *State v. Rosillo*,[11] *D*, a police informant, agreed to testify against a suspected drug dealer. Prior to trial, however, he was threatened by armed assailants, and nearly run over on the street. As a result, he feared for his life and that of his family, and as a further consequence, he gave false testimony at the trial of the alleged narcotics dealer. When *D* was prosecuted for perjury, he claimed duress. The court held, however, that the facts did not support the claim, as he was not in fear of *imminent* harm at the moment he testified falsely at the trial. According to the court, a duress claim would have been available if *D* had reasonably feared being shot through a courthouse window.

Fourth, there is some question as to whether a person may claim the common law defense if the threat is directed at a person unrelated to the actor. Fairly clearly, however, a threat directed at a family member of the defendant is sufficient.[12] For

---

[5] See *People v. Merhige*, 180 N.W. 418, 422 (Mich. 1920); *State v. Toscano*, 378 A.2d at 760-63; Dressler, Note 1, *supra*, at 1335-43; Fingarette, Note 1, *supra*, at 67 n.9.

[6] See § 22.02, *supra*.

[7] See § 18.03[A], *supra*.

[8] E.g., *United States v. Palmer*, 458 F.2d 663 (9th Cir. 1972) ("financial ruin" insufficient threat); *People v. Ricker*, 262 N.E.2d 456 (Ill. 1970) (threat of loss of job insufficient).

[9] *People v. Luther*, 232 N.W.2d 184, 187 (Mich. 1975).

[10] See *United States v. Contento-Pachon*, 723 F.2d 691, 694 (9th Cir. 1984).

[11] 282 N.W.2d 872 (Minn. 1979).

[12] *People v. Pena*, 197 Cal. Rptr. 264, 269 (Super. Ct. 1983); *State v. Toscano*, 378 A.2d at 762.

example, if C kidnaps the child of D, a bank teller, and threatens to kill the child immediately unless D steals money from her employer, the duress defense applies.

Even if the defendant acts as the result of a threat that satisfies all of the preceding elements, the defense is unavailable to her if she was at fault for being in the coercive situation. For example, if D voluntarily joins a criminal organization that she knows or has reason to know is likely to subject her to coercive threats at a later time, she will not be permitted to claim the defense if that foreseeable event arises.[13]

If the elements of the defense are satisfied, the coerced actor will be acquitted of the non-homicide offense that she committed. The *coercing* party, however, may be held responsible for the actions of the coerced actor.[14]

[C]—Duress: Justification or Excuse?

Some scholars, courts, and statutes treat duress as a subspecies of the justification defense of necessity, or treat the two defenses interchangeably.[15] There is superficial logic in this position: according to common law principles, the defense only applies if the coercing party threatens to use deadly force; and the defense is only available if the coerced actor commits a non-homicide offense. Therefore, at first blush—but only at first blush—it appears that a coerced party always commits the lesser of two evils; therefore, she is *justified* in acceding to the threat. Following this reasoning, the only significant difference between necessity and duress is that the former entails natural threats like fires and tornadoes, whereas the latter involves human threats.

It is not true, however, that *every* common law example of duress involves a lesser-evils situation. For example, if C threatens to cut off D's left arm unless D cuts off V's left arm, the harms are of equal severity, yet D is entitled to raise the duress defense if she complies with C's demand.

Furthermore, it is unlikely that the concept of duress as a justification for criminal activity conforms with common intuitions. For example, suppose that C orders D to rape V, and backs up the order by threatening grievous harm to X, D's young child (e.g., C threatens to sexually abuse X, cut off X's left hand, or make X blind). If D complies with C's threat and rapes V, it is unlikely that the decision whether to acquit D of rape will be based on a balancing of the harms threatened and inflicted.

---

[13] Williams at 758-59; English Law Commission, No. 83, Criminal Law: Report on Defences of General Application 13-14 (1977); American Law Institute, Comment to § 2.09, at 379 n.47.

[14] In common law terminology, the coercer is a "principal in the first degree" who used the coerced party as her "innocent instrumentality" in committing the offense. See § 30.03[A][2][b], *infra*.

[15] E.g., Wayne LaFave & Austin Scott, Criminal Law 433, 443 (2d ed. 1986) (treating duress as a subspecies of the necessity defense); *United States v. Bailey*, 444 U.S. 394, 410 (1980) (observing that "[m]odern cases have tended to blur the distinction between duress and necessity," and thereafter treating the two defenses alike); Ariz. Rev. Stat. Ann. § 13-412 (1989) (describing duress in justificatory language).

Instead, the issue is apt to be whether *D* should be blamed—excused—for the harm suffered by *V*.

In conformity with this analysis, most scholars, courts, and states criminal codes that draw distinctions between justifications and excuses, treat duress as an excuse defense.

§ 23.02 Rationale of the Defense (as an Excuse)

[A]—Utilitarian Arguments

The traditional utilitarian argument in support of the duress defense is straightforward: when a person is "in thrall to some [coercive] power" the threat of criminal punishment is ineffective.[16] As Hobbes has reasoned:

If a man, by the terror of present death, be compelled to do a fact against the law, he is totally excused, because no law can oblige a man to abandon his own preservation. And supposing such a law were obligatory, yet a man would reason thus: *If I do it not, I die presently; if I do it, I die afterwards; therefore by doing it, there is time of life gained . . . .*[17]

Moreover, a utilitarian may argue that the victim of coercion is just that—a victim. The coercing party, and not she, possesses a criminal disposition. Therefore, the coercing party, and not she, requires incapacitation and rehabilitation.

Not all utilitarian arguments support the defense. Sir James Stephen has presented the most famous utilitarian argument against the excuse. According to Stephen, recognition of the defense dangerously undermines the moral clarity of the criminal law and invites fraud: "Surely it is at the moment when the temptation to [commit] crime is strongest . . . that the law should speak most clearly and emphatically to the contrary." He conceded that it is unfortunate when an innocent person is "placed between two fires," but he believed that it is a much greater misfortune for society if the coercing party could confer immunity on her "agents by threatening them with death or violence if they refused to execute . . . [her] commands." Such a rule would open "a wide door . . . to collusion, and encouragement would be given to associations of malefactors, secret or otherwise."[18]

[B]—Retributive Arguments

Most arguments in support of the duress defense are founded on the retributive principle that a coerced actor does not deserve to be punished for her actions. In order to understand why this is so, it is useful first to consider various incorrect or potentially misleading explanations frequently given in support of the defense.

---

[16] Williams at 756.

[17] Thomas Hobbes, Leviathan, Pt. II, ch. 27 (1651).

[18] 2 James Stephen, A History of the Criminal Law in England 107-08 (1883).

First, some courts suggest that a coerced actor lacks the requisite *mens rea* to be convicted of an offense.[19] In almost all circumstances, however, this explanation is false.[20] As one court explained:

> One who acts under . . . duress faces an agonizing choice: the defendant simultaneously . . . perceives the need to defend himself and understands that he can negate the threat to himself by performing a specific unlawful act against an innocent third party. To protect himself, he must both . . . intend to perform the unlawful act and act on that . . . intent. There is no inconsistency here but a concurrence of act and intent.[21]

Second, courts frequently state that a coerced party should be excused because "commission of the alleged offense was no longer the voluntary act of the accused."[22] In the narrow willed-contraction-of-a-muscle sense of the term "voluntary act,"[23] however, this statement is incorrect. Stephen has correctly observed:

> A criminal walking to execution is under compulsion if any man can be said to be so, but his motions are just as much voluntary actions as if he was going to leave his place of confinement and regain his liberty. He walks to his death because he prefers it to being carried.[24]

That is, the coerced actor wills her muscles to commit the crime, e.g., to strike *V* or to steal *V*'s automobile. Coercion, therefore, does not negate the voluntary act requirement of the criminal law.

Third, it is not precisely correct to say that a person is excused for violating the law because she "lacked free will." The coerced actor has the capacity to choose, i.e., she is not an automaton controlled by the coercing party. More to the point, the coerced actor *in fact* chooses to violate the law; she chooses to commit an offense rather than to accept the threatened consequences. In a sense she "self-consciously subordinates [the law] to the primacy of the person who is the subject of desire,"[25] i.e., she chooses to make the coercing party's desires her own for present purposes.

[19] E.g., *State v. Tanner*, 301 S.E.2d 160, 163 (W.Va. 1982) ("In general an act which would otherwise constitute a crime may be excused on the ground that it done under compulsion or duress, since the necessary ingredient of intention . . . is then lacking.").

[20] In rare circumstances, a coerced actor may lack the specific intent required to commit a particular offense. For example, suppose that *C* coerces *D* to steal a Picasso painting from City Museum. *D* does as she is told, but as soon as the coercion is removed, she contacts the police. Under such circumstances, although *D* intended to take and carry away the Picasso, the prosecutor may not be able to prove that she did do so with the intent to permanently deprive the museum of its property. As such an intent is an element of the crime of larceny, *D* may be acquitted. Thus, in limited circumstances, duress serves as a failure-of-proof claim, see § 16.02, *supra*, rather than an ordinary excuse.

[21] *People v. King*, 2 Cal.Rptr.2d 197, 204 (Ct. App. 1991).

[22] *Regina v. Hudson*, [1971] 2 All E.R. 244, 246.

[23] See § 9.02[C][2], *supra*.

[24] 2 Stephen, Note 18, *supra*, at 102.

[25] Alan Brudner, *A Theory of Necessity*, 7 Oxford J. Legal Stud. 339, 349 (1987).

Although the free-will explanation is not precisely on target, it brings us very close to understanding why it is unjust to punish one who acts under duress. Although the coerced actor possesses free will, she does not possess a *fair opportunity* to exercise her will to act lawfully.[26]

Of course, society does not excuse an actor for violating the law whenever she must make a hard choice. Duress only excuses when the available choices are not only hard but also unfair.[27] Choices-making opportunities are unfair when the alternative to committing an offense is so awful that "judges are not prepared to affirm that they . . . could comply with [the law] if their turn to face the problem should arise."[28] The defense of duress recognizes that human frailty exists; as long as an actor's conduct demonstrates ordinary and expectable human frailty, society is prepared to excuse a coerced actor's unlawful conduct.

§ 23.03 Distinguishing Duress from Necessity

As noted earlier,[29] some commentators and courts treat duress as a subspecies of the justification defense of necessity, in which case the only true distinction between the defenses is that duress involves human threats, whereas the necessity defense applies to natural forces.

However, as long as duress is recognized as an excuse defense, which it should be,it is important to see how the defenses differ. The necessity defense—as one of its alternative names ("lesser evil" defense) reminds us—applies "when a person is faced with a choice of two evils and must then decide whether to commit a crime or an alternative act that constitutes a greater evil,"[30] and the person makes the right choice. In contrast, duress applies when the coercing actor's threats overwhelm the actor's will so that she makes the wrong choice, i.e., perpetrates an equal or greater evil.[31]

This difference has practical consequences.[32] When a person commits the lesser of two evils, nobody is subject to prosecution, because no social harm has actually ensued. For example, suppose that *D1* justifiably takes *V*'s parked automobile without permission, in order to drive a gravely injured child to the hospital. Even if it later turns out that the child was in that condition as the result of some wrongful

---

[26] This is an example of the free-choice or personhood theory of excuses. See § 17.03[E], *supra*.

[27] Dressler, Note 1, *supra*, at 1365.

[28] American Law Institute, Comment to § 2.09, at 374-75. Compare this remark to Lord Coleridge's observation in *Regina v. Dudley and Stephens*, 14 Q.B.D. 273 (1884), that judges "are often compelled to set up standards that we cannot reach ourselves, and to lay down rules which we could not ourselves satisfy." See § 22.04[B], *supra*. This statement, however, was made in the context of "justification" rather than "excuse."

[29] See § 23.01[C], *supra*.

[30] *United States v. Contento-Pachon*, 723 F.2d 691, 695 (9th Cir. 1984).

[31] See *United States v. Lopez*, 662 F.Supp. 1083, 1086 (N.D. Cal. 1987).

[32] The necessity/duress distinction may have additional practical implications. See § 23.05[C][2], *infra*.

conduct by *X*, it would be odd to say that *X* should be held criminally responsible for *D1*'s proper act of taking the child to the hospital in *V*'s car. [33] If a defendant is *excused*, however, the person who coerced her to commit the offense may be prosecuted for the harm caused. For example, if *D2* robs a bank because *C* threatens serious harm to a family member, *C* may be prosecuted for the robbery. This result follows from the fact that duress is an excuse rather than a justification, and that there is a culpable human being who may properly be held responsible for the social harm.

§ 23.04   Duress as a Defense to Homicide

[A]—General Rule

The common law rule, expressly adopted by statute in various states, [34] is that duress is not a defense to an intentional killing. [35] A very few states recognize an imperfect duress defense, which reduces the offense of the coerced actor to manslaughter. [36]

There is a division of thought regarding whether the duress defense may be raised in felony-murder prosecutions. [37] A few states provide that a person coerced to commit a felony, during which she or an accomplice unintentionally kills the victim, may raise the duress defense. [38] The reasoning is that since duress ordinarily is a defense to the underlying felony, it should also apply if someone unforeseeably dies during the commission of the crime. Other states disallow the defense in all murder prosecutions, regardless of the defendant's *mens rea* regarding the death. [39]

[B]—Is the No-Defense Rule Sensible?

What are the arguments for the common law rule that duress does not excuse a murder? Why is a defendant entitled to claim duress if she complies with a gun-to-the-head demand that she steal a car, but the defense is unavailable to her if she

---

[33] Of course, *X* may be prosecuted for any crime committed in relation to the child.

[34] E.g., Wash. Rev. Code Ann. 9A.16.060(2) (1988).

[35] E.g., *Wright v. State*, 402 So.2d 493, 498 (Fla. Dist. Ct. App. 1981); *Jackson v. State*, 558 S.W.2d 816, 819-20 (Mo. Ct. App. 1977) (quoting dictum in *State v. St. Clair*, 262 S.W.2d 25, 27 (Mo. 1953)); *Regina v. Howe*, [1987] 2 W.L.R. 568, 575 ("[A]n unbroken tradition of authority dating back to Hale and Blackstone seems to have been . . . that duress was not available to a defendant accused of murder.").

[36] *Wentworth v. State*, 349 A.2d 421, 427-28 (Md. Ct. Spec. App. 1975); Minn. Stat. 609.20(3) (1987 & Supp. 1994).

[37] See § 31.06, *infra*, for discussion of the felony-murder doctrine.

[38] The defense is more likely to be allowed if the coerced actor was an accomplice in the homicide, rather than the actual killer. E.g., *State v. Hunter*, 740 P.2d 559, 569 (Kan. 1987); *Tully v. State*, 730 P.2d 1206, 1210 (Okla. Crim. App. 1986); see *State v. Lassen*, 679 S.W.2d 363, 369 (Mo. Ct. App. 1984) (in dictum, stating that "[p]erhaps an argument can be made that the defense of duress ought to be allowed as a defense to felony-murder when the defendant did not do the killing").

[39] E.g., *State v. Lassen*, 679 S.W.2d at 369; *State v. Ng*, 750 P.2d 632, 636-37 (Wash. 1988).

kills as the result of precisely the same threat? From a utilitarian perspective, it would seem that the traditional justification for the defense, i.e., that a threat of future punishment will not deter an actor confronted by an immediate deadly threat,[40] applies as much to coerced murders as it does to coerced thefts.

Some scholars, however, defend the no-defense rule on utilitarian grounds. According to Jerome Hall, it is wrong to claim that "the drive of self-preservation is irresistible, that conduct in such situation is inexorably fixed for all human beings."[41] Lord Hailsham of the English House of Lords agrees:

> Doubtless in actual practice many will succumb to temptation [and kill] . . . . But many will not . . . . I have known in my own lifetime of too many acts of heroism by ordinary human beings of no more than ordinary fortitude to [reject the common law position].[42]

If Hall and Hailsham are correct, the argument proceeds, the law ought to be drafted to induce coerced parties to resist "kill-or-be-killed" orders.

The retributivist argument for the no-defense position is also debatable. Blackstone offered a religious explanation for the rule: murder is a crime against God; human laws, therefore, can never excuse such a crime.[43] In non-religious terms, the no-defense rule supports the moral imperative that, "if a man be desperately assaulted, and in peril of death, and cannot otherwise escape, unless to satisfy his assailant's fury he will kill an innocent person then present . . . he ought rather to die himself than kill an innocent."[44] The difficulty with this argument, is that it supports the proposition that a coerced actor is *unjustified* in taking an innocent life, but it does not necessarily demonstrate that she should not be *excused* for violating the moral imperative.

From a retributive perspective, the question should come down to "whether a coerced person who unjustifiably violates the moral principle [against taking an innocent life] *necessarily*, *unalterably*, and *unfailingly* deserves to be punished as a murderer, as the common law insists."[45] The answer would seem to be that she does not deserve to be treated as a murderer: one who is compelled to kill has no greater (or lesser) opportunity to act freely than one who is ordered to steal a car, assuming that the coercive threat is the same in both circumstances.[46] If a person

---

[40] See § 23.02[A], *supra*.

[41] Hall at 445-46.

[42] *Regina v. Howe*, [1987] 2 W.L.R. at 579.

[43] 4 Blackstone at *30.

[44] 1 Hale at *51.

[45] Dressler, Note 1, *supra*, at 1372.

[46] Indeed, notice that the prevailing common law rule regarding coerced homicides is in apparent conflict with the provocation doctrine of homicide law. See generally § 31.07, *infra*. Why should a person who kills in sudden *anger* as the result of adequate provocation be able to mitigate her offense to manslaughter, while one who kills out of *fear* for her own or another's life receives no formal mitigation? Sometimes this apparent inconsistency is explained in terms of the position of the victims: in the case of duress the victim is wholly innocent; in the provocation case she is to blame for provoking her own death. The difficulty

of reasonable moral strength might comply with a kill-or-be-killed threat (or, perhaps more compellingly, a kill-or-I-will-kill-a-loved-one threat), the case for denying the defense, as a matter of law, is weakened considerably.

[C]—The Rule is Questioned and Reaffirmed: the *Lynch-Howe* Saga

Despite the antiquity of the rule that duress never excuses murder, English courts briefly departed from it in the context of accomplices to murder in *Director of Public Prosecutions for Northern Island v. Lynch.*[47] In *Lynch*, D was coerced to drive a car carrying armed terrorists to the scene of an intentional homicide. D was prosecuted for murder as a "principal in the second degree," i.e., as an accomplice present during the commission of the homicide. Pursuant to the common law rule, the trial court rejected D's request for a jury instruction on duress. The House of Lords disagreed: without disturbing the rule that the defense is unavailable to principals in the *first* degree, i.e., perpetrators of murder, it ruled that the defense should be made available to persons charged as principals in the *second* degree.

The House of Lords failed to provide a clear justification for the distinction between perpetrators and accessories. In *Lynch*, D claimed to have been just a minor participant in the homicide, which made his case a comparatively sympathetic one for allowing the defense, but there was—and is—no reason to assume that all coerced accomplices are less dangerous or less culpable than all coerced perpetrators of homicides. Thus, the House of Lords created an arbitrary distinction, one that could not easily withstand scrutiny if, for example, another case came along in which the accomplice, although coerced, was a dangerous and hardened criminal who actively participated in the crime, but who did not pull the trigger in the murder.

Many observers believed that *Lynch* was simply a first step, leading to the outright abrogation of the common law no-defense rule. A dozen years later, however, in *Regina v. Howe,*[48] the House of Lords not only reaffirmed the common law rule in the context of principals in the first degree, but it overruled *Lynch*. In *Howe*, D and others brutally beat up V, after which D strangled V. At trial, D claimed that if he had not killed V, X, a partner in the crime, would have beaten D to death. The House of Lords heard D's appeal in order to answer the question: "Is duress available as a defence to a person charged with murder as a principal in the first degree (the actual killer)?"

The court answered the question in the negative. In defending the common law rule, Lord Hailsham observed:

> I do not at all accept in relation to the defence of murder it is either good morals, good policy or good law to suggest, as did the majority in *Lynch* . . .

---

with this reasoning, however, is that by focusing on whether the victim, by her conduct, "deserves to die," rather than on the defendant's choice-making capacities or opportunities, the law treats the two defenses as if they were justifications rather than excuses. Because of the apparent inconsistency in the rules, a few states recognize a partial defense in coerced homicide cases. See § 23.04[A], *supra.*

[47] [1975] App. Cas. 653.

[48] [1987] App. Cas. 417.

that the ordinary man of reasonable fortitude is not to be supposed to be capable of heroism if he is asked to take an innocent life rather than sacrifice his own.

Lord Hailsham asserted that if the House of Lords allowed *D*'s appeal in the present case, it would also have to say that *Regina v. Dudley and Stephens*,[49] the necessity case in which desperate seamen on a lifeboat killed one of their number so that they could eat his flesh to survive, was wrongly decided. In that case, the defendants' claim was denied, and they were convicted of murder. According to Hailsham, the only distinction between the cases was that in *Howe*, *D* reacted to a wrongful human threat, whereas in the former case, the actors responded to a natural threat, "a distinction without a relevant difference." What Lord Hailsham failed to note, however, was that the necessity case was resolved on the ground that the killing was unjustified, whereas in *Howe* the issue was whether to excuse *D*.

The House of Lords was not called upon in *Howe* to reconsider *Lynch*, but it did. Lord Hailsham stated that he continued to believe that a valid distinction could be drawn between a person who "participates in the irrevocable act of murder," and one who "simply participates before or after the event in the necessary preparation for it or the escape of the actual offender." Nonetheless, because *Lynch* was contrary to prior authority, the Lords believed that it was preferable to "restore the law to the condition it was almost universally thought to be prior to *Lynch*." In essence, the judicial members of the House of Lords were unwilling to support a distinction between perpetrators and accomplices; having reaffirmed the common law rule as to the former, it felt obliged to deny the defense to the latter.

§ 23.05   Escape from Intolerable Prison Conditions[50]

[A]—The Issue

Supreme Court Justice Harry Blackmun once wrote that "[t]he atrocities and inhuman conditions of prison life in America are almost unbelievable; surely they are nothing less than shocking."[51] Among the conditions that prisoners face are physical and sexual assaults from fellow inmates,[52] brutality at the hands of prison guards, fires in their cells, excessive cold and heat, and inadequate medical attention.

Occasionally, a prisoner seeks to avoid harsh prison conditions by escaping confinement. She may later be prosecuted for the crime of escape; in such circumstances, the escapee may defend her conduct on the ground that she fled due

----

[49] 14 Q.B.D. 273 (1884). See § 22.04[B], *supra*.

[50] See generally David Dolinko, Comment, *Intolerable Conditions as a Defense to Prison Escapes*, 26 UCLA L. Rev. 1126 (1979); Fingarette, Note 1, *supra*; George P. Fletcher, *Should Intolerable Prison Conditions Generate a Justification or an Excuse for Escape?*, 26 UCLA L. Rev. 1355 (1979); Martin R. Gardner, *The Defense of Necessity and the Right to Escape from Prison—A Step Towards Incarceration Free from Sexual Assault*, 49 S. Cal. L. Rev. 110 (1975).

[51] *United States v. Bailey*, 444 U.S. 394, 420 (1980) (dissenting opinion).

[52] Justice Blackmun stated: "A youthful inmate can expect to be subjected to homosexual gang rape his first night in jail, or, it has been said, even in the van on the way to jail." *Id.*

to intolerable prison conditions. Sometimes such a claim is based on the defense of duress; other times the justification defense of necessity is advanced.

[B]—The Law

At the policy level, courts are concerned that if an inmate who flees due to alleged intolerable prison conditions avoids conviction on this ground, other inmates will be emboldened to attempt to escape. As a result, a few courts have refused to recognize a defense in such circumstances.[53] Most modern courts, however, recognize the right of an escapee to assert an intolerable-prison-condition claim. They split, however, on whether the inmate should raise the defense of necessity or of duress.[54]

As either a necessity or duress defense, courts frequently place special restrictions on its use. From a practical perspective, the most significant limitation placed on the defense is the requirement that the escapee make "a bona fide effort to surrender or return to custody as soon as the claimed duress or necessity ha[s] lost its coercive force."[55] That is, once the prisoner attains a point of safety outside the prison, the escapee must turn herself in; if she fails to do so, the defense of duress or necessity is unavailable as a matter of law. Some courts do not go this far, instead treating the actor's failure to turn herself in as merely one factor in assessing the escapee's claim.[56]

[C]—Necessity versus Duress

[1]—The Conceptual Problem

Neither necessity nor duress neatly covers all intolerable-prison-condition cases. For example, when an inmate flees as the result of a threatened sexual assault, a necessity claim is inappropriate in jurisdictions that limit that defense to emergencies created by non-human forces. On the other hand, the defense of duress ordinarily is triggered when a coercer orders another person to commit the crime for which the latter is prosecuted. In prison cases, however, threats may spur an inmate to flee, but nobody commands her to escape.

[2]—Why the Nature of the Defense Is Significant

[a]—The Message of Acquittal

An inmate does not care whether she is acquitted on the basis of necessity or duress. Courts, lawyers, and prison officials, however, understandably worry about the message sent in prison escape cases.

---

[53] E.g., *State v. Davis*, 14 Nev. 439, 444-45 (1880).

[54] E.g., *People v. Lovercamp*, 118 Cal. Rptr. 110 (Ct. App. 1974) (necessity); *People v. Unger*, 362 N.E.2d 319 (Ill. 1977) (same); *State v. Reese*, 272 N.W.2d 863 (Iowa 1978) (same); *State v. Kinslow*, 799 P.2d 844 (Ariz. 1990) (duress); *People v. Harmon*, 220 N.W.2d 212 (Mich. Ct. App. 1974), *aff'd*, 232 N.W.2d 187 (Mich. 1975) (same); *State v. Tuttle*, 730 P.2d 630 (Utah 1986) (same).

[55] *United States v. Bailey*, 444 U.S. at 415.

[56] E.g., *People v. Unger*, 362 N.E.2d 319 (Ill. 1977).

The two defenses send different messages. Acquittal on the basis of necessity implies that it is right or, at least, tolerable, for a prisoner to escape confinement in specified circumstances; acquittal on the ground of duress implies only that the escapee should not be blamed for fleeing. A prison official is apt to consider the label of justification unacceptable; advocates of prison reform are likely to prefer this description.

[b]—Ability to Obtain Acquittal

Normally, a necessity claim is a harder defense to prove than a claim of duress. With necessity, the prisoner must convince the jury that her flight from confinement was a lesser evil than what was facing her behind bars. Once the balancing process begins, many factors weigh against the inmate. For example, prison escapes jeopardize discipline within the institution, a factor that a jury will weigh against the defendant. Also, if the inmate is an habitual violent criminal, her prior criminal record, which ordinarily would not be admissible at her trial, becomes relevant to her lesser-evil defense claim. Juries are likely to conclude that it is better that a dangerous criminal suffer in prison, than that she be free from confinement, even for a short time.

In duress cases, juries are not asked to balance evils. Neither prison discipline nor the inmate's prior criminal record is material. The determinative factor ought to be whether the conditions in the prison that motivated the flight were so extreme and imminent that the jurors could reasonably imagine themselves fleeing under similar circumstances.

[c]—Liability of Those Who Assist in the Escape

The line between duress and necessity may be critical in determining the criminal responsibility of persons who assist escapees. Consider the facts in *United States v. Lopez*:[57] D landed a helicopter on the grounds of a women's prison in order to effect the escape of X, his girlfriend, whose life allegedly had been unlawfully threatened by prison officials. D and X were apprehended ten days later; as a consequence of their actions, X was charged with escape, and D was charged with aiding in X's escape. The prosecution agreed that X was entitled to introduce evidence supporting her claim that her life was threatened in prison; but it sought to bar D from introducing the same evidence on his own behalf.

The propriety of the prosecutor's motion to bar the evidence depends on whether X's claim is properly identified as one of necessity (justification) or of duress (excuse). A justified act is a proper, or at least non-wrongful, act. Therefore, assuming that X was justified in escaping, D was also justified in assisting in the escape. In such circumstances, D should be permitted to raise X's necessity claim in his own behalf.

In contrast, with excuse defenses, the act is wrongful, but the actor is not held responsible for it because she is the victim of an excusing condition. Therefore, even if X were acquitted on the ground of duress, the prosecution could still show that D aided and abetted a wrongful-albeit-excusable act. Since D's life was not

---

[57] 662 F.Supp. 1083 (N.D. Cal. 1987).

threatened—he did not personally experience the excusing condition—he should not be allowed to raise X's duress claim.[58]

[d]—Liability of Those Who Resist the Escape

Assume the following not-unlikely scenario: D seeks to escape confinement due to intolerable prison conditions; X, a prison guard, exercises her responsibility to prevent the escape. Is X acting justifiably? If X uses force upon D, should X be prosecuted for battery? May D use force against X in self-defense? The answers to these questions may depend on the nature of D's defense.

If the proper defense to escape is duress, X is justified in preventing D from committing the wrongful act of escaping. X should also be allowed to use reasonable force to prevent the escape, and D would not be entitled to use force against her in the conflict.

If D's escape is justifiable, however, matters become more complicated. Either the law must recognize incompatible justifications—justify D's escape, yet also justify X's effort to prevent D's justified flight—or it must deny X, the prison guard, the right to use force to resist the escape. Under the latter reasoning, as well, D would be justified in using reasonable force, if necessary, to prevent resistance by the guard.

[3]—Concluding Comments

There is no reason why a jurisdiction should fit all prison-escape cases within just one defense category. Occasionally, a defendant-escapee will wish to assert that she (or the person she was assisting) acted properly in escaping, in which case the necessity defense should be permitted, whether or not the threat was human or natural in origin. For example, in *People v. Unger*,[59] D was a thief serving his sentence on an honor farm when his life was threatened by a fellow inmate. The court in *Unger* considered necessity to be the appropriate defense in the case.

But, why should an inmate always be forced to prove that the escape was the lesser of two evils? An inmate should be permitted to raise a duress claim instead of, or in conjunction with, the necessity claim. If a jury is unwilling to treat an escape as the lesser of two evils, but it does not believe that the inmate should be blamed for escaping, the jury should be allowed this option.

§ 23.06 Situational Duress: Brief Observations

[A]—The Simplest Case: Necessity as an Excuse[60]

Consider the following case: D and V are shipwrecked passengers on a lifeboat. A leak springs in the vessel and it is clear that it will sink unless one person departs

---

[58] In *Lopez*, the trial court concluded that X's defense "most clearly resemble[d]" a necessity claim. Therefore, it permitted D to introduce evidence at his trial regarding the purported threats on X's life.

[59] 362 N.E.2d 319 (Ill. 1977).

[60] See generally Brudner, Note 25, *supra*; Edward M. Morgan, *The Defence of Necessity: Justification or Excuse?*, 42 U. Toronto Fac. L. Rev. 165 (1984).

the boat. Therefore, *D* pushes *V* into the ocean, where she drowns. Does *D* have a valid defense?

At common law, *D* is guilty of murder. As *V* was not an aggressor, self-defense does not apply. Furthermore, even if the justification defense of necessity applies in homicide cases, a highly debatable issue,[61] this is not a case like *Dudley and Stephens*,[62] in which one person was killed in order to save a greater number of innocent lives.

Nor may *D* escape conviction on the ground of duress. Not only is duress not a common law defense to murder,[63] but even if it were, it would not apply here because duress applies to human threats,[64] whereas this case involved a threat emanating from a natural source.

Is a conviction for murder just, assuming for the moment that the defense of duress would (or should) apply in the case of a human threat? If a defense were recognized in the lifeboat case, it might be called "situational duress," to distinguish it from duress claims involving human-induced coercion; or the defense of necessity could be enlarged to include an excuse component, to deal with natural forces that compel a person to commit an equal or greater evil, rather than a lesser one.

The argument for the defense is that natural circumstances can be as compelling as human threats; therefore, situational duress should excuse in precisely the same circumstances that human coercion excuses conduct. Thus, in *Dudley and Stephens*, even if the defendants were not justified in the killing the youth, they could be excused for their behavior because of the compelling circumstances they experienced.[65]

Opponents of such a defense argue that in ordinary duress cases "the basic interests of the law may be satisfied by prosecution of the agent of unlawful force,"[66] namely, the coercer. Thus, if *C* compels *D* to rob a bank, *D* will be excused, but *C* can be convicted of the crime. In the case of situational duress, however, there is nobody who can be subjected to the law's application.

[B]—Going Beyond Natural Threats

Suppose that *X* uses physically and psychologically coercive techniques over an extended period of time ("brainwashing"), in order to render *D1* submissive to *X*.

---

[61] See § 22.04, *supra*.

[62] *Regina v. Dudley and Stephens*, 14 Q.B.D. 273 (1884). See § 22.04[B], *supra*.

[63] See § 23.04, *supra*.

[64] See § 23.02, *supra*.

[65] See *Perka v. The Queen*, [1984] 2 S.C.R. 232 (Canada Supreme Court) (recognizing a residual excuse defense of necessity, the essential criterion of which is the moral involuntariness of the actor's conduct, as measured by society's expectation of appropriate and normal resistance to pressure).

[66] American Law Institute, Comment to § 2.09, at 379.

Later, *X* noncoercively suggests to *D1* that she rob the State Bank. *D1* commits the crime. Should *D1* be excused?[67]

Suppose further that *D2* lives in a neighborhood dominated by vicious gangs, in which youths must join a gang or else suffer violence for failing to do so.[68] *D2* spends most of her time with gang members, who teach her a code of conduct including robbery, arson, and murder. One day, *D2* decides to prove her devotion to gang ideals by robbing a liquor store, during which offense she kills the owner. Should *D2* be excused for her crimes?

At common law, of course, neither defendant would be acquitted. *D1* and *D2* knew what they were doing; they intended to violate the law; and their actions were voluntary in the willed-contraction-of-a-muscle sense of that term. Moreover, the defense of duress is unavailable to them. In the first case, *D1* acted on the basis of *X*'s uncoerced suggestion, rather than a deadly threat. In *D2*'s case, there was no threat or suggestion of any kind; the decision to commit the offense was *D2*'s.

Are the results in these cases just? Some would say that they are not. *D1* seems to be of a victim (of *X*), rather than a criminal. *D2*, too, is a victim, if not of a particular person, then of an environment that shaped her attitudes toward the rest of the world. Few people can say with genuine confidence that, but for the luck of being born into a better environment, they would not have turned out as *D2* did.

Some commentators believe that the law should recognize new defenses, e.g, "brainwashing" and "rotten social background,"[69] to deal with the particular excusing conditions suggested here. Another solution is to recognize a more general excuse, which would provide that a person is excused for committing a crime if, through no fault of her own, she is placed in a situation so harsh that a person of ordinary moral firmness in her situation would have committed the crime.[70] In essence, this defense would be founded on the principle that a person is not responsible for her conduct if it is the result of a condition (e.g., brainwashing or a bad environment) beyond her control.[71]

Critics argue that recognition of such a defense would undermine the most basic principle of the criminal law, namely, that humans ordinarily possess sufficient free will to be held responsible for their actions. Although we should feel compassion

---

[67] See generally Richard Delgado, *Ascription of Criminal States of Mind: Toward a Defense Theory for the Coercively Persuaded ("Brainwashed") Defendant*, 63 Minn. L. Rev. 1 (1978) (favoring exculpation) with Joshua Dressler, *Professor Delgado's "Brainwashing" Defense: Courting a Determinist Legal System*, 63 Minn. L. Rev. 335 (1979) (rejecting Delgado's reasoning).

[68] The example is a variation on one provided by Richard Delgado, *A Response to Professor Dressler*, 63 Minn. L. Rev. 361, 365 (1979); see generally Richard Delgado, *"Rotten Social Background": Should the Criminal Law Recognize a Defense of Severe Environmental Deprivation?*, 3 Law & Inequality 9 (1985).

[69] E.g., Delgado, Note 67, *supra* (brainwashing); Delgado, *"Rotten Social Background"* Note 68, *supra*.

[70] See Dressler, Note 67, *supra*, at 359 (suggesting, but not advocating, such a defense).

[71] This is an application of the causation theory of excuses. See § 17.03[C], *supra*.

for victims of situational duress, critics maintain, there is nothing inconsistent with the claim that victims can also be victimizers who deserve to be blamed and punished for their unjustifiable conduct.[72]

§ 23.07 Battered Women Under Duress[73]

A battered woman who kill her abusive living partner may seek to defend her actions on the basis of self-defense. Self-defense law has undergone significant change as a result of a flurry of battered-woman self-defense cases that have made their way through the appellate courts in the past decade.[74] Now, a new legal problem is developing: How should the law deal with battered women who commit crimes under the domination of abusive men? Under what circumstances should they be permitted to claim duress?

Two special problems arise in this context. First, the man may order or simply expect the woman to commit a crime, or assist him in its commission, without issuing an immediate threat. Instead, the woman interprets his remarks or actions as threatening, in light of her battering experiences. The issue here is whether she may claim duress, although no threat has been issued or the threat occurred at a much earlier time. Second, under ordinary duress principles, a person is not excused for committing a crime if she could have escaped the situation. Likewise, the defense is unavailable to one who is at fault in exposing herself to the coercive situation. In many battered-woman cases, the woman may have an avenue of escape, yet she does not take it, out of fear or as the result of "learned helplessness," a symptom of battered woman syndrome.

Case law in the area is still comparatively slight.[75] However, in light of the willingness of courts to consider battered woman syndrome testimony in

---

[72] See Joshua Dressler, *Reflections on Excusing Wrongdoers: Moral Theory, New Excuses and the Model Penal Code*, 19 Rutgers L.J. 671, 682-89 (1988).

[73] See generally Meredith Blake, Note, *Coerced Into Crime: The Application of Battered Woman Syndrome to the Defense of Duress*, 9 Wis. Women's L.J. 67 (1994); Beth I.Z. Boland, *Battered Women Who Act Under Duress*, 28 New Eng. L. Rev. 603 (1994).

[74] See § 18.06[B], *supra*.

[75] E.g., *State v. Neelley*, 531 So.2d 69 (Ala.App. 1988), *aff'd*, 642 So.2d 494 (Ala. 1993) (*D* killed two girls whom she procured for her abusive husband, after he raped and sexually abused them; *D* was convicted and sentenced to death; held: conviction and sentence affirmed); *People v. Romero*, 13 Cal.Rptr.2d 332, 339 (App. Ct. 1992), *revs'd on procedural grounds*, 8 Cal.4th 728 (1994) (*D* committed a robbery in order to avoid a beating by her partner; held: *D*'s post-conviction petition for writ of *habeas corpus* was granted on the ground that her counsel did not investigate the possibility that she was suffering from battered woman syndrome); *State v. Dunn*, 758 P.2d 718 (Kan. 1988), *habeas granted, Dunn v. Roberts*, 768 F. Supp. 1442 (D. Kan. 1991), *aff'd*, 963 F.2d 308 (10th Cir. 1992) (*D* participated with *X* in two-and-a-half-week crime spree, in which two persons were kidnapped and murdered, and a robbery occurred; *D* was convicted; the state supreme court affirmed the conviction; her conviction was overturned by a federal court on the ground that she was entitled to payment for expert psychiatric services in support of her battered woman syndrome claim); *United States v. Homick*, 964 F.2d 899 (9th Cir. 1992) (*D* was convicted of conspiracy to commit wire fraud; held: conviction upheld on the ground that she failed to establish "battered woman" duress defense).

self-defense cases, it would seem that courts ought to be willing to consider such evidence in duress cases, as well.[76]

At least two factors support such a conclusion. First, duress is an excuse; if a battered woman may *justify* her actions when she kills her abuser in non-imminent circumstances, her experiences with the batterer are at least as significant in a duress case, in which she merely seeks to *excuse* her actions. Second, a woman who kills her abuser and claims self-defense based on battered woman syndrome testimony often finds herself in a Catch-22 situation: she claims that she is suffering from a psychologically paralyzing condition; yet she is seeking to justify an act—the killing of the abusive man—that demonstrates that, at least on this occasion, she was not as helpless as the syndrome suggests.[77] In contrast, when a battered woman asserts duress, her learned helplessness buttresses her duress claim.

Beyond the defense issue, a battered woman who is convicted of the crimes she committed at the behest of the abusive man should be permitted to introduce evidence of her condition in mitigation of her sentence.[78]

§ 23.08 Model Penal Code

[A]—General Rule

Duress is an affirmative defense to unlawful conduct by the defendant if: (1) she was compelled to commit the offense by the use, or threatened use, of unlawful force by the coercer upon her or another person;[79] and (2) a person of reasonable firmness in her situation would have been unable to resist the coercion.[80] The defense of defense is recognized in such circumstances, the Commentary explains, because the "law is ineffective in the deepest sense, indeed . . . it is hypocritical if it imposes on the actor . . . a standard that . . . judges are not prepared to affirm that they should and could comply with . . . ."[81]

The defense is unavailable if the actor recklessly placed herself in a situation in which it was probable that she would be subjected to coercion. If she negligently placed herself in such a situation, however, the defense is available to her for all

---

[76] See *People v. Romero*, 13 Cal.Rptr.2d at 338 ("With the two defenses thus juxtaposed, it is clear that a rule permitting expert testimony about [battered woman syndrome] in a self-defense case must necessarily permit it in a case where duress is claimed . . . .").

[77] Stephen Schulhofer, *The Gender Question in Criminal Law*, 7 Soc. Phil. & Policy, Spring 1990, at 105, 122.

[78] *United States v. Johnson*, 956 F.2d 894 (9th Cir. 1992) (held: Ds in drug case were entitled to raise "incomplete duress" claim for purposes of sentencing; sentencing court may consider testimony of experts on battered woman syndrome).

[79] Although the Code does not expressly so provide, the defense is also available if the defendant reasonably, but erroneously, believed that a threat to use unlawful force was issued. The defense is unavailable, however, if her mistake in this regard was reckless or negligent, and she is prosecuted for a crime of similar culpability. American Law Institute, Comment to § 2.09, at 380.

[80] Model Penal Code § 2.09(1).

[81] American Law Institute, Comment to § 2.09, at 374-75.

offenses except those for which negligence suffices to establish culpability.[82] The Commentary provides virtually no insight into the drafters' reason for the distinction between crimes of recklessness (for which the defense is lost) and crimes of negligence (for which the defense is partially unavailable). This provision differs from § 3.02, the Model Code choice-of-evils defense, which is available in some circumstances to a person who recklessly causes the emergency.[83]

[B]—Comparison to the Common Law

[1]—In General

The Code's duress defense is broader than the common law in various respects. First, it abandons the common law requirements of deadly force and imminency; the defendant is excused as long as a person of reasonable firmness would have committed the offense. Second, the defense is one of general applicability, so the defense may be raised in murder prosecutions.[84] Third, the Code does not require that the imperiled person be the defendant or a member of her family.

The Code defense is similar to the common law in two significant ways. First, the defense is limited to threats or use of "unlawful" force; therefore, it does not apply to coercion emanating from natural sources. This results in an anomaly: if D is compelled by X to run her car over the body of V, who is lying on a narrow mountain road, D may successfully claim duress; but if she runs over V because her brakes give out and she prefers to kill V than to die herself by driving over the cliff, D may be convicted of criminal homicide.[85]

Second, in conformity with the common law, the Code does not recognize the defense when any interest other than bodily integrity is threatened. The Commentary simply states that other threats, perils to property or reputation, "cannot exercise sufficient power over persons of 'reasonable firmness' to warrant consideration."[86]

[2]—Escape from Intolerable Prison Conditions[87]

The common law defense of duress applies when the coercer orders another person to commit a specified crime. Under the Code, however, the defense also applies if the coercer's use of unlawful force causes the coerced party to perform a different criminal act.

Therefore, the Model Code defense of duress applies in the typical intolerable-prison-condition escape case. For example, if X threatens to sexually assault D, a prison inmate, D may be excused for committing the different criminal act of

---

[82] Model Penal Code § 2.09(2).

[83] See § 22.05, *supra*.

[84] Even if a murder defendant is not acquitted, her duress claim may result in conviction of the lesser offense of manslaughter, on the ground that she committed the crime due to an "extreme emotional disturbance" for which there was a "reasonable explanation or excuse." Model Penal Code § 210.3(1)(b). See § 31.10[C][3], *infra*.

[85] American Law Institute, Comment to § 2.09, at 378.

[86] *Id.* at 375.

[87] See § 23.05, *supra*.

escaping confinement, assuming that a person of reasonable firmness in *D*'s situation would have fled.[88] Moreover, the Code provides that a coerced act may also be *justified* under § 3.02, the Code's choice-of-evils provision.[89] Therefore, a prisoner may be able to assert both defenses in an escape prosecution.

[3]—"Situational Duress"[90]

Because the duress defense only applies to human threats, "situational duress" claims, based on compelling natural circumstances, fall outside the scope of the defense.[91]

On the other hand, a brainwashing claim of duress might be available in a Model Penal Code jurisdiction. The duress defense applies if the actor commits an offense in response to prior use of unlawful force, assuming that a person of reasonable firmness in the actor's situation would have committed the crime; therefore, a victim of brainwashing could claim coercion on the ground that the prior force rendered her subconsciously fearful of more force if she did not accede to the suggestion that she commit a crime.[92]

[4]—Battered Women and the Nature of the "Person of Reasonable Firmness"[93]

A battered woman should find features of the Code's duress defense helpful to her coercion claim. First, as there is no imminency requirement, she may defend herself on the basis of an earlier threat by the abuser. Second, as with the brainwashing cases discussed immediately above, a woman who has suffered from prior abuse may be able to excuse her conduct when she commits a crime at the "suggestion" of her abusive partner.

A battered woman is measured by the objective standard of the "person of reasonable firmness" in the defendant's situation. Does this mean that the "reasonable person" is a woman suffering from battered woman syndrome? Perhaps not, as the Code intends for the standard to remain objective. The Commentary provides that a defendant's incapacity should be "based upon the incapacity of men *in general* to resist the coercive pressures."[94] The Code drafters believed that it was impractical to "vary legal norms with the individual's capacity to meet the standards they prescribe." Therefore, except when a person suffers from a "gross and verifiable" disability that may otherwise establish irresponsibility, e.g., insanity, the

---

[88] American Law Institute, Comment to § 2.09, at 377.

[89] Model Penal Code § 2.09(4).

[90] See § 23.06, *supra*.

[91] Thus, in the lifeboat case described in § 23.06[A], *supra*, the Code would leave *D* without an applicable defense. The drafters permitted this gap because they were concerned that if *D* were excused no one would be subject to prosecution for *V*'s unjustified death. See American Law Institute, Comment to § 2.09, at 379.

[92] American Law Institute, Comment to § 2.09, at 376-77.

[93] See § 23.07, *supra*.

[94] American Law Institute, Comment to § 2.09, at 374 (emphasis added).

Code leaves consideration of an actor's subjective weaknesses to the discretion of the sentencing judge.[95]

---

[95] See *Marx v. State*, 724 S.W.2d 456 (Ark. 1987) (under a duress statute based on the Model Penal Code, the court held that *D* was properly barred from introducing evidence regarding his peculiar mental and emotional conditions at the time of the coercion) .

CHAPTER 24

INTOXICATION

§ 24.01 Subject Matter Overview[1]

[A]—"Intoxication": Definition

The term "intoxication" may be defined as a "disturbance of mental or physical capacities resulting from the introduction of any substance into the body."[2] As this definition suggests, the law pertaining to intoxication does not distinguish between alcohol and other foreign substances, such as prescribed medications and illegal drugs.

[B]—Intoxication Law In Its Social and Historical Context

The relationship of intoxicants—primarily, alcohol and drugs—to crime is a close one. Intoxicants distort judgment. Alcohol, in particular, reduces an actor's ability to control his aggressive feelings and anti-social impulses; and persons addicted to narcotics often commit crimes in order to support their habit. The English House of Lords has observed:

> Self-induced alcoholic intoxication has been a factor in crimes of violence . . . throughout the history of crime in this country. [Now] voluntary drug taking with the potential and actual dangers to others it may cause has added a new dimension to the old problem with which the courts have had to deal in their endeavour to maintain order . . . .[3]

In light of the social damage caused by intoxicated actors, it is perhaps unsurprising that intoxication rarely serves as a basis for acquittal in criminal prosecutions. Common law rules relating to intoxication as a "defense"[4] are quite strict; and the modern trend has been for legislatures to reduce the scope of the defense still further or, in some circumstances, to abolish it completely. Particularly in the latter

---

[1] See generally Hall at 529-57; Williams at §§ 168, 178-83; Jerome Hall, *Intoxication and Criminal Responsibility*, 57 Harv. L. Rev. 1045 (1944); Chester N. Mitchell, *The Intoxicated Offender—Refuting the Legal and Medical Myths*, 11 Int'l. J. L. & Psychol. 77 (1988); Monrad G. Paulsen, *Intoxication as a Defense to Crime*, 1961 U. Ill. L.F. 1.

[2] *People v. Low*, 732 P.2d 622, 627 (Colo. 1987) (quoting Model Penal Code § 2.08(5)(a)).

[3] *Director of Public Prosecutions v. Majewski*, [1976] 2 All E.R. 142, 146 (opinion of Lord Ellwyn-Jones).

[4] The word "defense" is in quotation marks because intoxication can potentially serve as an excuse defense or, somewhat more often, as a failure-of-proof claim. See § 16.02, *supra*. A failure-of-proof claim is not a true defense.

circumstance, intoxication law borders, if it does not cross, the line of unconstitutional unfairness to criminal defendants.

[C]—Intoxication Cases: Issues to Consider

When a defendant is intoxicated at the time of the alleged criminal conduct, a lawyer must consider at least the following three questions. First, how did the defendant become intoxicated? Intoxication law is divisible into two general categories: rules pertaining to conduct that was the result of "voluntary" (or "self-induced") intoxication, and the law pertaining to "involuntary" (or "innocent") intoxication. The vast majority of cases concern the former condition.

Second, in what way does the defendant claim that his intoxication affected his culpability? In most cases, the actor claims that he did not form the requisite state of mind to be convicted of the offense. Occasionally, however, the defendant's intoxication is so gross that he may seek to show that he was unconscious when he acted, i.e., that his conduct did not include a voluntary act. Or, the defendant may assert that, although he had the requisite *mens rea* to commit the offense and was conscious when he was acting, the intoxicants made him temporarily insane.

Third, of what type of offense is the defendant charged—general intent, specific intent, or strict liability? The common law rules differ considerably depending on the nature of the *mens rea*, if any, that must be proved.

[D]—Intoxication Claims: Relationship to Other Defenses

Intoxication claims can confusingly parallel other defenses. First, as the previous comments suggest, under limited circumstances[5] an *intoxication* defense is recognized when an actor becomes "temporarily insane" as the result of the introduction of drugs, alcohol, or other foreign substances into the body. In other cases, as the result of long-term intoxication, a person may suffer from permanent (or, at least, continuing) insanity; in these circumstances a traditional *insanity* defense claim may lie.[6]

Second, in many states, the defenses of diminished capacity[7] and intoxication operate similarly, except that the former defense applies when the actor suffers from mental illness rather than intoxication. However, occasionally, a state will recognize a defense in one circumstance, but not in the other.[8]

Third, claims of intoxication and mistake-of-fact[9] frequently overlap. For example, in *Regina v. Cogan and Leak*,[10] *L* fraudulently convinced *C*, who was

---

[5] See § 24.06[B], *infra*.

[6] See § 24.05[B], *infra*.

[7] See Chapter 26, *infra*.

[8] *Easley v. State*, 629 So.2d 1046 (Fla. Ct. App. 1993) (recognizing a limited voluntary intoxication defense, although the state supreme court had previously rejected the defense of diminished capacity).

[9] See Chapter 12, *supra*.

[10] [1976] Q.B. 217.

intoxicated, that *V*, *L*'s wife, desired intercourse with *C*, despite *V*'s protestations to the contrary. Charged with rape, *C* claimed mistake-of-fact regarding *V*'s lack of consent. Because *C* was intoxicated, however, his claim might be described as an "intoxicated mistake"[11] claim. Often the two defenses operate similarly, so that the label attached to the claim will not matter. However, in some jurisdictions, the "mistake" defense is broader than the counterpart "intoxication" claim, so that the mixture of the two claims may result in conceptual confusion.

§ 24.02   Voluntary Intoxication: General Principles[12]

[A]—Definition of "Voluntary Intoxication"

[1]—In General

The term "voluntary intoxication" rarely is defined by the courts, which prefer instead to provide examples of the very few circumstances in which intoxication is involuntary. Basically, intoxication is "voluntary" if the actor is culpable for becoming intoxicated. Such culpability exists if the person knowingly ingests a substance that he knows or should know can cause him to become intoxicated, unless the substance was a prescribed medication or he was coerced to ingest it.[13]

Once an actor voluntarily ingests a known intoxicant, courts are unsympathetic to claims that the substance had an unexpected effect on the actor. For example, in *People v. Velez*,[14] *D* knowingly puffed on a marijuana cigarette at a social gathering, unaware that it was laced with phencyclidine (PCP), which caused *D* to become legally unconscious, during which period he assaulted *V* with a deadly weapon. The court held that for purposes of intoxication law, *D* was "voluntarily" intoxicated, because it was "common knowledge that unlawful street drugs do not come with warranties of purity or quality associated with lawfully acquired drugs, such as alcohol."

---

[11] Kenneth L. Campbell, *Intoxicated Mistakes*, 32 Crim. L.Q. 110 (1987).

[12] See generally J. Reid Meloy, *Voluntary Intoxication and the Insanity Defense*, 20 J. Psychiatry & L. 439 (1992); John Sellers, *Mens Rea and the Judicial Approach to "Bad Excuses" In the Criminal Law*, 41 Mod. L. Rev. 245 (1978); Alan R. Ward, *Making Some Sense of Self-Induced Intoxication*, 45 Cambridge L.J. 247 (1986); see also the sources in Note 1, *supra*.

[13] See Model Penal Code § 2.08(5)(b) (defining "self-induced intoxication").

[14] 221 Cal. Rptr. 631 (Ct. App. 1985).

[2]—Alcoholism, Drug Addiction, and "Voluntary Intoxication"[15]

Intoxication resulting from alcoholism or drug addiction is considered voluntary under common law principles. In general, "an irresistable [sic] compulsion to consume intoxicants caused by a physiological or psychological disability does not render the ensuing intoxication involuntary."[16] That is, the law treats the alcoholic's first drink of the day, and the drug addict's first use of narcotics on a particular occasion, no differently than it does the actions of the ordinary drinker and casual user of drugs.

As a matter of constitutional law, a state may not punish a person for the status of being addicted to narcotics[17] or, one may assume, of being an alcoholic. On the other hand, an alcoholic may be punished for the offense of public drunkenness;[18] and a drug addict may not use his condition as a defense to the crime of drug possession or, presumably, offenses committed in support of his drug habit.[19] Constitutional law in this regard is discussed elsewhere in the Text and should be considered at this point.[20]

[B]—General Rules

[1]—No Excuse

Courts commonly state that voluntary intoxication never excuses criminal conduct.[21] This is a somewhat misleading statement: although it is true that self-induced intoxication *as such* never excuses wrongdoing, the condition that intoxication causes, e.g., a clouded mental state, unconsciousness, or insanity, may serve as an exculpatory basis in limited circumstances. Nonetheless, the no-excuse rule is a good starting point from which to appreciate how few are the circumstances in which a voluntarily intoxicated actor may avoid criminal conviction.

One English justice expressed well the traditional attitude toward self-induced intoxication claims when he stated that "a man who by his own voluntary act

---

[15] See generally Herbert Fingarette, Heavy Drinking—The Myth of Alcoholism as a Disease (1988); Richard C. Boldt, *The Construction of Responsibility in the Criminal Law*, 140 U. Pa. L. Rev. 2245 (1992); Herbert Fingarette, *Alcoholism: Can Honest Mistake About One's Capacity for Self Control Be an Excuse?*, 13 Int'l. J. L. & Psychiatry 77 (1990); Warren Lehman, *Alcoholism, Freedom, and Moral Responsibility*, 13 Int'l. J. L. & Psychiatry 103 (1990); Stanton Peele, *Does Addiction Excuse Thieves and Killers from Criminal Responsibility?*, 13 Int'l J. L. & Psychiatry 95 (1990); Steven S. Nemerson, *Alcoholism, Intoxication, and the Criminal Law*, 10 Cardozo L. Rev. 393 (1988).

[16] *See v. State*, 757 S.W.2d 947, 950 (Ark. 1988); see *People v. Downey*, 515 N.E.2d 362, 371 (Ill. App. Ct. 1987); *State v. Bishop*, 632 S.W.2d 255, 258 (Mo. 1982).

[17] *Robinson v. California*, 370 U.S. 660 (1962).

[18] *Powell v. Texas*, 392 U.S. 514 (1968).

[19] See *United States v. Moore*, 486 F.2d 1139, 1147-48 (D.C. Cir. 1973).

[20] See § 9.04, *supra*.

[21] E.g., *People v. Langworthy*, 331 N.W.2d 171, 172 (Mich. 1982) ("Every jurisdiction in this country recognizes the general principle that voluntary intoxication is not any excuse for crime") (footnote omitted); *Commonwealth v. Graves*, 334 A.2d 661, 663 (Pa. 1975).

debauches and destroys his will power [should] be no better situated in regard to criminal acts than a sober man."[22] And, as an American court put it, the law should "not allow [the defendant] to avail himself of the excuse of his own gross vice and misconduct to shelter himself from the legal consequences of [his] crime."[23]

[2]—When Voluntary Intoxication May Be Exculpatory

Subject to clarification in the following three chapter sections, a person may be acquitted of an offense, if at the time of his conduct, as the result of self-induced intoxication: (1) he did not harbor the specific state of mind provided for in the definition of the offense; or (2) he suffered from long-term intoxication-induced "fixed" insanity. In general, however, issues of *mens rea* aside, a defendant is not able to escape conviction on the ground that, as the result of voluntary intoxication, he was unconscious at the time that he committed the social harm.

§ 24.03 Voluntary Intoxication: *Mens Rea*

[A]—In General

The most common voluntary intoxication "defense" raised in criminal trials is not a true defense at all, but is a failure-of-proof claim, or a "defense" that seeks to negate an element of the crime, in this case, the *mens rea* of the offense.

Today, there are as many as six different common law and statutory approaches to *mens rea* claims,[24] ranging from the rule that voluntary intoxication that negates an actor's *mens rea* is a defense to all crimes,[25] to the opposite (and increasingly popular) position that it is not recognized for any offense.[26] The traditional common law rules fall between these two extremes.

[B]—Traditional Common Law Rules

[1]—Overview

In matters relating to voluntary intoxication, the common law draws a distinction between general-intent and specific-intent crimes. Indeed, as the California Supreme Court once pointed out, the concepts of "general intent" and "specific intent" "evolved as a judicial response to the problem of the intoxicated offender." The distinction represents the law's "compromise between the conflicting feelings of sympathy and reprobation for the intoxicated offender."[27]

---

[22] *Director of Public Prosecutions v. Beard*, 1920 A.C. 479, 494 (opinion of Lord Birkenhead).

[23] *People v. Lewis*, 36 Cal. 531, 531-32 (1869), *overruled in part*, *People v. Gorshen*, 336 P.2d 492 (Cal. 1959).

[24] 1 Robinson at § 65(a)(2).

[25] E.g., Wis. Stat. Ann. § 939.42(2) (1982 & Supp. 1993).

[26] E.g., *White v. State*, 717 S.W.2d 784 (Ark. 1986).

[27] *People v. Hood*, 462 P.2d 370, 377 (Cal. 1969).

[2]—General-Intent Offenses

Voluntary intoxication is not a defense to general-intent crimes.[28] For example, if *D* rapes *V*, he will not be entitled to claim that, as a result of voluntary intoxication, his mind was so clouded that he did not or could not form the intent to have sexual intercourse with *V*.[29] Likewise, *D* is not permitted to introduce evidence that, because he was intoxicated, he became confused and believed that *V* consented to the intercourse.[30]

This rule made sense when the intoxication doctrine was first formulated. At that time, "general intent" referred to an offense for which the only *mens rea* required was a culpable state of mind.[31] Consistent with this meaning of the term "*mens rea*," the voluntary act of impairing one's mental faculties with intoxicants is a morally blameworthy course of conduct that renders the actor culpable for the ensuing harm.[32] By this view, a person's voluntary intoxication *proves*, rather than negatives, his "*mens rea*."

In modern language, self-induced intoxication typically constitutes reckless conduct.[33] The effect of alcohol and drugs on the human body is now sufficiently well known that the law may assume that when an ordinary person chooses to ingest intoxicating substances, he knows that he will suffer temporary impairment of his powers of perception, judgment, and control; therefore, he knows that he will jeopardize the safety of others while in that condition.

[3]—Specific-Intent Offenses

Voluntary intoxication is a defense to specific-intent crimes.[34] That is, a person is not guilty of an offense if, as the result of his intoxication at the time of the crime, he was incapable of forming[35] or did not in fact form,[36] the specific intent required in the definition of the offense.[37]

---

[28] *State v. Hurst*, 606 So.2d 965, 968 (La. Ct. App. 1992).

[29] See *State v. McDaniel*, 515 So.2d 572, 575 (La. Ct. App. 1987); *People v. Langworthy*, 331 N.W.2d at 177.

[30] American Law Institute, Comment to § 2.08, at 355.

[31] See §§ 10.02[B] and 10.06, *supra*.

[32] *Hendershott v. People*, 653 P.2d 385, 396 (Colo. 1982).

[33] *People v. Register*, 457 N.E.2d 704, 709 (N.Y. 1983); *Director of Public Prosecutions v. Majewski*, [1976] 2 All E.R. 142, 150 (Lord Elwyn-Jones, L.C.).

[34] *People v. Low*, 732 P.2d 622, 628 (Colo. 1987); *Linehan v. State*, 476 So.2d 1262, 1264 (Fla. 1985).

[35] *Commonwealth v. Henson*, 476 N.E.2d 947, 953 (Mass. 1985); *State v. Hicks*, 538 N.E.2d 1030, 1034 (Ohio 1989); *United States v. Zink*, 612 F.2d 511, 515 (10th Cir. 1980).

[36] E.g., *People v. Crittle*, 212 N.W.2d 196, 199 (Mich. 1973); Cal. Penal Code. § 22(b) (1988); *Regina v. Garlick*, 1981 Crim. L. Rev. 178.

[37] The difference in language between "lacking capacity to form" and "not forming" a specific intent is significant. Logically, one who lacks the capacity to form a specific intent, does not in fact form it. The converse, however, does not necessarily follow. As a practical matter, acquittal should be more difficult to obtain in an "incapacity" jurisdiction because intoxication rarely renders a person so insensible that he lacks the ability to intend. The

For example, suppose that D becomes intoxicated and sexually assaults V, a woman. He is arrested during the assault and charged with the specific-intent crime of assault with intent to rape. Under the common law, D is entitled to introduce evidence regarding his intoxication in order to prove that, because of his condition, he lacked the specific intent to rape V, either because he was too intoxicated to know what he was doing, or because he mistakenly believed that V was consenting. [38] D is entitled to introduce this evidence because "[w]here the legislature, in its definition of a crime, has designated a particular state of mind as a material element of the crime, evidence of intoxication becomes relevant if the degree of inebriation has reached that point" where he did not form the required intent. [39]

[4]—Criticism of the Traditional Approach

[a]—The Defense Is Too Narrow

Some critics of the common law rule believe that voluntary intoxication should serve as a potential defense to all criminal offenses. The applicability of the defense "should not depend on whether a court chooses to characterize an element of the crime charged as separate from the element of general intent." [40]

Notice the oddity with the present law: if D has nonconsensual sexual intercourse with V because he drunkenly believes V is consenting, D may *not* introduce evidence of his intoxication to support his *mens rea* claim in a general-intent rape prosecution. However, if D is arrested seconds before the intercourse occurs. and he is charged with the specific-intent offense of "assault with intent to rape," D may now introduce evidence of his drunkenness, in order to negate the specific intent ("intent to rape").

Nothing commends this dual approach. D's intoxication is the same in both cases. He is equally drunk. He is equally culpable for becoming drunk. His mind is equally clouded. His capacity to form a mental state is equally undermined (or not undermined). And, "neither common experience nor psychology knows of any such phenomenon as 'general intent' distinguishable from 'specific intent.'" [41] Nor do utilitarian concerns favor separate approaches: D is equally dangerous in the two cases; and principles of general deterrence demand equal treatment.

If D's voluntary intoxication should be treated the same regardless of whether the crime committed is specific-intent or general-intent in nature, advocates of the broader defense argue that the logic of the law regarding specific-intent offenses

---

"incapacity" language is undesirable because a jury may convict because it determines that the defendant had the capacity to form the specific intent, without resolving the pertinent question—*did* the defendant form the intent?

[38] See *People v. Guillett*, 69 N.W.2d 140, 143 (Mich. 1955).

[39] *Commonwealth v. Graves*, 334 A.2d at 663.

[40] *People v. Kelley*, 176 N.W.2d 435, 443 (Mich. Ct. App. 1970).

[41] *Id.* Indeed, as the Chief Justice Roger Traynor observed for the California Supreme Court, "[t]here is no real difference [between a general intent and a specific intent], . . . only a linguistic one, between an intent to do an act already performed and an intent to do the same act in the future." *People v. Hood*, 462 P.2d at 378.

should apply to all crimes: either the defendant did, or did not, form the state of mind required in the definition of the offense. Whatever we may think of the intoxicated actor for becoming inebriated, he should only be convicted if every element of the crime, including *mens rea*, is proven.

[b]—The Defense Should Be Abolished

Advocates for repeal of the defense contend that because "the aim of the law is to protect the innocent from injury by the sick as well as the bad,"[42] the intoxication defense "is detrimental to the welfare and safety of the citizens . . . in that criminals are at times excused from the consequences of their criminal acts merely because of their voluntary intoxication."[43] Unlike insane people, who are usually institutionalized on the basis of an insanity acquittal,[44] intoxicated persons who are acquitted, many of whom are alcoholics and drug addicts, return to the street where they may commit new offenses.

The no-defense rule, however, is wrong as a matter of principle. Even if an intoxicated actor is dangerous, this fact does not prove that he possessed the state of mind required in the definition of the offense. When a lawmaking body expressly includes a mental state in the definition of a crime, as common law courts did with specific-intent offenses and which legislatures now do with most non-strict-liability crimes, it does so because it believes that the particular *mens rea* incorporated therein renders the actor more deserving of punishment or more dangerous than if that mental state were absent. The law's refusal to recognize a claim that the defendant lacked the statutorily required state of mind, therefore, defeats the purpose of including the element in the definition of the offense.

The no-defense rule is of questionable constitutionality. The due process clause of the United States Constitution requires the prosecution to prove every element of an offense beyond a reasonable doubt.[45] The criminal process is not fair, i.e., the defendant is denied his "due" process, if the state includes a mental element in the definition of a crime, permits the prosecutor to put on evidence supporting the claim that the defendant acted with the required state of mind, and then prohibits the defendant from producing relevant evidence that might raise a reasonable doubt as to his *mens rea*.[46]

To permit a defendant the opportunity to use his intoxication as a potential defense does not mean that he will be acquitted. As already observed, the act of becoming intoxicated is itself a culpable act. For any crime for which negligence

---

[42] *State v. Maik*, 287 A.2d 715, 720 (N.J. 1972), *overruled on other grounds*, *State v. Krol*, 344 A.2d 289 (N.J. 1975).

[43] *White v. State*, 717 S.W.2d at 786 (quoting an emergency clause in an Act adopted by the state legislature repealing the defense).

[44] See § 25.05, *infra*.

[45] See § 7.03[B], *supra*.

[46] *Commonwealth v. Graves*, 334 A.2d at 665.

or, perhaps, recklessness[47] is sufficient to convict, the defendant's effort to negate his *mens rea* will fail.

[C]—Special Problem: Intoxication and Homicide

Some states only recognize the defense of voluntary intoxication in murder prosecutions.[48] Even in states that recognize the defense in the prosecution of all specific-intent crimes, the voluntary intoxication rules pertaining to criminal homicide merit special attention.

Many jurisdictions separate murder into degrees, in which first-degree murder includes "wilful, deliberate, premeditated" killings.[49] In virtually all states with this type of statutory system, a defendant may introduce evidence that, because his mental faculties were clouded by intoxicants, he did not premeditate and deliberate the killing.[50] In such circumstances, the defendant is entitled to have his crime reduced to second-degree murder.[51]

A defendant's intoxication may also arise as an issue in a felony-murder prosecution.[52] If the felony underlying the murder prosecution is one of specific-intent, a defendant is entitled to introduce evidence that he did not form the requisite felonious intent because of intoxication. If the defendant lacked the specific intent, he is not guilty of the felony, in which case the felony-murder rule does not apply.[53]

---

[47] Getting drunk is a reckless act in the sense that the actor knows that as the result of ingesting alcohol or drugs he will lose some command of his faculties. This does not necessarily mean, however, that a voluntarily intoxicated actor who causes social harm has done so recklessly, because the latter type of recklessness only occurs if the actor consciously disregarded a substantial and unjustifiable risk that the particular social harm of the criminal offense would result from his conduct. Most states, however, treat these two forms of recklessness—recklessly losing command of one's senses, and recklessly causing the social harm of the offense—equivalently. That is, a person who is charged with a crime requiring proof of recklessness cannot escape liability on the ground that, due to his voluntary intoxication, he was unaware of a risk of which he would have been aware had he not been in an intoxicated condition. E.g., *State v. Shine*, 479 A.2d 218, 223 (Conn. 1984).

[48] E.g., *Griggs v. Commonwealth*, 255 S.E.2d 475, 479 (Va. 1979).

[49] See § 31.03[C], *infra*.

[50] E.g., *Commonwealth v. Henson*, 476 N.E.2d at 953; *State v. Stasio*, 396 A.2d 1129, 1131 (N.J. 1979).

[51] Even if the intoxication also negates the element of "wilfulness"—intent to kill—the crime is only reduced to second-degree murder because a person who becomes so intoxicated that he cannot form the requisite intent for first-degree murder has acted recklessly in becoming so insensible; therefore, his actions fall within the recklessness or "depraved heart" form of murder that typically constitutes second-degree murder. See § 31.05 [A], *infra*. "Thus, the erosion, through voluntary intoxication, of the specific intent to kill . . . moves the crime *down* and *over* from a murderous *mens rea* requiring a specific intent to a different murderous *mens rea* not requiring such specific intent." *Cirincione v. State*, 540 A.2d 1151, 1153 n.1 (Md. Ct. Spec. App. 1988).

[52] The felony-murder doctrine is considered at § 31.06, *infra*.

[53] See *Commonwealth v. Parker*, 522 N.E.2d 924, 926 (Mass. 1988).

For example, suppose that *D*, in an extremely intoxicated condition, takes property from *V* by force. *V* dies of a heart attack brought on by the crime. If *D* was so intoxicated that did he not form the specific intent to steal *V* property, *D* is not guilty of robbery or, therefore, felony-murder.

§ 24.04 Voluntary Intoxication: Voluntary Act

Occasionally, a person will become so intoxicated that he is rendered unconscious, in which condition his body may move in an automatic, i.e., unwilled, manner and cause harm to others. At his trial, the defendant may seek to avoid conviction by asserting the general principle of criminal responsibility that a person may not be convicted of a crime unless his conduct includes a voluntary act, i.e., a willed, conscious, muscular contraction.[54]

This argument, as stated, inevitably fails. Although the voluntarily intoxicated actor may have been unconscious at the moment that he committed the offense, he is held responsible because of his prior conscious decision to ingest the intoxicants.[55]

Unconsciousness may serve as a defense in two contexts, but neither basis implicates the voluntary act requirement, as such. First, courts sometimes state that evidence of unconsciousness produced by voluntary intoxication may be introduced when "his defense is that he did not physically accomplish the act of which he is accused."[56] In other words, the defendant may use his intoxication-induced unconsciousness to prove that he did not commit the criminal act, but not to show that he committed it involuntarily.

Second, an unconscious person can have no actual intent to cause harm while in that state. Therefore, unconsciousness may serve as a proxy for a *mens rea* claim. In a common law jurisdiction, a person may introduce evidence of unconsciousness to prove that he lacked the specific intent required to be convicted of the offense.[57]

§ 24.05 Voluntary Intoxication: Insanity[58]

[A]—"Temporary" Insanity

Suppose á person becomes so intoxicated that, at the time he commits an offense, he is so out of touch with reality that he does not appreciate the wrongfulness of his conduct, or he cannot conform his conduct to the law. If his condition were caused by a mental disease, rather than by intoxication, he could raise the excuse

---

[54] See § 9.02[A], *supra*.

[55] *People v. Velez*, 221 Cal. Rptr. at 637 ("[C]riminal responsibility is justified on the theory that having chosen to breach one's duty to others of acting with reason and conscience, one may not entirely avoid criminal harm caused by one's breach of duty.").

[56] *Linehan v. State*, 442 So.2d 244, 250 (Fla. 1983).

[57] *People v. Kelly*, 516 P.2d 875, 881 (Cal. 1973).

[58] See generally Lawrence P. Tiffany, *The Drunk, The Insane, and the Criminal Courts: Deciding What to Make of Self-Induced Insanity*, 69 Wash. U.L.Q. 221 (1991).

of insanity.[59] As mental illness is not involved, however, the defendant may wish to claim that because of his voluntary ingestion of drugs or alcohol, he experienced something like "temporary insanity," or what Hale called "temporary phrenzy."[60]

The common law does not recognize such a defense. To the extent that an actor's intoxication was voluntary, "any degree of insanity thus produced would be a part of the consequences of such voluntary intoxication."[61] In contrast to mental illness, which is a condition that ordinarily is contracted involuntarily, one who voluntarily introduces alcohol or drugs into his system is the victim of "artificial voluntarily contracted madness."[62] As such, he is not entitled to the law's dispensation.[63]

[B]—"Fixed" Insanity

Habitual use of intoxicants can result in permanent brain damage, resulting in a substance-induced mental disorder that persists, i.e., the disorder remains even when the actor is not under the influence of intoxicants.[64]

The law distinguishes between mental impairment that does not extend beyond the period of voluntary intoxication, for which no defense is available, and insanity resulting from long-term use of drugs or alcohol. If the unsoundness of mind, although produced by long-term alcohol or drug abuse, has become "fixed" or "settled," the nearly universal rule is that the defendant may assert a traditional insanity defense.[65] Although the defense is usually asserted when the defendant was sober at the time of the offense, the insanity defense applies even if the actor was intoxicated at the time of the crime.[66]

In light of the unsympathetic view of common law jurists regarding intoxication-caused criminal conduct, it is surprising that "madness . . . contracted by the vice and will of the party"[67] would excuse. Indeed, one court has rejected the defense, stating:

> There is no principled basis to distinguish between the short-term and long-term effects of voluntary intoxication by punishing the first and excusing the second. If anything, the moral blameworthiness would seem to be even greater with

---

[59] The definition of "insanity" varies by jurisdiction. See § 25.04, *infra*. The comments in this chapter regarding intoxication-induced "insanity" apply to all definitions of the term.

[60] 1 Hale at *32.

[61] *Roberts v. People*, 19 Mich. 401, 422 (1870); see *Evans v. State*, 645 P.2d 155, 158-60 (Alaska 1982); *State v. Wicks*, 657 P.2d 781, 782 (Wash. 1983).

[62] 4 Blackstone at *25.

[63] However, a person suffering from such a mental condition may be incapable of forming a required *mens rea*, and be able to avoid conviction on this ground.

[64] See American Psychiatric Association, Diagnostic and Statistical Manual of Mental Disorders 192 (4th ed. 1994).

[65] 1 Hale at *32; *People v. Kelly*, 516 P.2d at 882; *Jones v. State*, 648 P.2d 1251, 1255 (Okla Crim. App. 1982); *State v. Wicks*, 657 P.2d at 782.

[66] *People v. Chapman*, 418 N.W.2d 658, 659 (Mich. Ct. App. 1987).

[67] 1 Hale at *32.

respect to the long-term effects of many, repeated instances of voluntary intoxication occurring over an extended period of time.[68]

The law's general willingness to recognize the defense is sometimes defended on the theory that it would constitute an impossible task to trace the chain of causation back to the original misconduct of abusive drinking or narcotics usage.[69] More likely, however, the law recognizes the fact that at some point a person's earlier voluntary decisions become morally remote.[70] One should not be blamed for every harmful act that can be linked to an earlier transgression.

§ 24.06   Involuntary Intoxication[71]

[A]—Definition

Intoxication is "involuntary" (or "innocent") if the actor is not to blame for becoming intoxicated. According to one scholar, if we judge the state of legal affairs from court opinions, involuntary intoxication is "simply and completely non-existent."[72] Although this is an exaggeration, cases of involuntary intoxication are exceedingly uncommon.

As described in *City of Minneapolis v. Altimus*,[73] intoxication is characterized as "involuntary" in four circumstances. First, coerced intoxication is involuntary, such as when *D*, a youth, is told that he will be left in the desert if he does not drink alcohol.[74] Second, intoxication by innocent mistake, e.g., *X* fraudulently induces *D* to ingest cocaine by telling him that it is a "breath freshener,"[75] is involuntary.

Third, blame is inappropriate if the actor becomes unexpectedly intoxicated from a prescribed medication, i.e., he does not know, and has no reason to know, that the medication is likely to have an intoxicating effect.[76] However, if the actor purposely takes more than the prescribed medication, the jury may find that the intoxication is voluntary.[77]

---

[68] *Bieber v. People*, 856 P.2d 811, 817 (Colo. 1993).

[69] Paulsen, Note 1, *supra*, at 23.

[70] See *Parker v. State*, 254 A.2d 381, 388 (Md. Ct. Spec. App. 1969) (distinguishing between "the direct results of drinking, which are voluntarily sought after, and its remote and undesired consequences").

[71] See generally Lawrence P. Tiffany & Mary Tiffany, *Nosologic Objections to the Criminal Defense of Pathological Intoxication: What Do the Doubters Doubt?*, 13 Int'l J. L. & Psychiatry, 49 (1990).

[72] Hall at 539.

[73] 238 N.W.2d 851, 856 (Minn. 1976).

[74] *Burrows v. State*, 297 P. 1029, 1035 (Ariz. 1931).

[75] *People v. Penman*, 110 N.E. 894, 900 (Ill. 1915).

[76] *City of Minneapolis v. Altimus*, 238 N.W.2d at 856-57.

[77] *People v. Chaffey*, 30 Cal.Rptr.2d 757 (Ct. App. 1994) (taking an overdose of prescription medicine in order to commit suicide may be deemed *voluntary* intoxication); but see *People v. Turner*, 680 P.2d 1290 (Colo. Ct. App. 1983) (as in the past, *D* took more than the prescribed medication for migraine headaches; in the past, he suffered drowsiness from

Fourth, "pathological intoxication" is involuntary. Pathological intoxication "is a temporary psychotic reaction, often manifested by violence, which is triggered by consumption of alcohol by a person with a pre-disposing mental or physical condition,"[78] e.g., temporal lobe epilepsy, encephalitis, or a metabolic disturbance. The defense only applies if the actor had no reason to know that he was susceptible to such a reaction.

[B]—General Rule

A person who is involuntarily intoxicated is entitled to acquittal in all of the circumstances in which *voluntary* intoxication is a defense. Because the actor's intoxication was contracted in a nonculpable manner, he should also be acquitted of a general-intent offense.[79]

A defendant is also excused for his conduct if, as the result of involuntary intoxication, he is "temporarily insane," i.e., he suffers from a temporary intoxication-induced mental condition that satisfies that jurisdiction's definition of insanity.[80]

§ 24.07　Model Penal Code[81]

[A]—General Rule

The Code distinguishes between three types of intoxication:[82] (1) self-induced intoxication; (2) pathological intoxication; and (3) intoxication that is not self-induced (i.e., involuntary intoxication).[83]

An actor's intoxicated condition at the time of a crime may exculpate him in two circumstances. First, any form of intoxication is a defense to criminal conduct if it negates an element of the offense.[84] Second, pathological intoxication and intoxication that was not self-induced are affirmatives defenses, if the intoxication

---

the overdose; on the present occasion it had an intoxicating effect; held: because the doctor had never warned him that an overdose might cause intoxication, and it had not caused this effect in the past, a jury could find that the intoxication was *involuntary*).

[78] Tiffany & Tiffany, Note 71, *supra*, at 49.

[79] To the extent that involuntary intoxication is a defense because it negates the required *mens rea* of an offense, it should not be a defense to a strict-liability crime, because there is no *mens rea* to negate. See *State v. Miller*, 788 P.2d 974 (Ore. 1990) (*D* drank coffee fixed for him by *X*, without knowledge that it had been spiked with alcohol; held: *D* may not claim involuntary intoxication in a strict-liability prosecution for driving under the influence of alcohol); contra, *People v. Koch*, 294 N.Y.S. 987 (N.Y. App. Div. 1937) (in prosecution for driving under the influence of alcohol, *D* may assert an involuntary-intoxication defense).

[80] *People v. Caulley*, 494 N.W.2d 853, 859 (Mich. Ct. App. 1992); *State v. Gardner*, 870 P.2d 900, 901-02 (Utah 1993).

[81] See generally Lawrence P. Tiffany, *Pathological Intoxication and the Model Penal Code*, 69 Neb. L. Rev. 763 (1990).

[82] For the MPC definition of "intoxication," see the text accompanying Note 2, *supra*.

[83] Model Penal Code § 2.08(4)-(5).

[84] Model Penal Code § 2.08(1).

caused the actor to suffer from a mental condition comparable to that which constitutes insanity under the Code.[85] These exculpatory claims are explained below.

[B]—Negation of an Element of an Offense

[1]—Mental State

[a]—In General

The Code does not distinguish between "general intent" and "specific intent" offenses.[86] Consequently, with one exception, a person is not guilty of an offense—regardless of whether it would be characterized as "general intent" or "specific intent" at common law—if, as the result of intoxication, he lacked the state of mind required in respect to an element of the crime.

For example, assume that under state law "rape" occurs when a male "knowingly has nonconsensual sexual intercourse with a female not his wife." Under this statute, *D* would be entitled to acquittal if, because of his self-induced intoxication, he did not have the knowledge required for the offense, e.g., he did not know that he was having intercourse, he did not know that the female did not consent, or he did not know that the victim was a "female not his wife."

[b]—Exception to the Rule

The Code recognizes one exception to the rule described above. The exception relates to crimes defined in terms of recklessness. Ordinarily, a person acts "recklessly" as defined by the Code if "he consciously disregards a substantial and unjustifiable risk that the material element of the offense exists or will result from his conduct."[87] However, in the case of self-induced intoxication, the Code provides that a person acts "recklessly" as to an element of the crime if, as the result of the self-induced intoxication, he was not conscious of a risk of which he would have been aware had he not been intoxicated.[88]

The practical effect of this provision is to permit a person who should be aware of a substantial and unjustifiable risk in his conduct, i.e., a negligent actor, to be punished for a crime based on recklessness, if the reason that he was unaware of the risk was that his self-induced intoxication clouded his mental faculties. The Commentary to the Code concedes that criticism of this rule is "worthy of respect," but the drafters concluded:

> [A]wareness of the potential consequences of excessive drinking on the capacity of human beings to gauge the risks incident to their conduct is by now so dispersed in our culture that it is not unfair to postulate a general equivalence between the risks created by the conduct of the drunken actor and the risks created by his conduct in becoming drunk.[89]

---

[85] Model Penal Code § 2.08(4).

[86] See § 10.07[A], *supra*.

[87] Model Penal Code § 2.02(2)(c).

[88] Model Penal Code § 2.08(2).

[89] American Law Institute, Comment to § 2.08, at 359.

[2]—Voluntary Act

The Code provides that a person is entitled to acquittal if his intoxication negates *any* element of the offense. Under the Code, a person is not guilty of an offense unless his conduct includes a voluntary act, or an omission in limited circumstances. [90]

Conduct during unconsciousness is involuntary. Therefore, a person who is unconscious as the result of intoxication, even if the intoxication is self-induced, may raise an involuntariness claim, although (as in common law jurisdictions), the requisite voluntary act may sometimes be found in conduct prior to the unconsciousness. [91]

[C]—Intoxication as an Affirmative Defense

Even if all of the elements of a crime are proved, the Code recognizes an affirmative defense based on intoxication if, at the time of his conduct: (1) the actor suffered from pathological intoxication or intoxication that was not self-induced; and (2) the actor's condition qualifies under the American Law Institute's test of insanity. [92]

If the criteria for the defense are satisfied, the actor's defense is that of intoxication, rather than insanity. The Code expressly provides that intoxication does not "in itself, constitute mental disease." [93] As is the case in common law jurisdictions, however, an actor is entitled to raise an *insanity* claim if, at the time of his conduct, he suffered from a mental disease caused by long-term use of alcohol or drugs. [94]

---

[90] Model Penal Code § 2.01(1). See § 9.05[A], *supra.*

[91] American Law Institute, Comment to § 2.08, at 353.

[92] For the Code definition of insanity, see Model Penal Code § 4.01(1). See § 25.04[C][3], *infra.*

[93] Model Penal Code § 2.08(3). The key words here are "in itself." The Institute does not preclude the possibility that experts will someday conclude that there is a disease giving rise to an uncontrollable urge to drink, in which case, an alcoholic whose intoxicated conduct meets the Code test of "insanity" would be entitled to raise the latter defense. American Law Institute, Comment to § 2.08, at 361.

[94] American Law Institute, Comment to § 2.08, at 362.

CHAPTER 25

INSANITY

§ 25.01 Subject Matter Overview[1]

Few doctrines of criminal law engender more controversy than the defense of insanity. From the time of Edward III in the fourteenth century, when "madness" became a complete defense to criminal charges,[2] English and American courts and, more recently, legislatures have struggled to define "insanity." No sooner is a definition propounded than critics, often from conflicting philosophical vantage points, attack it. Some criticism runs deeper, in the form of calls for abolition of the excuse.

The issue of the proper relationship of mental disease to criminal responsibility is controversial for various reasons. First, although the insanity defense is rarely raised,[3] it is offered in some unusually heinous and well publicized cases: e.g., in attacks upon public officials, such as when John Hinckley attempted to kill President Ronald Reagan;[4] in mass and serial killings; and in especially bizarre homicides.[5] These crimes shock the community and create a tension between society's desire to punish aggravated wrongdoers and its intuitive sense that punishment, as distinguished from psychiatric treatment, of such persons may be inappropriate, because people who commit such awful acts probably are seriously mentally ill.

Second, the insanity defense suffers from the conceptual intermingling of psychiatry and the law, or of what one mental health professional has called the "war between lawyers and psychiatrists."[6] The two groups, it is said, "speak two different languages in regard to professional matters."[7] A legal defense based at its core on a medical conception, therefore, is inevitably difficult to administer.

---

[1] See generally Herbert Fingarette, The Meaning of Criminal Insanity (1972); Herbert Fingarette & Ann Fingarette Hasse, Mental Disabilities and Criminal Responsibility (1979); Abraham S. Goldstein, The Insanity Defense (1967); Hall at 449-528; Michael S. Moore, Law and Psychiatry: Rethinking the Relationship (1984); Norval Morris, Madness and the Criminal Law (1982).

[2] Perkins & Boyce at 950.

[3] See § 25.07[B][1], infra.

[4] United States v. Hinckley, 525 F.Supp. 1342 (D.D.C. 1981), aff'd, 672 F.2d 115 (D.C. Cir. 1982).

[5] Contrary to the common impression that the insanity defense is raised virtually exclusively in homicide cases, as many as 86 percent of insanity pleas occur in the prosecution of nonviolent offenses. National Mental Health Association, Myths & Realities: A Report of the National Commission on the Insanity Defense 20-21 (1983).

[6] Karl Menninger, The Crime of Punishment ch. 4 (1966). See § 25.07[B][3], infra.

[7] Id. at 96.

This chapter addresses the principal issues regarding the insanity defense in its various forms, and considers the underlying arguments regarding its abolition or reform.

§ 25.02 Insanity Defense: Procedural Context

[A]—Competency to Stand Trial[8]

[1]—General Rule

A person may not be tried, convicted, or sentenced for an offense if, during the criminal proceedings, she: (1) lacks the capacity to consult with her attorney "with a reasonable degree of rational understanding"; or (2) lacks "a rational as well as factual understanding of the proceedings" against her.[9] Incompetency may be the result of a physical handicap (e.g., an inability to speak) or temporary or permanent mental disability (e.g., mental illness, mental retardation, or amnesia).

The trial of an incompetent defendant may not proceed because, if it did, the outcome would be unreliable. An incompetent person is unable to provide needed assistance to her attorney, e.g., to discuss strategy, explain her side of the case, and provide the names of potential witnesses. She is also unable meaningfully to confront her accusers at trial, and rationally to testify in her own behalf. Moreover, two justifications for punishment of offenders, retribution and some aspects of specific deterrence, may be frustrated if an incompetent defendant does not understand the nature of the proceedings against her.[10]

[2]—Procedures for Determining Competency

The issue of competency to stand trial may be raised by the prosecutor, the defense, or by the trial court on its own motion,[11] and is independent of any insanity plea that the defendant might later raise.[12]

Typically, a defendant's competency to stand trial is treated as an issue of law to be determined by the trial judge, rather than a question of fact for jury consideration.[13] Whenever the issue of competency is raised, the defendant is

---

[8] See generally Bruce J. Winick, *Presumptions and Burdens of Proof in Determining Competency to Stand Trial: An Analysis of Medina v. California and the Supreme Court's New Due Process Methodology in Criminal Cases*, 47 U. Miami L. Rev. 817 (1993); Bruce J. Winick, *Restructuring Competency to Stand Trial*, 32 UCLA L. Rev. 921 (1985).

[9] *Dusky v. United States*, 362 U.S. 402, 402 (1960) (internal quotation marks omitted).

[10] American Law Institute, Comment to § 4.04, at 230 n.1. Assaultive retribution (see § 2.03[C][2], *supra*) is frustrated if the person against whom vengeance is sought cannot understand why society is bringing the proceedings against her. Specific deterrence by intimidation (see § 2.03[B][2], *supra*) will fail if the party is so irrational that she cannot see the cause-and-effect relation between her conduct and the pain that would be inflicted.

[11] The defendant's competency must be investigated, even over her objection, if the trial judge believes that she may be incompetent. *Pate v. Robinson*, 383 U.S. 375, 385-86 (1966).

[12] The insanity defense pertains to a defendant's mental condition at the time of the crime, rather than during the criminal proceedings.

[13] Model Penal Code § 4.06(1). Prior to the promulgation of the Code, most states allowed a jury trial on the issue. American Law Institute, Comment to § 4.06, at 241-42.

required to submit to a psychiatric examination during which time she may be committed to a mental facility. The report of the examination is filed with the court.

If the findings of the report are not disputed by the parties, the judge may act on it. If the findings are disputed, a hearing is held at which the parties may present evidence on the matter of competency. State laws vary on the burden of proof at the hearing: some states place the burden on the defendant to prove that she is not competent to stand trial; others require the prosecutor to demonstrate the defendant's competency; and still other jurisdictions allocate the burden of proof to the party who raised the competency issue.[14]

[3]—Effect of an Incompetency Finding

If it is determined that the defendant is incompetent to stand trial, criminal proceedings must be suspended until she is competent.[15] In some cases, particularly if the defendant's incompetency is based on a permanent condition, such as severe mental retardation, a criminal trial may never be held.

An incompetency ruling usually results in the defendant's commitment to a mental facility. The Supreme Court has held, however, that the due process clause of the United States Constitution is violated when a criminal defendant is committed indefinitely, solely on the basis of her incompetency to stand trial.[16] A person may not be restrained "more than the reasonable period of time necessary to determine whether there is a substantial probability that [s]he will attain . . . capacity in the foreseeable future."[17] If it is determined that this is likely, her continued commitment "must be justified by progress toward that goal." If not, the defendant must be released or committed pursuant to customary civil procedures.[18] Even with these protections, the length of pretrial commitment will frequently extend beyond the possible maximum sentence for the crime.[19]

[B]—Pre-Trial Assertion of the Insanity Plea[20]

Many states and federal rules require a defendant to provide the prosecutor with notice prior to trial of her intention to raise the defense of insanity.[21] She may also be required to provide the prosecutor with a list of witnesses who will testify on behalf of her insanity claim. The purpose of the rule is to provide the prosecutor adequate time to prepare a rebuttal to the defense at trial, and to allow the court an

---

[14] *Medina v. California*, 112 S.Ct. 2572, 2578 (1992).

[15] Model Penal Code § 4.06(2).

[16] *Jackson v. Indiana*, 406 U.S. 715, 731 (1972).

[17] *Id.* at 738.

[18] As a result, Model Penal Code § 4.06(2), which authorizes indefinite commitment without a civil hearing, is unconstitutional. American Law Institute, Explanatory Note to § 4.06, at 241; see *Foucha v. Louisiana*, 112 S.Ct. 1780, 1787 n.6 (1992).

[19] Winick, *Restructuring Competency to Stand Trial*, Note 8, *supra*, at 926.

[20] See generally David S. Cohn, *Offensive Use of the Insanity Defense: Imposing the Insanity Defense Over the Defendant's Objection*, 15 Hastings Const. L.Q. 295 (1988).

[21] E.g., Model Penal Code § 4.03(2); Fed. R. Crim. Proc. 12.2(a).

opportunity to require the defendant to submit to a psychiatric examination, as described in the next subsection.

Courts are divided on the question of whether a trial court may interpose an insanity plea over a competent defendant's objections. [22]

[C]—Court-Imposed Psychiatric Examinations

In most states, a trial court has statutory authority to order a defendant to submit to a pretrial psychiatric examination if she plans to raise an insanity defense. [23] Under such rules, the defendant is committed to a mental facility for a specified period of time, usually 60 to 90 days, during which period the examination is conducted. In some states, a psychiatrist retained by the defendant may witness or even participate in the examination process. [24] In order to avoid the possibility of violating the defendant's constitutional privilege against compelled self-incrimination at trial, some jurisdictions prohibit the introduction at trial of the defendant's statements to the government's psychiatrist, except on the matter of insanity. [25]

If the report supports the defendant's claim of insanity, the prosecutor will frequently dismiss the charges against the defendant, on the condition that the accused agrees to civil commitment to a mental facility.

[D]—Jury Verdicts

In most states, the factfinder may return one of three verdicts in a criminal trial in which the defendant pleads insanity: "not guilty" (NG); "not guilty by reason of insanity" (NGRI); or "guilty." [26]

A verdict of NGRI implies that the prosecution proved all of the elements of the crime, including the defendant's *mens rea*, beyond a reasonable doubt, that all of the defendant's non-insanity defenses were rejected, but that the accused was insane at the time of the crime.

Logically, a jury should consider a NG verdict before it considers a NGRI verdict. Indeed, an instruction to the jury to consider the insanity defense *before* it considers the accused's guilt or innocence may violate the due process clause. [27] Such an instruction is inappropriate because it permits the jury to reach a NGRI verdict, which usually results in civil commitment of the insanity acquittee, [28] without determining whether the prosecution has satisfied its constitutional responsibility of proving every element of the crime beyond a reasonable doubt.

---

[22] Compare *Whalem v. United States*, 346 F.2d 812, 818 (D.C. Cir. 1965) (permitting it) with *Frendak v. United States*, 408 A.2d 364, 367 (D.C. 1979) (prohibiting it).

[23] Model Penal Code § 4.05(1); Fed. R. Crim. Proc. 12.2(c).

[24] Model Penal Code § 4.05(1).

[25] Model Penal Code § 4.09; Fed. R. Crim. Proc. 12.2(c).

[26] In a few states the jury may return a fourth verdict, "guilty but mentally ill." See § 25.08, *infra.*

[27] *State v. McMullin*, 421 N.W.2d 517, 519-20 (Iowa 1988).

[28] See § 25.05, *infra.*

[E]—Bifurcated Trial

A few states[29] require, and most states permit, a trial court to bifurcate a criminal trial in which the insanity defense is raised. During the first phase of the trial, all aspects of the case except the defendant's sanity are litigated. At the completion of the first phase, the factfinder deliberates and returns a verdict of guilty or not guilty (NG). If the verdict is NG, the defendant is acquitted and the trial is over.

If the defendant is found guilty, the second phase is conducted. Here, the sole issue is the accused's claim of insanity. After introduction of the testimony, most notably expert psychiatric evidence,[30] the factfinder deliberates and returns a second verdict of guilty or not guilty by reason of insanity.[31]

The purpose of bifurcation is four-fold. First, time may be saved. If the jury returns a NG verdict in the first phase, time consuming psychiatric testimony is avoided. Second, confusion may be reduced. The jury can reach a verdict in the first phase without considering complicated psychiatric evidence.

Third, the bifurcated system may decrease the possibility of compromise verdicts. In a unitary system, the jury deliberates once. If it has doubts regarding the defendant's involvement in the crime, but is convinced that she is insane, the jury may improperly compromise and find her insane, rather than acquit her outright.

Finally, the bifurcated system protects a defendant's privilege against compelled self-incrimination. In a unitary system, she may be forced to testify about her mental condition at the time of the crime in order to support her insanity defense. In the process, she opens herself up to questioning on issues unrelated to her mental condition. In a bifurcated system she may remain silent during the first phase, and force the prosecutor to prove her participation in the crime by independent evidence.

The bifurcated system has not worked as expected. Evidence of mental illness sometimes is introduced at the first phase, in order to demonstrate that the defendant lacked the mental state required in the definition of the offense.[32] The same evidence, therefore, is introduced twice, although the testimony is phrased slightly differently at each stage. In the first phase, the psychiatrist may testify regarding whether, as the result of a mental disease or defect, the defendant was capable of forming or did form the requisite intent for the criminal offense, e.g., whether D intended to kill V. In the second phase, the same witness is questioned regarding whether the accused was insane at the time of the crime, e.g., whether D knew right

---

[29] E.g., Cal. Pen. Code § 1026(a) (1994); Wis. Stat. § 971.165 (1993).

[30] Although uncommon, the issue of insanity may be raised, and an insanity verdict justified, solely on the basis of nonexpert testimony of the defendant's mental condition. *Pacheco v. State*, 770 S.W.2d 834, 835 (Tex. Ct. App. 1989).

[31] As long as there is competent lay testimony in support of the verdict, a jury may disregard the opinions of mental health experts, even if they reach a unanimous conclusion regarding the defendant's sanity. *People v. Banks*, 308 N.E.2d 261, 267-68 (Ill. Ct. App. 1974); *State v. Sanders*, 587 P.2d 893, 899 (Kan. 1978).

[32] Not all states that use the bifurcated system permit the introduction of psychiatric evidence to disprove *mens rea* in the first phase. E.g., *Steele v. State*, 294 N.W.2d 2, 3 (Wis. 1980).

from wrong when she intentionally killed *V*. The effect is that time is wasted, not saved; and juries are apt to be confused, not benefited, by the system.

[F]—Burden of Proof

Insanity is an affirmative defense. The defendant has the initial burden of producing evidence regarding her mental condition in order to raise the insanity defense. Furthermore, the legislature may constitutionally require the defendant to persuade the jury that she was insane at the time of the crime.[33]

Until the 1980s, most states and the federal courts required the prosecutor to prove the defendant's sanity beyond a reasonable doubt.[34] However, as the result of the insanity acquittal of John Hinckley for the attempted murder of President Ronald Reagan,[35] a majority of states and the federal system now require the defendant to shoulder the burden of persuasion regarding her insanity claim.

Most states that require a defendant to prove her insanity provide that she must do so by a preponderance of the evidence. Since 1984, however, defendants in federal courts must prove insanity by clear and convincing evidence.[36] No state presently requires the defendant to prove her insanity beyond a reasonable doubt, although such a burden was upheld by the Supreme Court in 1952.[37]

§ 25.03   Rationale of the Insanity Defense[38]

[A]—Utilitarian Theory

To the extent that the insanity defense is limited to persons who suffer from serious cognitive or volitional disorders,[39] punishment of an insane person may be "pointless or counter-productive."[40] A person who does not know what she is doing or who cannot control her conduct cannot be deterred by the threat of criminal sanction.

---

[33] *Leland v. Oregon*, 343 U.S. 790, 799 (1952); *State v. Box*, 745 P.2d 23, 25-28 (Wash. 1987).

[34] 2 Robinson at 284-85; e.g., Model Penal Code § 4.03(1).

[35] See Note 4, *supra*.

[36] 18 U.S.C. § 17(b) (1988).

[37] *Leland v. Oregon*, 343 U.S. at 798-99; but see *Jones v. United States*, 463 U.S. 354, 368 n.17 (1983) (describing the law is somewhat more cautious terms: "[a] defendant [may] be required to prove his insanity *by a higher standard than a preponderance of the evidence*") (emphasis supplied).

[38] See generally R.B. Brandt, *The Insanity Defense and the Theory of Motivation*, 7 Law & Phil. 123 (1988); Stephen J. Morse, *Excusing the Crazy: The Insanity Defense Reconsidered*, 58 S. Cal. L. Rev. 777 (1985); Benjamin B. Sendor, *Crime as Communication: An Interpretive Theory of the Insanity Defense and Mental Elements of Crime*, 74 Geo. L.J. 1371 (1986).

[39] A *cognitive* disorder is one that undermines a person's ability to perceive reality accurately. A *volitional* disorder is one that undermines a person's ability to control her conduct.

[40] American Law Institute, Comment to § 4.01, at 168 n.12. This argument discounts the various counter-utilitarian effects of recognizing the defense. See § 25.07[B][2], *infra*.

Incapacitation of an insane person normally is socially desirable, but acquittal by reason of insanity need not, and ordinarily does not, result in her liberty, inasmuch as the acquittal may form the basis for civil commitment.[41] There is no need, therefore, to convict and stigmatize an insane person in order to ensure her segregation from society.

Similarly, rehabilitation is not furthered by convicting an insane person and sending her to prison. It is more rational to separate her from the penal system and treat her condition as a medical problem.

[B]—Retributive Theory

Although utilitarian arguments are sometimes posited in support of the insanity defense, the underlying rationale of the defense is primarily retributive in nature. As one scholar has observed, "[w]e . . . put up with the bother of the insanity defense because to exclude it is to deprive the criminal law of its chief paradigm of free will."[42]

The role that free will plays in the recognition of the defense can be appreciated by paying attention to our feelings and intuitions. First, we make judgments about people, based on their actions. We condemn people who commit crimes, and blame them for their wrongdoing. At the same time, we applaud courage; we praise those who perform acts of benevolence. These reactions, however, are unjustifiable unless we acknowledge the concept of free will—that people can and do choose to do good or to do evil, that human behavior is not scripted by other persons or by non-human forces.

Another human feeling cannot be denied: severely mentally ill people do not seem to be like the rest of us. They seem odd or "crazy." We pity them (sometimes, too, we fear them), because they lack the capacity to do what other humans are able to do: to act rationally or to control their behavior. Ordinarily, we do not blame the insane person for her wrongdoing or, if we do, we sense that such negative expressions are wrong. To blame the insane person for her acts is much like blaming a sick person for sneezing or an infant for dropping her glass of milk.

Our impressions of the mentally diseased actor reinforce our basic belief in human free will. The exception of the insane person serves as proof of the general rule. Her oddness validates our normality; her inability to reason and act freely reinforces the fact that the rest of us make rational choices. The fact that we do not blame the insane person serves to justify the fact that we blame the sane wrongdoer. The insanity defense, therefore, serves as a distinguishing point between the bad and the mad, between evil and sickness, between those who possess free choice and those whose free choice is seriously undermined.

As one scholar has demonstrated,[43] we can place these feelings into a rational set of retributivist premises: just punishment is dependent on moral desert; moral

---

[41] See § 25.05, *infra.*

[42] Packer at 132.

[43] Morse, Note 38, *supra,* at 783.

desert is dependent on moral responsibility for one's actions; and moral responsibility for one's actions is dependent on the essential attributes of personhood, namely rationality and self-control. Insane people, however, lack essential attributes of personhood. Therefore, they are "no more the proper subjects of moral evaluation than are young infants, animals, or even stones."[44] Or, as one court put it:

> To punish a man who lacks the power to reason is as undignified and unworthy as punishing an inanimate object or an animal. A man who cannot reason cannot be subject to blame. Our collective conscience does not allow punishment where it cannot impose blame.[45]

§ 25.04　Definitions of "Insanity"[46]

[A]—Historical Overview

Generally speaking, five tests of insanity, discussed fully in subsection [C], *infra*, have gained support in the United States: the *M'Naghten*[47] rule; the "irresistible impulse" test; the "product" or *Durham*[48] standard; the American Law Institute's (ALI) Model Penal Code definition; and the federal statutory definition of insanity.

The first insanity test of modern relevance was enunciated by the English House of Lords in the *M'Naghten* case. It quickly became the generally accepted standard in this country. Criticism of the *M'Naghten* rule, however, was immediate and has been unending. As a result of the perceived narrowness of the test, a few courts expanded the standard of insanity, by coupling the *M'Naghten* rule with the irresistible impulse test.

In 1954, the influential United States Court of Appeals for the District of Columbia promulgated the *Durham* or "product" rule of insanity. Based on an 1870 New Hampshire case,[49] the *Durham* test was exceedingly broad, and was intended

---

[44] Michael S. Moore, *Causation and the Excuses*, 73 Cal. L. Rev. 1091, 1137 (1985).

[45] *Holloway v. United States*, 148 F.2d 665, 666-67 (D.C. Cir. 1945).

[46] See generally Jodie English, *The Light Between Twilight and Dusk: Federal Criminal Law and the Volitional Insanity Defense*, 40 Hastings L.J. 1 (1988); Stephen J. Morse, *Crazy Behavior, Morals, and Science: An Analysis of Mental Health Law*, 51 S. Cal. L. Rev. 527 (1978); see also the sources in Note 1, *supra*.

For discussion of jury behavior in insanity trials, see Norman J. Finkel & Sharon F. Handel, *How Jurors Construe "Insanity"*, 13 Law & Hum. Behav. 41 (1989); James R.P. Ogloff, *A Comparison of the Insanity Defense Standards on Juror Decision Making*, 15 Law & Hum. Behav. 509 (1991); Michael L. Perlin, *Psychodynamics and the Insanity Defense: "Ordinary Common Sense" and Heuristic Reasoning*, 69 Neb. L. Rev. 3 (1990); Caton Roberts & Stephen Golding, *The Social Construction of Criminal Responsibility and Insanity*, 15 Law & Hum. Behav. 349 (1991); Caton Roberts, Stephen Golding, & Frank Fincham, *Implicit Theories of Criminal Responsibility*, 11 Law & Hum. Behav. 207 (1987).

[47] *M'Naghten's Case*, 10 Cl. & F. 200, 8 Eng. Rep. 718 (1843).

[48] *Durham v. United States*, 214 F.2d 862 (D.C. Cir. 1954), *overruled* by *United States v. Brawner*, 471 F.2d 969 (D.C. Cir. 1972).

[49] *State v. Pike*, 49 N.H. 399 (1870).

to give mental health professionals considerable freedom in their testimony. As a consequence, *Durham* represented a dramatic departure in the jurisprudence of insanity. No other court, however, adopted the standard.

The *Durham* court encountered various problems with the product rule, which it struggled to resolve. In 1972, however, it abandoned the rule and substituted for it a version of the ALI insanity defense, originally promulgated by the Institute in 1962. The ALI test quickly attracted support from courts and legislatures. In less than two decades, it was adopted by ten of the eleven federal circuit courts and by approximately one-half of the states. [50]

The trend in favor of the ALI test seemed unstoppable until the attempted assassination of President Ronald Reagan. Public fury following John Hinckley's acquittal on the ground of insanity [51] resulted in pressure to abolish the defense. [52] Although the abolitionist movement generally failed, it had a significant effect on the law. Courts and legislatures began to reconsider their support for the comparatively broad ALI rule. For example, California, which originally adopted the *M'Naghten* test, and then shifted to the ALI standard, reversed itself again and returned to *M'Naghten*. [53] Congress, too, enacted a *M'Naghten*-like definition of insanity. At the same time, a few states abolished the insanity defense. [54]

The long-term future of the insanity defense cannot be predicted with confidence. However, in the short-term, most states appear willing to apply an insanity standard—*M'Naghten*—that was developed a century and a half ago, at a time when medical knowledge of the workings of the mind was exceedingly limited.

[B]—"Mental Disease or Defect"

[1]—In General

The terms "mental illness," "mental disorder," and "mental disease or defect," on the one hand, and "insanity," on the other hand, are not synonymous. The first set of terms is used by the mental health community; the word "insanity" is a legal term. Thus, it is incorrect to say that "mental illness" is a criminal defense; "insanity" is the excusing defense.

"Mental illness" is a more encompassing term than "insanity." A person can be mentally ill without being insane; insanity, however, presupposes a mental disease or defect.

---

[50] American Law Institute, Comment to § 4.01, at 175-76.

[51] See Note 4, *supra*.

[52] For example, an Associated Press-National Broadcasting Company poll found that 69 percent of the respondents favored abolition of the insanity defense. Minneapolis Tribune, Oct. 25, 1981, at 9a. See generally Valerie P. Hans, *An Analysis of Public Attitudes Toward the Insanity Defense*, 24 Criminology 393 (1986).

[53] Cal. Pen. Code § 25(b) (1988). The saga of California's insanity law, culminating in the passage of a statewide initiative designed to eliminate the ALI standard, is chronicled in *People v. Skinner*, 704 P.2d 752 (Cal. 1985).

[54] See § 25.07[C][1], *infra*.

[2]—Medical Definition of "Mental Disorder"

The American Psychiatric Association's manual of mental disorders concedes that "no definition adequately specifies precise boundaries for the concept of 'mental disorder.' "[55] A mental disorder is not a discrete entity. There are no sharp boundaries between "mental disorder" and "no mental disorder." And, as the manual admits, "[a] compelling literature documents that there is much 'physical' in 'mental' disorders and much 'mental' in 'physical' disorders."[56] That being said, the manual defines a "mental disorder" as a:

> clinically significant behavioral or psychological syndrome or pattern that occurs in an individual and that is associated with present distress (e.g., a painful symptom) or disability (i.e., impairment in one or more important areas of functioning) or with a significantly increased risk of suffering death, pain, or disability, or an important loss of freedom. In addition, this syndrome or pattern must not be merely an expectable and culturally sanctioned response to a particular event.[57]

Notice that this conceptualization of the term "mental disorder" treats mental illness in an atheoretical manner: whereas symptoms may point to the existence of a *physical* disease, a symptom or a cluster of symptoms *is* a mental disorder. Also, unlike physical disorders, the concept of "mental disorder" is culture-bound, i.e., one cannot identify a cluster of symptoms as a disorder without also considering the society in which the behavior pattern arises.

[3]—Legal Definition of "Mental Disease or Defect"

All of the insanity tests presuppose that the actor suffers from a "mental disease or defect" or "disease of the mind," yet courts rarely define the terms.[58] The Model Penal Code insanity defense, as well, provides no general definition of the critical phrase, preferring instead to leave the issue "open to accommodate developing medical understanding."[59]

Only the now-defunct *Durham* test of insanity included a definition of the term: a mental disease or defect is "any abnormal condition of the mind which substantially affects mental or emotional processes and substantially impairs behavior controls."[60] Under *Durham*, a "disease" is a condition capable of improving or deteriorating; a "defect" is a condition incapable of changing, which may be congenital (e.g., retardation), the result of injury to the brain, or the residual effect of a physical or mental illness.[61]

---

[55] American Psychiatric Association, Diagnostic and Statistical Manual of Mental Disorders xxi (4th. ed. 1994).

[56] *Id.*

[57] *Id.*

[58] See Goldstein, Note 1, *supra*, at 47-48.

[59] American Law Institute, Explanatory Note to § 4.01, at 164.

[60] *McDonald v. United States*, 312 F.2d 847, 851 (D.C. Cir. 1962).

[61] *Durham v. United States*, 214 F.2d at 875.

[C]—The Tests

[1]—*M'Naghten* Test[62]

[a]—Rule

The *M'Naghten* rule focuses exclusively on cognitive disability. According to *M'Naghten*, a person is insane if, at the time of her act, she was laboring under such a defect of reason, arising from a disease of the mind, that she: (1) did not know the nature and quality of the act that she was doing; or (2) if she did know it, she did not know that what she was doing was wrong, i.e., the accused at the time of doing the act did not know the difference between right and wrong.

Various features of the test should be observed. First, the word "know" used in both prongs of the test may be defined narrowly or broadly. Some courts apply the word narrowly: a person may be found sane if she can describe what she is doing ("I was strangling her") and can acknowledge the forbidden nature of her conduct ("I knew I was doing something wrong"). This may be referred to as "formal cognitive knowledge." Some courts, however, require a deeper meaning of "knowledge" ("affective knowledge"), which is absent unless the actor can evaluate her conduct in terms of its impact on others and appreciate the total setting in which she acts.

Second, the phrase "nature and quality of the act" is, potentially, an exceedingly narrow concept. If *D* squeezes *V*'s neck, believing that she is squeezing a lemon, she does not know the nature and quality of her act. However, if she knows that she is squeezing the neck of a human being, but does not appreciate that her act is causing pain, she may be sane insofar as the first prong of *M'Naghten* is concerned, at least in jurisdictions that apply a narrow meaning of the word "knowledge." Frequently, this prong is omitted from jury instructions, because anyone who does not know what she is doing (e.g., cannot distinguish between a neck and a lemon) will also "fail" the right-and-wrong test, the second prong of the insanity definition.

Third, it is unclear whether the word "wrong" in the right-and-wrong prong refers to legal or moral wrongdoing. There is language in *M'Naghten* to support either interpretation. Lord Tindal, for example, stated early in the opinion that M'Naghten could be punished if he "knew . . . that he was acting contrary to law; by which expression we . . . mean the law of the land." Subsequently, however, he stated that if the jury were instructed "exclusively with reference to the law of the land it might tend to confound the jury by inducing them to believe that an actual knowledge of the law was essential." Rather, Lord Tindal stated, the question is whether M'Naghten knew that his "act was one which he ought not to do, and if the act was at the same time contrary to the law of the land, he is punishable."

The distinction between legal and moral right-and-wrong will rarely affect the outcome of a trial. However, suppose that *D*, due to mental illness, believes that

---

[62] *M'Naghten's Case*, 10 Cl. & F. 200, 8 Eng. Rep. 718 (1843). The spelling of the defendant's name is almost as controversial as the test that is named after him. Four variations in spelling are found in the literature.

God has instructed her to kill *V*, an act that *D* knows violates the secular law. In view of God's edict, however, *D* believes that it is morally right to kill *V*. On these facts, *D* is sane if the right-and-wrong test is based on awareness of the illegality of an act; she should be found not guilty by reason of insanity, however, if *M'Naghten* requires knowledge of the immorality of her actions.

England has removed this ambiguity in the test by declaring that it refers to awareness that an act is legally wrong.[63] American law is sharply divided.[64] In jurisdictions that apply a "moral right-and-wrong" standard, however, the issue is not whether the defendant personally and subjectively believed that her conduct was morally proper; the question is whether she knowingly violated *societal* standards of morality.[65] Therefore, *D* is sane under this prong of *M'Naghten* if she commits an offense that she knows society will condemn, but which she is convinced is morally proper.

Fourth, a few *M'Naghten* jurisdictions that apply the "moral right-and-wrong" standard, also apply the so-called "deific decree" doctrine. Under this principle, a person who, as the result of a mental disorder, believes that she is acting under the direct command of God, is deemed legally insane. Sometimes this doctrine is treated as an *exception* to the general rule, i.e., it applies when "a party performs a criminal act, knowing it is morally and legally wrong, but believing, because of a mental defect, that the act is ordained by God."[66] However, other courts believe that the doctrine "is not so much an exception to the right-wrong test measured by the existing societal standards of morality as it is an integral factor in assessing a person's cognitive ability to distinguish right from wrong with respect to the act charged."[67] That is, a person who believes that God has decreed her act is likely to believe that society would approve of her conduct.

[b]—Criticisms of the Rule

The *M'Naghten* rule has been subjected to severe criticism. First, the test is considered "grossly unrealistic" because, by its terms, it does not recognize degrees of incapacity. A person must wholly lack cognition. Yet, "our mental institutions, as any qualified psychiatrist will attest, are filled with people who *to some extent* can differentiate between right and wrong,"[68] or who can tell the difference between a human neck and a lemon, but who still are out of touch with reality to a significant degree. Because of the apparent absolutism of the test, some

---

[63] *R. v. Windle*, [1952] 2 All E.R. 1, 2.

[64] See *People v. Serravo*, 823 P.2d 128 (Colo 1992) (noting the division of the courts, and concluding that "moral" right-and-wrong is the correct standard in that state).

[65] *Id.* at 137; *People v. Stress*, 252 Cal.Rptr. 913, 923 (Ct. App. 1988).

[66] *State v. Crenshaw*, 659 P.2d 488, 494 (Wash. 1983).

[67] *People v. Serravo*, 823 P.2d at 139; see also *State v. Potter*, 842 P.2d 481, 486-89 (Wash. Ct. App. 1992) (concluding that notwithstanding language in prior Washington cases treating the deific-decree doctrine as an "exception," the doctrine is instead an "elaboration[] of the second prong of the insanity rule").

[68] *United States v. Freeman*, 357 F.2d 606, 618 (D.C. Cir. 1966) (emphasis supplied).

psychiatrists are tempted to shape their testimony to fit the definition of insanity, although few of them believe that incapacity is ever complete.

Second, some critics believe that *M'Naghten* places "unrealistically tight shackles"[69] upon expert psychiatric testimony. If a trial court refuses to permit a psychiatrist to testify on any matter that falls outside the narrow confines of the test, the jury is unable to learn the full background of the defendant's state of mind.

Third, the test is outdated in that it disregards mental illnesses that affect *volition*. By focusing solely on cognitive disability, the rule disregards the possibility that a person may be able to distinguish good from evil, and yet be unable to control her behavior.

Finally, closely tied to the latter point, is the suggestion that the test is too narrow in terms of penological theory. If a person knows what she is doing but cannot control her conduct, she is undeterrable; therefore, punishment is inefficacious. Moreover, it is morally obtuse to punish a person who, due to mental illness, lacks sufficient free-will to control her conduct.

[2]—"Irresistible Impulse" Test

[a]—Rule

In order to broaden the scope of *M'Naghten*, some states (and, for a while, federal courts) formulated a third prong to the insanity test, which encompasses mental illnesses affecting volitional capacity. The latter prong has come to be known as the "irresistible impulse" test.

The precise language of the test varies by jurisdiction. Generally speaking, a person is insane if, at the time of the offense: (1) she "acted from an irresistible and uncontrollable impulse";[70] (2) she "lost the *power to choose* between the right and wrong, and to avoid doing the act in question, as that [her] free agency was at the time destroyed";[71] or (3) the "[defendant's] will . . . has been otherwise than voluntarily so completely destroyed that [her] actions are not subject to it, but are beyond [her] control."[72]

[b]—Criticisms of the Rule

Some objections to this rule parallel criticism of *M'Naghten*: the test is psychologically naive by requiring total incapacity (i.e., an *irresistible* impulse), and by excluding from its boundaries behavior that is the result of extended internal conflict (i.e., is "non-impulsive"). These criticisms, although valid in theory, are not ordinarily relevant in practice. The label "irresistible impulse" has proven to be a misnomer.[73] Most courts that apply the test do not exclude evidence that the defendant planned her behavior, as long as she lacked the ability to control her conduct, and most courts do not require proof of total volitional incapacity.

---

[69] *Id.* at 619.

[70] *Commonwealth v. Rogers*, 48 Mass. 500, 502 (1844).

[71] *Parsons v. State*, 2 So. 854, 866 (Ala. 1887).

[72] *Davis v. United States*, 165 U.S. 373, 378 (1897).

[73] Goldstein, Note 1, *supra*, at 67-79.

The test is also criticized on the ground that "a majority of psychiatrists now believe that they do not possess sufficient accurate scientific bases for measuring a person's capacity for self-control or for calibrating the impairment of that capacity."[74] According to the American Psychiatric Association, "[t]he line between an irresistible impulse and an impulse not resisted is probably no sharper than between twilight and dusk."[75]

[3]—American Law Institute (Model Penal Code) Test

[a]—Rule

The Model Penal Code provides that a person is not responsible for her criminal conduct if, at the time of the conduct, as the result of a mental disease or defect, she lacked substantial capacity to: (1) appreciate the "criminality" (or, in the alternative, at the option of the legislature adopting the Code, the "wrongfulness") of her conduct; or (2) to conform her conduct to the requirements of the law.[76] This test, described by most courts as the "American Law Institute" (ALI) test, is a revised version of the *M'Naghten* and irresistible-impulse tests. It consists of the second, and more significant, cognitive prong of the former test, and restates the volitional aspects of the latter standard.

Notice the differences between the ALI test and its antecedents. First, it uses the term "appreciate" rather than "know," in order to avoid a narrow interpretation of the *M'Naghten*-like cognitive prong. Second, the test avoids the word "impulse," in order to sidestep the potential pitfalls arising from using that word. Most significantly, both prongs of the test are modified by the words "lacks substantial capacity." This avoids the criticism that the earlier tests unrealistically required total incapacity.

[b]—Criticisms of the Rule

The ALI test has received little criticism independent of the objections raised regarding the earlier tests on which it is founded. Those who favor a broader test and who believe that psychiatric knowledge is unduly restricted in the courtroom have criticized the ALI definition because they believe that it is based on an outdated psychological assumption that the human mind is divisible into "volitional" and "cognitive" functions. In contrast, persons who favor a narrow definition of insanity are critical of the fact that the ALI standard includes a volitional prong, even though psychiatrists now question their ability to provide reliable data on the subject.

---

[74] *United States v. Lyons*, 731 F.2d 243, 248 (5th Cir. 1984).

[75] American Psychiatric Association, Statement on the Insanity Defense 11 (December, 1982).

[76] Model Penal Code § 4.01(1).

[4]—The Product (*Durham*) Test

[a]—Rule

The product (or *Durham*) test of insanity provides that a person is excused if her unlawful act was the product of a mental disease or defect.[77] Pursuant to this rule, the jury must determine whether the defendant was suffering from a mental disease or defect at the time of the offense and, if she was, whether the criminal conduct would have occurred but for the condition. Thus, the causal link between the act and her mental illness is the key.

[b]—Criticisms of the Rule

An early criticism of *Durham* was that the test failed to define the critical phrase "mental disease or defect." As such, it left the matter solely in the hands of mental health professionals. If a psychiatrist testified that the condition that caused the defendant's behavior was a mental disease, the accused was entitled to be acquitted; if the expert stated that the same condition fell outside the parameters of any recognized disease model, the defendant lost her insanity claim. Yet, the causal connection between the condition and the conduct was the same in both circumstances. After an embarrassing situation, in which a psychiatrist "flip-flopped" on whether a particular condition was a mental illness,[78] the Court of Appeals for the District of Columbia provided a working definition, set out elsewhere in this Chapter.[79]

Second, some lawyers criticized the test because they believed it allowed psychiatrists to usurp the jury's authority. As the *Durham* rule was applied, psychiatrists were called by the defense and the prosecution; the competing psychiatrists would testify that *D* suffered (or did not suffer) from condition X, that condition X was (or was not) a mental disease or defect, and that *D* would not (or would) have committed the crime but for condition X. Essentially, the expert's testimony "proved" that *D* was (or was not) insane. There was nothing for the jury to do other than to decide which experts to believe. The jury's moral judgment regarding *D*'s conduct was suppressed.[80]

A third criticism of *Durham* was that it excluded from criminal responsibility deterrable and morally blameworthy actors. For example, assume that *D* suffers from a delusion (brought on by a mental disease) that *X*, *V*'s husband, will marry her if *V* is dead. As a result, *D* kills *V*. Pursuant to the product rule, *D* is insane: but for her delusion, she would not have killed *V*.

---

[77] *Durham v. United States*, 214 F.2d 862, 874-75 (D.C. Cir. 1954), *overruled by United States v. Brawner*, 471 F.2d 969 (D.C. Cir. 1972); *State v. Abbott*, 503 A.2d 791, 794 (N.H. 1985) (quoting *State v. Pike*, 49 N.H. 399, 438 (1870)) ("whether an individual had a mental disease, and whether an act was the product of that disease").

[78] *In re Rosenfield*, 157 F. Supp. 18 (D.D.C. 1957) (a psychiatrist testified on Friday that *D*'s condition was not a mental disease; over the weekend, as the result of an administrative change in the witness's hospital policy, the condition was reclassified as a mental disease).

[79] See § 25.04[B][3], *supra*.

[80] The court later acknowledged this problem and set limits on psychiatric testimony, by preventing experts from testifying directly in terms of "products," "results" or "causes." *Washington v. United States*, 390 F.2d 444, 455-56 (D.C. Cir. 1967).

But, *D*'s acquittal on these facts is indefensible on utilitarian grounds. *D* knew what she was doing, knew that her conduct was legally and morally wrong, and, presumably, could have controlled her conduct. Therefore, *D* was deterrable.

From a retributive perspective, *D* may also be blamed for her conduct. At least under the free-choice theory of excuses,[81] a person who appreciates the illegality or immorality of her conduct, and is able to control her behavior, is a moral agent who may justifiably be held accountable for her actions.

[5]—Federal Test

The United States Congress enacted a statutory definition of insanity in 1984. Under the law, a person is excused if she proves by clear and convincing evidence that, at the time of the offense, as the result of a severe mental disease or defect, she was unable to appreciate: (1) the nature and quality of her conduct; or (2) the wrongfulness of her conduct.[82]

Various features of the federal test are noteworthy. First, unlike prior standards, the federal law requires proof that the actor suffers from a "severe" mental disease or defect. However, this word may be superfluous, since any mental disease or defect that satisfies either of the two prongs of the test is apt to be severe. Second, like *M'Naghten*, but unlike the ALI standard, cognitive incapacity must be total.

One feature of the federal rule is patterned on the ALI test: the word "appreciate," rather than "know," modifies both prongs of the defense. This should render the test broader than *M'Naghten* in this regard.

§ 25.05   Effect of an Insanity Acquittal

[A]—General Comments

Contrary to the common conception, a person found not guilty by reason of insanity (NGRI) is rarely released upon acquittal.[83] One scholar has gone so far as to state that the defense of insanity is not an excuse in the ordinary sense, but is actually a direction to punish the insane person in a noncriminal context.[84]

Although the latter use of the word "punish" conflicts with its ordinary criminal law meaning,[85] the statement is correct to the extent that a person found NGRI is almost always involuntarily committed to a mental facility for an indefinite period of time. In practice, an insanity-acquittee may remain in a mental hospital for a

---

[81] See § 17.03, *supra*.

[82] 18 U.S.C. § 17(a) (1988).

[83] National Mental Health Association, Note 5, *supra*, at 24-25. Moreover, a defendant who pleads insanity in a federal court is not entitled to an instruction informing the jury of the procedural consequences of a NGRI verdict. *Shannon v. United States*, 114 S.Ct. 2419, 2424 (1994).

[84] Packer at 134; see also Joseph Goldstein & Jay Katz, *Abolish the "Insanity Defense" -Why Not?* 72 Yale L.J. 853, 868 (1963) ("[T]he insanity defense is not a defense, it is a device for triggering indeterminate restraint.").

[85] See § 2.02, *supra*.

longer period of time than she would have served in a prison, had she been convicted of the crime.

[B]—Commitment Procedures

[1]—Automatic Commitment

In many states, a person found NGRI is automatically committed to a mental facility on the basis of the verdict. [86] Under automatic-commitment laws, the NGRI-acquittee is not entitled to a hearing to determine whether she continues to suffer from a mental illness, [87] or to determine whether her institutionalization is necessary for her protection or for that of society.

In this respect, NGRI-acquittees are provided fewer procedural rights than are granted to people who may be subjected to civil commitment. The Supreme Court has held that a person may not be committed to a mental institution in a civil proceeding unless the state proves by clear and convincing evidence that she is mentally ill and that she is dangerous to herself or others. [88] In contrast, with NGRI-acquittees in automatic-commitment jurisdictions, the insanity verdict at the criminal trial is considered a sufficiently reliable finding of current mental illness and dangerousness to dispense with a hearing. [89]

[2]—Discretionary Commitment

In many states and in the federal courts, commitment of an insanity-acquittee is not automatic. Typically, however, the trial judge has authority to require a person found NGRI to be detained temporarily in a mental facility for observation and examination, in order to determine whether she should be committed indefinitely.

Under federal law, a commitment hearing must be held within 40 days of an NGRI verdict, during which time the acquittee is detained in a mental hospital. [90] If the offense for which the defendant was acquitted involved bodily injury to another, serious damage to property, or a substantial risk to either, she must prove by clear and convincing evidence that she is entitled to release, i.e., that "release would not create a substantial risk of bodily injury to another person or serious damage of property of another due to a present mental disease or defect." [91] With less serious crimes, she must meet the same standard by a preponderance of the evidence.

---

[86] E.g., Model Penal Code § 4.08(1).

[87] It should be remembered that a finding of insanity only demonstrates that the defendant was mentally ill *at the time of the crime.*

[88] *Addington v. Texas,* 441 U.S. 418, 426-27 (1979).

[89] *Jones v. United States,* 463 U.S. 354, 363-64 (1983).

[90] 18 U.S.C. § 4243(c) (1988).

[91] 18 U.S.C. § 4243(d) (1988).

[C]—Release

[1]—Criteria for Release

An insanity-acquittee may be detained as long as she is *both* mentally ill and dangerous to herself or others. Put differently, she is constitutionally entitled to release from a mental facility if she is no longer mentally ill (even if she remains dangerous to herself or others) or is no longer dangerous (even if she continues to suffer from a mental illness).[92] State laws based on the Model Penal Code,[93] which authorizes the continued commitment of dangerous persons who are *not* mentally ill, violate the due process clause of the United States Constitution.[94]

[2]—Length of Confinement

An insanity-acquittee's commitment is of an indeterminate length, i.e., until she meets the criteria for release. She is not entitled to be released merely because she has been institutionalized for a period of time longer than she could have been imprisoned had she been convicted of the offense that triggered her commitment.[95] The concept of proportionality between a criminal offense and the length of detention is irrelevant in such circumstances, because the purpose of her confinement is "treatment," rather than "punishment."

[3]—Release Procedures

Release procedures vary by jurisdiction.[96] In many states, the court that ordered the insanity-acquittee's commitment retains jurisdiction over her. She or the mental facility may petition the court to release her based on the state's criteria for release.[97] In most jurisdictions, the acquittee may not petition for release for a specified period of time, ranging from 90 days to one year after initial commitment.[98] Thereafter, subsequent petitions for release may be limited to stated time intervals.

The institutionalized party is entitled to a hearing on her petition for release. In nearly all states, the burden of proof is placed on the committed party to demonstrate that she is either no longer mentally ill or dangerous. The burden of proof varies from a preponderance of the evidence to clear and convincing evidence.

§ 25.06   Execution of the Mentally Incompetent

A person who is sane at the time of the crime and competent to stand trial may be sentenced to death for murder. The common law rule, however, is that she may not be executed if she becomes insane while awaiting execution.

---

[92] *Foucha v. Louisiana*, 112 S.Ct. 1780, 1786-87 (1992).

[93] Model Penal Code § 4.08.

[94] See *Foucha v. Louisiana*, 112 S.Ct. at 1787 n.6.

[95] *Jones v. United States*, 463 U.S. at 370.

[96] See generally American Law Institute, Comment to § 4.08, at 262-65.

[97] Model Penal Code § 4.08(2)-(3).

[98] Under the Model Code, a six month waiting period is required before a person may petition for release. Model Penal Code § 4.08(5).

This rule is followed in every state that permits executions. Various reasons have been provided for the rule: (1) it offends humanity to execute the insane; (2) execution of an incompetent person does not provide an example to others; (3) an execution in such circumstances is religiously uncharitable; and (4) there is no purpose in punishing the insane ("madness is its own punishment").[99]

The execution of the presently insane also constitutes cruel and unusual punishment, in violation of the Eighth Amendment of the United States Constitution.[100] The Supreme Court has not determined what standard of insanity applies to the determination of incompetency for purposes of execution. However, apparently, at a minimum, "the Eighth Amendment forbids the execution . . . of those who are unaware of the punishment they are about to suffer and why they are to suffer it."[101] Some states,[102] along with Blackstone[103] and the American Bar Association,[104] are of the view that a defendant may also not be executed if she is unable to assist in her own defense, i.e., if she cannot convey to her attorney facts that might exist that would make the death penalty unjust or unlawful.

§ 25.07 Abolition of the Insanity Defense[105]

[A]—Introductory Comments

Opponents of the insanity defense (abolitionists, for short) come from different ideological and philosophical vantage points. Some abolitionists are political "hawks" who favor abolition of the defense as part of a broader effort to reduce the number of excuse defenses recognized in the criminal law. In contrast, some abolitionists are "doves" who would like to expand the law of excuses, but for reasons of equity do not want to treat mentally ill people any differently than other morally blameless actors who currently are punished for their wrongdoing. Public opinion surveys also suggest that opposition to the insanity defense is founded on both retributive and utilitarian grounds.[106]

---

[99] See *Ford v. Wainwright*, 477 U.S. 399, 407-08 (1986).

[100] *Id.* at 410.

[101] *Id.* at 422 (Powell, J., concurring).

[102] E.g., *Singleton v. State*, 437 S.E.2d 53, 55-58 (S.C. 1993).

[103] 4 Blackstone at *389.

[104] ABA Criminal Justice Mental Health Standards 7-5.6(b) (1986).

[105] See generally Morris, Note 1, *supra*; National Mental Health Association, Note 5, *supra*; Goldstein & Katz, Note 84, *supra*; Norval Morris, *The Criminal Responsibility of the Mentally Ill*, 33 Syracuse L. Rev. 477 (1982); Morse, Note 38, *supra*; Stephen J. Morse, *Justice, Mercy, and Craziness*, 36 Stan. L. Rev. 1485 (1984); Michael L. Perlin, *Unpacking the Myths: The Symbolism Mythology of Insanity Defense Jurisprudence*, 40 Case West. Res. L. Rev. 599 (1990); Jonas Robitscher & Andrew Ky Haynes, *In Defense of the Insanity Defense*, 31 Emory L.J. 9 (1982); Joseph H. Rodriguez, Laura M. LeWinn, & Michael S. Perlin, *The Insanity Defense Under Siege: Legislative Assaults and Legal Rejoinders*, 14 Rutgers L.J. 397 (1983); Ernest van den Haag, *The Insanity Defense*, Criminal Justice Ethics, Winter-Spring 1984, at 3.

[106] See Hans, Note 52, *supra*.

[B]—Abolitionist Arguments

[1]—Abuse

Abolitionists assert that the insanity defense results in abuse of the criminal justice system. They claim that the defense is frequently asserted and too often successful. [107] Implicit in this argument is that insanity claims, including successful ones, are often fraudulent in nature. As a result, wrongdoers "walk free" because they are able to persuade psychiatrists and gullible juries of their nonexistent madness.

According to the American Law Institute, however, there is little empirical support for this proposition. [108] According to one team of commentators, "[a]ll empirical analyses . . . have been consistent: the public, legal profession and . . . legislators 'dramatically' and 'grossly' overestimate both the frequency and the success rate of the insanity plea." [109]

Although statistics regarding use of the insanity plea are sketchy, it appears that the defense is rarely invoked; when it is invoked, there is often agreement among the experts that the defendant suffers from a mental illness; and the success rate for the insanity plea, although variable, is usually extremely low. [110] For example, in one reported New Jersey study, NGRI verdicts were secured in only 1/20 of 1 percent of all cases handled by the Office of Public Defenders. [111] As a consequence of jury antipathy to insanity claims, many criminal defense lawyers treat the defense as a "plea of last resort."

[2]—Counter-Deterrence

Although the insanity defense may serve a valid utilitarian purpose with genuinely insane people, [112] abolitionists fear that the defense may have a socially negative impact on those who are *not* mentally ill, and on those whose illnesses are not severe enough to qualify for acquittal. They reason that awareness by such people that the law recognizes an insanity defense may reduce the deterrent effect of the criminal sanction. A would-be wrongdoer may believe, although perhaps inaccurately, that if she is caught for her crime she will be able to avoid conviction or commitment by raising the insanity defense.

Defenders of the insanity plea contend that even if this argument is correct—although there is no empirical evidence to support it—the solution is not to abolish the defense, but instead is to educate the public regarding the true effect of the insanity defense (e.g., that long-term civil commitment usually follows the rare acquittal).

---

[107] See National Mental Health Association, Note 5, *supra*, at 14-15. A national survey in 1981 found that 87 percent of the public believed that the defense was over-used and too often successful. Minneapolis Tribune, Oct. 25, 1981, at 9a.

[108] American Law Institute, Comment to § 4.01, at 182.

[109] Rodriguez, LeWinn, & Perlin, Note 105, *supra*, at 401 (footnotes omitted).

[110] See Perlin, Note 105, *supra*, at 648-49, 651-53.

[111] National Mental Health Association, Note 5, *supra*, at 15.

[112] See § 25.03[A], *supra*.

[3]—Conflict of Perspectives

Some abolitionists contend that the criminal law and psychiatry cannot mix any more than oil and water does. They point out that the criminal law and psychiatry look at human conduct in contradictory fashion. On the one hand, criminal law doctrine is premised on the belief that humans possess free will; on the other hand, psychiatrists frequently contend that all conduct is the result of causes beyond human control. From the point of view of psychiatry, "the sick and the wicked [are] . . . equally free of blame";[113] the distinction that the criminal law seeks to draw between the mad and the bad, therefore, is an illusion.

Psychiatrist Karl Menninger agrees with the claim that lawyers and psychiatrists have conflicting perspectives on human conduct. He states that "[t]he Law—with a capital L—has no real relation to the affairs of men." He observes disparagingly that lawyers are interested in placing or rebutting "blame," and that "the word *justice*, which is so dear to lawyers, is one which the doctor *qua* scientist simply does not use or readily understand."[114]

The conflict-of-perspectives argument has much to commend it, but it may prove too much. Although psychiatrists are less apt to blame wrongdoers than are lawyers and the general public, the idea that some people are too sick to be blamed for their conduct is not antithetical to the criminal law, nor does it endanger the paradigm of free will. The criminal law is based on the view that, although humans *generally* possess free will, some people are so ill that they lack the basic attributes of personhood that make them morally accountable for their actions. Therefore, the present claim is more an argument for limiting psychiatric testimony in criminal trials than it is for abolishing the insanity defense.

[4]—"Mental Illness" as a Myth

Perhaps psychiatric disorders do not exist; they are merely constructed in the minds of psychiatrists. Indeed, according to some abolitionists, the concept of "mental illness" is a myth.

One advocate of this position is psychiatrist Thomas Szasz.[115] He contends that the term "mental illness" is little more than a phrase for describing abnormal behavior. But, "abnormality" means no more than that the conduct is unusual, odd, or atypical in a particular environment. Ultimately, he suggests, the term "mental disease" is attached to behavior that society considers strange, frightening, or disagreeable.

Historical support for this premise can be found. For example, before feminism became socially acceptable, some Freudian psychologists described female advocates of women's rights as "neurotics . . . compensating for masculine trends . . . [or] more or less successfully sublimating sadistic and homosexual [trends]."[116]

---

[113] *Insanity as a Defense: A Panel Discussion*, Annual Judicial Conference (2d Cir. 1964), reprinted in 37 F.R.D. 365, 371 (1964) (Weintraub, C.J.).

[114] Menninger, Note 6, *supra*, at 96.

[115] E.g., Thomas S. Szasz, The Myth of Mental Illness (1961); and Thomas S. Szasz, Ideology and Insanity (1970).

[116] See Mary P. Ryan, Womanhood in America 276 (1975) (quoting H. W. Frink).

Likewise, the psychiatric establishment labelled homosexuality as a mental disease until 1973, at which time the Board of Trustees of the American Psychiatric Association voted to remove homosexuality from that category. Yet, no new medical knowledge intervened in the 1970s to justify the change. Instead, social attitudes changed and pressure was placed on the psychiatric community to reconsider its earlier views: "[a] more recent moral judgment simply replaced an older one."[117]

Advocates of the insanity defense assert that the preceding criticisms of psychiatry, even if valid, are beside the point. In the typical case in which the insanity defense is raised, e.g., in which the defendant hallucinates or experiences exceeding strong urges to commit criminal acts, there is little doubt that she is suffering from an abnormal mental or physical condition, and is not simply a person out of place in her culture.

[5]—Equity

Some abolitionists contend that various conditions, e.g., a poor social environment, are as much or more criminogenic than psychoses, and yet they are not considered legitimate bases for exculpation.

Advocates of the "equity" position concede that a defense based on social adversity is politically unacceptable at this time. Therefore, since morally similar cases should be treated alike, they contend that until society recognizes an excuse for the grossly deprived, and for others who can prove non-psychosis-based causes for their criminal behavior, insane people should also be punished.[118]

[C]—Legislative Efforts to Abolish the Defense

[1]—*Mens Rea* Approach

Three states have abolished the insanity defense, but permit a defendant to introduce evidence of her mental disease or defect in order to rebut the prosecution's claim that she possessed the mental state required in the definition of the crime.[119] For example, if D is prosecuted for intentionally killing V, D may introduce evidence that, due to mental illness, she believed that she was squeezing a lemon rather than strangling V and, therefore, that she lacked the intent to kill. Evidence of D's mental condition would be inadmissible, however, to show that she did not realize that taking a human life is morally or legally wrong, that she acted on the basis of an irresistible impulse to kill, or even that she killed V because she hallucinated that V was about to kill her.

These state laws have been declared constitutional.[120] Although defendants have argued that "the insanity defense is so embedded in our legal history that it should

---

[117] Van den Haag, Note 105, *supra*, at 4.

[118] Norval Morris & Gordon Hawkins, The Honest Politician's Guide to Crime Control 179 (1970).

[119] Idaho Code § 18-207 (1987); Mont. Code Ann. § 46-14-102 (1993); Utah Code Ann. § 76-2-305(1) (1994).

[120] *State v. Searcy*, 798 P.2d 914 (Idaho 1990) (abolition of the insanity defense does not violate the due process clause); *State v. Korell*, 690 P.2d 992 (Mont. 1984) (abolition of the

be afforded status as a fundamental right,"[121] the United States Supreme Court has stated that:

> [t]he doctrines of *actus reus, mens rea*, insanity, . . . justification, and duress have historically provided the tools for a constantly shifting adjustment of the tension between the evolving aims of the criminal law and changing religious, moral, philosophical, and medical views of the nature of man. This process of adjustment has always been thought to be the province of the States.[122]

Specifically, the *mens rea* approach to insanity does not violate the due process clause, which requires that the prosecutor retain the burden of proof regarding all of the elements of a criminal offense.[123] Since the due process clause does not prohibit a legislature from abandoning the basic requirement of *mens rea*,[124] it should follow that it may take the less drastic approach of retaining the element of *mens rea*, while repealing the *defense* of insanity, as long as the prosecution is required to prove beyond a reasonable doubt that the defendant had the requisite mental state.

[2]—Sentencing Approach

In the early part of the twentieth century, a few legislatures not only abolished the insanity defense, but they barred evidence of the defendant's mental illness in order to rebut the prosecution's case-in-chief. For example, under these laws, *D* would not be permitted to introduce evidence during the guilt phase of the trial that, due to mental illness, she believed that she was squeezing a lemon when, in fact, she was strangling *V*. Instead, such testimony could only be considered after conviction, in the sentencing phase of the trial.

Without exception, state courts have declared such laws unconstitutional.[125] This outcome is sensible. Although states have wide latitude in defining criminal offenses and in determining what defenses will be recognized, once a legislature determines that a particular mental state is an element of a crime, it violates the due process clause to lessen the prosecutor's burden of proof by denying the defendant the opportunity to introduce evidence that might raise a reasonable doubt regarding her *mens rea* at the time of the offense.

---

defense neither deprives a defendant of her right of due process nor violates the Eighth Amendment bar on cruel and unusual punishment).

[121] *State v. Korell*, 690 P.2d at 998 (stating, but rejecting, the argument); but see *State v. Joyner*, 625 A.2d 791, 800 (Conn. 1993) (stating in dictum that "[w]e agree with the defendant that our common law tradition provides considerable support for the proposition that . . . the state could not entirely eradicate such a defense from the penal code").

[122] *Powell v. Texas*, 392 U.S. 514, 536 (1968).

[123] See § 7.03[B][1], *supra*.

[124] See § 11.04[A], *supra*.

[125] *State v. Lange*, 123 So. 639 (La. 1929); *Sinclair v. State*, 132 So. 581 (Miss. 1931); *State v. Strasburg*, 110 P. 1020 (Wash. 1910).

§ 25.08   "Guilty But Mentally Ill"[126]

In response to criticisms of the insanity defense, thirteen states have adopted an alternative verdict, "guilty but mentally ill" (GBMI).[127] In all but two of these states, the insanity defense has been retained, but a jury may now choose from among four, rather than the usual three, verdicts: guilty, not guilty, not guilty by reason of insanity (NGRI), and GBMI.[128] In these states, the jury returns a NGRI verdict if the defendant was insane at the time of the crime; it returns a GBMI verdict if she is guilty of the offense, was sane at the time of the crime, but is "mentally ill," as the latter term is defined by statute.

The effect of a GBMI verdict is that the convicted party receives the sentence that would otherwise be imposed if she were found guilty; after sentencing, however, she may receive psychiatric care in the prison setting or in a mental institution. If she is cured while in custody, she must complete her prison sentence.[129]

Proponents of the GBMI verdict claim the following benefits of the system: (1) inappropriate insanity findings will be reduced; (2) treatment of mentally ill, but sane, offenders is provided; and (3) the public receives greater protection from mentally disordered and dangerous offenders.

Critics of the verdict raise the following objections. First, the distinction between mental illness and insanity may be too fine for a jury to distinguish. Second, the GBMI verdict is unnecessary: any person convicted of a crime may receive psychiatric care, if the state wishes to provide it. Third, persons who are found GBMI are not guaranteed treatment. Especially during state budgetary crises, insufficient funds may be allocated to mental health agencies. Finally, juries may

---

[126] See generally Ingo Keilitz, Daina Farthing-Capowich, Bradley D. McGraw, & Adams, The Guilty But Mentally Ill Verdict: An Empirical Study (1984); Kurt M. Bumby, *Reviewing the Guilty But Mentally Ill Alternative: A Case of the Blind "Pleading" the Blind*, 21 J. Psychiatry & L. 191 (1993); Michael Davis, *Guilty But Insane?*, 10 Soc. Theory & Prac., Spring 1984, at 1; R.D. MacKay & Jerry Kopelman, *The Operation of the "Guilty But Mentally Ill" Verdict in Pennsylvania*, 16 J. Psychiatry & L. 247 (1988); Donald W. Morgan, Thomas M. McCullough, Peter L. Jenkins, & William M. White, *Guilty But Mentally Ill: The South Carolina Experience*, 16 Bull. Am. Acad. Psychiatry & L. 41 (1988); Gare A. Smith & James A. Hall, Project, *Evaluating Michigan's Guilty But Mentally Ill Verdict: An Empirical Study*, 16 U. Mich. J. L. Ref. 77 (1982); Roger George Frey, Note, *The Guilty But Mentally Ill Verdict and Due Process*, 92 Yale L.J. 475 (1983).

[127] Bumby, Note 126, *supra*, at 192-93.

[128] E.g., Mich. Comp. Laws Ann. § 768.36 (1982).

[129] Remarkably, various courts have held that, in a murder prosecution, a person found GBMI may be sentenced to death, notwithstanding her mental illness. *Sanders v. State*, 585 A.2d 117 (Del. 1990) (a GBMI verdict establishes a mitigating factor as a matter of law, but it does not preclude a death sentence if this mitigating factor is outweighed by aggravating factors); *State v. Wilson*, 413 S.E.2d 19 (S.C. 1992) (the fact that the defendant was found GBMI at the guilt phase of the trial is irrelevant in the sentencing phase).

compromise and return GBMI verdicts when NGRI verdicts should be reached, i.e., the GBMI alternative may reduce the number of *appropriate* insanity acquittals.[130]

---

[130] With one exception, however, studies have found that the GBMI option has not resulted in a decrease in NGRI verdicts. See MacKay & Kopelman, Note 126, *supra* (reviewing four previous studies that found no reduction in insanity acquittals, but reporting a reduction in Pennsylvania).

CHAPTER 26

DIMINISHED CAPACITY

§ 26.01 "Diminished Capacity": A Term of Confusion[1]

The term "diminished capacity" is used and misused by courts and commentators alike to describe two different concepts, neither one of which is adequately characterized by the term. One commentator has aptly depicted the state of affairs in this field as "undiminished confusion in diminished capacity."[2] Because of the confusion pervading this area of the law, any generalization about it is just that—a generalization subject to exceptions and inconsistencies.

With this caveat in mind, it may be said that "diminished capacity" is a term used to describe two categories of circumstances in which an actor's abnormal mental condition, short of insanity, will exonerate him or, more often, result in his conviction of a crime or degree of crime less serious than the original charge.

First, there is a *mens rea* form of diminished capacity. As explained in § 26.02, the *mens rea* model of diminished capacity functions as a failure-of-proof "defense," i.e., a defense that negates an element of a crime, rather than a true defense. As such, it ought to be, but is not, recognized as a potential basis for exculpation for any crime.

The second form of diminished capacity, which is a true defense (or, a true *partial* defense), will be called "partial responsibility" in this chapter.[3] This defense is more controversial than the *mens rea* variant. Recognized now in only a few states, and only for the crime of murder, this defense mitigates a criminal homicide to manslaughter.

§ 26.02 Diminished Capacity: *Mens Rea* Defense

[A]—Nature of the "Defense"

Consider three hypothetical cases. First, *D1* is charged with first-degree murder based on the claim that he intentionally killed *V*. *D1* wishes to introduce expert

---

[1] See generally 1 Robinson at §§ 64, 101, 102(d); Peter Arenella, *The Diminished Capacity and Diminished Responsibility Defenses: Two Children of a Doomed Marriage*, 77 Colum. L. Rev. 827 (1977); Joshua Dressler, *Reaffirming the Moral Legitimacy of the Doctrine of Diminished Capacity: A Brief Reply to Professor Morse*, 75 J. Crim. L. & Criminology 953 (1984); Stephen J. Morse, *Undiminished Confusion in Diminished Capacity*, 75 J. of Crim. L. & Criminology 1 (1984); Henry Weihofen & Winfred Overholser, *Mental Disorder Affecting the Degree of a Crime*, 56 Yale L.J. 959 (1947).

[2] Morse, Note 1, *supra*.

[3] It is also called "diminished responsibility." See Arenella, Note 1, *supra*.

testimony that at the time he killed *V* he was suffering from a mental illness. Although the testimony will not show that *D1* was insane at the time of the crime, it is intended to prove that, as a result of his abnormal mental condition, he did not form the intent to kill *V*.

Second, suppose that *D2* is prosecuted for rape and wishes to introduce evidence that as a result of mental retardation, he genuinely believed that the female with whom he was having intercourse was consenting.

Finally, suppose that *D3* is prosecuted for assault with intent to commit rape, but wishes to prove that due to a delusion he believed that the woman he was forcibly attacking was his wife.

In each of these cases, the proffered expert testimony forms the basis of what has come to be known as the "diminished capacity defense," or, more specifically, the *mens rea* version of the latter "defense." The testimony that each defendant seeks to introduce speaks to the "question of whether the defendant in fact possessed a particular mental state [intent to kill, by *D1*; intent to have nonconsensual intercourse, by *D2*; intent to rape, by *D3*] which is an element of the charged offense."[4] In these circumstances, the word "defense" is a "legal colloquialism," because the doctrine "is not designed to defeat a case the State has otherwise established."[5] That is, "the 'diminished capacity defense' . . . does not provide any grounds for acquittal not provided in the definition of the offense. Properly understood, [diminished capacity] is not a defense at all but merely a rule of evidence."[6] As one court has explained the defense/rule, "[f]or the purpose of determining criminal guilt, diminished capacity either negates the state of mind required for a particular offense, if successful, or it does not."[7]

[B]—Law

[1]—Overview

American law is sharply divided on the extent to which evidence of an abnormal mental condition not amounting to legal insanity may be introduced for the purpose of negating the *mens rea* of an offense. A few states, including those that follow the Model Penal Code, admit such evidence to negate the *mens rea* of any crime. Many more states limit the admissibility of such evidence to some or all specific-intent offenses. Other states do not recognize the defense at all.

[2]—Defense-to-All-Crimes (Model Penal Code) Approach

Perhaps as many as a dozen states[8] follow the reasoning of the Model Penal Code, which provides that evidence that the defendant suffered from a mental

---

[4] *United States v. Pohlot*, 827 F.2d 889, 896 (3rd Cir. 1987).

[5] *State v. Humanik*, 489 A.2d 691, 697 (N.J. App. Div. 1985).

[6] *United States v. Pohlot*, 827 F.2d at 897.

[7] *State v. Breakiron*, 532 A.2d 199, 208-09 (N.J. 1987).

[8] 1 Robinson § 64(a)-(b) (listing 12 American states); but see *State v. Provost*, 490 N.W.2d 93, 99 n.3 (Minn. 1992) (according to the court's research, only 7 states allow expert evidence of mental illness in the prosecution of all crimes).

disease or defect at the time of his conduct is admissible whenever it is relevant to prove that he lacked a mental state that is an element of the charged offense.[9]

The Colorado Supreme Court in *Hendershott v People*[10] has succinctly explained the reasoning behind the rule:

> Once we accept the basic principles that an accused is presumed innocent and that he cannot be adjudicated guilty unless the prosecution proves beyond a reasonable doubt the existence of the mental state required for the crime charged, it defies both logic and fundamental fairness to prohibit a defendant from presenting reliable and relevant evidence that, due to a mental impairment beyond his conscious control, he lacked the capacity to entertain the very culpability which is indispensable to his criminal responsibility in the first instance.

Applying the Model Penal Code rule to the hypotheticals posited in subsection [A], the defendants would be entitled to introduce evidence of their respective mental abnormalities. The effect of the evidence, if believed, would be to acquit the defendants of the crimes charged, although they might still be guilty of lesser offenses.[11] In contrast, a murder defendant who seeks to show, for example, that he is very mildly retarded and, as a consequence, is a follower of stronger-willed persons, would not be permitted to introduce expert evidence in this regard in an intent-to-kill prosecution, because the testimony, even if believed, would not negate the required element of intent.[12]

[3]—Limited-Use Approach

Some states arbitrarily limit the introduction of mental-condition evidence to murder prosecutions.[13] Thus, in the hypotheticals in subsection [A], *D1* would be permitted to introduce evidence of his mental illness in order to reduce the degree of murder for which he could be convicted, but *D2* and *D3* would not be allowed to introduce evidence of their abnormal mental conditions.

Many states recognize the defense as appropriate to negate the specific-intent element of any specific-intent offense, but refuse to permit the introduction of evidence of mental abnormality in the prosecution of general-intent crimes.[14] Thus, *D1* could raise his diminished capacity claim to prove that he lacked the capacity

---

[9] Model Penal Code § 4.02(1).

[10] 653 P.2d 385, 393-94 (Colo. 1982).

[11] *D1* could be convicted of any form of criminal homicide for which intent to kill is not an element. *D2*'s situation is more problematic: because of his mental condition *D2* believed he was having consensual intercourse; probably, therefore, he would be guilty of no offense, unless the state recognizes an offense of fornication. *D3* would be guilty of assault or battery since, as he perceived the situation, he was sexually attacking his own wife. Only the specific intent to rape would be negated by his mental condition.

[12] *State v. Watson*, 618 A.2d 367, 372 (N.J. Super. Ct. App. Div. 1992).

[13] E.g., *Commonwealth v. Weinstein*, 451 A.2d 1344, 1347 (Pa. 1982).

[14] According to *State v. Provost*, 490 N.W.2d at 99 n.3, seventeen states expressly limit mental-abnormality testimony to specific-intent crimes. E.g., *State v. Jackson*, 714 P.2d 1368, 1372-73 (Kan. 1986); *State v. Doyon*, 416 A.2d 130, 136 (R.I. 1980).

to form, or did not in fact form,[15] the specific intent to kill. *D3* could introduce evidence to prove that he lacked the specific intent to rape *V*. *D2*, however, would not be permitted to introduce evidence of his mental condition to disprove rape, because rape is a general-intent crime.

As a practical matter, this version of diminished capacity functions only as a partial defense, because there is almost always a crime for which a person with diminished capacity can be convicted, even if he succeeds in proving that he lacked a specific intent.[16] Thus, the defense will reduce a defendant's guilt from one degree of murder to a lower degree of criminal homicide, or from a non-homicide specific-intent offense to a general-intent crime, e.g., from burglary to criminal trespass, but outright acquittal is rare.

[4]—No-Defense Approach

A few jurisdictions permit introduction of evidence of the defendant's mental illness or defect in order to prove insanity, but refuse to admit such evidence for the purpose of negating the *mens rea* of the offense charged, regardless of whether the crime is one of "specific intent" or "general intent."[17]

In some states, the preceding rule leads to an anomaly: a defendant may introduce evidence of his self-induced, and thus culpable, *intoxication* in order to show that he lacked the specific intent to commit an offense, but he is barred from introducing expert testimony regarding an abnormal mental condition, which he did not culpably contract, for the same purpose. The stated justification for the distinction is that "[u]nlike the notion of partial or relative insanity, conditions such as intoxication, medication, epilepsy, infancy or senility are, in varying degrees susceptible to quantification or objective demonstration."[18] Or, according to one court:

> It takes no great expertise for jurors to determine whether an accused was so intoxicated as to be mentally unable to intend . . . whereas the ability to assimilate and apply the finely differentiated psychiatric concepts associated with diminished capacity demands a sophistication (or as critics would maintain a

---

[15] In a manner reminiscent of the law pertaining to voluntary intoxication, see § 24.03[B][3], *supra*, some jurisdictions speak of the defense in "lack of capacity" terms, e.g., *State v. Galloway*, 628 A.2d 735, 743 (N.J. 1993) ("the claimed deficiency . . . affect [ed] the defendant's cognitive capacity to form the mental state necessary for the commission of the crime"), whereas others states are concerned with whether the actor actually formed the state of mind in question. In California "capacity" evidence is inadmissible, but "actuality" testimony is admissible. Cal. Pen. Code § 28(a) (1988).

[16] Some courts expressly limit the defense in this regard. E.g., *State v. Doyon*, 416 A.2d at 137 ("Acceptance of the doctrine requires that there must be some lesser-included offense which lacks the requisite specific intent of the greater offense charged.").

[17] E.g., *Chestnut v. State*, 538 So.2d 820, 820 (Fla. 1989); *Bethea v. United States*, 365 A.2d 64, 89-90 (D.C. 1976).

[18] *Bethea v. United States*, 365 A.2d at 88. Based on this purported distinction, Florida bars "mental abnormality" evidence, *Chestnut v. State*, 538 So.2d 820 (Fla. 1989), but permits evidence of epilepsy, *Bunney v. State*, 603 So.2d 1270, 1273 (Fla. 1992), to show lack of specific intent.

sophistic bent) that jurors (and officers of the court) ordinarily have not developed. [19]

[C]—Arguments Against Full Recognition of the Defense

[1]—No Need for the Defense

Some observers contend that if psychiatrists accurately testify, and courts faithfully apply, the *mens rea* version of the diminished capacity defense it will virtually never be needed. [20] The thesis of this argument is that forming an intent is a simple, exceedingly basic process. Indeed, it is easier to prove that a defendant is insane than that he lacks the requisite *mens rea* because of mental illness. For example, a mentally ill person may kill on orders from God, or because of a compelling urge to do so. In both cases, the defendant may be insane (depending on the state's insanity rules), but in both circumstances he has the requisite intent to kill. On the other hand, if a person fails to form a required intent due to a mental disease or defect and, therefore, would be entitled to raise a diminished capacity claim— e.g., *D* strangles *V*, believing that he is squeezing a lemon—he is also insane, i.e., he does not appreciate the nature and quality of his conduct.

The preceding observations are accurate. Nonetheless, in the rare case in which a person is sufficiently mentally disordered that he lacks the *mens rea* of an offense, *whether or not he is insane*, he is entitled to acquittal, because an essential element of the crime has not been proved. Moreover, because the issue is one of *mens rea*, and not the excuse of insanity, the prosecutor, rather than the defendant, should be required to carry the burden of persuasion. [21]

[2]—Imprecision of Psychiatric Testimony

Many courts are distrustful of psychiatric testimony. As the remarks at the end of subsection [B] [4], *supra*, suggest, some courts are hesitant to allow juries to consider "finely differentiated psychiatric concepts" regarding intent. Opponents of the defense reason that when a defendant's mental condition is sufficiently extreme to merit an insanity defense, the law is prepared to assume that the actor is not responsible for his actions; but in the less extreme cases of diminished capacity (or "partial insanity," as some critics like to put it), mental health experts are unable to provide sufficiently objective verification of this intermediate condition.

This argument runs counter to the approach taken by the law in other contexts. For example, if the law is prepared to consider an expert's claim that the defendant has an uncontrollable urge to kill or is receiving orders from God, there does not appear to be any justification on the basis of comparative objectivity or quantification to deny the factfinder the opportunity to consider expert testimony regarding the defendant's lack of capacity to form a criminal intent.

---

[19] *State v. Wilcox*, 436 N.E.2d 523, 530 (Ohio 1982) (internal quotation marks and citations omitted).

[20] E.g., Arenella, Note 1, *supra*, at 833-35.

[21] See *State v. Breakiron*, 532 A.2d 199, 210 (N.J. 1987).

[3]—Fear of Crime

A person who is adjudged insane confronts "the very real possibility of prolonged therapeutic confinement."[22] In contrast, a successful diminished capacity claim may result in "outright acquittal";[23] thus, mentally disturbed and dangerous persons may be set free. As a reaction to the fear of releasing dangerous persons to the street, most jurisdictions limit the applicability of diminished capacity claims to specific-intent crimes, for which there exists a lesser crime, usually a general-intent offense, for which the defendant may be convicted.

The half-way approach of most states is illogical. A person who suffers from a mental disease is as apt to be unable to form the "general" intent of the lesser offense for which he is convicted as he is to be unable to form the "specific" intent for which he is acquitted. Moreover, logically, diminished capacity is like *involuntary intoxication*.[24] In both cases, the actor involuntarily suffers from a condition that prevents him from forming a criminal intent; therefore, just as with the latter condition, a mental illness should apply to general-intent offenses.

The upshot of the fear-of-crime argument is that, because a mentally disturbed person is dangerous, he should be convicted, even if he does not possess the *mens rea* required in the definition of the offense. However, this position is one of very questionable constitutionality.[25] The solution to the problem is not to deny the defendant the opportunity to negate the requisite culpability of the offense, but is to seek civil commitment of the defendant, on the basis that he is dangerous and mentally disordered.[26]

§ 26.03   Diminished Capacity: "Partial Responsibility" Defense

[A]—Overview

The defense described in this chapter section, which only applies in murder prosecutions to mitigate the offense to manslaughter, is very controversial in the United States. As discussed below, the California Supreme Court promulgated the United States version of the doctrine in the 1960s.[27] Only four other state courts

---

[22] *Bethea v. United States*, 365 A.2d at 90.

[23] *Id.* at 91.

[24] *State v. Provost*, 490 N.W.2d 93, 99 n.3 (Minn. 1992).

[25] See *United States v. Pohlot*, 827 F.2d 889, 901 (3rd Cir. 1987) (observing that although the Supreme Court has stated that a state may allocate to the defendant the burden of proving insanity, "it did not sanction, and probably would not sanction, a jury charge that prevented a jury from considering evidence of mental abnormality in determining whether the state had proven" the requisite *mens rea*).

[26] *Hendershott v. People*, 653 P.2d 385, 395 (Colo. 1982). The irony is that a mentally ill person has fewer procedural rights in the civil system than he does in the criminal justice system, and he may be institutionalized for a longer period of time than he would have been imprisoned for the offense. See § 25.05, *supra*.

[27] The common law defense was first recognized in the nineteenth century in Scotland, to reduce the offense of the "partially insane" from murder to the non-capital offense of "culpable homicide." Arenella, Note 1, *supra*, at 830 n.16. It is codified was England in the Homicide Act of 1957, 5 & 6 Eliz. 2, ch. 11, Part I, § 2.

adopted the defense. [28] Although it is hard to measure current support for the doctrine, at least two states, based on the Model Penal Code version of the principle, appear to recognize a partial responsibility defense. [29]

[B]—Rule

[1]—The California Approach

The partial responsibility defense was adopted "through the judicial back door," [30] in order to allow mitigation of some homicides from first-degree to second-degree murder; later the mitigation process extended to reducing murder to manslaughter. California courts led this movement.

In order to avoid the appearance of encroaching on legislative authority, the California courts (primarily, the state supreme court) dressed the partial responsibility defense in "*mens rea* clothing." [31] That is, the judges developed strained definitions of *mens rea* terms; then the courts concluded that mentally impaired actors lacked the requisite mental state (under the new definitions) to be convicted of first-degree or second-degree murder. In fact, however, the true rationale of the partial responsibility doctrine was—and is—that a person who does not meet the state's definition of insanity, but who suffers from a mental abnormality, is less blameworthy, and therefore less deserving of punishment, than a killer who acts with a normal state of mind.

For example, in *People v. Conley*. [32] *D* shot his ex-lover and her husband after planning their deaths over a weekend. According to psychiatric testimony, *D* suffered from "personality fragmentation" and was in a "disassociative state" on the fatal weekend. Nonetheless, the jury found that at the time of the crime, *D* killed the victims intentionally and with premeditation and deliberation. In short, the *mens rea* variant of the diminished capacity defense apparently did not apply.

The California Supreme Court overturned *D*'s first-degree murder conviction, although it accepted the jury's findings. It stated that the judge had failed to instruct the jury properly on the element of "malice aforethought," the mental element of murder that distinguishes the offense from manslaughter. To act with "malice aforethought," the court stated, a person must be aware of his "obligation to act within the general body of laws regulating society." If *D*, although sane, lacked this awareness, he did not act with malice aforethought and, therefore, lacked the required *mens rea* of murder; under such circumstances, *D* was guilty only of manslaughter.

Of course, a person who is unaware of his obligation to act within the law because he suffers from a mental disease or defect is probably insane because he does not know right from wrong. What the court really was doing was creating a

---

[28] American Law Institute, Comment to § 210.3, at 70 n.77.

[29] See § 26.03[B][2], *infra*.

[30] Morse, Note 1, *supra*, at 24.

[31] Arenella, Note 1, *supra*, at 831.

[32] 411 P.2d 911 (Cal. 1966).

mini-insanity defense, so that a jury could mitigate a defendant's guilt when it was unwilling to find insanity.

Later, the California Supreme Court extended the doctrine. Probably because the state legislature had not codified the irresistible-impulse test of insanity, the court further redefined "malice," by including a volitional feature: according to the court, "malice" is absent if, as the result of a mental abnormality, the defendant is "unaware of or *unable to act* in accordance with the law."[33]

In response to controversial verdicts involving the diminished capacity defense, the California legislature and the state's electorate abolished the partial responsibility form of the diminished capacity doctrine in the 1980s.[34]

[2]—Model Penal Code

The Model Penal Code provides that a homicide that would otherwise constitute murder is manslaughter if it is committed as the result of "extreme mental or emotional disturbance for which there is a reasonable explanation or excuse." The reasonableness of the actor's explanation or excuse for the "extreme mental or emotional disturbance" (EMED) is "determined from the viewpoint of a person in the actor's situation under the circumstances as he believes them to be."[35]

The EMED provision has two purposes: (1) it codifies in expanded form the common law "sudden heat of passion" doctrine;[36] and (2) it permits, but does not require, courts in states that adopt the EMED language to recognize a partial responsibility defense.[37] It is unclear how many states that have codified the EMED provision allow for a partial responsibility defense, but courts in at least two jurisdictions do recognize the defense.[38] The Commentary to the Model Code explains the partial responsibility doctrine this way:

> [The defense] looks into the actor's mind to see whether he should be judged by a lesser standard than that applicable to ordinary men. It recognizes the defendant's own mental disorder or emotional instability as a basis for partially excusing his conduct . . . . To the extent that the abnormal individual is judged as if he were normal, to the extent that the drunk man is judged as if he were sober, to the extent, in short, that the defective person is judged as if he were someone else, the moral judgment underlying criminal conviction is undermined.[39]

As a practical matter, the EMED provision is very difficult to apply in the context of diminished capacity, because the latter concept is subjective—the defendant is

---

[33] *People v. Poddar*, 518 P.2d 342, 348 (Cal. 1974) (emphasis supplied).

[34] For a thorough discussion of California law, including the abandonment of the doctrine, see *People v. Saille*, 820 P.2d 588 (Cal. 1991).

[35] Model Penal Code § 210.3(1)(b).

[36] See §§ 31.07 (common law), 31.10[C][3] (Model Penal Code), *infra*.

[37] American Law Institute, Comment to § 210.3, at 72-73.

[38] *State v. Dumlao*, 715 P.2d 822 (Haw. Ct. App. 1986); *State v. Counts*, 816 P.2d 1157 (Ore. 1991).

[39] American Law Institute, Comment to § 210.3, at 71.

not like an ordinary person because he suffers from an abnormal mental condition—yet the EMED standard is partially objective, i.e., the provision includes the "*reasonable* explanation or excuse" language. More specifically, the issue in partial responsibility cases is not whether there is a reasonable explanation or excuse for the defendant's homicidal act, but rather whether there is a reasonable explanation or excuse for the defendant's EMED that caused him to take a life.[40]

To see how the EMED doctrine works in the context of mental abnormalities, consider *State v. Dumlao*:[41] *D* introduced testimony at his trial that he suffered from "paranoid personality disorder," a condition that caused him to experience "unwarranted suspiciousness" of other people's actions and to be hypersensitive to criticism. As a result of his condition, *D* irrationally believed that his wife was being unfaithful to him, and he became enraged when his brother-in-law and father sought to counsel him about his suspicions. *D* took a life while in the preceding emotional state.

According to the appellate court, this evidence was sufficient to justify an instruction on EMED manslaughter. In determining whether there was a reasonable explanation or excuse for *D*'s disturbance, the court concluded that the jury should consider:

> the subjective, internal situation in which the defendant found himself and the external circumstances as he perceived them at the time, however inaccurate that perception may have been, and assess[] from that standpoint whether the explanation . . . for his emotional disturbance was reasonable.[42]

That is, to summarize: the issue is not whether there was a reasonable explanation or excuse for the homicide or for *D*'s paranoid condition (as to the latter, unless a defendant can be blamed for "contracting" a mental abnormality, there will *always* be a reasonable explanation or excuse); instead, the issue is whether there was a reasonable explanation or excuse, based on *D*'s psychological characteristics, for his emotional disturbance at the time of the crime. As to the latter matter, *D*'s abnormalities are considered because the Code provides that the reasonableness of the explanation should be considered "from the viewpoint of a person *in the actor's situation*," i.e., with his paranoid delusions and hypersensitivity, "under the circumstances as he believes them to be" (i.e., based on the assumption that his wife *was* being unfaithful to him).

The Commentary to the Code warns, however, that the fact that an actor suffers from a mental disorder does not preclude a finding that he is morally depraved. Moreover, it states that "surely" cases will exist (although it offers no examples) in which the defendant's mental condition, although abnormal, "should be regarded as having no just bearing on his liability" for the intentional homicide.[43]

---

[40] See *People v. Casassa*, 404 N.E.2d 1310, 1316 n.2 (N.Y. 1980).

[41] 715 P.2d 822 (Haw. Ct. App. 1986).

[42] *Id.* at 830 (quoting *People v. Casassa*, 404 N.E.2d at 1316).

[43] American Law Institute, Comment to § 210.3, at 72.

[C]—Controversy Regarding the Defense

Many objections to the partial responsibility defense parallel those pertaining to the *mens rea* form of diminished capacity. As the American Law Institute concedes, the partial responsibility defense "brings formal guilt more closely into line with moral blameworthiness, but only at the cost of driving a wedge between dangerousness and social control."[44] Indeed, the very factor that mitigates an actor's blameworthiness—his mental abnormality—aggravates his dangerousness.[45]

Also, critics of psychiatry are troubled by the recognition of this defense. Even if agreement exists that at some gross level mental disease can be so severe that it is fair to excuse the defendant, they believe that the subtle gradations that this defense implies—the distinction between full, partial, and no mental abnormality—cannot be determined reliably.

Psychiatric testimony aside, there are line-drawing concerns: if this defense is recognized, why are other forms of mitigation, such as economic adversity, not recognized? Some critics of the defense want all people equally disadvantaged treated alike, but they fear that this solution would undermine the traditional view that a sane person is morally and legally responsible for his intentional acts.[46]

Finally, one opponent of the partial responsibility defense, Professor Stephen Morse, contends that the question society should ask is: "How hard is it not to offend the law?" His answer is: "Not hard at all." The criminal law does not require people to live up to a high moral standard; all it demands of citizens is that they not rob, rape, kill, and commit other serious offenses. Morse reasons that even if a person has a mental health problem (short of insanity), it is not difficult for him to avoid offending society's laws. Therefore, Morse would abolish *all* partial excuses to murder, and would treat *all* sane intentional killers alike, "without regard to differences in background, mental or emotional condition, or other factors often thought to necessitate mitigation."[47]

But, even though it is true that it is not hard to avoid killing persons, it remains true that it *is* harder for some people to avoid violating the law than it is for others. For example, in *Fisher v. United States*,[48] D, a person of subnormal intelligence and a victim of a mental condition that made him highly aggressive, intentionally strangled V to death, after V uttered a racial epithet. D was convicted of murder. Applying Professor Morse's standard, D's murder conviction was proper. But, an advocate of the partial responsibility defense might respond that, although D deserved to be punished for his acts, his mental condition, for which he was not culpable, rendered him less blameworthy than a "normal" person, because it was harder for D to avoid taking a life than it would be for the ordinary person.[49] In

---

[44] *Id.* at 71-72.

[45] Arenella, Note 1, *supra*, at 857.

[46] *Id.* at 858-59.

[47] Morse, Note 1, *supra*, at 30.

[48] 328 U.S. 463 (1946).

[49] For a full exposition of this argument see Dressler, Note 1, *supra*.

the case of murder, in which the most severe penalties are imposed (in *Fisher*, D was executed), it may be appropriate to investigate an actor's mental condition with great care, and mitigate the offense when justice seems to require it, i.e., when the defendant's choice-making capacities are undermined by a mental disease or defect.

CHAPTER 27

ATTEMPT

§ 27.01 Chapter Overview[1]

When a person intentionally commits a crime, it is the result of a six-stage process.[2] First, the actor conceives the idea of committing a crime. Second, she evaluates the idea, in order to determine whether she should proceed. Third, she fully forms the intention to go forward. Fourth, she prepares to commit the crime, for example, by obtaining any instruments necessary for its commission. Fifth, she commences commission of the offense. Sixth, she completes her actions, thereby achieving her criminal goal. In some cases, of course, this process takes only seconds to transpire; in other circumstances, the six stages may take days, weeks, or even years, to complete.

Anglo-American law does not punish a person during the first three stages of the process. Until the third step occurs, the actor lacks a *mens rea*. Even after the *mens rea* is formed, she is not punished if there is no *actus reus*: people are not punished for thoughts alone.[3]

Activity in the middle ranges, i.e., after the formation of the *mens rea* but short of attainment of the criminal goal, is described as "inchoate"—imperfect or incomplete—conduct. Anglo-American law expressly[4] recognizes various inchoate offenses, the most notable of which are attempt, solicitation, and conspiracy. This chapter focuses on the inchoate crime of attempt.

Criminal attempts are of two varieties: "complete" or "imperfect"; and "incomplete."[5] A complete, but imperfect, attempt occurs when the actor performs all of the acts that she set out to do, but fails to attain her criminal goal. For example, if *D*, intending to kill *V*, purchases a gun, loads it, drives to *V*'s home, waits for *V*

---

[1] See generally Hall at 558-99; Katz at 276-99; Williams at §§ 197-209; Thurman W. Arnold, *Criminal Attempts—The Rise and Fall of an Abstraction*, 40 Yale L.J. 53 (1930); Joseph H Beale, Jr., *Criminal Attempts*, 16 Harv. L. Rev. 491 (1903); Edwin R. Keedy, *Criminal Attempts at Common Law*, 102 U. Pa. L. Rev. 464 (1954); Rollin M. Perkins, *Criminal Attempt and Related Problems*, 2 UCLA L. Rev. 319 (1955); Francis Bowes Sayre, *Criminal Attempts*, 41 Harv. L. Rev. 821 (1928); Paul Kichyun Ryu, *Contemporary Problems of Criminal Attempts*, 32 N.Y.U. L. Rev. 1170 (1957). Citations to specific criminal attempt topics are set out below, at the beginning of appropriate sections and/or subsections.

[2] See Hall at 576.

[3] See § 9.01[B], *supra*.

[4] Some non-inchoate crimes are inchoate offenses in disguise. See § 27.02[F], *infra*.

[5] Andrew Ashworth, *Criminal Attempts and the Role of Resulting Harm Under the Code, and in the Common Law*, 19 Rutgers L.J. 725, 734 (1988).

to arrive, and then fires the weapon at V, but misses her target, this is a complete, but imperfect, attempt. In contrast, an incomplete attempt occurs when the actor does some of the acts necessary to achieve the criminal goal, but she desists or is prevented from continuing, e.g., a police officer arrives before completion of the attempt.

Most, although not all, of the controversial features of attempt law relate to incomplete attempts. The earlier the police intervene to arrest for inchoate conduct, the greater the risk that suspicious looking, but actually innocent, conduct will be punished, or that a person with a genuine criminal intent will be arrested before she has the opportunity to reconsider her plans and voluntarily desist. On the other hand, the longer the law requires law enforcement officers to abstain from intervention, the greater are the chances that the actor will successfully complete the offense.

§ 27.02   General Principles

[A]—Historical Background

Although language favoring punishment of inchoate conduct can be found in judicial opinions as early as the middle of the fourteenth century, the general offense of attempt was not recognized until 1784.[6] Until then, "in those forthright days, a miss was as good as a mile."[7]

At common law, attempt was a misdemeanor, regardless of the nature or seriousness of the offense that the person sought to commit (i.e., the "target" or "substantive" offense).

[B]—Definition of "Attempt"

Until the Model Penal Code was drafted, most states punished, but did not define, criminal attempts.[8] However, subject to substantial clarification in subsequent sections of this chapter,[9] a criminal attempt occurs when a person, with the intent to commit an offense, performs any act that constitutes a substantial step toward the commission of that offense.[10] For current purposes, the "substantial step" required for a criminal attempt is conduct that has reached the fifth stage of criminality described in § 27.01, i.e., conduct that has passed the stage of preparation, and has moved to the point of perpetration, of the offense.

In common law parlance, attempt is a specific-intent crime.

[C]—Punishment of Attempts

As noted in subsection [A], a criminal attempt was a misdemeanor at common law, even when the target offense was a felony. Thus, an attempt to commit a felony was punished less severely than the target crime.

---

[6] *Rex v. Scofield*, Caldecott 397 (1784).

[7] Hall at 560.

[8] American Law Institute, Comment to § 5.01, at 300.

[9] See especially §§ 27.05-27.06, *infra*.

[10] Ill. Ann. Stat. ch. 38, § 8-4 (Smith-Hurd 1993 & Supp. 1994); *Townes v. State*, 548 A.2d 832, 834 (Md. 1988).

Today, an attempt to commit a felony is graded as a felony, but typically is treated as a lesser offense than the substantive crime.[11] Almost always, the penalty for an attempt to commit a capital crime or an offense for which the penalty is life imprisonment is set at a specific term of years of imprisonment. An attempt to commit a less serious felony is usually punished at one-half of the maximum allowed for the target crime (or by some similar formula).

[D]—Relationship of an Attempt to the Target Offense

According to a few statutes and court opinions, failure to consummate the target offense is an essential element of a criminal attempt.[12] The implication of this statement is that a criminal attempt and the substantive offense are mutually exclusive crimes: a wrongdoer either commits a crime or unsuccessfully attempts to commit it, but she never does both.

In contrast to the preceding analysis, most jurisdictions provide that a failed attempt to commit the target offense is not an essential element of a criminal attempt.[13] Indeed, with crimes of intent, the successful commission of the target crime logically involves an attempt to commit it.[14] This point is significant for two reasons: (1) in a prosecution for a crime of intent, a jury may properly return a guilty verdict for the lesser offense of an attempt to commit the substantive crime;[15] and (2) in every case where an attempt is charged, proof of its actual commission establishes the attempt.[16]

If a person commits the target offense, she may not be convicted of both it and the criminal attempt.[17] If she was charged with the substantive offense, and the jury convicts her of this offense, the criminal attempt *merges* with the substantive crime; the lesser offense of attempt is absorbed by the greater offense.[18]

[E]—"Assault": "Attempt" in Different Clothing

[1]—"Assault" versus "Attempt"

In the early common law, a criminal assault was defined as an attempted battery.[19] Today, most states have broadened the offense to include the tort version

---

[11] This is not the case in jurisdictions that follow the lead of the Model Penal Code. See § 27.09, *infra*.

[12] E.g., Cal. Penal Code § 664 (West 1988) ("Every person who attempts to commit any crime, but fails, . . . is punishable . . ."); *People v. Lardner*, 133 N.E. 375, 376 (Ill. 1921) ("The essentials of the attempt are the intent to commit the crime, the performance of some overt act toward its commission, and a failure to consummate the crime.").

[13] *Townes v. State*, 548 A.2d at 834.

[14] *People v. Vanderbilt*, 249 P. 867, 868 (Cal. 1926).

[15] E.g., Cal. Penal Code § 1159 (West. 1985).

[16] Cal. Penal Code § 663 (West 1985); *People v. Townes*, 548 A.2d at 834; *Berry v. State*, 280 N.W.2d 204, 208 (Wis. 1979).

[17] *United States v. York*, 578 F.2d 1036, 1040 (5th Cir. 1978).

[18] Williams at § 208.

[19] Perkins & Boyce at 159. A battery is any unlawful application of force to the person of another. American Law Institute, Comment to § 211.1, at 175.

of assault, i.e., intentionally placing another in apprehension of an imminent battery. Thus, today an assault ordinarily is proved if *D* attempts to batter *V* or, even if she does not, if she intentionally places *V* in imminent apprehension of a battery. Today, as at common law, a simple assault is a misdemeanor. [20]

Although a common law assault is an attempted battery, the law pertaining to criminal attempts does not apply to assaults. This is the result of an historical accident: assault law developed earlier and, therefore, independently of the crime of attempt. Specifically, for a criminal assault to occur, a greater degree of proximity to completion of the offense is required than in the case of non-assault attempts. For example, although an attempted murder may occur before the victim is in the would-be assailant's sights, a common law assault does not occur until the defendant is within apparent reach of the victim. [21]

Another difference between assault and attempt pertains to the doctrine of "impossibility." As described more fully below, [22] a person may be convicted of an attempt even if consummation of the target offense is factually impossible. For example, *D* may be convicted of attempted murder if, with the intention of killing *V*, she pulls the trigger of a faulty or unloaded gun. In contrast, some statutes define "assault" as "an unlawful attempt, *coupled with the present ability*, to commit [a battery]." [23] Under this definition, *D* would not be guilty of assault if she fired an unloaded weapon at *V*.

[2]—Attempted Assault

Inasmuch as a criminal attempt is a substantial step toward the commission of any offense, and assault is a criminal offense, the question arises whether a person may be convicted of "attempted assault." Since a common law assault is an attempted battery, an attempted assault would be an attempt to attempt to commit a battery, i.e., a substantial step toward committing a substantial step toward committing a battery.

Some courts have upheld convictions for attempted common law assault. [24] They reason that because an assault does not occur unless the assailant is near enough to the victim that she can immediately batter her, it should be possible to convict a person of *attempted* assault if she endeavors to place herself in this position, but fails to do so. [25]

Other courts consider the concept of an "attempted attempted battery" absurd, and do not recognize the crime. [26] They fear "a perversion of the law of

---

[20] Aggravated assaults, e.g., "assault with the intent to kill" and "assault with the intent to rape," are felonies.

[21] E.g., *State v. Boutin*, 346 A.2d 531 (Vt. 1975) (in a scuffle, *D* walked toward *V* with a bottle raised over his head, apparently with the intention of striking *V* with it; the police intervened when *D* and *V* were ten feet apart; held: assault conviction was reversed).

[22] See § 27.07, *infra*.

[23] E.g., Cal. Penal Code § 240 (West 1988) (emphasis added).

[24] E.g., *State v. Wilson*, 346 P.2d 115, 121 (Or. 1959).

[25] *People v. O'Connell*, 14 N.Y.S. 485 (1891).

[26] *Wilson v. State*, 53 Ga. 205, 206 (1874) (describing the concept of attempted assault as "absurd"). Of course, there is nothing absurd or illogical about the crime of "attempted

attempt."[27] whereby a person might be convicted of an offense on the basis of little more than a bare desire to commit a crime, or on the basis of innocent, but suspicious appearing, conduct.[28]

[F]—Inchoate Crimes in Disguise

Some common law and statutory offenses, although defined as if they were complete crimes, are inchoate offenses in disguise. Indeed, some such offenses prohibit conduct less proximate to completion than is required for a criminal attempt. For example, burglary is defined as "breaking and entering the dwelling house of another at night with the intent to commit a felony therein." To the extent that the purpose of burglary law is to prohibit trespasses to dwellings and to protect dwellers from the emotional distress of home-invasions, the specific intent of the offense—intent to commit a felony inside the dwelling—is superfluous.

In fact, the crime of burglary serves the additional purpose of compensating for stringencies found in the law of attempt. The act of breaking into another person's home in order to commit a felony inside will often fall short of a criminal attempt to commit the in-dwelling crime. For example, if D intends to break into V's residence, obtain a kitchen knife, and then go to V's second-floor bedroom and kill her, D is probably not guilty of attempted murder when she enters the home. Recognition of the independent substantive crime of burglary, therefore, allows a police officer who observes D's conduct to arrest her as she enters the house, while she still is within the practical reach of the officer.[29] Indeed, recognition of the crime of burglary allows for preventive law enforcement *before* D enters, when she is guilty of an *attempted* burglary.

Other offenses serve the same purpose. For example, statutes prohibiting stalking,[30] possession of burglars' tools,[31] and acts preparatory to arson[32] punish conduct that is merely preparatory to a criminal attempt. Even the common law offense of larceny has an inchoate aspect to it. A person is guilty of larceny if she

---

assault" if the assault is of the tort variety. *People v. Jones*, 504 N.W.2d 158, 164 (Mich. 1993).

[27] American Law Institute, Comment to § 211.1, at 179.

[28] Cf., *McQuirter v. State*, 63 So. 2d 388, 390 (Ala. Ct. App. 1953) (D was convicted of "attempted assault with intent to rape," based on evidence that he, a black man, followed V, a white woman, somewhat closely down the street; the court affirmed the conviction, stating that "the jury may consider social conditions and customs founded upon racial differences, such as that the prosecutrix was a white woman and defendant was a Negro man").

[29] American Law Institute, Comment to § 221.1, at 62-63.

[30] E.g., Cal. Penal Code § 646.9(a) (West Supp. 1994) ("Any person who willfully . . . and repeatedly follows or harasses another person and who makes a credible threat with the intent to place that person in reasonable fear for his or her safety . . . is guilty of the crime of stalking.").

[31] E.g., Cal. Penal Code § 466 (West 1988).

[32] E.g., Cal. Penal Code § 455 (West 1988) ("Any person who . . . commits any act preliminary [to arson], or in furtherance thereof, is punishable [as a felony].").

takes and carries away the personal property of another with the intent to permanently deprive the other of the property.[33] In essence, larceny occurs the instant the thief wrongfully moves the property even an inch, long before the permanent loss results.

§ 27.03 "Subjectivism" and "Objectivism"[34]

According to Austin, "[g]enerally, attempts are perfectly innocuous, and the party is punished . . . in respect of what he intended to do."[35] In other words, a person who attempts a crime is punished for possessing a *mens rea*; no social harm is required.

On its face, Austin's perception seems correct. Many incomplete attempts, and even some complete but imperfect ones,[36] appear to be harmless. For example, suppose that *D1* lies in wait outside *V1*'s house, in order to kill *V1* when she returns home. Just as *V1* shows up, a police officer drives by and arrests *D1* for attempted murder. Or, suppose that *D2*, intending to kill *V2*, her husband, points a gun at *V2*, who is asleep in bed, and pulls the trigger, only to discover that the gun is unloaded. *V2* sleeps through the attempt, and goes on with his life oblivious of *D2*'s efforts. *D1* and *D2* are guilty of attempted murder, but *V1* and *V2* have suffered no harm.

But, this does not end the analysis. As earlier defined,[37] there is social harm whenever a person "negates, *endangers* or destroys" an individual, group, or state interest that is socially valuable. When a person lies in wait in order to kill another, or pulls the trigger of a gun, she endangers another person's bodily security, jeopardizes the interest of loved ones in the intended victim's well-being, and impairs society's interest in a safe community in which to live. Likewise, when a person comes close to violating one of society's moral and legal commandments, she tears the fabric of society, if only slightly. Contrary to Austin's assertions, therefore, criminal attempts are not innocuous; criminal attempts *do* cause social harm.

Notwithstanding the deficiency, Austin's statement serves as a useful starting point for considering two conflicting perceptions of the proper roles of social harm and culpability in attempt law. The competing philosophies may be characterized as "subjectivism" and "objectivism." As will become evident in later sections of this chapter, some aspects of the common law, and the criminal attempt provisions of the Model Penal Code, are based on subjectivist views of inchoate liability. Some

---

[33] See Chapter 32, *infra*.

[34] See generally Fletcher at 115-22, 135-84; Ashworth, Note 5, *supra*; Lawrence Crocker, *Justice in Criminal Liability: Decriminalizing Harmless Attempts*, 53 Ohio St. L.J. 1057 (1992); Stephen J. Schulhofer, *Harm and Punishment: A Critique of Emphasis on the Results of Conduct in the Criminal Law*, 122 U. Pa. L. Rev. 1497 (1974); Thomas Weigend, *Why Lady Eldon Should Be Acquitted: The Social Harm in Attempting the Impossible*, 27 DePaul L. Rev. 231 (1977).

[35] 1 John Austin, Lectures on Jurisprudence 523 (4th ed. 1873).

[36] For the definition of "incomplete" and "complete" attempts, see § 27.01, *supra*.

[37] See § 9.10[B], *supra*.

strands of objectivism, however, are also discoverable in the common law of attempt.

Subjectivists, i.e., believers in subjective criminality, assert that, in determining guilt and calibrating punishment, the criminal law in general, and attempt law in particular, should focus on an actor's subjective intentions (her *mens rea*), which bespeak her dangerousness and bad character, rather than on her conduct (the *actus reus*), which may or may not result in injury on a particular occasion. With inchoate offenses, a subjectivist believes that "the act of execution is important [only] so far as it verifies the firmness of the [actor's] intent."[38] In a purely subjectivist system, therefore, any act—*no matter how innocuous*—that verifies the actor's commitment to carry out a criminal plan, or which corroborates her confession or other incriminating evidence, is sufficient to justify punishment for an inchoate crime.

In contrast, objectivists believe that conduct should not be punished unless its criminality is "objectively discernible at the time that it occurs,"[39] i.e., the defendant's "acts performed, without any reliance on the accompanying *mens rea*, [must] mark [her] . . . conduct as criminal in nature."[40] According to George Fletcher, "[t]he assumption is that a neutral third-party observer could recognize the activity as criminal even if [she] had no special knowledge about the offender's intention."[41]

In the realm of many substantive offenses, e.g., forcible rape, the criminality of the actor's conduct is easily discernible. With inchoate conduct, however, criminality will not always be obvious. As a practical matter, therefore, inchoate conduct in an objectivist system is often not punishable, unless the defendant's actions manifest criminality and, therefore, cause social harm by "disturbing the public repose,"[42] "unnerving . . . the community,"[43] or causing apprehension, fear or alarm in the community because the actor has patently "set out to do serious damage . . . and to break the accepted rules of social life."[44] Once this social harm has been identified, the actor's *mens rea* is relevant in order to determine whether she should be held accountable for the societal apprehension that she has caused. That is, if she did not intend to commit a crime—it just looked that way—she should not be punished.

Subjectivists and objectivists will frequently reach the same result regarding criminal liability, but for different reasons. For example, reconsider the two hypotheticals at the beginning of this chapter section. Subjectivists and objectivists alike would convict *D1* and *D2* of attempted murder. Subjectivists would favor conviction on the basis of the defendants' *mens rea*. The actors' conduct would be of limited significance, i.e., to verify the fact that their homicidal intentions were

---

[38] Fletcher at 138.

[39] *Id.* at 116.

[40] *United States v. Oviedo*, 525 F.2d 881, 885 (5th Cir. 1976).

[41] Fletcher at 116.

[42] *Clark v. State*, 8 S.W. 145, 147 (Tenn. 1888).

[43] Fletcher at 144.

[44] Weigend, Note 34, *supra*, at 264 (footnote omitted).

genuine and fixed. Conduct less proximate to the outcome would have been sufficient to justify punishment.

From an objectivist perspective, the criminality of the defendants' conduct is
easily discernible to a hypothetical observer on the basis of their conduct alone.
Therefore, assuming sufficient evidence of the actors' *mens rea*, objectivists would
punish *D1* and *D2*. However, if the actors' conduct had terminated at an earlier
stage—e.g., while *D1* was driving to *V1*'s house, or after *D2* loaded the gun but
before she pointed it at her husband[45]—the criminality of their conduct might not
have been manifest, in which case objectivists would not have favored conviction
and punishment.

The difference between subjectivism and objectivism may be seen more dramatically if one considers the following simple event: *D3* puts sugar in spouse-*V3*'s
coffee. Is this attempted murder? Of course not. Suppose, however, that we learn
that *D3* had told a friend a day earlier that she intended to put a lethal dose of poison
in *V3*'s coffee the next morning, and suppose further that *D3* thought that the sugar
was arsenic. If we are convinced beyond a reasonable doubt from this new
information that *D3* intended to kill *V3*, and that the act of putting sugar in the coffee
was an act in execution of this plan, the subjectivist would punish *D3* for attempted
murder. The innocuous conduct of putting sugar in *V3*'s coffee verifies *D3*'s
criminal intent.

An objectivist, however, seemingly would not convict *D3*. An objectivist would
look at the conduct, without consideration of *D3*'s prior statements about killing *V3*
or *D3*'s subjective belief that the substance was arsenic. Based on conduct alone,
the act of placing sugar in coffee does not demonstrate criminality. Therefore, in
the absence of knowledge of *D3*'s intentions and beliefs, her conduct would not
cause public alarm or unnerve the hypothetical observer.[46] Notwithstanding
evidence of *D3*'s *mens rea*—and thus of her dangerousness—the objectivist would
not punish *D3*, for want of social harm.

The underlying advantages and weaknesses of subjectivism and objectivism are
developed in later sections of this chapter in the context of specific legal issues.

---

[45] Since *D2* and *V2* live in the same house together, as wife and husband, there is nothing
manifestly criminal about one spouse loading a firearm in their home.

[46] Of course, the issue will not always be as simple for the objectivist as is described in
the text. How does the hypothetical observer know that the white substance put in the coffee
is sugar, rather than arsenic? Suppose that the sugar is spooned into the coffee cup from a
container labelled "poison," but which strangely contains sugar? Would the hypothetical
observer know that the substance is sugar, or would she believe that it is poison? Objectivists
do not have a settled answer to questions of this sort, but one scholar has suggested that "our
hypothetical observer, if he is to be of any help at all, must be thought of as having a correct
notion of all objective circumstances of the defendant's act which can be observed from
outside." Weigend, Note 34, *supra*, at 267. Under this view, the observer would know that
the substance is sugar, although it is being removed from a poison container.

§ 27.04   Punishing Attempts: Why, and How Much?[47]

[A]—Rationale for Punishing Attempts

[1]—Utilitarian Analysis

Professor H.L.A. Hart has written that "[i]t is not obvious . . . on some versions of utilitarian theory, why attempts should be punishable, as they are, in most legal systems."[48] After all, it may be argued, an attempt is merely conduct targeted at the commission of a substantive crime. Those who set out to commit a crime expect to succeed. Therefore, any deterrent effect of threatened punishment emanates from the substantive offense; the penalty threatened for an attempt has no additional influence. As it is inefficacious, it should not be inflicted.

As Hart has demonstrated, this argument is fallacious. First, a person may assume that if she is successful in her conduct she will avoid detection, so she will be willing to risk the penalty for the targeted crime. On the other hand, she may figure that if she fails in her attempt it will be because she executed the crime poorly, in which case her poor execution may result in arrest. Therefore, she may consider and be deterred by the punishment imposed for an attempt.

Second, applying subjectivist theories,[49] anyone who attempts to commit a crime is dangerous. Whether or not she succeeds in her criminal venture, she is likely to represent an ongoing threat to the community. Therefore, her incapacitation is justifiable.

Third, inchoate offenses provide a basis for official police intervention in order to prevent the consummation of an offense. Thus, separate from the justifications for punishment, attempt laws serve a valuable preventive law enforcement purpose.

[2]—Retributive Analysis

Punishment of attempts makes sense under retributive theory, although retributivists differ in their basis for defending attempt laws. Some retributivists (they might be termed subjective-retributivists) focus on the culpability of criminal attempters.

---

[47] See generally Fletcher at 472-83; Hart at 125-35; Ashworth, Note 5, *supra*; Bjrn Burkhardt, *Is There a Rational Justification for Punishing an Accomplished Crime More Severely Than an Attempted Crime?*, 1986 B.Y.U. L. Rev. 553; Michael Davis, *Why Attempts Deserve Less Punishment Than Complete Crimes*, 5 Law & Phil. 1 (1986); David D. Friedman, *Impossibility, Subjective Probability, and Punishment for Attempts*, 20 J. Leg. Stud. 179 (1991); Sanford H. Kadish, *The Criminal Law and the Luck of the Draw*, 84 J. Crim. L. & Criminology 679 (1994); Mordechai Kremnitzer, *Is There a Rational Justification for Punishing an Accomplished Crime More Severely than an Attempted Crime? A Comment on Prof. Dr, Bjrn Burkhardt's Paper*, 4 B.Y.U. J. Pub. L. 81 (1990); David Lewis, *The Punishment That Leaves Something to Chance*, 18 Phil. & Pub. Aff. 93 (1989); Yoram Shachar, *The Fortuitous Gap in Law and Morality*, 6 Crim. Just. Ethics, Summer/Fall 1987, at 12; J.C. Smith, *The Element of Chance in Criminal Liability*, 1971 Crim. L. Rev. 63; and the sources in Note 34, *supra*.

[48] Hart at 128.

[49] For an examination of subjectivist and objectivist theories, which relate to the discussion in this section, see § 27.03, *supra*.

They argue that a person who shoots but misses her intended victim is as morally culpable as one who succeeds in her endeavor. The only difference is the actor's aim or the fortuity of the victim's movement. The attempter, therefore, deserves to be punished. It would be "unthinkable" that the law would allow the lucky attempter off, while it punishes the successful wrongdoer. [50]

A second group of retributivists (call them objective-retributivists) defend punishment of attempts on the ground that an attempter, by her actions, "disturbs the order of things ordained by law." [51] By disturbing the public's repose and otherwise causing social harm, "punishment is necessary so as to restore, at least symbolically," the public order. [52]

[B]—Less or Equal Punishment?

As stated earlier in this chapter, [53] at common law and in nearly all non-Model Penal Code jurisdictions today, an attempt to commit a felony is punished less severely than the substantive offense. Is this traditional rule justifiable, or should an attempt be graded and punished at the same level as a successful criminal enterprise? Few issues in the criminal law have elicited more thoughtful debate.

[1]—Utilitarian Analysis

Advocates of equal punishment argue that a person who attempts to commit a crime is no less dangerous or in need of rehabilitation than one who succeeds in her criminal endeavor. Assume three persons, A, B, and C, each intending to kill another person. A aims a gun at $V1$, but is arrested before she pulls the trigger. B shoots $V2$, but through the heroic efforts of hospital personnel, $V2$ survives the attack. C kills $V3$. Utilitarian advocates say that nothing distinguishes the actors here except simple luck. The actors' intentions are the same; their criminal resolve is the same; they are equally dangerous. Punishment, therefore, should be the same.

Blackstone disagrees in part with the latter argument. He argues that "[f]or evil, the nearer we approach it, is the more disagreeable and shocking, so that it requires more obstinacy and wickedness to perpetrate an unlawful action, than barely to entertain the thought of it." [54] By this reasoning, "from the moment the defendant's conduct crosses the threshold of an attempt, up until the completion of the attempt, the punishments should ideally be graded with increasing severity." [55] In other words, a complete, but imperfect, attempt should be punished at the same level as the target offense, whereas incomplete attempts should be graded less severely.

The best utilitarian argument for lesser punishment of attempts—more specifically, of incomplete attempts—is that mitigated punishment provides "an encouragement to repentance and remorse," [56] i.e., the reduced punishment serves as an

---

[50] American Law Institute, Comment to Article 5, at 294.

[51] Ashworth, Note 5, *supra*, at 735.

[52] *Id.*

[53] See § 27.02[C], *supra*.

[54] 4 Blackstone at *14.

[55] Ashworth, Note 5, *supra*, at 739.

[56] 4 Blackstone at *14.

incentive to the actor to desist before completing the attempt.[57] For example, if a person entering a bank to rob it already is subject to the punishment imposed for a successful robbery, she has one less reason to stop short.[58]

[2]—Retributive Analysis

Most subjective-retributivists believe that a failed attempt should be punished as severely as an accomplished crime. They reason that luck—whether the attempt succeeds or fails—should have no role to play in setting the punishment of a wrong-doer: a person should be punished depending on her desert; and "desert [is] the same whether or not the harm occurs."[59] Under this view, a person deserves punishment proportional to her culpability, and "fault depends on [the] choice to do the wrongful action, not on what is beyond [her] control,"[60] i.e., whether the intended harm results.

Objective-retributivists disagree. They reason that punishment should be apportioned according to culpability *and* harm. After all, the criminal law punishes for external results, not merely for culpable thoughts; it is the harm that an actor culpably causes that generates the debt that she must symbolically repay through her punishment. Since the harm caused by a failed attempt necessarily is less than that caused by the successful commission of the targeted crime, the debt owed by the attempter is less than that of the successful wrongdoer. Therefore, the traditional approach to attempt law is correct: it should always be a lesser offense than the consummated crime.[61]

---

[57] Jeremy Bentham, Theory of Legislation 427 (C. Ogden ed. 1931).

[58] The same analysis would apply in some completed attempts: if *D* sends *V* a mail bomb which is set to explode in 24 hours, the attempt is complete (she has done every act in her power to commit the offense); but if her punishment for attempted murder is less than for murder, she has a powerful incentive to prevent the bomb from killing *V*.

[59] Kadish, Note 47, *supra*, at 688.

[60] *Id.*

[61] Critics say that this argument "confuse [s] punishment with compensation, the amount of which should indeed be fixed in relation to harm done." Hart at 130-31. According to Hart, the retributive basis for lesser punishment is that victims feel less resentment when an attempt fails than when it succeeds. Hart concedes that this resentment has "deep instinctive roots," but he questions whether the law should give effect to these harm-based sentiments. However, these sentiments may be appropriate: by attempting to commit an offense, a criminal sends the demeaning message to the victim that the wrongdoer's rights and interests are more valuable than the victim's; however, by committing the offense, the victim or her property is *actually* degraded and her rights are diminished. See Jean Hampton, *Correcting Harms Versus Righting Wrongs: The Goal of Retribution*, 39 UCLA L. Rev. 1659, 1677-80 (1992); Benjamin B. Sendor, *Restorative Retributivism*, 5 J. Contemp. Leg. Issues 323 (1994). Consider the case of a rape victim: is she not justified in feeling greater resentment because she has *in fact* been mastered by the rapist than if he had failed? Moreover, to "annul" the crime, society needs to bring the rapist "down" *to the extent that he has actually mastered the victim.*

§ 27.05   *Mens Rea* of Criminal Attempts[62]

[A]—General Rule

It is sometimes said that the mental state required for a criminal attempt is "the intent to commit some other crime."[63] This is an accurate statement, as far as it goes. It is more complete to say, however, that a criminal attempt involves two "intents": the actor (1) must intentionally commit the acts that constitute the *actus reus* of an attempt (as the latter concept is explained in § 27.06, *infra*), i.e., she must intentionally perform acts that bring her in proximity to the commission of a substantive offense (or which otherwise constitute a substantial step in that direction); and (2) she must perform these acts with the specific intention of committing the substantive crime. As the latter intent suggests, an attempt is a specific-intent offense, *even if the substantive crime is a general-intent offense.*

To see how the dual "intents" work, suppose that *D* fires a gun at a target range just as *V* walks in front of the target, and is nearly struck by a bullet from *D*'s gun. *D* is guilty of attempted murder if: (1) she pulled the trigger of the gun intentionally (as this would satisfy the first "intent" required above); and (2) she did so for the purpose of killing *V* (the second, and specific, intent). If *D* intentionally pulled the trigger of the gun, but she did not intend to kill *V* by her intentional acts, e.g., *V*'s presence was unexpected to *D*, then *D* is not guilty of attempted murder.

Although this rule is straightforward, various issues arise that require clarification.

[B]—"Result" Crimes

[1]—In General

A "result" crime is an offense defined in terms of a prohibited result. For example, the offense of criminal homicide prohibits the result of the death of a human being at the hands of another. For crimes of this nature, the ordinary rule is that a person is not guilty of an attempt unless her actions in furtherance of the prohibited result are committed with the specific purpose[64] of causing the

---

[62] See generally Arnold N. Enker, *Mens Rea and Criminal Attempt*, 1977 Am. B. Found. Res. J. 845.

[63] *State v. Green*, 480 A.2d 526, 534 (Conn. 1984).

[64] Suppose that a person does not want the result to occur but *knows* that it will take place. Is knowledge, rather than purpose, sufficient *mens rea* for attempt? Reconsider a hypothetical discussed earlier in the Text at § 10.04[A] [1], *supra*: *D* plants a bomb in an airplane so that it will explode in air and kill *V*, *D*'s spouse. *D* knows that every passenger on the airplane will die. At common law, *D*'s mental state as to their deaths is "intentional," i.e., a person causes a result "intentionally" if it is her conscious object to cause the result (she causes it "purposely") or if she knowingly causes the result. Therefore, if the bomb explodes, *D* may be convicted of "intentionally" killing each passenger. If the bomb fails to go off, however, is *D* guilty of attempted murder of the passengers? The common law answer to this question is uncertain. American Law Institute, Comment to § 5.01, at 305. The Model Penal Code resolution of this hypothetical is described at § 27.09[C], *infra*.

result.[65]

Because of the specific-intent nature of a criminal attempt, the prosecutor in an attempt prosecution is sometimes required to prove that the actor possessed a higher degree of culpability than is required to commit the target offense. For example, if *D* blindfolds herself and fires a loaded pistol into a room that she knows is occupied, she may be convicted of murder if someone is killed. Such a killing, although unintentional, is malicious (the *mens rea* of murder), because it evinces a reckless disregard for the value of human life.[66] However, if *D*'s reckless act does *not* kill anyone in the room, she is *not* guilty of attempted murder: *D* purposely aimed and fired the gun, i.e., she intentionally performed the acts that brought her close to taking a human life; but she lacked the specific intent to kill anyone in the room.[67]

The same result follows if *D* intends to severely injure *V*. *D*'s intent constitutes malice, so she may be convicted of murder if she unintentionally kills *V*. If *V* does not die from the attack, however, *D* is not guilty of attempted murder, as she lacked the specific intent to kill.[68]

[2]—Rationale of Intent Requirement

The requirement of intent makes etymological sense. The word "attempt" means "to try," which in turn means "to seek to do." This justification of the common law intent requirement, however, cannot take us very far. If the only obstacle to permitting guilt for unintentional attempts were the meaning of the word "attempt," we could simply change the name of the crime. The more important question is whether the requirement of specific intent make good penal sense. Or, turning the question around: Should the law permit a person to be convicted of an attempt if she acts with the same level of culpability as to the prohibited result as would be sufficient to convict her for the completed offense?

Those who would answer the preceding question in the affirmative contend that the policies underlying the target offense should apply to criminal attempts. For example, since the common law considers reckless indifference to the value of human life a sufficiently culpable frame of mind to justify a murder conviction if a person dies, it should also be adequate for a conviction of attempted murder, if nobody dies.[69]

But, there is a strong argument for maintaining the intent requirement, which is founded on the heightened dangerousness of intentional wrongdoers. A person who

---

[65] Care must be taken in stating the *mens rea* rule of attempt. The purpose required for an attempt is the purpose to cause the result that constitutes the crime. It is not necessary that the actor know that the result desired is a crime. American Law Institute, Comment to § 5.01, at 301 n.8.

[66] See § 31.05, *infra*.

[67] *Thacker v. Commonwealth*, 114 S.E. 504, 506 (Va. 1922) (shooting into a tent without the specific intent to kill does not constitute attempted murder); see *People v. Lee*, 738 P.2d 752, 754 (Cal. 1987) (specific intent to kill is a required element of attempted murder; lesser forms of malice are insufficient); *People v. Gentry*, 510 N.E.2d 963, 966 (Ill. App. Ct. 1987) (same).

[68] *State v. Hawkins*, 631 So.2d 1288, 1290 (La. Ct. App. 1994).

[69] J.C. Smith, *Two Problems in Criminal Attempts*, 70 Harv. L. Rev. 422, 434-35 (1957).

intends to commit an offense, takes substantial steps in that direction, but fails in its commission or is required temporarily to desist, remains a danger, i.e., "the actor's unspent intent is itself a source of harm independent of his conduct."[70] The danger is that after the failed attempt or involuntary desistance, the actor is likely to try again to commit the crime.

In contrast, one who acts recklessly or negligently in achieving a particular goal may not represent an ongoing threat. For example, a person who drives negligently in order to get to the airport for a flight, but who luckily kills nobody in the process, has no "unspent" intent that is apt to recur. Having satisfied her goal of reaching the airport, there is less reason to fear that the actor will repeat her dangerous conduct. Although the law may punish the driver for her negligent driving, she should not be treated as if she were as dangerous or culpable as a person who attempts to kill.

[3]—Special Homicide Problems

[a]—Attempted Felony Murder

Suppose that D intentionally commits a felony, during the perpetration of which another person unintentionally dies. At common law, D is guilty of murder as the result of the felony-murder rule.[71] Suppose, however, D accidentally fires a gun during the felony, and V is wounded. May D be convicted of *attempted* felony-murder?

Nearly all states that have considered this issue have held that attempted felony-murder is not a cognizable offense.[72] This is consistent with the principle that the offense of attempted murder requires a specific intent to kill; the defendant's intent to commit a felony does not substitute for the former intent.

A few states do recognize an offense of attempted felony-murder. The reasoning in support of this position is sparse, but apparently courts that allow for such a crime believe that the underlying policies of the felony-murder rule should override ordinary criminal attempt doctrines.[73]

In jurisdictions recognizing the offense, it is difficult to determine at what point an attempted felony-murder occurs. Certainly the doctrine applies if the felon wounds a person. But, in one case in which a conviction of attempted felony-murder was allowed, the victim was not wounded.[74] Indeed, one may question whether the firing of a weapon is necessary. Suppose that a felon simply points a gun at V in a threatening manner, and V suffers a non-lethal heart-attack? Suppose V does *not*

---

[70] Enker, Note 62, *supra*, at 855.

[71] See § 31.06, *infra*.

[72] *Bruce v. State*, 566 A.2d 103, 105 (Md. 1989) (reversing the conviction of attempted felony-murder on the basis of the facts described in the preceding paragraph).

[73] *Amlotte v. State*, 456 So.2d 448, 450 (Fla. 1984) (reasoning that "as under the felony murder doctrine, [the law] presumes the existence of the specific intent required to prove attempt").

[74] E.g., *White v. State*, 585 S.W.2d 952 (Ark. 1979).

suffer a heart attack? One court that recognizes the offense of attempted felony-murder has limited the crime to circumstances in which the felon commits "a specific overt act which could, but does not, cause the death of another."[75] This limitation, however, arguably could allow for a conviction of attempted felony-murder in all of the preceding hypothetical cases.

[b]—Attempted Manslaughter

A person who intentionally kills another in sudden heat of passion, as the result of adequate provocation, is guilty of voluntary manslaughter.[76] If a person in such an emotional state attempts to kill the provoker, but fails, the actor may properly be convicted of attempted voluntary manslaughter.[77] No reason of logic precludes this result, as the provoked actor possesses the specific intent to kill.

Logically, a person may not be convicted of attempted *involuntary* manslaughter, when the latter offense is based on a *mens rea* of criminal negligence or some other state of mind other than intent-to-kill.[78] It would be odd, indeed illogical, to say that a person can intentionally commit an unintentional crime.[79]

[C]—"Conduct" Crimes

The problems described in the preceding subsection must be distinguished from those pertaining to "conduct" crimes, i.e., crimes whose *actus reus* are defined in terms of harmful conduct rather than injurious results. For example, statutes penalizing reckless driving seek to deter or punish dangerous conduct, even if such conduct does not result in tangible harm.

Although little case law exists on the point, there is no logical reason why a person should not be convicted of an attempt to commit a conduct crime, as long as she possesses the specific intent to engage in the conduct that, if performed, constitutes the substantive offense. For example, suppose that *D* drives her car blindfolded, as a practical joke. This conduct would constitute an offense, such as reckless endangerment. Therefore, if *D* enters her car, blindfolds herself, turns on the ignition, and is arrested at that moment, she should be convicted of attempted reckless endangerment: she has intentionally committed the *actus reus* of the attempt by purposely blindfolding herself and turning on the car ignition; and she has the specific intent to drive the car in a manner that would be reckless.[80]

---

[75] *Amlotte v. State*, 456 So.2d at 450.

[76] See § 31.07, *infra*.

[77] E.g., *Cox v. State*, 534 A.2d 1333, 1336 (Md. 1988); *State v. Robinson*, 643 A.2d 591, 597 (N.J. 1994).

[78] *Cox v. State*, 534 A.2d at 1336.

[79] *Commonwealth v. Griffin*, 456 A.2d 171, 177 (Pa. Super. Ct. 1983).

[80] Williams at 619-20; *but see Minshew v. State*, 594 So.2d 703, 713 (Ala. Crim. App. 1991) (stating that the offense of attempted reckless endangerment "is legally impossible").

[D]—Attendant Circumstances

Suppose that D, believing that V is 18 years of age, has sexual intercourse with her. In fact, V is 16, under the age of legal consent for intercourse. In a prosecution for statutory rape, D's mistake of fact, even if reasonable, will not excuse him in most jurisdictions. One reason for this rule is that the attendant circumstance of the girl's age requires no *mens rea*; it is a strict-liability offense, at least as to that element.

Suppose that D is arrested immediately before intercourse occurs. Is D guilty of *attempted* statutory rape? That is, what *mens rea* regarding an attendant circumstance is required for the offense of attempt? Virtually all commentators agree that the ordinary specific-intent requirement of attempt law should not apply to attendant circumstances.[81] Some commentators favor the proposition that a person should be convicted of a criminal attempt if she is reckless with regard to any attendant circumstance.[82] Thus, in the statutory rape case, D would not be guilty of attempted statutory rape unless he knew that there was a substantial risk that the girl was underage.

Other commentators would not impose a special *mens rea* requirement regarding attendant circumstances in attempt prosecutions.[83] For them it is sufficient that the actor is as culpable regarding the attendant circumstance as is required for that element of the substantive crime. These scholars reason that as long as the actor has the specific intent to engage in the conduct, or to cause the result, that is prohibited by the statute defining the substantive crime, the law should not artificially require culpability greater than is necessary to commit the target offense. The policy supporting the latter offense should preempt attempt doctrines.

Following this reasoning, D would be guilty of attempted statutory rape: the target offense is one of strict liability with regard to the girl's age, so the same analysis would apply to the attempt.[84] Or, assume that D is charged with attempted trafficking in stolen property. If the substantive offense requires proof that the actor was at least reckless in regard to the attendant circumstance that the property was stolen, D may be convicted of attempted trafficking in stolen property if she purposely trafficked in the stolen property (the conduct element of the offense), and she was reckless in regard to the fact that the property was stolen.[85]

---

[81] See Enker, Note 62, *supra*, at 867 n.58.

[82] E.g., Williams at 619-20.

[83] E.g., J.C. Smith, *Two Problems in Criminal Attempts Reexamined -I*, 1962 Crim. L.R. 135, 143.

[84] *Simmons v. State*, 10 So.2d 436, 438 (Fla. 1942)

[85] *State v. Galan*, 658 P.2d 243, 244-45 (Ariz. Ct. App. 1982).

§ 27.06 *Actus Reus* of Criminal Attempts[86]

[A]—Policy Context

Neither the common law nor most statutes provide a clear vision of the *actus reus* of a criminal attempt. Unhelpful conclusory statements are frequently expressed: for example, an attempt involves "perpetration" rather than "preparation"; or the defendant's conduct must be "proximate" to completion, rather than "remote." Beyond this, courts have developed a myriad of rules or tests, many of which partially overlap each other, to identify when a criminal attempt occurs.

Part of the difficulty in drawing the proper line between noncriminal preparation and a criminal attempt is that courts are torn by competing policy considerations. On the one hand, some courts believe that "[t]he real question is whether acts of preparation when coupled with intent have reached a point at which they pose a danger to the public so as to be worthy of the law's notice."[87] On the other hand, if courts allow for too early police intervention, innocent persons, and those with still barely formed criminal intentions—persons who might voluntarily turn back from criminal activity—may be improperly or needlessly arrested.

The struggle to find the line of demarcation is also a function of the debate between subjectivists (i.e., those who believe that liability should attach as soon as the actor verifies her commitment to carrying out her plan) and objectivists (i.e., advocates of the view that liability should not attach until a person's conduct, without consideration of her intentions, manifests criminality, and thus would create apprehension in a hypothetical observer).[88]

Generally speaking, subjectivists favor an *actus reus* test of attempt that allows for early attachment of guilt. This generalization follows from the underlying premises of the doctrine. For subjectivists, proof of an actor's dangerousness, as evidenced by her *mens rea*, is paramount. Intention, however, can be proved through confessions, independent evidence of the actor's motive to commit the offense, and other third-party testimony regarding the defendant's state of mind. It follows from this that any conduct, no matter how slight, that corroborates the defendant's alleged *mens rea*, should suffice for a criminal attempt.

For objectivists, the *actus reus* element has independent significance, because adherents to this theory do not believe that society should use its coercive power against inchoate conduct unless the actor has caused some social harm, at least in the form of societal apprehension of criminal activity. Often, however, conduct does not lose its ambiguity and result in societal apprehension until well into the criminal transaction.

---

[86] See generally American Law Institute, Comment to § 5.01, at 321-29; Herbert Wechsler, William Kenneth Jones, & Harold L. Korn, *The Treatment of Inchoate Crimes in the Model Penal Code of the American Law Institute: Attempt, Solicitation, and Conspiracy [Pt. 1]*, 61 Colum. L. Rev. 571, 573-621 (1961).

[87] *State v. Otto*, 629 P.2d 646, 653 (Idaho 1981) (Bakes, C.J., dissenting).

[88] For a fuller explanation of these doctrines, see § 27.03, *supra*.

Objectivists believe that unchecked subjectivism, with its emphasis on *mens rea* and de-emphasis on conduct, endangers civil liberties, and too easily results in the conviction of innocent persons. They fear that subjectivism may result in criminal liability for little more than bad thoughts. Moreover, guilt will too often be based on unreliable confessions, and other circumstantial evidence of an actor's alleged motivations. In contrast, subjectivists reason that if a society must wait until conduct unambiguously demonstrates its criminality, crime prevention will be frustrated.

[B]—The Tests

[1]—General Observations

"Much ink has been spilt in an attempt to arrive at a satisfactory standard for telling where preparation[] ends and attempt begins."[89] The most common tests or factors that have developed over the years are described below. Generally speaking, the tests fall into two categories: those that focus on how much remains to be done before the crime is committed; and those that consider how much has already occurred.

In light of the conflicting policy considerations relating to attempt law, there is little or no way to predict with certainty where a court will draw the critical line between preparation and perpetration in a particular case. However, various factors come into play, including: (1) whether the act in question appears to be dangerously close to causing tangible harm, so that police intervention cannot realistically be delayed;[90] (2) the seriousness of the threatened harm, i.e., "the more serious the crime attempted . . ., the further back in the series of acts leading up to the consummated crime should the criminal law reach in holding the defendant guilty for an attempt"[91] and (3) the strength of the evidence of the actor's *mens rea*, i.e., the more clearly the intent to commit the offense is proven, the less proximate the acts need to be to consummation of the offense.[92]

[2]—"Last Act" Test

Some courts used to state that a criminal attempt only occurred when the person performed all of the acts that she believed were necessary to commit the target offense.[93] Applying this standard, an attempted murder-by-shooting does not occur until *D* pulls the trigger of the gun; an attempted theft of a museum painting does not take place until *D* begins to remove the property from the wall; and an attempted arson does not occur unless *D* sets on fire the dwelling that she hopes to destroy. Today, there is general agreement that an attempt occurs *at least* by the time of the last act, but no jurisdiction *requires* that it reach this stage on all occasions.

Little commends the last-act standard, except for its bright-line nature. As the examples of its application suggest, the police would be stymied by the rule; it

---

[89] *Mims v. United States*, 375 F.2d 135, 148 (5th Cir. 1967).

[90] Arnold N. Enker, *Impossibility in Criminal Attempts—Legality and the Legal Process*, 53 Minn. L. Rev. 665, 674 (1969).

[91] Sayre, Note 1, *supra*, at 845.

[92] See *People v. Berger*, 280 P.2d 136, 138 (Cal. Ct. App. 1955).

[93] E.g., *Regina v. Eagleton*, 6 Cox Crim. Cas. 559, 571 (1855).

would virtually be impossible to prevent commission of a substantive crime. Also, to the extent that subjectivist principles are important, an actor's dangerousness can be identified well before the last act; and, from an objectivist viewpoint, social harm can occur, and the criminality of an actor's conduct can often be discerned, before the final act.

[3]—"Physical Proximity" Test

Some courts state that, while it need not reach the last act, the actor's conduct must be "proximate" to the completed crime, in that "it must approach sufficiently near to it to stand either as the first or some subsequent step in a *direct movement* toward the commission of the offense after the preparations are made."[94] Or, as another court has explained, for an act to be indicted as an attempt, "it must go so far that it would result, or apparently result in the actual commission of the crime it was designed to effect, if not extrinsically hindered or frustrated by extraneous circumstances."[95]

In essence, according to this test, an attempt does not arise unless an actor has it within her power to complete the crime almost immediately. For example, *D* would be guilty of attempted robbery if, weapon in hand, she has her victim in view and can immediately proceed to rob her, absent external factors (such as the intervention of the police). On the other hand, one court held that an attempt did *not* occur when two men, intending to trick the victim out of his money, convinced him to go to the bank and withdraw some of his cash, but the men were arrested before he withdrew the cash, and before they made overtures to secure the money from him.[96]

[4]—"Dangerous Proximity" Test

In a series of cases,[97] Justice Oliver Wendell Holmes formulated a test that incorporates the physical-proximity standard, but which is somewhat more flexible: according to this standard, a person is guilty of an attempt when her conduct is in "dangerous proximity to success,"[98] or when an act "is so near to the result that the danger of success is very great."[99] There is no clear point of proximity, but Holmes observed that courts consider three factors: the "nearness of the danger, the greatness of the harm, and the degree of apprehension felt."[100]

Applying the dangerous-proximity standard, one state court has held that a person who, with intent to possess cocaine, orders contraband from a supplier, meets a courier at her home, examines the goods, but rejects them on quality grounds, is guilty of attempted possession of a controlled substance;[101] in contrast, a person

---

[94] *State v. Dowd*, 220 S.E.2d 393, 396 (N.C. Ct. App. 1975) (emphasis added).

[95] *Commonwealth v. Kelley*, 58 A.2d 375, 377 (Pa. Super. Ct. 1948).

[96] *Id.*

[97] *Commonwealth v. Kennedy*, 48 N.E. 770 (Mass. 1897); *Commonwealth v. Peaslee*, 59 N.E. 55 (Mass. 1901); *Hyde v. United States*, 225 U.S. 347 (1912) (dissenting opinion).

[98] *Hyde v. United States*, 225 U.S. at 388.

[99] *People v. Rizzo*, 158 N.E. 888, 889 (N.Y. 1927).

[100] Holmes at 68.

[101] *People v. Acosta*, 609 N.E.2d 518, 519 (N.Y. 1993).

who tells the courier that she will buy the drugs once she obtains sufficient funds, and schedules a later meeting to consummate the sale, but who is arrested immediately, is not guilty of an attempt.[102]

One of the most famous—and controversial—applications of this standard arose in *People v. Rizzo*,[103] in which four armed men drove around looking for *V*, whom they expected would be withdrawing a large sum of money from the bank. They entered various buildings looking for *V*. Suspicious, two police officers placed the men under surveillance. Finally, the suspects were arrested when one of them entered another building. *V* was not present where the arrest occurred.

With apparent embarrassment, the court overturned the conviction. While commending "[t]he police of the city of New York [for their] excellent work in this case by preventing the commission of a serious crime," and expressing their "great satisfaction to realize that we have such wide-awake guardians of our peace," the court concluded that in the absence of a victim, the armed suspects were not dangerously close to success.[104]

The beneficial feature of Holmes' test is its flexibility in comparison to the strict physical-proximity standard. On the other hand, the test provides little guidance to police officers on the street, who must determine at what point they may properly arrest a suspect. Indeed, if *Rizzo* was rightly decided, the "wide-awake guardians of the peace" should not have arrested the defendants for attempted robbery.[105] Yet, the defendants in *Rizzo* were dangerous, and their conduct manifested criminality (indeed, that is apparently why the police began to follow them).[106]

[5]—"Indispensable Element" Test

In determining proximity, some courts will not find an attempt if the actor has not yet obtained control of an indispensable feature of the criminal plan. For example, according to this standard, an actor who does not yet possess a necessary instrumentality for the crime, e.g., a gun for a murder or the equipment needed to manufacture illegal drugs, has not yet crossed the line from preparation to perpetration;[107] and an offense that requires action by an innocent person cannot be

---

[102] *People v. Warren*, 489 N.E.2d 240, 241-42 (N.Y. 1985).

[103] 158 N.E. 888 (N.Y. 1927).

[104] *Rizzo* raises interesting questions. For example, in light of *Rizzo*, may a person be convicted of attempted sexual assault, if he drives along with an undercover police officer to a building at which the accused expects to have sexual relations with a child he selected from a collection of pictures of girls supplied by the officer, but who in fact is not at the site and never would have been? See *Van Bell v. State*, 775 P.2d 1273 (Nev. 1989) (affirming a conviction based on a "proximity approach" to attempt law).

[105] Arrest for some other crime, including conspiracy to commit robbery, might have been proper.

[106] On the other hand, based on conduct alone, *of what offense* were they manifestly guilty of attempting—armed robbery, murder, kidnapping?

[107] E.g., *State v. Wood*, 103 N.W. 25 (S.D. 1905) (no attempt without a dangerous weapon); *State v. Addor*, 110 S.E. 650 (N.C. 1922) (no attempt without equipment to manufacture illegal whiskey).

attempted until that action is completed.[108]

This test, although easier to apply than the dangerous-proximity standard, is arbitrary. The presence or absence of an indispensable element often says little regarding the actor's culpability, the firmness of her intentions, or the degree to which prior conduct may have disturbed the public's repose.[109]

[6]—"Probable Desistance" Test

The preceding tests focus on the actor's proximity to successful completion of the crime, i.e., on how much remains to be done. In contrast, the Commentary to the American Law Institute has described another standard, which it terms the "probable desistance" test, that centers on how far the defendant has already proceeded. Specifically, a court will not find an attempt unless, in the ordinary course of events, "the actor . . . reached a point where it was unlikely that he would have voluntarily desisted from his effort to commit the crime."[110]

Courts called upon to make the necessary judgment do not try to determine whether the defendant reached her own psychological point of unlikely desistance; instead they try to identify the "point of no return" of an ordinary person. However, since ordinary people do not prepare to commit serious crimes, this test is fallacious.

[7]—"Unequivocality" Test

According to the unequivocality (or *res ipsa loquitur*) test, an act does not constitute an attempt until it ceases to be equivocal. That is, an attempt occurs when a person's conduct, standing alone, unambiguously manifests her criminal intent. It is as if the jury observed the conduct in video form with the sound off (so as not to hear the actor's potentially incriminating remarks), and sought to decide from the conduct alone whether the accused was attempting to commit the offense for which she was prosecuted.[111]

For example, in *People v. Miller*,[112] D threatened to kill V, whom D accused of harassing his wife. Later that day, D went armed with a rifle to a field where C, the local constable, and V, standing approximately 30 yards further away, were working. D walked in the direction of C and V, stopped, loaded his rifle but did not aim it, and resumed his approach. At some point either before or after D loaded his weapon, V fled at a right angle from D's line of approach. Ultimately, C took possession of the rifle without resistance. The court held that D was not guilty of attempted murder, because "up to the moment the gun was taken from the

---

[108] E.g., *In re Schurman*, 20 P. 277 (Kan. 1889) (D, with the intent to defraud a life insurance company, feigned death; X, the beneficiary under the policy, and an innocent party to the scheme, had not yet filed a claim; held: D is not guilty of an attempt to defraud the company).

[109] For example, the indispensable element can involve innocent conduct by a non-participant in the crime. See *id*. In such a case, this essential element adds nothing to the proof of the actor's criminal intentions or the harmfulness of her conduct.

[110] American Law Institute, Comment to § 5.01, at 325.

[111] See J.W. Cecil Turner, *Attempts to Commit Crimes*, 5 Cambridge L.J. 230, 236-38 (1934).

[112] 42 P.2d 308 (Cal. 1935).

defendant, no one could say with certainty whether [he] had come into the field to carry out his threat to kill [V] or merely to demand his arrest by [C]."

The unequivocality test is in general harmony with the objectivist goal of reserving criminal liability for those whose conduct manifests criminality and, as a consequence, causes social apprehension. The test, however, has been attacked as impractical. For example, in the leading case in support of the doctrine,[113] the court stated that buying a box of matches to burn a haystack is too ambiguous to justify conviction for attempted arson, but that "he who takes matches to a haystack and there lights one of them," acts unambiguously. However, as one scholar has shown,[114] the unequivocality standard fails to work in this case as intended, because a person who lights a match near a haystack may only intend to light a pipe. Thus, in this example, either we must say that the actor's conduct is equivocal (in which case, police intervention would be improper until the last act occurs, e.g, when the match is tossed into the hay), or we must concede that after conduct manifests criminality, a later act may render it ambiguous again (in which case the standard may not adequately protect the innocent from arrest).

[8]—"Substantial Step" Test

The "substantial step" test formulated by the American Law Institute and included in the Model Penal Code is described at § 27.09, *infra*.

§ 27.07   Defense: Impossibility[115]

[A]—The Issue

D wants to kill V. Standing outside V's house, she fires a gun at the bed in which she believes V is sleeping. V is not killed because she is not at home. Is D guilty of attempted murder?

Our intuitions almost certainly tell us that D should be convicted of an attempt. She has the requisite *mens rea*, and she has performed every act in her power to kill V. From a policy perspective, too, D merits punishment—she is dangerous, culpable, and has acted in a manner that would cause societal apprehension. The law confirms our moral intuitions and legal analysis: D is guilty of attempted murder.[116]

However, suppose that we change the facts slightly. Suppose that when D fires the gun, V is in the bed, but is already dead from a coincidental heart attack. That

---

[113] *King v. Barker*, [1924] N.Z.L.R. 865.

[114] Williams at 630.

[115] See generally Larry Alexander, *Inculpatory and Exculpatory Mistakes and the Fact/ Law Distinction: An Essay in Memory of Myke Bayles*, 12 Law & Phil. 33 (1993); Crocker, Note 34, *supra*; Enker, Note 90, *supra*; George P. Fletcher, *Constructing a Theory of Impossible Attempts*, Criminal Justice Ethics, Winter/Spring 1986, at 53; Graham Hughes, *One Further Footnote on Attempting the Impossible*, 42 N.Y.U. L. Rev. 1005 (1967); Ira P. Robbins, *Attempting the Impossible: The Emerging Consensus*, 23 Harv. J. Legis. 377 (1986); Kenneth W. Simons, *Mistake and Impossibility, Law and Fact, and Culpability: A Speculative Essay*, 81 J. Crim. L. & Criminology 447 (1990); Weigend, Note 34, *supra*.

[116] E.g., *State v. Mitchell*, 71 S.W. 175, 177-78 (Mo. 1902).

is, *V* is a corpse, rather than a "human being," as defined by homicide law. Is *D* now guilty of attempted murder? No, according to dicta in various court opinions.[117] Is this dicta wrong, or can this example be distinguished in a principled manner from the "empty bed" case?

Or, suppose that we move our case to a forest. *D* and *V* are hunting together; *D* wants to use this opportunity to kill *V*, so she shoots at *V* in the woods. As it turns out "*V*" is a tree stump. Or *V*, sensing danger, displays a wax facsimile of herself, and it this object that *D* shoots. Attempted murder? No, according to dicta and a holding in equivalent circumstances.[118]

Consider, finally, these two cases. In each one, a male has sexual intercourse with a 17-year-old female in a jurisdiction that sets the age of consent for intercourse at 16. In other words, in both cases statutory rape has *not* occurred. *D1*, however, believed that the girl was 15, so he thought that he was committing statutory rape.[119] *D2* knew that the girl was 17, but he incorrectly believed that the lawful age of consent was 18.[120] Should either or both of these cases constitute attempted statutory rape?

The real cases, and imaginative hypotheticals, go on and on. All of them raise the same issue: whether a person should be convicted for an "impossible attempt," i.e., for an attempt that cannot succeed. In each of these cases, the actor presumably has the requisite *mens rea*, and has done everything in her power to commit the target offense. If we disallow conviction in any of these cases, therefore, it will be because the law recognizes a defense of impossibility.

[B]—General Rule

The common law rule regarding impossible attempts is easy to state. It distinguishes between two types of impossibilities: "factual impossibility" and "legal impossibility." *At common law, legal impossibility is a defense; factual impossibility is not.*[121]

---

[117] *State v. Taylor*, 133 S.W.2d 336, 341 (Mo. 1939); *State v. Guffey*, 262 S.W.2d 152, 156 (Mo. Ct. App. 1953); see *State v. Logan*, 656 P.2d 777, 778 (Kan. 1983).

[118] See *State v. Guffey*, 262 S.W.2d 152, 156 (Mo. Ct. App. 1953) (*D*, a hunter, was not guilty of attempting to kill a deer out of season when he shot at a wax-dummy deer); *Regina v. M'Pherson*, 7 Cox Crim. Cas. 281, 284 (1857) (dictum, tree stump); *Rex v. Osborn*, 84 J.P. 63, 64 (Central Crim. Ct. 1919) (same).

[119] Notice that this is a mirror image of the typical mistake-of-fact case, in which *D* believes that the female is old enough to consent, but she is not. In the typical case, therefore, the *actus reus* of statutory rape is committed; at issue is *D*'s *mens rea*. In the present case, however, the *actus reus* of statutory rape did not occur, but *D* possessed a culpable mental state.

[120] Notice that this is a mirror image of the usual mistake-of-law case, in which an actor believes that her conduct is lawful, but it is not; here, the actor believed that he was violating a law, but he was not. If ignorance of the law does not ordinarily exculpate, may it nonetheless inculpate?

[121] American Law Institute, Comment to § 5.01, at 307-17; Hall at 586-87; Williams §§ 206-07; *Bandy v. State*, 575 S.W.2d 278, 279-80 (Tenn. 1979); *United States v. Oviedo*, 525 F.2d 881, 883 (5th Cir. 1976); *United States v. Thomas*, 32 C.M.R. 278, 283-84 (1962).

When one moves from the hornbook rule to specific cases, however, the law becomes exceedingly complex. Many pages of court opinions and scholarly literature have been filled in a largely fruitless effort to explain (and justify) the difference between the two types of impossible attempts. Perhaps no aspect of the criminal law is more perplexing than the common law of impossible attempts.

[C]—Factual Impossibility

[1]—In General

"Factual impossibility" exists when a person's intended end constitutes a crime, but she fails to consummate the offense because of an attendant circumstance unknown to her or beyond her control.[122] Examples of factual impossibility are: (1) a pickpocket putting her hand in the victim's empty pocket;[123] (2) an abortionist beginning the surgical procedure on a nonpregnant woman;[124] (3) an impotent male trying to have nonconsensual sexual intercourse;[125] (4) an assailant shooting into an empty bed where the intended victim customarily sleeps,[126] or pulling the trigger of an unloaded gun aimed at a person who is present.[127]

In each of these examples the actor was mistaken regarding some fact relating to the victim, herself or himself, and/or the method of commission. More specifically, the target offense was not consummated because the actor chose the wrong victim (the pickpocket and abortion cases), the victim was not present (the empty bed case), the actor was not physically capable of committing the offense (the impotency case), or inappropriate means were used to commit the crime (the unloaded gun case). Had the circumstances been as the actors believed them to be, or hoped that they were (e.g., the pocket contained property; the woman was pregnant; the victim was in the bed; the actor was physically capable of having intercourse; the gun was loaded), the crimes would have been consummated.

It should not be surprising that lawmakers are unsympathetic to claims of factual impossibility. In each of the cases described above, the actor has demonstrated her or his dangerousness (critical to subjectivists) and manifested criminality (important to objectivists). No good reason exists to recognize a defense merely because a person chooses her victim badly, does not use proper means to commit the crime, or for some other reason unrelated to her culpability does not successfully commit the offense.

[2]—"Inherent" Factual Impossibility

Although factual impossibility is not a defense to a criminal attempt, "inherent impossibility" (or, more completely, "inherent *factual* impossibility") may be a

---

[122] *United States v. Berrigan*, 482 F.2d 171, 188 (3d Cir. 1973); see Robbins, Note 115, *supra*, at 380 n.13 (quoting similar definitions).

[123] E.g., *People v. Twiggs*, 35 Cal. Rptr. 859 (Ct. App. 1963).

[124] E.g., *State v. Moretti*, 244 A.2d 499 (N.J. 1968).

[125] E.g., *Waters v. State*. 234 A.2d 147 (Md. Ct. App. 1967).

[126] E.g., *State v. Mitchell*, 71 S.W. 175 (Mo. 1902).

[127] E.g., *State v. Damms*, 100 N.W.2d 592 (Wis. 1960).

defense. The doctrine of inherent impossibility has arisen primarily in scholarly literature and judicial dictum, but it is recognized as a statutory defense in at least one state,[128] and, following the lead of the Model Penal Code,[129] may serve as a statutory basis for downgrading an offense or for dismissing the prosecution. To the extent that the defense is recognized, it applies if the method to accomplish the crime was one that "a reasonable person would view as completely inappropriate to the objectives sought."[130]

What is an example of an inherently impossible attempt? In one of the earliest cases to discuss the topic, an example was suggested: a " 'voodoo doctor' . . . [who] actually believed that his malediction would surely bring death to the person on whom he was invoking it."[131] However, this is a poor example, as it is not the case that incantation is a "completely inappropriate" means of killing another, e.g., if the intended victim believes in hexes and, as a consequence, dies of fright. A better example of the doctrine is attempting to sink a battleship with a pop-gun.[132] And, the doctrine has arisen recently as a real-life issue in a small number of attempted murder prosecutions involving persons suffering from acquired immune deficiency syndrome (AIDS) who bit, spat on, scratched, or sprayed blood at, their intended victims, purportedly in order to infect and kill them.[133]

Should the law recognize an inherent impossibility defense? For an objectivist, the answer is clear: if conduct would appear harmless to a person of normal understanding, no societal apprehension will occur and, therefore, punishment is unjustified. For subjectivists, the nagging question—one for which there is no obvious answer—is whether a person who endeavors to commit a crime in an inherently impossible manner is dangerous or, at least, whether she is dangerous to

---

[128] Minn. Stat. Ann. § 609.17(2) (West. 1987) (providing an impossibility defense, if "such impossibility would have been clearly evident to a person of normal understanding").

[129] See § 27.09[F][2], *infra.*

[130] *State v. Bird*, 285 N.W.2d 481, 482 (Minn. 1979).

[131] *Commonwealth v. Johnson* 167 A. 344, 348 (Pa. 1933) (Maxey, J., dissenting).

[132] *State v. Logan*, 656 P.2d 777, 779 (Kan. 1983).

[133] E.g., *State v. Haines*, 545 N.E.2d 834 (Ind. Ct. App. 1989) (*D* spat at, attempted to bite, and caused blood to spray at three paramedics; medical testimony was introduced that the paramedics were "put at risk" by *D*'s conduct; the jury convicted *D* of three counts of attempted murder; the appellate court approved the verdicts, stating that "the evidence presented at trial renders any defense of inherent impossibility inapplicable to this case"); *State v. Smith*, 621 A.2d 493 (N.J. Sup. Ct. App. Div. 1993) (*D*, a jail inmate, bit a guard, and was convicted of attempted murder; the court doubted that the proposition that AIDS cannot be transmitted by a bite "is presently provable scientifically, given the current state of medical knowledge"; held: conviction affirmed, and the judge did not abuse his discretion by refusing to downgrade the offense on the ground that the attempt was "inherently unlikely to result or culminate in the commission of a crime"); see also *Weeks v. State*, 834 S.W.2d 559 (Tex. Ct. App. 1992) (*D* spat on a prison guard; conviction for attempted murder was affirmed on the ground that the controverted evidence supported a jury finding that the AIDS virus could be spread by saliva).

an extent commensurate with the punishment that applies to an ordinary criminal attempt.[134]

[D]—Legal Impossibility

[1]—Introductory Comments

The term "legal impossibility" is an unfortunate one, for two reasons. First, there are two different categories of attempts that have been identified by courts as implicating "legal impossibility." Those two versions may be termed "pure" and "hybrid" legal impossibility. The failure of courts to distinguish between them creates unnecessary confusion.

Second, neither version of legal impossibility should be identified as such. As is developed below, hybrid legal impossibility cannot be distinguished from factual impossibility in any principled manner, and may properly be merged with it. On the other hand, pure legal impossibility may more accurately be identified as an application of the principle of legality.[135]

Largely as the result of the influence of the Model Penal Code, the overwhelming modern trend has been to abolish hybrid legal impossibility as a defense.[136] So-called pure legal impossibility remains a basis for exculpation.

[2]—Pure Legal Impossibility

"Pure legal impossibility" arises "when the law does not proscribe the goal that the defendant sought to achieve."[137]

The simplest case of pure legal impossibility occurs when a person performs a lawful act with a guilty conscience, i.e., she believes that she is committing a crime, but she is not. For example, as Jerome Hall has observed, "it is not a crime to throw even a Kansas steak into a garbage can."[138] If D commits this dastardly act she is guilty of no offense. And, even if she believes that there is such an offense, she is not guilty of attempting to commit this fanciful crime. Just as a person may not ordinarily escape punishment on the ground that she is ignorant of a law's existence,[139] it is also true that "we cannot punish people under laws that are purely the figments of their guilty imaginations."[140] Similarly, D is not guilty of a criminal attempt if, unknown to her, the legislature has repealed a statute that D believes that she is violating. For example, if D attempts to sell "bootleg" liquor after the repeal

---

[134] It *is* a nagging question, because it may be posited that a person who is so far out of touch with reality that, for example, she believes that she can sink a battleship with a pop-gun, may later commit some other irrational and dangerous act, or such a person may come upon a more sensible way to accomplish her criminal task.

[135] See § 5.01, *supra.*

[136] *State v. Logan*, 656 P.2d at 779.

[137] Robbins, Note 115, *supra*, at 389; see also Hall at 586; Williams at § 205.

[138] Hall at 595.

[139] See § 13.01[A], *supra.*

[140] Alexander, Note 115, *supra*, at 46.

of the Prohibition laws, she is not guilty of an attempt even though she is unaware of their repeal.

A somewhat more problematic case of pure legal impossibility arose in *Wilson v. State*.[141] *D* was prosecuted for forgery because he added the number "1" to a check made out to him in the sum of "$2.50," so that he could receive "$12.50." Under state law, however, this did not constitute forgery because he tampered with a legally "immaterial" part of the check.[142] Consequently, the trial judge informed the jury that it could not convict *D* of forgery, but that it could convict him of the lesser offense of attempted forgery, which it did.

D's conviction was reversed, as it should have been. What he sought to do did not constitute the crime of forgery.[143] Even if someone had asked *D* what it was that he thought he was doing, and even if he had said, "I am forging a check," this would have been irrelevant. Wisely or not, state lawmakers had excluded his conduct (making an immaterial change on a document) from the ambit of the crime of forgery. Therefore, Wilson may not be convicted of attempting to forge a check in this manner.[144]

Although courts may treat *Wilson* and the Kansas steak and bootleg-liquor hypotheticals as "legal impossibility" cases, the true basis for acquittal is the principle of legality. That is, conduct that neither the legislature nor a court has identified as criminal can serve as the foundation for a conviction, simply because the actor's mental state was bad or vicious. If we punished a person in such circumstances, it would be because she has demonstrated her general willingness to ignore society's legal prohibitions, or because of her general moral culpability. The legality principle provides, however, that we may not punish people—no matter culpable or dangerous they are—for conduct that is not unlawful at the time of the action.

[3]—Hybrid Legal Impossibility

[a]—In General

Hybrid legal impossibility (or what courts will simply call "legal impossibility") exists if the actor's goal is illegal (thus, distinguishing itself from pure legal impossibility), but commission of the offense is impossible due to a *factual* mistake by her regarding the *legal* status of some attendant circumstance relevant to her conduct.[145] As the preceding definition implies and as is clarified immediately

---

[141] 38 So. 46 (Miss. 1905).

[142] When there is a discrepancy between the written words and the figures on a check, the former apply. As a result, *D*'s alteration of the numbers without changing the words constituted an immaterial change.

[143] Wilson was guilty of some other offense, such as false pretenses or attempted false pretenses (if the money was not handed over).

[144] Thus, too, in the hypothetical described in subsection [A], *supra*, in which *D2* knew the age of the female with whom he had intercourse, but he mistakenly believed that his conduct constituted statutory rape, he would not be guilty of attempted statutory rape.

[145] Robbins, Note 115, *supra*, at 389-90.

below, this is a hybrid version of impossibility: the actor's impossibility claim includes both legal and factual aspects to it.

Courts have recognized a defense of legal impossibility or have stated that it would exist if *D*: (1) receives *un*stolen property believing that it was stolen;[146] (2) tries to pick the pocket of a stone image of a human;[147] (3) offers a bribe to a "juror" who is not a juror;[148] (4) tries to hunt deer out of season by shooting a stuffed animal;[149] (5) shoots a corpse believing that it is alive;[150] or (6) shoots at a tree stump believing that it is a human.[151]

Notice that each of the mistakes in these cases affected the legal status of some aspect of the defendant's conduct. A person is not guilty of "receiving stolen property with knowledge that it is stolen" unless the property is "stolen" in character. Likewise, one cannot legally bribe a juror unless the person bribed is a juror. The status of a victim as a "human being," rather than as a corpse, tree stump, or statue, legally is necessary to commit the crime of murder or to "take and carry away the personal property *of another.*" Finally, putting a bullet into a stuffed deer cannot legally constitute the crime of killing a deer out of season.

On the other hand, in each of the preceding examples of hybrid legal impossibility, *D* was mistaken about a fact: whether the property had been stolen; whether a person was a juror; whether the victims were living human beings; or whether the victim was an animal subject to being hunted out of season.[152]

Ultimately any case of hybrid legal impossibility may reasonably be character-ized as factual impossibility.[153] That is, applying the definition of "factual impossibility" set out above in subsection [C] [1], in each case *D*'s intended end (e.g., to receive stolen property; to pick a human pocket; to bribe a juror; to kill a human; to hunt a deer out of season) constituted a crime, but she failed to consummate the offense because of some fact of which *D* was unaware or was beyond her control. Thus, by skillful characterization, one can describe virtually any

---

[146] E.g., *People v. Jaffe*, 78 N.E. 169 (N.Y. 1906); *Booth v. State*, 398 P.2d 863 (Okla Crim. App. 1964).

[147] *Trent v. Commonwealth*, 156 S.E. 567, 569 (Va. 1931) (dictum).

[148] *State v. Taylor*, 133 S.W.2d 336 (Mo. 1939).

[149] E.g., *State v. Guffey*, 262 S.W.2d 152 (Mo. Ct. App. 1953); but see *State v. Walsh*, 870 P.2d 974, 975 (Wash. 1994) (on largely the same facts, held: *D* may be convicted of the offense of "spotlighting," i.e., "hunt[ing] big game with a spotlight or other artificial light").

[150] *State v. Taylor*, 133 S.W.2d 336 (Mo. 1939) (dictum).

[151] See the citations at Note 118, *supra.*

[152] Consider, as well, the hypothetical in subsection [A], *supra*, in which *D1* had inter-course with a female old enough to consent, although he believed that she was underage. This example involves hybrid legal impossibility: *D1* was mistaken about a fact (the girl's age); but her age is of legal significance in that sexual intercourse with a 17-year-old female (her true age) does not constitute statutory rape.

[153] The converse is not necessarily true. For example, there is no realistic issue of legal impossibility when *D* tries to fire an unloaded gun or puts her hand in an empty pocket in order to pick it.

case of hybrid legal impossibility, which is a common law defense, as an example of factual impossibility, which is *not* a defense.[154]

[b]—Modern Approach: Abolition of the Defense

Most states have abolished the defense of hybrid legal impossibility on the subjectivist ground that an actor's dangerousness is "plainly manifested"[155] in such cases. In most jurisdictions, therefore, lawyers and courts no longer have to distinguish between hybrid legal impossibility and factual impossibility.[156]

Is abolition a good idea? Two objections to the modern trend deserve attention. First, many cases of legal impossibility involve objectively innocuous conduct, or conduct that manifests criminality less serious than the offense for which the defendant ultimately is prosecuted. For example, shooting a tree stump, putting one's hands near the "pocket" of a statue, and receiving unstolen property are innocuous acts. Moreover, they do not manifest criminality of any kind. Putting a bullet into a corpse demonstrates criminality, but it is the wrongdoing of mutilating a corpse, a crime of its own and one less serious than attempted murder. Without the manifestation of criminality, a person is punished primarily for her thoughts, and not as the result of any societal apprehension caused by her conduct. For objectivists, but not subjectivists, this is a troubling feature of the abolitionist movement.

Second, when conduct is objectively innocent (e.g., firing a gun at a tree stump when nobody else is present), it is more difficult to infer criminal intent than when conduct manifests criminality (e.g., pointing a gun at the victim and firing it).[157] In such circumstances, therefore, the prosecutor's case will consist almost exclusively of evidence of the defendant's alleged *mens rea*, typically proven through the admission of the suspect's incriminating statements to the police or others, and evidence regarding the defendant's possible motive for committing the crime. In itself there is nothing wrong with such evidence, but any prosecution largely dependent on confessions, hearsay testimony, and other circumstantial evidence of a defendant's intent, runs a higher than normal risk of resulting in conviction of an innocent person[158] or of someone guilty of a lesser offense than the attempt charged.

---

[154] E.g., when *D* shoots a corpse, believing that it is a human being, *D* would describe this as a case of legal impossibility: "It is not legally possible for me to be guilty of murder when I shoot a corpse, because the offense of criminal homicide only applies to the killing of human beings." The prosecutor, however, would couch the claim in factual impossibility terms: "If the factual circumstances had been as *D* believed them to be—that the victim was alive when *D* shot him—he would be guilty of murder."

[155] American Law Institute, Comment to § 5.01, at 309.

[156] By 1979, 26 states had abolished the defense. Indeed, according to the American Law Institute, little modern authority exists for retention of the impossibility defense. American Law Institute, Comment to § 5.01, at 317.

[157] Enker, Note 90, *supra*, at 679-82.

[158] For example, there is a risk that the confession may have been coerced; and hearsay testimony is often unreliable, e.g., the third party may have misunderstood the defendant's words or the way in which they were expressed (e.g., jokingly).

Proponents of abolition of the legal impossibility defense believe that people will not be prosecuted on the basis of admissions alone, so that the risk of punishment of a person for wholly innocuous conduct "is more theoretical than practical."[159] But, sometimes, prosecutions of this sort do occur. For example, in *Anderton v. Ryan*,[160] D purchased a video recorder at a deep discount. Because of its price, D believed that it had been stolen and, therefore, she believed that she was guilty of the offense of "handling stolen property." Later, her house was burglarized. When the police routinely questioned her about the lost goods, including the video recorder, D admitted to the officers that she had purchased what she believed at the time was a stolen recorder. Based on her admission, she was prosecuted for attempted handling of stolen property. Apparently because the recorder was never retrieved, no effort was made at trial to prove that it actually was stolen property when she purchased it. As far as can be ascertained, therefore, D purchased unstolen property. Consequently, her guilt for the attempt was based exclusively on her guilty feelings, truthfully admitted to police officers.[161]

§ 27.08 Defense: Abandonment[162]

Once a person crosses the line from preparation to perpetration of an offense, i.e., once a criminal attempt has commenced, may the actor avoid conviction for the attempt if she abandons her criminal conduct before consummation of the target offense? For example, in *People v. McNeal*,[163] D, with the intention of raping V, grabbed V from a bus stop, took her at knifepoint to his home, pushed her onto a couch, and then began to fondle V. In an effort to prevent her rape, V begged him to let her go, explaining that she was trying to finish her education and that she was on the way to school to take two examinations. After V promised not to report him if he let her go, D apologized, took her to the bathroom so that she could fix her hair, and then walked her back to the bus stop. Clearly, D's acts satisfied any reasonable test of attempted rape, but should he be entitled to defend his actions on the ground that he abandoned the rape before consummation?

---

[159] American Law Institute, Comment to § 5.01, at 319-20.

[160] [1985] 2 All E.R. 355 (House of Lords).

[161] In *Anderton*, the House of Lords ruled that D was not guilty of the offense, although it had to provide a very strained interpretation of a statute that appeared to abolish the defense of legal impossibility. Subsequently, the House of Lords overruled *Anderton*. *Regina v. Shivpuri*, [1986] 2 All E.R. 334. Much as in *Anderton*, the defendant in *Shivpuri* was convicted on the basis of an admission to customs officers that the suitcase he was attempting to bring into the country contained prohibited drugs, when the substance in the suitcase actually turned out to be a harmless vegetable matter. His convicted was upheld.

[162] See generally Paul R. Hoeber, *The Abandonment Defense to Criminal Attempt and Other Problems of Temporal Individuation*, 74 Cal. L. Rev. 377 (1986); Daniel G. Moriarty, *Extending the Defense of Renunciation*, 62 Temple L. Rev. 1 (1989).

[163] 393 N.W.2d 907 (Mich. Ct. App. 1986) (affirming a conviction for attempted criminal sexual conduct).

Although there is disagreement on the matter, most scholars believe that abandonment was not a common law defense to attempt,[164] and many courts today continue to decline to recognize the defense.[165] To the extent that a defense of abandonment is recognized today, however, it applies only if the defendant *voluntarily* and *completely* renounces her criminal purpose. Abandonment by the defendant is voluntary when it is the result of repentance or a genuine change of heart.[166] Abandonment is not voluntary if the actor is motivated by unexpected resistance, the absence of an instrumentality essential to the completion of the crime, or some other circumstance that increases the likelihood of arrest or unsuccessful consummation of the offense.[167] And, the abandonment is not complete if the actor merely postpones her criminal endeavor until a better opportunity presents itself.[168]

There is also some support for the proposition that a person may not claim abandonment as a defense, even if the actor's desistance is motivated by genuine remorse and is complete, once she has performed the last act necessary to commit the offense, or has already caused serious harm to the victim. For example, in one case,[169] *D* stabbed *V*, his uncle, became remorseful and wept, and rushed *V* to a hospital. In an ensuing attempted murder prosecution, the court held that *D*'s abandonment could not be claimed in these circumstances.

The common law no-defense rule is motivated by objectivist principles, namely, that once the social harm of an attempt has occurred, a person should no more be able to avoid conviction for the harm caused than if a thief were to apologize for her actions and return the property after the crime has transpired. Although abandonment of an attempt, like voluntary restitution by a thief, may be relevant in sentencing, renunciation of a criminal purpose cannot undo the harm already inflicted.[170]

Jurisdictions that recognize the defense do so on subjectivist grounds. First, the defense encourages desistance by the attempter. Second, by voluntarily and completely abandoning an offense, an actor demonstrates that she possesses a less

---

[164] Hoeber, Note 162, *supra*, at 381; Williams at § 199; but see American Law Institute, Comment to § 5.01, at 356-57 (stating that there is uncertainty on the matter, but suggesting that the prevailing rule favored a limited defense).

[165] E.g., *United States v. Shelton*, 30 F.3d 702, 706 (6th Cir. 1994).

[166] *Pyle v. State*, 476 N.E.2d 124, 126 (Ind. 1985) (permitting a defense on the basis of repentance or "rising revulsion for the harm intended").

[167] *People v. Cross*, 466 N.W.2d 368, 370 (Mich. Ct. App. 1991); *State v. Mahoney*, 870 P.2d 65, 71 (Mont. 1994).

[168] American Law Institute, Comment to § 5.01, at 356.

[169] *State v. Smith*, 409 N.E.2d 1199, 1201 (Ind. Ct. App. 1980); accord, *State v. Mahoney*, 870 P.2d at 71.

[170] On the other hand, separate from the issue of a defense, an actor's abandonment may be relevant to the *prima facie* case: the abandonment may support a claim that the actor was not close enough to consummation to justify a finding that the *actus reus* of the attempt occurred, e.g., *Commonwealth v. McCloskey*, 341 A.2d 500 (Pa. 1975); and the defendant's abandonment may support a claim that she never intended to commit the offense in the first place.

dangerous character than an ordinary attempter or person who quits the offense out of fear of arrest.[171]

§ 27.09   Model Penal Code[172]

[A]—Introductory Comments

According to the Commentary to § 5.01, the Model Code provision on criminal attempts:

> The literature and the decisions dealing with the definition of a criminal attempt reflect ambivalence as to how far the governing criterion should focus on the dangerousness of the actor's conduct, measured by objective standards, and how far it should focus on the dangerousness of the actor, as a person manifesting a firm disposition to commit a crime.[173]

That is, the law has struggled with the competing principles of objectivism and subjectivism. The drafters of the Code, however, are not ambivalent: "[The proper focus of attention is the actor's disposition. The Model Code provisions are accordingly drafted with this in mind."[174]

The Model Code's approach to criminal attempts—indeed, to all of the inchoate offenses—is subjectivist nearly throughout. It defines a criminal attempt in a manner that "make[s] amenable to the corrective process those persons who have manifested a propensity to engage in dangerous criminal activity."[175] Its treatment of defenses to criminal attempts (it abolishes the defense of hybrid legal impossibility, but recognizes the defense of abandonment), and the punishment it imposes for inchoate offenses (in general, it grades an inchoate crime at the same level as the completed offense), are similarly motivated by subjectivist goals.

Section 5.01 has had significant impact on attempt law. Most of the federal courts apply the doctrines of § 5.01, although Congress has not enacted the provision; and a large number of states have adopted the Code provision in its entirety or in part.[176]

---

[171] *Sheckles v. State*, 501 N.E.2d 1053, 1056 (Ind. 1986); *People v. Taylor*, 598 N.E.2d 693, 699 (N.Y. 1992)

[172] See generally Wechsler, Jones, & Korn, Note 86, *supra*.

[173] American Law Institute, Comment to § 5.01, at 298 (footnote deleted).

[174] *Id.* (footnote deleted).

[175] *United States v. Dworken*, 855 F.2d 12, 16 (1st Cir. 1988).

[176] By 1979, 15 states had adopted § 5.01 in its entirety, and other states had adopted the Code's "substantial step" test, without defining it. American Law Institute, Comment to § 5.01, at 300 n.7. As noted earlier, the overwhelming trend is to abolish the legal impossibility defense, as the Code recommends; and most recently revised criminal codes include the Model Code's renunciation (abandonment) defense. *Id.* at 360.

[B]—Criminal Attempt: In General

[1]—Elements of the Offense

Generally speaking, a criminal attempt under the Code contains two elements: (1) the purpose to commit the substantive offense; and (2) conduct constituting a "substantial step" toward the commission of the substantive offense. These elements are explained more fully in subsections [C] and [D] below.

[2]—Explaining Section 5.01, Subsection (1)

Section 5.01, subsection (1), which defines an attempt, is a complicated provision. It reads:

> A person is guilty of an attempt to commit a crime if, acting with the kind of culpability otherwise required for commission of the crime, he:
>
> > (a) purposely engages in conduct that would constitute the crime if the attendant circumstances were as he believes them to be; or
> >
> > (b) when causing a particular result is an element of the crime, does or omits to do anything with the purpose of causing or with the belief that it will cause such result without further conduct on his part; or
> >
> > (c) purposely does or omits to do anything that, under the circumstances as he believes them to be, is an act or omission constituting a substantial step in a course of conduct planned to culminate in his commission of the crime.

To analyze an attempt issue under subsection (1), it is necessary to ask and answer one or two questions. First, does the case involve a complete or incomplete attempt? Second, if the case involves a complete attempt, is the target offense a "result" crime (e.g., murder) or a "conduct" crime (e.g., driving an automobile under the influence of alcohol)?

Subsections (1)(a) and (1)(b) pertain to *completed* attempts. Specifically, subsection (1)(a) should be considered when the target offense of the completed attempt is a conduct crime; subsection (1)(b) applies to result offenses. If the prosecution involves an *incomplete* attempt, subsection (1)(c) is used. However, this subsection must be read in conjunction with subsection (2), which elaborates on the meaning of "substantial step."

[C]—*Mens Rea*

In general, a person is not guilty of a criminal attempt unless it was her purpose, i.e., her conscious object, to engage in the conduct or cause the result that would constitute the substantive offense.

There are two exceptions to the requirement of purpose. First, subsection (1)(b) expressly and subsection (1)(c) implicitly [177] provide that a person is guilty of an attempt to cause a criminal result if she *believes* that the result will occur, even if it were not her conscious object to cause it. For example, if *D* plants a bomb on an airplane in order to kill *V*, her husband, and the bomb fails to go off (or if the

---

[177] American Law Institute, Comment to § 5.01, at 305 n.17.

bomb is defused), she is guilty of attempted murder of *V*, because it was her conscious object to take *D*'s life; but she would also be guilty of attempted murder of the other passengers in the airplane if she believed that they would die in the bombing.[178] The common law outcome in this case is uncertain.[179]

Second, the Commentary to § 5.01 explains that the prefatory phrase in subsection (1)—"acting with the kind of culpability otherwise required for the commission of the crime"—means that the *mens rea* of "purpose" or "belief" does not necessarily encompass the attendant circumstances of the crime.[180] For these elements, it is sufficient that the actor possesses the degree of culpability required to commit the substantive offense.

For example, if *D* may be convicted of statutory rape on proof that he was reckless as to the girl's age (the attendant circumstance), then he may convicted of *attempted* statutory rape if he were reckless, but not if he were negligent or innocent, as to the girl's age. If the material element of the girl's age is one of strict liability, i.e., *D* may be convicted of statutory rape although he reasonably believed that she was old enough to consent, then he may also be convicted of *attempted* statutory rape although he lacked a culpable mental state as to this attendant circumstance. The common law rule on this matter is uncertain.[181]

[D]—*Actus Reus*

[1]—In General

The Code shifts the focus of attempt law from what remains to be done, i.e., the actor's proximity to consummation of the offense, to what the actor has already done.[182] Subsection (1)(c) provides that, to be guilty of an offense, an actor must have done or omitted to do something that constitutes a "substantial step in a course of conduct planned to culminate in his commission of the crime." The premise of the Code is that one who engages in such purposive conduct is sufficiently dangerous to justify state intervention, even if she is not yet close to consummation of the offense. The "substantial step" standard is intended to "broaden the scope of attempt liability."[183]

Section 5.01(2) provides further content to the imprecise term "substantial step." First, it indicates that conduct is not a substantial step unless it strongly corroborates the defendant's criminal intent. This language is meant to reduce the risk of conviction of innocent persons. It incorporates some aspects of the common law unequivocality test of attempt,[184] without including its potential stringencies. Specifically, this subsection does not require that the defendant's conduct *by itself*

---

[178] *Id.* at 304-05.

[179] See Note 64, *supra*.

[180] American Law Institute, Comment to § 5.01, at 301-03.

[181] See § 27.05[D], *supra*.

[182] American Law Institute, Comment to § 5.01, at 329.

[183] *Id.*

[184] See § 27.06[B][7], *supra*.

manifest criminality, as objectivists favor. Rather, the key words in the provision are "strongly corroborative": the actor's conduct, considered in light of all the circumstances, must add significantly to other proof of her criminal intent, such as a confession or other incriminating statement.[185]

Second, subsection (2) provides a list of recurrent factual circumstances in which an actor's conduct, if strongly corroborative of her criminal purpose, "shall not be held insufficient as a matter of law." That is, if any of the enumerated instances are established, the jury is entitled to determine whether the defendant has taken a substantial step; and if the jury convicts the defendant of an attempt, this verdict may not be overturned on the ground that the step was insubstantial. The circumstances set out in subsection (2), drawn primarily from common law decisions in the field, include: lying in wait; searching for or following the contemplated victim of the crime; reconnoitering the contemplated scene of the crime; unlawful entry into a structure or building in which the crime will be committed; and possession of the materials to commit the offense, if they are specially designed for a criminal purpose.

[2]—Attempt to Aid

Suppose that *D1* furnishes a gun to *X1* so that *X1* can kill *V*. If *X1* attempts to kill *V*, *D1* is guilty of attempted murder as an accomplice.[186]

Compare the preceding example to the following: *D2* performs the same acts as *D1*, but *X2* is arrested before she attempts the crime, or *X2* voluntarily abandons her criminal endeavor. In this example, *D2* is not guilty of aiding and abetting a murder or attempted murder, since *X2* did not commit either of these offenses. Is *D2* guilty of *any* offense?

Conceptually, *D1* aided and abetted an attempt; *D2* attempted to aid and abet. Although *D1*'s liability is clear at common law, *D2* is guilty of no common law offense. However, the Model Penal Code expressly covers the circumstance in which *D2* finds herself. Under § 5.01(3), a person may be convicted of a criminal attempt, *although a crime was neither committed nor attempted by another*, if: (1) her conduct is intended to aid another in the commission of the offense; and (2) such assistance would have made her an accomplice in the commission of the crime under the Code's complicity statute,[187] if the offense had been committed or attempted. Thus, in the hypothetical, *D2* is guilty of attempted murder, although *X2* did not attempt to commit a murder: *D2* furnished the gun to *X2* with the purpose that the offense be committed; and this conduct would have made her an accomplice if the offense had occurred.

The rationale of the rule is straightforward: a person who attempts to aid in the commission of an offense is as dangerous as one who personally commits an offense or who aids in its commission or attempted commission.[188] Therefore, under subjectivist principles, her conduct justifies punishment.

---

[185] American Law Institute, Comment to § 5.01, at 331.

[186] See generally Chapter 30, *infra*.

[187] Model Penal Code § 2.06. See § 30.09, *infra*.

[188] American Law Institute, Comment to § 5.01, at 356.

[E]—Defenses

[1]—Impossibility

[a]—Hybrid Legal Impossibility

Section 5.01(1), as reprinted in subsection [B] above, is designed to abolish the defense of hybrid legal impossibility.

This outcome may be seen by considering three examples. First, assume that *D1* receives unstolen property, believing that it was stolen,[189] and is prosecuted for attempting to receive stolen property. As this case involves a completed attempt, and the offense charged is a conduct crime, subsection (1)(a) applies. Based on the language of subsection (1)(a), *D1* is guilty if she purposely engaged in conduct (receiving the property) that would constitute a crime "*if the attendant circumstances were as [s]he believes them to be.*" In this case, the attendant circumstance is the "stolenness" of the property. *D1* believed that the property was stolen. Had the circumstance been as she believed it to be, she would be guilty of the offense of receiving stolen property; therefore, she is guilty of attempting to receive stolen property.

Second, suppose that *D2* shoots to kill *V*, unaware that *V* is already dead. Although this might constitute hybrid legal impossibility, and a defense at common law,[190] *D2* is guilty of attempted murder under the Model Code.[191] Because this involves a result crime, subsection (1)(b) applies. Here, *D2* performed an act—firing a gun at *V*—"with the purpose of causing or with the belief that it [would] cause such result [*V*'s death] without further conduct on [*D2*'s] part." The fact that *V* was a corpse rather than a human being does not exculpate *D2*.

Finally, suppose that in either of these examples, the defendant is arrested prior to completion of the last act, but after commission of a substantial step. For example, suppose that *D1* prepares to receive the property but is arrested immediately before she takes possession; or, suppose that *D2* is arrested with the gun aimed at the corpse. Because further actions were intended in these cases, subsection (1)(c), rather than (1)(a) or (1)(b), applies. Still, *D1* and *D2* will be convicted because they performed acts that, "under the circumstances as [they] believe[d] them to be"—the property was stolen, *V* was alive—constituted "a substantial step in a course of conduct planned to culminate in . . . commission of the crime[s]."

The abrogation of the impossibility defense conforms with subjectivist principles. One who intends to commit a crime, but who fails to consummate it because of a circumstance of which the person is unaware, is as dangerous as one who successfully commits the crime or who does not commit it because of police intervention.

One aspect of the Code's treatment of impossibility cases deserves special attention. Observe that only in subsection (1)(c) cases, i.e., in cases of *incomplete*

---

[189] E.g., *People v. Jaffe*, 78 N.E. 169 (N.Y. 1906) (under common law, held: *D* is not guilty of an attempt).

[190] See § 27.07[D][3][a], *supra*.

[191] *People v. Dlugash*, 363 N.E.2d 1155 (N.Y. 1977).

attempts, does the Code require that the actor's conduct be strongly corroborative of her criminal purpose. The typical impossibility case, however, involves a *completed* attempt, in which event subsection (1)(a) or (1)(b) applies. In the usual impossibility case, therefore, corroboration of the actor's criminal purpose is *not* required.

This anomaly has been criticized. As discussed earlier,[192] many impossibility cases involve objectively innocuous conduct. Thus, if *D* buys a radio on the street believing that it is stolen, her conduct objectively is innocent and manifests no criminal intent. Nonetheless, she may be convicted under the Code of an attempt to receive stolen property, although the radio was not stolen, on the basis of circumstantial evidence of criminal purpose. The danger of conviction of an innocent person, therefore, is unmitigated.[193]

[b]—Pure Legal Impossibility

Although the Code does not expressly so provide, the Institute did not intend to abolish the defense of pure legal impossibility. The Commentary states that "it is of course necessary [pursuant to the principle of legality] that the result desired or intended by the actor constitute a crime."[194]

[2]—Renunciation (Abandonment)

The Code recognizes an affirmative defense of "renunciation of criminal purpose." A person is not guilty of an attempt if: (1) she abandons her effort to commit the crime or prevents it from being committed; and (2) her conduct manifests a complete and voluntary renunciation of her criminal purpose.[195]

Under this provision, renunciation is not complete if it is wholly or partially motivated "by a decision to postpone the criminal conduct until a more advantageous time or to transfer the criminal effort to another but similar objective or victim." For example, *D* is guilty of attempted bank robbery, if she arrives at the bank, but leaves without committing the offense because she determines that it is too risky to go ahead until she secures the assistance of an accomplice.[196] *D* would also be guilty of an attempt if, after taking a substantial step toward robbing Bank A, she shifted her efforts to Bank B.[197]

Renunciation is not voluntary if it is partially or wholly motivated by "circumstances, not present or apparent at the inception of the actor's course of conduct, that increase the probability of detection or apprehension or that make more difficult

---

[192] See § 27.07[D][3][b], *supra.*

[193] The Commentary's response to this criticism is that it is "unlikely . . . that persons will be prosecuted on the basis of admissions alone." American Law Institute, Comment to § 5.01, at 319-20. However, prosecutions of this sort do occur. See § 27.07[D][3][b], *supra.*

[194] American Law Institute, Comment to § 5.01, at 318.

[195] Model Penal Code § 5.01(4).

[196] E.g., *United States v. Jackson,* 560 F.2d 112 (2nd Cir. 1977).

[197] If *D* went on to rob Bank B, she would be guilty of attempted robbery of Bank A and of robbery of Bank B. If she were arrested before completing the Bank B robbery, *D* would be guilty of two counts of attempted robbery.

the accomplishment of the criminal purpose." Under this provision, *D1* is not entitled to the defense if she desists from a theft because she is aware that she is being observed by a police officer. Similarly, *D2* is guilty of attempted rape if he desists due to *V*'s resistance.

[F]—Grading of Criminal Attempts and Other Inchoate Crimes

[1]—In General

In a significant departure from common law tradition, the Code provides that the crimes of attempt, solicitation, and conspiracy are offenses of the same grade and degree, i.e., subject to the same punishment, as the offense attempted, solicited, or that is the object of the conspiracy.[198] This is consistent with the Code's subjectivist view of inchoate crimes.

The only exceptions to this system of grading are so-called "felonies of the first degree,"[199] which are crimes that carry a maximum penalty of life imprisonment.[200] An attempt (or solicitation or conspiracy) to commit one of these crimes constitutes a felony of the *second* degree,[201] the maximum penalty of which is ten years.[202]

[2]—Special Mitigation

The Code grants the trial judge authority to dismiss a prosecution of an inchoate offense, or to impose a sentence for a crime of a lower degree than is otherwise allowed, if the actor's conduct was so inherently unlikely to result in a crime that neither she nor her conduct represents a danger to society justifying her conviction and punishment at ordinary levels.[203] This provision provides flexibility to a judge in the rare case of an inherently impossible attempt, e.g., when *D* attempts to sink a battleship with a pop-gun.[204]

---

[198] Model Penal Code § 5.05(1).

[199] Model Penal Code § 6.01(1)(a).

[200] Model Penal Code § 6.06(1). Felonies of the first degree are expressly designated as such by the Code. Murder (§ 210.2), kidnapping (§ 212.1), rape (§ 213.1(1)), and robbery (§ 222.1) are felonies of the first degree.

[201] Model Penal Code § 5.05(1).

[202] Model Penal Code § 6.06(2).

[203] Model Penal Code § 5.05(2).

[204] See § 27.07[C][2], *supra*.

CHAPTER 28

SOLICITATION

§ 28.01 General Principles[1]

[A]—Definition

[1]—In General

Subject to clarification below, "solicitation," a common law misdemeanor, occurs when a person invites, requests, commands, hires, or encourages another to engage in conduct constituting any felony, or a misdemeanor relating to obstruction of justice or a breach of the peace.

Until the adoption of the Model Penal Code, most state penal codes did not contain a general criminal solicitation statute.[2] Instead, solicitations to commit specific offenses, such as murder and prostitution, were prohibited.

[2]—*Mens Rea*

Common law solicitation is a specific-intent crime. A person is not guilty of solicitation unless he intentionally commits the *actus reus* of the inchoate offense, i.e., he intentionally invites, requests, commands, hires, or encourages another to commit a crime, with the specific intent that the other person successfully consummate the solicited crime. For example, D is not guilty of solicitation if he jokingly suggests to X that X steal V's television set, even if X takes the suggestion seriously and commits the crime.

Or, suppose that D encourages X to pick V's pocket. D knows that V's pocket is empty, but X is unaware of this. If X follows D's suggestion and puts his hand in V's empty pocket, X will be guilty of attempted larceny, as the factual impossibility of committing the larceny does not serve as a defense to X's conduct.[3] D, however, will *not* be guilty of solicitation: he knew that X could not succeed in the larceny; therefore, he lacked the specific intent for guilt of solicitation.[4]

In contrast to the preceding example, suppose that D, like X, is unaware of the fact that V's pockets are empty when he encourages X to pick V's pocket. Under these changed circumstances, D is guilty of solicitation, because he believed that

---

[1] See generally Williams at §§ 193-95; John W. Curran, *Solicitation: A Substantive Crime*, 17 Minn. L. Rev. 499 (1933).

[2] American Law Institute, Comment to § 5.02, at 367.

[3] See § 27.07[C][1], *supra*.

[4] Williams at 611. Conceptually, D has solicited an *attempted* larceny, but the common law apparently did not recognize such an offense.

the crime could be committed. As with an attempt, factual impossibility is not a defense to the crime of solicitation.[5]

[3]—*Actus Reus*

The *actus reus* of a solicitation takes place when one person invites, requests, commands, hires, or encourages[6] another to commit a particular offense. For a solicitation to occur, neither the solicitor nor the solicited party needs to perform any act in furtherance of the substantive crime: the solicitation is complete the instant the actor communicates the solicitation to the other person. Thus, a solicitation occurs if *D* asks *X* to commit a crime but *X* refuses, or even if *X* agrees but does not intend to commit the crime (e.g., if *X* is an undercover police officer feigning intent).

In the absence of clarifying statutory language, courts have struggled to determine how to deal with uncommunicated solicitations. For example, in *State v. Cotton*,[7] *D*, a jail inmate, wrote letters to *X*, his wife, in which he solicited criminal activities on her part. Although *D* attempted to mail or forward the letters to *X*, there was no evidence that they actually reached her. The court held that, on this evidence, *D* could not be convicted of solicitation, although it suggested that a charge of *attempted* solicitation might have been allowed.[8]

[B]—Relationship of the Solicitor to the Solicited Party

[1]—In General

A typical solicitation occurs when *D* importunes *X* to perpetrate the substantive offense. In common law terms,[9] *D* intends for *X* to be the "principal in the first degree" of the solicited crime; *D* wishes to be the "principal in the second degree" or "accessory before the fact."[10] Put less technically, a solicitor wants another

---

[5] *Benson v. Superior Court*, 368 P.2d 116, 118 (Cal. 1962)

[6] The idea of the offense need not originate with the solicitor; it is enough that he encourages another to commit an offense that the other person already plans to commit. In light of the *mens rea* requirement, however, a person is not guilty of solicitation if his comments are not uttered for the purpose of encouraging the commission of the crime. For example, if *X* asks *D*, a devoted pacifist, whether *X* should register for the draft as required by law, and *D* remarks that registration is immoral, *D* is not guilty of solicitation unless his comments were made with the specific purpose of encouraging or inciting *X* to break the law. American Law Institute, Comment to § 5.02, at 371.

[7] 790 P.2d 1050 (N.M. 1990).

[8] Accord, American Law Institute, Comment to § 5.02, at 380-81. The same analysis would apply if a solicitor sends a message in a language that the other party does not understand, or if the soliciting party communicates the message orally, but the other party does not hear the words.

[9] See § 30.03, *infra*.

[10] Williams at § 198.

persun to perpetrate the offense; the solicitor intends to be in the background as an accomplice in the commission of the crime.[11]

At common law, no solicitation occurs if the solicitor intends to commit the substantive offense himself, but requests assistance by another. For example, if *D* requests *X* to kill *V*, *D* has solicited a murder. However, if *D* asks *X* to furnish him with a gun so that he (*D*) may kill *V*, a criminal solicitation has not transpired.

[2]—Use of an Innocent Instrumentality

A person may sometimes use another as his "innocent instrumentality"[12] in the commission of an offense. It is critical to appreciate the difference between solicitation of another to commit an offense, on the one hand, and use of an innocent instrumentality, on the other hand.

For example, if *D1* suggests to *X1* that the latter steal *V*'s television set, *D* is guilty of solicitation. This fits the solicitation paradigm: if *X1* does as requested, *X1* is the perpetrator of the offense; *D1* is an accomplice. In contrast, suppose that *D2* fraudulently says to *X2*: "My television set is at *V*'s house; he asked me to pick it up—would you do me a favor and get it for me?" In this example, *D2* is *not* guilty of solicitation to commit larceny, because *D2* is not requesting *X2* to engage in conduct that would constitute a crime *by X2*. Instead, *D2* is attempting to perpetrate the offense himself, by using *X2* as his innocent instrumentality. *X2* is *D2*'s "innocent instrumentality" because, if *X2* believes *D2*'s representations and takes *V*'s property, *X2* is not guilty of larceny since he lacks the specific intent to steal.

[C]—Relationship of a Solicitation to the Target Offense

Solicitation is not only an inchoate offense but is also a basis for accomplice liability. That is, one way in which a person may assist another in the commission of a crime and, as a consequence, be held accountable for the other's criminal acts, is by soliciting the substantive offense.[13]

For example, if *D* solicits *X* to murder *V*, and *X* does so, *D*'s solicitation makes him an accomplice in the commission of the murder. However, if *D* is convicted and punished for murder as an accomplice, he will not be punished for the solicitation, as the latter offense merges with the murder.[14] Similarly, if *X* attempts to murder *V* at *D*'s request, but fails in the effort, *D*'s solicitation merges with the attempt. On the other hand, if *D* solicits *X* to murder *V*, and *X* agrees, but *X* does not commit or attempt the substantive offense, *D* may be convicted with *X* of conspiracy to murder *V*. As before, the solicitation merges with the conspiracy. Finally, if *X* refuses to commit the crime solicited, *D* is guilty of solicitation.

---

[11] Occasionally, *D* may solicit *X* to solicit *Y* to commit an offense. Although this falls outside the usual definition of solicitation, courts often ignore this fact. E.g., *People v. Bloom*, 133 N.Y.S. 708 (App. Div. 1912); *State v. Davis*, 6 S.W.2d 609 (Mo. 1928) (reversing conviction on other grounds).

[12] See § 30.03[A][2][b], *infra*.

[13] See § 30.04[A], *infra*.

[14] *Lewis v. State*, 404 A.2d 1073, 1083 (Md. 1979).

[D]—Policy Considerations

Solicitation is a controversial offense. Some commentators believe that solicitations should not be punished because the offense suppresses conduct at too early a stage. Indeed, no common law crime (except an *attempted* solicitation) punishes conduct more preparatory to a substantive offense than the crime of solicitation. According to Glanville Williams, the purpose of the offense is to enable police to "nip criminal tendencies in the bud."[15] In fact, however, his metaphor would be more accurate if he had stated that its purpose is to nip criminal tendencies at the stem.

The extremely inchoate nature of the crime of solicitation is evident if one carefully analyzes the offense. Essentially, solicitation is an attempted conspiracy.[16] That is, when *D* solicits *X* to commit an offense, he wants *X* to agree to commit the offense solicited; if *X* agrees, they have formed a conspiracy. In turn, a conspiracy can exist long before a crime is attempted. Thus, solicitation is an attempt to conspire to commit an offense, a double inchoate crime.

The contrasting view is that solicitations are dangerous precisely because they are attempted conspiracies. As discussed more fully elsewhere,[17] one rationale for punishing conspiracies is that there is more danger in two persons agreeing to commit a crime than in one or two persons separately planning to commit the same offense. Therefore, when a solicitor attempts to create such a dangerous grouping, his conduct represents a threat that advocates of the offense believe society has a legitimate interest in deterring.

§ 28.02　Comparison of Solicitation to Other Inchoate Offenses

[A]—Conspiracy

A conspiracy is an agreement between two or more persons to commit an unlawful act or series of unlawful acts.[18] As noted in the preceding subsection, a solicitation is an attempted conspiracy. However, a solicitation is not a necessarily-included offense of conspiracy. That is, it is possible to have a conspiracy without a prior solicitation. For example, suppose that *A*, intending to kill *V*, requests *B*'s assistance in the crime. If *B* agrees to help, they have formed a conspiracy; however, as *A* did not request *B* to perpetrate the offense, no common law solicitation has occurred.[19]

Or, suppose that *C* informs *D* that he (*C*) intends to kill *V*. *D* tells *C* that, he, too, wishes *V* dead. As a consequence of their common goal, they form a pact to kill

---

[15] Williams at 609.

[16] *State v. Sexton*, 657 P.2d 43, 44 (Kan. 1983). However, solicitation is not a necessarily-included offense of conspiracy. See § 28.02[A], *infra*.

[17] See § 29.02[B], *infra*.

[18] See § 29.01[A], *infra*.

[19] See § 28.01[B][1], *supra*.

V. The latter agreement would constitute a conspiracy, although *C* never solicited the offense. [20]

[B]—Criminal Attempt [21]

An issue that has perplexed courts is whether a solicitation can *in itself* constitute an attempt to commit the crime solicited. That is, if *D* solicits *X* to rob *V*, under what circumstances, if any, may *D* be convicted of attempted robbery, rather than of solicitation? The matter is of considerable significance in jurisdictions in which criminal attempts are punished more severely than solicitations.

Courts have taken four approaches to this issue. [22] First, some cases treat all solicitations as potential attempts, subject to the usual attempt doctrines. On this basis, a solicitation that is proximate to the target offense may constitute an attempt to commit it. For example, if *D* solicits unarmed *X* to murder *V* when the latter returns to town in a week, *D*'s conduct does not constitute an attempt because the crime is too remote. On the other hand, if *D* solicits *X*, who is already armed and in *V*'s presence, to commit the offense immediately, *D*'s solicitation could constitute an attempt.

Second, some courts hold that solicitation coupled with a "slight act" in furtherance of it *by the solicitor* is an attempt. [23] For example, in jurisdictions that follow this rule, if *D* solicits an offense, and then pays *X* money to commit the crime or furnishes *X* with a weapon to commit the offense, *D* is guilty of an attempt even if *X* does nothing further, and even if *X* is an undercover police officer who would never have committed the crime. [24]

Third, some courts hold that a solicitation is not an attempt unless the solicitor's overt acts would constitute an attempt if he had intended to commit the crime himself. For example, if *D* pays *X* money to commit a crime or furnishes him with an instrumentality to commit the offense, *D* is not guilty of attempt. However, if *D* solicits *X* to burglarize *V*'s home, and then opens a window at *V*'s house for *X*'s later entry, *D* would be guilty of attempted burglary, even if *X* never arrives at the scene.

Finally, many courts hold that solicitation is never an attempt to commit a crime, because the solicitor does not intend personally to commit the offense.

These situations must be distinguished from the case in which a person seeks to use another as his innocent instrumentality to commit an offense. Suppose, as hypothesized earlier, [25] *D* tries to convince *X* to take *V*'s property by convincing him

[20] See *Monoker v. State*, 582 A.2d 525, 528 (Md. Ct. Spec. App. 1990); *People v. Stroner*, 449 N.E.2d 1326, 1328 (Ill. 1983).

[21] See Williams at § 198.

[22] American Law Institute, Comment to § 5.02, at 368-69 (and citations therein).

[23] See *Stokes v. State*, 46 So. 627, 629 (Miss. 1908).

[24] E.g., *State v. Gay*, 486 P.2d 341, 345 (Wash. Ct. App. 1971); *contra State v. Otto*, 629 P.2d 646, 650 (Idaho 1981).

[25] See § 28.01[B][2], *supra*.

that the property belongs to D. In this circumstance, D is not guilty of solicitation because he is not requesting X to commit larceny, but instead is trying to commit the offense himself with an innocent tool, X.

Although the request is not a solicitation, it may constitute an *attempt* by D to commit the offense solicited. D has committed the last act in his power to cause the property to be taken. Moreover, his conduct is more proximate to the theft than a solicitation, because X is more apt to agree to take the property when he believes that he is acting lawfully than when he is asked to commit a knowingly criminal act.

§ 28.03   Model Penal Code [26]

[A]—Definition

Pursuant to the Model Penal Code, a person is guilty of solicitation to commit a crime if: (1) the actor's purpose is to promote or facilitate the commission of a substantive offense; and (2) with such purpose, he commands, encourages or requests another person to engage in conduct that would constitute the crime, an attempt to commit it, or would establish the other person's complicity in its commission or attempted commission. [27]

This definition of solicitation is broader than the common law version in four key respects. First, it applies to the solicitation of all crimes and not simply of felonies and serious misdemeanors.

Second, unlike the common law, the Code recognizes a solicitation to commit an attempt. Reconsider the case discussed earlier, [28] in which D solicits X to put his hand in what D knows is an empty pocket of V. If X does as requested, X is guilty of attempted larceny; D would be guilty of no common law offense, however, because he did not intend for X to commit larceny. Under the Code, however, D would be guilty of solicitation of an *attempted* larceny. In the language of the solicitation provision, D solicited X to "engage in specific conduct [picking V's empty pocket] that would constitute . . . an attempt to commit such crime [of larceny]."

Third, the relationship of the solicitor to the solicited party need not be that of accomplice to perpetrator. Suppose that D asks X to provide him with a weapon so that D may kill V. At common law, D has not solicited a murder, because he has not requested X to perpetrate the offense. Under the Code, D is guilty of solicitation because X would be held accountable for the offense were it completed: that is, he has requested X to "engage in specific conduct [provide a weapon to D] that would . . . establish [X's] complicity [as an accomplice] in its commission or attempted commission."

---

[26] See generally Herbert Wechsler, William Kenneth Jones, & Harold L. Korn, *The Treatment of Inchoate Crimes in the Model Penal Code of the American Law Institute: Attempt, Solicitation, and Conspiracy (Pt. 1)*, 61 Colum. L. Rev. 571 (1961).

[27] Model Penal Code § 5.02(1).

[28] See § 28.01[A][2], *supra*.

Finally, an uncommunicated solicitation, i.e., an attempted solicitation at common law, is itself a solicitation under the Code.[29]

[B]—Defense: Renunciation

The Model Code establishes a defense to solicitation of "renunciation of criminal purpose." A person is not guilty of solicitation if he: (1) completely and voluntarily renounces his criminal intent; and (2) either persuades the solicited party not to commit the offense or otherwise prevents him from committing the crime.[30]

This defense is recognized for the same reason that it applies to the other inchoate offenses of attempt and conspiracy: a person who abandons his criminal purpose and thwarts the commission of the offense demonstrates thereby that he is no longer dangerous. Establishment of the defense also serves as an incentive to the solicitor to prevent the crime from being committed.

[C]—Punishment

At common law, solicitation was a misdemeanor, even when the solicited offense was a felony. The Model Code takes the untraditional approach of grading nearly all inchoate crimes, including solicitation, at the same level as the substantive offense.[31] Very few states have adopted this sentencing system, although some states now treat solicitation to commit a felony as a felony of a lesser degree than the substantive crime.[32]

---

[29] Model Penal Code § 5.02(2).

[30] Model Penal Code § 5.02(3).

[31] Model Penal Code § 5.05(1). See § 27.09[F][1], *supra.*

[32] American Law Institute, Comment to § 5.05, at 487-88.

CHAPTER 29

CONSPIRACY

§ 29.01 Definition of the Crime[1]

[A]—Common Law

A common law conspiracy is an agreement by two or more persons to commit a criminal act or a series of criminal acts, or to accomplish a legal act by unlawful means.[2] Formulated by the English Star Chamber in 1611,[3] conspiracy was a common law misdemeanor. As discussed below,[4] the offense is punished more severely today than it was at common law.

As so defined, conspiracy is an extremely controversial crime. Some courts and many scholars have called for its reform or abolition.[5] The nature of the controversies become evident in subsequent sections of this chapter. Three interrelated criticisms of the crime, however, may be emphasized here. First, the "crime of conspiracy is so vague that it almost defies definition."[6] Second, a person may be convicted of the offense well before she commits any act in perpetration of a substantive crime. Finally, and closely related to the last point, the crime "is always 'predominantly mental in composition' because it consists primarily of a meeting of minds and an intent."[7]

---

[1] See generally Katz at 260-75; Peter Buscemi, Note, *Conspiracy: Statutory Reform Since the Model Penal Code*, 75 Colum. L. Rev. 1122 (1975); *Developments in the Law—Criminal Conspiracy*, 72 Harv. L. Rev. 920 (1959); Abraham S. Goldstein, *Conspiracy to Defraud the United States*, 68 Yale L.J. 405 (1959); Phillip E. Johnson, *The Unnecessary Crime of Conspiracy*, 61 Cal. L. Rev. 1137 (1973); Paul Marcus, *Criminal Conspiracy Law: Time To Turn Back From An Ever Expanding, Even More Troubling Area*, 1 Wm. & Mary Bill Rts. J. 1 (1992); Francis B. Sayre, *Criminal Conspiracy*, 35 Harv. L. Rev. 393 (1922); Herbert Wechsler, William Kenneth Jones, & Harold L. Korn, *The Treatment of Inchoate Crimes in the Model Penal Code of the American Law Institute: Attempt, Solicitation, and Conspiracy (Pt. 2)*, 61 Colum. L. Rev. 957 (1961).

[2] *People v. Carter*, 330 N.W.2d 314, 319 (Mich. 1982).

[3] *Poulterers' Case*, 9 Co. Rep. 55b, 77 Eng. Rep. 813 (1611).

[4] See § 29.03[A], *infra*.

[5] For an example of the latter position see Johnson, Note 1, *supra*.

[6] *Krulewitch v. United States*, 336 U.S. 440, 446 (1949) (Jackson, J., concurring). Justice Jackson also described the crime as "chameleon-like." *Id.* at 447. Another critic has compared the crime to Einstein's theory of relativity, stating that the concept is "so far removed from ordinary human experience or modes of thought . . . [that] it escapes just beyond the boundaries of the mind." Jessica Mitford, The Trial of Dr. Spock 61 (1969).

[7] *Krulewitch*, 336 U.S. at 447-48 (Jackson, J., concurring) (footnote omitted).

The formlessness of the crime of conspiracy has served as a powerful tool of prosecutors—Judge Learned Hand once described the crime as the "darling of the modern prosecutor's nursery"[8] —to suppress inchoate conduct that they consider potentially dangerous or morally undesirable.

Because of conspiracy law's emphasis on *mens rea*, and its consequent de-emphasis on conduct, there exists a greater than normal risk that "persons will be punished for what they say rather than for what they do, or for associating with others who are found culpable."[9] Indeed, as an historical matter, conspiracy laws have often been used to suppress controversial activity, such as strikes by workers and public dissent against government policies.[10]

[B]—Model Penal Code

Section 5.03(1) of the Model Penal Code defines "conspiracy" as follows:

A person is guilty of conspiracy with another person or persons to commit a crime if with the purpose of promoting or facilitating its commission he:

(a) agrees with such other person or persons that they or one or more of them will engage in conduct that constitutes such crime or an attempt or solicitation to commit such crime; or

(b) agrees to aid such other person or persons in the planning or commission of such crime or of an attempt or solicitation to commit such crime.

This definition and other features of the Code's treatment of criminal conspiracies are explored throughout this chapter.

§ 29.02 Punishing Conspiracies: Why?

[A]—"Conspiracy" as an Inchoate Offense: Preventive Law Enforcement

As with other inchoate offenses, the bar on conspiratorial agreements provides police officers with a basis for arresting people before they commit other criminal offenses.

Conspiracy law allows police intervention at a much earlier point than is permitted under attempt law. As is explained below,[11] a common law conspiracy is formed the moment two or more persons agree that one of them will later commit an unlawful act. At common law, no conduct in furtherance of the conspiracy is required; even when an act in furtherance of the conspiracy is statutorily required, the act may be wholly preparatory to the commission of the target offense. Consequently, advocates of conspiracy laws believe that the offense unfetters police and fills in the gaps in the "unrealistic" law of criminal attempts.[12] They also justify

---

[8] *Harrison v. United States*, 7 F.2d 259, 263 (2d Cir. 1925).

[9] Johnson, Note 1, *supra*, at 1139.

[10] See Mitford, Note 6 *supra*, at 61-72.

[11] See § 29.04[A], *infra*.

[12] Bernard Chernos, Note, 14 U. Toronto Fac. L. Rev. 56, 61 (1956).

conspiracy law on the ground that an agreement to commit a criminal act is concrete and unambiguous evidence of the actors' dangerousness and the firmness of their criminal intentions.[13]

However, the agreement that serves as the "concrete" and "unambiguous" evidence of the defendants' dangerousness and culpability is often proved inferentially.[14] Moreover, even if an agreement is conclusively proved to exist, the potential temporal remoteness of the agreement to the target offense increases the likelihood that some conspirators who would later renounce their intentions, or whose intentions were not strongly held when the agreement was formed, will be punished.

[B]—Special Dangers of Group Criminality

According to advocates of conspiracy laws, two people united to commit a crime are more dangerous than one or both of them separately planning to commit the same offense: "the strength, opportunities and resources of many is obviously more dangerous and more difficult to police than the efforts of a lone wrongdoer."[15]

The purported dangers inherent in collective criminal action are many.[16] First, as a result of fear of co-conspirators, loyalty to them, or enhanced morale arising from the collective effort, a party to a conspiracy is less likely to abandon her criminal plans than if she were acting alone. Other special dangers are said to inhere in conspiracies: collectivism promotes efficiency through division of labor; group criminality makes the attainment of more elaborate crimes possible; and the "[c]ombination in crime makes more likely the commission of crimes unrelated to the original purpose for which the group was formed."[17]

The assumption that the whole is greater than the sum of its parts has never been verified empirically. As one scholar has noted,[18] it is as likely that conspiracies will frustrate as that they will promote crime: with more people involved, there is an enhanced risk that someone will leak information about the offense, turn against others, or try to convince colleagues to desist from their criminal endeavor.

§ 29.03   Punishing Conspiracies: How Much?

[A]—In General

[1]—Common Law and Non-Model Penal Code Statutes

At common law, a conspiracy to commit a felony or a misdemeanor was a misdemeanor.[19] Modern statutory treatment of the offense varies widely among the

---

[13] American Law Institute, Comment to § 5.03, at 387-88.

[14] See § 29.04[A], *infra*.

[15] *Krulewitch v. United States*, 336 U.S. 440, 448-49 (1949) (Jackson, J., concurring) (footnote omitted).

[16] See generally *Developments in the Law*, Note 1, *supra*, at 923-25.

[17] *Callanan v. United States*, 364 U.S. 587, 593-94 (1961).

[18] Goldstein, Note 1, *supra*, at 414.

[19] Williams at § 220.

states.[20] Some states continue to treat all conspiracies, regardless of the seriousness of their objectives, as misdemeanors. More often, however, the sanction for conspiracy is graded in relationship to the contemplated crime. Many states punish conspiracies to commit felonies as felonies, and conspiracies to commit misdemeanors as misdemeanors. In most states, a conspiracy to commit a felony is punished less severely than the target offense.[21]

[2]—Model Penal Code

The Model Penal Code grades a conspiracy to commit any crime other than a felony of the first degree at the same level as the object of the conspiracy.[22] If a conspiracy has multiple objects, e.g., to rape and to steal,[23] the conspiracy is graded on the basis of the more or most serious target offense. As with the other inchoate offenses, the Code takes the subjectivist view that people who agree to commit crimes but are arrested before consummation are as dangerous as those who commit the offenses that are the objects of the conspiracy.

[B]—Punishment When the Target Offense is Committed

[1]—Common Law

Unlike the crimes of attempt and solicitation, the offense of conspiracy does not merge into the attempted or completed offense that was the object of the conspiracy.[24] For example, if *D1* and *D2* conspire to rob *V*, and later consummate or attempt to commit the robbery, they may be convicted and punished for both the conspiracy and the robbery or its attempt.[25]

The non-merger doctrine is unsupportable if the main purpose of conspiracy law is to provide the police with an opportunity to prevent the commission of the target offense. Once the object of the conspiracy is committed or attempted, this purpose of conspiracy law evaporates. Similarly, if the focus of the offense is on the dangerousness of the individual conspirator, her punishment should be calibrated

---

[20] See American Law Institute, Comment to § 5.05, at 488-89.

[21] At least one state authorizes *more severe* punishment of a conspiracy than of the substantive offense. E.g., Cal. Penal Code § 182a (West Supp. 1994) (treating conspiracy to commit specified misdemeanors as a felony); *People v. Tatman*, 24 Cal.Rptr. 2d 480 (Ct. App. 1993) (upholding felony conviction for a conspiracy to commit misdemeanor offenses relating to unlawful possession of red abalone, in violation of the Fish and Game Code).

[22] Model Penal Code § 5.05(1). See § 27.09[F][1], *supra*.

[23] As is explained more fully at § 29.08, *infra*, an agreement to commit multiple crimes constitutes only one conspiracy.

[24] *Callanan v. United States*, 364 U.S. 587, 593-94 (1961). At early common law, conspiracy merged with the target offense if the latter crime was a felony. *Developments in the Law*, Note 1, *supra*, at 968.

[25] E.g., *People v. Jones*, 601 N.E.2d 1080, 1088 (Ill. App. Ct. 1992) (upholding conviction of attempted armed robbery and conspiracy to commit armed robbery); *United States v. Boykins*, 966 F.2d 1240, 1245 (8th Cir. 1992) (upholding against constitutional attack, punishment for conspiracy to possess cocaine and attempted possession, based on the same incident).

to the crime that she threatened to commit; punishing her for both crimes is duplicative. The non-merger rule makes sense, however, if one focuses on the alternative rationale of conspiracy law, i.e., to attack the special threats that conspiratorial groupings represent.

[2]—Model Penal Code

The Code diverges from the common law. It provides that a person may not be convicted and punished for both conspiracy and the object of the conspiracy or an attempt to commit the target offense, unless the prosecution proves that the conspiracy involved the commission of additional offenses not yet committed or attempted. [26]

For example, if *D1* and *D2* conspire to rob Bank *V* and then do so, they may be convicted and punished for robbery or conspiracy, but not for both offenses. In contrast, if *D1* and *D2* conspire to rob Banks *V1*, *V2*, and *V3*, and they are arrested after robbing Bank *V1*—thus, before their other criminal objectives were satisfied— the conspiracy does *not* merge with the completed offense. The drafters of the Code believed that, in these circumstances, the special dangers inherent in collective action justify independent punishment of the conspiracy.

§ 29.04 Conspiracy: The Agreement

[A]—In General

The gist of a conspiracy is the agreement to commit an unlawful act or series of such acts. An express agreement, however, need not be proved. [27] Indeed, a physical act of communication of an agreement (e.g., a nod of the head or some verbal exchange) is not required. Furthermore, an agreement can exist although not all of the parties to it have knowledge of every detail of the arrangement, as long as each party is aware of its essential nature. [28]

Nonetheless—and this is the essence of the agreement—there must be present "on the part of each conspirator communion with a mind and will outside [herself]." [29] In this very limited sense, the conspiracy is externalized; that is, the agreement takes the law beyond the individual mental states of the parties, in which each person separately intends to participate in the commission of an unlawful act, to a shared intent and mutual goal, to a spoken or unspoken understanding by the parties that they will proceed in unity toward their shared goal.

How does a prosecutor prove the existence of this amorphous but critical agreement? Although, as one scholar has pointed out, "[a] conspiracy is not merely a concurrence of wills but a concurrence resulting from agreement," [30] it cannot be

---

[26] Model Penal Code § 1.07(1)(b). See American Law Institute, Comment to § 1.07, at 109.

[27] *United States v. James*, 528 F.2d 999, 1011 (5th Cir. 1976).

[28] *Blumenthal v. United States*, 332 U.S. 539, 557-58 (1947); *United States v. Pintado*, 715 F.2d 1501, 1503 (11th Cir. 1983).

[29] *Developments in the Law*, Note 1, *supra*, at 926.

[30] Williams at 667.

gainsaid that "[c]onspiracy is by nature a clandestine offense,"[31] one in which the agreement that constitutes the crime "is seldom born of 'open covenants openly arrived at.'"[32] The difficulty in demonstrating an agreement has proven to be the prosecutor's greatest advantage because, "in their zeal to emphasize that the agreement need not be proved directly, the courts sometimes neglect to say that it need be proved at all."[33]

A conspiratorial agreement may be established directly or through entirely circumstantial evidence.[34] Indeed, as one court has acknowledged, "because of the clandestine nature of a conspiracy and the foreseeable difficulty of the prosecution's burden of establishing the conspiracy by direct proof, the courts have permitted broad inferences to be drawn . . . from evidence of acts, conduct, and circumstances."[35]

A conspiracy "may be inferred from a 'development and a collocation of circumstances.'"[36] That is, a crime committed as the result of a prior agreement is apt to look choreographed. For example, in one case,[37] the prosecution proved the following: D1 was driving an automobile in which D2 and D3 were passengers; as the car drove by V, a pedestrian, D1 stopped the car; D2 called V over to the curb; D2 and D3 got out of the vehicle leaving their car doors open, and robbed V; D2 and D3 re-entered the car; and D1 drove away. Based on these facts, the court held that a jury could rationally find, beyond a reasonable doubt, that a conspiracy to rob V had been formed, and that D1, the driver of the vehicle, was a party to the agreement. Countless cases based on far less evidence than this have found conspiratorial agreements.[38]

When the choreography is missing, however, a court is less likely to find an agreement, absent more direct evidence. For example, in another case,[39] D1 and D2, two males, conversed with V, a female, on a street. When D1 said he was out of cigarettes, the three began walking toward a nearby convenience store. Along the way, V slipped and fell to the ground, at which moment D1 jumped on top of V in order to rape her. D1 handed his trouser belt to D2, who encouraged D1 in the rape.

---

[31] *Developments in the Law*, Note 1, *supra*, at 933.

[32] *Lacaze v. United States*, 391 F.2d 516, 520 (5th Cir. 1968).

[33] *Developments in the Law*, Note 1, *supra*, at 933 (footnote omitted).

[34] *United States v. Blasco*, 702 F.2d 1315, 1330 (11th Cir. 1983).

[35] *People v. Persinger*, 363 N.E.2d 897, 901 (Ill. App. Ct. 1977).

[36] *Glasser v. United States*, 315 U.S. 60, 80 (1942) (quoting *United States v. Manton*, 107 F.2d 834, 839 (2d Cir. 1939).

[37] *Commonwealth v. Azim*, 459 A.2d 1244 (Pa. Super. Ct. 1983).

[38] E.g., *People v. Persinger*, 363 N.E.2d 897 (Ill. App. Ct. 1977) (*O*, an undercover officer, purchased barbiturates from D1 at the latter's residence; during the meeting, D1 turned to D2, her husband, and requested a pocket knife to scratch the prescription label off the container in which the pills were enclosed; D2 was also present at other illegal purchases; held: there was sufficient evidence of a D1-D2 conspiracy).

[39] *Commonwealth v. Cook*, 411 N.E.2d 1326 (Mass. App. Ct. 1980).

D2's conduct—holding the belt and encouraging *D1*—constituted assistance in the rape. As such, he was properly charged as an accomplice in the commission of the rape. Based on this evidence, however, an appellate court concluded that *D2* was not properly convicted of conspiracy with *D1* to rape *V*.

The court's conclusion was sound. It was a chance meeting of the two men with the victim; the rape occurred in an apparently spontaneous, unplanned manner, i.e., *V* slipped and *D1* suddenly attacked her. As the court reasoned, it was as likely that *D2* became involved as an accomplice after the rape began as it was "to infer that the minds of the parties had met in advance," as part of an agreement to commit the rape.

[B]—Distinguishing the Agreement from the Group That Agrees

The term "conspiracy" describes the agreement that constitutes the offense for which the parties may be punished. However, a common but often misleading use of the word "conspiracy" is to describe *the group itself* that intends to commit the unlawful acts.

These two different uses of the term are often blurred by commentators and courts. Thus, one treatise states that "the gist of a conspiracy is the combination which is formed."[40] Some courts repeat the unfortunate characterization of a conspiracy as a "combination" of people.[41] Holmes, too, has described a conspiracy as "a partnership in criminal purposes."[42]

The crime of conspiracy should not be described in this fashion. One danger in failing to distinguish between the agreement and the group is that conspiracy convictions may be improperly affirmed. For example, suppose that *D* intentionally aids *X* and *Y* to commit a crime. *D* may be convicted of the target offense as the result of her accomplice relationship to the other parties. If *X* and *Y* were conspirators, however, may *D* also be convicted of conspiracy with them?

If "conspiracy" is the *X-Y* group rather than their agreement, then it follows logically that when *D* aids *X* and *Y* she aids the "conspiracy" (i.e., the group). Therefore, pursuant to complicity law, *D* is an accomplice of the "conspiracy" and, consequently, is guilty of the crime of conspiracy. Some courts, perhaps a majority, follow this approach.[43]

This analysis is wrong.[44] The essence of a conspiracy is the agreement—the union of wills—and not the group of conspirators. In order to aid and abet a conspiracy, therefore, *D* must intentionally aid and abet the formation of the agreement,[45]

---

[40] Perkins & Boyce at 682; see also *id.* at 683 ("the conspiracy is the combination resulting from the agreement, rather than the mere agreement itself").

[41] E.g., *Commonwealth v. Cook*, 411 N.E.2d at 1328.

[42] *United States v. Kissel*, 218 U.S. 601, 608 (1910).

[43] *Developments in the Law*, Note 1, *supra*, at 934 n.77.

[44] *Id.* at 934-35; American Law Institute, Comment to § 5.03, at 420-21.

[45] E.g., *D* arranges a meeting between *X* and *Y* so that they can reach an agreement. See *People v. Strauch*, 88 N.E. 155, 159 (Ill. 1909).

rather than aid the parties after the latter have formed the conspiratorial arrangement. A person who performs the latter type of assistance should be convicted of the substantive offense aided, but not of conspiracy.

[C]—Object of the Agreement

At common law, the object[46] of a conspiracy must be "to do either an unlawful act or a lawful act by criminal or unlawful means."[47] As this quote may suggest, the contemplated act that is the basis of the conspiratorial agreement need not constitute a crime; "it will be enough if the acts contemplated are corrupt, dishonest, fraudulent, or immoral."[48] Thus, it is possible for two people to be guilty of the offense of conspiracy because they have agreed to perform an act that is not criminal if performed by one of them. For example, under this doctrine, it is a conspiracy for two or more persons to agree to perform a civil wrong (i.e., an act that would subject them to civil damages),[49] or to agree to perform an act that is not a civil wrong but is otherwise considered immoral or dangerous to the public health or safety.[50]

This feature of common law conspiracy, followed in many pre-Model Penal Code statutes,[51] has been strongly criticized by commentators as violative of the principle of legality.[52] People are entitled to fair notice that their planned conduct is subject to criminal sanction. In an age in which legislatures rather than courts define criminal conduct, people should be able to turn to a written code for reasonable guidance in the conduct of their lives. If the legislature has not made a specified act criminal it is unfair to surprise people by punishing the *agreement* to commit the *non*criminal act.

Fair notice is also a constitutional requirement. Although the Supreme Court has never ruled on the validity of this feature of conspiracy law, it has strongly hinted that the breadth of the "unlawfulness" element violates due process.[53] State court rulings on the subject are mixed.[54]

---

[46] For purposes of clarity it is assumed here that the conspirators have a single objective. However, a single agreement may include multiple objectives. See § 29.08, *infra*.

[47] *State v. Parker*, 158 A. 797, 799 (1932) (quoting 12 Corpus Juris, 547).

[48] *Id.*

[49] E.g., *State v. Loog*, 179 A. 623 (N.J. 1935) (conspiracy to defame another).

[50] E.g., *Shaw v. Director of Public Prosecutions*, [1962] A.C. 220 (H.L.) (affirming a conviction for conspiracy to corrupt public morals, based on the publication of a lawful "Ladies' Directory" that contained the names and telephone numbers of prostitutes); *Commonwealth v. Donoghue*, 63 S.W.2d 3 (Ky. 1933) (affirming a conviction for conspiracy to exact usurious rates of interest, although usury was not a crime).

[51] American Law Institute, Comment to § 5.03, at 395.

[52] *Commonwealth v. Bessette*, 217 N.E.2d 893, 896 n.5 (Mass. 1966) (noting the criticism).

[53] *Musser v. Utah*, 333 U.S. 95, 96-97 (1948).

[54] E.g., compare *State v. Bowling*, 427 P.2d 928, 932 (Ariz. Ct. App. 1967) (unconstitutional) with *People v. Sullivan*, 248 P.2d 520, 526 (Cal. Ct. App. 1952) (constitutional).

[D]—Overt Act

A common law conspiracy is complete upon formation of the unlawful agreement. No act in furtherance of the conspiracy is required.[55] Nonetheless, many statutes diverge from the common law, and require an allegation in the indictment and proof at trial of the commission of an overt act in furtherance of the conspiracy.

The overt act need not represent the commencement of the consummation of the target offense. Instead, any act (and, in some cases, even an omission[56]), no matter how trivial, is sufficient, if performed in pursuance of the conspiracy.

The overt act need not be illegal.[57] For example, the act of writing a letter or making a telephone call pursuant to the unlawful agreement, the lawful purchase of an instrumentality to commit the offense, or attendance at a lawful meeting,[58] can qualify as the overt act.

Furthermore, the allegation and proof of a single overt act by *any* party to a conspiracy is sufficient basis to prosecute *every* member of the conspiracy,[59] including those who may have joined in the agreement after the act was committed.[60]

To the extent that an overt act is an element of the offense of conspiracy,[61] it reflects the view that a mere agreement does not represent a sufficient danger to society to be punished.[62] The overt act requirement, "like the substantial-step component of the law of attempt, helps to separate truly dangerous agreements from banter and other exchanges that pose less risk."[63]

[E]—Model Penal Code

[1]—In General

Section 5.03, subsection (1), the Model Code definition of conspiracy,[64] "rests on the primordial conception of agreement as the core of the conspiracy idea."[65]

---

[55] *United States v. Shabani*, 115 S.Ct. 382, 384 (1994); *People v. Von Villas*, 15 Cal.Rptr.2d 112, 153 (Ct. App. 1992).

[56] E.g., *United States v. Offutt*, 127 F.2d 336 (D.C. Cir. 1942) (failure by a conspirator to report for induction into the military).

[57] See *People v. Diaz*, 24 Cal. Rptr. 367, 373 (Ct. App. 1962).

[58] *Yates v. United States*, 354 U.S. 298, 333-34 (1957), *overruled on other grounds*, *Burks v. United States*, 437 U.S. 1 (1978) (attendance at a meeting of the Communist Party may constitute the overt act in furtherance of a conspiracy to overthrow the government).

[59] *Bannon v. United States*, 156 U.S. 464, 469 (1895).

[60] *Kaplan v. United States*, 7 F.2d 594, 596 (2nd Cir. 1925).

[61] In some jurisdictions, an overt act, although required, is not an element of the offense. Instead, the act "merely affords a *locus penitentiae*, so that before the act done either one or all of the parties may abandon their design, and thus avoid the penalty prescribed by the statute." *United States v. Britton*, 108 U.S. 199, 204-05 (1883).

[62] *Developments in the Law*, Note 1, *supra*, at 948.

[63] *United States v. Sassi*, 966 F.2d 283, 284 (7th Cir. 1992).

[64] The definition is set out in full in § 29.01[B], *supra*.

[65] American Law Institute, Comment to § 5.03, at 421.

The American Law Institute rejected the confusing conception of conspiracy as a "combination" or as a "partnership."[66]

Four types of agreement fall within the definition of conspiracy. A person is guilty of conspiracy if she agrees to: (1) commit an offense (i.e., "engage in conduct that constitutes such crime"); (2) attempt to commit an offense;[67] (3) solicit another to commit an offense;[68] or (4) aid another person in the planning or commission of the offense.[69]

[2]—Object of the Agreement

In a significant departure from the common law, the Model Code provides that the object of the conspiratorial agreement must be a criminal offense. All but three state penal code revisions since the adoption of the final draft of the Code in 1962 have agreed with the American Law Institute in this regard.[70]

[3]—Overt Act

The Code provides that a person may not be convicted of conspiracy to commit a misdemeanor or a felony of the third degree[71] unless she or a fellow conspirator committed an overt act in pursuance of the conspiracy. With felonies of the first and second degree, however, no overt act is required.[72]

As a result of this feature of the Code, the overt-act requirement has gained wide acceptance among the states. Most penal code revisions, however, have gone beyond the Code and apply the overt-act rule to all crimes.[73]

§ 29.05   Conspiracy; *Mens Rea*

[A]—In General

Common law conspiracy is a specific-intent offense. A criminal conspiracy does not occur unless two or more persons intend to agree *and* intend that the object of their agreement be achieved.[74] Absence of either intent renders the defendants' conduct non-conspiratorial. Thus, if O, an undercover police officer, agrees with D to murder V, O has the requisite intent to form an agreement with D, but she lacks the specific intent that the murder be consummated. As a result, O is not guilty of

---

[66] See § 29.04[B], *supra.*

[67] The purpose of this aspect of the definition is examined at § 29.09[A][2], *infra.*

[68] E.g., *D1* may be convicted of conspiracy if she agrees with *D2* that *D2* will solicit *X* to steal *V*'s painting.

[69] E.g., *D1* agrees to provide *D2* with a gun to be used to kill *V*. *D1* is guilty of conspiracy to commit murder, although she did not agree to commit the offense herself.

[70] American Law Institute, Comment to § 5.03, at 397.

[71] All felonies under the Code are of the third degree unless another degree is specified. Model Penal Code § 6.01(1).

[72] Model Penal Code § 5.03(5).

[73] American Law Institute, Comment to § 5.03, at 455-56.

[74] *People v. Horn*, 524 P.2d 1300, 1302-03 (Cal. 1974).

conspiracy. And, as discussed more fully elsewhere,[75] since *O* is not guilty of conspiracy, *D* cannot be convicted, because there are not "two or more persons" with the requisite intent.

It follows from the specific-intent nature of conspiracy that the culpability required for conviction of conspiracy at times must be greater than is required for conviction of the object of the agreement. For example, suppose that *D1* and *D2* agree to set fire to an occupied structure in order to claim the insurance proceeds. If the resulting fire kills occupants, they may be convicted of murder on the ground that the deaths, although unintentional, were recklessly caused. They are not guilty of conspiracy to commit murder, however, because their objective was to destroy the building, rather than to kill someone. Put another away, as a matter of logic, one "cannot agree to accomplish a required specific result unintentionally."[76]

[B]—Special Issues

[1]—"Purpose" versus "Knowledge": The Meaning of "Intent"

The specific intent of conspiracy is the "intent" that the object of the agreement be achieved. In most cases, the word "intent" suffices to define the state of mind required. Sometimes, however, it does not.

It will be remembered that the term "intent" encompasses within it two close but still different mental states, namely, what the Model Penal Code describes as "purpose" and "knowledge."[77] That is, *D* "intends" a result to occur if it is her conscious object (i.e., *purpose*) to cause the result, or if she *knows* that it will occur from her conduct. The question that lurks, therefore, is whether the specific mental state of conspiracy is proved if either concept of "intent" exists, or whether conspiracy can be demonstrated only if each party has as her *purpose* that the conspiratorial objective be achieved.

---

[75] See § 29.06[A], *infra*.

[76] *State v. Beccia*, 505 A.2d 683, 684 (Conn. 1986) (holding that conspiracy to commit reckless arson is not a cognizable offense); but see *State v. Wheeler*, 496 A.2d 1382 (R.I. 1985) (reversing a conviction of conspiracy to commit negligent homicide on the ground of insufficient evidence, but not suggesting that such an offense was a logical impossibility).Is it possible to conspire to commit voluntary manslaughter? On first glance, it would seem not. For example, two people cannot conspire to commit a *sudden* heat-of-passion killing. But, consider *People v. Horn*, 524 P.2d 1300 (Cal. 1974): *D1* and *D2*, while severely intoxicated, agreed to kill *V*. Had they gone through with their plans, *D1* and *D2* would have been guilty of voluntary manslaughter, rather than murder, on the basis of the diminished capacity doctrine as it then existed in California. The issue in *Horn* was how the diminished capacity doctrine applied to the crime of conspiracy. The majority in *Horn* held that the defendants were entitled to have the jury return a verdict of conspiracy to commit voluntary manslaughter: just as diminished capacity reduces the culpability of a homicide, it reduces the level of the actors' guilt for the conspiracy. The dissent argued that the defendants' diminished capacity was relevant in determining whether they formed the conspiratorial agreement. If they did, they conspired to commit murder; if they lacked the intent to agree, they did not conspire at all.

[77] See § 10.04[A][1], *supra*.

Usually this issue arises in a narrow context: a person or business furnishes goods or services to another person or group *knowing* that the goods or services will be used for illegal purposes. For example, X goes to *D1*, a gun dealer, and states that she wishes to purchase a gun so that she can kill her husband, *V*. *D1* agrees to sell X a gun although she knows X's criminal purpose. Or, consider these cases: *D2* sells sugar to persons whom she knows are the producers of illicit whiskey; [78] *D3*, the operator of a telephone answering service, provides telephone messages to known prostitutes; [79] and *D4*, a drug wholesaler, sells large quantities of legal drugs to X, knowing that X is using them for unlawful purposes. [80] In each of these cases, the person furnishing goods or services is aware of her customer's criminal intentions, but she may not care whether the crime is committed.

The argument for requiring proof of criminal purpose is that, in view of the highly inchoate nature of the offense, conspiracy laws should be reserved for those with criminal objectives, rather than to "seek to sweep within the drag-net of conspiracy all those who have been associated in any degree whatever with the main offenders." [81] In particular, the law should not be broadened to punish those whose primary motive is to conduct an otherwise lawful business in a profitable manner.

The argument in favor of permitting conviction on the basis of knowledge is that society has a compelling interest in deterring people from furnishing their wares and skills to those whom they know will use them unlawfully. Free enterprise should not immunize an actor from criminal responsibility in such circumstances; unmitigated desire for profits or simple moral indifference should not be rewarded at the expense of crime prevention.

Case law is divided on this issue. [82] The courts are consistent in stating, however, that even if purpose is required, it may often be inferred from *D*'s knowledge of X's plans. [83] The requisite purpose may be inferred if *D* promotes the venture and has a "stake in its outcome," [84] such as when she furnishes goods or services at a grossly inflated price. Similarly, purpose may be inferred from knowledge if a grossly disproportionate share of *D*'s business is with X, [85] or with separate customers whose planned conduct is illegal. [86] Finally, purpose may be proved from knowledge if *D* provides goods or services for which there is no lawful use.

---

[78] *United States v. Falcone*, 109 F.2d 579 (2d Cir.), *aff'd*, 311 U.S. 205 (1940).

[79] *People v. Lauria*, 59 Cal. Rptr. 628 (Ct. App. 1967).

[80] *Direct Sales Co. v. United States*, 319 U.S. 703 (1943).

[81] *United States v. Falcone*, 109 F.2d at 581.

[82] American Law Institute, Comment to § 5.03, at 404 & n.67 (and cases cited therein).

[83] See *People v. Lauria*, 59 Cal. Rptr. at 632-34

[84] *United States v. Falcone*, 109 F.2d at 581.

[85] E.g., *Direct Sales Co. v. United States*, 319 U.S. 703 (1943) (*D*, a drug wholesaler, sold morphine sulfate to X, a physician, in quantities 300 times the amount required for lawful purposes).

[86] E.g., *Shaw v. Director of Public Prosecutions* [1962] A.C. 220 (H.L.) (*D* sold space in a telephone and address directory to prostitutes).

[2]—*Mens Rea* Regarding Attendant Circumstances

The specific-intent element of conspiracy applies to the proscribed conduct or results of conduct that are the object of the agreement, but what mental state is required regarding attendant circumstances of an offense? For example, consider the essential facts of *United States v. Feola*:[87] *D1* and *D2*, drug dealers, agreed to attack *V*, a federal officer engaged in his official duties disguised as a drug customer. Clearly, *D1* and *D2* intended the prohibited result (battery), but were they guilty of the more serious federal offense of conspiracy to assault a federal officer in the performance of his official duties? That is, does the specific-intent requirement of conspiracy apply to the attendant circumstance of the victim's status as a law enforcement officer?

According to the Supreme Court, the substantive offense (assault upon a federal officer) requires no culpable state of mind regarding the attendant circumstance. That is, a person may be convicted of assault upon a federal officer as long as she has the requisite intent to commit the assaultive acts, even if she does not know or have reason to know that the intended victim is an officer engaged in official duties. In light of this, the prosecution argued for symmetry: the *mens rea* required for conviction of the substantive offense should apply to the conspiracy to violate the substantive offense. Thus, in this case, no *mens rea* would be required as to the victim's status.

The defendants argued that even if a person may be convicted of assault upon a federal officer without knowledge of the victim's federal status, one can hardly *conspire* to assault a federal officer without knowledge of his identity. In support of this proposition they quoted the reasoning of Judge Learned Hand, who provided this example:

> While one may, for instance, be guilty of running past a traffic light of whose existence one is ignorant, one cannot be guilty of conspiring to run past such a light, for one cannot agree to run past a light unless one supposes that there is a light to run past.[88]

Although Judge Hand's "attractive, but perhaps seductive"[89] reasoning "seems difficult to overcome,"[90] the Supreme Court in *Feola* rejected his reasoning, and held that the federal conspiracy statute does not require any greater *mens rea* as to an attendant circumstance than is embodied in the substantive offense itself (in this case, no *mens rea*).

Was the Court correct in rejecting Hand's traffic light analogy? Arguably, the circumstances in *Feola* were distinguishable from it. First, Hand's traffic offense was a *malum prohibitum* strict-liability crime, whereas an assault requires a wrongful intent to injure another. A court might wish to be more protective of defendants when the underlying offense is of the *malum prohibitum* variety.

---

[87] 420 U.S. 671 (1975).

[88] *United States v. Crimmins*, 123 F.2d 271, 273 (2nd Cir. 1941).

[89] *Feola*, 420 U.S. at 689.

[90] American Law Institute, Comment to § 5.03, at 413.

Second, the moral-wrong doctrine[91] supports a distinction. As the Supreme Court said in *Feola*:

> This interpretation [that no *mens rea* is required as to the victim's status as a law enforcement officer] poses no risk of unfairness to defendants. It is no snare for the unsuspecting. Although the perpetrator of a narcotics [offense], such as the one involved here, may be surprised to find that his intended victim is a federal officer in civilian apparel, he nonetheless knows from the very outset that his planned course of conduct is wrongful.

The same cannot be said in the case of Judge Hand's traffic violator, who was not committing a wrongful act based on the facts as she reasonably believed them to be.

Third, in *Feola* the attendant circumstance was a so-called "jurisdictional" element of the crime. That is, the fact that a victim is a federal officer performing her official duties is not a material element of the offense: it is included in the definition of the crime solely to provide the federal courts with authority to prosecute assaults that would otherwise constitute state crimes only. According to *Feola*, Congress did not intend for this jurisdictional-only feature of the law to stand in the way of conspiracy prosecutions based on the federal assault statute. In Hand's traffic light example, however, the issue of federal jurisdiction was not implicated; the fact that a traffic light is on the road has no jurisdictional significance.

Feola is not a constitutionally-based decision. As such, states are not required to follow the principles of the case in interpreting their own conspiracy statutes. Thus, it remains an open question, on a state-by-state basis, whether the offense of conspiracy may require a higher level of culpability regarding an attendant circumstance than is embodied in the underlying offense.

[3]—Corrupt-Motive Doctrine

Some jurisdictions apply what has come to be known as the "corrupt-motive doctrine."[92] This doctrine states that in addition to the usual *mens rea* requirements of conspiracy (i.e., intent to agree, and intent to commit the substantive offense), the parties to a conspiracy must also have a corrupt or wrongful motive for their actions.[93]

When the objective of a conspiracy is a *malum-in-se* offense, e.g., murder, rape, or larceny, the effect of this requirement is minimal, in that it only requires that the parties have sufficient knowledge of the relevant facts that they can appreciate that their conduct is wrongful. Thus, if we reconsider *Feola*,[94] in which *D1* and *D2*

---

[91] See § 12.06[B], *supra*.

[92] At one time, the doctrine was said to have "won general acceptance." *Developments in the Law*, Note 1, *supra*, at 936. However, the Commentary to the Model Penal Code states that the current status of the doctrine in most jurisdictions is uncertain. American Law Institute, Comment to § 5.03, at 418.

[93] E.g., *Commonwealth v. Benesch*, 194 N.E. 905, 910 (Mass. 1935); *People v. Powell*, 63 N.Y. 88, 92 (1875).

[94] *United States v. Feola*, 420 U.S. 671 (1975). See § 29.05[B][2], *supra*.

agreed to assault *V*, an undercover police officer, the parties had the requisite corrupt motive to commit a wrongful act (assault a human being), although they did not realize the degree of seriousness of their wrongful plan (i.e., they did not know that *V* was a law enforcement officer).

When the criminal objective is a *malum prohibitum* offense, however, the corrupt-motive doctrine serves as an exception to the usual rule that ignorance of the law is no excuse. Thus, in a jurisdiction that applies this doctrine, if *D1* and *D2* agree to do X, a morally innocent but illegal act, they cannot be convicted of conspiracy to commit X if they did not realize that X was illegal. In the absence of knowledge of the law, the parties lacked a corrupt motive.[95]

[C]—Model Penal Code

A person is not guilty of conspiracy under the Code[96] unless the conspiratorial agreement was made "with the purpose of promoting or facilitating" the commission of the substantive offense. As at common law, this means that a person is not guilty of conspiracy unless the object of the agreement was to bring about the prohibited result or to cause the prohibited conduct to occur, even if such purpose is not an element of the target offense. For example, suppose that *D1* and *D2* agree to burn down an occupied building for the insurance proceeds and, in the ensuing fire, an occupant dies. The defendants are guilty of murder, based on their reckless indifference to the value of human life.[97] However, they are not guilty of conspiracy to commit murder, unless an object of their agreement was to take human life.[98] The express requirement of purpose resolves a common law debate: a conspiracy does *not* exist if a provider of goods or services is aware of, but fails to share, another person's criminal purpose.[99]

The Model Penal Code does not recognize the corrupt-motive doctrine.[100] Section 2.04, subsection (3), of the Code specifies the circumstances in which

---

[95] E.g., *Commonwealth v. Gormley*, 77 Pa. Super 298 (1921) (*D1* and *D2*, election officials, were not guilty of conspiracy to violate a *malum prohibitum* election law when they agreed to commit acts that violated the substantive offense, because they were unaware that their activities fell within the offense).

[96] "Conspiracy" is defined in full at § 29.01[B], *supra*.

[97] Model Penal Code § 210.2(1)(b).

[98] American Law Institute, Comment to § 5.03, at 407-08. However, *D1* and *D2* may be convicted of conspiracy to recklessly endanger the occupants of the building. Model Penal Code § 211.2. This result is possible because their *purpose*, in the language of § 5.03(1)(a), was to "engage in conduct [setting fire to the building] that constitutes such crime [placing another person in danger of death or serious bodily injury, the offense of reckless endangerment]."

[99] See generally American Law Institute, Comment to § 5.03, at 403-04. The issue is raised in 29.05[B][1], *supra*.

[100] See § 29.05[B][3], *supra*.

ignorance of the law is a defense. The drafters of the Code did not believe that a special ignorance defense in the case of conspiracy was justified. [101]

The Code does not determine what culpability, if any, regarding the attendant circumstances of a substantive offense is required to convict for the offense of conspiracy. [102] The Commentary states that this issue is "best left to judicial resolution." [103]

§ 29.06   "Plurality" Requirement

[A]—Common Law

According to Justice Cardozo, "[i]t is impossible . . . for a man to conspire with himself." [104] This observation follows from the fact that a conspiracy is an agreement, and an agreement is a group act. Unless two or more people form an agreement, no one does. As a consequence, a prosecution of common law conspiracy must fail in the absence of proof that at least two persons possessed the requisite *mens rea* of a conspiracy. This is the so-called "plurality" requirement; it is founded on the premise that "conspiracy" is a bilateral concept.

As a result of the plurality principle, there can be no common law conspiracy if one of two parties to an agreement lacks the specific intent to commit the substantive offense. For example, no conspiracy conviction is possible if one of the two persons is an undercover agent feigning agreement, [105] or lacks the capacity to form the agreement due to mental illness. [106] Indeed, the acquittal of all but one alleged conspirator in a joint conspiracy trial requires the discharge of the remaining defendant, [107] regardless of the jury's reason for acquittal.

The plurality rule does not require that two persons be prosecuted and convicted of conspiracy. It is enough that the prosecutor proves beyond a reasonable doubt that two people are guilty of conspiracy. Thus, the conviction of a conspirator is not in jeopardy simply because the other person involved in the arrangement is unapprehended, dead, or unknown, or cannot be prosecuted because he has been

---

[101] They reasoned that the real purpose of the corrupt-motive doctrine was to "import fair mens rea requirements into [strict liability] statutes." American Law Institute, Comment to § 5.03, at 417 (footnote deleted). Although the drafters agreed with this goal, they favored promoting it directly through changes in general culpability requirements, rather than through conspiracy doctrine.

[102] See § 29.05[B][2], *supra*.

[103] See American Law Institute, Comment to § 5.03, at 413.

[104] *Morrison v. California*, 291 U.S. 82, 92 (1934).

[105] E.g., *State v. Pacheco*, 882 P.2d 183, 186 (Wash. 1994); *United States v. Escobar de Bright*, 742 F.2d 1196, 1199-1200 (9th Cir. 1984).

[106] See *Regle v. State*, 264 A.2d 119 (Md. Ct. Spec. App. 1970) (the prosecutor alleged a four-person conspiracy, but one party was a police informant, the second was a police officer, and the third was insane, leaving only one defendant with the requisite *mens rea*; held: conspiracy conviction could not stand).

[107] See *Commonwealth v. Campbell*, 390 A.2d 761, 764 (Pa. Super. Ct. 1978).

granted immunity.[108] And, although the rule used to be to the contrary,[109] the modern rule is that a convicted conspirator is not automatically entitled to relief because of the acquittal of the remaining conspirators in a separate trial.[110] As long as the evidence at the first trial was "sufficient unto itself to support its verdict"[111] —that is, the prosecutor proved that there was a conspiratorial agreement between two or more persons, one of whom was the defendant—the failure to convince the second jury of the conspiracy does not impair the validity of the first conviction, since the acquittal at the second trial may have been the result of a multitude of factors, such as the unexpected absence of a critical state witness.[112]

The plurality requirement has been criticized. First, the rule undermines the law enforcement purpose of conspiracy laws. For example, if *O*, an undercover police officer, feigns willingness to assist *D* in the commission of a murder, the plurality rule prevents *O* from arresting *D* until the latter's conduct reaches the potentially dangerous stage of an attempt. Second, the fact that a co-conspirator is a police officer or for some other reason is not subject to conviction for conspiracy, does not negate the dangerousness or culpability of the remaining guilty actor.[113]

[B]—Model Penal Code

The Model Code departs significantly from the common law by establishing a unilateral approach to conspiracy liability. Unlike the common law definition of conspiracy, which is phrased in terms of "two or more persons," the Code "focuses inquiry on the culpability of the actor whose liability is in issue, rather than on that of the group of which [she] is alleged to be a part."[114] That is, although the gist of the offense, as at common law, is the agreement, "conspiracy" is defined in terms of the guilt of a single party. This is evident from the Code's definition of "conspiracy,"[115] which starts, "*A person* is guilty of conspiracy with another person" if "*he agrees* with such other person" to commit an offense.

The unilateral nature of the Code's conspiracy provision affects legal analysis in various ways, some of which are discussed later in this chapter.[116] Its effect regarding the plurality doctrine, however, is straightforward. Although the prosecution may not convict a person of conspiracy in the absence of proof of an agreement, it is no defense that the person with whom the actor agreed: (1) has not been or cannot be convicted; or (2) is acquitted in the same or subsequent trial on the ground

---

[108] See *Commonwealth v. Byrd*, 417 A.2d 173, 176-77 (Pa. 1980).

[109] E.g., *Sherman v. State*, 202 N.W. 413, 414 (Neb. 1925), *overruled* in *Platt v. State*, 8 N.W.2d 849, 855 (Neb. 1943); *Developments in the Law*, Note 1, *supra*, at 972-73.

[110] *Commonwealth v. Byrd*, 417 A.2d at 177.

[111] *Gardner v. State*, 408 A.2d 1317, 1322 (Md. 1979).

[112] *Platt v. State*, 8 N.W.2d at 855.

[113] G.H.L. Friedman, *Mens Rea in Conspiracy*, 19 Mod. L. Rev. 276, 282-83 (1956).

[114] American Law Institute, Comment to § 5.03, at 393; see generally *id.* at 398-402.

[115] See § 29.01[B], *supra*, for the full definition.

[116] See §§ 29.07[E], 29.09[D][2], *infra*.

that she did not have the intent to go forward with the criminal plan (e.g., she feigned agreement in an effort to frustrate the endeavor[117] or is insane[118]).

The unilateral approach has been adopted in all but a very few recent revisions of state penal codes.[119]

§ 29.07   Parties to a Conspiracy

[A]—The Issue

Frequently, the facts surrounding an incident demonstrate that a conspiracy is afoot, but what is unclear is whether there is a single conspiracy involving many defendants, or multiple conspiracies involving fewer persons in each group. Four well-known cases illustrate the issue. They will be discussed throughout this section.

[1]—*Kotteakos v. United States*[120]

Brown served as a broker for 31 persons in obtaining fraudulent loans from the government. He and the loan recipients were indicted on one count of conspiracy. The evidence at trial demonstrated that the loan recipients were part of eight or more independent groups, none of which had any connection with any other group except that each used Brown as its broker.

The issue in the case was whether the 32 defendants were parties to a single conspiracy (as the prosecutor contended), or whether there existed eight or more smaller conspiracies, each consisting of a different group of loan recipients and Brown (as the loan recipients asserted).

[2]—*Blumenthal v. United States*[121]

In *Blumenthal*, the unnamed owner of a liquor wholesale agency distributed whiskey through two men, Weiss and Goldsmith, who arranged with Feigenbaum and Blumenthal to sell the whiskey to local tavern owners at a price in violation of the law.

The prosecutor alleged one conspiracy, the parties being the unidentified owner, the two distributors, and the salesmen. The salesmen claimed, however, that they never dealt with the owner or knew his identity. If they participated in a conspiracy, they asserted, it was one with the distributors alone; in turn the distributors were in a separate conspiracy with the owner.

---

[117] E.g., *State v. St. Christopher*, 232 N.W.2d 798 (Minn. 1975).

[118] Model Penal Code § 5.04(1)(b) expressly provides that it is no defense that the person with whom the defendant conspired is "irresponsible or has an immunity to prosecution or conviction." However, this result is already implicit in the unilateral conception. American Law Institute, Comment to § 5.03, at 399-400.

[119] *Id.* at 398-99.

[120] 328 U.S. 750 (1946).

[121] 332 U.S. 539 (1947).

[3]—*United States v. Peoni*[122]

Peoni sold a small quantity of counterfeit money to Regno, who in turn sold the money to Dorsey, who passed the money in commerce to innocent persons. The prosecutor alleged that the three men were parties to a single conspiracy. Peoni contended that if he was a party to any conspiracy it was with Regno alone, who in turn conspired with Dorsey.

[4]—*United States v. Bruno*[123]

Bruno and 87 other persons were prosecuted for conspiracy to import, sell, and possess narcotics. The evidence showed that a group of persons whose object it was to smuggle narcotics into the country through the Port of New York distributed the drugs through middlemen to retailers in New York and other retailers serving the Texas-Louisiana region. The retailers distributed the drugs to individual addicts.

No communication between the importers and any of the retailers or between the New York retailers and the Texas-Louisiana retailers was proved. The importers did know, however, that the middlemen dealt with retailers, and the retailers knew that the middlemen obtained their drugs from importers.

On appeal, the petitioners claimed that instead of a single conspiracy, there were at least three conspiracies: one between the importers and the middlemen; a second between the middlemen and the New York retailers; and a third between the middlemen and the Texas-Louisiana retailers.

[B]—Why the Issue Matters

[1]—Liability for Conspiracy

The most obvious reason why the structure of a conspiracy is important is that it will affect the number of counts of conspiracy of which a particular person may be prosecuted and convicted. For example, in *Kotteakos*, as the prosecutor conceived of the case, Brown was guilty of one conspiracy with 31 loan recipients; but from the loan recipients' perspective, he was potentially guilty of eight or more counts of conspiracy, each involving a smaller number of parties.[124]

[2]—Liability of Parties for Substantive Offenses

As is discussed more fully elsewhere,[125] a conspirator is guilty of every offense committed by every other conspirator in furtherance of the unlawful agreement. The structure of the conspiracy, therefore, may dramatically affect an individual conspirator's liability for the substantive crimes of others.

For example, if the prosecutor in *Kotteakos* were correct in treating the 32 defendants as parties to a single conspiracy, each party could be convicted of 31

---

[122] 100 F.2d 401 (2d Cir. 1938).

[123] 105 F.2d 921 (2d Cir.), *rev'd on other grounds*, 308 U.S. 287 (1939).

[124] The prosecutor conceptualized the case as involving one large conspiracy, which was beneficial to Brown in this regard. However, other factors (such as those discussed immediately below) may have affected the prosecutor's decision regarding how to frame the conspiracy indictment.

[125] See § 30.08, *infra*.

separate counts of fraud (assuming that the fraudulent loans were obtained); if the loan recipients' theory were correct, however, each of them was guilty of only a few fraudulently obtained loans, namely those obtained by the group composing the smaller conspiracy.

Similarly, in *Bruno* the prosecutor's theory could result in New York retailers being held accountable for every drug sale on the Texas-Louisiana streets (and vice-versa); their liability would be considerably less if the petitioners' theory of the structure of the conspiracy were correct.

[3]—Use of Hearsay Evidence

"Hearsay evidence" is evidence of a statement made other than by a witness while testifying at the hearing, which is offered to prove the truth of the matter stated. Subject to many exceptions, hearsay testimony is inadmissible at trial. That is, under this rule, W, a witness, may not testify that X told her that she saw D commit an offense.[126]

The hearsay rule is subject to two exceptions relevant here. First, an out-of-court admission by D, e.g., an assertion by D stating that she killed V, may be introduced at D's trial through the hearsay testimony of W, someone to whom D made the statement or who overheard her remarks. Second, and more importantly, an out-of-court statement of a conspirator made by her while participating in the conspiracy may be introduced in evidence against the other conspirators. Thus, a statement by $D1$ to W that she and $D2$ murdered V may be introduced against both $D1$ and $D2$ and any other co-conspirators.

The structure of the alleged conspiracy, therefore, is critical to determination of the admissibility of hearsay testimony. For example, under the prosecutor's theory of the conspiracy in *Bruno*, an out-of-court statement made by a New York retailer that "we and the Texans and Louisianans are getting a rotten deal from the importers and middlemen," could be introduced into evidence against the importers, middle-men, Texas and Louisiana retailers, and every other New York retailer. If the retailers' theory of the conspiracy were correct, however, the New York retailer's remarks would be inadmissible against the Texas-Louisiana retailers, because they were not parties to the New York conspiracy.

[4]—Joint Trial

Generally speaking, prosecutors prefer to bring every member of an alleged conspiracy to trial in a single proceeding, rather than to prosecute the conspirators in separate trials. Joint trials are more efficient (e.g., all of the evidence may be introduced once to a single jury). Perhaps equally importantly, however, a joint trial makes it more difficult for innocent or barely culpable defendants to separate themselves from guilty co-defendants. As Justice Jackson has observed:

> A co-defendant in a conspiracy trial occupies an uneasy seat. There generally will
> be evidence of wrongdoing by somebody. It is difficult for the individual to make

---

[126] Hearsay testimony is inadmissible because if it were allowed, a defendant would be denied her constitutional right to cross-examine her accuser (X in the example in the text), and because it would render the trial less reliable than if the accuser were required to testify directly.

his own case stand on its own merits in the minds of jurors who are ready to believe that birds of a feather are flocked together.[127]

Thus, in *Bruno*, the most culpable importers were joined with the comparatively small-time street retailers; even if some of the 88 persons charged with conspiracy were innocent of wrongdoing, they faced substantial difficulties of proof.

[5]—Overt-Act Requirement

The structure of a conspiracy is critical in jurisdictions recognizing an overt-act requirement.[128] In these jurisdictions, an act of one conspirator in furtherance of the agreement renders a prosecution permissible against every other party to the same agreement.

Thus, in *Kotteakos* proof of a single overt act by one person, for example by Brown, pertaining to a single fraudulent loan, would be sufficient to bring the conspiracy prosecution against all 32 defendants. If the loan recipients' argument were correct, however, at least eight separate conspiracies were involved, and proof of an overt act in each of these cases would be required.

[6]—Venue

In general, a trial may be held in any jurisdiction in which the crime was committed. With conspiracies, a trial may be brought not only where the agreement was formulated, but also in any jurisdiction in which any member performed any act in its furtherance.

The effect of this venue rule is especially dramatic in federal cases. The larger the conspiracy alleged by the prosecutor, the greater are the number of federal districts in which it is permissible to bring the prosecution. The prosecutor, therefore, has an incentive to shape the conspiracy in a manner that will allow her to bring the case in a sympathetic venue. It also permits her to compel a defendant in a conspiracy prosecution "to defend at great distance from any place he ever did any act because some accused confederate did some trivial and by itself innocent act in the chosen district."[129]

[C]—Structure of Conspiracies

In conspiracy prosecutions involving multiple layers of actors, it is useful for a lawyer to conceptualize the alleged conspiracy in diagrammatic fashion. Usually the diagramming will demonstrate that a conspiracy looks something like a wheel, a chain, or a combination of the two.

[1]—Wheel Conspiracies

Some conspiracies look like wheels. In the center of the wheel (*the hub*) is one person or group who transacts illegal dealings with various other persons or groups (*the spokes*). As the prosecutor conceptualized it, *Kotteakos* was a wheel conspiracy. Brown was the hub. Each of the persons for whom he obtained loans or, at least, each of the eight groups of persons with whom he dealt, was a spoke.

---

[127] *Krulewitch v. United States*, 336 U.S. 440, 454 (1949) (concurring opinion).

[128] See generally § 29.04[D], *supra*.

[129] *Krulewitch v. United States*, 336 U.S. at 453 (Jackson, J., concurring).

However, for a wheel conspiracy to be complete, i.e., for it to be fair to say that there exists a single conspiracy that includes the hub and all of the spokes, there must be a rim around the wheel. That is, one must be able to draw a line around the wheel connecting the spokes. If this cannot be done, then there is no wheel conspiracy; rather there exist as many chain conspiracies as there are spokes, with the membership of each conspiracy consisting of the hub and the individual spoke. The process of how the spokes are connected together to create a genuine wheel conspiracy is considered in subsection [D].

[2]—Chain Conspiracies

A chain conspiracy ordinarily involves "several layer of personnel dealing with a single subject matter, as opposed to a specific person."[130] These conspiracies most often occur in business-like criminal activities, in which each person or group in the conspiracy has specialized responsibilities that link together the various aspects of the unlawful conduct.

As the prosecutors alleged the facts, *Blumenthal* and *Peoni* were three-link chain conspiracies. In *Blumenthal* the unidentified owner of the wholesale agency was linked to Weiss and Goldsmith, the distributors, who in turn were linked to Feigenbaum and Blumenthal, who sold the whiskey to taverns. In *Peoni*, Peoni was linked to Regno who was linked to Dorsey.

The issue with chain conspiracies is how many people or groups may properly be linked together. The longer the chain, the more tenuous the relationship between the distant links.

[3]—Chain-Wheel Conspiracies

It is not unusual to find that the structure of a very large conspiracy has features of both a wheel and a chain.[131] *Bruno* potentially fits this description. Notice that it was basically a chain consisting of smugglers, middlemen, and retailers. However, there existed at least two geographically disparate groups of retailers. It is possible, therefore, to conceptualize the conspiracy either as two chain conspiracies (in which the importers, middlemen, and the separate state retailers are linked) or as a chain conspiracy with spokes at the end (thus, the importers are linked to the middlemen, at which point the various retail groups become spokes connected to the middlemen).[132]

---

[130] *People v. Macklowitz*, 514 N.Y.S.2d 883, 886 (N.Y. Sup. Ct. 1987).

[131] "Perhaps a more accurate way to visualize a complex conspiracy case would be to view it as a three dimensional organic chemistry molecule with each party interacting continuously with another thereby forming and adhering to the whole, for a common purpose." *Id.*

[132] Of course, the New York and Texas-Louisiana spokes consisted of many individual retailers no more likely to be connected to one another than one state group was connected to the retailers in the other region. Thus, if one were inclined to do so, one could break up the two spokes into many more individual spokes.

[D]—Common Law Analysis

[1]—In General

There is no simple method for determining the proper structure of a conspiracy. Many factors, including the nature of the criminal activity, the number of defendants, the size of the business, and the extent of contact between the parties, will affect the ultimate result. One matter is clear, however: to be regarded as a co-conspirator, a person does not need to know the identity, *or even of the existence*, of every other member of the conspiracy, although she must "have a general awareness of both the scope and the objective of the enterprise."[133] It follows, therefore, that a prosecutor's theory of a conspiracy is not fatally flawed solely because one party to the alleged agreement never communicated with certain other members.

[2]—Wheel Conspiracies

Hubs and spokes frequently perceive events differently. The hub views each spoke as part of a broader criminal enterprise; the spokes, however, often interpret the situation more narrowly. For example, in *Kotteakos*, Brown was in the business of obtaining fraudulent loans for his customers. He sought each customer—each spoke—as a part of a broader plan. The customers, however, were interested only in their own loans.

A rim does not exist, i.e., there is no wheel conspiracy, unless the prosecutor demonstrates that the spokes viewed their contacts with the hub as part of a plan broader than any individual spoke's relationship with the hub: "[w]hat is required is a *shared*, single criminal objective, not just similar or parallel objectives between similarly situated people."[134]

In *Kotteakos*, the appellate court concluded that the spokes lacked this shared objective. No community of interest existed among the spokes: each loan recipient wanted a loan, received it, and moved on. Each loan was independent of the others. Each fraudulent application stood or fell on the basis of the false claims asserted in that particular application. Thus, the spokes were correct in concluding that, rather than one wheel conspiracy, there existed multiple chain conspiracies involving Brown and each spoke.

An example of a genuine wheel conspiracy is *Anderson v. Superior Court*:[135] *D*, an illegal abortionist, hired as many as 17 persons, to whom he paid "finder's fees," to refer pregnant women to him. The court upheld an indictment charging the 18 persons (*D*, the hub; and the 17 spokes) as parties to a single conspiracy. Here, unlike in *Kotteakos*, the spokes had an ongoing relationship with the hub. And, arguably, each of the spokes shared a common objective, since their continued employment depended on the success of the illegal venture.

---

[133] *United States v. Evans*, 970 F.2d 663, 670 (10th Cir. 1992).

[134] *Id.* at 670.

[135] 177 P.2d 315 (Cal. Ct. App. 1947).

[3]—Chain Conspiracies

Large chain conspiracies are easier to prove than wheel conspiracies. This follows from the fact that chain conspiracies ordinarily involve unlawful plans that cannot succeed unless each link successfully perform her responsibilities in the arrangement.

Thus, in *Blumenthal*, the Supreme Court found that the prosecutor properly charged a single conspiracy. Although the salesmen claimed that they did not know of the owner's existence (much less his identity), the Court pointed out that they knew that the persons with whom they dealt were not the true owners of the whole-sale agency. Therefore, the "salesmen knew or must have known that others unknown to them were sharing in so large a project." Each salesman "by reason of [his] knowledge of the plan's general scope, if not its exact limits, sought a common end, to aid in disposing of the whiskey."

This does not mean that every chain is a single conspiracy. *Peoni*, for example, was not a single conspiracy. Here, Peoni apparently sold only a small number of counterfeit bills to Regno. Peoni did not care whether Regno passed the money himself or, as he did, sold it to another person to pass. Peoni had no common interest, therefore, with Dorsey. Instead, there were two independent conspiracies, one between Peoni and Regno and a second one between Regno and Dorsey. If larger numbers of bills had been involved—enough that Peoni needed Regno to obtain assistance in passing the money—a single conspiracy might have been proved.[136]

[4]—Chain-Wheel Conspiracies

Quite arguably, *Bruno* involved a chain-wheel conspiracy. The court ruled that the importers, middlemen, and geographically disparate retailers were all part of a single chain conspiracy. The retailers knew that smugglers existed (and vice-versa). More importantly, each link had a stake in the larger venture. The court failed to explain, however, why and how the retailers—the separate spokes—were drawn together. The court properly analyzed the chain feature of the conspiracy, but it ignored the wheel aspect.

[E]—Model Penal Code

[1]—Relevant Provisions

The Model Penal Code provides a complex but potentially fairer approach to the party dimension of a conspiracy. Two aspects of the Code are relevant. First, § 5.03(1), as reprinted above,[137] and discussed earlier,[138] adopts the unilateral approach to conspiracy, and provides that a person is guilty of conspiracy if, with the purpose of promoting or facilitating the commission of a crime, she agrees with another to commit the offense.

---

[136] E.g., *United States v. La Vecchia*, 513 F.2d 1210 (2d Cir. 1975).

[137] See § 29.01[B], *supra*.

[138] See §§ 29.04[E], 29.05[C], 29.06[B], *supra*.

Second, § 5.03(2) provides additional guidance in determining when parties to separate agreements to commit the same crime may be linked together:

Scope of Conspiratorial Relationship. If a person guilty of conspiracy . . . knows that a person with whom he conspires to commit a crime has conspired with another person or persons to commit the same crime, he is guilty of conspiring with such other person or persons, whether or not he knows their identity, to commit such crime.

[2]—Example of the Code Approach: *United States v. Bruno* [139]

The Commentary to the Code explains how some of the cases discussed earlier in this section would be analyzed under the Model Code. [140] The most interesting questions arise regarding *Bruno*, in which the Code would require a very different mode of analysis and, very likely, would reach a different outcome. In order to understand how the Code provisions are applied, we may simplify the *Bruno* facts by assuming the existence of a single importer, a single middleman, and one retailer each in New York and Texas-Louisiana; also, for sake of clarity, certain facts not clear in *Bruno* will be assumed.

Here is the *Bruno*-inspired hypothetical scenario: Importer meets with Middleman and agrees that Importer will smuggle narcotics into the country, in violation of Statute X. In their meeting, they further agree that Middleman will find retailers to sell the narcotics in their states, which sales would violate Statute Y. Middleman proceeds to meet with New York Retailer and, on another date, with Texas-Louisiana Retailer, and agrees with each of them that the retailers will sell drugs in their respective states, in violation of Statute Y. Neither retailer knows that Middleman is dealing with another retailer, nor do the retailers know the details of the Importer-Middleman dealings.

Based on these facts a lawyer would start by applying § 5.03(1), in order to identify each agreement to commit a crime that occurred. Doing this, the evidence supports the existence of four agreements: (1) Importer and Middleman, to violate Statute X; (2) Importer and Middleman, to violate Statute Y; (3) Middleman and New York retailer, to violate Statute Y; (4) Middleman and Texas-Louisiana retailer, to violate Statute Y.

Based on § 5.03(1) alone, therefore, we have four two-person agreements. At this point, however, § 5.03(2) may be applied to add additional links to the conspiracies. Importer knew that Middleman, with whom she had conspired to violate Statute Y, would also conspire with New York Retailer and Texas-Louisiana Retailer to commit the same offense. Consequently, Importer is guilty of conspiring with both retailers to violate Statute Y.

The retailers, however, did not know that Middleman, with whom they dealt, had conspired with Importer to violate Statute Y; therefore, in light of the Code's unilateral approach to conspiracy, the retailers are not guilty of conspiring with Importer

---

[139] 105 F.2d 921 (2d Cir.), *rev'd on other grounds*, 308 U.S. 287 (1939). See § 27.07[A][4], *supra.*

[140] See American Law Institute, Comment to § 5.03, at 425-35.

to violate Statute Y (although, as just seen, Importer is guilty of conspiring *with them* to commit the same offense). Moreover, there is probably no basis for finding that the New York and Texas-Louisiana retailers had the requisite purpose of promoting or facilitating the commission of the sales in the other region, so neither retailer should be joined in any conspiracy relating to the violation of Statute Y outside their own area.

Thus, we reach this conclusion. Importer conspired with Middleman to violate Statute X; and she conspired with Middleman, New York Retailer, and Texas-Louisiana retailer to violate Statute Y. The same result applies to Middleman. New York Retailer is guilty of conspiring with Middleman to violate Statute Y, but is guilty of no other offense. Similarly, Texas-Louisiana Retailer conspired with Middleman to violate Statute Y.

Notice the difference between this analysis and the common law. The *Bruno* court described the conspiracy broadly to be "to smuggle narcotics into the Port of New York and distribute them to addicts both in [New York] and Texas and Louisiana." That was a fair description of the situation from the viewpoint of Importer and Middleman, but it was not either retailer's perception. Given the bilateral nature of common law conspiracy, however, once it is concluded in a common law jurisdiction that Importer and Middleman conspired with the retailers to import and sell drugs, the retailers are guilty of conspiring with them to violate the same laws.

The result under the Code, however, more accurately represents the divergent culpabilities of the parties: Importer and Middleman, who were deeply involved in the events, are guilty of conspiring with everyone; the retailers, who cared little about anything other than the sales in their respective region, would be guilty of conspiracy with Middleman to sell drugs in their region, but no more.

§ 29.08   Objectives of a Conspiracy

[A]—The Issue

Suppose that *D1* and *D2* rob *V1* on Day 1, rob *V2* on Day 2, and rob and rape *V3* on Day 3. Assuming that these crimes were committed as the result of a conspiratorial relationship between *D1* and *D2*, a critical question remains: how many conspiracies were there? That is, do we say that there were four conspiracies, one for each crime (to rob *V1*, to rob *V2*, to rob *V3*, and to rape *V3*)? Or were there three conspiracies, one for each victim? Are there two conspiracies based on the statutes violated (robbery and rape)? Or, is there just one conspiracy to commit all of the criminal acts?

[B]—Common Law Analysis

Although various approaches to the issue have developed, the Supreme Court in *Braverman v. United States*[141] announced the following rule regarding federal conspiracy prosecutions:

---

[141] 317 U.S. 49, 53 (1942).

[T]he precise nature and extent of the conspiracy must be determined by reference to the agreement which embraces and defines its objects. Whether the object of a single agreement is to commit one or many crimes, it is in either case that agreement which constitutes the conspiracy which the statute punishes. The one agreement cannot be taken to be several agreements and hence several conspiracies because it envisages the violation of several statutes rather than one.

It follows in the case discussed above, therefore, that the fact that *D1* and *D2* planned to violate two criminal statutes, or to violate a particular statute multiple times, does not in itself convert a single conspiracy with multiple objectives into multiple conspiracies with a single objective each.

Ultimately, under *Braverman*, the issue is whether a single agreement or many distinct ones were formed. In the hypothetical, for example, it is possible that *D1* and *D2* got together once and agreed to commit each of the offenses, in which case there was one conspiracy. On the other hand, they may have met various times, each time reaching a new and independent agreement to rob, and the rape may have been a spur-of-the moment group decision, in which case *D1* and *D2* are guilty of four conspiracies. It is also possible that the co-conspirators originally agreed to conduct robberies together (without specifying the number or identity of the victims), and (as in the last scenario) the rape of *V3* was a last-moment decision. Under these circumstances, there were two conspiracies.

It may also be observed that, in light of the supposed special dangers in group criminality, the preceding scenarios result in different policy outcomes. If it were to turn out that *D1* and *D2* robbed *V1*, split the proceeds, and disbanded, only later to get together again and repeat the process, then the social harm of their unification occurred multiple times. On the other hand, if they conspired to rob people—if they planned to stay together and keep victimizing others—the special dangers of unity occurred only once.

Because of inherent difficulties of proof, and in order not to "place a premium upon foresight in crime,"[142] many courts avoid careful inquiry into the events and, instead, treat the initial agreement between the parties as implicitly incorporating later objectives.

[C]—Model Penal Code

Under the Code, a person with multiple criminal objectives is guilty of only one conspiracy if the multiple objectives are: (1) part of the same agreement; or (2) part of a continuous conspiratorial relationship.[143] Thus, in the *D1-D2* example, each person would be guilty of only one count of conspiracy, even if the crimes resulted from multiple agreements, as long as "there was a single and continuous association for criminal purposes."[144]

---

[142] *Developments in the Law*, Note 1, *supra*, at 930.

[143] Model Penal Code § 5.03(3).

[144] American Law Institute, Comment to § 5.03, at 439.

§ 29.09 Defenses

[A]—Impossibility

[1]—Common Law

Issues of factual and legal impossibility, matters of considerable complexity in the realm of criminal attempts,[145] also arise (although much less often) in conspiracy prosecutions. For example, are *D1* and *D2* guilty of conspiracy if they agree to: (1) perform an abortion on a nonpregnant woman;[146] (2) kill a non-existent person;[147] (3) receive stolen property that was not actually stolen;[148] or (4) kill an enemy by voodoo.[149]

Case law on the subject is thin, but it has been stated that the majority, but not universal, rule is that neither factual impossibility nor legal impossibility is a defense to a criminal conspiracy.[150] In jurisdictions that recognize an impossibility defense, many of the difficulties in distinguishing between legal impossibility (a defense) and factual impossibility (no defense) reassert themselves.[151] For example, the courts are divided on whether a conspiracy to perform an illegal abortion on a nonpregnant woman is an example of factual or hybrid legal impossibility.[152]

The rationale for denying a hybrid legal impossibility defense in the conspiracy context is, arguably, at least as strong as with criminal attempts. Like people who attempt crimes, those who conspire to commit unlawful acts are dangerous, even if their conduct in the present case will be fruitless. Indeed, the impossibility that the defendants' conduct will result in consummation of the contemplated crime may be *less* relevant to a conspiracy, which is primarily a *mental* offense, than to an attempt, in which the primary focus is on the proximity of the *conduct* to the consummation of the target crime.[153]

On the other hand, the fact that conspiracy *is* primarily a mental offense—and, as a consequence, involves highly inchoate activity—may be an argument for a *broader* impossibility defense. When the objective circumstances do not support the

---

[145] See § 27.07, *supra*.

[146] E.g., *People v. Tinskey*, 228 N.W.2d 782 (Mich. 1975) (defense is recognized); *State v. Moretti*, 244 A.2d 499 (N.J. 1968) (no defense is recognized).

[147] *State v. Houchin*, 765 P.2d 178 (Mont. 1988) (conspiracy).

[148] *United States v. Petit*, 841 F.2d 1546 (11th Cir. 1988).

[149] See *Voodoo Priest Scheme*, Washington Post, Feb. 18, 1989, at A18; and *Officials Say 2 Tried to Put Hex on Judge*, Chicago Tribune, May 28, 1989, at 6 (reporting that two Mississippi brothers were indicted on the charge of conspiracy to murder a judge who had sentenced one of the alleged conspirators to prison; the plan was to obtain a lock of the judge's hair and have a Jamaican voodoo priest cast a death curse with it).

[150] *State v. Houchin*, 765 P.2d at 179-80 (stating the majority rule, but interpreting the state's conspiracy statute as allowing for a defense of legal impossibility).

[151] There is no published appellate court opinion determining whether "inherent impossibility" (see § 27.07[C][2] *supra*) is a defense to conspiracy.

[152] See Note 146, *supra*.

[153] *State v. Moretti*, 244 A.2d at 502.

claim that a criminal objective can be achieved, e.g., performing an abortion on a woman who is not pregnant, the risk of punishing innocent people is enhanced.

[2]—Model Penal Code

The Model Penal Code does not recognize a defense of factual or hybrid legal impossibility in conspiracy cases. The Code's definition of conspiracy states that a person is guilty of an offense if she agrees with another that "they or one of them will engage in conduct that constitutes . . . *an attempt* . . . to commit such crime," or if she "agrees to aid such other person or persons in . . . *an attempt* . . . to commit such crime."[154]

Of course, people do not conspire to attempt crimes; they conspire to commit them. This language is meant to take account of the impossibility situation.[155] Thus, as the Commentary suggests, if *D1* and *D2* agree to rob a bank that they incorrectly believe is federally insured, they may be convicted of conspiracy to rob a federally insured bank, although commission of such offense is impossible, because they would have been guilty of criminal attempt had they proceeded with the plan.

[B]—Abandonment

[1]—Common Law

The crime of conspiracy is complete the moment the agreement is formed or, in some jurisdictions,[156] once an overt act is committed in furtherance of a criminal objective. Once the offense is complete, abandonment of the criminal plan by a party to the conspiracy is not a defense to the conspiracy.[157] The reasoning is the same as with attempts: once a crime has occurred, a person cannot undo that offense.

An actor's abandonment of the conspiratorial objective, however, is not without relevance. If a person withdraws from a conspiracy, she may avoid liability for subsequent crimes committed in furtherance of the conspiracy by her former co-conspirators. Also, once a person withdraws, the statute of limitations for the conspiracy begins to run in her favor.

Courts are strict in their requirement of proof of abandonment. Usually they require that the abandoning party communicate her withdrawal to each of her fellow co-conspirators.[158] Some courts go further and require her successfully to dissuade the others from pursuing their criminal objectives.[159]

[2]—Model Penal Code

The Model Code provides an affirmative defense to the crime of conspiracy if the conspirator renounces her criminal purpose, and thwarts the success of the

---

[154] Model Penal Code § 5.03(1) (emphasis added).

[155] American Law Institute, Comment to § 5.03, at 421.

[156] See § 29.04[D], *supra*.

[157] American Law Institute, Comment to § 5.03, at 457.

[158] *People v. Sconce*, 279 Cal.Rptr. 59, 63 (Ct. App. 1991).

[159] See *Eldredge v. United States*, 62 F.2d 449, 451-52 (10th Cir. 1932).

conspiracy under circumstances demonstrating a complete and voluntary renunciation of her criminal intent.[160]

The drafters of the Code rejected the no-defense rule on the same ground that it recognizes the abandonment defense to other inchoate offenses,[161] namely, that a voluntary renunciation of a criminal purpose negates the actor's dangerousness. On the other hand, in light of the special dangers inherent in conspiratorial groupings, it is insufficient for a conspirator merely to withdraw; she must also negate the danger of the group that she joined.

[C]—Wharton's Rule

[1]—Common Law

[a]—In General

An agreement by two persons to commit an offense that, *by definition*, requires the voluntary participation of two persons, cannot be prosecuted as a conspiracy. This is "Wharton's Rule."[162]

The offenses of adultery, bigamy, and incest classically fall within the scope of Wharton's Rule. These offenses, by definition, require the willing participation of two persons; there is no way one person can commit these offenses. Other examples of crimes for which Wharton's Rule applies are: dueling; sale of contraband;[163] and receipt of a bribe.[164] A person cannot duel with herself, sell contraband in the absence of a willing buyer, or receive a bribe without a briber.

On the other hand, Wharton's Rule is not a bar to a conspiracy prosecution for: (1) possession of a controlled substance with the intent to deliver;[165] (2) "bartering, exchanging, or offering" an illegal narcotic to another;[166] or (3) unlawfully "receiving or disposing" of another person's property.[167] In each of these cases it is theoretically possible for the offense to be committed in the absence of an agreement.[168]

---

[160] Model Penal Code § 5.03(6).

[161] See §§ 27.09[E][2], 28.03[B], *supra*.

[162] 2 Francis Wharton, Criminal Law § 1604 (12th ed. 1932); *Iannelli v. United States*, 420 U.S. 770, 773 n.5 (1975); *Developments in the Law*, Note 1, *supra*, at 954.

[163] *People v. Urban*, 553 N.E.2d 740, 741-42 (Ill. App. Ct. 1990).

[164] *People v. Wettengel*, 58 P.2d 279, 281 (Colo. 1935).

[165] *Johnson v. State*, 587 A.2d 444, 452-53 (Del. 1991).

[166] *State v. Cavanaugh*, 583 A.2d 1311, 1314 (Conn. App. Ct. 1990).

[167] *Guyer v. State*, 453 A.2d 462, 466 (Del. 1982).

[168] In (1), it takes only one person to *possess* a controlled substance, and actual delivery (as distinguished from the intent) is not an element of the crime. In (2), it requires two persons to *barter* or *exchange*, but it takes only one willing person to *offer* an illegal narcotic. As the offense is defined in the disjunctive, Wharton's Rule does not apply. In (3), a person can *receive* property by finding it on the street; likewise, she can *dispose* of property by throwing it away.

The rationale of Wharton's Rule is that if a substantive offense cannot be committed in the absence of an agreement, the added dangers relating to group criminality are absent. This reasoning ignores the other rationale of conspiracy: the concern regarding inchoate conduct. That is, even if there is no increased danger resulting from, for example, two persons agreeing to duel, Wharton's Rule prevents the police from arresting the would-be duelers until they reach the more dangerous stage of an attempt.

Because Wharton's Rule can frustrate law enforcement, some courts limit the applicability of the doctrine to cases in which the substantive offense has been consummated or attempted. [169] For example, if *D1* and *D2* agree to commit adultery, the conspirators may be arrested, convicted, and punished for conspiracy, notwithstanding Wharton's Rule. However, if the offense is attempted or completed before they can be arrested, *D1* and *D2* may not be convicted and punished for the conspiracy. Instead, contrary to the usual rule, [170] the conspiracy merges into the substantive offense.

Although Wharton's Rule was described as recently as 1959 as "firmly entrenched" [171] in American common law jurisprudence, the Supreme Court in 1975 ruled that the doctrine "has current vitality [in the federal courts] only as a judicial presumption, to be applied in the absence of legislative intent to the contrary." [172]

[b]—Exceptions to the Rule

Two exceptions to Wharton's Rule are recognized. First, the "third–party exception" provides that if more than the minimum number of persons necessary to commit an offense agree to commit the crime, Wharton's Rule is not triggered. [173] For example, if *D1*, *D2*, and *D3* agree that *D1* and *D2* will commit adultery, one person more than is necessary to commit adultery is involved in the conspiracy. Now, the added dangers of collective criminality return, so that all three persons may be convicted of conspiracy. [174]

Second, Wharton's Rule does not apply if the two persons involved in the conspiracy are not the two people involved in committing the substantive offense.

---

[169] See, e.g., *United States v. Kohne*, 347 F. Supp. 1178, 1185-86 (W.D. Pa. 1972).

[170] See § 29.03[B][1], *supra*.

[171] *Developments in the Law*, Note 1, *supra*, at 955.

[172] *Iannelli v. United States*, 420 U.S. at 782.

[173] *Gebardi v. United States*, 287 U.S. 112, 122 n.6 (1932); *Brown v. Commonwealth*, 390 S.E.2d 386, 389 (Va. Ct. App. 1990).

[174] See *Brown v. Commonwealth*, 390 S.E.2d at 389 (*D1* contacted *D2* with instructions that the latter contact *D3* to purchase heroin, which *D2* did; held: charge of conspiracy to distribute heroin is not barred by Wharton's Rule). Wharton's rule can combine with the plurality doctrine to cause anomalous results. For example, if three people conspire to duel, but one of the three is acquitted because she was insane or for some other reason lacked the requisite specific intent, only two guilty persons remain in the conspiracy. In such a case, Wharton's rule re-emerges, and neither of the remaining duelers may be convicted of conspiracy.

For example, if *D1* and *D2*, two males, conspire for *D2* to commit adultery with *X*, a conviction of *D1* and *D2* for conspiracy to commit adultery is proper. [175]

[2]—Model Penal Code

Wharton's Rule is not recognized under the Code. The drafters believed that the doctrine improperly "overlooks the functions of conspiracy as an inchoate crime." [176] On the other hand, as described earlier in this chapter, [177] a conspirator may not ordinarily be convicted and punished for both a conspiracy to commit a crime and for its attempt or successful commission. Therefore, the absence of a "Wharton's Rule" defense does not result in additional punishment of a conspirator who implements her criminal objectives.

[D]—Legislative-Exemption Rule

[1]—Common Law

A person may not be convicted of conspiracy to violate an offense if her conviction would frustrate a legislative purpose to exempt her from prosecution for the substantive crime.

A classic example of the application of the legislative-exemption rule is *Gebardi v. United States*. [178] *Gebardi* involved a prosecution under the Mann Act, [179] which makes it an offense to "knowingly transport . . . any woman or girl [in interstate commerce] for the purpose of prostitution . . . or for any other immoral purpose." Although violation of this law can involve the willing concurrence of the female in her transportation across interstate boundaries, the offense can also occur as the result of transportation of the female against her will. The Mann Act, therefore, does not come within the ambit of Wharton's Rule. [180]

This does not end the analysis, however. As *Gebardi* explained, the purpose of the Mann Act is to protect females from sexual exploitation. Thus, a female who willingly or unwillingly crosses state lines for immoral purposes is perceived by the legislature as the victim of the transporter's conduct. It would frustrate this purpose if a female were subject to prosecution as an accomplice in the Mann Act violation, or if she were convicted of conspiracy in her own transportation. The legislative-exemption rule precludes such a prosecution. [181]

The legislative-exemption rule can result in an anomaly when it is applied in conjunction with the plurality doctrine. In *Gebardi*, for example, one defendant (a

---

[175] *State v. Martin*, 200 N.W. 213, 214 (Iowa 1924).

[176] American Law Institute, Comment to § 5.04, at 482-83.

[177] See § 29.03[B][2], *supra*.

[178] 287 U.S. 112 (1932).

[179] 18 U.S.C. § 2421 (1949 Supp. 1986).

[180] *Gebardi*, 287 U.S. at 122-23.

[181] The same analysis applies to statutory rape. This offense is meant to protect young unmarried females from a less-than-fully informed decision to have sexual intercourse. It would frustrate legislative intent, therefore, if the girl could be convicted as an accomplice in her own statutory rape, or if she were subject to prosecution for conspiracy in her own victimization. See *Queen v. Tyrrell*, [1894] 1 Q.B. 710.

male) conspired with a female for her to cross interstate boundaries for immoral purposes. The female was not subject to prosecution for conspiracy under the legislative-exemption rule. Therefore, the court treated the male as if he had conspired with himself, a logical impossibility. Because "two or more persons" were not involved in the offense, the plurality doctrine precluded conviction of the non-immunized male defendant.

[2]—Model Penal Code

Unless the legislature otherwise provides, a person may not be prosecuted for conspiracy to commit a crime under the Model Code if she would not be guilty of the consummated substantive offense: (1) under the law defining the crime; or (2) as an accomplice in its commission.[182] A person is not guilty as an accomplice in the commission of an offense if she was the victim of the prohibited conduct, or if her conduct was "inevitably incident to its commission."[183]

For example, in the absence of express legislative authority to the contrary, if a male and an underage female have sexual intercourse, the female may not be convicted as an accomplice in her own "victimization." Similarly, in the absence of contrary legislative intent, a pregnant woman may not be convicted as an accomplice in a criminal abortion of her own fetus, because her conduct is "inevitably incident" to the commission of the crime. And, because underage females and pregnant women cannot be convicted as *accomplices* in these offenses, they are also immune from prosecution for *conspiracy* to commit these offenses upon themselves.

However, because conspiracy is a unilateral offense under the Model Code, one who conspires with the immunized party remains subject to conviction for conspiracy.[184]

---

[182] Model Penal Code § 5.04(2).

[183] Model Penal Code § 2.06(6)(a)-(b).

[184] Model Penal Code § 5.04(1)(b).

CHAPTER 30

LIABILITY FOR THE ACTS OF OTHERS: COMPLICITY

§ 30.01 Chapter Overview[1]

This chapter is concerned with multi-party criminal conduct or, more specifically, the circumstances under which a person who does not personally commit a proscribed harm may be held accountable for the conduct of another person with whom he has associated himself.

Two theories of complicity will be described in this chapter. First and foremost, a person may be held accountable for the conduct of another person if he assists[2] the other in committing an offense. Liability of this nature is called "accomplice" or "accessory" liability. Second, in many jurisdictions, a person may be held accountable for the conduct of a co-conspirator who commits a crime in furtherance of their agreement. In the latter case, the mere existence of the conspiracy is sufficient to justify liability; assistance in the commission of the crime is not required.

The common law of complicity uses special terms to distinguish between parties to offenses. These terms are discussed later in this chapter.[3] For purposes of overall clarity, however, two general terms will often be used: the "primary party" (*P*, for short); and the "secondary party" (*S*).

The "primary party" is the person who personally commits the physical acts that constitute an offense. For example, in a criminal homicide, *P* is the one whose acts directly cause the death of *V*, e.g., the person who shoots or poisons *V*.[4] Any person

---

[1] See generally Fletcher at §§ 8.5-8.8; Katz at 252-75; K.J.M. Smith, A Modern Treatise on the Law of Criminal Complicity (1991); Williams at §§ 118-41; Peter Alldridge, *The Doctrine of Innocent Agency*, 2 Crim. L.F. 45 (1990); Joshua Dressler, *Reassessing the Theoretical Underpinnings of Accomplice Liability: New Solutions to an Old Problem*, 37 Hastings L.J. 91 (1985); Sanford H. Kadish, *Complicity, Cause and Blame: A Study in the Interpretation of Doctrine*, 73 Cal. L. Rev. 323 (1985); David Lanham, *Complicity, Concert and Conspiracy*, 4 Crim. L.J. 276 (1980); David Lanham, *Accomplices, Principals and Causation*, 12 Melb. U. L. Rev. 490 (1980); Rollin M. Perkins, *Parties to Crime*, 89 U. Pa. L. Rev. 581 (1941); Paul H. Robinson, *Imputed Criminal Liability*, 93 Yale L.J. 609 (1984); and Francis Bowes Sayre, *Criminal Responsibility for the Acts of Another*, 43 Harv. L. Rev. 689 (1930).

[2] The word "assists" is used here in a very general sense. For more specifics, see § 30.04, *infra*.

[3] See § 30.03, *infra*.

[4] More than one person can be a primary actor, e.g., if *P1* and *P2* each shoot *V*, who dies as the result of both wounds.

who is not the primary party, but who is associated with him in the commission of an offense, is a "secondary party." Generally speaking, S is the person who assists P in the commission of an offense. It is S's liability for P's acts that is the focus of this chapter.

§ 30.02 Accomplice Liability: General Principles

[A]—General Rules

[1]—Definition of an "Accomplice"

Subject to substantial clarification below, S is an accomplice of P in the commission of an offense if he intentionally assists P to engage in the conduct that constitutes the crime. The term "assists" is used here as a general term to encompass many forms of conduct, including aiding, abetting, encouraging, soliciting, advising, and procuring the commission of the offense.

[2]—Criminal Responsibility of an Accomplice: Derivative Liability

Accomplice liability is derivative in nature.[5] That is, an accomplice is not guilty of an independent offense of "aiding and abetting";[6] instead, he derives his liability from the primary party with whom he has associated himself.[7] The primary party's acts become his acts.[8] In general, S may be convicted of any offense committed by P with S's intentional assistance.[9]

For example, if S intentionally assists P to rob V, S is liable for the robbery committed by P. If P fails in his effort to rob V, but is guilty of attempted robbery, S is also guilty of attempted robbery.[10] If P's conduct does not proceed sufficiently far to constitute an attempt, S is guilty of no offense as an accomplice;[11] since P committed no crime, there is no liability for S to derive from P.[12]

[B]—Theoretical Foundations of Accomplice Liability

The doctrine of accomplice liability is so old and widely accepted that few scholars and even fewer lawyers have sought to consider why a person who does not directly engage in conduct that constitutes an offense should be held accountable for the wrongful behavior of others.

---

[5] Kadish, Note 1, *supra*, at 337.

[6] *State v. Estrada*, 603 A.2d 1179, 1189 (Conn. App. Ct. 1992).

[7] *People v. Carter*, 330 N.W.2d 314, 322 (Mich. 1982).

[8] *United States v. Gooding*, 25 U.S. 460, 469 (1827).

[9] As described in § 30.05[B][5], *infra*, there is considerable authority for the view that S is also liable for any crime committed by P that was a natural and probable consequence of the criminal activity in which S intentionally assisted.

[10] See *People v. Rehkopf*, 370 N.W.2d 296, 298 n.3 (Mich. 1985).

[11] See *People v. Genoa*, 470 N.W.2d 447 (Mich. Ct. App. 1991) (S furnished money to X, an undercover police agent, so that X would purchase drugs for him; X did not do so; held: S cannot be convicted as an accomplice, as the underlying crime was not committed or attempted).

[12] However, S may be guilty of the offense of conspiracy with P to commit robbery.

At first glance, the premise that a person may be held criminally responsible for the conduct of another should prove surprising, if not also disturbing. After all, the concept of personal, as distinguished from vicarious, responsibility is "deeply rooted" in criminal law jurisprudence.[13] Yet Anglo-American courts impute the acts of the primary party to the secondary actor. That is, once a person is deemed to be an accomplice of another, his identity as a person subject to criminal punishment is subsumed in that of the primary party.

There are at least two ways to defend accomplice liability. First, accomplice liability is analogous to civil agency law.[14] In civil law, a person may be held accountable for the actions of another if he "consent[s] to be bound by the actions of his agent, whom he vests with authority for this purpose."[15] In criminal law, an accomplice is held accountable for the conduct of the primary party because, by intentionally assisting the primary party, the accomplice voluntarily identifies himself with the other. His intentional conduct, therefore, is "equivalent to manifesting consent to liability under the civil law."[16]

Second, accomplice liability may be perceived in terms of "forfeited personal identity."[17] That is, we may euphemistically describe accomplice liability in agency terms, but underlying this language is the belief that "she who chooses to aid in a crime forfeits her right to be treated as an individual."[18] In essence, the accomplice authorizes the primary party's conduct: the accomplice says, as it were, "your acts are my acts." The law treats the accomplice, therefore, as if he were no more than an incorporeal shadow of the primary party.

§ 30.03 Accomplice Liability: Common Law Terminology

[A]—Parties to a Felony[19]

[1]—General Comments

At common law, there were four categories of parties to felonies other than treason.[20] As discussed in subsection [B], the distinctions between the parties were of considerable practical significance. Today, however, virtually every state has repealed most or all of the common law distinctions. Despite statutory reforms, however, many courts persist in using common law language and, in some cases, stubbornly have resisted the procedural changes. Therefore, lawyers are well served to be mindful of the common law terminology.

---

[13] Sayre, Note 1, *supra*, at 702.

[14] Civil rules of agency do not perfectly coincide with accomplice liability doctrine. See Dressler, Note 1, *supra*, at 110-11.

[15] Kadish, Note 1, *supra*, at 354.

[16] *Id.* at 355.

[17] Dressler, Note 1, *supra*, at 111; *People v. Luparello*, 231 Cal. Rptr. 832, 850 (Ct. App. 1987) (quoting Dressler).

[18] Dressler, Note 1, *supra*, at 111.

[19] See generally 4 Blackstone at *34-39.

[20] The common law treated all parties to treason as "principals."

[2]—Principal in the First Degree

[a]—In General

A "principal in the first degree" is the person who, with the *mens rea* required for the commission of the offense: (1) physically commits the acts that constitute the offense; or (2) as described in subsection [b] below, commits the offense by use of an "innocent instrumentality."[21] In modern cases, the principal in the first degree is often described as the "perpetrator" of the offense. It is his conduct from which all secondary parties' liability derives.

In most cases, the principal in the first degree is the individual who personally commits the crime. He is the one who strangles *V1*, has sexual intercourse with *V2*, or takes and carries away the personal property of *V3*, i.e., he is the person who performs the proscribed physical acts.

[b]—Innocent-Instrumentality Rule

[i]—In General

The innocent-instrumentality rule provides that a person is the principal in the first degree if, with the *mens rea* required for the commission of the offense, he uses a non-human agent or a non-culpable human agent to commit the crime.

For example, suppose that *D* trains his dog to pick up his neighbor's newspaper every morning from the front lawn, and bring it to *D*, who keeps the newspaper as his own. *D* is guilty of petty larceny: he is the principal in the first degree of the theft. Because the dog is not a human being and, therefore, does not have the capacity to form a culpable mental state or act with "free will" as we understand that concept, the animal is *D*'s innocent instrumentality. We no more treat the dog as the perpetrator of the theft than we would say that a gun is the "perpetrator" of a murder and that the person pulling the trigger is the gun's "accomplice."

A human being may also be an innocent instrumentality. Common law jurisprudence in this regard is not entirely clear, but it appears that a person is the principal in the first degree of an offense if he uses or manipulates another to commit an offense, such that the other person is subject to acquittal on the basis of lack of *mens rea* or the existence of an excusing condition.

For example, suppose that *D* falsely informs *X* that *V*'s lawn mower belongs to *D*. Based on the false representation, *D* convinces *X* to "retrieve" the property from *V*'s front lawn. On these facts, *X* is not guilty of larceny, because he lacked the specific intent to steal. Instead, *D* is guilty of the theft, as the principal in the first degree. In this case, *X* is like the dog in the preceding hypothetical: he is a non-culpable agent being manipulated by a culpable party to commit an offense.

A party is also the principal in the first degree if he causes *X*, an insane person[22] or a child,[23] to commit an offense, or if he coerces *X* to commit the crime. In these

---

[21] *State v. Ward*, 396 A.2d 1041, 1046 (Md. 1978).

[22] 4 Blackstone at *35 (a party is a principal if he kills another by "inciting a madman to commit murder").

[23] *Queen v. Manley*, 1 Cox Crim. Cas. 104 (1844) (by dictum, *D* is the principal in the first degree if he convinces a child to take money from his father).

circumstances, X is innocent of the offense as the result of an excuse (insanity, infancy, or duress).

[ii]—Difficulties in Application of the Rule [24]

Some offenses, by definition, only prohibit conduct of designated classes of persons. For example, as ordinarily defined, perjury can only be committed by one who falsely testifies as a witness in an official proceeding, such as a criminal or civil trial.

With certain other offenses, the nature of the proscribed action appears (at least in the minds of some courts) to be "nonproxyable," [25] i.e., an action that cannot be committed through an agent. For example, "acting drunk and disorderly," "marrying," and "carnally knowing another," may be actions that must be performed by the principal in the first degree, and not by another.

Consider a few cases that fall into these special problem areas. Suppose that $D1$, by deception, causes W, a witness in a judicial proceeding, to give false testimony as to certain material facts. W is not guilty of perjury, due to lack of *mens rea*. But, can we say that $D1$ is guilty of the offense through the innocent-instrumentality doctrine? To do so is to suggest that $D1$ perpetrated the offense, but *he* did not perjure himself, i.e., $D1$ was not a witness under oath in a judicial proceeding.

Or, consider a case of a potentially nonproxyable act: Adam gave Eve an apple to eat, which Adam alone knew was forbidden, are we prepared to hold Adam guilty through his innocent instrumentality? If so, we are holding him guilty of "eating the apple," which he did not do. [26]

Or, more seriously, consider the offense of rape, which may fall victim of both categories of offenses under discussion. First, as the offense is defined, a husband cannot be convicted of raping his own wife, nor can a woman be convicted of raping another woman, although either can be convicted as accomplices in a rape. [27] Thus, the prohibited action only applies to a designated class of persons—men who have sexual intercourse with women other than their wives. It may also be the case that "sexual intercourse" or "carnally knowing another" (as the common law sometimes put it) is a nonproxyable action. What happens, then, if $D2$ coerces X to rape $D2$'s wife? To convict $D2$ through the innocent-instrumentality doctrine means that he is guilty of raping his own wife, a legal impossibility. And, it suggests that he had intercourse with his wife, when he did not.

---

[24] See generally Kadish, Note 1, *supra*, at 372-85.

[25] *Id.* at 374.

[26] See Glanville Williams, Textbook on Criminal Law 317 (1978) (finding it improbable that a court would convict Adam as the principal in the first degree).

[27] E.g., *Cody v. State*, 361 P.2d 307, 319 (Okla. Crim. App. 1961), *affirmed*, 376 P.2d 625 (Okla. Crim. App. 1962) (a husband may be an accomplice in the rape of his wife); *People v. Reilly*, 381 N.Y.S.2d 732, 739 (N.Y. County Ct. 1976) (a woman may be convicted as an accessory in the rape of another woman).

In such cases, some,[28] but by no means all,[29] courts will refuse to convict a person as a principal in the first degree, through the innocent-instrumentality doctrine. In such circumstances, a court may stretch to interpret the facts in a manner that allows the defendant to be treated as a secondary party,[30] or it must permit the party to escape punishment for the offense.

[3]—Principal in the Second Degree

A "principal in the second degree" is one who is guilty of an offense "by reason of having [intentionally assisted in] . . . the commission thereof in his presence, either actual or constructive."[31] A person is "constructively" present if he is situated in a position to assist the principal in the first degree during the commission of the crime, e.g., if S serves as a "lookout" or "getaway" driver outside a bank that P robs.

[4]—Accessory Before the Fact

An "accessory before the fact" does not differ appreciably from a principal in the second degree, except that he is *not* actually or constructively present when the crime is committed.[32] An accessory before the fact often is the person who solicits, counsels, or commands (short of coercing[33]) the principal in the first degree to commit the offense.

[5]—Accessory After the Fact

An "accessory after the fact" is one who, with knowledge of another's guilt, intentionally assists the felon to avoid arrest, trial, or conviction.[34] The line between a principal in the second degree, on the one hand, and accessory after the fact, on the other hand, is a thin one: for purposes of accomplice liability, the commission

---

[28] E.g., *People v. Enfeld*, 518 N.Y.S.2d 536, 537-38 (N.Y. Sup. Ct. 1987) (*D*, a private party, fraudulently induced *X*, a public servant, to issue a false certificate; due to lack of *mens rea*, *X* was not guilty of violating a statute that prohibited public servants from issuing false certificates; held: *D* could not be convicted of the offense); *Dusenbery v. Commonwealth*, 263 S.E.2d 392, 394 (Va. 1980) (*D*, who coerced *X* and *Y* to have sexual intercourse with each other, was prosecuted for rape of the female (*Y*); the court overturned *D*'s conviction as a principal in the first degree of *Y*'s rape, because prior state rulings "establish[ed] that one element of rape is the penetration of the female sexual organ by the sexual organ of the principal in the first degree").

[29] E.g., *People v. Hernandez*, 96 Cal. Rptr. 71, 74 (Ct. App. 1971) (*D* compelled her husband to have sexual intercourse with a nonconsenting woman; the court upheld *D*'s conviction as the principal in the first degree of the rape on the basis of the innocent–instrumentality doctrine); *Morrisey v. State*, 620 A.2d 207, 210-11 (Del. 1993) (*D* forced a couple to engage in sexual intercourse; held: *D* was guilty of unlawful sexual intercourse); *United States v. Walser*, 3 F.3d 380, 387-88 (11th Cir. 1993) (by deception, *D* caused *W* to testify falsely at a trial; held: *D* may be convicted of perjury); *People v. Sadacca*, 489 N.Y.S.2d 824, 847 (N.Y. Sup. Ct. 1985) (same).

[30] See § 30.06[B][3][a], *infra*.

[31] *State v. Ward*, 396 A.2d at 1046.

[32] *Id.* at 1046-47.

[33] If *D* coerces *X* to commit the offense, *D* is the principal in the first degree through an innocent instrumentality. See § 30.03[A][2][b], *supra*.

[34] *State v. Ward*, 396 A.2d at 1047.

of an offense continues—and, therefore, those who aid are principals in the second degree—until all of the acts constituting the crime have ceased. For example, in a bank robbery, the offense is not complete until the principal in the first degree takes possession of another's property and carries it to a place of temporary safety. [35] Therefore, the driver of the "getaway" car is a principal in the second degree rather than an accessory after the fact; once the property has reached a point of temporary safety, anyone who intentionally assists the robber to avoid prosecution is an accessory after the fact.

At common law, an accessory after the fact was guilty of the original felony, although he did not assist in its commission. His knowing involvement after the fact "tainted him with guilt of that very offense." [36] Today, nearly all jurisdictions treat accessoryship after the fact as an offense *separate* from, and *less* serious than, the felony committed by the principal in the first degree. [37] As a result, this chapter does not consider further the liability of accessories after the fact.

[B]—Principals versus Accessories: Procedural Significance [38]

[1]—General Comments

Although the common law distinguished between principals in the first and second degree, no matter of procedural significance depended on this dichotomy. However, the line between principals and accessories was of profound significance, as discussed below.

Why did the distinctions develop? As with other areas of substantive criminal law, the specter of the death penalty distorted legal doctrine. At common law, all felons were subject to the death penalty. As the number of felonies expanded, courts invented devices for reducing the number of people subject to execution. According to Professor Perkins, "[w]ithout doubt, the principal-accessory distinction was one of those devices, and because of this it is not surprising to find the development along lines which tended to prevent conviction in spite of clear evidence of guilt." [39] In short, the procedural devices served to protect many accomplices from the fate suffered by principals.

[2]—Jurisdiction

At common law, a principal was prosecuted in the jurisdiction in which the crime was perpetrated. An accessory had to be tried in the jurisdiction in which the accessorial acts occurred. If the prosecutor was unsure where the acts took place, he ran the risk of losing the conviction of the accessory.

For example, assume that *D* murdered *V*, and that *S* solicited the crime. If the prosecutor believed that the solicitation occurred in State X, where the homicide took place, and, therefore, he brought *S* to trial in that jurisdiction, *S*'s conviction

---

[35] *People v. Cooper*, 811 P.2d 742, 747 (Cal. 1991).

[36] Perkins, Note 1, *supra*, at 589.

[37] E.g., Wash. Rev. Code § 9A.76.050 ("Rendering Criminal Assistance"); Model Penal Code § 242.3 (Hindering Apprehension or Prosecution).

[38] See generally Perkins, Note 1, *supra*, at 607-14.

[39] *Id.* at 607.

could not stand if it turned out that S solicited the crime while he and D were eating lunch in a neighboring jurisdiction.

[3]—Rules of Pleading

At common law, an indictment had to state correctly whether the party charged was a principal or an accessory. If the prosecutor alleged that X was the principal in the first degree and that Y was the principal in the second degree, but evidence at trial demonstrated that the roles of the parties were reversed, both defendants could still be convicted. On the other hand, if the evidence demonstrated that Y was not the principal in the second degree as alleged, but was an accessory before the fact, his conviction could not stand. Likewise, if a person were indicted as an accessory, but it was proved at trial that he was a principal, an acquittal was required.

[4]—Timing of the Trial of Accessories

At common law, principals and accessories could be tried jointly (assuming that the court had jurisdiction over all of the parties) or separately. However, under no circumstances could the accessory be tried in advance of the principal's trial. Consequently, if the principal could not be brought to trial, for example, because he had died, fled the jurisdiction, or was immune from prosecution, the accessory could not be brought to justice.

[5]—Effect of the Acquittal of a Principal

Closely related to the preceding point, an accessory could not be convicted of a crime unless and until the principal were convicted. If the principal were acquitted in a separate trial, the accessory could not be prosecuted; if they were prosecuted jointly, the accessory could not be convicted if the jury failed to convict the principal. This rule applied regardless of the reason for the principal's acquittal, even if it were based on a jury finding that, although the crime occurred and the accessory assisted in it, the principal was not guilty of the offense by reason of insanity or because another person committed the crime.

[6]—Degree of Guilt of the Parties

The common law rule was that an accessory could not be convicted of a more serious offense, or higher degree of an offense, than his principal. For example, if P were convicted of assault, the accessory could not be convicted of the more serious offense of assault with intent to kill.

One exception to this rule existed: an accessory could be convicted of a higher degree of criminal homicide than the principal.[40] For example, an accessory could be convicted of murder, although the principal was guilty of the lesser offense of voluntary manslaughter. This outcome was possible if the principal killed in sudden heat of passion,[41] but the accomplice acted with malice aforethought, i.e., he calmly and intentionally assisted the enraged principal to kill the victim.[42]

---

[40] Williams at § 130; 1 Hale at *438.

[41] See § 31.07, *infra*.

[42] *Parker v. Commonwealth*, 201 S.W. 475, 478 (Ky. 1918).

§ 30.04 Accomplice Liability: Assistance

[A]—Types of Assistance

[1]—In General

An accomplice is a person who, with the requisite *mens rea*, assists the primary party in committing an offense. There are three basic types of assistance: (1) assistance by physical conduct; (2) assistance by psychological influence; and (3) assistance by omission (assuming that the omitter has a duty to act).

[2]—Physical Conduct

The most straightforward cases of assistance involve physical conduct. For example, *S* may assist *P* by furnishing him with an instrumentality to commit an offense,[43] "casing" the scene in advance,[44] holding the victim down while *P* kills him, or driving a "getaway" car from the scene of the crime.

[3]—Psychological Influence

Assistance by psychological influence occurs if *S* incites, solicits, or encourages *P* to commit the crime. The most controversial cases involve assistance by encouragement, because juries and courts must often speculate as whether the secondary party has psychologically influenced the primary party by his presence or words.

May mere presence at the scene of a crime constitute encouragement? It is sometimes said that presence and passive acquiescence while an offense is committed does not *in itself* make a person an accomplice in the crime.[45] Indeed, presence at the scene, *coupled with the hidden intent to aid if necessary*, is insufficient if such assistance proves unnecessary.[46] Thus, it has been held that an indictment founded simply on the allegation that *S* accompanied *P* to the location of a crime and watched as the offense occurred, was insufficient to sustain an accomplice prosecution.[47] And, a conviction was reversed where the evidence showed that *S*, the driver of a car containing his wife and two children, said and did nothing while *P*, a back seat passenger, robbed a hitchhiker whom *S* has previous picked up.[48]

The latter holding in particular is surprising in light of a line of cases that suggest that, while presence alone may be insufficient to justify conviction as an accomplice, presence coupled with *very little else* will justify (although not require) a finding of accomplice liability based on psychological encouragement. For example, encouragement may be found from the assurance of a bystander that he will not

---

[43] *Hensel v. State*, 604 P.2d 222, 239 (Alaska 1979) (furnishing fuses used to destroy a structure as part of a burglary).

[44] *State v. Arillo*, 553 A.2d 281, 283 (N.H. 1988).

[45] E.g., *Pace v. State*, 224 N.E.2d 312, 313 (Ind. 1967); *State v. Flint H.*, 544 A.2d 739, 741 (Me. 1988); *State v. Vaillancourt*, 453 A.2d 1327, 1328 (N.H. 1982).

[46] See *Hicks v. United States*, 150 U.S. 442, 450 (1893).

[47] *State v. Vaillancourt*, 453 A.2d 1327 (N.H. 1982).

[48] *Pace v. State*, 224 N.E.2d 312 (Ind. 1967).

interfere with the perpetrator's plans; [49] liability may even be found from the *failure* of the party to disapprove of, or oppose, the criminal action, if he is an acquaintance of the principal. [50] Likewise, proof of presence, *coupled with a prior agreement to assist*, will support a claim of encouragement, even if such assistance is not rendered. [51] Thus, assistance-by-encouragement serves as a powerful, and yet highly speculative, basis for allowing accomplice liability.

[4]—Assistance by Omission

As noted immediately above, a person is not an accomplice simply because he knowingly fails to prevent the commission of an offense, but such failure to act may serve as a critical factor in determining that he assisted by psychological influence.

The failure of a person to try to prevent the commission of an offense may also justify a finding of assistance through omission, if the omitter has a duty to intervene. For example, a parent is an accomplice in the commission of a criminal homicide if, with the requisite *mens rea*, he allows another person to kill his child. [52] Likewise, a property owner may have a legal duty to prevent the commission of a crime on his property, e.g., *D*'s knowing failure to prevent the sale of illegal drugs on his property would justify a finding of assistance-by-omission. [53] Similarly, the failure of a police officer to stop a crime, if coupled with the requisite *mens rea*, would support a conviction on the basis of accomplice liability.

[B]—Amount of Assistance Required

[1]—In General

A person is not an accomplice unless his conduct (or omission) *in fact* assists in the commission of the offense. Thus, *S* is not an accomplice in the commission of a robbery if he is present at the scene of the crime in order to aid *P* if necessary, but his assistance is not called upon, and there are no additional facts to support a claim of assistance by encouragement. [54] Likewise, *S* is not an accomplice of *P* if he performs an act to assist *P*, but his conduct is wholly ineffectual. For example,

---

[49] *State v. Doody*, 434 A.2d 523, 530 (Me. 1981).

[50] See *State v. Parker*, 164 N.W.2d 633, 641-42 (Minn. 1969) (prior association with the principal, presence at the scene without disapproval, and flight with the principal thereafter, justified conviction).

[51] *Hicks v. State*, 150 U.S. at 450. The prior agreement to assist will also justify liability on the basis of conspiratorial, as distinguished from accomplice, liability, in jurisdictions that recognize this separate form of complicity. See § 30.08, *infra*.

[52] See *State v. Walden*, 293 S.E.2d 780, 786-87 (N.C. 1982) (crime of assault). Guilt in such circumstances may also be founded on *direct*, rather than accomplice, liability. See generally § 9.07, *supra*. The determination of whether to prosecute an omitter directly or as an accomplice may depend on whether the omission *caused* the prohibited social harm. As discussed at § 30.04[B] [2], *infra*, a person may be held accountable as an accomplice although his assistance did not cause the ultimate harm; if the party is prosecuted directly, however, the omission must be an actual and proximate cause of the result.

[53] *Porter v. State*, 570 S.2d 823, 826-27 (Ala. Crim. App. 1990).

[54] See *Hicks v. United States*, 150 U.S. at 450.

S is not an accomplice if he utters words of encouragement to *P* who fails to hear them, or if *S* opens a window to allow *P* to enter a dwelling unlawfully, but *P* (unaware of the open window) enters through a door.[55]

Once it is determined that *S* assisted *P*, however, the degree of aid or influence provided is immaterial.[56] Any aid, *no matter how trivial*, suffices. For example, *S* may be deemed an accomplice of *P* if, acting with the requisite *mens rea*, he applauds *P*'s criminal activities,[57] or if his presence at the scene of the offense encourages *P* by adding apparent numerical strength to the criminal venture.[58] Likewise, one may be considered an accomplice in an offense by holding *P*'s child while *P* commits the crime,[59] by preparing food for *P* to give him sustenance during the planning or commission of the crime,[60] or by providing moral support by asking *P* to bring home bananas from the grocery store that he plans to rob.[61]

[2]—Accomplice Liability and the Doctrine of Causation[62]

[a]—The Law

A secondary party is accountable for the conduct of the primary party even if his assistance was causally unnecessary to the commission of the offense. That is, *S* is guilty of an offense as an accomplice even if, but for his assistance, *P* would have committed the offense anyway.[63] Thus, it would be immaterial to *S*'s liability in each of the examples of trivial assistance noted in the preceding subsection, that *P* would have committed the crime when he did without *S*'s minor aid or encouragement.

The absence of a causation requirement is consistent with the underlying rationale of accomplice liability. It will be remembered that accomplice liability is derivative in nature:[64] *S* is not guilty of a substantive offense of aiding and abetting; instead, his guilt is derived from that of *P*. Therefore, once it is determined that *S* assisted *P* with the requisite *mens rea* (i.e., *S* is *P*'s accomplice), "proof that the *principal* [*P*] caused the [social harm] satisfies the requirement of establishing the causal relationship of the *accomplice*."[65] Since *S* is an accomplice and, as such, forfeits his personal identity in the criminal transaction,[66] it is no longer relevant whether

---

[55] Kadish, Note 1, *supra*, at 358-59.

[56] *Fuson v. Commonwealth*, 251 S.W. 995, 997 (Ky. 1923).

[57] See *Wilcox v. Jeffery*, [1951] 1 All E.R. 464, 465 (*S* met *P* at the airport and was present and applauded when *P*, a saxophonist, performed at an illegal concert; the court noted that *S*'s presence was not accidental, but was meant to encourage *P*; it opined that the result might have been different had *S* booed at the concert).

[58] *Fuller v. State*, 198 So.2d 625, 630 (Ala. Ct. App. 1966).

[59] See *State v. Duran*, 526 P.2d 188 (N.M. Ct. App. 1974).

[60] See *Alexander v. State*, 102 So. 597 (Ala. Ct. App. 1925).

[61] See *State v. Helmenstein*, 163 N.W.2d 85, 89 (N.D. 1968).

[62] See generally Dressler, Note 1, *supra*.

[63] *State ex rel. Martin, Att'y Gen. v. Tally*, 15 So. 722, 739 (Ala. 1894).

[64] See § 30.02[A][2], *supra*.

[65] *Commonwealth v. Smith*, 391 A.2d 1009, 1011 (Pa. 1978) (emphasis added).

[66] See § 30.02[B], *supra*.

S's assistance caused the harm. It is enough that he assisted someone else who caused the harm.

[b]—Criticism of the Law

The requirement of a causal relationship between a person's conduct and the social harm for which he is being punished is a fundamental feature of criminal responsibility.[67] Its irrelevance to accomplice liability, therefore, is troubling.

Causality serves two important functions in the criminal law. First, it guarantees that criminal liability will be personal rather than vicarious. Second, causation is a tool by which to calibrate the appropriate level of a wrongdoer's punishment.

The element of causation could serve the same valuable purposes in the field of accomplice law. First, as previously shown,[68] a person whose connection to a crime is exceedingly remote can be ensnared as an accomplice. For example, because there is no causation requirement, any person present at an illegal event (e.g., a criminal battery at a sporting event) is subject to liability as an accomplice if he assists in the commission of the crime by encouraging the primary party through applause. If a causal connection between *S*'s assistance and *P*'s criminal conduct were required, however, the risk of attenuated liability would be greatly reduced.

Second, accomplice law can result in disproportionate punishment. At common law and under modern statutes, accomplices are treated alike in terms of punishment: one whose participation in an offense is substantial and one whose conduct is insignificant are subject to the same punishment. This approach, however, may be inconsistent with the retributive principle of just deserts. In this context, recall how the common law treats inchoate conduct: although one who unsuccessfully attempts to commit a crime is as dangerous and morally culpable as one who commits the offense, the unsuccessful criminal is punished less severely than the successful one. One reason for this outcome is that the harm actually caused by the would-be murderer, robber, or rapist is less than the harm caused by the successful murderer, robber, or rapist.[69]

The same principle arguably ought to apply to accomplices. The accomplice whose assistance was a *sine qua non* factor in the harm caused by the primary party should be punished proportionally to the harm that he and the primary party intentionally caused. Thus, if *S* solicits *P* to commit an offense, *S* should be punished at the same level as *P*. Similarly, if *S* provides essential assistance to *P*— aid but for which the crime would not have occurred when it did—*S* may fairly be punished as severely as *P* is punished. Non-causal accomplices, however, should be punished less than causal accomplices and primary parties. For example, if *S* provides encouragement to *P*, but *P* would have committed the crime when he did notwithstanding the psychological aid, *S* should be punished less than *P*.

---

[67] See § 14.01, *supra*.

[68] See § 30.04[B][1], *supra*.

[69] See § 27.04[B][2], *supra*.

§ 30.05 Accomplice Liability: *Mens Rea*

[A]—In General

Courts frequently state that a person is an accomplice in the commission of an offense if he intentionally aids the primary party to commit the offense charged.[70] This statement is sometimes broken down into "dual intents": (1) the intent to assist the primary party; and (2) the intent that the primary party commit the offense charged.[71]

These formulations are adequate to deal with most cases. However, in some cases, particularly when a person is charged as an accomplice in the commission of an offense for which recklessness or negligence suffices for liability,[72] it is necessary to be somewhat more precise about the mental state. Therefore, although not all courts and commentators agree on the matter, it is probably more accurate to state that an accomplice must possess two states of minds: (1) the intent to assist the primary party to engage in the conduct that forms the basis of the offense; and (2) the mental state required for commission of the offense, as provided in the definition of the substantive crime.[73] Almost always,[74] the second mental state may be inferred upon proof of the first.

For example, suppose that S is a customer in a bank when Ṗ enters and announces that he is robbing it. S, startled, unthinkingly exclaims, "you'll never succeed because the guard is right behind you." Alerted, P disarms the guard and robs the bank. Based on these facts, it is evident that S assisted P in the robbery by providing a warning to P that facilitated him in the commission of the crime.

Nonetheless, S is not an accomplice of P because he lacked both mental states required of an accomplice. First, he did not intend for his words to assist P to engage in the robbery. At most, he was reckless in this regard. Second, and following almost inextricably from the first point, S did not want the bank robbed, i.e., it was not his objective to have the bank deprived permanently of its property, the specific intent required for the offense.[75]

---

[70] E.g., *People v. Burns*, 242 Cal.Rptr. 573, 577 (Ct. App. 1987); *Virgilio v. State*, 834 P.2d 1125, 1127 (Wyo. 1992) (to be an accomplice "a person must intend that his acts or words secure the commission of the crime") (quoting Wyoming Pattern Jury Instruction— Criminal 3.203); see Kadish, Note 1, *supra*, at 346 ("he must act with the intention of influencing or assisting the primary party to engage in the conduct constituting the crime").

[71] *State v. Harrison*, 425 A.2d 111, 113 (Conn. 1979).

[72] See § 30.05[B][3], *infra*.

[73] *State v. Foster*, 522 A.2d 277, 283 (Conn. 1987).

[74] But see § 30.05[B][1], *infra*.

[75] See *People v. Tewksbury*, 544 P.2d 1335, 1340-41 (Cal. 1976) (S aided P to commit a robbery by supplying pencil and paper on which to draw a diagram of the site of the robbery, and by driving P to a rendezvous point near the crime; S was not an accomplice unless she performed these acts with the purpose of aiding in the offense).

[B]—Significant *Mens Rea* Issues

[1]—The Feigning Accomplice

It is usually reasonable to infer that when a person intentionally assists another to engage in the conduct that constitutes an offense, he does so because he wants the other person to succeed in his endeavor, i.e., he shares the criminal intent of the primary party. Sometimes, however, this inference is inaccurate. Matters of some complexity arise, for example, when a police officer or private person joins a criminal endeavor as an "accomplice" and feigns a criminal intent in order to obtain incriminating evidence against the primary party or in order to ensnare the other in criminal activity.

Consider the classic case of *Wilson v People.*[76] *S* and *P*, drinking partners, got into an argument over *S*'s assertion that *P* had stolen his watch. A conversation followed in which the two men agreed to steal property from *V*'s drugstore. In furtherance of the agreement, *S* assisted *P* to enter *V*'s store. While *P* was inside, *S* called the police and then returned to the drugstore and took property handed to him by *P*. Before the parties could leave, the police arrived and arrested *S* and *P* for burglary and larceny.

S's conviction as an accomplice was overturned by the state supreme court. Some of its reasoning was unpersuasive. It analogized *S*'s conduct to that of a detective who enters an existing criminal endeavor in order to "explode" it. *S*, however, hardly fit that characterization. He did not join a crime already in play; he helped devise the plan, apparently in order to set up *P* for arrest, in retaliation for the latter's alleged theft of *S*'s watch.

Nonetheless, *S* was properly acquitted. *S* had the intent to assist *P* to engage in the conduct that constituted burglary and larceny; that is, he intended to assist *P* to enter *V*'s store and to take property out of it. What *S* lacked was the second *mens rea* of an accomplice, namely, the mental states required for commission of the offenses of larceny and burglary.

Larceny requires a specific intent to deprive another person of his property permanently. Although *P* possessed this intent, *S*'s act of calling the police demonstrated that he did not intend for *V* to be deprived of the property permanently. Consequently, *S* lacked the specific intent of larceny. Because he did not intend for a larceny to occur, *S* also lacked the specific intent of burglary, i.e., the intent that a felony (larceny) occur inside the building.

Wilson does not provide a ready-made escape hatch for law enforcement officers who join crimes in order to arrest suspects. *Wilson* was an unusual case because both of the offenses charged required a specific intent that *S* did not possess. However, if *S* had intentionally assisted *P* to kill *V*, rather than to burglarize his building, *S* would be guilty of murder because he intended to kill *V*. The fact that *S*'s motive for wanting *V* dead was to set up *P* for arrest would not negate the requisite *mens rea*.

---

[76] 87 P.2d 5 (Colo. 1939).

[2]—"Purpose" versus "Knowledge": The Meaning of "Intent"

The *mens rea* of accomplice liability is usually described in terms of "intention." As with the crime of conspiracy, however, there is considerable debate regarding whether a person may properly be characterized as an accomplice if he *knows* that his assistance will aid in a crime, but he lacks the *purpose* that the crime be committed. For example, suppose that S rents his house to P, the manager of an illegal gambling enterprise.[77] Is S an accomplice in P's illegal activities if he rented the property with knowledge of his tenant's intended activities, or must it be proved that he shared P's criminal purpose?

The arguments for and against imposing liability on the basis of knowledge, rather than purpose, have been summarized elsewhere in the context of conspiracy law.[78] As in that area, the case law is mixed. Most courts, however, hold that a person is not an accomplice in the commission of an offense unless he "shares the criminal intent of the principal; there must be a community of purpose in the unlawful undertaking."[79]

[3]—Liability for Crimes of Recklessness and Negligence

As already observed, courts and statutes frequently express the culpability requirement for accomplice liability in terms of "intent," e.g., the "intent to promote or facilitate the commission of the offense."[80] The implication of these words is that the accomplice must want the crime to be committed by the other party (or, at least, know that it will take place). If so, it is logically impossible for a person to be an accomplice in the commission of a crime of recklessness or negligence.

For example, suppose that S encourages P to drive at an exceedingly high rate of speed on a busy public road near a school. While speeding, P loses control of his car and strikes and kills V, a child leaving school for the day. We may assume that P is guilty of manslaughter as the result of his criminal negligence. Of what is S guilty? Based on a statute interpreted to require an intent to commit the substantive office, S cannot be convicted as an accomplice in the negligent manslaughter. If S must "intend that the offense be committed," then he must "intend that the offense [of negligent manslaughter] be committed." However, how can one *intend* a *negligent* killing? Essentially, that would mean that S intended V to die in a negligent manner, which simply means that S intended P to kill V. In the latter case, the offense would be murder, not negligent homicide.

Some courts analyze accomplice liability in this manner. Thus, in these jurisdictions, as a matter of law, a person cannot be convicted as an accomplice in the

---

[77] *United States v. Giovannetti*, 919 F.2d 1223 (7th Cir. 1990).

[78] See § 29.05[B][1], *supra*.

[79] *State v. Duran*, 526 P.2d 188, 189 (N.M. Ct. App. 1974); see *People v. Beeman*, 674 P.2d 1318, 1326 (Cal. 1984); *State v. Gladstone*, 474 P.2d 274, 278 (Wash. 1970).

[80] Alaska Stat. § 11.16.110 (1962) (as discussed in *Echols v. State*, 818 P.2d 691, 692 (Alaska Ct. App. 1991)).

commission of a crime of negligence or recklessness.[81] The majority rule, however, is that guilt is allowed in such circumstances.[82]

Conviction of an accomplice in the commission of a crime of recklessness or negligence should be permitted as long as the secondary party has the two mental states described in the second paragraph of subsection [A]: (1) the intent to assist the primary party to engage in the conduct that forms the basis of the offense; and (2) the mental state required for commission of the substantive offense.

In the present hypothetical, S should be treated as an accomplice in the negligent death. First, he intended to encourage P to engage in the conduct that formed the basis of the offense, i.e., he intended to encourage P to drive at a high rate of speed on a public road near a school, which speeding resulted in V's death. Second, S was criminally negligent in relation to V's death by encouraging P to drive in this manner. This outcome is sensible: S is as culpable as P; as long as criminal negligence is sufficient to convict P, it should be adequate to hold S accountable.

On the other hand, if P, while speeding at S's encouragement, had negligently turned the wrong way on a one-way street, thereby striking and killing V, S might not be an accomplice in *this* negligent homicide. It is quite arguable that the conduct that formed the basis of this homicide was the act of wrong-way driving, and not the conduct that S intentionally encouraged, i.e., the speeding.[83]

[4]—Attendant Circumstances

Suppose that S intentionally assists P to have sexual intercourse with V, a nonconsenting female. P realizes that V is not consenting (and, therefore, is guilty of rape), but S negligently believes that V is consenting. Is S guilty of rape as P's accomplice? Notice the unusual situation: S intended to assist P in the conduct, i.e., sexual intercourse, that constituted the rape; however, S did not intend to assist in a *nonconsensual* act of intercourse, i.e., he did not share P's knowledge of the attendant circumstance of the victim's lack of consent.

---

[81] E.g., *Echols v. State*, 818 P.2d at 694-95 (S cannot be convicted as an accomplice in a reckless assault); *State v. Etzweiler*, 480 A.2d 870, 874-75 (N.H. 1984) (quashing an indictment of S as an accomplice of P in a negligent homicide). As noted in *Echols*, however, it may be possible to convict the "accomplice" *directly*, i.e., as the principal in the first degree, for an unintentional result. For example, suppose that D and X are competitors in a drag race on a highway, during which race X crosses the center-line and strikes and kills V, the driver of a car proceeding in the opposite direction. As a result of the collision, V dies. Even if D cannot be convicted as X's accomplice in the negligent or reckless homicide, D might be convicted as a principal in the offense. As long as all of the elements of the crime are proved—a voluntary act by D (e.g., encouraging the racing), the requisite *mens rea*, social harm, and causation (actual and proximate)—D may be convicted *directly* for V's death. The major stumbling block in such a prosecution would be that X's voluntary decision to cross the center line might be treated as a superseding cause of V's death.

[82] E.g., *People v. Wheeler*, 772 P.2d 101, 103 (Colo. 1989) (approving the conviction of S as an accomplice in a negligent homicide, as long as S intended to promote or facilitate the act or conduct of P that negligently resulted in the death); *State v. Foster*, 522 A.2d at 283 (affirming a conviction for negligent homicide, on the ground that S aided P with the mental state required for the commission of the crime).

[83] Kadish, Note 1, *supra*, at 347-48.

The issue here—whether the intent requirement of accomplice liability applies as well to attendant circumstances—is one that courts have rarely considered. In the absence of statutory guidance, it is submitted that the better rule is that, as long as the secondary party acts with the purpose of assisting the principal in the conduct that constitutes the offense, he should be held as an accomplice if his culpability as to the attendant circumstance would be sufficient to convict him as a principal, i.e., the *mens rea* policies regarding the substantive offense should control the accomplice's situation. For example, in a jurisdiction in which the rape statute is interpreted to require proof of recklessness regarding the female's lack of consent, the secondary party should be held responsible for the rape if he acted with at least that level of culpability as to the attendant circumstances, but not if his culpability was less than that of recklessness. [84]

[5]—Natural-and-Probable-Consequences Doctrine

Although a person is not an accomplice in the commission of an offense unless he acts with the intent to assist in the conduct that constitutes the crime, many jurisdictions apply the so-called "natural-and-probable-consequences doctrine," which provides that an accomplice "is guilty not only of the offense he intended to facilitate or encourage, but also of any reasonably foreseeable offense committed by the person he aids and abets." [85] That is, once the prosecutor proves that a person is an accomplice in the commission of *a* crime (call it Crime A), he is also responsible for every other criminal act (e.g., Crimes B and C) perpetrated by the primary party that was a reasonably foreseeable consequence of Crime A. [86] This doctrine is most often applied in homicide cases. [87]

Thus, to apply the natural-and-probable-consequences doctrine, one must ask four questions: (1) Did *P* commit crime A?; (2) If yes, did *S* intentionally assist in the commission of Crime A, i.e., was *S* an accomplice in the commission of that offense?; (3) If yes, did *P* commit any other crimes?; and (4) If yes, were these crimes, although not contemplated or desired by *S*, reasonably foreseeable consequences of Crime A? [88]

For example, suppose that *S* intentionally aids *P* in the commission of an armed bank robbery, by driving *P* to the bank and serving as a lookout from that position. During the robbery, *P* forcibly moves *V*, a teller, to a back room, which action constitutes kidnapping; and *P* intentionally kills *X*, a bank guard attempting to prevent the robbery. On these facts, *P* is guilty of robbery; and *S* is guilty as an accomplice. *P* is also guilty of the offenses of kidnapping and murder. And, in a jurisdiction applying the natural-and-probable-consequences doctrine, *S* is also

---

[84] *Bowell v. State*, 728 P.2d 1220, 1222-23 (Alaska Ct. App. 1986), *overruled on other grounds in Echols v. State*, 818 P.2d 691 (Alaska Ct. App. 1991).

[85] *People v. Croy*, 710 P.2d 392, 398 n.5 (Cal. 1985); see *State v. Fitch*, 600 A.2d 826, 827-28 (Me. 1991).

[86] *People v. Houston*, 629 N.E.2d 774, 779 (Ill. App. Ct. 1994); *State v. Linscott*, 520 A.2d 1067, 1069 n.2 (Me. 1987).

[87] American Law Institute, Comment to § 2.06, at 312.

[88] *People v. Woods*, 11 Cal.Rptr.2d 231, 239 (Ct. App. 1992).

guilty of these offenses, because they were reasonably foreseeable consequences of the armed bank robbery in which S assisted. Thus, S is guilty of crimes in which he did not assist, and of which he may not have approved.

On the other hand, if P had taken the opportunity of the robbery to sexually assault a customer in the bank, S would not be guilty of the latter offense, as this was not a reasonably foreseeable consequence of a bank robbery. P's actions would be treated as separate and distinct from the robbery in which S assisted. [89]

The natural-and-probable-consequences doctrine has aptly been described as "incongruous and unjust," [90] and "obnoxious . . . to the basic precepts and purposes of our criminal law." [91] Notice the effect of the rule: an accomplice may be convicted of a crime of intent although his culpability regarding its commission may be no greater than that of negligence. Thus, the effect of the rule is to permit conviction and punishment of an accomplice whose culpability is *less* than is required to prove the guilt of the primary party. [92] In view of the relative roles of the primary and secondary parties, one would assume that an accomplice should not be convicted unless he has the same or higher level of culpability than is required to convict the perpetrator. [93]

---

[89] See 4 Blackstone at *37 ("But if A. commands B. to burn C.'s house and he, in so doing, commits a robbery; now A., though accessory to the burning, is not accessory to the robbery, for that is a thing of a distinct and unconsequential nature.").

[90] American Law Institute, Comment to § 2.06, at 312 n.42.

[91] *People v. Langston*, 273 N.W.2d 99, 100 (Mich. Ct. App. 1978).

[92] This feature of the doctrine has been subjected to constitutional attack, on the ground that it violates the due process clause, which requires that the prosecution prove every element of the offense—in this case, the *mens rea* of intent in the substantive offense—beyond a reasonable doubt. E.g., *State v. Linscott*, 520 A.2d 1067 (Me. 1987) (rejecting the due process attack). However, this argument should fail: the prosecution *is* required to prove every element of the substantive offense in the trial of the primary party; the secondary party's liability is derived from the primary party. As long as the prosecution proves all of the "elements" of accomplice liability, it has satisfied the constitutional obligation.

A more serious constitutional claim is that the doctrine may result in disproportional punishment, since the punishment for the offense is graded on the assumption that the actor committed the crime intentionally, whereas the accomplice may have been merely negligent in regard to the offense. Thus, it is conceptually possible under the doctrine for an accomplice to a low-penalty misdemeanor to be punished as a murderer, e.g., if S assists P to brandish a firearm (a misdemeanor), during which conduct P intentionally or recklessly kills V. See *People v. Mouton*, 19 Cal.Rptr.2d 423 (Ct. App. 1993) (allowing for such a possibility, but reversing a murder conviction on other grounds).

[93] American Law Institute, Comment to § 2.06, at 312 n.42.

§ 30.06 Liability of the Secondary Party In Relation to the Primary Party[94]

[A]—General Comments

At common law, an accessory could not be convicted of the crime in which he assisted until the principal was convicted and, with the limited exception of criminal homicide, could not be convicted of a more serious offense or degree of offense than that of which the principal was convicted.[95] Nearly all states have abrogated these rigid common law rules. It does not follow from this, however, that issues regarding the relationship between the primary party and secondary parties no longer arise, for they do.

Accomplice liability is derivative in nature.[96] This means that for an accomplice to be liable for an offense, there must be a primary party. It is still true that "a defendant may not be convicted as an [accomplice] where the guilt of a principal has not been shown."[97] Or, put another way, logically, for an accomplice to be guilty of a crime, there must have been a crime committed by another person from whom the accomplice's liability originates.

What does it mean, however, to say that the primary party "has committed a crime" for which the accomplice may be held accountable? Some cases are straightforward. For example, ordinarily it is no longer a procedural bar to the conviction of a secondary party that the primary party was not prosecuted for the offense. The non-prosecution of the alleged perpetrator of an offense does not in itself suggest that a crime did not occur. His non-prosecution might be the result of any one of countless factors extraneous to his guilt (e.g., death, flight from the jurisdiction, or immunity from prosecution).

Difficulties arise, however, when the primary party is acquitted of the offense. Does an acquittal imply that a crime was not committed? Not necessarily. For example, if *P* and *S* are charged with raping *V*, and *V* is unable to identify her attacker, but provides a clear identification of his accomplice, a jury could logically acquit *P* and convict *S*. *P*'s acquittal does not imply that a crime did not occur, only that *P* was not the perpetrator of it.[98]

Some acquittals do suggest that a crime has not occurred. For example, if *P* is charged with stealing *V*'s car, and he proves at trial that *V* consented to the taking, then no larceny occurred. Conceptually, *P*'s acquittal precludes the conviction of an accomplice to this *non*-offense.[99]

---

[94] See generally Alldridge, Note 1, *supra*; Lanham, *Accomplices, Principals and Causation*, Note 1, *supra*.

[95] See § 30.03[B][5]-[6], *supra*.

[96] See § 30.02[A][2], *supra*.

[97] *People v. Vaughn*, 465 N.W.2d 365, 369 (Mich. Ct. App. 1990).

[98] *Id.* (although there must be a principal for there to be an accomplice, the "evidence need not establish that a specifically named individual was the guilty principal").

[99] However, courts are hesitant to disapprove of inconsistent jury verdicts, because it is rarely possible to determine why the jury acquitted one defendant while convicting another.

The following subsections deal with other acquittal-based circumstances in which it may be argued that a "crime" has not occurred in some sense: the *actus reus* of the offense was committed, but *P* did not have the requisite *mens rea*; or all of the elements of the crime were proven, but *P* has a valid claim of defense to his conduct. Under which of these circumstances, if any, should *S* be allowed to escape conviction? Also, under what circumstances, if any, may *S* derive *more* guilt than arises from *P*'s conviction?

[B]—Liability When the Primary Party is Acquitted

[1]—"Primary Party" As An Innocent Instrumentality

If *D* coerces *X* to commit a theft by threatening *X*'s life, *X* will be acquitted of larceny on the ground of duress. Today, and according to common law principles, *D* may be convicted of larceny. *X* was *D*'s innocent instrumentality. Therefore, at common law, *D* was the principal in the first degree of the offense.[100] Conceptually, *D's guilt is not founded on accomplice-liability principles.* Instead, *D* is *directly* liable for committing the crime through the instrumentality; *D*'s guilt is not derived from another culpable person. *X*'s acquittal, therefore, presents no bar to the conviction of the only culpable party.

[2]—Acquittal on the Basis of a Defense

[a]—Justification Defenses

Suppose that *V* unlawfully threatens *P*'s life. *S* assists *P* to kill *V*. *P* is acquitted of murder on the ground of self-defense. Is *S* guilty in the homicide? Although case law in this area is understandably sparse, the proper result seems evident: as *P* was acquitted because his actions were justified, *S* should also be acquitted. Although *V* was killed, recognition of the justification defense of self-defense implies that no crime has occurred, or even that a positive good has resulted. In the absence of wrongdoing by *P*, there is no crime to impute to *S*.[101]

[b]—Excuse Defenses

When the primary party is acquitted on the basis of an excuse (e.g., insanity, involuntary intoxication, or duress), his acquittal should not bar a successful prosecution of a secondary party to whom the excuse does not extend. An acquittal on the ground of an excuse means that the actions of the primary party *were* wrongful, but that he was not responsible for them because of the excusing condition.[102] If the primary party is guilty of all of the elements of the crime, and his conduct is otherwise wrongful, there is no reason why the secondary party should not be

---

This hesitancy is particularly strong when the accomplice is convicted in a separate trial—in front of a different jury, possibly based on different evidence—after the acquittal of the principal. E.g., *People v. Wilkins*, 31 Cal.Rptr.2d 764, 766-68 (Ct. App. 1994) (permitting the conviction of an accomplice following the acquittal of the primary party).

[100] See § 30.03[A][2][b], *supra.*

[101] See *Patton v. State*, 136 S.W. 459, 460 (Tex. Crim. App. 1911); see also *United States v. Lopez*, 662 F.Supp. 1083 (N.D. Cal. 1987) (discussed in subsection [b], *infra*).

[102] See §§ 16.03[C] and 17.03, *supra.*

convicted of assisting in the wrongful conduct, assuming that he has no personal excuse of his own.[103]

For example, in *United States v. Lopez*,[104] *S* assisted *P* to escape from prison. *P* sought to show at her trial that she fled the prison because of unlawful threats on her life. The prosecution did not object to *P* seeking to defend her actions on this ground, but it did resist *S*'s efforts to introduce evidence of the threats as a basis for acquittal in *S*'s prosecution as an accomplice.

The court held that *S*'s right to introduce such evidence depended on whether *P*'s defense claim was founded on necessity (justification) or duress (excuse).[105] As the court explained, and as considered in subsection [a], "[a] third party has the right to assist an actor in a justified act." Therefore, if *P*'s claim was that she did the right thing by escaping, *S* was entitled to show that he assisted in this justified act. On the other hand, "[e]xcuses are always personal to the actor."[106] If *P*'s claim was that she did the wrong thing by escaping, but that she was not to blame because she was coerced, this was *her* personal excusing condition. As *S* was not coerced, he was not entitled to avoid conviction for assisting in an *unjustified* escape.[107]

[3]—Acquittal on the Basis of Lack of *Mens Rea*

[a]—In General

Suppose that a culpable secondary party assists a primary party to commit a wrongful act, but the primary actor is acquitted because he lacked the requisite *mens rea*. For example, consider *Regina v. Cogan and Leak*.[108] Leak convinced Cogan to have sexual intercourse with Leak's wife by falsely telling him that she would agree to the intercourse. In fact, Leak compelled his wife to submit to Cogan. Cogan was acquitted of rape on the basis of the *Morgan*[109] principle that his unreasonable mistake of fact regarding the wife's consent negated the *mens rea* of the offense.

In light of Cogan's acquittal, was Leak guilty of rape? The court answered the question affirmatively, providing two alternative theories. First, since Leak caused Cogan to misunderstand the attendant circumstances, Cogan was Leak's innocent instrumentality. Thus, Leak was the principal in the first degree who used Cogan's "body as the instrument for the necessary physical act."[110] The difficulty with this analysis, however, is that it makes Leak guilty of raping his own wife, a conclusion that some courts are unwilling to reach.[111]

---

[103] See Fletcher at 664-67; Kadish, Note 1, *supra*, at 380-81; accord, *United States v. Azadian*, 436 F.2d 81, 82-83 (9th Cir. 1971).

[104] 662 F. Supp. 1083 (D.C.N.D. Cal. 1987).

[105] See § 23.05, *supra*.

[106] *Lopez*, 662 F. Supp. at 1086.

[107] In *Lopez*, however, the court concluded that *P*'s defense more nearly resembled a justification claim; therefore, it permitted *S* to raise *P*'s defense.

[108] [1976] Q.B. 217.

[109] *Regina v. Morgan*, [1976] App.Cas. 182 (H.L.). See § 12.06[D], *supra*.

[110] *Cogan and Leak*, Q.B. at 223.

[111] See § 30.03[A][2][b][ii], *supra*.

Second, the court opined that there was no reason why Leak should not be viewed as an accomplice of Cogan: "The fact that Cogan was innocent . . . does not affect the position that she was raped." It said further, "[n]o one outside a court of law would say that she had not been [raped]." In essence, the *actus reus* of rape was committed: the victim was forced to have sexual intercourse against her will. Therefore, a "crime" occurred. Cogan committed it. Leak encouraged it. Cogan's "crime" may be imputed to Leak.

This analysis, however, is not without serious conceptual difficulties. Can we truly say that the "crime" of rape occurred? As Professor Glanville Williams has observed, "this will not do at all. [The court] uses popular . . . language, on the question whether the *fact* of 'rape' has occurred, instead of legal language, on the question whether the *crime* of rape has occurred."[112] Certainly, the most common legal understanding of the term "crime" is that it involves an *actus reus and a mens rea*—that is, after all, what the prosecutor must prove (beyond a reasonable doubt) against a perpetrator. But, Cogan did not commit "rape" in *that* sense, as he lacked a *mens rea*. Therefore, this case is not like that of a party who commits the *actus reus* with the requisite *mens rea* (i.e., commits all of the elements of a crime), but is acquitted on the ground of an excuse. Since Leak's liability must be derived from that of Cogan, and Cogan committed no "crime" on *this* understanding of the term, it is highly questionable whether Leak should be convicted of rape as an accomplice.

Some scholars would permit conviction of a secondary party, as long he assists in the commission of the *actus reus* of an offense. For example, Professor Peter Alldridge, while disagreeing with the *Cogan and Leak* court's use of the innocent-instrumentality doctrine in that case,[113] sees no difficulty in treating Leak as an accomplice:

> The answer appropriate to the case . . .is to say that the norm laid down by the law relating to rape is that it is wrongful for a man to have intercourse with a woman who does not in fact consent. *That wrongful act is rape.* The excuse [lack of *mens rea* of Cogan] . . . is personal to [Cogan], and there is no reason why there should not be liability [of Leak] as an accessory.[114]

Thus, under this view, the "wrongful act" (as distinguished from a "crime") of the primary party is imputed to the secondary party, which when coupled with the secondary party's own *mens rea*, creates the "crime."

But, this analysis seems misguided. It is one thing to impute a crime to the accomplice, and then measure the culpability of the respective parties on the basis of each person's *mens rea*;[115] it is quite another matter to derive criminal liability from a person who has committed no offense. It would be sensible, following Professor Alldridge's reasoning, to convict Leak *as a perpetrator*, *rather than an*

---

[112] Williams, Note 26, *supra*, at 320 (emphasis added).

[113] "[T]o allege . . . that [Leak] had intercourse with his wife without her consent . . . is not what happened and . . ., had this been what had happened, it would not have constituted a crime." Alldridge, Note 1, *supra*, at 52.

[114] *Id.* (emphasis added) (footnote omitted).

[115] See § 30.06[C], *infra*.

accomplice, of a new crime, such as "causing or encouraging a wrongful act by another."[116] But, it is inaccurate to say that there was a *crime* committed by *Cogan* that may be imputed to Leak.

[b]—Special Problem: The Feigning Primary Party

Earlier in this chapter we considered the liability of a putative accomplice to a crime whose purpose for participation with the primary party was to ensnare the latter in criminal activity.[117] Suppose that the converse occurs: consider the classic case of *State v. Hayes*.[118]

S proposed to *P* that he join *S* in the burglary of *V*'s store. *S* was unaware of the fact that *P* was a relative of *V*. With *V*'s approval, *P* agreed to the plan. *S* assisted *P* into the building, and took possession of property handed to him by *P*. Before they could leave the scene, *S* was arrested for burglary. *S* was convicted of the offense, but the state supreme court overturned the conviction.

At first glance the court's ruling seems incorrect: *S* intentionally assisted *P*; and *S* had the requisite felonious intent. On a closer look, however, the result is unexceptionable. *P* was the primary party: he committed the acts that arguably constituted the burglary. *S*'s liability, therefore, had to derive from *P*. Yet, *P* was not guilty of burglary, because he entered the building with the express approval of the owner.

Is there any way to justify *S*'s conviction? One possible theory would be to suggest that *he* was the primary party, who used *P* as his innocent instrumentality. The innocent-instrumentality doctrine, however, does not apply here because that rule is limited to circumstances in which the instrumentality is used or manipulated by another person. In this case *P* was not *S*'s puppet; if anything, *S* was duped by *P*.

Alternatively, we could say that *P* committed the *actus reus* of burglary. Therefore, a crime occurred for which *S* may be held accountable. This argument, however, is subject to the criticism noted in subsection [a], namely that it is inappropriate to say that a burglary has occurred when a person commits the *actus reus* of an offense without the requisite *mens rea*. This criticism is especially compelling here since *P* not only lacked the requisite *mens rea* of burglary, but he had an antagonistic mental state, i.e., the intent to cause *S*'s arrest. Moreover, it is not even clear that we can say that the *actus reus* of the offense was committed by *P*: in view of the owner's permission for *P* to enter, there was no unlawful breaking and entering by *P*.

[C]—Liability of an Accomplice When the Primary Party is Convicted

At common law, except with criminal homicides, an accessory before the fact could not be convicted of a crime more serious than that of the principal. Now that

---

[116] See Kadish, Note 1, *supra*, at 382.

[117] See § 30.05[B][1], *supra*.

[118] 16 S.W. 514 (Mo. 1891), *overruled on other grounds, State v. Barton*, 44 S.W. 239 (Mo. 1898).

this procedural bar no longer exists, many commentators have concluded that there is no conceptual obstacle to convicting a secondary party of a more serious offense than is proved against the primary party. As they reason, once it is proved that "the principal has caused an *actus reus*, the liability of each of the secondary parties should be assessed according to his own *mens rea*."[119] That is, although joint participants in a crime are tied to a "single and common *actus reus*,"

> the individual *mentes reae* or levels of guilt of the joint participants are permitted to float free and are not tied to each other in any way. If their *mentes reae* are different, their independent levels of guilt . . . will necessarily be different as well.[120]

In the case of homicide, courts follow this approach. An accomplice may be convicted of first-degree murder, even though the primary party is convicted of second-degree murder or of voluntary manslaughter. This outcome follows, for example, if the secondary party, premeditatedly, soberly and calmly, assists in a homicide, while the primary party kills unpremeditatedly, drunkenly, or in provocation. Likewise, it is possible for a primary party negligently to kill another (and, thus, be guilty of involuntary manslaughter), while the secondary party is guilty of murder, because he encouraged the primary actor's negligent conduct, with the intent that it result in the victim's death.

This approach makes sense as long as we view "criminal homicide" as a single offense—that of causing the death of another with a culpable mental state—involving multiple levels of blameworthiness. It is fair to say, then, that when *P* commits the offense of criminal homicide, this crime is imputed to *S*, whose own liability for the homicide should be predicated on his own level of *mens rea*, whether it is greater or less than that of the primary party.

It does not necessarily follow, however, that this analysis should be applied in all non-homicide circumstances. Consider, for example, the case of *Regina v. Richards*:[121] *S* procured two men—we will call them, together, *P*—to severely beat up her husband, *V*. However, *P* did not do as procured, but instead committed the lesser offense of "unlawful wounding" (essentially, a minor battery). Of what is *S* guilty? Is it "unlawful wounding" or, as the jury concluded, the more serious offense of "unlawful wounding with the intent to commit grievous bodily harm"?

The *Richards* court held that *S* was guilty of the lesser offense, although she had a more culpable state of mind than *P*. *Richards* was the subject of both ardent criticism and support by commentators.[122] Ultimately, it was overruled.[123]

---

[119] J.C. Smith & Brian Hogan, Criminal Law 140 (5th ed. 1983).

[120] *Oates v. State*, 627 A.2d 555, 558 (Md. Ct. Spec. App. 1993) (stated, however, in a criminal homicide prosecution).

[121] [1974] Q.B. 776.

[122] Compare Williams, Note 26, *supra*, at 322-23, and Smith & Hogan, Note 119, *supra*, at 132-36 (condemning the decision) with Kadish, Note 1, *supra*, at 388-91, and Fletcher at 672-73 (providing support for the court's analysis).

[123] *Regina v. Howe*, [1987] App. Cas. 417 (H.L.).

At first (and perhaps later) glance, the problem in *Richards* seems indistinguishable from the homicide cases. Although the crimes of "wounding" and "wounding with the intent to cause grievous bodily harm" were separate offenses, they could as easily have been treated as different degrees of the same offense, much as criminal homicide is divided into degrees and/or separate offenses severable only in terms of *mens rea*. Therefore, we can say that *P* committed the crime—not just the *actus reus* of the offense—of wounding, and we can then treat *S* and *P* as guilty of different degrees of this offense, based on their respective levels of culpability. So interpreted, *Richards* was properly overruled.

But, notice this: what *S* wanted *P* to do was to commit a *different* social harm than was actually perpetrated. If *P* had done as *S* had wanted, she would have been guilty as an accomplice of some aggravated form of bodily harm (a felony, rather than the misdemeanor committed by *P*). That is, she wanted one offense to occur (one with a different *actus reus*), and she did what she could to cause such a result (by procuring *P* to commit the greater offense), but the greater harm never occurred. Thus, this is *not* like a homicide case, in which the secondary party wants precisely what has occurred—the wrongful death of another—and in which the only difference between the parties is their degree of culpability *as to the harm that has been inflicted.*

A person cannot be an accomplice to a crime that has never occurred, as there is no crime for which to derive liability. In *Richards*, if we permit conviction of *S* for the greater offense, are we not effectively convicting her for a non-existent crime? At least in a legal system in which attempts are punished less severely than completed offenses because less harm has occurred, it is submitted that a person who assists in a "mini-crime" (unlawful wounding), but with the intent that it result in a "maxi-crime" (an aggravated battery), should not be convicted of the greater offense simply because she desired the commission of the greater offense. The actor's heightened culpability (and dangerousness) can be handled through an additional solicitation charge.

§ 30.07 Limits to Accomplice Liability

[A]—Legislative-Exemption Rule

A person may not be prosecuted as an accomplice in the commission of a crime if he is a member of the class of persons for whom the statute prohibiting the conduct was enacted to protect. For example, the statutory rape law was enacted to protect young females from immature decisions to have sexual intercourse; the legislature considers her to be the victim of the offense. It would conflict with legislative intent, therefore, if she could be prosecuted as a secondary party to her own statutory rape.[124]

[B]—Abandonment

As with the law of conspiracy,[125] many courts hold that a person who provides assistance to another for the purpose of promoting or facilitating the offense, but

---

[124] The legislative-exemption rule is discussed more fully at § 29.09[D], *supra.*
[125] See § 29.09[B], *supra.*

who subsequently abandons the criminal endeavor, can avoid accountability for the subsequent criminal acts of the primary party.

A spontaneous and unannounced withdrawal will not do.[126] Instead, the accomplice must communicate his withdrawal to the principal and make bona fide efforts to neutralize the effect of his prior assistance. For example, one who provides an instrumentality for use in the crime must regain possession of it or otherwise neutralize its effect. Thus, a person who provides a fuse for dynamiting a building, must remove the fuse; and, "if it has been set, he must step on the fuse."[127] On other hand, one who has offered nothing more than mild encouragement may be able to neutralize his effect by communicating his objection to the crime, unless he provides it at the point at which the event is virtually unstoppable.

§ 30.08   Conspiratorial Liability: The *Pinkerton* Doctrine

[A]—"Accomplice" versus "Conspiratorial" Liability"

It is often important to distinguish between *accomplice* liability, the subject of the preceding sections of this chapter, and complicity based solely on a *conspiratorial* relationship, the topic of this chapter section. As discussed in subsections [B] and [C], many jurisdictions hold that a person, simply because he is a party to a conspiracy, may be held responsible for the actions of his "partner[s] in crime."[128] And, as will be seen, conspiratorial liability is a potentially broader form of liability than accomplice doctrine.

In most circumstances, an accomplice is also a conspirator with the primary party in the commission of the crime. For example, if S drives P to a bank which P robs, serves as a lookout, and drives P away from the bank, it is reasonable to infer a conspiratorial meeting of the minds of S and P. Indeed, even when a conspirator does not actively participate in the planning or commission of an offense, the sheer act of agreeing may serve as encouragement to the primary party, and thereby render the conspirator an accomplice in the commission of the crime.

Nonetheless, one can be a conspirator without being an accomplice. For example, in *Pinkerton v. United States*,[129] S and P conspired to violate certain provisions of the Internal Revenue Code. Thereafter, P violated the Revenue Code provisions. However, he did so while S was in prison for unrelated reasons. The prosecutor did not claim that S assisted P in the planning or commission of the substantive offenses. And, S's presence in prison negated any reasonable inference that his earlier act of agreeing encouraged P when he committed the crimes. S's responsibility in P's conduct, therefore, was not based on accomplice principles, and had to find its source, if any, in conspiracy law.

---

[126] *State v. Thomas*, 356 A.2d 433, 442 (N.J. Super. Ct. App. Div. 1976), *reversed on other grounds*, 387 A.2d 1187 (N.J. 1978).

[127] *Eldredge v. United States*, 62 F.2d 449, 451 (10th Cir. 1932) (discussing withdrawal from a conspiracy).

[128] *Pinkerton v. United States*, 328 U.S. 640, 647 (1946).

[129] 328 U.S. 640 (1946).

Accomplice liability in the absence of a conspiracy is also possible. For example: *P* enters a bank to rob it; *S*, a customer, observes *P*'s actions and decides to assist in the crime by disabling a bank security camera. Here, *P* and *S* never agreed to commit the robbery together. But, *S* is *P*'s accomplice in light of his assistance.[130]

Thus, in many cases a person may be held responsible for the actions of another either as an accomplice or a co-conspirator; sometimes, only one theory of complicity will apply.

[B]—Rule of Conspiratorial Liability

According to the so-called "*Pinkerton* doctrine," a party to a conspiracy is responsible for any criminal act committed by an associate if it: (1) falls within the scope of the conspiracy; or (2) is a foreseeable consequence of the unlawful agreement.[131] This rule of complicity is independent of accomplice liability: a conspirator's accountability exists *even if he did not assist the party whose conduct is imputed to him.*

It is unclear how many states have adopted the *Pinkerton* doctrine. Many courts have expressed approval of it, but often such support comes in cases in which the result would have been the same had traditional accomplice rules been invoked.[132] Nonetheless, at least one court insists that the *Pinkerton* rule is the majority principle in states that have considered the issue.[133]

[C]—Comparison of Liability

In many cases, accomplice and conspiracy liability overlap completely. For example, suppose that *S* and *P* agree to commit an armed robbery and work together in its planning stages. *P* commits the offense. *S* will be held accountable for the robbery under either theory of liability: he intentionally assisted *P* to rob the bank; and, as the robbery was the object of the conspiracy, he is liable for it under conspiracy rules.

Similarly, if *P* kills *V* during the robbery, *S* is accountable for the death under either theory: the killing was a natural and probable consequence of the crime in which *S* intentionally assisted; and the homicide was a foreseeable consequence of the conspiracy to commit the robbery.

The rules potentially diverge in dramatic ways, however, when the *P-S* conspiracy is broad or open-ended. Notice that under *Pinkerton*, a person may be held accountable for the natural and probable consequences of the conspiracy, which may result in extensive liability if the agreement is a broad one; under accomplice law, however, a person is only responsible for the natural and probable consequences of the particular crimes in which the person has intentionally assisted.

---

[130] For another example of accomplice liability in the absence of a conspiracy, see *Commonwealth v. Cook*, 411 N.E.2d 1326 (Mass. App. Ct. 1980), discussed at § 29.04[A], *supra*.

[131] *Pinkerton v. United States*, 328 U.S. at 647-48.

[132] *Developments in the Law—Criminal Conspiracy*, 72 Harv. L. Rev. 920, 993-95 (1959).

[133] *State v. Walton*, 630 A.2d 990, 998 (Conn. 1993).

To see the difference, suppose that *D1* and *D2* conspire to run a prostitution ring and live off the earnings of the prostitutes.[134] Assuming that the conspiracy includes the prostitutes, *D1* and *D2* would clearly be guilty under *Pinkerton*, and less clearly under doctrines of accomplice liability, of every act of prostitution committed by every prostitute.[135]

But, consider the prostitutes' position in the far-flung conspiracy. It is unlikely that any prostitute assisted in the acts of prostitution by other women. Under accomplice liability doctrine, therefore, a prostitute would not be guilty of any substantive offenses except her own. Pursuant to *Pinkerton*, however, once it is determined that she was a party to an open-ended agreement to commit prostitution, she would be liable for every act of prostitution performed by every other prostitute, *and of every other offense committed by D1 and D2 and by any other prostitute that was committed in furtherance of the broad conspiracy.* Rigid application of the *Pinkerton* rule, therefore, may result in extensive liability of comparatively minor parties to a criminal agreement.

Critics of the *Pinkerton* doctrine believe that the law "lose[s] all sense of just proportion if simply because of the conspiracy itself each [conspirator is] held accountable for thousands of additional offenses of which he was completely unaware and which he did not influence at all."[136] Defenders of the rule state that "such harshness may be considered as an occupational hazard confronting those who might be tempted to engage in a criminal conspiracy within a jurisdiction that adheres to the so-called *Pinkerton* rule."[137]

§ 30.09 Model Penal Code

[A]—Forms of Liability

[1]—In General

Under the Model Penal Code a person is guilty of an offense if he commits it "by his own conduct or by the conduct of another person for which he is legally accountable, or both."[138] In other words, a person can be convicted of an offense if he personally commits the crime, or if his relationship to the person who commits it is one for which he is legally accountable. Three forms of accountability for the acts of others are recognized by the Code and are described below.

[2]—Accountability Through an Innocent Instrumentality

The Code adopts the accepted principle that one is guilty of the commission of a crime if he uses an innocent instrumentality to commit the crime. A person (*D*) is legally accountable for the conduct of "an innocent or irresponsible person" (*X*)

---

[134] *People v. Luciano*, 14 N.E.2d 433 (N.Y. 1938).

[135] In *id.*, Luciano was convicted of 62 counts of prostitution.

[136] American Law Institute, Comment to § 2.06, at 307.

[137] *State v. Barton*, 424 A.2d 1033, 1038 (R.I. 1981).

[138] Model Penal Code § 2.06(1).

if he (D): (1) has the mental state sufficient for commission of the offense; and (2) causes the innocent or irresponsible person to engage in the criminal conduct.[139]

It should be observed that the Code is explicit where the common law is implicit: the innocent-instrumentality doctrine applies only if D *causes X* to engage in the conduct in question. Thus, this section does not apply merely because X is insane or otherwise "innocent or irresponsible." D must have done something to manipulate or otherwise use X, so that it may fairly be said that, but for D's conduct, X would not have engaged in the conduct for which D is being held accountable.

If D causes X, an innocent or irresponsible person, to engage in criminal conduct, D is responsible for X's conduct if, but only if, D possessed the mental state sufficient for the commission of the crime. For example, if D coerces X to have nonconsensual sexual intercourse with V, D is guilty of rape, because he possessed the mental state required for that offense.[140] Or, suppose that D provides his car to X, an insane person with a known "penchant for mad driving."[141] If X proceeds to drive D's car in a dangerous manner, D may be convicted of reckless endangerment, on the basis of D's recklessness in providing the car to a known mad driver. However, if D is unaware of X's dangerous tendencies, D would not be guilty of reckless endangerment: he has caused X to engage in the conduct, but he does not possess the mental state (recklessness) sufficient for commission of the offense.

[3]—Miscellaneous Accountability

A person may be held accountable for another person's conduct if the law defining an offense so provides.[142] This provision is not of broad importance, but it does recognize that a legislature may wish to enact special laws of accomplice liability, as, for example, when it prohibits aiding and abetting a suicide attempt,[143] or knowingly causing or facilitating a prison escape.[144]

[4]—Accomplice Accountability

A person is legally accountable for the conduct of another person if he is an accomplice of the other in the commission of the criminal offense.[145]

Two features of accomplice liability should initially be observed. First, it is a form of liability independent of the innocent-or-irresponsible-person doctrine described in subsection [2], i.e., the rules of accomplice liability described below have no bearing on the situation in which a person uses an innocent instrumentality.

Second, accomplice liability is dependent on the relationship of the parties in the commission of a *specific offense*. In other words, if S is prosecuted for robbery

---

[139] Model Penal Code § 2.06(2)(a).

[140] *Morrisey v. State*, 620 A.2d 207, 211 (Del. 1993) (under a complicity statute based on the Model Penal Code, D was convicted of unlawful sexual intercourse, after he forced X and V to have sexual intercourse).

[141] American Law Institute, Comment to § 2.06, at 302.

[142] Model Penal Code § 2.06(2)(b).

[143] Model Penal Code § 210.5(2).

[144] Model Penal Code § 242.6.

[145] Model Penal Code § 2.06(2)(c).

because he allegedly served as *P*'s accomplice, the issue that must be resolved is whether *S* was *P*'s accomplice *in that robbery*, and not whether *S* was *P*'s accomplice in the commission of some other crime or of crimes in general.

[5]—Rejection of Conspiratorial Liability

The Model Code rejects the *Pinkerton*[146] doctrine of conspiratorial liability. That is, under the Code, a person is not accountable for the conduct of another solely because he conspired with that person to commit an offense. The liability of one who does not personally commit an offense must be based on one of the preceding forms of accountability, most often on the basis of accomplice liability. The drafters of the Code rejected the *Pinkerton* doctrine because they believed there was "no better way to confine within reasonable limits the scope of liability to which conspiracy may theoretically give rise."[147]

[B]—Nature of an "Accomplice"

[1]—Conduct

[a]—In General

S is an accomplice of *P* in the commission of an offense if, with the requisite *mens rea*, he: (1) solicits *P* to commit the offense; (2) aids, agrees to aid, or attempts to aid *P* in the planning or commission of the offense; or (3) has a legal duty to prevent the commission of the offense, but makes no effort to do so.[148]

[b]—Accomplice Liability by Solicitation

S is an accomplice of *P* in the commission of an offense if he solicits *P* to commit the crime. The complicity section does not define the term "solicits." Rather, accomplice liability exists if *S*'s conduct would constitute criminal solicitation, as that offense is defined elsewhere in the Code.[149]

[c]—Accomplice Liability by Aiding

The Code dispenses with the many common law and statutory terms used to describe the conduct that may constitute assistance in the commission of an offense, and replaces them with the single word "aids." It should be observed, however, that in the Model Code, "soliciting" a crime is *not* a form of "aiding"; it is an independent basis for accomplice liability. This distinction can prove significant, as discussed in the next two subsections.

[d]—Accomplice Liability by Agreeing to Aid

S is an accomplice of *P* if he agrees to aid *P* in the planning or commission of an offense. This requirement is met, for example, if *S* tells *P* that he will help to plan the commission of the offense, or if he agrees to provide *P* with an instrumentality for the commission of the crime, *even if S does not fulfill his promise.*

---

[146] *Pinkerton v. United States*, 328 U.S. 640 (1946). See § 30.08, *supra*.

[147] American Law Institute, Comment to § 2.06, at 307.

[148] Model Penal Code § 2.06(3)(a).

[149] Model Penal Code § 5.02. See generally § 28.03, *supra*.

However, because this form of accomplice liability is based on "aiding," rather that "soliciting," S is *not* an accomplice of P merely because he agrees to solicit the commission of an offense but fails to do so.

This feature of the Code differs at least in form from the common law. In most cases, S's agreement to aid in the commission of an offense serves as encouragement to P and, therefore, functions as a basis for common law accomplice liability. The Code does not require proof of such encouragement, however; it is enough that S manifested his participation in the offense by agreeing to aid.

On the other hand, "agreeing to aid" is *not* equivalent to conspiring to commit an offense. That is, this is not the *Pinkerton* doctrine in disguise. One can conspire to commit an offense (and, therefore, be guilty of conspiracy) and yet not "agree to aid" another person in a particular offense (and, therefore, not be an accomplice of a co-conspirator in the commission of that crime).

For example, suppose that S agrees to aid P to rob Bank A. In furtherance of their conspiracy, P steals a "getaway" car. Under *Pinkerton* doctrine, S is guilty of the theft, as that offense was committed in furtherance of their conspiracy to rob Bank A. However, under the Code, S is not guilty of the car theft, as he did not agree to aid (or, for that matter, solicit, aid, or attempt to aid) P in the commission of that offense.

[e]—Accomplice Liability by Attempting to Aid

[i]—In General

In a significant departure from the common law,[150] the Code provides that S may be held accountable as an accomplice of P in the commission of an offense if he attempts to aid in the planning or commission of the crime, even if his aid proves ineffectual. For example, if S opens a window so that P may enter to commit a felony inside the building, S is an accomplice in the burglary, even if P enters by the door. In such circumstances, S has "attempted" to aid P, i.e., he has taken a substantial step in a course of conduct intended to culminate in assistance in the commission of an offense.

[ii]—The Relationship of § 2.06 (Complicity) to § 5.01 (Criminal Attempt)

It is useful to see how § 2.06, the Model Code's complicity provision, relates to § 5.01, which prohibits criminal attempts. In particular, § 5.01(3), discussed elsewhere in this Text,[151] should be considered here.

Suppose that S sterilizes medical instruments in order to assist P in the commission of an illegal abortion. If P performs the abortion, S is guilty as an accomplice of P in its commission. Similarly, if P is in the midst of an illegal abortion but is arrested before he can complete it, P is guilty of an *attempted* abortion under the Code's criminal attempt provision. In turn, S would be guilty of the attempt under the Code's complicity statute.

---

[150] See § 30.04[B][1], *supra.*

[151] See § 27.09[D][2], *supra.*

However, suppose that *P* is arrested *before* he takes a substantial step in a course of conduct intended to result in an abortion. Under these circumstances, *P* is not guilty of attempting an illegal abortion.[152] In this case, *S* is not accountable under the complicity statute, because the person from whom he would derive his liability committed no crime. Nonetheless, *S* is guilty of a criminal attempt by *his own conduct* (i.e., *not* through the doctrine of complicity), by application of Model Penal Code § 5.01(3), which provides that a person who engages in conduct designed to aid[153] in the commission of an offense "that would establish complicity under Section 2.06 if the crime were committed by such other person, is guilty of an attempt . . . although the crime is not committed or attempted by such other person."

Notice the irony in this result: *S* is guilty of an attempt to perform an illegal abortion; *P*, the primary participant, is not guilty of attempt.

[f]—Accomplice Liability By Omission

Ordinarily, one cannot be an accomplice in the commission of an offense by failing to act. The rule is to the contrary, however, if the omitter has a duty to prevent the commission of the offense, such as, for example, if he is a police officer standing by while a crime is committed in his presence.

It should be remembered, however, that the omitter must possess the mental state required of an accomplice, i.e., he must have failed to act with the purpose of promoting or facilitating the commission of the offense. An omission that is the result of fright or ignorance, rather than dereliction of duty, would not result in accomplice liability.

[2]—Mental State

[a]—In General

A person is an accomplice if he assists "with the purpose of promoting or facilitating the commission of the offense."[154] This provision conforms with common law precedent. For example, if *S* drives *P* to a liquor store where *P* commits a robbery, *S* is guilty of robbery if his act of assistance (driving the automobile) was committed with the purpose of facilitating the commission of the offense; however, he is not guilty if he did not know what *P* intended to do in the store.

After considerable debate, the American Law Institute rejected the argument that complicity liability should apply to one who knowingly, but not purposely, facilitates the commission of an offense.[155] For example, if *S*, a merchant, sells dynamite to *P*, with knowledge that *P* intends to use the explosives to blow open

---

[152] He may be guilty of another offense, e.g., conspiring with *S* to commit the abortion.

[153] Notice that § 5.01(3) uses the word "aid" in relationship to the complicity statute; thus, this provision does not apply if *S solicits* another to commit an offense, which offense is neither committed nor attempted.

[154] Model Penal Code § 2.06(3)(a).

[155] See American Law Institute, Comment to § 2.06, at 314-19.

a safe, *S* is not an accomplice in the subsequent crime, unless it was his conscious object to facilitate the commission of the offense.

[b]—Liability for Crimes of Recklessness and Negligence

The requirement of purposeful conduct set out in § 2.06 triggers the same question that confronts courts interpreting the common law and pre-Model Code statutes: under what circumstances, if any, is a person an accomplice in the commission of a crime of recklessness or negligence?

The Code expressly deals with this issue. Section 2.06(4) provides that, when causing a particular result is an element of a crime, a person is an accomplice in the commission of the offense if: (1) he was an accomplice in the *conduct* that caused the *result*; and (2) he acted with the culpability, if any, regarding the *result* that is sufficient for commission of the offense.

Reconsider an earlier hypothetical:[156] *S* encourages *P* to speed on a public road near a school. *P* loses control of the car and strikes and kill *V*, a child. *S* and *P* are prosecuted for negligent homicide. On these facts, *S* may be held accountable for the death caused by *P*.

To see this, one must go through a three-step process. First, determine *P*'s potential responsibility. For sake of discussion, assume that *P* is guilty of negligent homicide. Second, ask whether *S* was an accomplice in the *conduct* that caused the *result* (rather than asking the ordinary question of whether *S* was an accomplice in the commission of the unlawful result). The answer is that *S* was an accomplice in the *conduct*: he assisted by encouraging the conduct (speeding) that caused the result (the death); and he uttered the words of encouragement with the purpose of promoting the conduct (the speeding). Third, ask whether *S* acted with the culpability in regard to the *result* (the death) that is sufficient for commission of the offense. In this case, *S* probably acted with the requisite culpability (negligence).

This provision has special significance in states that recognize the common law doctrines of felony-murder and misdemeanor-manslaughter.[157] These common law rules allow the primary party in a homicide to be convicted if the death occurs accidentally while he is committing a felony or misdemeanor. The effect of § 2.06(4) is to make the accomplice in the *conduct* that causes the result (i.e., an accomplice in the underlying felony or misdemeanor) strictly liable for the ensuing death, on the ground that he possessed the level of culpability in regard to the *result* that is sufficient for commission of the offense, i.e., no culpability.

[c]—Attendant Circumstances

Reconsider an earlier case:[158] *S* purposely assists *P* to have sexual intercourse with *V*, a nonconsenting female. *P* realizes that *V* is not consenting (and, therefore, is guilty of rape), but *S* unreasonably believes that *V* is consenting. Is *S* guilty of rape as *P*'s accomplice?

---

[156] See § 30.05[B][3], *supra*.

[157] See §§ 31.06 and 31.09, *infra*. Although the Code rejects these doctrines, a state could adopt § 2.06(4) and yet retain one or both of these homicide rules.

[158] See § 30.05[B][4], *supra*.

The Code does not address this question. The Commentary states that "[t]here is deliberate ambiguity"[159] in this regard. Thus, a court might determine that the requirement of purpose extends to the attendant circumstances, in which case S is not guilty of the rape. Alternatively, the policy of the substantive offense might control, i.e., S would be guilty of the offense if he has the culpable state of mind regarding the victim's nonconsent that is sufficient to convict the perpetrator of that offense.

[d]—Natural-and-Probable-Consequences Doctrine

The Code does not recognize the common law natural-and-probable-consequences rule.[160] As a result, the liability of an accomplice does not extend beyond the purposes that he shares. For example, suppose that S aids P in the commission of a bank robbery by furnishing P with the details of the bank's security system. Later, P steals an automobile, which he uses as his "getaway" vehicle in the robbery. Although S is an accomplice of P in the commission of the robbery (he aided P with the purpose of promoting that offense), he is not an accomplice in the commission of the theft, although it may have been a natural consequence of the offense in which he was an accomplice, because he did not purposely aid in the car theft.

[C]—Liability of the Accomplice In Relation to the Perpetrator

The Model Code provides that an accomplice in the commission of an offense may be convicted of a crime, upon proof of its commission by another, regardless of whether the other person is convicted, acquitted, or not prosecuted. Furthermore, an accomplice may be convicted of a different offense or different degree of offense than is the primary party.[161] Thus, the fact that P is acquitted of an offense does not preclude the conviction of S for that offense, as long as the prosecutor shows that *someone* committed the crime in question, and that S aided that person.[162] It is also possible to convict S of assault with intent to kill, and P of simple assault, if S has a more culpable frame of mind regarding the attack.

The Code also expressly provides that a person who is legally incapable of committing an offense personally may be held accountable for the crime if it is committed by another person for whom he is legally accountable.[163] For example, although a husband cannot legally rape his own wife at common law or under the Model Penal Code,[164] he may be convicted as an accomplice in her rape.

---

[159] American Law Institute, Comment to § 2.06 at 311 n.37.

[160] See § 30.05[B][5], *supra*. However, with homicides, the natural-and-probable-consequences rule can come in the back door as the result of the convergence of the felony-murder and misdemeanor-manslaughter rules and Model Penal Code § 2.06(4), as described at § 30.09[B][2][b], *supra*.

[161] Model Penal Code § 2.06(7).

[162] Although the acquittal of the perpetrator is not a bar to conviction of an accomplice, as noted, the Code does require proof of "the commission of the offense." The Code does not indicate, however, what it means by the word "offense" in this context. Thus, the Code does not resolve the issues raised in § 30.06[B][2]-[3], *supra*.

[163] Model Penal Code § 2.06(5).

[164] Model Penal Code § 213.1.

[D]—Limits to Accomplice Liability

Section 2.06(6) states that, unless the Code expressly provides to the contrary, a person is not an accomplice in the commission of an offense if any one of three circumstances exist. First, S may not be convicted as an accomplice if he is the victim of the offense. For example, the parent of a kidnapped child who pays a ransom may not be convicted as an accomplice in the kidnapping of his own child.

Second, S is not an accomplice of P if S's conduct is "inevitably incident" to the commission of the offense. For example, a purchaser of narcotics is not an accomplice in the commission of a sale of the controlled substance.[165]

Third, the Code establishes a defense of abandonment. A person is not an accomplice in the commission of a crime if he terminates his participation before the crime is committed, and if he: (1) neutralizes his assistance; (2) gives timely warning to the police of the impending offense; or (3) in some other manner attempts to prevent the commission of the crime.[166]

---

[165] *Robinson v. State*, 815 S.W.2d 361 (Tex. Ct. App. 1991) (*S*, a purchaser, is not guilty as an accomplice in the offense of delivery of a controlled substance by *P*, the seller).

[166] See § 30.07[B] for general discussion of how the defense is applied.

CHAPTER 31

CRIMINAL HOMICIDE

§ 31.01 Homicide[1]

[A]—Definition of "Homicide"

At very early common law, "homicide" was defined as "the killing of a human being by a human being."[2] This definition includes suicide within its compass. However, the later common law definition of "homicide," followed in modern statutes, is "the killing of a human being by *another* human being." Suicide, therefore, is no longer a form of homicide.[3]

"Homicide" is a legally neutral term. That is, a homicide may be innocent or criminal. The duly authorized execution of a convicted felon, for example, is no less a homicide than the most "cold-blooded" murder.

[B]—Definition of "Human Being"

[1]—The Beginning of Human Life[4]

At common law, a fetus must be born alive to be considered a "human being" within the meaning of that term in criminal homicide law.[5]

This rule is anomalous. Following the common law approach, a homicide occurs when one causes the death of a being that is not considered human at the time of the death-producing act, as long as it is "human" when it dies. Thus, if *D* strikes *V*, a pregnant woman, in the abdomen causing lethal injury to the fetus, a homicide occurs if the fetus is expelled from the womb alive and dies from the blow seconds

---

[1] See generally Fletcher at 235-390; Herbert Wechsler & Jerome Michael, *A Rationale of the Law of Homicide (Pts. I & II)*, 37 Colum. L. Rev. 701, 1261 (1937).

[2] Royal Commission on Capital Punishment Report, (Cmd. 8932) para. 72 (1953).

[3] At common law, attempted suicide was a misdemeanor. Today, a person who assists another to commit suicide may be charged with aiding and abetting a suicide, an independent statutory offense in many jurisdictions. E.g., Model Penal Code § 210.5; see Juliana Reno, Note, *A Little Help From My Friends: The Legal Status of Assisted Suicide*, 25 Creighton L. Rev. 1151 (1992) (summarizing statutory and case law to date).

[4] See generally Clarke D. Forsythe, *Homicide of the Unborn Child: The Born Alive Rule and Other Legal Anachronisms*, 21 Val. U. L. Rev. 563 (1987); Patricia A. King, *The Juridical Status of the Fetus: A Proposal for Legal Protection of the Unborn*, 77 Mich. L. Rev. 1647 (1979); Jeffrey A. Parness, *Crimes Against the Unborn: Protecting and Respecting the Potentiality of Human Life*, 22 Harv. J. on Legis. 97 (1985).

[5] See *Meadows v. State*, 722 S.W.2d 584, 585 (Ark. 1987); *Keeler v. Superior Court*, 470 P.2d 617, 622 (Cal. 1970); *State v. Beale*, 376 S.E.2d 1, 3 (N.C. 1989).

after birth. Yet, if the same act is more efficient, in that it causes immediate death of the fetus in the womb, a homicide has not occurred.

Some commentators and judges argue that the common law rule is outdated. The stated basis of the "born alive" rule was that a live birth was needed to prove that the "unborn child" was alive at the time of the accused's actions, and that these acts were the cause of its death.[6] In light of advances in modern medical technology, the argument proceeds, it is now possible to determine whether a fetus is alive in the mother's womb, to determine with much greater likelihood of accuracy its chances of being born alive, and to identify the cause of its death if it is born dead. Therefore, the definition of "human being" should include viable, and perhaps even nonviable, fetuses.[7]

Whatever the merits of the issue, most courts have held that any redefinition of the term "human being" to include a fetus within its scope must come from the legislature, rather than from the judiciary.[8] Two arguments support this view. First, the suggested change in the definition of "human being" would represent a substantive enlargement of criminal homicide law: what was once feticide would become the far more serious offense of murder or manslaughter. In the modern era, creation of new offenses and expansion of old ones are considered to be legislative functions.[9]

Second, the issue is one of profound moral significance, and one that raises weighty policy considerations. Although everyone would agree that a fetus—indeed, even an embryo—is alive, there is considerable dispute as to when that living thing should be deemed a "human being," and thus entitled to the full protection of society's homicide laws. Matters of such deep moral complexity, especially when there are sharp societal divisions, are better resolved by legislative bodies, which are likely to be more closely in touch with social attitudes than the judiciary.

---

[6] *Commonwealth v. Cass*, 467 N.E.2d 1324, 1328 (Mass. 1984); *Hughes v. State*, 868 P.2d 730, 732 (Okla. Crim. App. 1994); cf *Keeler v. Superior Court*, 470 P.2d at 633 (Burke, Acting C.J., dissenting) ("The common law reluctance to characterize the killing of a quickened fetus as a homicide was based solely upon a presumption that the fetus would have been born dead.").

[7] See *People v. Davis*, 872 P.2d 591, 597-600 (Cal. 1994) (the state murder statute, which expressly prohibits the malicious killing of a fetus, applies to the killing of any fetus that has progressed beyond the embryonic stage of seven to eight weeks, except in the case of a constitutionally or statutorily protected therapeutic abortion).

[8] E.g., *Vo v. Superior Court*, 836 P.2d 408, 415 (Ariz. Ct. App. 1992); *Keeler v. Superior Court*, 470 P.2d at 633-34; *Hollis v. Commonwealth*, 652 S.W.2d 61, 63 (Ky. 1983); *State v. Beale*, 376 S.E.2d at 4; contra, *Commonwealth v. Cass*, 467 N.E.2d at 1329-30; *Hughes v. State*, 868 P.2d at 733-34; *State v. Horne*, 319 S.E.2d 703, 704 (S.C. 1984) (redefining the term "human being," but applying the change prospectively only).

[9] See § 3.02[A], *supra*.

[2]—The End of Human Life[10]

When does a person cease to be a "human being" for purposes of homicide law, i.e., what constitutes the legal death of a human being? The traditional rule, based on then-prevailing medical standards, recognized a cardiopulmonary definition of "death": a human being was dead when there was a complete and permanent stoppage of the circulation of the blood and the "cessation of the animal and vital functions consequent thereon, such as respiration, pulsation, etc."[11]

Since the development of life-support devices and procedures, this definition has proven unsatisfactory. It is now possible artificially to maintain the heart and lung activities of persons who have lost the spontaneous capacity to perform these "animal and vital functions." As one court put it, "human bodies can be made to breathe and blood to circulate even in the utter absence of brain function."[12] The effect of the machinery, therefore, is to keep some people legally "alive" long after their capacity for independent life has ceased.

In 1968, an influential Harvard Medical School committee reported that the medical conception of death was changing.[13] It concluded that cessation of brain function is a more suitable measure of death, especially when a patient's respiration and circulation are being supported artificially. The committee set forth a multi-step test designed to identify "brain death syndrome."

As is now understood, the brain anatomically is divided into three parts. The cerebrum (the "higher brain") controls cognitive functions, including consciousness. The cerebellum ("middle brain") controls motor coordination. And the brain stem ("lower brain") provides the "animal functions," i.e., reflexive and spontaneous activities such as breathing and swallowing.[14] "Brain death" exists when the whole brain—all three portions—irreversibly cease to function. The fact that respiration and pulsation can be or are artificially induced by machinery does not affect the conclusion.

In 1970, the Kansas legislature enacted the first statute recognizing termination of brain functions as a basis for determining legal death.[15] The law provided in part that death occurs when, according to accepted medical standards, the individual

---

[10] See generally Susan L. Brennan & Richard Delgado, *Death: Multiple Definitions or a Single Standard?*, 54 S. Cal. L. Rev. 1323 (1981); Alexander Morgan Capron & Leon R. Kass, *A Statutory Definition of the Standards for Determining Human Death: An Appraisal and a Proposal*, 121 U. Pa. L. Rev. 87 (1972); Report of the Ad Hoc Committee of the Harvard Medical School to Examine the Definition of Brain Death, *A Definition of Irreversible Coma*, 205 J.A.M.A. 337 (1968); Task Force on Death and Dying of the Institute of Society, Ethics, and the Life Sciences, *Refinements in Criteria for the Determination of Death: An Appraisal*, 221 J.A.M.A. 48 (1972).

[11] *Smith v. Smith*, 317 S.W.2d 275, 279 (Ark. 1958) (quoting Black's Law Dictionary 488 (4th ed. 1951)).

[12] *In re T.A.C.P.*, 609 So.2d 588, 591 (Fla. 1992).

[13] See Report of the Ad Hoc Committee of the Harvard Medical School, Note 10, *supra*.

[14] *People v. Eulo*, 472 N.E.2d 286, 291-92 (N.Y. 1984).

[15] Kan. Stats. Ann. § 77-202.

experiences an irreversible cessation of breathing and heartbeat (the common law definition), or there is an absence of spontaneous brain activity. Since then, a majority of states, either by statute or judicial decision,[16] have incorporated "brain death" in their definition of "death."[17]

[C]—Year-and-a-Day Rule[18]

According to Blackstone, "[i]n order . . . to make the killing murder, it is requisite that the party die within a year and a day after the stroke received, or cause of death administered . . . ."[19] That is, if D shoots V on January 1, 1994 and V dies on January 1, 1995 a homicide has resulted; but, if V dies on or after January 2, 1995, a criminal homicide prosecution is barred, although a non-homicide prosecution, such as for assault with intent to kill,[20] is permitted.

The year-and-a-day rule dates back to 1278,[21] and is "well established"[22] in Anglo-American common law. The rule apparently "reflects the judgment that proof of causation for murder 'should not be unduly speculative.' "[23] In light of the inexactitude of medical science at the time the rule originated, there was virtually no way to ensure that a death after an extended passage of time was attributable to human rather than to natural causes. Consequently, the arbitrary time limitation was devised.[24]

The year-and-a-day-rule is now anachronistic.[25] As a result of advances in medical technology, an assault victim can be kept alive indefinitely, well past the year-and-a-day line. And, medical science can now determine the cause of death with considerable precision, even if the person suffers a lingering death.

As a consequence, the clear trend is to abrogate the rule or apply a longer time limitation.[26] Because the rule is part of the American common law, some courts believe they have authority to abolish it. Other courts contend that the rule is substantive in nature, i.e., an implicit, but nonetheless "constituent element of the

---

[16] E.g., *People v. Eulo*, 472 N.E.2d at 288-89.

[17] See also Unif. Determination of Death Act § 1, 12 U.L.A. 340 (Supp. 1991) (stating that death occurs when there is either irreversible cessation of circulatory and respiratory functions or of "all functions of the entire brain, including the brain stem").

[18] See generally Donald E. Walther, Comment, *Taming a Phoenix: The Year-and-a-Day Rule in Federal Prosecutions for Murder*, 59 U. Chi. L. Rev. 1337 (1992); D.E.C. Yale, *A Year and a Day in Homicide*, 48 Cambridge L.J. 202 (1989).

[19] 4 Blackstone at *197.

[20] E.g., *Commonwealth v. Pinnick*, 234 N.E.2d 756 (Mass. 1968).

[21] Statutes of Gloucester, 6 Edward 1, ch. 9 (1278).

[22] *People v. Stevenson*, 331 N.W.2d 143, 145 (Mich. 1982).

[23] *United States v. Jackson*, 528 A.2d 1211, 1216 (D.C. 1987) (quoting *State v. Young*, 390 A.2d 556, 562 (N.J. 1978).

[24] This is not a statute of limitations in the ordinary sense. If a victim dies within 366 days, the prosecution may commence after that time.

[25] *State v. Gabehart*, 836 P.2d 102, 105 (N.M. Ct. App. 1992).

[26] E.g., Cal. Penal Code § 194 (West 1988) (applying a three-years-and-a-day rule).

crime of murder [or manslaughter]," [27] and therefore may only be abolished by legislative action. [28]

§ 31.02   Criminal Homicide: General Principles

[A]—"Murder" and "Manslaughter": Common Law Definitions

A criminal homicide is one committed without justification or excuse. In very early English legal history, "criminal homicide" was a single offense, punishable by death; later, it was divided by statute into "murder" and the lesser non-capital offense of "manslaughter." These two offenses are part of the American common law.

The common law definition of "murder" is "the killing of a human being by another human being with malice aforethought." [29] Manslaughter is "an unlawful killing of a human being by another human being *without* malice aforethought." [30] Thus, as Blackstone has put it, "malice aforethought" is the "grand criterion which now distinguishes murder from other killing." [31]

At common law, there were no degrees of murder or manslaughter. However, for purpose of clarity, judges often distinguished between "voluntary" (really, "intentional") and "involuntary" ("unintentional") manslaughter. These terms have persisted to this day. Originally, the punishment for the two forms of manslaughter was the same. [32]

[B]—Murder: Definition of "Malice Aforethought"

[1]—"Aforethought"

In very early English history, the word "aforethought" probably required that a person think about, or premeditate, the homicide long before the time of the killing. [33] It gradually lost this meaning, so that the term "aforethought" is now superfluous in English homicide law. [34]

---

[27] *State v. Young*, 390 A.2d at 559.

[28] *State v. Gabehart*, 836 P.2d at 105 (noting the debate and citing cases in support of both positions).

[29] See *United States v. Wharton*, 433 F.2d 451, 454 (D.C. Cir. 1970); American Law Institute, Comment to § 210.2, at 13-14. Coke defined murder as follows: "When a man of sound memory and of the age of discretion unlawfully kills any reasonable creature in being, and under the King's peace, with malice aforethought, either express or implied by the law, the death taking place within a year and a day." Quoted in *id.* at 14 n.1.

[30] 4 Blackstone at *191 (emphasis added).

[31] *Id.* at *198-99.

[32] Perkins & Boyce at 83.

[33] *Id.* at 57.

[34] Royal Commission, Note 2, *supra*, at para. 74.

The word "aforethought" has always been superfluous to the definition of murder in American law. Therefore, unless a statute modifies the common law by requiring proof of premeditation,[35] a spur-of-the-moment killing may constitute murder.[36]

[2]—"Malice"

"Malice" is a legal term of art with little connection to its non-legal meaning. As the term has developed, a person who kills another acts with the requisite "malice" if she possesses any one of four states of mind: (1) the intention to kill a human being; (2) the intention to inflict grievous bodily injury on another; (3) an extremely reckless disregard for the value of human life; or (4) the intention to commit a felony during the commission or attempted commission of which a death results.[37] These four mental states are discussed in subsequent sections of this chapter.

These disparate mental states are believed to have one feature in common: in the absence of justification (e.g., self-defense), excuse (e.g., insanity), or mitigating circumstance[38] (e.g., adequate provocation), each mental state involves an extreme indifference to the value of human life. In the first case—intent-to-kill murder—the malice is said to be "express"; the other forms involve "implied" malice.

[C]—Manslaughter: Types of "Unlawful Killings"

Manslaughter is an unlawful killing that does not involve malice aforethought or, as the Commentary to the Model Penal Code puts it, it is a "homicide without malice aforethought on the one hand and without justification or excuse on the other."[39]

Traditionally, three types of unlawful killings constitute manslaughter. First, an intentional killing committed in "sudden heat of passion" as the result of "adequate provocation" is voluntary manslaughter.

Second, an unintentional killing that is the result of "an act, lawful in itself, but [done] in an unlawful manner, and without due caution and circumspection"[40] is involuntary manslaughter. In modern terminology, this is a homicide committed in a criminally negligent manner.

Third, an unintentional killing that occurs during the commission or attempted commission of an unlawful act may constitute involuntary manslaughter. If the killing occurs during the commission of an unlawful act amounting to a felony, the homicide is murder, "but if no more was intended than a mere trespass [i.e., a non-felony], [the homicide] will amount only to manslaughter."[41] This type of

---

[35] Frequently, such a requirement exists. See generally § 31.03[C], *infra*.

[36] *State v. Heidelberg*, 45 So. 256, 258 (La. 1907).

[37] *People v. Aaron*, 299 N.W.2d 304, 319-20 (Mich. 1980); American Law Institute, Comment to § 210.2, at 14-15. Some scholars include a fifth form of malice: a homicide that results from resisting a lawful arrest. Whatever may have been the law in England, this is not an independent form of "malice" in the United States. *Id.* at 15 n.13.

[38] The term "mitigating circumstance," as used in homicide law, is any factor the existence of which results in conviction of the wrongdoer for a lesser homicide offense than murder.

[39] American Law Institute, Comment to § 210.3, at 44.

[40] 4 Blackstone at *192.

[41] *Id.* at *193.

manslaughter is sometimes dubbed "unlawful-act manslaughter" or "misdemeanor-manslaughter."

[D]—Statutory Reformulation of Criminal Homicide Law

[1]—In General

At common law, murder was a capital offense. Over time, efforts were made to ameliorate the harshness of the law; it was not believed that every homicide committed with malice aforethought deserved the death penalty.

American reform of homicide law began in Pennsylvania in 1794, when that state's legislature passed a statute dividing murder into two degrees: murder in the first degree, for which the death penalty remained intact; and murder in the second degree, for which a lesser sentence was imposed. The state did not materially change the nature of manslaughter law, although it formally divided the offense into "voluntary" and "involuntary" components. Whereas the common law graded both forms of manslaughter equally, Pennsylvania imposed a more severe penalty for voluntary manslaughter than for involuntary manslaughter. By 1953, 37 states and the District of Columbia had divided murder into degrees, with most of them adopting verbatim the "Pennsylvania model" of criminal homicide. [42]

In more recent years, reform of the common law has taken three separate paths. Many states continue to follow the Pennsylvania approach, discussed immediately below. A few states have modified the Pennsylvania model by dividing murder into *three* degrees. [43] And, some states have followed the path of the Model Penal Code, discussed later in this chapter, [44] which rejects the degrees-of-murder approach, divides criminal homicide into three offenses (murder, manslaughter, and negligent homicide), and significantly reformulates the offenses.

[2]—The Division of Murder Into Degrees ("Pennsylvania Model")

In interpreting a murder statute modeled on the Pennsylvania system, a lawyer must first determine whether a murder (as distinguished from a lesser offense or no offense) has occurred. That is, one does not divide murder into degrees until a determination is made that the killing is properly characterized as a murder. Common law principles apply at this level: that is, a murder is a killing of another human being with "malice aforethought"; and "malice aforethought" consists of any one of the four mental states described in this chapter.

Assuming that a murder has occurred, three types of murder fall within the first-degree category in the Pennsylvania model. First, murders that are perpetrated in a specified manner (in the original Pennsylvania statute, there were two: by means of poison; or lying in wait) are considered sufficiently morally heinous to merit the state's highest penalty. [45] Second, a "wilful, deliberate, and premeditated" killing

---

[42] *Smith v. State*, 398 A.2d 426, 434 (Md. Ct. Spec. App. 1979).

[43] In fact, Pennsylvania now divides murder into three degrees. 18 Pa. Cons. Stat. Ann. § 2502 (1983).

[44] See generally § 31.10, *infra*.

[45] There is some dispute regarding whether this category is independent of the "wilful, deliberate, premeditated" category mentioned in the text immediately below. The "Pennsylva-

is first-degree murder.[46] Third, a killing that occurs during the perpetration or attempted perpetration of an enumerated felony (in the original version: arson, rape, robbery, and burglary) is treated as murder in the first degree.

All other forms of murder constitute second-degree murder. That is, within the class of homicides that constitute "murder" under common law principles, any killing that does not fall within the preceding three categories is treated as the lesser form of murder. In general, this means that the following murders would constitute second-degree: intentional killings that are not premeditated and deliberate; intent-to-inflict-grievous-bodily-injury killings; reckless killings; and deaths that occur during the commission of felonies other than those enumerated in the first-degree section.

§ 31.03   Murder: Intent to Kill[47]

[A]—In General

One who intentionally[48] kills another human being without justification (e.g., self-defense), excuse (e.g., insanity), or mitigating circumstance (e.g., sudden heat of passion) is guilty of killing with "malice aforethought"—"express malice"— and, therefore, is guilty of common law murder.[49] Typically, a murder involving the specific intent to kill is first-degree murder in states that grade the offense by degrees, at least if the homicide was also "deliberate" and "premeditated," as the latter terms are defined in subsection [C].

---

nia Model" reads: "all murder, which shall be perpetrated by means of poison, or by lying in wait, or *by any other kind of wilful, deliberate and premeditated killing* . . . ." On the face of it, therefore, poisoning and lying-in-wait are examples of wilful, deliberate, premeditated killings. As such, the first category is subsumed by the second. Nonetheless, courts have usually interpreted the statute to mean that any murder that occurs by means of poison or lying in wait is first-degree, even if the actor did not intend to kill the victim. Thus, a person who lies in wait in order to inflict serious bodily injury, but who inadvertently kills the victim, is guilty of first-degree murder: the defendant's *mens rea* constitutes one of the four forms of "malice" recognized at common law; therefore, the killing is "murder"; and, since the killing occurred by lying-in-wait, it is first-degree. *People v. Laws*, 15 Cal.Rptr.2d 668, 673-74 (Ct. App. 1993) (holding *D* guilty of first-degree murder for a reckless lying-in-wait murder).

[46] See § 31.03[C], *infra*.

[47] See generally Samuel H. Pillsbury, *Evil and the Law of Murder*, 24 U.C. Davis. L. Rev. 437 (1990).

[48] At common law, one "intends" a result if it is her purpose to cause the result or if she knows that it is virtually certain to occur. See § 10.04[A][1], *supra*.

[49] 4 Blackstone at *199.

[B]—Proving the Intent to Kill

[1]—In General

[a]—Natural-and-Probable-Consequences Rule

The intent-to-kill form of "malice aforethought" involves subjective fault, i.e., the prosecutor must prove that the defendant formed the intent to kill another person, rather than that, simply, a reasonable person would have known that the conduct would result in death.

How is this subjective fault proved? Often it is proved by means of a syllogism: (1) ordinary people intend the natural and probable (or "foreseeable") consequences of their actions; (2) the defendant is an ordinary person; and (3) therefore, she intended the natural and probable consequences of her actions in this case.

When the probable consequence of the defendant's conduct is that someone will die, this syllogism invites the jury to infer the requisite specific intent. For example, if *D* savagely beats *V*, causing *V*'s death, the prosecution may seek to prove that *D* intended to kill *V* by demonstrating to the jury (and emphasizing in closing arguments) that the probable consequence of such a beating was *V*'s death; therefore, in the absence of evidence that *D* was not an ordinary person, the jury may infer that *D* intended the natural and probable consequence of her conduct, i.e., *V*'s death.

[b]—Deadly-Weapon Rule

When a person kills another with a deadly weapon, proof of intent-to-kill is buttressed further. The more general proposition that a person intends the natural and probable consequences of her actions is supported by the somewhat more specific proposition that when she intentionally uses a deadly weapon [50] or, more precisely, intentionally uses a deadly weapon directed at a vital part of the human anatomy, an intention to kill may properly be inferred. [51] This is sometimes called the "deadly-weapon rule."

[2]—Constitutional Limitation

In the past, judges instructed juries on the rules described above, by stating that, in essence, "the law *presumes* that a person intends the natural and probable consequences of her voluntary acts," or that "the law *presumes* that a person intends to kill another if she intentionally uses a deadly weapon on a vital part of the human anatomy."

---

[50] A "deadly weapon" is variously defined as anything "designed, made, or adapted for the purpose of inflicting death or serious physical injury," Ala. Code § 13A-1-2(11) (1994), or that is "likely to produce," *People v. Rodriguez*, 123 Cal.Rptr. 185, 188 (Ct. App. 1975), or "capable of causing," Alaska Stat. § 11.81.900(b)(11) (1989 & Supp. 1994) such harm. The Model Penal Code defines it as an animate or inanimate substance that, as used or intended, is capable of causing death or serious physical injury. Model Penal Code § 210.0(4).

[51] *Glenn v. State*, 511 A.2d 1110, 1126-28 (Md. Ct. Spec. App. 1986); *Commonwealth v. Webster*, 59 Mass. 295, 305 (1850), *overruled on other grounds, Commonwealth v. McLeod*, 326 N.E.2d 905 (Pa. 1975); *Commonwealth v. O'Searo*, 352 A.2d 30, 35-37 (Pa. 1976).

Although it is permissible, even desirable, for jurors to draw common sense *inferences* from objective circumstances, a jury instruction of the sort just described violates the due process clause of the United States Constitution. It is violative because the instruction requires or might cause a reasonable juror to shift the burden of persuasion regarding an element of the offense—here, intent—to the defendant, notwithstanding the rule that the prosecutor must prove every element of the crime beyond a reasonable doubt.[52]

[C]—"Wilful, Deliberate, Premeditated" Killings

[1]—Overview of the Issue

Nearly all states that grade murder by degrees provide that a "wilful, deliberate, premeditated" killing is murder in the first degree. Unfortunately, courts have had untold difficulty agreeing on the meaning of this phrase. One matter is fairly clear: although the term "wilful" has various definitions in the criminal law,[53] in this context it means, simply, "a specific intent to kill."

But, what do the other two words—"deliberate" and "premeditated"—add to this? A few courts expressly treat the terms as if they were superfluous, i.e., the phrase "wilful, deliberate, and premeditated" is a single mental state amounting, simply, to the intent to kill.[54]

Most jurisdictions understand this phrase to mean more than this, i.e., that the division of murder into degrees is meant to separate the most heinous forms of murder, which deserve the most severe penalties, from "those which, although 'intentional' in some sense, lack the gravity associated with first degree murders."[55] However, some courts draw such a razor thin line between a "wilful" (intentional) killing, on the one hand, and a "wilful, deliberate, premeditated" one, on the other hand, that the distinction loses practical significance: nearly every intentional killing constitutes first-degree murder.

In contrast, some states treat the terms "wilful," "deliberate" and "premeditated" as genuinely independent elements of first-degree murder.[56] In these states, a significant line is drawn between a spur-of-the-moment, albeit intentional, killing, and what lay people might describe as a "cold-blooded" killing, i.e., a homicide committed after calm and careful reflection by the wrongdoer. The view of these jurisdictions is that one who acts "cold-bloodedly" is "more dangerous, more culpable [,] or less capable of reformation than one who kills on . . . impulse."[57]

---

[52] *Sandstrom v. Montana*, 442 U.S. 510, 524 (1979). See § 8.02, *supra*.

[53] See § 10.04[C], *supra*.

[54] See *Smith v. State*, 398 A.2d 426, 443 (Md. Ct. Spec. App. 1979) ("[t]his is not a series of distinct mental states but a repetitive stressing of the same mental state—the requirement that the killing itself and not merely the murder-producing act, be intentional"); *Powell v. State*, 838 P.2d 921, 927 (Nev. 1992) (stating that "[o]ther jurisdictions have held that the terms . . . are a single phrase, meaning simply that the actor intended to commit the act and intended death to result").

[55] *State v. Garcia*, 837 P.2d 862, 865 (N.M. 1992).

[56] E.g., *People v. Morrin*, 187 N.W.2d 434, 436 (Mich. Ct. App. 1971).

[57] *Bullock v. United States*, 122 F.2d 213, 214 (D.C.Cir. 1941).

But, is it true that a person who intentionally kills upon careful reflection is a more dangerous or culpable person than one who acts on impulse? Premeditation and deliberation might only reflect "the uncertainties of a tortured conscience rather than exceptional depravity."[58] Contrast, for example, the case of a person who impulsively pushes a small child sitting on a bridge into the river with an adult who kills his terminally ill father after long and careful consideration, in order to end his parent's torment.[59] If "premeditation" means anything, the impulsive killer is guilty of second-degree murder, and the mercy killer could be convicted of first-degree murder. Yet, as a function of depravity or dangerousness, most people would reverse the results.

[2]—"Deliberate"

Some courts treat "deliberate" as a synonym for "intentional," as when the statement "I *deliberately* did X" means "I *intentionally* did X."[60]

The better view is that "deliberate"—as in "to deliberate"—means "to measure and evaluate the major facets of a choice or problem."[61] As such, deliberation presupposes a "*cool* purpose."[62] This state of mind is "characterized by . . . unhurried, careful, thorough, and cool calculation and consideration of effects and consequences."[63] It is the term "deliberation" that brings to first-degree murder the idea that the most heinous killings are those that are "cold-blooded."

Obviously, it takes time to deliberate. Therefore, it is impossible for a person to deliberate unless she premeditates.[64] Nonetheless, it is possible to premeditate (as that concept is explained below) without possessing the frame of mind characteristic of the concept of "deliberation." Whereas "premeditation" involves the *quantity* of time that a person put into formulating her design, "deliberation" speaks to the *quality* of the thought processes.

Thus, one who kills in a sudden rage may be guilty of manslaughter if her anger is the result of adequate provocation.[65] But, even if her anger does not mitigate the homicide to manslaughter, it should reduce the degree of murder, because the killing is "hot-blooded," rather than "cold-blooded." Similarly, a severely intoxicated

---

[58] American Law Institute, Comment to § 210.6, at 127-28.

[59] See *State v. Forrest*, 362 S.E.2d 252 (N.C. 1987) (upholding a conviction for first-degree murder in a "mercy killing").

[60] E.g., *Commonwealth v. Carroll*, 194 A.2d 911, 917 (Pa. 1963) (in which the state supreme court found adequate evidence that the killing was wilful, deliberate, and premeditated from the fact that *D* testified that he "remembered the gun, *deliberately* took it down, and *deliberately* fired two shots into the head of his sleeping wife").

[61] *People v. Morrin*, 187 N.W.2d at 449.

[62] *State v. Brown*, 836 S.W.2d 530, 538 (Tenn. 1992) (emphasis added).

[63] Webster's Third New International Dictionary 1789 (1966).

[64] *Smith v. State*, 398 A.2d at 444.

[65] See § 31.07, *infra*.

person might not be able to act with sufficient reflection to be guilty of first-degree murder, no matter how long she premeditates.[66]

[3]—"Premeditated"

To "premeditate" means "to think about beforehand."[67] The law is sharply divided, however, on how much prior thought must go into a homicide before it is considered premeditated. At one extreme is a line of cases that finds its origins in an 1868 court opinion that stated that "if sufficient time be afforded to enable the mind fully to frame the design to kill, and to select the instrument, or frame the plan . . ., it is premeditated."[68] Specifically, "*no* time is too short for a wicked man to frame in his mind the scheme of murder."[69] As well, no time is too short for a *non-*wicked man to form the intent.[70]

Courts following this line of reasoning state that the time required to premeditate is not "days or hours, or even minutes."[71] It may be no more than "a brief moment of thought."[72] Indeed, according to this view, "[t]he time required to establish premeditation may be of the shortest possible duration and may be so short that it is instantaneous," as long as the intent is formed *before* the homicide is committed.[73] Thus, this approach effectively equates premeditation with any intentional killing. It undermines one of the principles underlying the legislative division of murder into degrees, namely, that a carefully considered and planned killing is worse than a spur-of-the-moment homicide.

In order to ensure that the element of premeditation retains independent significance, some courts provide that it takes "some appreciable time" to premeditate.[74] No specific period of time is required, but the essence of the term is preserved by requiring proof that the killer had time not only to form the intent, but also to turn

---

[66] This might explain the outcome in *Midgett v. State*, 729 S.W.2d 410, 413 (Ark. 1987), in which *D*, while disciplining his child, beat the youth to death, *D* was convicted of first-degree murder. The state supreme court overturned the conviction. It stated that even if *D* intended to kill his child in the "overheated" and "drunken disciplinary beating . . .," there [was] still . . . no evidence whatever of a premeditated and deliberate killing." What was missing, if anything, was the calm (not "overheated" or "drunken") reflection implicit in the concept of "deliberation."

[67] *People v. Morrin*, 187 N.W.2d at 449; but see *Powell v. State*, 838 P.2d at 926 (approving a jury instruction that defined "premeditation" as "a determination to kill, distinctly formed in the mind at any moment before or *at the time of the killing*") (emphasis added). The italicized words in *Powell* render the term "premeditation" meaningless. "Instantaneous premeditation," ultimately, is a "contradiction in terms." *Bullock v. United States*, 122 F.2d at 213-14.

[68] *Commonwealth v. Drum*, 58 Pa. 9, 16 (1868).

[69] *Id.*

[70] *Commonwealth v. Carroll*, 194 A.2d at 916.

[71] *Bostic v. United States*, 94 F.2d 636, 639 (D.C. Cir. 1937).

[72] *Government of Virgin Islands v. Lake*, 362 F.2d 770, 776 (3d Cir. 1966); see *Watson v. United States*, 501 A.2d 791, 793 (D.C. 1985) ("as brief as a few seconds").

[73] *State v. Lyle*, 513 N.W.2d 293, 299 (Neb. 1994).

[74] *State v. Moore*, 481 N.W.2d 355, 361 (Minn. 1992).

the matter over in her mind and to give the matter at least a second thought.[75] Obviously, the greater the substance of the "deliberation" requirement, the longer the period of premeditation must be. It is not possible to conduct unhurried, careful, thorough, and cool calculation and consideration of effects and consequences—the essence of the deliberative process[76] —in a matter of a few seconds.

The California Supreme Court was once among the leaders in requiring rigorous proof of deliberation and premeditation. In a landmark decision, *People v. Anderson*,[77] the court identified three categories of evidence pertinent to the determination of these elements: (1) planning activity; (2) motive; and (3) manner of killing. The latter category focuses on whether the method of killing was "so particular and exacting" that a jury could infer a preconceived design. Thus, a single knife wound to the heart is better evidence of premeditation than multiple, "indiscriminate" stab wounds.[78]

According to *Anderson*, a finding of first-degree murder ordinarily involves: (A) all three types of evidence just described; (B) extremely strong category (1) evidence; or (C) category (2) evidence, along with either category (1) or (3). However, *Anderson*, "although not overruled . . ., has been construed to insignificance."[79] According to a later opinion of the state supreme court, "[t]he *Anderson* factors, while helpful for purposes of review, are not a sine qua non to finding first degree premeditated murder, nor are they exclusive."[80]

§ 31.04 Murder: Intent to Inflict Grievous Bodily Injury

Malice aforethought is implied if a person intends to cause grievous bodily injury to another, but death results.[81] In states that grade murder by degree, this form of malice nearly always constitutes second-degree murder.

The term "grievous bodily injury" (or, equivalently, "great bodily harm," or "serious bodily injury") is not often defined in the murder context, but the term is often explained in case law or statutes in relation to other offenses, such as battery, and these definitions are usually carried over to implied-malice murder prosecutions.

---

[75] *People v. Morrin*, 187 N.W.2d at 449.

[76] See § 31.03[C][2], *supra*.

[77] 447 P.2d 942 (1968).

[78] Accord, *Watson v. United States*, 501 A.2d at 795 (in sustaining a first-degree murder conviction, the court observed that the defendant "did not fire a series of shots, as though in a panic, but a single shot, which went directly into the [victim's] chest"). Evidence of multiple stab wounds or gun shots may also suggest lack of calmness, which would negate deliberation. On the other hand, multiple wounds might suggest a more depraved state of mind; and, with multiple wounds, the actor has time to consider her actions "during the interval between the injuries imposed." *Baker v. State*, 632 A.2d 783, 795 (Md. 1993).

[79] *People v. Caldwell*, 11 Cal.Rptr.2d 752, 756 (Ct. App. 1992), *review denied, opinion withdrawn by order of California Supreme Court* (opinion may not be cited as precedent, see Cal. Rules of Court 976, 977).

[80] *People v. Perez*, 831 P.2d 1159, 1163 (Cal. 1992).

[81] 3 James Stephen, A History of the Criminal Law in England 80-81 (1883).

"Grievous bodily injury" is an injury that "must be grave, not trivial," but need *not* be "such as may result in death."[82] It is an injury that "gives rise to the apprehension of danger to life, health, or limb."[83] According to one statute, it is an injury involving:

> serious impairment of physical condition, including, but not limited to: loss of
> · consciousness; concussion; bone fracture; protracted loss of impairment of func-
> tion of any bodily member or organ; a wound requiring extensive suturing; and
> serious disfigurement.[84]

Thus, a person who must be treated in a hospital emergency room for abrasions to her hands and knees and for a fracture of the jawbone,[85] or who experiences a broken rib, a black eye, and a two-and-a-half inch cut in the back of her head requiring stitches,[86] has experienced serious bodily injury. It follows, therefore, that a person who unjustifiably and inexcusably *intends* to cause these injuries is guilty of murder, if the victim dies as a result of the attack.

Serious issues regarding this form of malice rarely arise in murder prosecutions. If the defendant intentionally used a deadly weapon on the victim, it is likely that the jury will find express malice, i.e., intent to kill, unless the injuries or wounds were directed at a non-vital part of the body, in which case implied malice is easily proven. Also, virtually any time a person intends to imperil life (but does not intend to kill) she acts with "extreme recklessness," still another version of "malice," discussed immediately below.

§ 31.05   Murder: Extreme Recklessness ("Depraved Heart" Murder)

[A]—In General

[1]—Terminology

Malice aforethought is implied if a person's conduct manifests an extreme indifference to the value of human life. In states that separate murder into degrees, this type of murder almost always constitutes second-degree murder.

At common law, this state of mind is often described colorfully—or, as one court put it, "more visceral[ly] than intellectual[ly]"[87] —as conduct demonstrating "an abandoned heart,"[88] "an abandoned and malignant heart,"[89] a "depraved heart,"[90]

---

[82] *Jackson v. State*, 323 S.W.2d 442, 443 (Tex. Crim. App. 1959) (defining "serious bodily injury").

[83] *Id.*

[84] Cal. Penal Code § 243(f)(5) (West 1988 & Supp. 1994) (defining "serious bodily injury" in the context of a battery statute).

[85] *State v. Miller*, 491 P.2d 481, 483 (Ariz. Ct. App. 1971).

[86] *State v. Perry*, 426 P.2d 415, 418 (Ariz. Ct. App. 1967).

[87] *People v. Love*, 168 Cal.Rptr. 407, 410 (Ct. App. 1980).

[88] 4 Blackstone at *200.

[89] Cal. Penal Code § 188 (West 1988).

[90] *Windham v. State*, 602 So.2d 798, 800 (Miss. 1992).

or (to change bodily organs) "a depravity of mind."[91] Some courts have characterized this form of malice in terms of both the heart and the mind: "wickedness of disposition, hardness of heart, cruelty, recklessness of consequences and a mind regardless of social duty."[92] For current purposes, it will be described as "depraved heart" murder.

In less colorful, but more precise and modern, terms, a depraved-heart murder is a "reckless" or "extremely reckless" homicide. The addition of the adverb "extremely" is useful because many court opinions antedating the Model Penal Code used the word "recklessness" as a synonym for "criminal negligence," the mental state required for one form of involuntary manslaughter.[93] If "recklessness" (as in "criminal negligence") is required for guilt of manslaughter, then "extreme recklessness" is the form of risk-taking that constitutes murder.

[2]—Facts Supporting a Finding of Extreme Recklessness

Cases falling within the depraved-heart category of murder "are not stereotyped."[94] However, each case involves conduct (or more specifically, risk-taking) that manifests such a high degree of indifference to the value of human life[95] that it may fairly be said that "the actor 'as good as' intended to kill his victim."[96]

For example, a jury may find implied malice if a person, without intending to kill or seriously injure another: (1) intentionally shoots a firearm in a crowded room;[97] (2) drives her car at a very high rate of speed in inclement weather and while highly intoxicated;[98] or (3) plays "Russian roulette" by loading a gun with one "live" and four "dummy" shells, spinning the revolver, and intentionally firing it at another person.[99] Malice may also be evidenced by an omission, such as when a parent, out of indifference, fails to feed her infant for two weeks.[100]

---

[91] People v. Register, 457 N.E.2d 704, 706 (N.Y. 1983).

[92] Commonwealth v. Malone, 47 A.2d 445, 447 (Pa. 1946) (quoting Commonwealth v. Drum, 58 Pa. 9, 17 (1868)).

[93] See § 31.08, infra.

[94] People v. Love, 168 Cal.Rptr. at 411.

[95] At one time, this form of murder required an act that manifested indifference to the value of human life in general, rather than to a particular person, but this is no longer the case. Windham v. State, 602 So.2d at 802.

[96] Lloyd Weinreb, Homicide: Legal Aspects in 2 Encyclopedia of Criminal Justice 859 (Sanford H. Kadish ed. 1983).

[97] E.g., People v. Register, 457 N.E.2d 704 (N.Y. 1983); see also People v. Jernatowski, 144 N.E. 497 (N.Y. 1924) (firing a gun into a crowded room).

[98] Davis v. State, 593 So.2d 145 (Ala. Crim. App. 1991) (D, with a blood-alcohol content of .237%, drove through a dense fog at a speed of 70 miles per hour, and crossed the center line, striking the victim's car head-on); see also People v. Whitfield, 868 P.2d 272 (Cal.' 1994) (D, with a blood-alcohol level more than three times the legal limit, became stuporous and crossed the center line, killing the victim).

[99] E.g., People v. Roe, 542 N.E.2d 610 (N.Y. 1989); see also Commonwealth v. Malone, 47 A.2d 445 (Pa. 1946) (D put one bullet in a five-chambered gun, spun the cylinder, and pulled the trigger three times; the gun discharged on the third effort).

[100] People v. Burden, 140 Cal.Rptr. 282 (Ct. App. 1977).

[B]—Distinguishing Murder from Manslaughter

Because there is no common law bright line between "negligence" and "reckless-ness,"[101] and there is no universally accepted common law definition of "reckless-ness,"[102] the line between unjustified risk-taking that constitutes involuntary manslaughter and that which constitutes murder has never been drawn with clarity.

In general, however, most present-day courts provide that implied malice is proven if the actor's conduct involves "the deliberate perpetration of a *knowingly* dangerous act with . . . unconcern and indifference as to whether anyone is harmed or not,"[103] or "where the killing was proximately caused by . . . an act, the natural consequences of which are dangerous to human life, which act was deliberately performed by a person who *knows* that his conduct endangers the life of another and who acts with *conscious* disregard for life."[104]

In more precise terms, therefore, a person kills "recklessly" if she consciously disregards a substantial and unjustifiable risk to human life. When such recklessness is extreme, i.e., when the risk of death is very great, and the justification for taking the risk is weak or non-existent, the actor is guilty of murder. In such circumstances, she has acted with a "depraved heart."

In contrast, when a person should be, but is not, aware that her conduct is very risky (and unjustifiably so), her behavior may justify the appellation of "criminal negligence," but the callousness that connotes "implied malice" is lacking. In these less culpable circumstances, a killing constitutes involuntary manslaughter.

---

[101] See § 10.04[D][1], *supra.*

[102] See § 10.04[D][3], *supra.*

[103] *DeBettencourt v. State,* 428 A.2d 479, 484 (Md. Ct. Spec. App. 1981) (emphasis added).

[104] *People v. Nieto-Benitez,* 840 P.2d 969, 975 (Cal. 1992) (quoting *People v. Phillips,* 414 P.2d 353 (Cal. 1966)) (internal quotations omitted) (emphasis added).

§ 31.06   Murder: Felony-Murder Rule[105]

[A]—The Rule

At common law, a person is guilty of murder if she kills another person during the commission or attempted commission of any felony.[106] This is the so-called "felony-murder rule." The rule was abolished by statute in England in 1957.[107] It never existed in France or Germany. The rule is richly criticized in this country.[108] Nonetheless, the rule "still thrives"[109] in the United States, and is retained in some form in nearly every state jurisdiction.[110]

Under most modern murder statutes, a death that results from the commission of an enumerated felony (usually a dangerous felony, such as arson, rape, robbery, or burglary) constitutes first-degree murder for which the maximum penalty is death or life imprisonment. If a death results from the commission of an unspecified felony, it is second-degree murder.

The felony-murder rule applies whether a felon kills the victim intentionally, recklessly, negligently, or accidentally and unforeseeably. Thus, the felony-murder rule authorizes strict liability for a death that results from a felony that is intentionally committed. Although some courts have candidly suggested that the felony-murder rule dispenses with the requirement of malice, the more usual explanation is that the intent to commit the felony constitutes the implied malice required for common law murder.

---

[105] See generally Kevin Cole, *Killings During Crime: Toward a Discriminating Theory of Strict Liability*, 28 Am. Crim. L. Rev. 73 (1990); David Crump & Susan Waite Crump, *In Defense of the Felony Murder Doctrine*, 8 Harv. J.L & Pub. Pol'y. 359 (1985); Norman J. Finkel & Kevin B. Duff, *Felony-Murder and Community Sentiment: Testing the Supreme Court's Assertions*, 15 Law & Hum. Behav. 405 (1991); George P. Fletcher, *Reflections on Felony-Murder*, 12 Sw. U. L. Rev. 413 (1981); Richard A. Rosen, *Felony Murder and the Eighth Amendment Jurisprudence of Death*, 31 B.C. L. Rev. 1103 (1990); Nelson E. Roth & Scott E. Sundby, *The Felony-Murder Rule: A Doctrine at Constitutional Crossroads*, 70 Cornell L. Rev. 446 (1985); Tamu Sudduth, Comment, *The Dillon Dilemma: Finding Proportionate Felony-Murder Punishments*, 72 Cal. L. Rev. 1299 (1984); James J. Tomkovicz, *The Endurance of the Felony-Murder Rule: A Study of the Forces That Shape Our Criminal Law*, 51 Wash. & Lee 1429 (1994).

[106] 4 Blackstone at 200-01 ("And if one intends to do another felony, and undesignedly kills a man, this is also murder."); *Commonwealth v. Balliro*, 209 N.E.2d 308, 312 (Mass. 1965); *Regina v. Serné*, 16 Cox Crim. Cas. 311, 312 (1887).

[107] Homicide Act, 1957, 5 & 6 Eliz. 2, ch. 11 § 1.

[108] See § 31.06[B][1], *infra*.

[109] *State v. Maldonado*, 645 A.2d 1165, 1171 (N.J. 1994).

[110] The rule is not recognized by statute in Hawaii, see Haw. Rev. Stat. § 707-701 (Supp. 1986); Kentucky, see Ky. Rev. Stat. Ann. § 507.020 (Baldwin 1984); and Michigan, see *People v. Aaron*, 299 N.W.2d 304, 321 (Mich. 1980) (interpretation of a statute that appears to recognize the rule). In New Mexico, the state supreme court ruled that the felony-murder statute requires an intent to kill. *State v. Ortega*, 817 P.2d 1196, 1204 (N.M. 1991).

In light of the strict-liability nature of the rule, *D1*, a robber, is guilty of murder if *V1* dies from fright caused by the robbery.[111] Similarly, *D2* is guilty of felony-murder if she accidentally shoots *V2* in the chest during the commission of a felony, and *V2* dies years later from a heart attack during a backyard basketball game, as the result of permanent damage to the heart produced by the original wound.[112] And, since the rule in its pure form applies to a homicide that occurs during the commission of *any* felony,[113] *D3* is guilty of murder if she attempts to steal *V3*'s watch from her purse and a gun concealed in it discharges, killing *V3*. Furthermore, the felony-murder rule extends implicitly (and sometimes expressly by statute) to accomplices in the commission of felonies. Therefore, if *S* were an accomplice in any of the hypothesized felonies, she would be guilty of murder, without regard to her own state of mind relating to the death.

[B]—Rationale of the Rule

[1]—Initial Observations

Consider these observations: (1) "[p]rincipled argument in favor of the felony-murder doctrine is hard to find";[114] (2) the "ancient rule . . . has been bombarded by intense criticism and constitutional attack";[115] and (3) "[c]riticism of the rule constitutes a lexicon of everything that scholars and jurists can find wrong with a legal doctrine."[116] What follows are the most common arguments in defense of the much condemned rule.

[2]—Deterrence

The most common defense of the felony-murder rule is that it is intended to deter negligent and accidental killings during the commission of felonies.[117] As Holmes explained this theory, the law ought to throw on the felon the peril that if a death results, even an unforeseeable one, she will be punished as a murderer.[118] This enhanced risk, the argument proceeds, will cause the felon to be more careful, i.e., she may commit the felony, but she will do so in a manner less likely to result in death.[119]

---

[111] See *People v. Stamp*, 82 Cal. Rptr. 598 (Ct. App. 1969) (*D* ordered *V* and others to lie down on the floor during a robbery; *V*, who had heart disease, died from fright); *State v. Dixon*, 387 N.W. 2d 682 (Neb. 1986) (*D* broke into *V*'s house; *V* suffered cardiac arrhythmia and died from the emotional trauma of the experience).

[112] See *People v. Harding*, 506 N.W.2d 482 (Mich. 1993) (in actual case, original shooting was not accidental).

[113] Many courts have limited the rule in this regard. See § 31.06[C][1]-[2], *infra*.

[114] American Law Institute, Comment to § 210.2, at 37.

[115] *State v. Maldonado*, 645 A.2d at 1171.

[116] Roth & Sundby, Note 105, *supra*, at 446.

[117] *People v. Washington*, 402 P.2d 130, 133 (Cal. 1965).

[118] Holmes at 59.

[119] It should be noticed that the felony-murder rule is *not* intended to deter the underlying felony. The rational way to deter *that* offense is to increase the penalty for the felony, and not to increase the penalty for the unintended, and perhaps unforeseeable, byproduct of it, the homicide.

Critics of the felony-murder rule reject the deterrence argument. They ask, "[q]uite simply, how does one deter an unintended act?"[120] Of course, the act of committing the felony *is* intended, but the *result* of the death is unintended, and may even be unforeseeable to the most rational and far-sighted felon.

Perhaps the most cogent criticism of the deterrence argument is empirical in nature. Homicides during the commission of felonies are exceedingly rare. For example, according to some data, only one-half of one percent of all robberies end up in a homicide.[121] Yet, even this figure overstates the case, because it does not differentiate between homicides intentionally or recklessly caused during the commission of robberies (i.e., cases in which murder convictions would be possible without the use of the felony-murder rule) and ones that accidentally or negligently occur. In short, it is hard to make the case for the need for the felony-murder rule on deterrence grounds.

[3]—Reaffirming the Sanctity of Human Life

Two commentators[122] defend the felony-murder rule on the ground that it reaffirms the sanctity of human life. The rule reflects society's judgment that the commission of a felony resulting in death is more serious—and, therefore, deserves greater punishment—than the commission of a felony *not* resulting in death. If a criminal is required to "pay her debt" to society, the felony-murderer has a greater debt to pay than the felon who does not take a life.

This argument proves too much. Even if a felony that results in a death should be punished more severely than one that does not result in a homicide, it hardly follows that a felon who accidentally takes a life should be subject to the severe penalties, including death or life imprisonment, reserved for murderers.

In order to calculate a wrongdoer's debt to society, and thus to set an appropriate punishment for an offense, legislators must consider the actor's culpability, and not simply the harm that she has caused.[123] In the context of felony-murder, it must be kept in mind that the offense involves two different social harms: the felony and the homicide. The culpability for each should be analyzed separately. The penalty for the felony serves to punish for the intentional social harm of that crime. The real issue, therefore, is whether it is fair to increase the felon's punishment for the social harm of a death that may have been caused unintentionally, non-recklessly, and non-negligently.

Consider two pickpockets, *P1* and *P2*. *P1* puts her hand in *V1*'s pocket and finds a wallet containing two hundred dollars. *P2* puts her hand in *V2*'s pocket and discovers a wallet with the same amount of money, but *V2* dies of shock from the experience. The property harm caused is the same—the loss of two hundred dollars. And, the culpability of *P1* and *P2* as to the thefts is identical. Therefore, as to the larcenies, they should be punished alike.

---

[120] Roth & Sundby, Note 105, *supra*, at 451.

[121] See *Enmund v. Florida*, 485 U.S. 782, 799-800 nn. 23-24 (1982) (reporting the data).

[122] Crump & Crump, Note 105, *supra*, at 361-69.

[123] See § 6.03, *supra*.

As for the social harm of the death, *P2* is no more culpable than *P1*, as the death was unforeseeable. It is true, of course, that *P2* caused a death, but in terms of *mens rea*, her culpability (as that of *P1*) is that of an intentional thief, and no more. Even if it were concluded that *P2* should pay some debt for the unforeseeable death, it surely violates ordinary concepts of just deserts to treat the unlucky pickpocket as deserving of punishment equal to that of an intentional, premeditated killer. Indeed, the rule may even conflict with constitutional principles of proportional punishment. [124]

[4]—Transferred Intent

The felony-murder rule is sometimes defended on the basis of the transferred-intent doctrine. The argument is that the felon's intent to commit a felony is transferred to the homicide. [125] Thus, the offense is not one of strict liability but one of intent.

This is a misuse of the transferred intent doctrine. The doctrine provides that an actor's intention to commit a particular social harm (call it Social Harm X) relating to a particular victim (call her Victim *A*) may be transferred to a different, unintended victim (Victim *B*) of the same social harm (Social Harm X). [126] Ordinarily, however, the law does not recognize a transference of intent to cause one social harm (Social Harm X) to a different and greater harm (Social Harm Y), involving the same victim. Thus, when *D* intends to steal rum in a boat (Social Harm X), and in the process accidentally sets fire to the boat (Social Harm Y), she is not guilty of intentionally burning the boat. [127] Yet, this is precisely what occurs with a felony-murder: the felon's intent to commit a felony (Social Harm X) is transferred to the different, and more serious, social harm of a homicide (Social Harm Y).

[5]—Easing the Prosecutor's Burden of Proof

Many felony-murder convictions do not involve innocent homicides. For example, a robber may intentionally shoot the victim or a police officer during the commission of the crime. In such a case one may infer that the felon intended to kill or seriously injure the victim. Thus, malice aforethought can be proven independent of the felony.

Even when a felon does not intend to kill or seriously injure another person, her felonious conduct will often manifest a depraved heart, i.e., extreme recklessness. For example, an arson may burn down a house knowing that the building is probably occupied, or a rapist may wound the victim in order to overcome her resistance.

Yet, even in felony cases involving one of these alternative forms of malice, prosecutors often charge the defendant on the basis of felony-murder. The effect

---

[124] See *People v. Dillon*, 668 P.2d 697, 719 (Cal. 1983) (holding that some felony-murders may not be punished as first-degree murder on the ground that it would constitute cruel and unusual punishment under the state and federal constitutions).

[125] *State v. O'Blasney*, 297 N.W.2d 797, 798 (S.D. 1980).

[126] See § 10.04[A][3], *supra*.

[127] *Regina v. Faulkner*, 13 Cox Crim. Cas. 550 (1877).

of the doctrine, therefore, if not its explicit rationale, is to ease the prosecutor's burden of proof regarding malice aforethought, by dispensing with the requirement that she show that the felon intended to kill or injure the victim grievously or that the felon was aware that her conduct was highly dangerous to human life. All that the prosecutor must do is prove that the defendant committed the felony and that the death occurred during its commission.

[C]—Limits on the Rule

Many courts have engrafted limitations on the felony-murder rule, the most significant of which are considered below.

[1]—Inherently-Dangerous-Felony Limitation

In order to avoid the potential harshness of the felony-murder rule, many states limit the rule to homicides that occur during the commission of felonies dangerous to human life. This is often described as the "inherently dangerous felony" limitation.

What is an "inherently dangerous" felony? Many courts do not classify a felony as dangerous unless, considering the elements of the offense in the abstract (that is, by looking at the offense as it defined by statute), rather than by considering the facts in the particular case, there is a substantial risk that the felonious conduct will result in death to an innocent person.[128] Applying this rule, one state court has held that theft is not an inherently dangerous felony, even though the felon in the particular case caused the death of a cancer-ridden child by falsely claiming that he had a cure for the disease, which induced the parents to forego traditional medical care.[129] Similarly, the offense of false imprisonment (defined as imprisonment "effected by violence, menace, fraud, or deceit") is not dangerous in the abstract, because the offense, as defined, is often committed in nonviolent fashion (by fraud or deceit).[130] The fact that the felon in the actual case used *force* to imprison the victim was immaterial to the analysis "in the abstract."

In contrast to the abstract approach, many states that apply the dangerous-felony limitation determine the dangerousness of a felony by considering "both the nature of the felony [in the abstract] and the circumstances surrounding its commission."[131] If the felony is dangerous under either approach, it may serve as the predicate for a felony-murder prosecution.

Either version of the inherently-dangerous-felony limitation brings felony-murder very close to the extreme-recklessness concept of malice. A felony the commission of which is likely to result in death is a crime the commission of which is apt to demonstrate the "wickedness of disposition, hardness of heart, cruelty, recklessness

---

[128] *People v. Burroughs*, 678 P.2d 894, 897 (Cal. 1984). How substantial must the risk be? In California, an act does not qualify as inherently dangerous unless there is " 'a high probability' that death will result." *People v. Patterson*, 778 P.2d 549, 558 (Cal. 1989).

[129] *People v. Phillips*, 414 P.2d 353 (Cal. 1966).

[130] See *People v. Henderson*, 560 P.2d 1180 (Cal. 1977).

[131] *State v. Harrison*, 564 P.2d 1321, 1324 (N.M. 1977).

of consequences and . . . mind regardless of social duty" that constitutes depraved-heart murder.[132] The reason there is not a perfect overlap is that the depraved-heart form of murder usually requires conscious risk-taking; it is theoretically possible (although rarely the case in real life) that a felon will be unaware of the dangerousness of her actions.

[2]—Independent-Felony (or "Merger") Limitation

In many states, the felony-murder rule does not apply if the underlying felony is an offense that is an "integral part"[133] or is "included in fact"[134] in the homicide itself. In such circumstances, the felony is not sufficiently independent of the death and, therefore, merges with it. For purposes of the felony-murder rule, such a felony disappears; it is subsumed by the homicide.

One aspect of this rule is easy to understand and appreciate. For example, suppose that *D* negligently kills *V*. A criminally negligent homicide constitutes involuntary manslaughter, which is a felony.[135] Because a death occurred during the commission of a felony—involuntary manslaughter—*D* would be guilty of murder under the felony-murder rule if there were no merger doctrine. That is, without some limitation on felony-murder, there could never be a manslaughter conviction, as the latter offense would always be bootstrapped into felony-murder.[136]

Now, consider this situation: *D* arrives home and discovers her husband in bed with *V*. In sudden heat of passion, she shoots and kills *V*. Under normal principles, *D* is guilty of voluntary manslaughter, a felony.[137] Just as with *involuntary* manslaughter, the felony of voluntary manslaughter should not serve as the basis for a felony-murder prosecution: it is an offense included in fact in the murder. But, may the prosecutor take this case one step further back? May she say that the predicate felony is not voluntary manslaughter, but is the felony of "assault with a deadly weapon"? May *that* felony be used to raise *D*'s offense to murder? Unless a jurisdiction applies the "independent felony" or "merger" limitation, the felonious assault may be used. Many, but not all,[138] jurisdictions hold that felonious assault may not serve as the basis for felony-murder.[139]

More difficult questions arise when a person commits a felony other than assault, but which offense includes assaultive behavior. For example, in *People v.*

---

[132] See § 31.05[A][1], *supra.*

[133] *People v. Ireland*, 450 P.2d 580, 590 (Cal. 1969); *Foster v. State*, 444 S.E.2d 296, 297 (Ga. 1994).

[134] *Richardson v. State*, 823 S.W.2d 710, 714 (Tex. Ct. App. 1992); see *State v. Essman*, 403 P.2d 540, 545 (Ariz. 1965).

[135] See § 31.08, *infra.*

[136] See *People v. Moran*, 158 N.E. 35, 36 (N.Y. 1927).

[137] See § 31.07, *infra.*

[138] E.g., *State v. Beeman*, 315 N.W.2d 770, 777 (Iowa 1982); *State v. Wanrow*, 588 P.2d 1320, 1322 (Wash. 1978) (not recognizing an independent-felony limitation).

[139] E.g., *State v. Essman*, 403 P.2d at 545; *People v. Ireland*, 450 P.2d at 590; *Edge v. State*, 414 S.E.2d 463, 465-66 (Ga. 1992); *State v. Fisher*, 243 P. 291, 293 (Kan. 1926) (recognizing an independent-felony limitation).

Wilson,[140] a man forcibly entered his estranged wife's home carrying a shotgun. The entry constituted burglary, as he entered with the purpose of committing a felony (assault with a deadly weapon) inside. The California Supreme Court held that the burglary in this case merged with the homicide. In essence, the fact that the assault took place inside a dwelling—and, thus, converted the offense to burglary—was coincidental and irrelevant to the analysis. Most states, however, have rejected this outcome.[141]

The *Wilson* opinion seemed to suggest that *any* felony that includes in fact an assault with a deadly weapon merges with the homicide and, therefore, will not support application of the felony-murder rule. The California Supreme Court later pulled back from this view, however, and held that a felony does not merge if the assaultive conduct involves "an independent felonious purpose."[142] Thus, if a death results during the commission of an armed robbery, the underlying assault does not merge with the homicide since the felonious purpose of the conduct—to take property—is independent of the homicide.

This version of the merger doctrine is sensible. Assuming that the rationale of felony-murder is to reduce the likelihood of accidental deaths occurring during the commission of felonies,[143] the felony-murder rule can only serve this deterrent function if the wrongdoer has a felonious purpose independent of the assault. That is, if *D*'s felonious purpose is to assault *V*, there is no way that the felony-murder rule can serve its function: there is no way to convince *D* to achieve her felonious purpose (attack *V*) safely. On the other hand, if *D*'s purpose is to take *V*'s property—a felonious intent independent of any assaultive conduct—she can seek to obtain the property violently (armed robbery) or nonviolently (theft). Assuming that the felony-murder rule has any deterrent effect, operation of the rule here makes sense as a warning to *D* that if she chooses to go ahead with her felonious plan to take another person's property, she should do so in a non-dangerous manner. If she fails to heed the message, and she takes property forcibly and a person dies during the robbery, it is appropriate to apply the felony-murder doctrine.

[3]—The *Res Gestae* Requirement

[a]—Overview

The felony-murder rule applies when a killing occurs *during the commission or attempted commission* of a felony. To give meaning to the italicized phrase, courts commonly state that, in order for the felony-murder rule to operate, the homicide must occur "within the *res gestae* of [things done to commit] the felony."[144] This requirement has two components: (1) a temporal and geographical proximity requirement; and (2) a causal aspect. Both of these features are discussed below. As

---

[140] 462 P.2d 22 (1969).

[141] *Commonwealth v. Claudio*, 634 N.E.2d 902, 905 (Mass. 1994) (describing *Wilson* as the minority view); e.g., *People v. Miller*, 297 N.E.2d 85 (N.Y. 1973).

[142] *People v. Burton*, 491 P.2d 793, 801 (Cal. 1971) (emphasis omitted).

[143] See § 31.06[B][2], *supra*.

[144] *State v. Leech*, 790 P.2d 160, 163 (Wash. 1990).

will be seen, the *res gestae* rule, if strictly construed, can serve as a limitation on the felony-murder rule; but if it is broadly applied, it serves as an *extension* of the rule.

[b]—Temporal/Geographical Proximity Requirement

In general, there must be a close proximity in terms of time and distance between the felony and the homicide.[145] This means that the *res gestae* period begins when the actor has reached the point at which she could be prosecuted for an attempt to commit the felony,[146] and it continues at least until all of the elements of the crime are completed. Thus, the felony-murder rule does not apply if the felony was conceived of after the homicide, i.e., as an afterthought of the killing.[147] For example,, if *D* accidentally kills *V*, after which she decides to take *V*'s property, the latter felony comes too late to meet the *res gestae* requirement.

On the other hand, for purposes of felony-murder, most courts provide that the *res gestae* of a felony continues, even after commission of the crime, until the felon reaches a place of temporary safety.[148] Thus, an armed robber who flees across urban roofs during the night, may be convicted of felony-murder if a police officer, in hot pursuit, falls into an airshaft on a roof and dies.[149] Likewise, a person who commits a robbery in a building, leaves, and is confronted outside by a victim of the crime, is guilty of felony-murder if she kills the resisting victim on the street.[150] However, the felony-murder rule is *not* operative if the felon kills a pedestrian the next day, 280 miles away from the scene of the crime.[151]

[c]—Causation Requirement

The *res gestae* requirement includes more than a connection in time and place: there must also be a causal relationship between the felony and the homicide.[152]

The but-for causal connection is often easy to satisfy. For example, if *V* suffers a fatal heart attack brought on by *D*'s felonious conduct, the connection is satisfied, even if the heart failure occurs two hours after the crime.[153] However, for the causation element to be met, the prosecutor must show that it was the *felonious nature* of the conduct that caused the death. For example, in *King v. Commonwealth*,[154] *D*, accompanied by accomplice *X*, piloted an airplane containing

---

[145] *People v. Dudrey*, 635 P.2d 750, 752 (Wash. Ct. App. 1982).

[146] *Payne v. State*, 406 P.2d 922, 924 (Nev. 1965).

[147] *Bouwkamp v. State*, 833 P.2d 486, 492 (Wyo. 1992); see *People v. Esquivel*, 34 Cal.Rptr.2d 324, 330-31 (Ct. App. 1994) (*X* killed *V*; thereafter, *X* and *D* took property belonging to *V*; *D* is not guilty of felony-murder if he did not form the intent to commit the felony under after *X* killed *V*).

[148] *People v. Salas*, 500 P.2d 7, 15 (Cal. 1972).

[149] *People v. Matos*, 634 N.E.2d 157 (N.Y. 1994). These facts also raise a causation issue, discussed in the next subsection.

[150] *Payne v. State*, 406 P.2d 922 (Nev. 1965).

[151] *Doane v. Commonwealth*, 237 S.E.2d 797 (1977).

[152] *State v. Adams*, 98 S.W.2d 632, 637 (Mo. 1936).

[153] *Stewart v. State*, 500 A.2d 676 (Md. Ct. Spec. App. 1985).

[154] 368 S.E.2d 704 (Va. Ct. App. 1988).

marijuana through a thick fog. A crash ensued, in which X died. The court held that the felony-murder rule did not apply: it observed that the crash would have resulted even if they had been transporting legal cargo. D was not flying unduly low to avoid radar sighting, or in any other dangerous manner; the accident was the result of the bad weather.

Even assuming a but-for connection, some courts apply general principles of *proximate* causation, in which case there is no felony-murder if an unforeseeable coincidental factor intervenes. Courts that are particularly hostile to the felony-murder doctrine sometimes require a more direct causal connection between the felony and the homicide than would be expected if the felon had intended to kill her victim.[155]

[4]—Killing by a Non-Felon[156]

[a]—The Issue

Suppose that *F1* and *F2* enter a liquor store in order to rob it. *F1* points a gun at *X*, a store employee, and threatens to kill her unless she hands over the money in the cash register. To prove her point, *F1* fires warning shots over *X*'s head. In response, *X* justifiably fires a weapon at *F1* to prevent the robbery. Two people—*F1* and *V*, a customer in the store—are struck and killed by the bullets. May *F2* be convicted of felony-murder of *F1* and *V*?

Notice the problem raised by these facts: the fatal shots were fired by *X*, rather than by one of the felons. In a literal sense, the killings occurred "during the commission or attempted commission of the felony," but they did not occur in *furtherance* of it. The question for consideration, therefore, is whether the felony-murder rule should apply in these circumstances.

[b]—The "Agency" Approach

The overwhelming majority of states that have considered the issue apply the so-called "agency" theory of felony-murder,[157] which provides that the felony-murder rule "does not extend to a killing, although growing out of the commission of the felony, if directly attributable to the act of one other than the defendant or those associated with him in the unlawful enterprise."[158] In short, the felony-murder rule does not apply if an adversary to the crime, rather than a felon, personally commits the homicidal act. Therefore, in the hypothetical described in subsection [a], *F2* may not be convicted of felony-murder for the deaths of *F1* and *V* at the hands of

---

[155] American Law Institute, Comment to § 210.2, at 33-34.

[156] See generally John S. Anooshian, Note, *Should Courts Use Principles of Justification and Excuse to Impose Felony-Murder Liability?*, 19 Rutgers L.J. 451 (1988); Norval Morris, *The Felon's Responsibility for the Lethal Acts of Others*, 105 U. Pa. L. Rev. 50 (1956).

[157] *State v. Oimen*, 516 N.W.2d 399, 407-08 (Wis. 1994) (rejecting the agency approach, but stating that it is the position of the "vast majority of state courts that have addressed this issue"); see *State v. Canola*, 374 A.2d 20, 29-30 (N.J. 1977) (applying the agency rule, and citing other cases in support of this approach); *State v. Bonner*, 411 S.E.2d 598 (N.C. 1992).

[158] *State v. Canola*, 374 A.2d at 23.

non-felon X. The same result would apply if the shooter were a bystander or police officer, rather than the direct victim of the felony.

Why should a felon escape punishment as a murderer when the shooter is not a felon? Conceptually, the explanation is this: generally speaking, a person is criminally responsible for her own acts, but not for the actions of others; therefore, a felon who does not shoot anyone ($F2$) is not responsible for the actions of a non-felon shooter (X). However, there is an exception to the rule against vicarious responsibility: a person is responsible for the acts of another if the primary actor—the shooter—is functioning as the agent of the secondary party—the non-shooting felon. This agency relationship exists when the secondary party is an accomplice of the primary party.[159] Under such circumstances, the primary party's acts are imputed to the secondary party. Therefore, in the ordinary felony-murder situation, in which a felon kills an innocent person, her co-felons are also responsible for the shooting. Here, however, $F2$ cannot be convicted of the homicides because the primary party was not a person with whom she was an accomplice. It is not possible, therefore, to impute the acts of the antagonistic party (X) to $F2$, on the basis of agency.

The agency approach is supported by two other arguments. First, the killing cannot truly be said to be within the *res gestae* of the offense, since the killing was not in furtherance of the crime, but in resistance to it. Second, the felony-murder rule can have little or no deterrent effect when the shooter is a non-felon, since the felon has no control over the actions of the innocent person.

[c]—The "Proximate Causation" Approach

[i]—In General

A few courts apply the "proximate causation" theory of felony-murder.[160] Following this approach, a felon is liable for any homicide that occurs during the commission of the offense, whether the shooter is a felon or a third party, if the killing was the proximate result of the felonious activity.

As with any other proximate-causation issue, the result will depend on the particular facts of the case, and the matter ultimately is one for the jury to decide. For example, in the hypothetical under discussion, $F1$ pointed a gun at X, threatened her life and fired warning shots; this conduct could be viewed as the proximate cause of X's reasonable and foreseeable response. If the circumstances were so viewed, $F2$ could be convicted of the death of her colleague, $F1$, and of V, the innocent bystander. In contrast, the felony-murder rule would probably not apply if a pickpocket took money and fled, and the crime victim pulled a gun and fired it at the felon, killing a bystander.

[ii]—Limited Version

Should a court that permits the operation of the felony-murder rule when the shooter is a non-felon take into consideration *who was shot*? In the hypothetical

---

[159] See § 30.02[B], *supra*.

[160] E.g., *People v. Hernandez*, 624 N.E.2d 661 (N.Y. 1993); *State v. Oimen*, 516 N.W.2d 399 (Wis. 1994).

under discussion, for example, should a proximate-causation jurisdiction distinguish between the deaths of V and F1, for purposes of F2's felony-murder responsibility? Pennsylvania once drew such a distinction: the rule was that F2 could be convicted of murder in V's death, but not as to F1.[161] Even today, there is apparent support for this distinction.[162]

This differentiation is based on the principle that when a non-felon kills a felon this homicide is *justifiable*, whereas the death of a bystander accidentally shot by a non-felon is *excusable* homicide. As these italicized words are explained elsewhere in this Text,[163] a justifiable homicide is a proper or permissible killing (i.e., no social harm has resulted); an excusable homicide involves a wrongful result for which the actor is not morally accountable. Courts that draw this distinction believe that a felon should not be found guilty in a justifiable homicide, because it would be as if she were being punished for causing a good result (i.e., the death of a co-felon). This reasoning is hardly self-evident, however, since the felon who would be convicted wrongfully assisted in creating the condition that made her co-felon's death justifiable.

[d]—Distinguishing Felony-Murder from Other Theories

Even in an agency jurisdiction, a felon may be held responsible for the death of another at the hands of a third party, as long as the basis for the charge is not felony-murder. For example, in the hypothetical in subsection [a], F1's conduct—pointing a loaded gun at X, threatening X's life, and shooting the weapon—quite arguably manifested an extreme indifference to the value of human life. Consequently, if F1 had unintentionally killed X when she fired the gun, F1 would have been guilty of reckless murder. And, F2 would have been guilty of murder as well, under traditional complicity principles, since F1's reckless acts would have been imputed to her.

It follows, therefore, that if F1 recklessly caused X to kill V, F2 may be held responsible for V's death, since F1's reckless acts will be imputed to F2, her accomplice.[164] On the other hand, F2 may *not* be convicted of F1's death at X's hands, because F1's malicious (reckless) conduct did not result in the unlawful killing of *another* human being, but rather in her own justifiable homicide. Therefore, in the case of F1's death, there is no criminal homicide to impute to F2.[165]

---

[161] See *Commonwealth v. Almeida*, 68 A.2d 595 (Pa. 1949) (police officer killed another police officer; held: felony-murder rule applies); *Commonwealth v. Redline*, 137 A.2d 472, 483 (Pa. 1958) (police officer killed co-felon; held: felony-murder does not apply); *Commonwealth ex rel. Smith v. Myers*, 261 A.2d 550 (Pa.1970) (overruling *Almeida*, and adopting agency theory).

[162] Compare *State v. Harrison*, 564 P.2d 1321, 1324 n.1 (N.M. 1977) (in dictum, the court stated that the felony-murder rule would apply if a police officer were to kill an innocent bystander while shooting at a felon) with *Jackson v. State*, 589 P.2d 1052 (N.M. 1979) (a co-felon was shot by a crime victim; held: felony-murder charge is properly dismissed when the victim of the felony kills a felon).

[163] See § 16.03[B]-[C], *supra*.

[164] *People v. Washington*, 402 P.2d 130, 133 (Cal. 1965).

[165] *People v. Antick*, 539 P.2d 43, 50 (Cal. 1975).

§ 31.07   Manslaughter: Provocation ("Sudden Heat of Passion")[166]

[A]—In General

Under common law principles, an intentional homicide committed in "sudden heat of passion" as the result of "adequate provocation" mitigates the offense to voluntary manslaughter.[167] Although the issue rarely arises, the so-called "provocation defense" may also negate other forms of malice aforethought, i.e.., cases in which the actor is provoked to inflict grievous bodily injury upon another or to act in an extremely reckless manner, in which death unintentionally results.[168]

The common law defense contains four elements, discussed in the next subsection: (1) the actor must have acted in heat of passion; (2) the passion must have been the result of adequate provocation; (3) the actor must not have had a reasonable opportunity to cool off; and (4) there must be a causal link between the provocation, the passion, and the homicide.[169]

[B]—Elements of the Defense

[1]—State of Passion

The provocation defense does not apply unless the defendant is in a state of passion at the moment of the homicide.[170] Although anger may be the emotion most often claimed in heat-of-passion cases, the defense is not so limited. "Passion" includes any "violent, intense, high-wrought, or enthusiastic emotion."[171] This term is "sufficiently broad to encompass a range of emotions[,] including fear,"[172] jealousy,[173] and "wild desperation."[174]

---

166 See generally Jeremy Horder, Provocation and Responsibility (1992); A.J. Ashworth, *The Doctrine of Provocation*, 35 Cambridge L.J. 292 (1976); Peter Brett, *The Physiology of Provocation*, 1970 Crim. L. Rev. 634; Donna K. Coker, *Heat of Passion and Wife Killing: Men Who Batter/Men Who Kill*, 2 Rev. L. & Women's Stud. 71 (1992); Joshua Dressler, *Rethinking Heat of Passion: A Defense in Search of a Rationale*, 73 J. Crim. L. & Criminology 421 (1982); Joshua Dressler, *Provocation: Partial Justification or Partial Excuse?*, 51 Mod. L. Rev. 467 (1988); Finbarr McAuley, *Anticipating the Past: The Defence of Provocation in Irish Law*, 50 Mod. L. Rev. 133 (1987).

167 *Comber v. United States*, 584 A.2d 26, 42 (D.C. Ct. App. 1990).

168 The defense does not apply in felony-murder cases. The " 'predictable conduct by a resisting victim' of a felony cannot 'constitute the kind of provocation sufficient to reduce a murder charge to voluntary manslaughter.' " *People v. Balderas*, 711 P.2d 480, 510 (Cal. 1985) (quoting *People v. Jackson*, 618 P.2d 149 (Cal. 1980)).

169 *Girouard v. State*, 583 A.2d 718, 721 (Md. Ct. App. 1991); *State v. Mauricio*, 568 A.2d 879, 883 (N.J. 1990).

170 *State v. Johnson*, 23 N.C. 354, 362 (1840) ("[P]rovocation furnishes no extenuation, unless it produces passion.").

171 *People v. Borchers*, 325 P.2d 97, 102 (Cal. 1958) (quoting Webster's New International Dictionary (2d ed. 1950)).

172 *LaPierre v. State*, 734 P.2d 997, 1001 (Alaska Ct. App. 1987).

173 *People v. Berry*, 556 P.2d 777, 781 (Cal. 1976).

174 *People v. Borchers*, 325 P.2d at 102.

[2]—Adequate Provocation

[a]—Early Common Law Categories

Early English case law defined "adequate provocation" as "an amount of provocation as would be excited by the circumstances in the mind of a reasonable man."[175] Common law courts developed a small and fixed list of categories that met this standard. These "paradigms of misbehavior"[176] were: (1) an aggravated assault or battery;[177] (2) mutual combat;[178] (3) commission of a serious crime against a close relative of the defendant;[179] (4) illegal arrest;[180] and (5) observation by a husband of his wife committing adultery.[181]

Among the provocative acts that were *not* considered adequate were: (1) a trivial battery;[182] (2) learning about (but not observing) adultery;[183] (3) observation of the sexual unfaithfulness of a fiance or other unmarried sexual partner;[184] and (4) words, no matter how insulting or offensive.[185]

[b]—Modern Law

[i]—In General

The rigid common law categories of "adequate provocation" have given way in many states to the view that the issue of what constitutes adequate provocation should be left to the jury to decide. As one court explained, "[w]hat is sufficient provocation . . . must vary with the myriad shifting circumstances of men's temper and quarrels."[186] No court can "catalogue all the various facts and combinations of facts which shall be held [sufficient]."[187]

---

[175] *Regina v. Welsh*, 11 Cox Crim. Cas. 336, 338 (1869).

[176] *Brown v. United States*, 584 A.2d 537, 540 (D.C. Ct. App. 1990).

[177] *Stewart v. State*, 78 Ala. 436 (1885); *Beasley v. State*, 8 So. 234 (Miss. 1887). The line between provocation and self-defense is subtle. If *V* unjustifiably strikes *D* with the intent to kill her, *D* is justified in killing *V* in self-defense, assuming that she reasonably believes that the attack will continue and that deadly force is necessary. If *V* commences a *non*deadly attack on *D*, *D* may justifiably use *non*deadly force to protect herself, and if an accidental death ensues she will not be guilty of any homicide offense. If *V* starts a *non*deadly assault and *D*, enraged, *intentionally* kills *V*, her disproportionate response impairs her claim of self-defense, but the provocation defense comes into play.

[178] Mutual combat is "a fight or struggle which both parties enter willingly or in which two persons, upon a sudden quarrel, and in hot blood, mutually fight upon equal terms and death results from the combat." *People v. Neal*, 446 N.E.2d 270, 274 (1983).

[179] E.g., *State v. Cooper*, 36 So. 350 (La. 1904) (rape of a close relative).

[180] See *John Bad Elk v. United States*, 177 U.S. 529 (1900).

[181] *Speake v. State*, 610 So.2d 1238, 1240 (Ala. Ct. Crim. App. 1992). The gender-bias of the common law rule would no longer apply today, of course.

[182] *Commonwealth v. Webb*, 97 A. 189, 191 (Pa. 1916).

[183] See *Holmes v. Director of Public Prosecutions*, [1946] 2 All E.R. 124, 127.

[184] See *Rex v. Greening*, 3 K.B. 846, 23 Cox Crim. Cas. 601 (1913).

[185] Perkins at 93.

[186] *Commonwealth v. Paese*, 69 A. 891, 892 (Pa. 1908).

[187] *Maher v. People*, 10 Mich. 212, 222-23 (1862).

Jurors are instructed that provocation is sufficient to mitigate an intentional killing to manslaughter: if it "would render any ordinary prudent person for the time being incapable of that cool reflection that otherwise makes it murder";[188] if it "might render ordinary men, of fair average disposition, liable to act rashly or without due deliberation or reflection, and from passion, rather than judgment";[189] or if "in the mind of a just and reasonable man [it would] stir resentment to violence."[190]

One common law rule that has persisted in most jurisdictions, however, is that words alone do not constitute adequate provocation.[191] This can prove to be a harsh rule. For example, in one incident, D, an African-American, killed V, his white neighbor, in a rage after V informed D that he had purposely shot D's dog a few weeks earlier, and that he had done so because "it was bad enough living around niggers, much less dogs."[192] Thus, two types of words were involved in this situation: informational words (words informing the listener of an incident—killing a dog—that might have constituted adequate provocation had it been observed); and highly insulting words. Applying the words-alone rule, D is not entitled to an instruction on voluntary manslaughter, even though this "ignores the fact that sometimes words may be even more inflammatory than aggressive actions."[193]

This rule is slowly breaking down. Some courts allow the defense to be raised in the case of informational, but not insulting, words.[194] Other courts have held open the possibility that insulting words may qualify in extreme circumstances.[195] Also, the "words alone" rule does not apply in jurisdictions following the Model Penal Code.[196]

---

[188] *Addington v. United States*, 165 U.S. 184, 186 (1897) (jury instruction apparently approved).

[189] *Maher v. People*, 10 Mich. at 220 (emphasis deleted).

[190] *Fields v. State*, 52 Ala. 348, 354 (1875).

[191] *Girouard v. State*, 583 A.2d 718, 722 (Md. Ct. App. 1991) (describing this as the "overwhelming" rule).

[192] *People v. Green*, 519 N.W.2d 853, 856 (Mich. 1994).

[193] *State v. Shane*, 590 N.E.2d 272, 277 (Ohio 1992).

[194] *Commonwealth v. Berry*, 336 A.2d 262 (Pa. 1975) (D killed V after being informed that V had assaulted X, D's mother); see *State v. Shane*, 590 N.E.2d at 278 (observing that some courts allow the defense to be applied to informational words regarding adultery).

[195] E.g., *People v. Pouncey*, 471 N.W.2d at 351; *State v. Shane*, 590 N.E.2d at 278.

[196] See § 31.10[C][3][b], *infra*.

[ii]—The Nature of the "Reasonable Person"[197]

Who is the "reasonable person" to whom the provoked defendant is compared, in order to determine what constitutes "adequate provocation"? First, it should be observed that the word "reasonable" is an odd, if not improper, term in this context, since the "reasonable man" is sometimes considered to be "the public embodiment of rational behavior,"[198] which is hardly an apt description of a provoked killer. It is more accurate, therefore, to describe the objective character in this context as an "ordinary" person.

Second, to the extent that one seeks to determine the nature of the "reasonable/ ordinary person" on the basis of traditional Anglo-American case law, we learn that the person is of average disposition,[199] i.e., not exceptionally belligerent;[200] sober at the time of the provocation;[201] and of normal mental capacity.[202]

As in other areas of the criminal law,[203] there has been a movement to subjectivize the standard, i.e., to merge the defendant's personal characteristics into the ordinary/reasonable person.[204] Increasingly, juries are instructed to test the defendant's reaction to a provocation by the standard of the ordinary person "in the actor's situation." Often this phrase is left unexamined, but sometimes the jury is instructed more specifically. For example, in an English case in which a 15-year-old male was provoked to kill a man who had sexually assaulted him, the jury was told

---

[197] See generally Joshua Dressler, *When "Heterosexual" Men Kill "Homosexual" Men: Reflections on Provocation Law, Sexual Advances, and the "Reasonable Man" Standard*, 85 J. Crim. L. & Criminology 726 (1995); J. Edwards, *Provocation and the Reasonable Man— Another View*, 1954 Crim L. Rev. 898; Colin Howard, *What Colour Is the "Reasonable Man"?*, 1961 Crim. L. Rev. 41; Robert B. Mison, Comment, *Homophobia in Manslaughter: The Homosexual Advance as Insufficient Provocation*, 80 Cal. L. Rev. 133 (1992); M. Naeem Rauf, *The Reasonable Man Test in the Defence of Provocation: What are the Reasonable Man's Attributes and Should the Test be Abolished?*, 30 Crim. L.Q. 73 (1987); Laurie J. Taylor, Comment, *Provoked Reason in Men and Women: Heat-of-Passion Manslaughter and Imperfect Self-Defense*, 33 UCLA L. Rev. 1679 (1986); Glanville Williams, *Provocation and the Reasonable Man*, 1954 Crim. L. Rev. 740; Stanley M.H. Yeo, *Lessons on Provocation from the Indian Penal Code*, 41 Int'l & Comp. L.Q. 615 (1992); Note, *Manslaughter and the Adequacy of Provocation: The Reasonableness of the Reasonable Man*, 106 U. Pa. L. Rev. 1021 (1958).

[198] Ronald K.L. Collins, *Language, History and the Legal Process: A Profile of the "Reasonable Man"*, 8 Rut.-Cam. L.J. 311, 315 (1977).

[199] *Maher v. People*, 10 Mich. at 220.

[200] *Mancini v. Director of Public Prosecutions*, [1941] 3 All E.R. 272, 277.

[201] *Regina v. McCarthy*, [1954] 2 All E.R. 262, 265.

[202] *Rex v. Lesbini*, [1914] 11 Crim. App. 7.

[203] See especially §§ 18.06[A]-[B], *supra*.

[204] See *State v. Thunberg*, 492 N.W.2d 534, 536 (Minn. 1992) (noting the trend). The Model Penal Code has been extremely influential in this regard. See § 31.10[C][3][a], *infra*.

that the "reasonable man" possesses the degree of self-control to be expected of a person of the same age and sex as the accused.[205]

How far should such subjectivization be permitted to go? Courts are struggling with this question. For example, in one case,[206] the defendant happened upon two women engaged in lesbian lovemaking at a campsite. Enraged, the defendant killed one of the women, and wounded the other. He sought to introduce psychiatric evidence at his trial that he was in sudden heat of passion because he had previously been rejected by women, including his mother who may have had a lesbian relationship of her own, and that he had been the prior victim of sexual abuse by other men. In essence, he sought to have his actions tested by the standards of a person who had previously experienced such trauma. The trial court refused to allow the testimony and convicted the defendant of first-degree murder. The appellate court affirmed.[207]

This decision seems proper. The heat-of-passion defense recognizes the ordinary human frailty of loss of self-control in provocative circumstances.[208] The defendant here, however, sought to show that he had *abnormal* human frailties. Although this might support a diminished capacity claim,[209] subjectivization of this degree is out of place in a provocation case.

In another prosecution,[210] the defendant, who had come to the United States from China a year earlier, brutally killed his wife because she refused to have sex with him and admitted that she had been seeing other men. The defense proffered expert testimony of an anthropologist, who asserted that the accused's reaction "would not be unusual at all . . . for a normal Chinese in that situation." He went on to state that, in part because of the shame or humiliation such a person would feel in the closed-knit Chinese community, "one could expect a Chinese to react in a much more volatile, violent way to those circumstances that someone from our own society." Even assuming arguendo the accuracy of this testimony, does this mean that the defendant's conduct should be measured by the standards of an "ordinary/reasonable man brought up in a Chinese culture"? The trial judge apparently thought so.[211]

---

[205] *Director of Public Prosecutions v. Camplin*, [1978] 2 All E.R. 168, 175. Is a gender-specific instruction, such as that recommended in *Camplin*, a good idea? If jurors believe that an ordinary woman is less likely than an ordinary man to respond violently to a provocation—a very plausible assumption—a gender-specific instruction might result in a standard prejudicial to a woman who "acts like a man," i.e., who responds violently to a provocation.

[206] *Commonwealth v. Carr*, 580 A.2d 1362 (Pa. Super. Ct. 1990).

[207] See also *Commonwealth v. Halbert*, 573 N.E.2d 975 (Mass. 1991) (*D*, a male, purportedly a prior victim of a gang rape, killed *V* after *V* touched him on the knee and asked "Josh, what do you want to do?"; held: court did not err in refusing to instruct the jury on voluntary manslaughter).

[208] See § 31.07[C][2][b], *infra*.

[209] See § 26.03, *supra*.

[210] *People v. Dong Lu Chen*, No 87-7774 (N.Y. Sup. Ct. Dec. 2, 1988) (discussed in Leti Volpp, *(Mis)identifying Culture: Asian Women and the "Cultural Defense"*, 17 Harv. Women's L.J. 57, 64-77 (1994)).

[211] The judge found the defendant guilty of manslaughter, based in considerable part on evidence of the defendant's culture.

Decisions of this sort put the law on a slippery slope. In an effort to take cognizance of cultural disparities in our multicultural society, and thus to be fair to persons who are not fully integrated into the dominant culture, the law runs the risk of trivializing the normative anti-killing message of the criminal law.

[3]—Cooling Off Time

The defense of provocation involves *sudden* heat of passion. The defense is unavailable if a reasonable person would have cooled off in the time that elapsed between the provocation and the fatal act.[212] As with the adequacy of the provocation, this element of the defense used to be determined by the judge, but today is a matter left to the jury.

Particularly in much earlier years, this element was strictly applied. It was said, for example, that the homicidal act had to occur "in the first transport of passion."[213] Under such a rule, the defense is unavailable to one who is subjected to multiple minor acts of provocation which, when combined, cause the individual to boil over, or to one who broods over a provocation before acting. In one famous case,[214] V committed sodomy on D while the latter was unconscious. For three weeks, V ridiculed D, by informing others of what had taken place. Finally, D could take no more of it, and he killed V in a rage. The appellate court held that D was not entitled to claim provocation, as too much time had elapsed because the original provocative act and the homicide. Modern courts have been somewhat more sympathetic to provocation claims of this sort.[215]

[4]—Causal Connection

Notwithstanding provocation by the decedent, the defense is unavailable to a person whose motivation for the homicide is unrelated to the provocation. For example, suppose that D calmly plans to kill V, her hated business partner. Coincidentally, at the time of the planned homicide, D discovers V committing adultery with X, D's husband. Angrily, D decides to use this opportunity to kill V. Under these circumstances, D is not entitled to the defense. Although observation of adultery is adequate provocation, and D was in a state of high emotion at the time of the offense, the preconceived design to kill, and not the provocation, was the impetus for the homicide.

[C]—Rationale of the Defense

[1]—Partial Justification or Partial Excuse?: Initial Inquiry

The provocation doctrine was developed in order to mitigate the harshness of the death penalty, which originally applied to all unjustifiable homicides.[216] This

---

[212] American Law Institute, Comment to § 210.3, at 59.

[213] *State v. Yanz*, 50 A. 37, 38 (Conn. 1901).

[214] *State v. Gounagias*, 153 P. 9 (Wash. 1915).

[215] E.g., *People v. Berry*, 556 P.2d 777 (Cal. 1976) (D was provoked by V on an on-and-off basis for two weeks; after the last provocative act, D remained in V's apartment for 20 hours awaiting her return; when she returned and began to scream at him he killed V; held: this was sufficient evidence to support a manslaughter conviction).

[216] Royal Commission on Capital Punishment Report, (Cmd. 8932) para. 144 (1953).

rationale, however, fails to explain the doctrine's continued vitality in England, which no longer has capital punishment, and in the United States, in which there are no more mandatory death penalty laws.[217]

Why should people who become angry enough to kill when provoked be given a defense (partial as it is) when they intentionally take a human life? The common law sheds little light on the subject. Indeed, as English courts and commentators have observed, the doctrine developed "largely [for] reasons of the heart and of common sense, not [for] reasons of pure juristic logic."[218] Put simply, the doctrine has lacked a clear and consistent rationale.

In an effort to identify a sensible rationale for the doctrine, it is useful to focus initially on the role of the provocative act in stirring the defendant's homicidal conduct. What is the relevance of the provocation? One philosopher has phrased the issue this way:

> Is [the provoker] partially responsible [for the homicide] because he roused a violent impulse or passion in me so that it wasn't truly or merely me "acting of my own accord"? Or is it rather that, he having done me such injury, I was entitled to retaliate?[219]

In essence, the issue come down to this: does a provocation serve as a partial justification or, instead, a partial excuse for a homicide?[220] In partial-justification terms, do we say that a heat-of-passion killing is a less serious offense than an ordinary homicide, because the decedent (partially) deserved to die or the defendant had an incomplete right to kill the decedent? Or, instead, do we partially *excuse* the killer because we believe that the passion she experienced at the moment of the fatal act makes her less responsible for her conduct?

The answer to the justification/excuse puzzle is that, unfortunately, courts have often failed to state which doctrinal path is involved; or worse, they have explained the doctrine under both theories.

[2]—Justification or Excuse: A Deeper Look

[a]—The Argument For Provocation as a Partial Justification

Various features of the defense, most notably, the original categories of "adequate provocation,"[221] suggest that a provoked killing is partially justified. For example,

---

[217] In general, mandatory death penalty statutes are unconstitutional. *Sumner v. Shuman*, 483 U.S. 66. 77 (1977); *Woodson v. North Carolina*, 428 U.S. 280, 304 (1976). Furthermore, in states that divide murder into degrees, a heat-of-passion killing should constitute no more than second-degree murder, a non-capital offense: a person who kills suddenly when provoked does not premeditate or act with the degree of calmness normally associated with first-degree murder. See § 31.03[C], *supra*.

[218] *Director of Public Prosecutions v. Camplin*, [1978] 2 All. E.R. 168, 180.

[219] J. Austin, *A Plea for Excuses*, "The Presidential Address to the Aristotelian Society, 1956," reprinted in Ordinary Language 43 (V. Chappel ed. 1964).

[220] For definitions of "justification defense" and "excuse defense," see § 16.03[B]-[C], *supra*; for consideration of the importance of distinguishing between the two types of defenses, see § 17.05, *supra*.

[221] See § 31.07[B][2][a], *supra*.

upon a husband witnessing his wife in an act of adultery, "if the husband shall stab the adulterer, or knock out his brains, that is bare manslaughter,"[222] but it is murder if a man kills after discovering his fiance in such a tryst. The common law explanation for the dichotomy was that "adultery is the highest invasion of property,"[223] whereas a man "has no such control" over his faithless lover.[224] In short, a husband is justified in protecting his "property" from a "trespasser."

The other categories of "adequate provocation," as well, involve affronts that, in an earlier era, "men of honour" were expected to respond to by "inflict[ing] proportional . . . retaliation . . . on the perpetrator of the injustice."[225] In other words, provokers deserved to be harmed, but homicide was an over-response; therefore, the provoked actor was only partially justified in taking a life.

Another justificatory feature of the defense is the "misdirected retaliation" rule, which provides that the defense may only be used if the defendant attempts to kill the "right" person, i.e., the person who performed the provocative act. For example, in *Rex v. Scriva*,[226] D observed P, a reckless driver, strike X, D's young child. Provoked, D attempted to attack P with a knife. V, a bystander, intervened. Therefore, D intentionally killed V. The court held that the issue of provocation was properly withdrawn from the jury. Although D was adequately provoked, the provoker—the person who (partially) deserved to die—was P, and not V.[227]

[b]—The Argument For Provocation as a Partial Excuse

Various arguments, and language from court opinions, support the proposition that the provocation defense is a partial excuse, and not a partial justification. It is helpful at the outset, however, to distinguish between the *anger* (or other passion) that the provoked party experiences and the *homicidal act* arising from it. Even if a person is justified in becoming angry when she is provoked, this does not mean that her homicidal reaction to the provocation is justified, even partially. Instead, as most modern courts have come to realize, the heat-of-passion defense is "the legal system's recognition of the weaknesses or infirmity of human nature and that those who kill [in sudden heat of passion] . . . are less morally blameworthy than those who kill in the absence of such influence."[228]

Why are provoked killers less blameworthy? Two explanations may be offered. First, a person who kills in such circumstances does not act from a "bad or corrupt

---

[222] *Regina v. Mawdridge*, [1707] Kel. J. 119, 137, 84 Eng. Rep. 1107, 1115.

[223] *Id.*

[224] *Rex v. Greening*, 3 K.B. at 849, 23 Cox. Crim. Cas. at 603.

[225] Horder, Note 166, at 51.

[226] [1951] Vict. L.R. 298.

[227] See also *Thibodeaux v. State*, 733 S.W.2d 668 (Tex. Ct. App. 1987) (X told D, her common law husband, that he was not the father of V, a two-month old baby; devastated by the news, D killed V; held: D was not entitled to an instruction on manslaughter because, under state law, the provocation that incites the homicide must come from "the individual killed or another acting with the person killed").

[228] *Simpson v. United States*, 632 A.2d 374, 377 n.8 (D.C. Ct. App. 1993).

heart, but from infirmity of passion to which even good men are subject."[229] The more serious the provocation, the more likely it is that the bad act can be explained by "the extraordinary character of the situation . . . rather than [by] any extraordinary deficiency in . . . [human] character."[230]

A more common way to explain the defense is in terms of voluntariness. The defense is a "concession to human weakness,"[231] in that the law recognizes that a person disturbed or obscured by passion is less able to control her actions than one who is in a normal state. Therefore, assuming that the provocation is of a nature that would cause a similar reaction in an ordinary person (so that the provoked person cannot be blamed for her emotional state), the provoked actor is not fully to blame for her homicidal act: she lacks sufficient free choice to be held fully accountable for her actions.[232]

[D]—Burden of Proof

In states in which criminal homicide is defined in common law terms, provocation is a failure-of-proof "defense,"[233] in that it negates the "malice aforethought" element of murder. Therefore, once the defendant satisfies her burden of production on the issue, the prosecution constitutionally is required to carry the burden of persuasion, i.e., it must prove beyond a reasonable doubt that it was not a sudden-heat-of-passion homicide.[234]

§ 31.08 Manslaughter: Criminal Negligence

According to Blackstone, a homicide is manslaughter when "a person does an act, lawful in itself, but in an unlawful manner *and without due caution and circumspection.*"[235] Although common law courts have used many terms to explain the italicized language—including "gross negligence," "culpable negligence," and, confusingly, "recklessness"—the best modern term is "criminal negligence." In states that distinguish between forms of manslaughter, a criminally negligent homicide is "involuntary" manslaughter, a lesser offense than "voluntary" ("sudden heat of passion") manslaughter.

As "criminal negligence" is generally defined,[236] involuntary manslaughter involves a gross deviation from the standard of care that reasonable people would exercise in the same situation.[237] Under this standard, "ordinary" negligence—an

---

229 *State v. Cook*, 3 Ohio Dec. Reprint 142, 144 (1859).

230 Wechsler & Michael, Note 1, *supra*, at 1281.

231 *Holmes v. Director of Public Prosecutions*, [1946] 2 All E.R. at 128; American Law Institute, Comment to § 210.3, at 55.

232 See Horder, Note 166, *supra*, at 72-110.

233 See § 16.02, *supra*.

234 *Mullaney v. Wilbur*, 421 U.S. 684 (1975). See § 7.03[B][2], *supra*.

235 4 Blackstone at *192 (emphasis added).

236 See § 10.04[D][2], *supra*.

237 *State v. Hernandez*, 815 S.W.2d 67, 70 (Mo. Ct. App. 1991).

amount sufficient to justify tort liability—is insufficient for criminal liability. A few states, however, allow conviction for manslaughter on the basis of tort-level negligence.[238]

On the other hand, as noted elsewhere,[239] the line most commonly drawn between criminal negligence and the sort of risk-taking that justifies a finding of malice aforethought (and consequent murder) is one founded on the consciousness of the actor's risk-taking. One who is aware that she is taking a substantial and unjustifiable risk to human life, but proceeds anyway, manifests the indifference to the value of human life that constitutes malice aforethought; one who should be aware of the risk, but is not, is negligent.

For example, one who playfully fires a gun that she knows has bullets in it, in the direction of another person, may be convicted of murder;[240] if the same person performs the same act believing that the gun is unloaded, she is guilty of manslaughter.[241] Or, if a parent knowingly ignores her child's need for food or medical care to survive, the ensuing death may constitute murder.[242] If the parent is unaware the peril, but should be, the offense is manslaughter.[243]

§ 31.09   Manslaughter: Unlawful-Act (Misdemeanor-Manslaughter) Doctrine

An accidental homicide that occurs during the commission of an unlawful act not amounting to a felony (or, at least, not amounting to felony that would trigger the felony-murder rule) constitutes involuntary manslaughter.[244] This is the analogue to the felony-murder rule and, as such, is often termed the "misdemeanor-manslaughter" rule. Depending on the law in a particular jurisdiction, however, it may be more accurate to describe the offense as "unlawful-act manslaughter."

The scope of the doctrine varies widely by jurisdiction. As with the felony-murder rule, some courts limit its applicability to inherently dangerous misdemeanors.[245] Limited in this manner, the offense will often overlap involuntary (criminally negligent) manslaughter. Other courts distinguish between misdemeanors *mala in se* and *mala prohibita*, limiting the homicide rule to offenses of the

---

[238] E.g., *State v. Williams*, 484 P.2d 1167 (Wash. 1971) (conviction of parents in negligent death of infant child, on the basis of a manslaughter statute authorizing conviction for ordinary negligence); see *People v. Olson*, 448 N.W.2d 845 (Mich. Ct. App. 1989) (holding that a statute permitting conviction on the basis of ordinary negligence does not violate due process).

[239] See § 31.05[B], *supra*.

[240] See § 31.05[A][2], *supra*.

[241] *In re Dennis M.*, 450 P.2d 296, 298 (Cal. 1969).

[242] E.g., *People v. Burden*, 140 Cal.Rptr. 282 (Ct. App. 1977) (failure to feed child who died of starvation).

[243] E.g., *State v. Williams*, 484 P.2d 1167 (Wash. Ct. App. 1971) (parent was unaware of seriousness of child's illness; failure to secure medical care constituted manslaughter).

[244] See 4 Blackstone at *192-93; *Comber v. United States*, 584 A.2d at 49.

[245] E.g., *Comber v. United States*, 584 A.2d at 51 ("if the manner of its commission entails a reasonably foreseeable risk of appreciable physical injury").

former variety.[246] Some states, however, apply the doctrine to all misdemeanors. In such jurisdictions, a driver who fails to stop at a stop sign, in violation of the law, may be convicted of manslaughter if she non-negligently causes the death of a pedestrian.[247] Or, it is manslaughter if a person lightly pushes an intoxicated person without justification (a battery), and the victim loses her balance, falls, and strikes her head on the pavement and dies.[248]

The unlawful-act doctrine is not always limited to misdemeanor conduct. In jurisdictions that do not apply the felony-murder rule to some felonies (e.g., non-dangerous felonies), a killing that occurs during the commission of an excluded felony should constitute manslaughter. On the other end of the spectrum, there is precedent for the view that morally wrongful, but legal, conduct may serve as the predicate for a manslaughter conviction. For example, if a person attempts to commit suicide (an immoral act), she may be convicted of manslaughter if a bystander dies successfully preventing the suicide.[249]

§ 31.10   Criminal Homicide: Model Penal Code[250]

[A]—In General

A person is guilty of criminal homicide under the Model Code if she unjustifiably and inexcusably takes the life of another human being[251] purposely knowingly, recklessly, or negligently.[252] The death need not occur within a year and a day of the homicidal act, as at common law.[253] The Code recognizes three forms of criminal homicide: murder, manslaughter, and (unlike the common law) negligent homicide.

---

246 E.g., *Mills v. State*, 282 A.2d 147 (Md. Ct. Spec. App. 1971).

247 E.g., *State v. Hupf*, 101 A.2d 355 (Del. 1953).

248 See *State v. Pray*, 378 A.2d 1322, 1324 (Me. 1977) (rejecting the doctrine on such facts, because it "is not based on sound principles").

249 *People v. Chrisholtz*, 285 N.Y.S.2d 231 (N.Y. Sup. Ct. 1967); accord, *Commonwealth v. Mink*, 123 Mass. 422 (1877), but see *Commonwealth v. Catalina*, 556 N.E.2d 973 (Mass. 1990) (limiting the offense to deaths arising from batteries).

250 Richard Singer, *The Resurgence of Mens Rea: I -Provocation, Emotional Disturbance, and the Model Penal Code*, 27 B.C. L. Rev. 243 (1986); Franklin E. Zimring & Gordon Hawkins, *Murder, the Model Code, and the Multiple Agendas of Reform*, 19 Rutgers L.J. 773 (1988).

251 The Code applies the common law born-alive definition of "human being." Model Penal Code § 210.0(1). See § 31.01[B][1], *supra*. The Code does not define legal death. See § 31.01[B][2], *supra*.

252 Model Penal Code § 210.1(1).

253 Neither the Code provisions on criminal homicide nor causation (§ 2.03) mention the year-and-a-day rule. According to the Commentary, therefore, it does not apply. American Law Institute, Comment to § 210.1, at 9. The common law rule is discussed at § 31.01[C], *supra*.

[B]—Murder

A criminal homicide constitutes murder when the actor unjustifiably, inexcusably, and in the absence of a mitigating circumstance, kills another: (1) purposely or knowingly; or (2) recklessly, under circumstances manifesting extreme indifference to the value of human life.[254] Thus, using common law terminology, a homicide is murder (defenses aside) if the actor intentionally takes a life, or if she acts with extreme recklessness (i.e., depraved-heart murder).

There are no degrees of murder under the Code. However, the offense of murder is graded as a felony of the first degree,[255] which means that the offense carries a minimum sentence of from one to ten years' imprisonment, and a maximum sentence of death[256] or life imprisonment.[257]

The Model Code definition of murder abandons the common law element of malice aforethought. As such, the common law mental state of "intent to commit grievous bodily injury"—one form of malice—has no independent significance under the Code. Any case involving this state of mind would constitute extreme recklessness (i.e., murder) or a lesser form of unintentional homicide (i.e., reckless manslaughter or negligent homicide).[258]

The Code's approach to felony-murder is a bit more complicated. The drafters of the Code were opposed in principle to the rule, but they considered it politically unfeasible to abolish it. Therefore, the Model Code provides that extreme recklessness (and, thus, murder) is presumed if the homicide occurs while the actor is engaged in, or is an accomplice in, the commission, attempted commission, or flight from one of the dangerous felonies specified in the statute.[259]

For example, under this provision, if D unintentionally kills V during the commission of a robbery, the jury should be instructed that it may, but need not, infer extreme recklessness from commission of the crime.[260] If the felony was committed in a manner that does not manifest an extreme indifference to the value of human life, however, the felon should not be convicted of murder.

---

[254] Model Penal Code § 210.2(1)(a)-(b).

[255] Model Penal Code § 210.2(2).

[256] Although the Reporters of the Model Penal Code favored abolition of the death penalty, see American Law Institute, Comment to § 210.6, at 111-17, the American Law Institute took no position on the issue. In order to accommodate pro-death penalty legislatures, procedures for implementing the death penalty for murder were adopted. Model Penal Code § 210.6.

[257] Model Penal Code § 6.06(1).

[258] American Law Institute, Comment to § 210.2, at 28-29.

[259] Model Penal Code § 210.2(1)(b).

[260] See American Law Institute, Comment to § 210.2, at 30.

[C]—Manslaughter

[1]—In General

A person is guilty of manslaughter if she: (1) recklessly kills another; or (2) kills another person under circumstances that would ordinarily constitute murder, but which homicide is committed as the result of "extreme mental or emotional disturbance" for which there is a "reasonable explanation or excuse."[261] These forms of manslaughter are discussed below. The Code does not recognize any form of criminal homicide based on the unlawful-act (misdemeanor-manslaughter) rule.

Manslaughter is a felony of the second degree. It carries a minimum punishment of imprisonment from one to three years and a maximum sentence of 10 years.[262]

[2]—Reckless Homicide

A person who kills another recklessly is guilty of manslaughter. It should be observed, however, that a homicide committed recklessly may also constitute murder under the Model Code. The difference between the two offenses is that, in the case of murder, the recklessness must manifest extreme indifference to the value of human life. This feature is not included in the definition of manslaughter.

Reckless manslaughter is a necessarily-included lesser offense of reckless murder.[263] That is, in any case in which a defendant is prosecuted for reckless murder, she is entitled to a jury instruction regarding reckless manslaughter, and may be convicted of the lesser offense if the jury determines that her conscious risk-taking, although unjustifiable and substantial, was not extreme enough to merit treatment as murder.

In another sharp departure from the common law, liability for manslaughter under the Code cannot be founded on criminal negligence. The drafters of the Code believed that no person should be convicted of an offense as serious as manslaughter in the absence of subjective fault, e.g, *conscious* disregard of a substantial and unjustifiable risk.

[3]—Extreme Mental or Emotional Disturbance

[a]—In General

A person who would be guilty of murder because she purposely or knowingly took a human life, or because she killed a person recklessly under circumstances manifesting an extreme indifference to the value of human life, is guilty of the lesser offense of manslaughter if she killed the victim while suffering from an "extreme mental or emotional disturbance" (EMED) for which there is "reasonable explanation or excuse." The reasonableness of the explanation or excuse regarding the EMED is "determined from the viewpoint of a person in the actor's situation under the circumstances as he believes them to be."

The Model Penal Code provides that the defendant has the burden of producing evidence regarding this affirmative defense, after which the prosecution must

---

[261] Model Penal Code § 210.3(1)(a)-(b).

[262] Model Penal Code § 6.06(2).

[263] American Law Institute, Comment to § 210.3, at 53.

disprove the defense beyond a reasonable doubt.[264] However, most states that have adopted this provision of the Code require the defendant to prove the affirmative defense by a preponderance of the evidence.[265]

The concept of EMED is intended to incorporate two common law doctrines: (1) sudden heat of passion (but in expanded form); and (2) partial responsibility (diminished capacity). The latter form of manslaughter in discussed elsewhere in the Text.[266]

This manslaughter provision has two components, one subjective and the other objective. The subjective component is the EMED. This condition need not involve "a state of mind so far from the norm as to be characteristic of a mental illness."[267] Instead, it is enough that the defendant experienced intense feelings, sufficient to cause loss of self-control, at the time of the homicide.[268]

Second, there must be a "reasonable explanation or excuse" for the EMED, which is the objective portion of the defense. It should be noted, however, that this standard relates to the mental condition, and not to the homicide, i.e., the defense is not based on the ground that there is a reasonable explanation or excuse for the homicide, but rather that there is a reasonable explanation or excuse for the EMED that caused the actor to lose her self-control and kill.[269] In turn, this objective standard is partially subjective, in that the reasonableness of the explanation is considered from the viewpoint of a person "in the actor's situation under the circumstances as he believes them to be."

The Commentary states that the phrase "the actor's situation" is intended to incorporate the accused's personal handicaps and other relevant external characteristics; however, in order to preserve the normative message of the criminal law, the "idiosyncratic moral values" of the defendant must be excluded.[270] The drafters took no position regarding less extreme personal characteristics, e.g., abnormal sensitivity to verbal attacks or "an abnormally fearful temperament." These factors are left to judicial interpretation.[271]

Although the Commentary is not specific in this regard, at least one jurisdiction has held that, upon a finding of EMED, the defendant is entitled to a jury instruction regarding manslaughter, i.e., the objective element of the defendant should always be left to the trier of fact to consider.[272]

---

[264] Model Penal Code § 1.12(2).

[265] 1 Robinson at 483; American Law Institute, Comment to § 210.3, at 63.

[266] See § 26.03[B][2], *supra.*

[267] *State v. Ott*, 686 P.2d 1001, 1011 (Or. 1984) (interpreting state statute based on Model Code).

[268] *Id.*; *State v. Dumlao*, 715 P.2d 822, 828 (Haw. 1986).

[269] *People v. Casassa*, 404 N.E.2d 1310, 1316 n.2 (N.Y. 1980).

[270] For example, if *V* touched *D* on the shoulder and made a homosexual proposition, *D* could not claim EMED manslaughter on the ground that her rage was brought on by her "moral" view that gay people who make sexual advances deserve to be killed.

[271] American Law Institute, Comment to § 210.3, at 62-63.

[272] *People v. Casassa*, 404 N.E.2d at 1317.

[b]—Comparison of Model Code to Common Law "Heat-of-Passion"

The EMED manslaughter provision is much broader than the common law provocation defense. First, a specific provocative act is not required to trigger the EMED defense.[273] All that must be proven is that the homicide occurred as the result of an EMED for which there is a reasonable explanation of excuse. For example, if a psychiatrist testifies that *D* killed *V*, his brother, under the influence of EMED, brought on by a combination of factors, including "child custody problems, the inability to maintain a recently purchased home and an overwhelming fear of his brother,"[274] a jury instruction on manslaughter is warranted, although *V* did nothing to provoke the incident.[275]

Second, even if there is a provocation, it need not involve "an injury, affront, or other provocative act perpetrated upon [the defendant] by the decedent."[276] Therefore, the person may successfully claim the defense if she simply believes, although incorrectly, that the decedent was responsible for the affront, or if there was a provocation and the defendant "strikes out in a blinding rage and kills an innocent bystander."[277]

Third, even if the decedent provoked the incident, it need not fall within any fixed category of provocations; and, contrary to the common law, words alone can warrant a manslaughter instruction. For example, if *D* kills *V* as a result of EMED, a jury instruction on manslaughter is warranted (although, of course, a *verdict* of manslaughter is not required) if the basis for the EMED was that: (1) *V* derided *D* because he was unable to have an erection when he attempted to have intercourse with her;[278] (2) *V* took *D*'s reserved parking space in an apartment building;[279] or (3) in a restaurant, *V* demanded money owed to him by *D* from an earlier drug transaction, a verbal argument ensued, and *V* placed his hand on *D*'s plate.[280]

Fourth, there is no rigid cooling-off rule. The suddenness requirement of the common law—the homicide must follow almost immediately the provocation—is absent here.[281]

---

[273] *State v. Elliott*, 411 A.2d 3, 7 (Conn. 1979).

[274] *Id.* at 5.

[275] See also *People v. Tabarez*, 497 N.Y.S.2d 80 (Sup. Ct. App. Div. 1985), *aff'd*, 503 N.E.2d 1369 (1986) (*D* shot at *V* while experiencing an EMED brought on by depression, prolonged unemployment, a very fragile personality, and an I.Q. of 66).

[276] American Law Institute, Comment to § 210.3, at 61.

[277] *Id.*

[278] *People v. Moye*, 489 N.E.2d 736 (N.Y. 1985) (murder conviction reversed on ground that evidence was sufficient to warrant manslaughter instruction).

[279] *State v. Raguseo*, 622 A.2d 519 (Conn. 1993) (EMED instruction given; *D* was convicted of murder; conviction upheld on sufficiency-of-evidence grounds).

[280] *People v. Walker*, 473 N.Y.S.2d 460 (Sup. Ct. App. Div.), *aff'd in memorandum*, 475 N.E.2d 445 (N.Y. 1984) (murder conviction affirmed; no jury instruction on EMED given; this ruling was upheld on ground that there was no evidence that *D* suffered from EMED; had he experienced EMED, instruction would presumably have been required).

[281] *State v. Elliott*, 411 A.2d at 7.

[D]—Negligent Homicide

A criminally negligent homicide—involuntary manslaughter at common law—constitutes the lesser offense of negligent homicide under the Code.[282] The offense is graded as a felony of the third degree, which carries a minimum sentence of one to two years' incarceration, and a maximum sentence of five years.[283]

---

[282] Model Penal Code § 210.4.

[283] Model Penal Code § 6.06(3).

CHAPTER 32

THEFT

§ 32.01 Subject Matter Overview[1]

This chapter considers three theft[2] offenses: larceny, embezzlement, and false pretenses. As is explained below, larceny is a common law felony; the other offenses find their origins in English misdemeanor statutes.

In very early English history, only *forcible* appropriation of property, i.e., robbery, was punished.[3] By the middle ages, however, jurists expanded the scope of the criminal law to prohibit nonviolent, albeit nonconsensual, dispossessions of personal property, i.e., larceny.

The law of larceny did not develop simply or smoothly. Various economic conditions, originating as early as the fifteenth century, placed pressure on the English courts to expand the scope of theft law in order to deter new forms of dishonest conduct. To a significant extent the courts cooperated with the economic interests of the time. Rather than create new theft offenses, however, the judges manipulated the elements of larceny to encompass the new conduct. The outcome was a law riddled with technicalities and intricacies.

At the same time, judicial displeasure with capital punishment, the penalty for all but the most petty larcenies, deterred English courts from broadening the law to the extent that economic conditions might have justified. Consequently, various gaps in the law of larceny developed. The "cure" for the lacunae was the enactment of statutory "gap-fillers," most importantly the misdemeanor offenses of false pretenses and embezzlement.

In recent years, many legislature have consolidated the three crimes discussed in this chapter into a single offense, often denominated, simply, as "theft." These efforts at consolidation are briefly noted later.[4] Notwithstanding the reform

---

[1] See generally Jerome Hall, Theft, Law and Society (2d ed. 1952); Kathleen F. Brickey, *The Jurisprudence of Larceny: An Historical Inquiry and Interest Analysis*, 33 Vand. L. Rev. 1101 (1980); George P. Fletcher, *The Metamorphosis of Larceny*, 89 Harv. L. Rev. 469 (1976); Lloyd L. Weinreb, *Manifest Criminality, Criminal Intent, and the "Metamorphosis of Larceny"*, 90 Yale L.J. 294 (1980).

[2] The word "theft" is used in this chapter to signify the involuntary and unlawful transfer of property. Unless otherwise noted, the term is not used to describe any particular common law or statutory offense.

[3] Robbery is larceny from the person by use or threatened use of force. *People v. Butler*, 421 P.2d 703, 706 (Cal. 1967).

[4] See § 32.11, *infra*.

movement, lawyers cannot confidently ignore the centuries of theft law that preceded consolidation. "History has its own logic."[5] Many of the substantive doctrines discussed below remain highly relevant today.

§ 32.02   Larceny: General Principles

[A]—Definition

Common law larceny is the trespassory taking and carrying away of the personal property of another with the intent to permanently deprive the possessor of the property.[6]

It is useful to break this definition down into its components and to become familiar with the different ways that each element is described by judges and commentators. The *actus reus* of larceny is the "trespassory taking and carrying away of the personal proprty of another." It should be observed that larceny is a "conduct," rather than a "result," crime. That is, it prohibits the conduct of taking and carrying away personal property; the offense is complete when those acts occur. It is not necessary that the property taken be damaged, destroyed or converted to the personal use of the wrongful taker. Instead, if the offender has the requisite *mens rea*, it is assumed that injury to the property or to the victim's interest in it will occur (if it has not already occurred). In this sense, larceny may be viewed as an inchoate offense.

The most complicated legal aspect of the *actus reus* of larceny is the requirement that there be a "trespassory taking." More specifically, the trespassory taking involves the nonconsensual taking *of possession* of the property in question.[7] A person who by trespass obtains title—ownership—to the property of another is guilty, if anything, of obtaining property by false pretenses, a different offense. The element of "taking" is frequently described in the case law as the "caption" of the property.

The element of "carrying away" is often described as the "asportation" of the property. Legal issues regarding this element rarely arise.

Larceny prohibits only the trespassory caption and asportation of another person's *personal* property. Real property is not the subject of larceny law. Moreover, only tangible forms of personal property are encompassed in the offense.

Larceny is a specific-intent crime. The actor who takes and carries away the personal property of another must do so with the specific intent to deprive the other of the property on a permanent basis. Sometimes this *mens rea* is described in shorthand, simply, as "the intent to steal," "felonious intent," or by the Latin words,

---

[5] American Law Institute, Comment to § 223.1, at 130.

[6] See *Lee v. State*, 474 A.2d 537, 539 (Md. Ct. Spec. App. 1984); *United States v. Waronek*, 582 F.2d 1158, 1161 (7th Cir. 1978); 4 Blackstone at *230 ("the felonious taking, and carrying away, of the personal goods of another").

[7] See *Bell v. United States*, 462 U.S. 356, 358 (1983) (noting that the original purpose of larceny law was to prevent breaches of the peace, and the concern of the courts was that violence was more apt to occur when property was taken from the possession of another).

"animus furandi." The wrongdoer must possess this intent at the time of the trespassory caption and asportation.

[B]—Grading of the Offense

The common law distinguished between grand and petit (now "petty") larceny. Grand larceny involved the stealing of goods above the value[8] of twelvepence.[9] This amount, now worth well less than ten American cents, equaled the value of a sheep.[10]

Although grand and petty larceny were felonies at common law, the death penalty applied only to grand larceny. In this country, grand larceny is a felony, and petty larceny (often involving property worth less than five hundred dollars) is a misdemeanor.[11]

§ 32.03   Larceny: Trespass

The act of taking and carrying away the personal property of another is not, in itself, an offense. The beginning point is that "[t]here can be no larceny without a trespass, and there can be no trespass unless the property was in the possession of the one from whom it is charged to have been stolen."[12]

The term "trespass" as used in this context is not related to the tort or crime of trespass to land. Rather, the origin of the term is the ancient writ of *trespass be bonis*

---

[8] The value of property for the purpose of determining whether the offense is "grand" or "petty" in nature is ordinarily based on the stolen item's current market value, or "the price at which the minds of a willing buyer and a willing seller would meet." *United States v. DiGilio,* 538 F.2d 972, 979 (3rd Cir. 1976). Although case law on the point is scant, apparently the thief's belief regarding the value of the property is irrelevant at common law. American Law Institute, Comment to § 223.1, at 145-46. That is, a thief is guilty of grand larceny, even if he reasonably believes that he is stealing a nearly worthless item; he is guilty of petty larceny if he takes cheap property, believing it is valuable.

The Model Penal Code departs from the common law in this regard. Take the case in which *D* steals an original Picasso painting, believing that he is taking a cheap duplicate. Under § 223.1(2), the value of property is determinined on the basis of the "highest value, by any reasonable standard, of the property . . . the actor stole or attempted to steal." Because this language is silent regarding the element of culpability, the standard of recklessness is assumed. Model Penal Code § 2.02(3). Therefore, *D* may be convicted of grand larceny if he recklessly believed that the painting was a cheap copy. However, if he was only negligent in this belief, his mistake of fact would negate the valuation element of the offense, and he could not be convicted of grand larceny. Model Penal Code § 2.04(1). He could be convicted, however, of petty larceny. Model Penal Code § 2.04(2). For fuller discussion of this situation, see American Law Institute, Comment of § 223.1, at 144–47.

[9] 4 Blackstone at *229.

[10] Perkins & Boyce at 290.

[11] The Model Penal Code applies a three-level classification of theft. The crime is a felony if the value of the property exceeds $500 or is a specified type of property (e.g., a firearm or automobile). A less serious theft is a misdemeanor or petty misdemeanor. Model Penal Code §§ 223.1(2)(a)-(b).

[12] *People v. Hoban,* 88 N.E. 806, 807 (Ill. 1909).

asportatis (trespass for goods carried away), which was the basis for the tort of trespass to chattel. In the context of larceny, a "trespass" occurs if one takes possession of the victim's personal property—he dispossesses the other of the property—without consent, or in the absence of a justification for the nonconsensual dispossession.[13]

Originally, the concept of trespass was limited to acts of stealth. The doctrine of *caveat emptor* ("let the buyer beware") prevailed: one who obtained possession of another person's property by fraud was viewed as a clever person, rather than as a wrongdoer deserving of the death penalty. Gradually this *laissez faire* attitude changed. In 1757, the Parliament enacted the misdemeanor offense of "obtaining property by false pretenses."[14] This offense, however, prohibited the use of deception to obtain *title* to another's property; mere dispossession of personal property by fraud was not covered by the statute.

Fraud became a part of larceny law in 1779 with *Pear's Case.*[15] In *Pear*, *D* rented *V*'s horse for a day with the fraudulent intent to take it and sell it immediately, which he did. Because stealth was not involved, the delivery of the horse to *D* by *V* was outwardly consensual. Nonetheless, a majority of judges in the case concluded that *D* was guilty of larceny or, as it is often identified by statute, "larceny by trick."

The reasoning of *Pear* is in some doubt.[16] Nonetheless, it is clear that obtaining possession of property by fraud constitutes a trespassory taking that may result in conviction for larceny.

§ 32.04 Larceny: Taking (Caption)

[A]—The Significance of "Possession"

Larceny involves the trespassory taking of personal property from the *possession* of another; ownership is not the key.[17]

"Possession" is a term of art in larceny law. As a result of competing pressures on the common law courts—the need to broaden the scope of larceny law to meet the economic needs of the time, and the desire of judges to avoid undue use of the death penalty[18]—various legal fictions developed in the law of possession.

In order to understand larceny law, therefore, one must distinguish between the doctrines of "possession" and "custody." It is also important to focus on the

---

[13] E.g., no trespass occurs if a law enforcement officer takes property pursuant to a court order.

[14] See § 32.10, *infra.*

[15] *King v. Pear*, 1 Leach 212, 168 Eng. Rep. 208 (1779).

[16] See § 32.04[B][5], *infra.*

[17] 2 Frederick Pollock & Frederic William Maitland, History of English Law 498 (2d ed. 1898) ("[T]he crime involves a violation of possession; it is an offence against a possessor and therefore can never be committed by a possessor."); *People v. Sheldon*, 527 N.W.2d 76, 77-78 (Mich. Ct. App. 1995).

[18] See § 32.01, *supra.*

relationship of the parties involved in the transfer of property, e.g., is there a "master-servant" (employer-employee) or bailor-bailee relationship.

[B]—"Custody" versus "Possession"

[1]—In General

A person has *possession* of property when he has sufficient control over it to use it in a reasonably unrestricted manner. Possession can be actual or constructive. It is *actual* if the person is in physical control of it; it is *constructive* if he is not in physical control of it but nobody else has actual possession of it, either because the property was lost or mislaid or because another person has mere "custody" of it (as that term is defined immediately below). *All non-abandoned property is in the actual or constructive possession of some party at all times.*

A person has mere "custody" of property if he has physical control over it, but his right to use it is substantially restricted by the person in constructive possession of the property. Unfortunately, the terms "possession" and "custody" largely represent legal conclusions regarding the comparative rights of the parties; there is no bright-line point at which the degree of control over property shifts from custody to possession.

Whenever a court must ascertain whether larceny has occurred, it must determine who initially had possession of the property that allegedly was stolen, and then it must decide whether, when, and to whom "possession" (as distinguished from "custody") was transferred. If the person charged with larceny *did* obtain possession from another, the issue will be whether such possession occurred trespassorily or lawfully.

As a starting point, a person in physical control of property ordinarily is in *possession* of it. However, a person in physical control of property has mere *custody* of the property if: (1) he has temporary and extremely limited authorization to use the property; (2) he received the property from his employer for use in the employment relation; (3) he is a bailee of goods enclosed in a container; or (4) he obtained the property by fraud.

[2]—Temporary and Limited Use of Property

A person with temporary and extremely limited authority to use a piece of property has mere custody of it.[19] Thus, D, a dinner guest, has only custody of the cutlery used at V's dining room table.[20] Similarly, if V, a jewelry merchant, hands a ring to D, a customer, for inspection, D has custody of the item; V retains constructive possession.[21]

The line between custody and possession can be fuzzy. A critical factor, however, is whether D uses the property in V's presence. Thus, if D test-drives an automobile, D's control over it largely depends on whether V, the car dealer, is in the vehicle

---

[19] *United States v. Mafnas*, 701 F.2d 83, 84 (9th Cir. 1983).

[20] 1 Hale at *506.

[21] *Chisser's Case*, 83 Eng. Rep. 142 (1678).

during the drive. If he is, *D* has *custody* of the car. If he is allowed to drive the car alone, *possession* of the car shifts from *V* to *D* when *D* leaves the lot.

Why does it matter whether *D* has "custody" or "possession"? Reconsider the test-drive hypothetical. Suppose that *D* test-drives the car in *V*'s presence (i.e., *D* has custody). When they return to the lot, *V* gets out of the car, but *D* speeds away in the vehicle. At the instant of this act, *D* has dispossessed *V* of the car; *D* no longer has mere custody of the automobile, because he is using the property in a manner far in excess of his limited right to test-drive it in *V*'s presence. Consequently, *D*'s act would represent a "taking" of the property, i.e., he has "taken possession" of the vehicle from *V*. As the taking was nonconsensual, it was "trespassory." Therefore, if *D* intended to steal the car when he drove away, *D* would be guilty of larceny.

On the other hand, suppose that *D* was permitted to test-drive the car alone. As he is driving the car, *D* decides he likes it so much that he is not going to return it, so he drives it out of town. In this case, there is *no* common law larceny. Here, *D* took possession of the car from *V* when he left the lot by himself for the test-drive. This taking was nontrespassory, because it was consensual. When he later decided to steal the car and drove it away, no trespassory taking occurred because he already had (lawful) possession of the property. Although not guilty of larceny, *D* could be guilty of the statutory offense of embezzlement, which generally prohibits the misappropriation of property by one who obtains possession of it in a nontrespassory manner. [22]

[3]—Employers and Employees

[a]—Employer to Employee

By necessity employers must frequently furnish their personal property to employees in furtherance of the employment relation. In such circumstances, the employer consensually transfers the property to his employee. This does not fit the paradigm of larceny, i.e., the use of stealth to obtain another's property.

In order to make sure that dishonest employees could be convicted of larceny of property furnished to them by their employers, the common law adopted the fiction that when a master furnishes property to his servant for use by the servant in the master-servant relationship, the master retains *constructive possession* of the property, and the servant has mere *custody* of it. [23]

For example, if *V*, the owner of a pizza-delivery franchise, furnishes *D*, his servant, with a car in order to deliver pizzas, *D* has mere custody of the automobile. [24] If *D* does not return with the car, he violates *V*'s possessory right to the property and, consequently, trespassorily takes possession of it. If the taking was felonious, i.e., with the intent to steal the car, *D* is guilty of larceny.

---

[22] See § 32.09, *infra.*

[23] 2 East, Pleas of the Crown 564-65 (1803); *United States v. Mafnas,* 701 F.2d at 84.

[24] Notice that if the *D-V* relationship were not that of employee-employer but that of customer-merchant as discussed in § 32.04[B][2], *supra, D* would have *possession* of the automobile when he drives away with it.

[b]—Third Person to the Employee for the Employer

The rule described in subsection [a] applies when an employer furnishes personal property to his employee. The premise that the employee has limited control over the property because of the employment relation does not apply when an employee receives property from a person who has no special authority over him, but who wants the property delivered to the employee's boss. Ordinarily, therefore, a servant who obtains property from a third person for delivery to the servant's master takes lawful *possession* upon delivery. Therefore, in the absence of some other legal fiction, the servant cannot be convicted of larceny of the property if he carries it away.

Notice how this situation plays out in a banking situation. In the famous *Bazeley* case,[25] *D*, a teller of Bank *X*, apparently took customer *V*'s deposit and immediately pocketed it. *D* was prosecuted for larceny. Essentially, this is what occurred: *V* had possession of the money when he entered the bank; *D* took actual possession of the property from *V* when it was delivered to him for the purpose of transferring it to *D*'s employer, *X*;[26] as this taking was consensual, it was not trespassory; therefore, no larceny occurred.[27] Instead, shortly after *Bazeley* was decided, the Parliament enacted an embezzlement statute encompassing *D*'s conduct.[28]

A slight change in the facts in *Bazeley*, however, would have changed the outcome. For example, assume that *D*, having no dishonest intention, places *V*'s deposit in *X*'s bank drawer, as is proper. At the end of the day, however, *D* decides to abscond with the cash, which he does. Now, *D* is guilty of larceny.[29] In these circumstances, possession of the money moved nontrespassorily from *V* to *D* to *X* (when it was placed in the drawer for the day). Then, when *D* removed the money from the drawer at the end of the day, possession shifted from *X* to *D*. The latter act, however, constituted a trespassory taking; the victim of the larceny, however, was Bank *X*, rather than *V*.

[4]—Bailors and Bailees

The fifteenth century marked a period of economic chaos in England as that country was transformed from a feudal, agricultural society into one in which manufacturing sprung up in every town, and international commercial ties developed.[30] As a result of these changes, members of the European mercantile class were forced to entrust their property to carriers who would transport their goods long distances. Unfortunately for the merchants, with the new industry came a new form of criminal conduct, committed by many carriers. Their *modus operandi* was to take containers, wrongfully open them, remove some or all of the contents so that they could be sold for personal profit, close the containers, and then deliver them.

---

[25] *King v. Bazeley*, 2 Leach 835, 168 Eng. Rep. 517 (1799).

[26] See 1 Hale at *667.

[27] See also *Commonwealth v. Ryan*, 30 N.E. 364 (Mass. 1892).

[28] See § 32.09[A], *infra*.

[29] *Nolan v. State*, 131 A.2d 851 (Md. 1957).

[30] Hall, Note 1, *supra*, at 21.

In terms of larceny law, this presented a problem. The merchant consensually entrusted the goods to the carrier, so there appeared to be a lawful transfer of possession. Beginning with the *Carrier's Case*,[31] therefore, the King's Council of the Star Chamber developed a new legal fiction, the "breaking bulk" doctrine, that expanded larceny law.

The precise reasoning of *Carrier's Case* is a matter of some dispute. The most common interpretation of the case, however, is that when a person is entrusted with a container for delivery in unopened condition, the bailee receives possession of the container but mere custody of its contents. When the bailee wrongfully opens the container and removes the contents, i.e., when he "breaks bulk," a trespassory taking of possession of the contents results.[32]

The significance of the breaking-bulk doctrine is that the timing and means used by the carrier to steal goods determines whether larceny has occurred. For example, suppose that *C*, a carrier, receives property belonging to the bailor, *B*, for delivery to *A*, but he improperly sells the unopened container to *X* (i.e., he does not break bulk). In this case, there is no larceny,[33] because *C* had lawful possession of the container, and he never took possession of the contents. On the other hand, if *C* opens the container prior to delivery and sells the contents to *X*, *C* has committed larceny. Similarly, if *C* delivers the container whole to *A*, and then takes it from *A*, larceny has occurred, although the victim is *A*, who was dispossessed, rather than *B*.[34]

[5]—Fraud

Pear's Case[35] involves another legal fiction regarding the nature of possession of property. In *Pear*, *D* rented a horse from *V* with the intent to sell it, which he did immediately. Eleven of twelve judges to whom the case was referred concluded that *D*'s fraudulent conduct constituted a trespass and that, therefore, the taking constituted larceny (or "larceny by trick").

The apparent reasoning of the judges was that, in light of *D*'s fraud, "the parting with the property had not changed the nature of the possession, but that it remained unaltered in the prosecutor [*V*] at the time of the conversion." In other words, because of *D*'s fraud, constructive possession of the horse remained with *V*; *D* received only custody of the steed. When he sold the horse in violation of the arrangement, therefore, *D* trespassorily took possession of the animal.[36]

---

[31] *Anon. v. The Sheriff of London (The Carrier's Case)*, Year Book 13 Edw. IV pl. 5 (1473), *reprinted in* 64 Selden Society 30 (1945). The case is discussed in great detail in Hall, Note 1, *supra*, at 3-33.

[32] Another interpretation of the case is that the bailee receives possession of *everything*, but that when he opens the container possession returns to the bailor, so that the subsequent act of taking the contents out of the container is a trespassory taking.

[33] Edmond Coke, Third Institute *107 (1644).

[34] 4 Blackstone at *230.

[35] *King v. Pear*, 1 Leach 212, 168 Eng. Rep. 208 (1779).

[36] There is another interpretation of this case. Perkins and Boyce assert that the proper reading of this case is, or should be, that *D* took possession of the horse when he rented it

Pear creates a substantial hurdle for a prosecutor in a common law jurisdiction, who must charge a defendant with the proper offense. Notice the prosecutor's quandary: if *D* receives property from *V*, based on a false promise to return it, he receives only custody of the property, and is guilty of larceny if he appropriates it. On the other hand, if *D* has an honest intent when he receives the property (and, thus, no fraud is involved), *D* receives *possession* of the property, and any subsequent misappropriation constitutes embezzlement or no offense.

In these two hypotheticals, the objective, external circumstances are the same. The difference—which will determine whether the offense is larceny or embezzlement (if anything)—is a function of when *D* formed the felonious intent. Even if we put aside the fact that *D*'s culpability is the same in either case [37] —so it ought not to matter what label is attached to the crime—the critical fact in the case is one likely to be known only by the defendant. Yet, an error by the prosecutor in charging the defendant with the wrong offense could result in acquittal or reversal of the conviction of an obviously dishonest person. [38]

§ 32.05 Larceny: Carrying Away (Asportation)

A person is not guilty of larceny unless he carries away the personal property that he took trespassorily from another. However, virtually any movement of the property—even a "hair's breadth" [39] —away from the point of caption is sufficient. [40] Thus, larceny, rather than attempted larceny, occurs if a shoplifter is caught with the merchant's property inside the premises, [41] or if a person pulls an earring from the victim's ear, and moves it only a few inches before it gets snagged in her hair. [42]

The asportation requirement is not satisfied, however, unless the movement of the property constitutes a "carrying away" motion. For example, if *D* moves a box from the floor to a table in order to open it and steal the contents, this change of

---

with the fraudulent intent; since this taking was deceitful, it was trespassory. Perkins & Boyce at 305. If Professors Perkins and Boyce are right, *D* was guilty of larceny the moment he rode away, although the authors concede that it would have been difficult to prove *D*'s felonious intent at that time. According to the reading of the case expressed in the text, however, larceny did not occur until *D* acted in violation of the rental agreement.

If Perkins and Boyce are right, there are other interesting implications. First, if *D* abandoned his felonious intent after renting the horse (but before he sold it) he would still be guilty of larceny (although it would be much harder to prove the felonious intent). Second, if *D* loaned the horse for one day to *X* before selling it, *X* would be guilty of receiving stolen property, assuming he knew of *D*'s intentions. Under the holding of the case described in the text, neither of these results would follow.

[37] However, at common law, embezzlement was a misdemeanor; larceny was a capital felony.

[38] This problem is considered in greater detail in § 32.11, *infra*.

[39] Hall, Note 1, *supra*, at 259.

[40] American Law Institute, Comment to § 223.2, at 164.

[41] *People v. Olivo*, 420 N.E.2d 40, 44 (N.Y. 1981).

[42] *Rex v. Lapier*, 1 Leach 320, 168 Eng. Rep. 763 (1784); see *Harrison v. People*, 50 N.Y. 518 (1872) (pickpocket moved a wallet in victim's pocket a few inches before he was caught).

position of the property does not meet the asportation requirement; instead, it is an act in furtherance of the process of taking possession of the contents of the container. Therefore, if *D* were arrested at this moment, he would be guilty of *attempted* larceny.[43]

In view of the nearly trivial nature of the "carrying away" requirement, one scholar has observed that "it is frequently difficult to see where taking ends and asportation begins."[44] As a consequence, the Model Penal Code does not require proof of asportation.[45] This feature of the Code has been followed by most states that have revised their theft laws.[46]

§ 32.06 Larceny: Personal Property of Another

[A]—Personal Property

[1]—Land and Attachments Thereto

The common law of larceny does not protect land.[47] By its nature, land is immovable; a wrongdoer cannot carry it away and thereafter damage, destroy or lose it. The underlying purpose of larceny law, therefore, does not apply to real estate. Moreover, land can only be "taken" in the sense that a person may come onto it and evict the rightful possessor, or obtain title to unoccupied land by adverse possession. These injuries can be righted adequately by civil action.

Items attached to the land, e.g., trees, crops, and inanimate objects affixed in the earth[48] also fall outside the scope of the offense. Once they are severed from the land, however, they become personal property and subject to larceny law.

Certain fictions were developed by the courts to deal with the taking and carrying away of trees and crops recently severed from the land. For example, suppose that *D* wrongfully enters *V*'s land and chops down a tree. Once the tree is severed from the land its legal nature changes from real to personal property. Because *D* is the first person to control the tree/timber after it has become personal property, he is in possession of it. Because *V* never had possession of the severed tree *as personal property*, *D* did not take possession of it trespassorily (or otherwise) from *V*. Even though the severed tree lies on *V*'s land, *D* retains constructive possession of it as long as he remains near it. If he takes the tree from *V*'s land at this time, therefore, he has committed no larceny, although he is liable in tort for trespass to the land.

On the other hand, suppose that *D* leaves the land with the intention of returning the next day to retrieve the timber. As soon as he leaves, *D* loses constructive

---

[43] See *Cherry's Case*, 168 Eng. Rep. 221 (1781) (*D* picked up a package containing cloth in order to remove the cloth; held: no larceny).

[44] Hall, Note 1, *supra*, at 259.

[45] E.g., Model Penal Code § 223.2(1) (providing that theft occurs if a person "unlawfully takes" another's property).

[46] American Law Institute, Comment to § 223.2, at 165.

[47] 4 Blackstone at *232.

[48] E.g., *Parker v. State*, 352 So.2d 1386 (Ala. Crim. App. 1977) (wires attached to poles embedded in the earth are real property).

possession of the timber; because it sits on *V*'s land in *D*'s absence, possession of the personal property immediately shifts to *V*. When *D* enters the land the next day, therefore, and carries away the timber with the intent of depriving *V* of it permanently, *D* is guilty of larceny. [49]

The Model Penal Code and many modern statutes dispense with these rules. The Model Code's theft laws cover all property ("anything of value" [50]), including "immovable" property, such as real estate, and "movable" property, "including things growing on, or found in land." [51]

[2]—Animals

At common law, animals in the state of nature or *ferae naturae* (e.g., wild deer, wild birds, fish in an open river) were not "property" within the meaning of larceny law. However, once an animal was confined by a person on his land or killed, it became his personal property, subject to the law's protection. [52]

Domesticated animals of a "base nature" also fell outside the scope of the common law definition of larceny. Horses and cattle were subject to larceny laws; dogs were "base." [53] Such distinctions were primarily based on economic factors, but today all domesticated animals and birds are protected by theft statutes.

[3]—Stolen Property and Contraband

It is larceny for a person to take and carry away the property of another, even if the "victim" also had no right to possess the property in question. Thus, it is larceny to steal stolen property from a thief, or to steal contraband, e.g., illegal narcotics, that no person has a lawful right to possess. [54]

It would be easy to rationalize a contrary result. It might plausibly be argued that thieves, persons who are not bona-fide purchasers of stolen goods, and possessors of contraband, should be deemed to have no possessory interest in wrongfully secured property. Instead, however, theft laws are applicable in order to deter the free-for-all that might ensue if criminals could steal from each other with impunity. [55]

---

[49] See 2 East, Pleas of the Crown 587 (1803).

[50] Model Penal Code § 223.0(6).

[51] Model Penal Code § 223.0(4). See American Law Institute, Comment to § 223.2, at 166-68.

[52] 4 Blackstone at *235.

[53] See 2 East, Note 49, *supra*, at 614.

[54] See *United States v. Benson*, 548 F.2d 42, 44 (2d Cir. 1977) (false pretenses prosecution involving the taking of stolen property); *People v. Otis*, 139 N.E. 562, 562-63 (N.Y. 1923) (involving theft of bootleg liquor during Prohibition); see also Model Penal Code § 223.0(7) (defining property "of another" broadly to include persons who would be precluded from civil recovery of the property because it was used in an unlawful transaction or was contraband).

[55] See *Commonwealth v. Crow*, 154 A. 283, 286 (Pa 1931) ("[t]o establish the rule that the owner of liquor, illegally held, had no property right therein, would lead to a condition of terror and bloodshed among rival bootleggers far worse than we have known"). Perhaps, however, such a "free-for-all" is a cost that criminals should be required to pay if they choose to violate the law. This cost would be considered by a rational criminal in determining the value of committing a property crime.

[4]—Intangible Personal Property

Because common law larceny involves the wrongful taking and carrying away of personal property, property without a corporeal existence, i.e., intangible property, is excluded from its coverage.[56] For example, labor or services are not the subject of traditional theft laws. Thus, if a college student wrongfully takes a computer print-out that lists the computer-access account numbers of other students, and then uses the numbers to obtain computer services to which he is not entitled, he is not guilty of theft of the computer services, although he is technically guilty of larceny of the sheet of paper on which the account numbers were found.[57]

Today the vast majority of larceny statutes follow the Model Penal Code's lead and prohibit the unlawful transfer of intangible personal property rights.[58]

[B]—Of Another

It is not common law larceny, of course, to take and carry away one's own personal property. However, because larceny involves the trespassory taking of *possession* of another person's property, a person may be convicted of larceny of property he owns.

For example, if *D*, landlord of an apartment building and owner of the furnishings therein, enters an apartment unit leased to *V*, and takes and carries away the furniture, in violation of the lease agreement, *D* has taken the personal property "of another" for purposes of larceny law.[59]

The Model Penal Code defines "property of another" broadly to include "property in which any person other than the actor has an interest."[60] This definition includes a possessory or ownership interest. It is also broad enough to make it a crime for a partner to steal partnership funds in which he shares an interest,[61] contrary to the common law rule.[62]

§ 32.07   Larceny: Intent to Steal (*Animus Furandi*)

[A]—Nature of the Felonious Intent

[1]—In General

Courts commonly state that a person is not guilty of larceny unless he takes and carries away the personal property of another with the "specific intent to steal" the

---

[56] 4 Blackstone at *234.

[57] See *Lund v. Commonwealth*, 232 S.E.2d 745 (Va. 1977); *People v. Tansey*, 593 N.Y.S.2d 426 (N.Y. Sup. Ct. 1992) (in prosecution for possession of stolen goods, *D* is not guilty if the "stolen" property is an intangible telephone authorization code).

[58] Model Penal Code § 223.2(2).

[59] See 4 Blackstone at *231 (it is larceny if *D* steals his own goods from a pawnbroker or from "any one to whom he hath delivered and entrusted them.").

[60] Model Penal Code § 223.0(7).

[61] American Law Institute, Comment to § 223.2, at 169.

[62] E.g., *People v. Zinke*, 555 N.E.2d 263 (N.Y. 1990).

property. In this context, "intent to steal" is a shorthand way of describing the felonious intent of larceny, which is the intent to deprive another person permanently of the property.[63] Thus, *D* is guilty of larceny if he trespassorily drives away in *V*'s automobile, with the intent of keeping the car. However, he is not guilty of larceny (although he would be guilty of a statutory offense of "joyriding"), if he intends to keep the vehicle temporarily and then return it.[64]

It should be observed that the felonious intent of larceny is *animus furandi* (intent to deprive), not *lucri causa* (for the sake of gain). That is, it is neither necessary nor sufficient that the thief intended to obtain personal benefit from the taking.[65] For example, if *D* takes and carries away *V*'s valuable vase with the intention of destroying it, he has committed larceny although he may gain nothing (except some nonpecuniary pleasure) from the act. On the other hand, if *D* takes *V*'s framed college diploma off the wall and carries it away with the purpose of using it for a day to fraudulently obtain money from another, *D* is not guilty of larceny of the diploma although he has taken it for personal gain.

[2]—Recklessly Depriving Another of Property Permanently

Not infrequently, a court will uphold a conviction for larceny under circumstances in which it is hard to draw the conclusion that the actor had the intent to steal the property. Instead, it is more accurate to infer that the actor knew that his conduct would create a substantial risk of permanent loss, i.e., that the actor was guilty of recklessly exposing the property to permanent loss.[66] Although this is a different *mens rea* than "intent to steal," many courts treat these two states of mind alike or, at least, infer the felonious intent from the actor's recklessness.[67]

For example, *D1* is guilty of the larceny of a car if he trespassorily takes *V*'s vehicle in City X, with the intention of driving it to City Y, two hundred miles away, and abandoning it there.[68] Although *D1* may hope that the car will be returned to *V*, there is a very high likelihood that the abandoned car will be re-stolen or its component parts taken, before it can be recovered. *D1*'s recklessness in this regard is enough to justify a larceny conviction. Similarly, the intent to steal may be

---

[63] *People v. Brown*, 38 P. 518, 519 (Cal. 1894).

[64] *Impson v. State*, 58 P.2d 523 (Ariz. 1936); see *People v. Kunkin*, 507 P.2d 1392 (Cal. 1973) (*A*, an employee of the state attorney general, unlawfully took a confidential state document to *B* and *C*, journalists, for their inspection, with the intention of returning the document; held: since *A* lacked the intent to steal the document, he did not commit theft; therefore, *B* and *C* were not guilty of possession of stolen property).

[65] See *Jupiter v. State*, 616 A.2d 412, 416 (Md. Ct. App. 1992); *State v. Gordon*, 321 A.2d 352, 356 (Me. 1974).

[66] *State v. Davis*, 38 N.J.L. 176, 178 (N.J. 1875).

[67] See *State v. Gordon*, 321 A.2d at 357-58; accord Model Penal Code § 223.0(1) (although a person is not guilty of theft unless he acts with the "purpose to deprive" the other of the property, § 223.2(1), the word "deprive" is defined broadly to include disposal of property "so as to make it unlikely that the owner will recover it").

[68] *United States v. Sheffield*, 161 F. Supp. 387, 390 (D. Md. 1958) (*D* is guilty of larceny, even if he intended to abandon the vehicle six blocks from the site of the original taking).

inferred if *D2* takes property which does not belong to him, with the intention of returning it only if he is paid a reward.[69]

[B]—Concurrence of *Mens Rea* and *Actus Reus*

[1]—In General

A larceny does not occur unless the actor possesses the intent to steal the property at the moment of commission of the *actus reus* of larceny. For example, if *D* takes and drives away *V*'s car, intending to steal it, *D* has committed larceny. On the other hand, if *D* obtains permission to use *V*'s automobile for the day and, hours later, decides to abscond with it, he is *not* guilty of larceny, because he did not have the felonious intent when he took possession of the car.

[2]—Continuing-Trespass Doctrine

Suppose that *D* nonconsensually takes *V*'s car with the intention of keeping it for the day and then returning it. Hours later, *D* decides to keep the automobile permanently and drives out of town with it. Is *D* guilty of larceny?

On its face, it would seem not. *D* initially took the car without permission, i.e., a trespassory taking occurred. At the time of the trespassory taking, *D* had a wrongful intent (intent to keep the car without permission for one day), but he did not have the intent to steal. The felonious intent was an afterthought. Consequently, it would seem that the requisite concurrence of *mens rea* and *actus reus* is missing.

Courts developed the legal fiction of "continuing trespass" to deal with such cases. According to this doctrine, when a person takes possession of another person's property by trespass, every moment that he retains possession of it constitutes a new trespassory taking that continues until he terminates possession of the property.[70] Therefore, in the hypothetical, *D*'s nonconsensual taking of the vehicle was trespassory; every moment he retained the car he was committing the *actus reus* of larceny anew; when he decided hours later to deprive *V* of the automobile permanently, this intent to steal concurred with the "new" trespassory taking. Therefore, *D* is guilty of larceny.

[C]—Claim of Right

[1]—In General

A person is not guilty of larceny if he takes property belonging to another person based on the belief that he has a right to possess the property.[71] The actor's belief negates the specific intent to steal.[72]

---

[69] *State v. Hauptmann* 180 A. 809, 819 (N.J. 1935) ("intent to return should be unconditional; and, where there is an element of coercion or of reward, as a condition of return, larceny is inferable"); see American Law Institute, Comment to § 223.2, at 174.

[70] *State v. Somerville*, 21 Me. 14, 19 (1842).

[71] *State v. Varszegi*, 635 A.2d 816, 818 (Conn. 1993); accord Model Penal Code § 223.1(3)(b). The Code's more expansive "claim of right" defense is discussed at American Law Institute, Comment to § 223.1, at 151-59.

[72] *People v. Butler*, 421 P.2d 703, 706 (Cal. 1967).

For example, suppose that *D*, a landlord, believes that *V*, a tenant, has failed to pay his rent. In fact, the rent was paid, but *D* failed to credit *V*'s account. As a result, *D* enters *V*'s premises and mistakenly impounds *V*'s furniture, pursuant to a default-clause in the lease that authorizes *D* to enter the premises, seize a tenant's property, and sell it as a way of recovering unpaid rent. Under these circumstances, *D* is not guilty of larceny: even if his mistake of fact were unreasonable, the mistake negates the intent to steal.

The same analysis would apply in the landlord-tenant hypothetical if *D*'s mistake related to a matter of law, rather than fact. For example, suppose that *V*, in fact, had defaulted on the rent. If *D* entered the premises and seized *V*'s property based on an *incorrect* reading of the lease, *D* would not be guilty of larceny: whether his mistake of law was reasonable or not, he believed that he had a right to take the property; therefore, he did not have the intent to steal *V*'s furniture. [73]

Although there is some contrary case law on the point, the generally accepted rule is that the specific intent to steal is negated even if a person uses force to retrieve the property to which he claims a right. For example, if *D* believes he is owed money by *V*, and seeks to obtain it at gunpoint, *D* is not guilty of robbery (i.e., larceny by force), [74] although he may be guilty of aggravated assault inasmuch as the latter offense does not require the intent to steal. [75]

[2]—Forced Sale

Suppose that *D* takes *V*'s property with the intention of paying fair market value for the item. In this circumstance, *D* intends to deprive *V* permanently of the specific property in question, but he does not intend to deprive *V* of its value. May *D* assert a claim-of-right defense, on the ground that he believed that he had a right to take the property as long as he paid for it?

If the property *D* takes was *not* for sale, *D* should be convicted of larceny, even if he intends to pay fair market value for the item. [76] Nonetheless, the law on the subject is sparse and inconsistent. The case for conviction is strongest, however, if *D* has reason to know that *V* would refuse to accept payment in lieu of the return of the item.

Suppose, however, a good is for sale, but the merchant does not want to sell it to *D*. For example, suppose that *D* attempts to purchase a beer from bartender *V*, who refuses to serve *D* because the latter is intoxicated. If *D* takes the beer (perhaps by force), and throws down change to pay for the drink, is *D* guilty of larceny (or

---

[73] See *State v. Varszegi*, 635 A.2d at 819.

[74] See *State v. Bonser*, 623 P.2d 1251, 1252 (Ariz. Ct. App. 1981); *People v. Butler*, 421 P.2d at 706-07. The Model Penal Code is in accord with this rule. Model Code § 222.1 defines "robbery" as the infliction of serious bodily injury or a threat thereof upon another "in the course of committing a theft." As no theft occurs if there is a claim of right, see Note 71, *supra*, there can be no robbery in such circumstances. For criticism of the prevailing rule, see *State v. Schaefer*, 790 P.2d 281 (Ariz. Ct. App. 1990).

[75] *Butts v. Commonwealth*, 133 S.E. 764, 768 (Va. 1926).

[76] See Perkins & Boyce at 345 (stating that it is robbery to require a person at gunpoint to "sell" property that is not for sale).

robbery, if force were used)? According to Blackstone, this would not be an offense;[77] and this is the prevailing, although non-unanimous,[78] American view.[79]

§ 32.08 Larceny: Lost and Mislaid Property

The law is confronted with competing policy concerns when a person loses or misplaces his property. On the one hand, there is the interest of the owner in regaining his property; on the other hand, society has an interest in promoting the relatively unrestricted use or transfer of property. As a result, courts have developed rules that seek to balance these competing interests.

The rights of a finder of lost property depend on two factors: (1) the possessory interest of the owner at the time the property is discovered; and (2) the finder's state of mind when he retrieves the lost property.

Regarding the first factor, an owner of property retains constructive possession of his lost property if there exists a reasonable clue to ownership of it when it is discovered. A reasonable clue to ownership exists if the finder: (1) knows to whom the lost property belongs; or (2) "has reasonable ground to believe, from the nature of the property, or the circumstances under which it is found, that if he . . . deals honestly with it, the owner will appear or be ascertained."[80] Thus, a court is more apt to rule that there exists a reasonable clue to ownership of an expensive piece of jewelry found on the floor of a grocery store, than a dollar bill aimlessly blowing down a street.

If there is *no* reasonable clue to ownership of the lost property, the finder may use the property as he wishes; the act of picking up the property and using or disposing of it is not a "taking" (trespassory or otherwise). However, if there is a reasonable clue to ownership of the property, the finder's state of mind upon discovery becomes critical. When *D*, the finder, picks up the lost (reasonable-clue-to-ownership) property, he takes possession of it from *V*, the owner. If *D* takes possession with the intent to steal the property, he is guilty of larceny.[81] If *D* picks up the article with the intent to find the owner, the taking is not trespassory. Therefore, if *D* subsequently absconds with the property, he is not guilty of larceny since the original taking was lawful. Moreover, because *V* did not entrust the property to *D*, *D*'s actions may fall outside the scope of a typical embezzlement statute.[82]

With *mislaid* property, the same two factors—the possessory interest of the owner in the property, and the finder's state of mind upon discovery—come into play. However, in regard to the first factor, the common law is more protective of the

---

[77] 4 Blackstone at *242 ("it is doubted, whether the forcing [of a merchant] . . . to sell his wares, and giving him the full value of them, amounts to so heinous a crime as robbery").

[78] See *Jupiter v. State*, 616 A.2d at 414 (noting and citing support for the contrary view, and taking no position on the matter).

[79] American Law Institute, Comment to § 223.1, at 158; Perkins & Boyce at 345.

[80] *Brooks v. State*, 35 Ohio. St. 46, 50 (1878).

[81] *Id.*

[82] See § 32.09[B], *infra*.

interests of a person who mislays, rather than loses, his property.[83] An object is "mislaid" if "it is intentionally put in a certain place for a temporary purpose and then inadvertently left there when the owner goes away."[84] Supposedly, there is *always* a clue to ownership of mislaid property: because it was misplaced, rather than lost, the owner knows where it is, and is likely to return to pick it up once he notices that he has left it behind.[85] Therefore, the lawfulness of the finder's actions depends entirely on his state of mind when he takes possession of the property from the owner: if he takes it with the intent to steal it, he is guilty of larceny;[86] if he picks it up with honest intentions, he is not guilty of any theft offense.

§ 32.09 Embezzlement

[A]—Historical Background

Embezzlement is not a common law offense. The offense is the result of eighteenth century legislative efforts to compensate for gaps in the law of larceny. As described earlier, common law jurists were willing to punish new forms of dishonest conduct by manipulating the meaning of the term "trespassory taking" to expand the scope of larceny law. But, there were limits to their willingness to stretch the law: in particular, they were not prepared to treat dishonest employees, who appropriated property lawfully entrusted to them by third persons for delivery to employers, as capital felons.

In 1799, shortly after the acquittal of a dishonest bank employee in the *Bazeley* case,[87] Parliament enacted the first general embezzlement statute.[88] The statute provided in pertinent part:

> [I]f any servant or clerk, or any person employed . . . by virtue of such employment receive or take into his possession any money, goods, bond, bill, note, banker's draft, or other valuable security, or effects, for or in the name or on the account of his master or masters, or employer or employers, and shall fraudulently embezzle, secrete, or make away with the same, or any part thereof . . . [he] shall be deemed to have feloniously stolen the same . . . .[89]

Subsequent embezzlement statutes were enacted to deal with other persons not encompassed by this law.

Under English law, embezzlement was a misdemeanor. In the United States today, embezzlement is a felony or misdemeanor, depending on the value of the property embezzled.

---

[83] The Model Penal Code treats lost and mislaid property similarly. See Model Penal Code § 223.5 ("Theft of Property Lost, Mislaid, or Delivered by Mistake").

[84] Perkins & Boyce at 310.

[85] *Id.* at 310-11.

[86] However, if the finder genuinely believes that the item was abandoned by its owner, he lacks the specific intent to steal it. See Model Penal Code § 223.1(3)(a); American Law Institute, Comment to § 223.5, at 227-28.

[87] *King v. Bazeley*, 2 Leach 835, 168 Eng. Rep. 517 (1799). See § 32.04[B][3][b], *supra*.

[88] Previously, it had enacted statutes prohibiting embezzlement by officers and servants of the Bank of England, South Sea Company, and the post office. Hall, Note 1, *supra*, at 39.

[89] 39 Geo. III, c. 85 (1799).

[B]—Elements of the Offense

Because of the statutory nature of the offense, and the piecemeal manner in which embezzlement laws were enacted, no single definition of the crime exists. At a minimum, however, embezzlement involves two basic ingredients: (1) that *D* came into possession of the personal property of another in a lawful manner; and (2) that *D* thereafter fraudulently converted the property (i.e., *D* performed some act that demonstrated his intent to deprive another of the property permanently). Most embezzlement statutes include a third element: that *D* came into possession of the property as the result of entrustment by or for the owner of the property.

[C]—Distinguishing Larceny from Embezzlement

The most significant distinction between larceny and embezzlement is that "[i]n embezzlement, the property comes lawfully into possession of the taker and is fraudulently or unlawfully appropriated by him; in larceny, there is a trespass in the unlawful taking of the property."[90] It is useful to summarize here some of the subtle differences between the two offenses, as developed in earlier sections of this chapter.

First, a person who fraudulently secures property from another obtains mere *custody* of the property. Consequently, the subsequent appropriation of the property, which constitutes a trespassory taking of possession thereof, renders the fraudulent actor guilty of larceny (by trick).[91]

Second, an employee who receives property from his employer for use in the employment relationship ordinarily obtains mere *custody* of the property. Therefore, if the employee takes and carries away the employer's property with the concurrent intent to steal it, he is guilty of larceny, rather than embezzlement.[92]

Third, an employee who receives property *for* his employer from a third person ordinarily receives *possession* of the property. Therefore, if he later decides to convert the property, he is guilty of embezzlement.[93]

Fourth, a bailee entrusted with property ordinarily obtains possession of it, except that if the property is enclosed in a container, he obtains possession of the container but only custody of its contents.[94] Therefore, if the bailee subsequently decides to sell or otherwise convert the entrusted property in the condition in which it was received (e.g., in its original container if there was one), he is guilty of embezzlement. In contrast, if the bailee wrongfully opens the container and converts the contents, he is guilty of larceny. If he is responsible for delivering the container to a third party, and he does so without opening it, and thereafter decides to steal the property, he is guilty of larceny.

---

[90] *State v. Smith*, 98 P.2d 647, 648 (Wash. 1939) (quoting 18 Am. Jur., Embezzlement § 3 (1938)), *overruled in part*, *State v. Smith*, 798 P.2d 1146 (Wash. 1990).

[91] See § 32.04[B][5], *supra*.

[92] See § 32.04[B][3][a], *supra*.

[93] See § 32.04[B][3][b], *supra*.

[94] See § 32.04[B][4], *supra*.

Finally, in jurisdictions in which entrustment is an element of the offense of embezzlement, a person who finds lost or mislaid property, takes it with the intent to find the true owner, and then changes his mind and converts the property to his own use, is guilty of no offense. It is larceny, however, if he had a wrongful intent when he found the property. [95]

§ 32.10 False Pretenses

[A]—In General

The offense of "obtaining property by false pretenses" or, simply, "false pretenses," is statutory in nature. Originally, it was a misdemeanor in England. In the United States, it is now a felony or misdemeanor, depending on the value of the property obtained.

The original false pretenses statute was enacted in England in 1757. [96] According to that statute, any person who "knowingly and designedly" by false pretenses obtains title to "money, goods, wares or merchandizes" from another person "with the intent to cheat or defraud" the other person is guilty of false pretenses. A "false pretense" is a false representation of an existing fact. [97]

[B]—Distinguishing False Pretenses From Larceny and Embezzlement

Larceny, embezzlement, and false pretenses may occur as the result of fraud. False pretenses is similar to larceny in one critical way: fraud is used to obtain the property; in contrast, an embezzler obtains the property lawfully, but thereafter fraudulently converts it to his own use. The primary difference between larceny and false pretenses is that a thief who uses trickery to secure *title*, and not simply possession, of property, is guilty of false pretenses; one who merely secures possession through fraud is guilty of larceny by trick. [98]

In some cases the line between larceny-by-trick and false pretenses is clear. For example, in *Pear's Case*, [99] D fraudulently rented a horse from V, intending from the outset to steal the animal. Clearly, this was not false pretenses: the existence of the rental arrangement demonstrates that title to the horse did not pass with possession.

Often the line between the two offenses is very thin. Frequently, a court will rule that, although the thief obtained *possession* of property through fraud, *title* to it did not transfer because some condition had not yet been satisfied. For example, in one case, [100] D drove his car into V's gas station and asked the operator to fill his tank.

---

[95] See § 32.08, *supra*.

[96] 30 Geo. II, c. 24 § 1 (1757).

[97] See *Lund v. Commonwealth*, 232 S.E.2d 745, 748 (Va. 1977); American Law Institute, Comment to § 223.3, at 184.

[98] *Bell v. United States*, 462 U.S. 356, 359 (1983).

[99] *King v. Pear*, 1 Leach 212, 168 Eng. Rep. 208 (1779).

[100] *Hufstetler v. State*, 63 So.2d 730 (Ala. Ct. App. 1953).

D did not intend to pay for the gasoline. After the tank was filled, *D* sped away without paying. The court determined that *D* committed larceny-by-trick rather than false pretenses: *V* did not intend title to the gas to pass until payment was made.[101] In contrast, if *D* had paid for the gasoline with counterfeit money, title would have passed, and the offense would have been false pretenses.

Similarly, one who provides money to another for a special purpose does not transfer title to it until that purpose is met. For example, in *Graham v. United States*,[102] *D*, a lawyer, obtained money from *V*, his client, for the stated purpose of bribing *X*, a police officer, for *V*'s benefit. Instead, *D* converted the cash to his own use. The court held that *D* was guilty of larceny: *V* did not intend to part with title to the money until it was delivered to *X* as a bribe.

[C]—Elements of the Offense

[1]—False Representation

False pretenses requires a false representation. The representation itself may be in writing, orally presented, or in the form of misleading conduct.[103] Usually, nondisclosure of a material fact does not constitute false pretenses, even if the omitter of the information knows that the other party is acting under a false impression.[104] However, nondisclosure constitutes misrepresentation if the omitter has a duty of disclosure, such as when he has a fiduciary relationship to the victim.

The representation, of course, must be false. A person is not guilty of false pretenses if he obtains title to property by making a "false" claim that turns out to be true. For example,, if *D* sells a book purporting to be the diary of Hitler, he cannot be convicted of false pretenses if the diary is genuine, although *D* believed that it was forged. Instead, *D* would be guilty of *attempted* false pretenses.

[2]—Existing Fact

[a]—Fact versus Opinion

The expression of an opinion, uttered with the intent to defraud another, does not constitute false pretenses.[105] For example, "seller's talk" or "puffing" (e.g., "this is the best product that has ever been manufactured") is not actionable. The justification for the rule is that such statements cannot be taken literally as fact, but must be considered to be the seller's opinion. As such, a listener should not rely on the utterance.

---

[101] Accord, *Jones v. State*, 322 So.2d 735 (Ala. Ct. App. 1975) (*D*, a cattle buyer at an auction, used fraud to secure a copy of the sales slip from the owner's clerk, upon the promise that he would return immediately with a check to pay for the cattle; held: *D* was guilty of larceny-by-trick, as the owner did not intend to transfer title until he received the money).

[102] 187 F.2d 87 (D.C. Cir. 1950).

[103] In one famous case, *D* obtained property from *V* by giving the false impression that he was an Oxford student by wearing a cap and gown identified with the college. *Rex v. Barnard*, 173 Eng. Rep. 342 (1837).

[104] *People v. Johnson*, 150 N.Y.S. 331 (N.Y. 1914).

[105] *Regina v. Bryan*, 7 Cox. Crim. Cas. 312, 317 (1857).

The fact/opinion distinction, however, may also preclude conviction of persons not involved in puffing. For example, a statement by a seller regarding the value of his property is traditionally treated as a non-actionable representation of opinion.[106] The basis for this rule is that the value of property is founded on the price at which the minds of willing buyers and sellers meet. A representation regarding value, therefore, is an expression of opinion by the speaker of the price he thinks the property would obtain in the market.

As the fact/opinion distinction would suggest, the ethic of *caveat emptor* was strong as the law of false pretenses developed. It is commonly acknowledged today, however, that if this distinction is inflexibly followed it will result in "the clever . . . be[ing] able to steal with impunity."[107] As a consequence, many states have expanded the scope of false pretenses. For example, Model Penal Code § 223.3 provides that a person is guilty of "theft by deception" (the Code's equivalent offense) if he creates or reinforces a false impression regarding the value of property. However, the Code expressly immunizes puffing, if the statement would not deceive an ordinary listener.

[b]—Fact versus Promise of Future Conduct

Suppose that *D* purchases an automobile on installment contract[108] and later fails to make payments. Or, suppose that *D* obtains a loan and later fails to meet his obligation of repayment. May *D* be convicted of false pretenses if he had no intention of paying his debt when he entered into the agreement?

Conceptually, a promise to make payment in the future is an assertion of the present fact of the speaker's intention to perform a future act. Nonetheless, common law courts were reluctant to treat a debtor's breach of contract as the basis for prosecution for false pretenses. The traditional explanation is that "the act complained of . . . is as consonant with ordinary commercial default as with criminal conduct . . . . Business affairs would be materially encumbered by the ever present threat that a debtor might be subjected to criminal penalties . . . ."[109] The majority rule, therefore, is that the offense of false pretenses does not apply to misrepresentations regarding future conduct.

In recent years, however, many states have redrafted their theft laws to encompass false promises. The Model Penal Code is typical of this trend. It prohibits deception regarding a person's "intention or other state of mind." The Code expressly provides, however, that deception regarding the intention to fulfill a promise cannot be inferred solely from the fact that the promisor did not perform as guaranteed.[110]

---

[106] E.g., *Commonwealth v. Quinn*, 111 N.E. 405, 407 (Mass. 1916).

[107] American Law Institute, Comment to § 223.3, at 192.

[108] Although title technically is retained by the vendor of property until full payment is received on an installment contract, the equitable interest obtained by the purchaser is sufficiently great that the offense of false pretenses applies. *Whitmore v. State*, 298 N.W. 194, 195 (Wis. 1941).

[109] *Chaplin v. United States*, 157 F.2d 697, 698-99 (D.C. Cir. 1946).

[110] Model Penal Code § 223.3(1).

[3]—*Mens Rea*

The original false pretenses statute and others modeled on it require proof not only that the actor uttered a false representation of an existing fact, but that it was uttered "knowingly and designedly" and with "the intent to defraud."

The phrase "knowingly and designedly" means only that the actor made the representation knowing that it was false. The phrase "intent to defraud" constitutes the specific intent of false pretenses; it approximates the meaning of "intent to steal" required in larceny prosecutions. Thus, *D* is not guilty of false pretenses if he knowingly utters a false statement in order to obtain property to which he believes he is entitled. In such circumstances, *D* lacks the intent to defraud another.[111]

§ 32.11   Consolidation of Theft Offenses

It is virtually impossible to justify theft law as it has developed. Many legal fictions complicate the law of larceny, embezzlement, and false pretenses; and the lines between the offenses are exceedingly thin. And, through all of this, there is no meaningful difference between the offenses in terms of the culpability of the actors, their dangerousness, or the seriousness of the harm caused.

Making matters worse, the fine distinctions between the offenses depend largely on the hidden intentions of the parties. The line between larceny and embezzlement, for example, depends on whether the defendant formed the wrongful mental state prior to, or after, the property was delivered to him. The line between larceny-by-trick and false pretenses, on the other hand, depends on whether title passed in a property transaction; yet this critical fact depends largely on the victim's intent at the time of transference.

These distinctions have served as mighty encumbrances in the prosecution of wrongdoers. At one time, a prosecutor of a theft offense was required to prove the commission of the form of theft alleged in the indictment. Thus, if the indictment charged larceny, the prosecutor could not obtain a conviction for embezzlement or false pretenses. In many jurisdictions, a prosecutor is allowed to allege alternative offenses in an indictment, but this is only a slight benefit: he must still convince all of the jurors as to which crime was committed. As a result, thieves sometimes escape punishment because the prosecutor is unable to prove beyond a reasonable whether the wrongdoer had a felonious intent at the time he took possession of property (larceny) or later (embezzlement), or whether the wrongdoer's admitted fraud resulted in transfer of title (false pretenses) or only possession (larceny).

As the result of difficulties of proof, most states have sought to ease the prosecutor's burden by consolidating the three theft crimes (and sometimes other property crimes) into a single theft offense. However, lawyers in jurisdictions that have reformed the law in this manner should be wary of what consolidation does and does not do.

Specifically, unless a theft statute provides to the contrary, the consolidation may do nothing more than bring the various theft crimes under a single statutory

---

[111] *People v. Thomas*, 3 Hill 169 (N.Y. Sup. Ct. 1842).

umbrella. Consequently, a prosecutor who alleges facts in the indictment that would support a claim of theft-by-larceny could be precluded from proving a different form of theft, e.g., theft-by-embezzlement, at trial.[112]

To avoid the latter difficulty some states have followed the lead of the Model Penal Code. The Code sets out separate forms of theft—e.g., theft by unlawful taking, theft by deception, theft by extortion—but the offenses are consolidated, in that the prosecutor may prove a different form of theft than was specified in the indictment, as long as the defendant's right to a fair trial is ensured.[113] Another approach is to allow the prosecutor to allege simply that the defendant "stole" the property in question, and to support the allegation at trial with evidence of any form of theft.[114]

---

[112] E.g., *People v. Dumar*, 13 N.E. 325 (N.Y. 1887).

[113] Model Penal Code § 223.1(1).

[114] Mass Ann. Laws ch. 277 § 41 (1972).

CHAPTER 33

RAPE

§ 33.01   Rape: General Principles[1]

[A]—Definition: Common Law

Blackstone defined *rape* as "carnal knowledge of a woman forcibly and against her will."[2] At common law, however, a husband who forced his wife to engage in sexual intercourse with him was not guilty of rape.[3] Common law rape is a general-intent offense.

An ancient English felony statute prohibited sexual intercourse by a male with a "woman child" under the age of ten years with or without her consent.[4] This offense has come to be known as "statutory rape," although it is a feature of the common law of the United States.

[B]—Definition: Modern Statutes

Modern American rape statutes vary considerably in their language.[5] Typically, rape is defined as sexual intercourse achieved "forcibly," "against the will" of the female, or "without her consent." Often, a rape statute contains all three phrases.[6]

Many rape statutes prohibit specified forms of nonforcible, but nonconsensual, sexual intercourse. For example, sexual intercourse by a male with an unconscious or drugged female,[7] and sexual intercourse procured by "fraud-in-the factum,"[8] may constitute rape.

Traditional rape statutes are gender-specific. That is, only males are legally capable of perpetrating the offense,[9] and only females are victims of the crime.

---

[1] See generally Susan Brownmiller, Against Our Will (1975); Susan Estrich, Real Rape (1987); Susan Estrich, *Rape*, 95 Yale L.J. 1087 (1986).

[2] 4 Blackstone at *210. "Carnal knowledge" is sexual intercourse, i.e., genital copulation. Sexual penetration by the penis of the vulva is necessary to constitute rape; sexual emission is neither sufficient nor necessary. 1 Hale at *628.

[3] 1 Hale at *628-29. See § 33.06, *infra*.

[4] 18 Eliz. ch. 7, § 4; see 4 Blackstone at *212.

[5] See generally American Law Institute, Comment to §213.1, at 275-78.

[6] E.g., Maryland Ann. Code of 1957 Art. 27, § 463(a)(1) (1992) ("[b]y force or threat of force against the will and without the consent of the other person").

[7] E.g., Cal. Penal Code § 261(a)(3)-(4) (1994).

[8] *Id.* § 261(a)(4)(C). See § 33.04[C], *infra*.

[9] However, a female may be convicted of rape as an accomplice of a male.

However, some states have redefined the offense in gender-neutral terms as to both the perpetrator and the victim.[10]

So-called "statutory rape" remains an offense, although all states have expanded the scope of the crime to include sexual intercourse with minor girls over the age of 10. Not uncommonly, states now apply a two-level approach to this offense: sexual intercourse with a very young girl (e.g., 14 or below) remains punishable at the level of forcible rape; intercourse with an older girl is a lesser felony.[11]

[C]—Grading of the Offense

Under the Saxon laws, rape was a felony punishable by death. For a short time in the thirteenth century, it was treated as only a trespass punishable by two years' imprisonment and a fine. Subsequently, the offense was treated again as a capital · crime.[12]

In the United States, as late as the mid-1920s, 18 states, the District of Columbia, and the federal government authorized capital punishment for rape. However, "the death penalty [was] reserved overwhelmingly for black defendants, especially those convicted of raping white women."[13] In 1977, however, the Supreme Court ruled that the penalty of death was constitutionally disproportionate for the rape of an adult woman.[14]

Today, rape is treated as a serious, often the most serious, non-homicide felony. Penalties vary, but most states set the maximum penalty at life imprisonment[15] or a substantial terms of years.[16]

§ 33.02 Statistics Regarding Rape

[A]—Rate of Reported Rapes

Accurate figures on the commission of rape are very hard to find.[17] The Uniform Crime Report, which records official crime statistics, only keeps records on crimes reported to the police. Because of the stigma attached to the crime, and the

---

[10] E.g., Mich. Comp. Laws Ann. §§ 750.520a-520l (1991).

[11] American Law Institute, Comment to § 213.1, at 324-26.

[12] 4 Blackstone at *211-12.

[13] James R. Acker, *Social Science in Supreme Court Death Penalty Cases: Citation Practices and Their Implications*, 8 Just. Q. 421, 431 (1991); see also Robert J. Hunter, Paige Heather Ralph, & James Marquart, *The Death Sentencing of Rapists in Pre-Furman Texas (1942-1971): The Racial Dimension*, 20 Am. J. Crim. L. 313 (1993).

[14] *Coker v. Georgia*, 433 U.S. 584 (1977). See § 6.05[B], *supra*.

[15] E.g., Mich. Comp. Laws Ann. § 750.520b (1991).

[16] E.g., N.Y. Penal Law §§ 130.35 (1987), § 70.02(3)(a) (1987) (authorizing imprisonment of from 6 to 25 years for rape in the first degree).

[17] For discussion of some of the problems in this regard, see Helen M. Eigenberg, *The National Crime Survey and Rape: The Case of the Missing Question*, 7 Just. Q. 655 (1990).

embarrassment that rape victims often suffer in the criminal process,[18] rape may be the most under-reported crime of violence in the United States.[19]

One government-financed survey of adult women claimed that approximately 683,000 adult women were raped in 1990, a figure more than five times as high as the number of such assaults reported for the same year by the Justice Department.[20] However, there is no way to determine the reliability of the survey, which extrapolated on the basis of telephone questioning of 4,008 women.

Another government survey, the National Crime Survey (NCS), estimates that only 53% of all attempted or completed rapes are reported to the police.[21] Completed rapes are reported more often than attempted rapes, and rapes by strangers are reported more frequently than rapes by acquaintances. Also, the presence of a weapon by the rapist increases the likelihood of the offense being reported. Overall, the NCS indicates that 155,000 women age 12 or older were victims of consummated or attempted forcible rapes each year between 1973 and 1987. If these figures are correct, one woman in 600 was a rape victim in each surveyed year.

[B]—Who Is Raped and By Whom

[1]—Victims

Based on government survey data, an African-American woman is nearly twice as likely to be raped as a white woman, although in absolute terms, white women are victims more often than non-whites.

Rape victims tend to be young. Females (of all races) age 16 to 24 are three times more likely to be raped than older women.

---

[18] In the initial police encounter, the victim, already traumatized, must describe how the rape occurred. In the past, the investigating officer almost always was a man; sometimes he would express the view or imply that he believed that the victim consented to the intercourse or was partially responsible for her own victimization. (Today, policewomen interview the victim in cities with well-staffed police departments.) Routinely, as well, the victim must have a medical examination, which may include fingernail scrapings, combing of the pubic hair, and vaginal smears. Hospital personnel also take photographs of the victim, including of her genitalia, if she suffered any injuries, no matter how minor. See Minnesota Program for Victims of Sexual Assault, Sexual Assault: A Statewide Problem 11-13 (E. Keller ed. 1978). At trial, the rape victim must testify regarding the events leading up to and including the rape. In the past, she was also subject to cross-examination by the defendant's attorney regarding her prior sexual conduct. Today, however, nearly every state has a "rape-shield" statute, which limits questioning regarding the victim's sexual history. See § 33.07[C], *infra*.

[19] American Law Institute, Comment to § 213.1, at 283.

[20] David Johnston, *Survey Shows Number of Rapes Far Higher Than Official Figures*, New York Times, April 14, 1992, at A9 (reporting on the National Women's Study, financed in part by the National Institute on Drug Abuse, which is a part of the Department of Health and Human Services).

[21] U.S. Department of Justice, Bureau of Justice Statistics, Female Victims of Violent Crime (NCJ-126826 Jan. 1991). The statistics reported in this chapter section *infra* are from this study.

Many rape victims are poor. Approximately one-half of the victims fall within the lowest third of the income distribution. Also, unemployed women are raped three times as often as those who have jobs; central-city residents are much more likely to be victimized than those living in suburban or rural regions.

Students are victimized disproportionately. They are 1 1/2 times more like to be raped than women overall. Women living in dormitories are especially subject to victimization.

[2]—Perpetrators

Rapists and their victims are usually of the same race. During the years 1973-1987, seven of every 10 white rape victims were raped by white offenders; the figure was 8 out of ten with black victims.

Rapists tend to be older than their victims. Approximately 75% of the offenders are over the age of 21.

[C]—When, Where, and How Rapes are Committed

About 65% of all rapes occur at night, most often after midnight and before 6:00 a.m. About 35% of the assaults occur in the victim's home; 20% occur in the street; and 15% at a friend's home. Other common sites for rape are automobiles and parking lots.

Most rapists are unarmed. However, in the years covered by the NCS, in approximately 35% of all completed or attempted rapes, the perpetrator either threatened the victim with a weapon and/or verbally threatened her with serious harm.

Most rape victims, as many as 80%, take self-protective measures. These figures remain constant, whether the perpetrator is a stranger or an acquaintance. Women who resist are somewhat less likely to be victims of completed rapes than those who fail to take self-protective measures. However, those who resist a forcible rape are more likely to be injured (58%) than those who do not resist (46%).

More than one-half of all victims of *completed* rapes receive medical attention, commonly in a hospital emergency room. Only 10% of the victims of *attempted* rape seek medical care.

§ 33.03   Social Attitudes Regarding Rape [22]

[A]—Social Harm of Rape

[1]—The Original Perspective

The law of rape is rooted in ancient male concepts of property. [23] A virgin daughter was a valuable commodity owned by her father; a wife was a chattel of

---

[22] See generally Michael Davis, *Setting Penalties: What Does Rape Deserve?*, 3 Law & Phil. 61 (1984); Lynne Henderson, *Rape and Responsibility*, 11 Law & Phil. 127 (1992); Catherine A. MacKinnon, *Feminism, Marxism, Method, and the State: Toward Feminist Jurisprudence*, 8 Signs: J. Women in Culture and Soc'y 635 (1983); Stephen J. Schulhofer, *Taking Sexual Autonomy Seriously: Rape Law and Beyond*, 11 Law & Phil. 35 (1992).

[23] Brownmiller, Note 1, *supra*, at 376; see generally, *id*, at 16-30.

her husband. As a consequence, rape was a property offense. For example, according to one Biblical passage, the punishment for rape of a virgin daughter was fifty shekels, to be paid to her "owner" (the father), and forced marriage to the victim. [24]

The marital immunity rule, [25] i.e., the doctrine that a husband is legally incapable of raping his wife, is a manifestation of the view that the husband "owned" sexual rights over his wife. According to this view, the husband had the right to sexual relations with his wife whenever he chose, regardless of her wishes.

[2]—Modern Perspective

Lawmakers and feminist scholars, in particular, have sought in recent years to provide a modern explanation of the loss suffered by rape victims. Generally speaking, rape is viewed as a crime of violence and a privacy/autonomy offense.

The conception of rape as a crime of violence is easy to understand. Any rape involves, at a minimum, a battery of the female. When it is committed forcibly, it has all the earmarks of an aggravated battery. According to this view, the social harm of rape is not the sex act itself, but the way in which it is executed: violently.

However, rape involves more than bruises or breaks to the body. [26] Rape is a sexual invasion of the woman's body, in which her "private, personal inner space" is violated without her consent. [27] It is an internal assault, an assault on her psyche, and a violation of the privacy of the victim. The act of rape denies the woman autonomy by abridging her right to determine when, with whom, and how she will have sexual intimacy. Perhaps as significantly, rape is a hostile, humiliating, degrading act of sexual domination by the man of the woman. [28]

[B]—Perceptions of the Seriousness of the Offense

[1]—In General

A person's view of the social harm of rape largely determines that individual's perception of the seriousness of the crime. Although rape is considered a serious offense in all states, [29] empirical evidence suggests that not all rapes are considered equally serious. Indeed, even if the force used in a sexual assault remains constant, the perceived character and background of the victim of the rape, and her

---

[24] See Deuteronomy 22:28-29.

[25] See § 33.06, *infra*.

[26] A male reader might imagine the experience of being sexually assaulted, for example, in a jail, by another inmate. It is unlikely that the male victim of a forcible sexual assault would feel that he was *only* battered.

[27] Brownmiller, Note 1, *supra*, at 376.

[28] *Id.* at 376-78; see *State v. Smith*, 148 N.J. Super. 219, 226, 372 A.2d 386, 389-90 (1977), *reversed*, 426 A.2d 38 (N.J. 1981) ("Rape is necessarily and essentially an act of male self-aggrandizement . . . . Rape subjugates and humiliates the woman . . . ."). One commentator has described rape as an "act of terrorism" that keeps women dependent on men. S. Griffin, *Rape: The All-American Crime* in Rape Victimology 36 (L. Schultz ed. 1975).

[29] See § 31.01[C], *supra*.

relationship, if any, to the rapist, affects public attitudes regarding the seriousness of the crime.

[2]—Blaming the Victim

Both men and women tend to attribute some blame for a rape to the victim, even when the circumstances of the assault do not suggest any causal responsibility on her part. To some extent, victim-blaming occurs with all offenses. One explanation for this phenomenon is that people want (and perhaps psychically need) to believe that the world is just. This belief is cast in doubt when innocent people are victims of crime. Therefore, when a person is victimized, the observer—and even the victim herself—wants to believe that the victim was partially responsible for her own fate. [30]

This phenomenon is exacerbated in rape cases. Various studies suggest that males and females, but especially males, assign significant weight for the occurrence of a rape to the character and behavior of the female victim. [31] For example, in one study, [32] college students were provided descriptions of two rapes. In each, the victim was forcibly attacked by a stranger, late at night, as she walked across a campus following an evening college class. In one rape, however, the victim was described as a divorced, topless dancer, out of jail awaiting trial on a drug charge. The other victim was a married social worker.

In terms of gender, the study demonstrated that the respectability of the victim— her supposed character—affected male perceptions of responsibility for the crime. Males placed more blame for the crime on a victim's "low" character (the topless dancer) than did women. In contrast, females were more likely to attribute responsibility for the crime to the victim's behavior, e.g., walking home late at night (the same in both cases), and on matters of chance (simply being in the wrong place at the wrong time).

As might be expected from these findings, when the students were asked to assign a penalty to the rapists, men and women responded differently. The females assigned penalties virtually alike in the two cases, approximately 46 years' imprisonment (on a 1 to 99 year scale). Male respondents were harsher than females in the case of the rape of the social worker, assigning an average penalty of 54 years. They were substantially more lenient, however, in setting the penalty for the rape of the topless dancer (an average 18 years).

How do we explain the male view that the rape of a topless dancer is three times less heinous (based on assigned penalties) than the rape of a social worker? In part,

---

[30] See generally M. Lerner, *The Desire for Justice and Reactions to Victims*, in Altruism and Helping Behavior (J. Macaulay & L. Berkowitz eds. 1970).

[31] E.g., L.G. Calhoun, J.W. Selby, A. Cann, and G.T. Keller, *The Effect of Victim Physical Attractiveness and Sex of Respondent on Social Reactions to the Victims of Rape*, 17 Brit. J. Soc. & Clinical Psychol. 191 (1978); James Luginbuhl & Courtney Mullin, *Rape and Responsibility: How and How Much Is the Victim Blamed?*, 7 Sex Roles 547 (1981); J.W. Selby, L.G. Calhoun, and T. Brock, *Sex Difference in the Social Perception of Rape Victims*, 3 Personality & Soc. Psychol. Bull. 412 (1977).

[32] Luginbuhl & Mullin, Note 31, *supra*.

the answer is that in the minds of the male respondents, she was partially responsible for the rape; therefore, somewhat like a comparative negligence analysis in tort law, the penalty is mitigated.

But, there is probably more. It may be that the male respondents did not believe that there is as much social harm in raping a person of "low" sexual character than one of "high" character. That is, it is possible that the property aspect of traditional rape law has not given way (or, at least, was prevalent at the start of the 1980s when this study was conducted). To many males, females may still be sexual objects—"prizes" to be won by a male.[33] If so, it would follow that a woman who is believed to be sexually promiscuous is a less valuable prize than a woman of good sexual character.[34] The female respondents, however, focused on the victims' right to physical integrity and sexual autonomy. These interests are not impaired by the woman's sexual history.

[3]—Victim's Relationship to Rapist

Other factors affect attitudes regarding rape. For example, in one study of public attitudes, rape of a stranger was considered a significantly more serious offense than rape of an acquaintance.[35] Respondents treated the forcible rape of a stranger in a park as an extremely serious crime (remarkably, even more serious than the assassination of a public official). On the other hand, the forcible rape of a neighbor, although still a serious offense, was considered less egregious. Both of these cases, however, were perceived as significantly more serious than the forcible rape of a former wife, which ranked well below "use of heroin," and somewhat below "seduction of a minor," "selling pep pills," and "advocating the overthrow of the government," in crime seriousness. Indeed, the offense was considered only slightly more serious than "driving while drunk" and "practicing medicine without a license."[36]

---

[33] Comment, *Forcible and Statutory Rape: An Exploration of the Operation and Objectives of the Consent Standard*, 62 Yale L.J. 55, 72 (1952) (There exists "a masculine pride in the exclusive possession of a sexual object. The consent [of the female] . . . awards the man a privilege of bodily access, a personal 'prize' whose value is enhanced by sole ownership.") (footnotes deleted).

[34] *United States v. Wiley*, 492 F.2d 547, 555 (D.C. Cir. 1973) (Bazelon, J., concurring) ("[p]enalties [for rape] are high because a 'good' woman is a valued possession of a man"). It should be noted that Judge Bazelon was critical of this view.

[35] Peter H. Rossi, Emily Waite, Christine E. Bose, & Richard E. Berk, *The Seriousness of Crimes: Normative Structure and Individual Differences*, 39 Am. Soc. Rev. 224, 228-29 (1974).

[36] An attitudinal study of college students, beginning law students, and students who had taken a course in criminal law, found that the victim's relationship to the rapist was much less important than in the study reported in the text. See Joshua Dressler, Peter N. Thompson, & Stanley Wasserman, *Effect of Legal Education Upon Perceptions of Crime Seriousness: A Response to Rummel v. Estelle*, 28 Wayne L. Rev. 1247 (1982). Students who had had a course in criminal law were least likely to consider the factor relevant.

§ 33.04   Rape: Means of Execution

[A]—In General

Generally speaking, sexual intercourse by *D*, a male, with *V*, a female not his wife, constitutes rape if it is committed: (1) forcibly; (2) by means of certain forms of deception; (3) while *V* is asleep or unconscious;[37] or (4) under circumstances in which *V* is not competent to give consent (e.g., she is drugged, mentally disabled, or too young).[38] The first two criteria are discussed below.

In forcible rape cases, which represent the vast majority of rape prosecutions, the law is undergoing change. It is useful, therefore, to distinguish between the traditional law, and the developing law in some jurisdictions, in which the scope of the offense has been greatly expanded.

[B]—Forcible Rape

[1]—Traditional Law

[a]—In General

The traditional rule is that a successful prosecution for forcible rape requires proof that the female did not consent to the intercourse *and* that the sexual act was "by force" or "against her will." That is, where there is lack of consent, but no showing of force, a forcible rape conviction is inappropriate.[39]

Generally speaking, nonconsensual intercourse is "forcible" if the male uses or threatens to use force likely to cause serious bodily harm to the female[40] or, possibly, a third person.[41] Intercourse secured by a *non*-physical threat does not ordinarily constitute forcible rape.[42] Thus, *D* is not guilty of forcible rape of *V*, if *V* submitted to sexual intercourse because *D* threatened to fire her or to deny her some pecuniary benefit unless she agreed to sexual relations with him.

Typically, the issues of nonconsent and force merge. The male's use (or threatened use) of grave force on the victim proves both elements. Moreover, the common law rule is that a conviction of forcible rape may not stand unless "the victim resisted [the male's aggression] and her resistance was overcome by force or that she was prevented from resisting by threats to her safety."[43] Thus, even if

---

[37] *State v. Moorman*, 358 S.E.2d 502, 505 (N.C. 1987).

[38] American Law Institute, Comment to § 213.1, at 301.

[39] *Commonwealth v. Berkowitz*, 641 A.2d 1161, 1164 (Pa. 1994); *State v. Alston*, 312 S.E.2d 470 (N.C. 1984) (forcible rape conviction overturned, notwithstanding that the victim did not consent to the intercourse).

[40] American Law Institute, Comment to § 213.1, at 308.

[41] *Fitzpatrick v. State*, 558 P.2d 630, 631 (Nev. 1977).

[42] But see *Commonwealth v. Rhodes*, 510 A.2d 1217, 1226 (Pa. 1986) (interpreting the statutory term "forcible compulsion" as including "not only physical force or violence but also moral, psychological or intellectual force used to compel a person to engage in sexual intercourse against that person's will").

[43] *Hazel v. State*, 157 A.2d 922, 925 (Md. 1960).

a sexual encounter does not begin in a forcible manner, the resistance requirement imposes on the female (if the male is to be prosecuted successfully for forcible rape) the obligation to act in a manner that, at once, demonstrates her lack of consent, and causes the perpetrator to use violence (or its threat) in order to overcome her will.

The resistance requirement has been expressed in different ways by courts but, in general, the female must "follow the natural instinct of every proud female"[44] to resist the sexual attacker, unless she is prevented from doing so by serious threats to her safety. She has to resist the rapist "to the utmost," resist "until exhausted or overpowered,"[45] or resist "the attack in every way possible and [continue] such resistance until she [is] overcome by force, [is] insensible through fright, or cease[s] resistance from exhaustion, fear of death or great bodily harm."[46]

[b]—"Fear" versus "Threat"

In order for a forcible rape charge to be upheld on the basis of "threat of force," as distinguished from actual force, it is not ordinarily enough for the prosecution to show that the female *feared* serious bodily injury if she resisted. *Fear* is a subjective emotion—a feeling in the mind of the victim—whereas a *threat* is an objective act (verbal or physical) emanating from another person. In general, both components—the female's subjective apprehension, and some conduct by the male that places her in reasonable apprehension for her safety, is required.[47]

However, a forcible rape prosecution is appropriate, even if the female's fears are unreasonable, if the male "knowingly takes advantage of that fear in order to accomplish sexual intercourse."[48] For example, in a sexual assault case, if a fearful female has intercourse with a male after telling him, "I know that you are going to kill me unless I cooperate," a forcible rape conviction would be allowed, even if the male never intended to seriously injure her, and even if the female's fears were unreasonable under the circumstances: a male has no right to exploit her fearful condition to have sexual relations with her.

[c]—Cases Applying the Traditional Doctrine

The strictness of the traditional definition of "forcible rape" is evident by considering three cases. In *Rusk v. State*,[49] *V* agreed to give *D*, a man she met at a bar, a drive home. When they arrived, *D* invited *V* upstairs. When she refused, *D* took the keys from the ignition and asked, "Now will you come up?" *D* agreed: it was

---

[44] *State v. Rusk*, 424 A.2d 720, 733 (1981) (Cole, J., dissenting).

[45] *People v. Dohring*, 59 N.Y. 374, 386 (1874).

[46] *King v. State*, 357 S.W.2d 42, 45 (Tenn. 1962).

[47] See *People v. Iniguez*, 872 P.2d 1183, 1188 (Cal. 1994); *Commonwealth v. Berkowitz*, 641 A.2d at 1164. However, if a rape statute requires proof of "force or *fear*," e.g., Kan. Stat. Ann. 21-3502(1)(a) (1993) (emphasis added), a threat is not required. *State v. Borthwick*, 880 P.2d 1261, 1270 (Kan. 1994) (upholding forcible rape conviction on the basis of the victim's subjective fear, in the absence of any threat by the defendant).

[48] *People v. Barnes*, 721 P.2d 110, 122 n.20 (Cal. 1986).

[49] 406 A.2d 624 (Md. Ct. Spec. App. 1979), *reversed*, 424 A.2d 720 (Md. 1981).

late at night; and, as she was in a strange neighborhood, she feared for her safety. Inside, *D* pulled her on the bed and began to remove her blouse. She took off the rest of her clothing when he asked her to do so. Throughout the process, *V* begged to be allowed to leave, and at one point, as he put his hands lightly on her throat, she asked *D*, "If I do what you want, will you let me go without killing me?" *D* said "yes," after which *V* "proceeded to do what he wanted me to do." *D* was convicted of forcible rape.

The Court of Special Appeals reversed *D*'s conviction. In the court's view, no forcible rape occurred: *V* did not physically resist *D*; nor did the evidence support the claim that she reasonably feared that if she had resisted, *D* would have harmed her. [50] This judgment was reversed, however, by the Court of Appeals, which sensibly held that the "reasonableness of [*V*'s] apprehension of fear was plainly a question of fact for the jury to determine."

In *State v. Alston*, [51] evidence was presented that *D* and *V* had participated in an abusive relationship, in which *V* sometimes had sexual relations with *D* "just to accommodate" his violent demands. On those occasions, *V* testified, "she would stand still and remain entirely passive while [*D*] undressed her and had intercourse with her." At the time of the alleged rape, however, *V* was no longer living with *D*; she wanted to end the relationship, but she was afraid to tell him. On the day of the incident, *D* grabbed *V* in a parking lot, and threatened to " 'fix' her face so that her mother could see he was not playing." When *V* agreed to walk with him if he let her go, *D* did so. The two walked along the street as *D* spoke of their relationship. They arrived at a house belonging to a friend of *D*, at which they had had sexual relations in the past. Inside, after additional conversation, *D* asked her if she was "ready." *V* told *D* that she did not want to have sex with him, but when *D* told her to lie down on a bed, she complied, after which *D* pushed apart her legs and had intercourse. *D* was convicted of forcible rape.

The appellate court overturned the conviction. It held that there was sufficient evidence that *V* had not consented to the intercourse, but there was no evidence that *D* "used force or threats to overcome the will of the victim *to resist the sexual intercourse*." That is, neither *V*'s general fear of *D*, nor his specific threats of force *not* linked directly to a demand for sexual intercourse on the present occasion, could support a forcible rape conviction.

Finally, consider *Commonwealth v. Berkowitz*, [52] a case involving sexual intercourse between two college students in the victim's dormitory room. *D*, who was a friend of *V*'s roommate, came by and, after some conversation, asked *V* to give him a back rub. She refused. While *V* was sitting on the floor, *D* came over and "kind of pushed" *V* down. She described it as a "leaning-type of thing." On the floor, *D* straddled *V*, lifted up her shirt and bra, and began fondling *V*. At various times,

---

[50] Even within the context of traditional rape doctrine, the court should have found that *V* knowingly took advantage of her expressed fear that *D* would kill her if she did not cooperate.

[51] 312 S.E.2d 470 (N.C. 1984).

[52] 609 A.2d 1338 (Pa. Super. Ct. 1992), *affirmed*, 641 A.2d 1161 (Pa. 1994).

V objected to his actions. *D* unsuccessfully attempted to put his penis in *V*'s mouth. Although *V* did not physically resist, she continued to say "no." *D* got off, locked the door, and then put *V* back on the bed ("kind of like a push"), straddled her, and had intercourse. *V* did not physically resist or cry out. *D* was convicted of forcible rape.

The conviction was overturned. As in *Alston*, there was no consent, but the element of force was found to be lacking. The prosecutor conceded that *D* had not threatened *V*, so the issue came down to the matter of actual force. The court ruled that *D* did not use force sufficient to prevent resistance by a person of reasonable resolution.

Thus, these three cases provide the following clues to the traditional rule in rape cases. First, nonconsent and force are not synonymous. Second, in order to prove force, the female must physically (not merely verbally) resist the male (i.e., "no" is not enough), or the male must use or threaten force on the present occasion to an extent that would cause a reasonable female to fear grievous injury if she were to resist.

[2]—The Law In Transition [53]

[a]—Departure From Resistance Requirement

The common law resistance rule is unjustifiable. First, as one court reported, [54] "studies have demonstrated that while some women respond to sexual assault with active resistance, others 'freeze' " and "become helpless from panic and numbing fear." Therefore, although a female's resistance is highly relevant in demonstrating her lack of consent, her lack of resistance indicates little in relation to consent.

Second, although a female who resists a sexual assault is less likely to be raped than one who takes no self-protective measures, research also shows that resistance increases the risk of aggravated injury to the female. [55] A legal system that intends to protect women from sexual assaults should not require them to perform acts that will enhance the risk of aggravated injury.

Although many states retain the resistance requirement, the trend is to reduce the significance of the rule or to abolish it entirely. Thus, some states no longer require a female to physically resist her attacker "to the utmost," although evidence of some

---

[53] See generally Beverly Balos & Mary Louise Fellows, *Guilty of the Crime of Trust: Non-stranger Rape*, 75 Minn. L. Rev. 599 (1991); Donald A. Dripps, *Beyond Rape: As Essay on the Difference Between the Presence of Force and the Absence of Consent*, 92 Colum. L. Rev. 1780 (1992); Donald Dripps, Linda Fairstein, Robin West, & Deborah Denno, *Panel Discussion: Men, Women and Rape*, 63 Fordham L. Rev. 125 (1994); Steven I. Friedland, *Date Rape and the Culture of Acceptance*, 43 Fla. L. Rev. 487 (1991); Lois Pineau, *Date Rape: A Feminist Analysis*, 8 Law & Phil. 217 (1989); Lani Anne Remick, Comment, *Read Her Lips: An Argument for a Verbal Consent Standard in Rape*, 141 U. Pa. L. Rev. 1103 (1993); Schulhofer, Note 22, *supra*; Robin L. West, *Legitimating the Illegitimate: A Comment on Beyond Rape*, 93 Colum. L. Rev. 1442 (1993).

[54] *People v. Barnes*, 721 P.2d at 118-119.

[55] See § 33.02[C], *supra*.

form of reasonable resistance may be required. Other jurisdictions, either by statute[56] or common law interpretation,[57] have abolished the requirement.

[b]—Expanding the Definition of "Force"

The critical statutory term, "force"—and, thus, the potential scope of forcible rape statutes—is undergoing judicial expansion. It is hard to know yet how far the expansion will proceed, and whether the changes will gain support in many, or only a few, jurisdictions.

In at least a few jurisdictions, a forcible rape prosecution may be proven on the basis of lack of consent by the female, coupled with nothing more than the physical force inherent in the act of penetration. For example, in *State v. Brown,*[58] *V* was asleep in a hospital bed when *D* entered her room, pulled up her gown, pulled down her panties, and pushed his finger into her vagina. *V* awoke while *D* was touching her abdomen; *V* believed that *D* was a nurse conducting an appropriate abdominal palpation, so she did not object. When *V* became aware that *D* was not dressed as a nurse, she asked, "Sir, may I help you." By then, *D* had completed the penetration, and was on his way out, stating, "No, ma'm, everything's okay, just go back to sleep."

The appellate court held that these facts supported a forcible rape prosecution. It stated that *D*'s "actions in pulling back the bedclothing, pulling up the victim's gown, and pulling her panties aside amount to actual physical 'force' as that term is to be applied in sexual offense cases." A concurring justice explained the ruling more narrowly: "force and lack of consent may be implied when the circumstances surrounding the attack are such the victim cannot resist or give consent," specifically, when "the attack was carried out by surprise."

But, a forcible rape prosecution is now possible in at least one jurisdiction, even in the absence of surprise, solely on the basis of the female's lack of permission for the sexual intercourse. The New Jersey Supreme Court ruled in *State in the Interest of M.T.S.*[59] that a person is guilty of forcible rape (actually, forcible "sexual assault" under the statute) if he commits an act of sexual penetration[60] of another person[61] in the absence of affirmative and freely given permission, either express or implied, for the specific act of penetration. Without such permission, *any* force used, even the force inherent in the sexual act itself, justifies a forcible rape prosecution. Thus, under *M.T.S.*, the female is not required to say "no"; nor may the male avoid conviction by proving, simply, that the female wanted to have

---

[56] E.g., Mich. Comp. Laws. Ann. § 750.520i (1991) ("A victim need not resist the actor in prosecution [for rape].").

[57] *People v. Barnes,* 721 P.2d at 121.

[58] 420 S.E.2d 147 (N.C. 1992).

[59] 609 A.2d 1266 (N.J. 1992).

[60] The statute prohibits unlawful "sexual penetration," and not simply male-female genital copulation. The emphasis here, however, will be on sexual intercourse.

[61] The sexual assault statute is gender-neutral as to the victim. For purposes of clarity, however, the discussion in the text will assume that the victim is female.

intercourse. Instead, a male commits forcible rape if he has intercourse without securing permission—a "yes" in words or action—before proceeding.

Whether or not *M.T.S.* is rightly decided as a matter of statutory construction,[62] it strikes at the core purpose of modern rape laws, namely, to protect the sexual autonomy of the female.[63] The underlying reasoning of *M.T.S.* seems to be this: just as a person is not required to say "no" when a thief takes her property—a thief cannot successfully claim, "I had the right to take *V*'s unlocked car because she did not object when I got in and drove away"—a female should not be required to object to the male's sexual advances in order to render a subsequent sexual act of penetration impermissible.

If *M.T.S.* is going to be followed—if the law is going to focus on the violation of a woman's autonomy rather than on the degree of physical force used—a number of difficult issues remain to be decided. First, what conduct short of an express "yes" is sufficient to prove permission? Is consensual heavy petting adequate, or must the female say or do something that demonstrates that she is willing to proceed to intercourse? In *M.T.S.*, *D* and *V*, two teenagers, were involved in consensual "kissing and heavy petting," but *V* did not give permission for the *specific* act of sexual penetration, and it was this failure that rendered *D*'s actions violative of the forcible rape statute, as interpreted by *M.T.S.*. So, again, what will suffice short of express permission to have sexual intercourse?

Second, as the permission must be given freely, the courts must determine what conduct by the male renders permission tainted. For example, if a female consents to intercourse with her male employer in order to avoid a wrongful reduction in her salary, is this freely–given consent? Does it matter whether the salary reduction is substantial or trivial? Suppose that a female gives permission because he offers her a raise to which she would not otherwise be entitled? Various rules come to mind. First, the rule could be that permission is invalid if it is secured as the result of *any* illegal or tortious act by the male, regardless of whether it has a coercive effect on the female. Or, second, the standard could be that permission is tainted if it is the result of a threat *or offer* that would cause a person of reasonable firmness to grant permission. Third, the latter standard could apply, but be limited to threats.[64]

[C]—Fraud[65]

At common law, a seducer is not a rapist.[66] That is, a male may use any nonforcible "sales technique," no matter how deceptive, to obtain the consent of a

---

[62] The statute required proof of "force or coercion," but "lack of consent" was not an express element. Yet, the practical effect of the decision is to write "force or coercion" out of the statute, and to replace it with an affirmative permission requirement.

[63] See § 33.03[A][2], *supra*.

[64] See Schulhofer, Note 22, *supra* (in which Professor Schulhofer defends broad expansion of the law, but does not believe that "nonpermission" cases should be equated to rape; rather, he would create a lesser offense that prohibits nonviolent impairment of sexual autonomy).

[65] See generally Vivian Berger, *Not So Simple Rape*, Crim. Just. Ethics, Winter/Spring 1988, at 69; Vicki Waye, *Rape and the Unconscionable Bargain*, 16 Crim. L.J. 94 (1992).

[66] *People v. Evans*, 379 N.Y.S.2d 912, 919 (N.Y. App. Div. 1975).

female to sexual intercourse, and escape criminal punishment as a rapist.[67] It is not rape, for example, for D, a look-alike of a famous actor, to induce V to have intercourse with him by claiming to be the actor. It is not rape for D to pay for intercourse with a prostitute with counterfeit money,[68] or for a doctor to induce a woman to have intercourse with him by falsely claiming that it will cure her of an illness.[69] Each of these example have one fact in common: the victim knew that she was consenting to sexual intercourse; the fraud was in the inducement to have intercourse.

In contrast, a female's consent to engage in sexual intercourse is invalid if, as a result of fraud, she is unaware that she has consented to the act of sexual intercourse. For example, D, a male physician, is guilty of rape if, by so-called "fraud-in-the-factum," he obtains consent from V, a female patient, to "insert an instrument" in her vagina while she is under anaesthesia, if the "instrument" used is his penis.[70]

Courts have struggled with the question of how to deal with a male who engages in sexual intercourse by deceiving a woman into believing that he is her husband. For example, suppose that D enters V's bed at night in the dark, under circumstances in which he knows that she believes that he is her husband. If she has intercourse with him, is it rape? Some courts treat this as fraud-in-the-inducement, since the victim knew that she was consenting to sexual intercourse.[71] Most courts, however, treat this deception as fraud-in-the-factum (and, therefore, rape), on the ground that the attendant circumstance that the male was not the female's husband was a fundamental aspect of the sexual act; therefore, the female did not know what it was that she was consenting to do.[72]

If the law of rape is meant to protect a woman's sexual autonomy, should fraud-in-the-inducement vitiate consent? The question poses difficult matters of line-drawing and policy. For example, if fraud converts every induced act of sexual intercourse into rape, a male would be subject to prosecution if, allegedly, he falsely claimed love or promised marriage in order to secure the female's consent to intercourse. Prosecutions in such circumstances would result in serious problems

---

[67] Obtaining sexual intercourse by fraudulent inducement may constitute an offense less serious than rape. E.g., Cal. Penal Code § 266 (1988) (procuring female for illicit intercourse by false pretenses; punishable by incarceration not exceeding one year).

[68] Perkins & Boyce at 1080.

[69] *Don Moran v. People*, 25 Mich. 356 (1872); see *Boro v. Superior Court*, 210 Cal.Rptr. 122 (Ct. App. 1985) (D falsely claimed to V that he was a doctor, that she had contracted a dangerous, perhaps fatal, disease, and that the only way to treat the disease was through surgery or sexual intercourse with an anonymous donor injected with a serum; V agreed to the latter "cure"; D had sexual intercourse with V; held: charge of rape, based on a rape statute that prohibited intercourse "[w]here a person is at the time unconscious of the nature of the act," dismissed on the ground that D committed fraud-in-the-inducement; V was conscious of the nature of the act to which she had consented).

[70] See *Pomeroy v. State*, 94 Ind. 96 (1883).

[71] E.g., *Regina v. Barrow*, 11 Cox Crim. Cas. 191 (1868).

[72] *Regina v. Dee*, 15 Cox Crim. Cas. 579 (1884).

of proof, and would expend finite judicial resources to deal with failed relationships. As Martha Chamallas has observed, "the most common risk in any sexual relationship is the risk that one party will end the relationship unilaterally . . . ."[73] Quite arguably, the law should not require a person who ends a relationship to bear the risk of a felony rape prosecution in such circumstances.

On the other hand, what if a man fraudulently claims that he is sterile,[74] or that he does not have a communicable disease,[75] in order to secure consent to intercourse. Arguably, cases of this sort should be resolved, as they are now, in tort actions. And, when the harm resulting from fraud is substantial, e.g., the female contracts AIDS, there may be adequate means to bring the male to justice, e.g., a prosecution for aggravated battery, reckless endangerment, or even attempted murder. The contrary claim is that these prosecutions do not directly redress the victim's interest in sexual autonomy. If fraud in a business context can result in a theft prosecution, fraud in this context should result in a sexual assault prosecution, albeit of a lesser degree of the offense than if force were used.

§ 33.05 Rape: *Mens Rea*[76]

Rape is a general-intent offense.[77] That is, although a specific intent to have *nonconsensual* intercourse is not an essential element of the crime,[78] a defendant is guilty of rape if he possessed a morally blameworthy state of mind regarding the female's lack of consent. Therefore, the general rule is that a person is not guilty of rape if he entertained a genuine *and reasonable* belief that the female voluntarily consented to intercourse with him.[79] This rule conforms with ordinary common law mistake-of-fact doctrine relating to general-intent offenses.[80] However, a minority view[81] in the United States is that even a defendant's *reasonable* mistake of fact

---

[73] Martha Chamallas, *Consent, Equality, and the Legal Control of Sexual Conduct*, 61 S. Cal. L. Rev. 777, 834-35 (1988).

[74] E.g., *Barbara A. v. John G.*, 193 Cal.Rptr. 422 (Ct. App. 1983) (battery and deceit action, in tort, resulting from pregnancy based on the defendant's claim of sterility).

[75] *Kathleen K. v. Robert B.*, 198 Cal.Rptr. 273 (Ct. App. 1984) (civil suit, based on defendant's false claim that he did not have a venereal disease).

[76] See generally Victoria J. Dettmar, *Culpable Mistakes in Rape: Eliminating the Defense of Unreasonable Mistake of Fact as to Victim Consent*, 89 Dick. L. Rev. 473 (1984); R.A. Duff, *Recklessness and Rape*, 3 Liverpool L. Rev. 49 (1981); James Faulkner, *Mens Rea in Rape: Morgan and the Inadequacy of Subjectivism or Why No Should Not Mean Yes in the Eyes of the Law*, 18 Melbourne U. L. Rev. 60 (1991); Douglas N. Husak & George C. Thomas, *Date Rape, Social Convention, and Reasonable Mistakes*, 11 Law & Phil. 95 (1992); Sakthi Murthy, Comment, *Rejecting Unreasonable Sexual Expectations: Limits on Using a Rape Victim's Sexual History to Show the Defendant's Mistaken Belief in Consent*, 79 Cal. L. Rev. 541 1991).

[77] *Steve v. State*, 875 P.2d 110, 115 (Alaska Ct. App. 1994); *State v. Cantrell*, 673 P.2d 1147, 1154 (Kan. 1993).

[78] *Commonwealth v. Grant*, 464 N.E.2d 33, 36 (Mass. 1984).

[79] *People v. Mayberry*, 542 P.2d 1337, 1345 (Cal. 1975).

[80] See § 12.06, *supra*.

[81] *Commonwealth v. Ascolillo*, 541 N.E.2d 570, 575 (Mass. 1989).

regarding the female's lack of consent is *not* a defense.[82] In contrast, in England, the defendant's honest but *unreasonable* mistake of fact *is* a defense, at least if he was not reckless in his belief.[83]

In traditional forcible rape prosecutions, the issue of the actor's *mens rea* rarely arises. As a practical matter, one who uses force to secure intercourse will be unable to claim successfully that he was mistaken—reasonably or otherwise—regarding the woman's lack of consent. Indeed, a defendant is not entitled to a mistake-of-fact instruction absent substantial evidence of equivocal conduct on the victim's part, such as would cause a reasonable person to believe that consent existed.[84]

The issue of *mens rea* is—or, at least, should be—a more significant issue in acquaintance-rape prosecutions, in jurisdictions in which the resistance rule has been abolished or in which a conviction may be obtained in the absence of force beyond that which is incidental to the sex act itself.[85] In such cases, as a practical matter, the defendant's guilt or innocence is likely to depend on his culpability in regard to the female's lack of consent.

First, the case for an instruction on mistake is strong if a couple has had an ongoing consensual intimate relationship, and the female does not express her opposition to sex, either in words or conduct, on the particular occasion. Second, according to at least one late 1980s study, a significant number of females engage in "token resistance" to sex, in order to avoid the appearance of promiscuity or so as to enhance the sexual experience.[86] At least at this time in our culture, therefore, a male who believes that "no" means "no?," "maybe," or "try harder" rather than "no," is likely to state a sufficient claim of mistake-of-fact to merit an instruction on the matter, absent use of force. The instruction leaves to the jury the duty to determine whether the male's mistake was *bona fide* and reasonable, in light of the circumstances of the situation and modern attitudes about sex relations.

Finally, in a jurisdiction in which a male is guilty of rape absent affirmative and freely given permission for intercourse, the mistake-of-fact rule must be slightly rephrased:

> [I]f there is evidence to suggest that the defendant reasonably believed that such permission had been given, the State must demonstrate [beyond a reasonable doubt] either that [the] defendant did not actually believe that affirmative

---

[82] The word "defense" is used here loosely. "Mistake-of-fact" is not a true defense. See § 16.02, *supra*.

[83] *Regina v. Morgan*, [1976] A.C. 182; see Sexual Offenses (Amendment) Act of 1976 (permitting conviction on the basis of knowledge or recklessness as to the victim's lack of consent). See § 12.06[D], *supra*.

[84] *People v. Williams*, 841 P.2d 961, 966 (Cal. 1992).

[85] See § 33.04[B][2], *supra*.

[86] E.g., Charlene L. Muehlenhard & Lisa C. Hollabaugh, *Do Women Sometimes Say No When They Mean Yes? The Prevalence and Correlates of Women's Token Resistance to Sex*, 54 J. Personality & Soc. Psychol. 872 (1988) (reporting that 39.3% of the respondent female college students admitted to engaging in "token resistance" at least once).

permission had been freely-given or that such a belief was unreasonable under all of the circumstances. [87]

§ 33.06 Marital Immunity Rule [88]

[A]—The Immunity and Its Rationales

[1]—Rule

In 1736, Sir Matthew Hale stated that a "husband cannot be guilty of rape committed by himself upon his lawful wife." [89] He cited no authority for this proposition as, indeed, there was none. [90] Nonetheless, the so-called marital immunity rule became a part of the common law, and was adopted by most American legislatures as part of the original definition of rape.

[2]—Rationales

[a]—Consent/Property Rationale

According to Hale, "by their matrimonial consent and contract the wife hath given up herself in this kind unto her husband, which she cannot retract." [91] However, the concept of irrevocable consent by the wife makes little sense in modern times, if it ever did. The general understanding of most marital partners today is that each consents generally to have sexual intercourse with the other, subject to the right of either to refuse on particular occasions. Moreover, if a husband uses force to secure intercourse with his wife, he is subject to prosecution for assault or battery upon her; the principle of consent does not carry over to these offenses.

The more accurate explanation of the common law marital immunity rule is that the wife was the virtual property of the husband. [92] She was "incorporated and consolidated into that of the husband." [93] Therefore, the husband possessed an unlimited right of sexual access to her.

[b]—Protection of the Marriage

Defenders of the marital immunity rule sometimes argue that it is needed to protect "against governmental intrusion into marital privacy," and to promote "reconciliation of the spouses." [94]

---

[87] *State in the Interest of M.T.S.*, 609 A.2d 1266, 1279 (N.J. 1992).

[88] See generally Diana H. Russell, *Rape in Marriage* (Rev. ed. 1990); Rene I. Augustine, *Marriage: The Safe Haven for Rapists*, 29 J. Fam. L. 559 (1991); John D. Harman, *Consent, Harm and Marital Rape*, 22 J. Fam. L. 423 (1983).

[89] 1 Hale at *629.

[90] *Regina v. R.*, [1991] 4 All E.R. 481, 483 ("[t]here is no similar statement in the works of any earlier English commentator").

[91] 1 Hale at *629.

[92] American Law Institute, Comment to § 213.1, at 343.

[93] 1 Blackstone at *430.

[94] *People v. Liberta*, 474 N.E.2d 567, 574 (N.Y. 1984) (rejecting the argument).

This argument vastly overstates the case for the immunity. If a husband's use of force to have intercourse with his wife is an isolated act in an otherwise salvageable marriage, it is unlikely that the wife will seek a rape prosecution of her husband. On the other hand, if the husband is guilty of ongoing physical and sexual abuse, there is little in the marriage worth saving. In any case, in such circumstances, the interest in protecting the safety of the woman certainly outweighs the privacy concern.

[c]—Protection of the Husband in Divorce Proceedings

Some advocates of the marital exemption rule assert that if a husband could be prosecuted for rape of his wife, she might use this threat as leverage in property settlement negotiations in divorce proceedings.

This argument is unpersuasive. There is no reason to believe that a woman's ability to take unfair advantage of her husband would be significantly heightened by the repeal of the marital immunity rule. Even in jurisdictions that apply the exemption, a husband may be prosecuted for assault or battery if he uses force to secure intercourse; therefore, a wife could always use the threat of prosecution for these offenses as leverage. Beyond this, it is odd at best for the law to take sides with a wrongdoer against his victim on the unproven assumption that the victims, as a group, will behave improperly in civil proceedings.

[d]—Less Serious Harm

Some advocates of the marital immunity doctrine contend that the existence of the marital relationship "is not irrelevant to the concerns of the law of rape."[95] They reason that an important aspect of the harm of rape is the degradation of the woman that results from forcing her to have sexual intimacy with someone with whom she does not wish such a relationship. Although a female's sexual autonomy, as a male's, should include the right to refuse sexual relations on any given occasion, the marital relationship implies a general willingness—indeed, desire—by the parties to have intercourse with each other. When intercourse is coerced on a given occasion in the marital relationship, therefore, the wife's autonomy is less seriously violated than if the perpetrator were a stranger or someone with whom the victim had not indicated a general willingness to have sexual relations.

Despite the plausibility of this argument (particularly in the case of nonforcible rapes), there are important reasons for treating nonconsensual sexual intercourse in the marital bedroom as a form of rape, albeit as a lesser offense. Even in the marriage context, rape causes harm not protected by the laws of assault and battery. Spousal rape impairs (albeit less so than in the case of stranger rape) the wife's sexual autonomy; and, particularly if the husband's conduct is ongoing, the sex act by the husband becomes a means of subordinating the wife within the marriage. These special violations should be denounced by the law; the offense of rape is better suited to do this than the laws of assault and battery.

---

[95] American Law Institute, Comment to § 213.1, at 344.

[B]—Breakdown of the Rule

The marital immunity rule was judicially abolished in England in 1991.[96] The law in the United States is in transition. According to one recent survey,[97] only two states maintain a total exemption for marital rape. At the other end of spectrum, 12 states have wholly abolished the rule. Most states retain a partial exemption, although its form varies. In general, however, the immunity does not apply if the parties are legally separated or are living apart at the time of the rape.

§ 33.07　Proving Rape at Trial[98]

[A]—Corroboration Rule[99]

At common law, the testimony of the "prosecutrix"—the alleged rape victim—was sufficient to uphold a conviction for rape; her testimony did not need to be corroborated.[100] However, a minority of states, by statute or case law, have instituted a corroboration requirement. That is, under such a rule, no person may be convicted of rape (or, often, of any other sex offense) upon the uncorroborated testimony of the alleged victim.

The corroboration requirement is the result of "legitimate concerns, out-dated beliefs, and deep-seated prejudices."[101] Defenders of the rule believe that there is a higher risk of conviction of an innocent person in the prosecution of a sex offense than in the prosecution of other crimes. Lord Hale asserted that rape "is an accusation easily to be made and hard to be proved, and harder to be defended by the party accused, though never so innocent."[102]

Why would some lawmakers believe that conviction of an innocent person is more likely in a rape case than, for example, a robbery? Some of the reasons given are based on entrenched notions of sexuality that suggest that the testimony of a woman in a rape prosecution is particularly suspect.[103] According to this view,

---

[96] *Regina v. R.*, [1991] 4 All E.R. 481.

[97] Augustine, Note 88, *supra*, at 578-84 (and citations therein).

[98] See generally Ronet Bachman & Raymond Paternoster, *A Contemporary Look at the Effects of Rape Law Reform: How Far Have We Really Come*, 84 J. Crim. L. & Criminology 554 (1983).

[99] See generally Note, *The Rape Corroboration Requirement: Repeal Not Reform*, 81 Yale L.J. 1365 (1972).

[100] American Law Institute, Comment to § 213.6, at 422; *State v. Matlock*, 660 P.2d 945, 946 (Kan. 1983).

[101] *United States v. Wiley*, 492 F.2d 547, 552 (D.C. Cir. 1973) (Bazelon, J., concurring).

[102] 1 Hale at *635. These words or a paraphrase of them commonly form the basis of a cautionary jury instruction given at the conclusion of rape trials in over half of the states. A. Thomas Morris, Note, *The Empirical, Historical and Legal Case Against the Cautionary Instruction: A Call For Legislative Reform*, 1988 Duke L.J. 154, 156. In recent years, however, various courts have jettisoned the instruction. E.g., *People v. Rincon-Pineda*, 538 P.2d 247, 256 (Cal. 1975); *State v. Bashaw*, 672 P.2d 48, 50 (Ore. 1983).

[103] *United States v. Wiley*, 492 F.2d at 550.

some women fantasize being raped and, therefore, genuinely come to believe that they were raped, when in fact the sexual contact was consensual.[104]

Other advocates of the corroboration rule believe that women have a strong motive to "cry rape" falsely. Traditionally, females were expected to avoid sexual relations until marriage; those who violated this moral code were subject to embarrassment, stigmatization, and even ostracism. Therefore, an unmarried female who had sexual intercourse or, more significantly, became pregnant, had a strong incentive to claim that she was raped, rather than to admit that she had consented to sexual intimacy.

Another aspect of the concern for the accused may be the unfortunate result of racism. Historically, society disapproved of interracial sexual relations. Racist stereotypes have also suggested that black men are prone to rape white women.[105] A white woman who was known or suspected to have had sexual relations with an African-American male, therefore, was under substantial social pressure to claim that she was raped. The corroboration requirement reduced the risk of racially-motivated convictions.

Opponents of the rule state that Lord Hale's "comment does not reflect contemporary thought or experience."[106] The premise that women commonly fantasize rape is unfounded; and the other concerns are overstated or outdated. For example, minority group members previously excluded from jury service now serve regularly on juries, which reduces the risk of racially-biased rape convictions. Moreover, today's society is far more tolerant of premarital sexual activity than it was in the past, so that women have little reason to claim rape when it is not true. Finally, rape remains an under-reported crime.[107] In light of the stigma attached to the crime, and the embarrassment that rape victims often suffer in the legal system, there is little reason to believe that false claims of rape will occur often enough to justify a corroboration requirement.

Opponents of the corroboration rule appear to be winning the day. A number of states that adopted the rule have since repealed it.[108]

---

[104] American Law Institute, Comment to § 213.6, at 426-27; see Brownmiller, Note 1, *supra*, 319-33 (describing this attitude); Comment, *Forcible and Statutory Rape: An Exploration of the Operation and Objectives of the Consent Standard*, 62 Yale L.J. 55, 66 (1952) ("[M]any women . . . require as a part of preliminary 'love play' aggressive overtures by the man . . . . [T]heir erotic pleasure . . . depend [s] upon an accompanying physical struggle."). Many feminists believe, however, that a more accurate psychological view is that men fantasize that women fantasize being raped.

[105] Statistics disprove this claim. See § 33.02[B][2], *supra*.

[106] *State v. Bashaw*, 672 P.2d at 49.

[107] See § 33.02[A], *supra*.

[108] American Law Institute, Comment to § 213.6, at 423 (citing nine states in which legislative repeal occurred by 1978).

[B]—Rape-Shield Statutes[109]

In a criminal trial, two basic principles determine the admissibility of proffered evidence: (1) no evidence is admissible unless it is relevant; and (2) subject to limited exceptions, relevant evidence is admissible. Evidence is relevant if it has the tendency to prove or disprove any disputed fact at issue, including the credibility of a witness. However, a judge has discretion to exclude relevant evidence if its probative value is outweighed by the risk that it will cause undue prejudice to an opposing party.

In rape trials, defense attorneys traditionally seek to introduce evidence relating to the alleged rape victim's sexual history and moral character. Specifically, three classes of evidence regarding the complainant might be proffered: (1) her prior consensual sexual acts with the accused; (2) her prior consensual sexual acts with persons other than the accused; and (3) her reputation for lack of chastity.

The first category of evidence has always been admissible if the defendant contends that the female consented to sexual intercourse with him on the present occasion. Thus, if *V* claims that she was raped by *D* on January 15, it is relevant to the issue of guilt that she consented to sexual relations with *D* on January 14. Of course, the fact that she consented on one day does not necessarily mean that she consented on another day; nonetheless, the evidence has the tendency to disprove *V*'s claim of lack of consent.[110] Therefore, the jury is entitled to consider the fact of their prior consensual sexual relations, and to give the evidence as much weight as it believes is justified. This remains the rule today.

The other two categories of evidence have always been more problematical. In the past, however, many states permitted testimony regarding the complaining witness's prior sexual history with other men and/or her reputation for lack of chastity as substantive evidence relevant to the issue of her consent to intercourse with the accused. The traditional justification for this rule was that:

> [no] court can overrule the law of human nature, which declares that one who has already started on the road of [sexual unchastity], would be less reluctant to pursue her way, than another who yet remains at her home of innocence and looks upon such a [pursuit] . . . with horror.[111]

Such evidence was also admissible in the past to impeach the female's credibility, apparently on the ground that there is a connection between sexual immorality and lack of veracity. The effect of these rules of evidence was to put the complaining witness on trial along with the defendant.

---

[109] See generally Ann Althouse, *Thelma and Louise and the Law: Do Rape Shield Rules Matter?*, 25 Loy. L.A. L. Rev. 757 (1992); Andrew Z. Soshnick, Comment, *The Rape Shield Paradox: Complainant Protections Amidst Oscillating Trends of State Judicial Interpretation*, 78 J. Crim. L. & Criminology 644 (1987); Cassia Spohn & Julie Horney, *"The Law's The Law, But Fair is Fair:" Rape Shield Laws and Officials' Assessments of Sexual History Evidence*, 29 Criminology 137 (1991).

[110] Their prior sexual relations are also relevant to the issue of *D*'s *mens rea* at the time of the alleged offense.

[111] *People v. Abbot*, 19 Wendell's Rep. 192, 196 (N.Y. 1838).

In the past two decades, however, so-called "rape-shield" laws have been enacted by virtually every state. Although the statutes vary, these laws generally deny a defendant in a rape case the opportunity, absent good cause to the contrary, to cross-examine the complainant, or to offer extrinsic evidence, concerning her prior sexual conduct with others or her reputation for chastity.

Although rape-shield laws reduce the risk of prejudice to rape victims, they also increase the risk that an accused person might be denied the opportunity to introduce evidence that would demonstrate his innocence. In an extreme case, enforcement of a rape-shield law may conflict with the Constitution: specifically, the Sixth Amendment provides that a defendant is entitled to confront and cross-examine his accusers (in this case, the alleged victim of the rape) and to present evidence in his own behalf. However, these constitutional rights are not absolute, and courts have resorted to a balancing test, in which the interests of the rape-shield law are weighed against the defendant's need to introduce the "shielded" evidence in the specific case.

For example, in *State v. Colbath*,[112] *D* and *V* were in a tavern. *V* directed "sexually provocative statements" toward *D* in the bar. While in the bar, *V* also allowed *D* to feel her breasts and buttocks, and she rubbed *D*'s penis. Later, the two left the bar together and went to *D*'s trailer, where they had sexual intercourse. When *D*'s live-in companion unexpectedly arrived, she assaulted *V*. *V* sought to explain the situation on the ground that *D* had raped her. In support of *D*'s claim that the sexual acts were consensual, *D* sought unsuccessfully at trial to introduce evidence of *V*'s public sexual behavior with other men in the tavern on the day of the incident, including the fact that she had left the bar with other men in the hours immediately preceding her actions with *D*.

The court held that the rape-shield law had to give way in this case to the defendant's constitutional rights to confront the witnesses against him and to present his own exculpatory evidence. The court emphasized that the evidence involved public acts by *V*: "[E]vidence of public displays of general interest in sexual activity can be taken to indicate a contemporaneous receptiveness to sexual advances that cannot be inferred from evidence of private behavior with chosen sex partners." The court stated that the evidence *D* sought to introduce was more than "merely . . . relevant." Instead, it strongly supported *D*'s claim that *V* had made a false accusation, in light of the "undignified predicament" in which she found herself when she was discovered by *D*'s live-in companion.

Rulings of this sort are rare.[113] In general, courts have ruled that "the probative-ness of the [defendant's proffered] evidence is so minuscule when weighed against

---

[112] 540 A.2d 1212 (N.H. 1988) (opinion of Souter, J.)

[113] Indeed, in a case not unlike *Colbath*, another court upheld the exclusion of evidence under a rape-shield law. In *People v. Wilhelm*, 476 N.W.2d 753 (Mich. Ct. App. 1991), *D* and *V* were at a bar, although not together. *D* wished to introduce evidence at the trial that he saw *V* expose her breasts to two men who were sitting at her table, and that she permitted one of them to fondle her breasts. Another witness also observed the activity. However, the court upheld the trial court's exclusion of the evidence. It stated that "we fail to see how a woman's consensual sexual conduct with another in public indicates to third parties that the

the potential prejudice to the complaining witness that . . . the sixth amendment rights must bend to protect the innocent victims."[114]

[C]—Rape Trauma Syndrome[115]

With increasing frequency, prosecutors in rape prosecutions seek to introduce expert testimony relating to "rape trauma syndrome" (RTS).[116] The syndrome is "the acute phase and long-term reorganization process that occurs as a result of forcible rape or attempted forcible rape."[117] According to those who have studied the subject, a rape victim is as apt to appear calm and subdued immediately after an attack as she is to manifest fear, anger, or anxiety. Many woman in the acute phase also experience physical symptoms, such as tension headaches, fatigue, and disturbed sleep patterns. In the long-term phase, many rape victims develop phobias related to the circumstances of the rape, e.g., a person raped in her home may develop a fear of the indoors.[118]

RTS research is controversial.[119] Critics allege a number of methodological problems, including that: the various RTS studies do not agree on the definition of "rape"; the studies involve unrepresentative or inadequate samplings of victims; and information is elicited from victims in an unscientific manner.[120]

Some jurisdictions permit expert testimony regarding RTS, but only for limited purposes. For example, some states allow RTS evidence in order to explain the

---

woman would engage in similar behavior with them." The court distinguished *Colbath* on the ground that the woman in that case had left the bar with various men during the afternoon in question, and that the beating she received from *D*'s girl friend provided a motive for fabrication.

[114] *State v. Herndon*, 426 N.W.2d 347, 361 (Wis. Ct. App. 1988).

[115] See generally Nicole Rosenberg Economou, Note, *Defense Expert Testimony on Rape Trauma Syndrome: Implications for the Stoic Victim*, 42 Hastings L.J. 1143 (1991); Patricia A. Frazier & Eugene Borgida, *Rape Trauma Syndrome: A Review of Case Law and Psychological Research*, 16 Law & Hum. Behav. 293 (1992).

[116] In rare circumstances, the *defense* has sought to introduce RTS evidence, in order to show that a rape did *not* occur, on the ground that the alleged victim did *not* manifest "typical" post-rape symptoms. E.g., *Henson v. State*, 535 N.E.2d 1189, 1191 (Ind. 1989) (held: in a case in which the complaining witness was observed drinking and dancing the night after the alleged rape, it was error to exclude RTS evidence that this was atypical behavior of a rape victim).

[117] *People v. Taylor*, 552 N.E.2d 131, 133 (N.Y. 1990) (quoting Ann Burgess & Lynda Holmstrom, *Rape Trauma Syndrome*, 131 Am. J. Psychiatry 981, 982 (1974)).

[118] A rape is also a stressor that can lead to post-traumatic stress disorder (PTSD). American Psychiatric Association, Diagnostic and Statistical Manual of Mental Disorders 424-29 (4th ed. 1994). A victim of PTSD will persistently reexperience the traumatic event in dreams, images, thoughts, or perceptions. She may experience feelings of detachment or estrangement from others, be unable to experience loving feelings, and manifest symptoms such as difficulty in concentrating, exaggerated startle response, and hypervigilance.

[119] See Frazier & Borgida, Note 115, *supra*.

[120] See *State v. Black*, 745 P.2d 12, 17 (Wash. 1987).

complainant's post-incident behavior,[121] e.g., calmness,[122] if such conduct would likely be viewed by jurors, as lay people, as inconsistent with a claim of rape.[123] On the other hand, when the prosecutor seeks to introduce RTS evidence to prove directly that a rape occurred, many jurisdictions disallow RTS evidence.[124]

§ 33.08 Model Penal Code

[A]—Sex Offenses, In General

Article 213 of the Model Penal Code sets out the sexual offenses recognized under the Code: rape; gross sexual imposition; deviate sexual intercourse; corruption of minors; sexual assault; and indecent exposure. Only rape, deviate sexual intercourse, and some forms of corruption of minors constitute felony offenses. Consensual sexual conduct between adults is not prohibited.

The offenses of rape and gross sexual imposition are summarized here. However, the Code's approach to these offenses has been followed in whole or in part by only a few states.[125]

[B]—Rape

[1]—In General

A male is guilty of rape if, acting purposely, knowingly, or recklessly regarding each of the material elements of the offense, he has sexual intercourse with a female under any of the following circumstances: (1) if the female is less than 10 years of age; (2) the female is unconscious; (3) he compels the female to submit by force or by threatening her or another person with imminent death, grievous bodily harm, extreme pain or kidnapping; or (4) he administers or employs drugs or intoxicants in a manner that substantially impairs the female's ability to appraise or control her conduct.[126]

The Code recognizes a partial marital exemption. The offense excludes conduct with a spouse, unless the parties are living apart under a formal decree of separation.

---

[121] The issue in RTS cases is whether *expert* evidence regarding the syndrome may be introduced. The prosecutor may always offer *non*-expert evidence of the complainant's post-incident conduct, in order to buttress her claim that a rape occurred. *State v. Alberico*, 861 P.2d 219, 223 (N.M. Ct. App. 1991) ("Apparently no court, not even those most hostile to expert testimony on RTS, disputes that the jury . . . should be entitled to hear testimony that after the incident the alleged victim began to suffer from sleeplessness, loss of appetite, fear of men, etc.").

[122] *People v. Taylor*, 552 N.E.2d at 135.

[123] See also, e.g., *People v. Hampton*, 746 P.2d 947 (Colo. 1987) (RTS evidence permitted where *V* waited 89 days to report an attack by an acquaintance, and expert would have testified that reluctance to report a rape is especially great in acquaintance-rape cases).

[124] E.g., *People v. Bledsoe*, 681 P.2d 291, 301 (Cal. 1984); *State v. Saldana*, 324 N.W.2d 227, 229 (Minn. 1982); *People v. Taylor*, 552 N.E.2d at 138.

[125] American Law Institute, Comment to § 213.1, at 299.

[126] Model Penal Code § 213.1(1).

Moreover, the immunity extends to persons "living as man and wife," although they are not formally married.[127]

Rape is a felony of the first degree (and, thus, graded as seriously as murder) in either of two circumstances: (1) the defendant inflicted serious bodily injury upon the female or another in the course of the rape; or (2) the female was *not* a "voluntary social companion" who had "previously permitted him sexual liberties." In all other circumstances, the offense is a felony of the second degree.

[2]—Comparison to Common Law

The Code's treatment of rape is traditional in various regards. First, it is gender-specific, i.e., legally only males can commit the offense, and only females are the victims. Second, the Code affirms the general principle that nonconsensual intercourse with a spouse is not rape.

The Code differs from the common law in various respects. First, the term "sexual intercourse" is defined broadly to include genital, oral, and anal sexual penetration by the male of the female.[128]

Second, rape is defined in terms of the male's acts of aggression or overreaching, rather than in the negative terms of the female's lack of consent. The drafters favored this approach because "[t]he deceptively simple notion of consent may obscure a tangled mesh of psychological complexity, ambiguous communication, and unconscious restructuring of the event by the participants."[129] By shifting the focus to the male's conduct, the Code avoids the common law's emphasis on objective proof of the victim's lack of consent. In particular, the Code does not require proof of resistance by the victim, although the Commentary recognizes that evidence of resistance may sometimes be required to convince the jury that the sexual act was compelled.[130]

Third, the definition of rape is broader than the common law in certain respects: the offense is committed if the female submits as the result of violence directed at a third party; and it is rape if the victim submits as a result of a threat to kidnap her or another. On the other hand, sexual intercourse obtained by fraud-in-the-*factum* does not constitute the offense of rape, although it does make up the offense of gross sexual imposition, as discussed below.

[C]—Gross Sexual Imposition

Subject to the exemptions discussed above relating to spouses and persons living together "as husband and wife," a male is guilty of gross sexual imposition, a felony of the third degree, if he has sexual intercourse with a female in any one of three circumstances. First, he is guilty if the female submits as the result of a "threat that would prevent resistance by a woman of ordinary resolution."[131]

---

[127] Model Penal Code § 213.6(2).

[128] Model Penal Code § 213.0(2).

[129] American Law Institute, Comment to § 213.1, at 303.

[130] *Id.* at 305.

[131] Model Penal Code § 213.1(2)(a).

This provision represents a sharp departure from the common law, which required proof of force or a threat of a physical nature.[132] Thus, a man who obtains intercourse by threatening a woman with loss of employment, is guilty of gross sexual imposition, but not of any common law sex offense, if his threat meets the objective standard defined in the law. The objective standard—"a woman of ordinary resolution"—is "not a staple of the law,"[133] but the drafters believed it was sufficiently clear to permit the jury to distinguish between serious threats (e.g., loss of a job) and trivial ones (e.g., a threat by a police officer to give the victim a parking ticket). It should also be noted that *offers* do not fall within the scope of the offense; for example, a man is not guilty of gross sexual imposition if he offers a poverty-stricken woman a high-paying job if she submits to intercourse.

Second, gross sexual imposition is committed if a male has sexual relations with a female with knowledge that, as the result of mental illness or defect, she is unable to appraise the nature of her conduct.[134]

Finally, a male is guilty of this offense if "he knows that [the woman] is unaware that a sexual act is being committed upon her or that she submits because she mistakenly supposes that he is her husband."[135] Essentially, this incorporates the common law approach to fraudulent rape.[136]

[D]—Proving A Sexual Offense

The Model Penal Code adheres to the highly questionable corroboration requirement, which is followed by a small (and diminishing) number of non-Code jurisdictions.[137] It also requires that juries be instructed to treat a complainant's testimony "with special care in view of the emotional involvement of the witness and the difficulty of determining the truth with respect to alleged sexual activities carried out in private."[138]

The Code also includes a dubious prompt-complaint rule. A prosecution is barred if an adult complainant fails to bring the offense to the attention of a law enforcement agency within three months of its occurrence.[139]

The Code is silent regarding two matters that have been the focus of post-Code legislation and litigation:[140] the admissibility of evidence of the complainant's sexual history or reputation for chastity; and the admissibility of expert testimony regarding rape trauma syndrome.

---

[132] See § 33.04[B][1], *supra.*

[133] American Law Institute, Comment to § 213.1, at 313.

[134] Model Penal Code § 213.1(2)(b).

[135] Model Penal Code § 213.1(2)(c).

[136] See § 33.04[C], *supra.*

[137] Model Penal Code § 213.6(5). The corroboration requirement is discussed at § 33.07[A], *supra.*

[138] Model Penal Code § 213.6(5).

[139] Model Penal Code § 213.6(4).

[140] See §§ 33.07[B]-[C], *supra.*

TABLE OF REFERENCES TO THE MODEL PENAL CODE

TABLE OF CASES

[References are to sections.]

D

[References are to sections.]

[References are to sections.]

[References are to sections.]

[References are to sections.]

[References are to sections.]

INDEX

A

ACCESSORY LIABILITY (See ACCOMPLICE LIABILITY)

ACCOMPLICE LIABILITY (See also CONSPIRATORIAL LIABILITY)

Accomplice, defined . . . § 30.02[A][1]

Assistance
    Amount of assistance required . . . .
    § 30.04[B]
    Causation, not required element . . . . . .
    § 30.04[B][2]
    Types . . . § 30.04[A]

Conspiracy (the crime), distinguished from . . . § 29.04[B]

Derivative liability, explained . . § 30.02[A][2]

General principles . . . § 30.02

Innocent-instrumentality doctrine
    Distinguished from accessory liability . . .
    § 30.03[A][2][b][i]
    Nonproxyable offenses . . . .
    § 30.03[A][2][b][ii]

Limits to liability
    Abandonment . . . § 30.07[B]
    Legislative-exemption rule . . § 30.07[A]

Mens rea
    Attendant circumstances . . § 30.05[B][4]
    Crimes of recklessness and negligence . .
    § 30.05[B][3]
    Feigning accomplices . . . § 30.05[B][1]
    Generally . . . § 30.05[A]
    Natural-and-probable-consequences doctrine . . . § 30.05[B][5]
    Purpose versus knowledge . . . .
    § 30.05[B][2]

Model Penal Code . . . § 30.09

Parties to a felony
    Common law terminology . . . § 30.03[A]
    Procedural significance of . . . § 30.03[B]

Rationale of . . . § 30.02[B]

Relationship of parties
    Acquittal of primary party, effect of . . . .
    § 30.06[B]
    Conviction of primary party for lesser offense, effect of . . . § 30.06[C]
    Generally . . . § 30.06[A]

ACTUS REUS
Defined . . . § 9.01[A]
General principles . . . § 9.01

Hypnotism
    Common law . . . § 9.02[C][3][a]
    Model Penal Code . . . § 9.05[A]

Multiple personality disorder . . § 9.02[C][3][b]

Omissions
    Criticisms of general rule . . . § 9.06[B]
    Exceptions to general rule . . . § 9.07
    Factor, in proximate causation analysis
    . . . § 14.03[C][7]
    General rule . . . § 9.06[A]
    Medical omissions . . . § 9.09
    Model Penal Code . . . § 9.08
    Rationale of general rule . . . § 9.06[C]

Rationale . . . § 9.01[B]

Social harm
    Constitutional limits . . . § 9.11
    Defined . . . § 9.10[B]
    General principles . . . § 9.10[A]
    Statutory analysis . . . § 9.10[C]
    Sub-categories . . . § 9.10[D]

Voluntary act
    "Act" defined . . . § 9.02[B]
    Alcoholism/addiction . . . § 9.04
    Burden of proof . . . § 9.02[E]
    Constitutional law . . . § 9.04
    Model Penal Code . . . § 9.05
    Possession, crimes of . . . § 9.03[C]
    Potential exceptions to requirement of . . .
    § 9.03
    Rationale . . . § 9.02[D]
    Rule . . . § 9.02[A]
    Time-framing problem . . . § 9.02[F]
    "Voluntary" defined . . . § 9.02[C]

ALCOHOLISM (See *ACTUS REUS* and INTOXICATION)

ARREST DEFENSE (See LAW ENFORCEMENT)

ASSAULT
Attempt, distinguished from . . . § 27.02[E][1]
Attempted assault . . . § 27.02[E][2]
Defined . . . § 27.02[E][1]

ATTEMPT
Actus reus
    Policy debate . . . § 27.06[A]
    Tests . . . § 27.06[B]

Complete and incomplete attempts, defined . . . § 27.01

Defenses

N

NECESSITY

NEGLIGENCE (See *MENS REA*)

O

OMISSIONS (See *ACTUS REUS*)

P

PRESUMPTIONS

PRINCIPLE OF LEGALITY (See LEGALITY)

PRIVACY, RIGHT OF

PROPORTIONALITY OF PUNISHMENT

PUBLIC-WELFARE OFFENSES (See STRICT LIABILITY)

PUNISHMENT (See also DENUNCIATION, RETRIBUTIVISM, and UTILITARIANISM)

R

RAPE

REASONABLE-PERSON TEST